PROFESSIONAL
ASP.NET DESIGN PATTERNS

PROFESSIONAL

ASP.NET Design Patterns

PROFESSIONAL

ASP.NET Design Patterns

Scott Millett

Wiley Publishing, Inc.

Professional ASP.NET Design Patterns

Published by
Wiley Publishing, Inc.
10475 Crosspoint Boulevard
Indianapolis, IN 46256
www.wiley.com

Copyright © 2010 by Wiley Publishing, Inc., Indianapolis, Indiana

Published simultaneously in Canada

ISBN: 978-0-470-29278-5
ISBN: 978-0-470-94445-5
ISBN: 978-0-470-95289-4
ISBN: 978-0-470-95301-3

Manufactured in the United States of America

10 9 8 7 6 5 4 3 2 1

For general information on our other products and services please contact our Customer Care Department within the United States at (877) 762-2974, outside the United States at (317) 572-3993 or fax (317) 572-4002.

Wiley also publishes its books in a variety of electronic formats. Some content that appears in print may not be available in electronic books.

Library of Congress Control Number: 2010929314

This book is dedicated to my wonderful wife Lynsey — not that she will read it, mind you.

ABOUT THE AUTHOR

SCOTT MILLETT is an enterprise software architect working in London for Wiggle.co.uk, an e-commerce company specializing in cycle and triathlete sports. He has been working with .NET since version 1.0 and was awarded the ASP.NET MVP in 2010. He is the co-author of Wrox's *Professional Enterprise .NET*, and when not writing about or working with .NET he can be found relaxing and enjoying the music at Glastonbury and all of the major music festivals in the UK during the summer. If you would like to talk to Scott about the book, anything .NET, or the British music festival scene, feel free to write to him at scott@elbandit.co.uk, or by giving him a tweet @ScottMillett.

CREDITS

ACQUISITIONS EDITOR
Paul Reese

PROJECT EDITOR
Brian Herrmann

TECHNICAL EDITOR
Joe Fawcett

PRODUCTION EDITOR
Eric Charbonneau

COPY EDITOR
Karen Gill

EDITORIAL DIRECTOR
Robyn B. Siesky

EDITORIAL MANAGER
Mary Beth Wakefield

ASSOCIATE DIRECTOR OF MARKETING
David Mayhew

PRODUCTION MANAGER
Tim Tate

**VICE PRESIDENT AND
EXECUTIVE GROUP PUBLISHER**
Richard Swadley

VICE PRESIDENT AND EXECUTIVE PUBLISHER
Barry Pruett

ASSOCIATE PUBLISHER
Jim Minatel

PROJECT COORDINATOR, COVER
Lynsey Stanford

COMPOSITOR
James D. Kramer,
Happenstance Type-O-Rama

PROOFREADER
Jen Larsen, Word One

INDEXER
Johnna VanHoose Dinse

COVER PHOTO
© Özgür Donmaz/istockphoto.com

ACKNOWLEDGMENTS

I WOULD LIKE TO THANK Brian Herrmann, Paul Reese, and all those at Wrox who have helped to create this book. I would also like to thank Joe Fawcett who did a sterling job as the technical editor.

Massive thanks to Imar Spaanjaars (http://imar.spaanjaars.com/) for giving up his personal time to review chapters and give me some great feedback.

I would also like to take the opportunity to thank a couple of people that I have learned a great deal from over the last couple of years. I attended JP Boodhoo's (http://blog.jpboodhoo.com/) .NET boot camp in the summer of 2009 and it was probably one of the most inspirational weeks I have ever had, and it reminded me why I love the job I do. Thanks, JP.

When MVC first came along, a fellow named Rob Conery (http://blog.wekeroad.com/) started a blogging series on creating an MVC store. He explored many great technologies and methodologies during the store's construction, including BDD, TDD, DDD, KanBan, and Continuous Integration to name but a few. I learned more than I could have possibly imagined, in no small part due to the down-to-earth, fun manner in which Rob presented the content. If this book is half as good as those videos, I will be a very happy man. Rob now has a company dedicated to providing great video resources for developers at www.tekpub.com/. It's well worth a look — top banana.

CONTENTS

FOREWORD

Houses get built, manufacturing plants create stuff, and automobiles come off assembly lines enabled by well-known and agreed upon patterns for building things. For well-understood tasks there's no reason to reinvent the wheel.

As Christopher Alexander said:

> *Each pattern describes a problem which occurs over and over again in our environment, and then describes the core of the solution to that problem, in such a way that you can use this solution a million times over, without ever doing it the same way twice.*

When the Gang of Four (that you'll learn about in a minute!) wrote the first Design Patterns book for software engineers, it was the first time that patterns had been formally expressed in our discipline. In this book, you'll learn not just about patterns, but also antipatterns and what we can learn from them as well.

Sometimes it's not always clear what the best practice is, and mapping design pattern language to tangible usage within ASP.NET can be a challenge. Scott Millett's book takes those time tested design patterns, teaches you how to read them, and then applies them in a concrete and specific way to the problems that we as ASP.NET programmers have to deal with every day.

Filled with lots of code, instead of endless prose like some books, this book strives to connect the dots and make these patterns real, applicable and relevant in your daily life as a developer. In doing so, Millett calls upon not just what comes out of the box with ASP.NET from Microsoft, but also shows us some of the gifts that open source software has given us like Castle ActiveRecord, StructureMap, AutoMapper, and NHibernate.

From the Gang of Four to Uncle Bob's S.O.L.I.D. to Fowler's Enterprise patterns, Scott (what a lovely name) connects timeless patterns to the timely technologies of today like jQuery and JSON, the Entity Framework, and WCF.

I hope you enjoy reading it as much as I did.

SCOTT HANSELMAN
Program Manager – Microsoft
http://hanselman.com *and* @shanselman *on Twitter*

INTRODUCTION

THIS BOOK IS ALL ABOUT showing you how to use the power of design patterns and core design principles in real ASP.NET applications. The goal of this book is to educate developers on the fundamentals of object oriented programming, design patterns, principles, and methodologies that can help you become a better programmer. Design patterns and principles enable loosely coupled and highly cohesive code, which will improve your code's readability, flexibility, and maintenance. Each chapter addresses a layer in an enterprise ASP.NET application and shows how proven patterns, principles, and best practices can be leveraged to solve problems and improve the design of your code. In addition, a professional-level, end-to-end case study is used to show how to use best practice design patterns and principles in a real website.

WHO THIS BOOK IS FOR

This book is for ASP.NET developers who are comfortable with the .NET framework but are looking to improve how they code and understand why design patterns, design principles, and best practices will make their code more maintainable and adaptable. Readers who have had experience with design patterns before may wish to skip Part 1 of the book, which acts as an introduction to the Gang of Four design patterns and common design principles, including the S.O.L.I.D. principles and Martin Fowler's enterprise patterns. All code samples are written in C# but the concepts can be applied very easily to VB.NET.

WHAT THIS BOOK COVERS

This book covers well-known patterns and best practices for developing enterprise-level ASP.NET applications. The patterns used can be applied to any version of ASP.NET from 1.0 to 4.0. The patterns themselves are language agnostic and can be applied to any object oriented programming language.

HOW THIS BOOK IS STRUCTURED

Professional ASP.NET Design Patterns can be used both as a step-by-step guide and as a continuous source of reference to dip into at your leisure. The book is broken into three distinct sections. Part 1 is an introduction to patterns and design principles. Part 2 examines how patterns and principles can be used in the various layers of an ASP.NET application. Part 3 represents an end-to-end case study showcasing many of the patterns covered in the book. You may find it useful to work through the chapters before reading the case study, or you may find it easier to see the patterns in action by reading the case study section first and referring back to Part 2 for a more detailed view on the patterns and principles used.

Part 1: Introducing Patterns and Principles

The first part of this book begins by introducing the concepts of design patterns, enterprise patterns, and design principles, including the S.O.L.I.D. design principles.

Chapter 1: The Pattern for Successful Applications

This chapter explores why, as a professional developer, you need to understand design patterns and principles, and more importantly, how to utilize them in a real-world enterprise-level application. It covers the origins of the Gang of Four design patterns, their relevance in today's world, and their decoupling from specific programming languages. An overview of some common design principles and the S.O.L.I.D. design principles follows, and the chapter ends with a description of Fowler's enterprise patterns.

Chapter 2: Dissecting the Pattern's Pattern

This chapter introduces you to the practical knowledge necessary to use a design pattern template, and how to read the GoF design patterns using the design templates. The chapter will then teach you how to understand the design pattern groupings and give information on knowing how to choose and apply a design pattern. The chapter finishes with an example on refactoring existing code to use design patterns and principles to increase maintainability.

Part 2: The Anatomy of an ASP.NET Application: Learning and Applying Patterns

Part two of the book shows how the patterns and principles introduced in the first two chapters can be applied to various layers of an enterprise-level ASP.NET application.

Chapter 3: Layering Your Application and Separating Your Concerns

This chapter describes the benefits of a layered design over the traditional ASP.NET web forms code-behind model. It goes on to cover the concepts of logical layering and the separation of your application's concerns. The chapter then defines the responsibilities of each distinct layer in an enterprise-level ASP.NET application that will be covered in the remaining chapters of this part. The chapter ends with an exercise in refactoring away from the Smart UI antipattern to a layered architectural approach.

Chapter 4: The Business Logic Layer: Organization

This chapter covers patterns designed to organize your business logic layer. The chapter begins with a description of the Transaction Script pattern followed by the Active Record, with an exercise to demonstrate the pattern using the Castle Windsor project. The last pattern this chapter looks at is the Domain Model pattern demonstrated in an exercise with NHibernate. The chapter ends with a review of the domain-driven design (DDD) methodology and how it can be used to focus your efforts on business logic rather than infrastructure concerns.

Chapter 5: The Business Logic Layer: Patterns

Chapter 5, like the previous chapter, focuses on the business layer, but this time on the patterns and principles that can be used construct your objects and how to make sure that you are building your application for scalability and maintainability. The patterns covered include Factory, Decorator, Template, State, Strategy, and Composite. Enterprise patterns are covered including Specification and Layer Supertype. The chapter ends with some design principles that can improve your code's maintainability and flexibility; these include Dependency Injection, Interface Segregation, and Liskov Substitution Principle.

Chapter 6: The Service Layer

This chapter covers the role that the service layer plays in an enterprise ASP.NET application. The chapter starts with a brief look at Service Oriented Architecture and why it's needed. The Facade design pattern is then examined. Messaging patterns such as Document Message, Request-Response, Reservation, and the Idempotent pattern are then covered. The chapter finishes with an exercise that utilizes WCF to demonstrate all of the patterns covered in the chapter.

Chapter 7: The Data Access Layer

How to persist the state of your business objects with your data store is a critical part of your application architecture. In this chapter, you will learn about design patterns utilized in this layer and how to incorporate them. Two data access strategies are demonstrated to help organize your persistence layer: Repository and Data Access Objects. The chapter then covers enterprise patterns and principles that will help you fulfill your data access requirement needs elegantly, including Lazy Loading, Identity Map, Unit of Work, and the Query Object. The chapter finishes with an introduction to Object Relational Mappers and the problems they solve. An enterprise Domain Driven exercise with POCO business entities utilizing both NHibernate and the MS Entity Framework completes the chapter.

Chapter 8: The Presentation Layer

This chapter introduces you to patterns designed to organize the presentation logic and to keep it separate from the other layers in your application. The chapter starts with an explanation of how you can tie your loosely coupled code together with Structure Map, and an Inversion of Control container. The chapter then moves on to describe a number of presentation patterns, including letting the view be in charge with the Model-View-Presenter pattern and ASP.NET web forms, the Front Controller presentation pattern utilizing the Command and Chain of Responsibility patterns, as well as the Model-View-Controller Pattern implemented with the ASP.NET MVC framework and Windsor's Castle Monorail framework. The final presentation pattern covered is PageController as used in ASP.NET web forms. The chapter ends with a pattern that can be used with organizational patterns, namely the ViewModel pattern and how to automate domain entities to ViewModel mapping with AutoMapper.

Chapter 9: The User Experience Layer

In the final chapter of Part 2 the focus is set on the user experience layer. The chapter starts with an explanation of what AJAX is and the technologies that make it possible. JavaScript libraries are then covered to show how you can simplify working with JavaScript with powerful libraries such as jQuery. The main part of the chapter describes some common Ajax patterns: the Ajax Periodic Refresh and Timeout patterns, maintaining history with the Unique URL pattern, client side data binding with JTemplate, and the Ajax Predictive Fetch pattern.

Part 3: Case Study: The Online E-Commerce Store

The final part of the book uses an end-to-end example application to demonstrate many of the patterns introduced in Part 2.

Chapter 10: Requirements and Infrastructure

The first case study chapter introduces Agatha's e-commerce store that you will build in the remaining four chapters. The chapter describes the requirements for the site as well as the base infrastructure and overall architecture that will be used. ASP.MVC is used for the presentation layer with a domain model employed for the middle layer organization and NHibernate is leveraged to persist and retrieve business entities from the database.

Chapter 11: Creating the Product Catalog

Chapter 11 builds the product catalogue browsing functionality of the store. jQuery is heavily used to give a rich web 2.0 look and feel. Json is utilized to communicate between the controllers and the ASPX views to provide Ajax functionality. ViewModels are used to provide the controllers with a flattened view of the domain. AutoMapper is employed to convert the domain entities into the ViewModels.

Chapter 12: Implementing the Shopping Basket

In this chapter the customer's shopping basket is implemented. The customer's cookie is used to store a summary of the basket contents and a service is created to abstract the access to cookie storage. Again the web 2.0 look and feel is kept, with all actions on the basket taking place via Ajax calls.

Chapter 13: Customer Membership

Chapter 13 tackles customer membership and authentication. The ASP.NET membership provider is used for onsite authentication but a second authentication method is used to allow customers to authenticate with their existing web based accounts such as Facebook and Google. The customer account screens are also developed.

Chapter 14: Ordering and Payment

The final chapter in the case study exercise sees the payment and checkout functions of the site created. PayPal is the chosen payment merchant but the code is abstracted away so that any online payment merchant can be swapped in easily. The chapter finishes by adding the ordering history to the customer's account section.

CONVENTIONS

To help you get the most from the text and keep track of what's happening, we've used a number of conventions throughout the book.

 The pencil icon indicates notes, tips, hints, tricks, or and asides to the current discussion.

As for styles in the text:

➤ We *highlight* new terms and important words when we introduce them.

➤ We show keyboard strokes like this: Ctrl+A.

➤ We show file names, URLs, and code within the text like so: `persistence.properties`.

➤ We present code in two different ways:

```
We use a monofont type with no highlighting for most code examples.
```

We use bold to emphasize code that is particularly important in the present context or to show changes from a previous code snippet.

SOURCE CODE

As you work through the examples in this book, you may choose either to type in all the code manually, or to use the source code files that accompany the book. All the source code used in this book is available for download at `www.wrox.com`. When at the site, simply locate the book's title (use the Search box or one of the title lists) and click the Download Code link on the book's detail page to obtain all the source code for the book. Code that is included on the Web site is highlighted by the following icon:

Available for download on Wrox.com

Listings include the filename in the title. If it is just a code snippet, you'll find the filename in a code note such as this:

Code snippet filename

Because many books have similar titles, you may find it easiest to search by ISBN; this book's ISBN is 978-0-470-29278-5.

Once you download the code, just decompress it with your favorite compression tool. Alternately, you can go to the main Wrox code download page at `www.wrox.com/dynamic/books/download.aspx` to see the code available for this book and all other Wrox books.

ERRATA

We make every effort to ensure that there are no errors in the text or in the code. However, no one is perfect, and mistakes do occur. If you find an error in one of our books, like a spelling mistake or faulty piece of code, we would be very grateful for your feedback. By sending in errata, you may save another reader hours of frustration, and at the same time, you will be helping us provide even higher quality information.

To find the errata page for this book, go to `www.wrox.com` and locate the title using the Search box or one of the title lists. Then, on the book details page, click the Book Errata link. On this page, you can view all errata that has been submitted for this book and posted by Wrox editors. A complete book list, including links to each book's errata, is also available at `www.wrox.com/misc-pages/booklist.shtml`.

If you don't spot "your" error on the Book Errata page, go to `www.wrox.com/contact/techsupport.shtml` and complete the form there to send us the error you have found. We'll check the information and, if appropriate, post a message to the book's errata page and fix the problem in subsequent editions of the book.

P2P.WROX.COM

For author and peer discussion, join the P2P forums at `p2p.wrox.com`. The forums are a Web-based system for you to post messages relating to Wrox books and related technologies and interact with other readers and technology users. The forums offer a subscription feature to e-mail you topics of interest of your choosing when new posts are made to the forums. Wrox authors, editors, other industry experts, and your fellow readers are present on these forums.

At `p2p.wrox.com`, you will find a number of different forums that will help you, not only as you read this book, but also as you develop your own applications. To join the forums, just follow these steps:

1. Go to `p2p.wrox.com` and click the Register link.

2. Read the terms of use and click Agree.

3. Complete the required information to join, as well as any optional information you wish to provide, and click Submit.

4. You will receive an e-mail with information describing how to verify your account and complete the joining process.

 You can read messages in the forums without joining P2P, but in order to post your own messages, you must join.

Once you join, you can post new messages and respond to messages other users post. You can read messages at any time on the Web. If you would like to have new messages from a particular forum e-mailed to you, click the Subscribe to this Forum icon by the forum name in the forum listing.

For more information about how to use the Wrox P2P, be sure to read the P2P FAQs for answers to questions about how the forum software works, as well as many common questions specific to P2P and Wrox books. To read the FAQs, click the FAQ link on any P2P page.

PART I
Introducing Patterns and Principles

1

The Pattern for Successful Applications

WHAT'S IN THIS CHAPTER?

➤ An introduction to the Gang of Four Design Patterns

➤ An overview of some common design principles and the SOLID design principles

➤ A description of Fowlers Enterprise Patterns

John Lennon once wrote, "There are no problems, only solutions." Now, Mr. Lennon never, to my mind, did much in the way of ASP.NET programming; however, what he said is extremely relevant in the realm of software development and probably humanity, but that's a whole other book. Our job as software developers involves solving problems — problems that other developers have had to solve countless times before albeit in various guises. Throughout the lifetime of object-oriented programming, a number of patterns, principles, and best practices have been discovered, named, and catalogued. With knowledge of these patterns and a common solution vocabulary, we can begin to break down complex problems, encapsulate what varies, and develop applications in a uniformed way with tried and trusted solutions.

This book is all about introducing you to design patterns, principles, and best practices that you can apply to your ASP.NET applications. By their very nature, patterns and principles are language agnostic, so the knowledge gained in this book can be applied to win forms, WPF and Silverlight applications, as well as other first-class object-oriented languages.

This chapter will cover what design patterns are, where they come from, and why it's important to study them. Fundamental to design patterns are solid object-oriented design principles, which will be covered in this chapter in the form of Robert Martin's S.O.L.I.D. principles. I will also introduce you to some more advanced patterns as laid out in Martin Fowler's *Patterns of Enterprise Application Architecture* book.

DESIGN PATTERNS EXPLAINED

Design patterns are high-level abstract solution templates. Think of them as blueprints for solutions rather than the solutions themselves. You won't find a framework that you can simply apply to your application; instead, you will typically arrive at design patterns through refactoring your code and generalizing your problem.

Design patterns aren't just applicable to software development; design patterns can be found in all areas of life from engineering to architecture. In fact, it was the architect Christopher Alexander who introduced the idea of patterns in 1970 to build a common vocabulary for design discussion. He wrote:

> *The elements of this language are entities called patterns. Each pattern describes a problem that occurs over and over again in our environment and then describes the core of the solution to that problem in such a way that you can use this solution a million times over without ever doing it the same way twice.*

Alexander's comments are just as applicable to software design as they are to buildings and town planning.

Origins

The origins of the design patterns that are prevalent in software architecture today were born from the experiences and knowledge of programmers over many years of using object-oriented programming languages. A set of the most common patterns were catalogued in a book entitled *Design Patterns: Elements of Reusable Object-Oriented Software*, more affectionately known as the *Design Patterns Bible*. This book was written by Erich Gamma, Richard Helm, Ralph Johnson, and John Vlissides, better known as the Gang of Four.

They collected 23 design patterns and organized them into 3 groups:

➤ **Creational Patterns:** These deal with object construction and referencing.

➤ **Structural Patterns:** These deal with the relationships between objects and how they interact with each other to form larger complex objects.

➤ **Behavioral Patterns:** These deal with the communication between objects, especially in terms of responsibility and algorithms.

Each pattern is presented in a template so readers can learn how to decipher and apply the pattern. We will be covering the practical knowledge necessary to use a design pattern template in Chapter 2 along with a brief overview of each pattern that we will be looking at in the rest of this book.

Necessity

Patterns are essential to software design and development. They enable the expression of intent through a shared vocabulary when problem solving at the design stage as well as within the source code. Patterns promote the use of good object-oriented software design, as they are built around solid object-oriented design principles.

Patterns are an effective way to describe solutions to complex problems. With solid knowledge of design patterns, you can communicate quickly and easily with other members of a team without having to be concerned with the low-level implementation details.

Patterns are language agnostic; therefore, they are transferable over other object-oriented languages. The knowledge you gain through learning patterns will serve you in any first-class object-oriented language you decide to program in.

Usefulness

The useful and ultimate value of design patterns lies in the fact that they are tried and tested solutions, which gives confidence in their effectiveness. If you are an experienced developer and have been programming in .NET or another object-oriented language for a number of years, you might find that you are already using some of the design patterns mentioned in the Gang of Four book. However, by being able to identify the patterns you are using, you can communicate far more effectively with other developers who, with an understanding of the patterns, will understand the structure of your solution.

Design patterns are all about the reuse of solutions. All problems are not equal, of course, but if you can break down a problem and find the similarities with problems that have been solved before, you can then apply those solutions. After decades of object-oriented programming, most of the problems you'll encounter will have been solved countless times before, and there will be a pattern available to assist in your solution implementation. Even if you believe your problem to be unique, by breaking it down to its root elements, you should be able to generalize it enough to find an appropriate solution.

The name of the design pattern is useful because it reflects its behavior and purpose and provides a common vocabulary in solution brainstorming. It is far easier to talk in terms of a pattern name than in detail about how an implementation of it would work.

What They Are Not

Design patterns are no silver bullet. You have to fully understand your problem, generalize it, and then apply a pattern applicable to it. However, not all problems require a design pattern. It's true that design patterns can help make complex problems simple, but they can also make simple problems complex.

After reading a patterns book, many developers fall into the trap of trying to apply patterns to everything they do, thus achieving quite the opposite of what patterns are all about — making things simple. The better way to apply patterns, as stated before, is by identifying the fundamental problem you are trying to solve and looking for a solution that fits it. This book will help with the identification of when and how to use patterns and goes on to cover the implementation from an ASP.NET point of view.

You don't always have to use design patterns. If you have arrived at a solution to a problem that is simple but not simplistic and is clear and maintainable, don't beat yourself up if it doesn't fit into one of the 23 Gang of Four design patterns. Otherwise, you will overcomplicate your design.

This talk of patterns might seem rather vague at the moment, but as you progress through the book, you will learn about the types of problems each pattern was designed to solve and work through implementations of these patterns in ASP.NET. With this knowledge, you can then apply the patterns to your applications.

DESIGN PRINCIPLES

Design principles form the foundations that design patterns are built upon. They are more fundamental than design patterns. When you follow proven design principles, your code base becomes infinitely more flexible and adaptable to change, as well as more maintainable. I will briefly introduce you to some of the more widely known design principles and a series of principles known as the S.O.L.I.D. principles. Later in the book we will look at these principles more deeply and implement them and best practices in ASP.NET.

Common Design Principles

There are a number of common design principles that, like design patterns, have become best practice over the years and helped to form a foundation onto which enterprise-level and maintainable software can be built. The following sections preview some of the more widely known principles.

Keep It Simple Stupid (KISS)

An all-too-common issue in software programming is the need to overcomplicate a solution. The goal of the KISS principle is concerned with the need to keep code simple but not simplistic, thus avoiding any unnecessary complexities.

Don't Repeat Yourself (DRY)

The DRY principle aims to avoiding repetition of any part of a system by abstracting out things that are common and placing those things in a single location. This principle is not only concerned with code but any logic that is duplicated in a system; ultimately there should only be one representation for every piece of knowledge in a system.

Tell, Don't Ask

The Tell, Don't Ask principle is closely aligned with encapsulation and the assigning of responsibilities to their correct classes. The principle states that you should to tell objects what actions you want them to perform rather than asking questions about the state of the object and then making a decision yourself on what action you want to perform. This helps to align the responsibilities and avoid tight coupling between classes.

You Ain't Gonna Need It (YAGNI)

The YAGNI principle refers to the need to only include functionality that is necessary for the application and put off any temptation to add other features that you may think you need. A design methodology that adheres to YAGNI is test-driven development (TDD). TDD is all about writing tests that prove the functionality of a system and then writing only the code to get the test to pass. TDD is discussed a little later in this chapter.

Separation of Concerns (SoC)

SoC is the process of dissecting a piece of software into distinct features that encapsulate unique behavior and data that can be used by other classes. Generally, a concern represents a feature or behavior of a class. The act of separating a program into discrete responsibilities significantly increases code reuse, maintenance, and testability.

The remainder of this book refers back to these principles so you can see how they are implemented and help form clean and maintainable object-oriented systems. The next group of design principles you will look at were collected together under the grouping of the S.O.L.I.D. design principles.

The S.O.L.I.D. Design Principles

The S.O.L.I.D. design principles are a collection of best practices for object-oriented design. All of the Gang of Four design patterns adhere to these principles in one form or another. The term S.O.L.I.D. comes from the initial letter of each of the five principles that were collected in the book *Agile Principles, Patterns, and Practices in C#* by Robert C. Martin, or Uncle Bob to his friends. The following sections look at each one in turn.

Single Responsibility Principle (SRP)

The principle of SRP is closely aligned with SoC. It states that every object should only have one reason to change and a single focus of responsibility. By adhering to this principle, you avoid the problem of monolithic class design that is the software equivalent of a Swiss army knife. By having concise objects, you again increase the readability and maintenance of a system.

Open-Closed Principle (OCP)

The OCP states that classes should be open for extension and closed for modification, in that you should be able to add new features and extend a class without changing its internal behavior. The principle strives to avoid breaking the existing class and other classes that depend on it, which would create a ripple effect of bugs and errors throughout your application.

Liskov Substitution Principle (LSP)

The LSP dictates that you should be able to use any derived class in place of a parent class and have it behave in the same manner without modification. This principle is in line with OCP in that it ensures that a derived class does not affect the behavior of a parent class, or, put another way, derived classes must be substitutable for their base classes.

Interface Segregation Principle (ISP)

The ISP is all about splitting the methods of a contract into groups of responsibility and assigning interfaces to these groups to prevent a client from needing to implement one large interface and a host of methods that they do not use. The purpose behind this is so that classes wanting to use the same interfaces only need to implement a specific set of methods as opposed to a monolithic interface of methods.

Dependency Inversion Principle (DIP)

The DIP is all about isolating your classes from concrete implementations and having them depend on abstract classes or interfaces. It promotes the mantra of coding to an interface rather than an implementation, which increases flexibility within a system by ensuring you are not tightly coupled to one implementation.

Dependency Injection (DI) and Inversion of Control (IoC)

Closely linked to the DIP are the DI principle and the IOC principle. DI is the act of supplying a low level or dependent class via a constructor, method, or property. Used in conjunction with DI, these dependent classes can be inverted to interfaces or abstract classes that will lead to loosely coupled systems that are highly testable and easy to change.

In IoC, a system's flow of control is inverted compared to procedural programming. An example of this is an IoC container, whose purpose is to inject services into client code without having the client code specifying the concrete implementation. The control in this instance that is being inverted is the act of the client obtaining the service.

Throughout this book, you will examine each of the S.O.L.I.D. principles in more detail. Next, however, you will investigate some enterprise-level patterns designed to deal with specific scenarios that are built upon common design principles and design patterns.

FOWLER'S ENTERPRISE DESIGN PATTERNS

Martin Fowler's *Patterns of Enterprise Application Architecture* book is a best practice and patterns reference for building enterprise-level applications. As with the GoF patterns book, experienced developers will no doubt already be following many of the catalogued patterns. The value in Fowler's work, however, is the categorization of these patterns along with a common language for describing them. The book is split into two sections. The first half deals with n-tier applications and the organizing of data access, middleware, and presentation layers. The second half is a patterns reference rather like the GoF patterns book but more implementation specific.

Throughout this book, you will be looking at the ASP.NET implementations of Fowler's patterns. The following sections examine what the rest of the book will tackle.

Layering

Chapter 3 covers the options at your disposal to layer an enterprise ASP.NET application. You will look at the problems with the traditional code behind the model of web forms, and how to separate the concerns of presentation, business logic, and data access with a traditional layered approach.

Domain Logic Patterns

Chapter 4 examines three popular methods for organizing your business logic: Transaction Script, Active Record, and Domain Model.

Transaction Script

Transaction Script is the organization of business logic in a linear, procedural fashion. It maps fine-grained business use cases to fine-grained methods.

Active Record

Active Record organizes business logic in a way that closely matches the underlying data structure, namely an object that represents a row in a table.

Domain Model

The Domain Model pattern is an abstraction of real domain objects. Both data and behavior are modeled. Complex relationships between objects can exist that match the real domain.

You will look at how to use each of these patterns in ASP.NET and when it is appropriate to choose one pattern over another.

Object Relational Mapping

In Chapter 7 your attention will turn to how you can persist the state of our business entities as well as how you can retrieve them from a data store. You will look at the enterprise patterns required for the infrastructure code to support persistence, including the patterns introduced in the following sections.

Unit of Work

The Unit of Work pattern is designed to maintain a list of business objects that have been changed by a business transaction, whether that be adding, removing, or updating. The Unit of Work then coordinates the persistence of the changes as one atomic action. If there are problems, the entire transaction rolls back.

Repository

The Repository pattern, by and large, is used with logical collections of objects, or *aggregates* as they are better known. It acts as an in-memory collection or repository for business entities, completely abstracting away the underlying data infrastructure.

Data Mapper

The Data Mapper pattern is used to hydrate an object from raw data and transfer information from a business object to a database. Neither the business object nor the database is aware of the other.

Identity Map

An Identity Map keeps tabs on every object loaded from a database, ensuring everything is loaded only once. When objects are subsequently requested, the Identity Map is checked before retrieving from the database.

Lazy Loading

Lazy or deferred loading is the act of deferring the process of obtaining a resource until it's needed. If you imagine a Customer object with an address book, you could hydrate the customer from the database but hold the population of the address book until the address book is needed. This enables the on-demand loading of the address book, thus avoiding the hit to the database if the address data is never needed.

Query Object

The Query Object pattern is an implementation of a Gang of Four interpreter design pattern. The query object acts as an object-oriented query that is abstracted from the underlying database, referring to properties and classes rather than real tables and columns. Typically, you will also have a translator object to generate the native SQL to query the database.

Web Presentation Patterns

In Chapter 8, you will turn your attention to the presentation needs of enterprise-level ASP.NET applications. The chapter focuses on patterns designed to keep business logic separate from presentation logic. First you will look at the problems with the code behind model that was prominent in early web forms development; then you will investigate patterns that can be used to keep domain and presentation logic separate, as well as allowing the presentation layer to be effectively tested.

Each of these patterns is tasked with separating the concerns of presentation logic with that of business logic. The patterns covered for ASP.NET presentation needs are:

➤ Model-View-Presenter

➤ Model-View-Controller

➤ Front Controller

➤ Page Controller

Base, Behavioral, and Structural Patterns

Throughout the book, you will be seeing how to leverage other enterprise patterns found in Fowler's book in enterprise ASP.NET applications. These patterns will include Null Object, Separated Interface, Registry, and Gateway.

Null Object Pattern

Also known as the Special Case pattern, this acts as a return value rather than returning null to the calling code. The null object will share the same interface or inherit from the same base class as the expected result, which alleviates the need to check for null cases throughout the code base.

Separated Interface

The Separated Interface pattern is the act of keeping the interfaces in a separate assembly or namespace to the implementations. This ensures that the client is completely unaware of the concrete implementations and can promote programming to abstractions rather than implementations and the Dependency Inversion principle.

Gateway

The Gateway pattern allows clients to access complex resources via a simplified interface. The Gateway object basically wraps the resource API into a single method call that can be used anywhere in the application. It also hides any API complexities.

All of the enterprise patterns introduced here will be covered in more detail throughout the book with exercises to see how they are implemented in an ASP.NET scenario. The next section wraps up the chapter with a brief look at design methodologies and practices that use the patterns and principles you have been introduced to in this chapter.

OTHER DESIGN PRACTICES OF NOTE

In addition to the design patterns, principles, and enterprise patterns that have been covered so far, I would like to introduce you to a few design methodologies: test-driven development, behavior-driven development, and domain-driven development. This section won't cover these topics deeply because they are out of the scope of this book. However, the sample code featured in each of the chapters to demonstrate patterns and principles that you can download from www.wrox.com has been designed using these methodologies.

Test-driven Development (TDD)

Contrary to the name, TDD is more of a design methodology than a testing strategy; the name simply just doesn't do it justice. The main concept behind it is to allow your tests to shape the design of a system. When creating a software solution you start by writing a failing test to assert some business logic. Then you write the code to get that test to pass; last, you clean up any code via refactoring. This series of steps has been coined the *red-green-refactor*. The red and green refer to the colors that testing frameworks use to show tests passing and failing.

By going through the process of TDD, you end up with a loosely coupled system with a suite of tests that confirm all behavior. A byproduct of TDD is that your tests provide a sort of living documentation that describes what your system can and can't do. Because it is part of the system, the tests will never go out of date, unlike written documentation and code comments.

For more information on TDD, take a look at these books:

➤ *Test Driven Development: By Example* by Kent Beck

➤ *The Art of Unit Testing: With Examples in .NET* by Roy Osherove

➤ *Professional Enterprise .NET* by Jon Arking and Scott Millett (published by Wrox)

Domain-driven Design (DDD)

In a nutshell, DDD is a collection of patterns and principles that aid in your efforts to build applications that reflect an understanding of and meet the requirements of your business. Outside of that, it's a whole new way of thinking about your development methodology. DDD is about modeling the real domain by fully understanding it first and then placing all the terminology, rules, and logic into an abstract representation within your code, typically in the form of a domain model. DDD is not a framework, but it does have a set of building blocks or concepts that you can incorporate into your solution.

You'll use this methodology when you build the case study application in Chapters 10 and 11. Some of the deeper aspects of DDD are examined in Chapter 4.

For more information on DDD, take a look at these books:

➤ *Domain-Driven Design: Tackling Complexity in the Heart of Software* by Eric Evans

➤ *Applying Domain-Driven Design and Patterns: With Examples in C# and .NET* by Jimmy Nilsson

➤ *.NET Domain-Driven Design with C#: Problem - Design - Solution* by Tim McCarthy

Behavior-driven Design (BDD)

You can think of BDD as an evolution of TDD merged with DDD. BDD focuses on the behavior of a system rather than just testing it. The specifications created when using BDD use the same ubiquitous language as seen in the real domain, which can be beneficial for both technical and business users.

The documentation that is produced when writing specifications in BDD gives readers an idea of how a system will behave in various scenarios instead of simply verifying that methods are doing what they are supposed to. BDD is intended to meet the needs of both business and technical users by mixing in aspects of DDD with core TDD concepts. BDD can be performed using standard unit testing frameworks, but specific BDD frameworks have emerged, and BDD looks to be the next big thing.

Again, if you download from www.wrox.com the code for the case study you will build in Chapters 10 and 11, you will find BDD specifications written to demonstrate the behavior of the system. Unfortunately, at the time of writing, there were no books on the subject of BDD. Therefore, my advice is to search for as much information on the Internet as possible on this great methodology.

SUMMARY

In this chapter, you were introduced to a series of design patterns, principles, and enterprise patterns that can be leveraged in ASP.NET applications.

➤ The Gang of Four patterns are 23 patterns catalogued into a book known as the *Design Patterns Bible*. These design patterns are solution templates to common recurring problems. They can also be used as a shared vocabulary in teams when discussing complex problems.

➤ Robert Martin's S.O.L.I.D. design principles form the foundations to which many design patterns adhere. These principles are intended to promote object-oriented systems that are loosely coupled, highly maintainable, and adaptable to change.

➤ Fowler's enterprise patterns are designed to be leveraged in enterprise-level applications. They include patterns to organize business logic, patterns to organize presentation logic, patterns to organize data access, as well as a host of base patterns that you can use throughout a system.

The introduction to these patterns and principles has been fairly high level, but as you progress through the book, you will find a deeper explanation of all of the concepts discussed in this chapter, and ASP.NET implementations from real-world scenarios that you can hopefully relate to and apply in your systems to solve problems.

The next chapter takes a closer look at the Gang of Four patterns that will be covered in this book. You will be introduced to the practical knowledge necessary to use a design pattern template and how to read a pattern.

2

Dissecting the Pattern's Pattern

WHAT'S IN THIS CHAPTER?

➤ How to read GoF design patterns using the design templates

➤ Learning and understanding the design pattern groupings

➤ Knowing how to choose and apply a design pattern

➤ A quick example on refactoring existing code to use design patterns and principles to increase maintainability

Many books on the market give an overview and a template for individual design patterns but leave it up to the developer to learn how to decipher and apply the pattern. In this chapter, you will gain the practical knowledge necessary to use a design pattern solution template and apply it to your code base. You will then learn about the 23 design patterns and the groups they belong to. Finally, you will run through a quick exercise in which you will implement some design principles and patterns that you have read about.

HOW TO READ DESIGN PATTERNS

In the original design patterns book by the Gang of Four, each pattern was presented in a pattern template. The idea behind the pattern template was to enable the reader to decipher a pattern and learn about what set of problems it was designed to solve. In this book, I use a simplified version of the GoF pattern template to describe the GoF patterns, Fowler's enterprise patterns, and the S.O.L.I.D. design principles.

Gang of Four Pattern Template

The GoF book described each pattern using the following template:

➤ **Pattern Name and Classification:** The Pattern Name is important because it helps to form the common pattern vocabulary. The Classification defines the job of the pattern, be it Creational, Structural, or Behavioral. These classifications are examined in more detail later in this chapter.

➤ **Intent:** The Intent section reveals the problems that the pattern sets out to solve and why it is useful.

➤ **Also Known As:** The Also Known As section details the other names that some patterns are known as.

➤ **Motivation:** The Motivation section describes a problem scenario and how to use a design pattern to solve it.

➤ **Applicability:** The Applicability section lists the situations when it is advantageous to apply the design pattern.

➤ **Structure:** The Structure section is a graphical representation of the pattern, including the collaborations and relationships between objects. Typically this is shown as a UML diagram.

➤ **Participants:** The Participants are all the objects involved in the design pattern.

➤ **Collaborations:** The Collaborations section details how the participants work together to form the design pattern.

➤ **Consequences:** The Consequences section lists any benefits and liabilities caused when implementing the design pattern.

➤ **Implementations:** The Implementations section details any gotchas and best practices when implementing the design pattern.

➤ **Sample Code:** The Sample Code section shows an implementation of the design pattern.

➤ **Known Uses:** The Known Uses section shows implementations of the pattern in real-life applications.

➤ **Related Patterns:** The Related Patterns section lists other patterns that collaborate or work well with the design pattern.

Simplified Template

To avoid duplicating what the GoF book already does and to present the design patterns, enterprise patterns, and design principles in a more concise and standard format, I will be using a simplified pattern template as set out next.

Name and Intent

As with the GoF section with the same name, the Name and Intent section will reflect the purpose of the pattern or principle, its uses, the benefits it can have on your application, as well as the motivation behind using the pattern or principle.

UML Diagram

Where applicable, a UML diagram will show a graphical representation of the pattern or principle structure. A graphical representation will display the generic solution template as well as an implementation detailed in the code example.

Code Example

To really understand a design pattern or principle, it's important to see an implementation of it. The code example will be specific to ASP.NET in its content and will be pulled from real-life projects, not Hello World samples.

There will be an enterprise-level case study in the third part of this book so you can see how to use design patterns in all aspects of an application. Now that you understand how the design patterns will be presented to you and how you can read them, you can start to look in more detail at the groups of patterns that the GoF covers.

DESIGN PATTERN GROUPS

Twenty-three design patterns are featured in the GoF design patterns book, falling within one of three subgroups: Creational, Structural, or Behavioral. This section will take a quick look at each group and the patterns within. Throughout this book, you will examine the patterns that are useful for ASP.NET development.

Creational

Creational patterns deal with object construction and referencing. They abstract away the responsibility of instantiating instances of objects from the client, thus keeping code loosely coupled and the responsibility of creating complex objects in one place adhering to the Single Responsibility and Separation of Concerns principles.

Following are the patterns in the Creational group:

➤ **Abstract Factory:** Provides an interface to create families of related objects.

➤ **Factory:** Enables a class to delegate the responsibility of creating a valid object. This pattern is covered in Chapter 5.

➤ **Builder:** Enables various versions of an object to be constructed by separating the construction for the object itself.

➤ **Prototype:** Allows classes to be copied or cloned from a prototype instance rather than creating new instances.

➤ **Singleton:** Enables a class to be instantiated once with a single global point of access to it.

Structural

Structural patterns deal with the composition and relationships of objects to fulfill the needs of larger systems.

Following are the patterns in the Structural group:

> ➤ **Adapter:** Enables classes of incompatible interfaces to be used together. This pattern is covered in this chapter.

> ➤ **Bridge:** Separates an abstraction from its implementation, allowing implementations and abstractions to vary independently of one another.

> ➤ **Composite:** Allows a group of objects representing hierarchies to be treated in the same way as a single instance of an object. This pattern is covered in Chapter 5.

> ➤ **Decorator:** Can dynamically surround a class and extend its behavior. This pattern is covered in Chapter 5.

> ➤ **Facade:** Provides a simple interface and controls access to a series of complicated interfaces and subsystems. This pattern is covered in Chapter 6.

> ➤ **Flyweight:** Provides a way to share data among many small classes in an efficient manner.

> ➤ **Proxy:** Provides a placeholder to a more complex class that is costly to instantiate. This pattern is covered in Chapter 7.

Behavioral

Behavioral patterns deal with the communication between objects in terms of responsibility and algorithms. The patterns in this group encapsulate complex behavior and abstract it away from the flow of control of a system, thus enabling complex systems to be easily understood and maintained.

Following are the patterns in the Behavioral group:

> ➤ **Chain of Responsibility:** Allows commands to be chained together dynamically to handle a request. This pattern is covered in Chapter 9.

> ➤ **Command:** Encapsulates a method as an object and separates the execution of a command from its invoker. This pattern is covered in Chapter 9.

> ➤ **Interpreter:** Specifies how to evaluate sentences in a language.

> ➤ **Iterator:** Provides a way to navigate a collection in a formalized manner.

> ➤ **Mediator:** Defines an object that allows communication between two other objects without them knowing about one another.

> ➤ **Memento:** Allows you to restore an object to its previous state.

> ➤ **Observer:** Defines the way one or more classes can be alerted to a change in another class.

> ➤ **State:** Allows an object to alter its behavior by delegating to a separate and changeable state object. This pattern is covered in Chapter 5.

> ➤ **Strategy:** Enables an algorithm to be encapsulated within a class and switched at run time to alter an object's behavior. This pattern is covered in Chapter 5.

> ➤ **Template Method:** Defines the control of flow of an algorithm but allows subclasses to override or implement execution steps. This pattern is covered in Chapter 5.

> ➤ **Visitor:** Enables new functionality to be performed on a class without affecting its structure.

You should now understand the role of each of the GoF patterns. You will examine many of these patterns in greater detail in the remainder of this book. With such a large menu to choose from, it's important to understand how to go about selecting and applying the most appropriate pattern for your problem. This is exactly what you will learn about in the next section.

HOW TO CHOOSE AND APPLY A DESIGN PATTERN

You can choose from many design patterns, so how do you identify which one is appropriate for your problem? To know which design pattern to use and how to apply the solution template to your specific problem, it's important to understand these guidelines.

> ➤ You can't apply patterns without knowing about them. The first important step is to expand your knowledge and study patterns and principles both in the abstract and concrete form. You can implement a pattern in many ways. The more you see different implementations of patterns, the more you will understand the intent of the pattern and how a single pattern can have varying implementations.

> ➤ Do you need to introduce the complexity of a design pattern? It's common for developers to try to use a pattern to solve every problem when they are studying patterns. You always need to weigh the upfront time needed to implement a pattern for the benefit that it's going to give. Remember the KISS principle: Keep It Simple, Stupid.

> ➤ Generalize your problem; identify the issues you're facing in a more abstract manner. Look at how the intent of each pattern and principle is written, and see if your problem fits with the problem that a particular pattern or principle is trying to solve. Remember that design patterns are high-level solutions; try to abstract your problem, and don't focus too hard on the details of your specific issue.

> ➤ Look at patterns of a similar nature and patterns in the same group. Just because you have used a pattern before doesn't mean it will always be the correct pattern choice when solving a problem.

> ➤ Encapsulate what varies. Look at what will likely change with your application. If you know that a special offer discount algorithm will change over time, look for a pattern that will help you change it without impacting the rest of your application.

> ➤ After you have chosen a design pattern, ensure that you use the language of your pattern along with the language of the domain when naming the participants in a solution. For example, if you are using the strategy pattern to provide a solution for costing various shipping couriers, name them accordingly, such as `FedExShippingCostStrategy`. By using the pattern's common vocabulary along with the language of your domain, you will immediately make your code more readable and understandable to other developers with patterns knowledge.

When it comes to design patterns, there is no substitute for studying. The more you know about each of the design patterns, the better equipped you will be at applying them. Scan the intent of each pattern to refresh your memory when you have a problem and are looking for a solution.

A great learning exercise is to try to identify patterns in the .NET Framework. For example, the ASP.NET Cache uses the Singleton pattern; creating a new Guid uses the Factory pattern; the .NET 2 XML classes use the Factory pattern whereas version 1.0 did not.

By now you should have an understanding of how to read and decipher a design pattern, an overview of the list of design patterns, and the knowledge of how to choose and apply a pattern. To help the cement this knowledge and make the abstract talk of patterns into something more concrete, you will walk through a quick example to see how you can apply design patterns and principles to legacy code.

A QUICK PATTERN EXAMPLE

It's all well and good to talk about how great patterns and principles are, but it's important to see them in action. With this in mind, this section examines how a simple piece of ASP.NET code that you have probably seen countless times before can be improved with the use of patterns and design principles.

You are going to look at a section of code that you might find in a typical e-commerce application — specifically, the code that retrieves all products within a given category. Figure 2-1 shows a class diagram containing a `ProductService` class with the single `GetAllProductsIn` method, a `Product` class that represents the store's products, and a `ProductRepository` class that is used to retrieve products from a database.

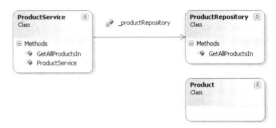

FIGURE 2-1

The job of the `ProductService` class is to coordinate the retrieval of a list of products from the repository for a given category ID and then store the results in cache so the next call can be executed faster.

Before going any further, you need to build the classes and look at the code.

1. Fire up Visual Studio and create a new solution named `ASPPatterns.Chap2`, as shown in Figure 2-2.

2. Add a new C# Class Library project to this solution by selecting File ➪ Add ➪ New Project, and name the project `ASPPatterns.Chap2.Service`. Delete the `Class1.cs` class file that visual studio creates for you by default.

3. Add a new class to the project named `Product`:

```
public class Product
{
}
```

4. Add a new class to the project named `ProductRepository` with the following code listing:

```
public class ProductRepository
{
    public IList<Product> GetAllProductsIn(int categoryId)
    {
        IList<Product> products = new List<Product>();

        // Database operation to populate products …

        return products;
    }
}
```

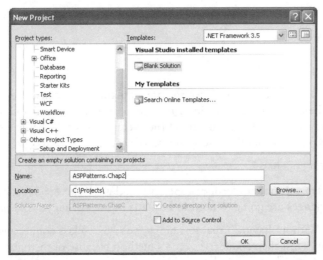

FIGURE 2-2

5. Add the `ProductService` class with the following definition. You also need to add a reference to the `System.Web` namespace because this class deals with the HTTP context cache API:

```
using System;
using System.Collections.Generic;
using System.Linq;
using System.Text;
using System.Web;

namespace ASPPatterns.Chap2.Service
{
    public class ProductService
    {
        private ProductRepository _productRepository;

        public ProductService()
        {
            _productRepository = new ProductRepository();
        }

        public IList<Product> GetAllProductsIn(int categoryId)
        {
            IList<Product> products;
            string storageKey = string.Format(
                                    "products_in_category_id_{0}", categoryId);

            products = (List<Product>)HttpContext.Current.Cache.Get(storageKey);

            if (products == null)
            {
                products = _productRepository.GetAllProductsIn(categoryId);
                HttpContext.Current.Cache.Insert(storageKey, products);
```

```
            }

            return products;
        }
    }
```

The `Product` and `ProductRepository` classes don't require any explanation because they are simple placeholders in this scenario. The `ProductService` single method is straightforward and it simply coordinates the retrieval of products from the cache, and in the event of the cache being empty, the retrieval of products from the repository and the insertion into the cache.

So what's wrong with the current codebase?

➤   The `ProductService` depends on the `ProductRepository` class. If the `ProductRepository` class changes its API, changes are going to need to be made in the `ProductService` class.

➤   The code is untestable. Without having a real `ProductRepository` class connecting to a real database, you're unable to test the `ProductService`'s method because of the tight coupling that exists between these two classes. Another problem related to testing is the dependency on the HTTP context for use in the caching of the products. It is hard to test code that is so tightly coupled to HTTP context.

➤   You're stuck with the HTTP context for caching. In its current state, using a different cache storage provider such as Velocity or Memcached would require altering of the `ProductService` class and any other class that uses caching. Velocity and Memcached are both distributed memory object caching systems that can be used in place of ASP.NET's default caching mechanism.

Now that you know what's wrong with the code, you can look at fixing it.

Refactoring to Principles

First, consider the problem of the `ProductService` class dependency on the `ProductRepository` class. In its current state, the `ProductService` class is fragile; if the API of the `ProductRepository` class changes, the `ProductService` class might need to be modified. This breaks the separation of concerns and single responsibility principle.

The Dependency Inversion Principle

> *Depend on abstractions, not on concretions.*

We can employ the Dependency Inversion principle to decouple the `ProductService` class from the `ProductRepository` by having both depend on an abstraction — an interface. Open the `Product Repository` class, right-click on the class name, and select Refactor ⇨ Extract Interface from the context menu that appears. When the Extract Interface dialog appear, check the box next to the method name to ensure that it is included in the interface, and click OK. A new interface is created for you named `IProductRepository`. Clean up the code produced by including the System.Collections.Generic namespace as a using statement and marking the interface as public, which can be seen in the following code listing:

```
using System;
using System.Collections.Generic;

namespace ASPPatterns.Chap2.Service
{
    public interface IProductRepository
    {
        IList<Product> GetAllProductsIn(int categoryId);
    }
}
```

The ProductRepository class is amended to implement the newly created interface, like so:

```
public class ProductRepository : IProductRepository
{
    public IList<Product> GetAllProductsIn(int categoryId)
    {
        IList<Product> products = new List<Product>();

        // Database operation to populate products …

        return products;
    }
}
```

The last thing you need to do is update the ProductService class to ensure that it references the interface rather than the concrete implementation:

```
public class ProductService
{
    private IProductRepository _productRepository;

    public ProductService()
    {
        _productRepository = new ProductRepository();
    }

    public IList<Product> GetAllProductsIn(int categoryId)
    {
        …
    }
}
```

What have you achieved by introducing a new interface? The ProductService class now depends only on an abstraction rather than a concrete implementation; this means that the ProductService class is completely ignorant of any implementation, ensuring that it is less fragile and the code base as a whole is less resilient to change.

However, there is one slight problem: the `ProductService` class is still responsible for creating the concrete implementation and currently it is impossible to test the code without a valid `ProductRepository` class. Dependency Injection can help here.

The Dependency Injection Principle

The `ProductService` class is still tied to the concrete implementation of the `ProductRepository` because it's currently the job of the `ProductService` class to create the instance. This can be seen in the `ProductService` class constructor. Dependency Injection can move the responsibility of creating the `ProductRepository` implementation out of the `ProductService` class and having it injected via the class's constructor, as can be seen in the following code listing:

```
public class ProductService
{
    private IProductRepository _productRepository;

    public ProductService(IProductRepository productRepository)
    {
        _productRepository = productRepository;
    }

    public IList<Product> GetAllProductsIn(int categoryId)
    {
        ...
    }
}
```

This enables a substitute to be passed to the `ProductService` class during testing, which enables you to test the `ProductService` class in isolation. By removing the responsibility of obtaining dependencies from the `ProductService`, you are ensuring that the `ProductService` class adheres to the Single Responsibility principle: it is now only concerned with the coordinating of retrieving data from the cache or repository and not for creating the concrete `IProductRepository` implementation.

Dependency Injection comes in three flavors: Constructer, Method, and Property. You have just used Constructor Injection. Dependency Injection is explored in more depth later in the book.

The last thing you need to do is sort out the dependency on the HTTP `Context` for your caching requirements. For this you will employ the services of a simple design pattern.

Refactoring to the Adapter Pattern

Because you don't own the source code to the HTTP `Context` class, you can't simply create an interface for it and have it implement it like you did for the `ProductRepository` class. Luckily, this type of problem has been solved countless times before, and there is a design pattern to help you out. The Adapter pattern basically translates one interface for a class into a compatible interface, so you can apply this pattern to change the HTTP `Context` caching API into a compatible API that you want to use. Then you can inject this via an interface into the `ProductService` class using the Dependency Injection principle.

Create a new interface named ICacheStorage with the following contract:

```
public interface ICacheStorage
{
    void Remove(string key);
    void Store(string key, object data);
    T Retrieve<T>(string key);
}
```

Now that you have the new interface, you can update the ProductService class to use it instead of the HTTP Context implementation:

```
public class ProductService
{
    private IProductRepository _productRepository;
    private ICacheStorage _cacheStorage;

    public ProductService(IProductRepository productRepository,
                          ICacheStorage cacheStorage)
    {
        _productRepository = productRepository;
        _cacheStorage = cacheStorage;
    }

    public IList<Product> GetAllProductsIn(int categoryId)
    {
        IList<Product> products;
        string storageKey = string.Format(
                              "products_in_category_id_{0}", categoryId);
        products = _cacheStorage.Retrieve<List<Product>>(storageKey);

        if (products == null)
        {
            products = _productRepository.GetAllProductsIn(categoryId);
            _cacheStorage.Store(storageKey, products);
        }

        return products;
    }
}
```

The problem now is that the HTTP Context Cache API can't implicitly implement the new ICacheStorage interface. How can the Adapter pattern help you out of this pickle?

The intent of the Adapter design pattern as stated by the Gang of Four is as follows:

Converts the interface of a class into another interface clients expect.

That sounds like exactly what you're after.

Figure 2-3 shows the UML representation of the Adapter pattern.

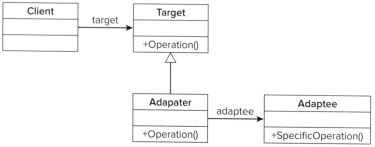

FIGURE 2-3

As you can see in Figure 2-3, a client has a reference to an abstraction — the `Target`. In this case this is the `ICacheStorage` interface. The `Adapter` is an implementation of the `Target` interface and simply delegates the `Operation` method to the `Adaptee`, which runs its own `SpecificOperation` method. You can see that the `Adapter` simply wraps an instance of the `Adaptee` and delegates the work off to it while implementing the contract of the `Target` interface.

Take a look at what the UML looks like for this specific problem. Figure 2-4 shows the classes you have and the `Adapter` class you need to implement the Adapter pattern with the HTTP `Context` cache API.

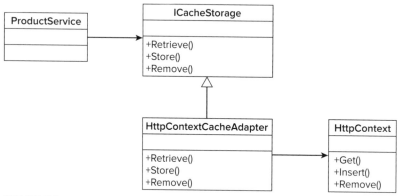

FIGURE 2-4

In Figure 2-4, you can see that a new class — `HttpContextCacheAdapter` — is needed. This class is a wrapper for the HTTP `Context` cache and delegates work to its methods.

To implement the Adapter pattern, you need to create the missing `HttpContextCacheAdapter`, so add a new class named `HttpContextCacheAdapter` with the following definition to the project:

```
using System;
using System.Collections.Generic;
using System.Linq;
using System.Text;
```

```csharp
using System.Web;

namespace ASPPatterns.Chap2.Service
{
    public class HttpContextCacheAdapter : ICacheStorage
    {
        public void Remove(string key)
        {
            HttpContext.Current.Cache.Remove(key);
        }

        public void Store(string key, object data)
        {
            HttpContext.Current.Cache.Insert(key, data);
        }

        public T Retrieve<T>(string key)
        {
            T itemStored = (T)HttpContext.Current.Cache.Get(key);
            if (itemStored == null)
                itemStored = default(T);

            return itemStored;
        }
    }
}
```

It is now easy to implement a new caching solution without affecting any existing code. For instance, if you wanted to use Memcached or MS Velocity, all you would need to do is create an `Adapter` that allows the `ProductService` class to interact with the caching storage provider via the common `ICacheStorage` interface.

The Adapter pattern is deceptively simple; its sole purpose is to let classes with incompatible interfaces work together.

The `Adapter` isn't the only pattern that can help with caching data. You will be looking at how the Proxy design pattern can help with caching later in the case study in Chapter 11.

Leveraging Enterprise Patterns

In the current design, to use the `ProductService` class you always have to provide the constructor with an implementation of `ICacheStorage`, but what if you don't want to cache data? One option is to provide a null reference, but that would mean littering the code with checks for a null `ICacheStorage` implementation. A far better way is to use the Null Object pattern for these special cases.

Null Object Pattern

The Null Object pattern, sometimes called the Special Case pattern, is another deceptively simple pattern. It's useful when you don't want to specify or can't specify a valid instance of a class, and you don't really want to pass around a `null` reference. The role of the `null` object is to replace the `null` reference and implement the same interface but with no behavior.

Here's how the Null Object pattern can help if you don't want to cache data in the `ProductService` class. Add a new class to the project named `NullObjectCache` with the following definition:

```
public class NullObjectCache : ICacheStorage
{
    public void Remove(string key)
    {
        // Do nothing
    }

    public void Store(string key, object data)
    {
        // Do nothing
    }

    public T Retrieve<T>(string storageKey)
    {
        return default(T);
    }
}
```

Code file NullObjectCache.cs in project ASPPatterns.Chap2.Service

The `NullObjectCache` can now be passed to the `ProductService`. When asked to cache data, it will do nothing and will always return `null` to the `ProductService`, ensuring no data will be cached.

In the code download that accompanies this book, you will find a second project of unit tests using the NUnit framework that verify the behavior of the `ProductService` class.

SUMMARY

This chapter delved a little deeper into the world of design patterns. Here's a recap of what was covered.

The chapter began with a discussion on how to read design patterns. You looked at the pattern template the GoF uses to describe each pattern in a consistent manner. You then discussed the more concise template that will be used to describe the patterns and principles that will be presented in the rest of this book.

The GoF design patterns belong to one of three groups: Creational, Structural, or Behavioral. Creational design patterns deal with the responsibility of constructing objects; Structural design patterns are concerned with getting objects to work together to produce new functionality; and Behavioral design patterns are all about algorithms and communication.

Knowing when, how, and which design pattern to apply is a hard task for beginners but one that gets significantly easier with experience. Design patterns are high-level abstract solutions; knowing when to apply them requires you to think about your problem in a high-level, abstract way. By generalizing your problem, you stand a much better chance of easily finding a solution that can resolve it. Design patterns are not appropriate to use for all problems; sometimes a simple solution will suffice, and the need to introduce complexity just to incorporate a design pattern is not necessary.

The chapter concluded with a brief look at how you can apply some of the patterns and principles that you have been introduced to. You looked at a small piece of code that's typical to a host of ASP.NET applications and showed how refactoring to some design principles and design patterns can improve the quality of the code without changing its behavior. You first refactored to the Dependency Inversion principle to remove tight coupling on dependent classes. To further improve loose coupling and to enable us to test the code in isolation, you employed the Dependency Injection principle to supply the dependent classes via the `ProductService` constructor. You then leveraged the Adapter design pattern to enable the HTTP `Context` cache API to implement a caching interface that we developed. Last, you looked at how the Null Object pattern can be used as a stand-in when we didn't want to cache data.

The second part of this book explores how patterns can be used in different parts of an ASP.NET application. In the next chapter, you will be introduced to the concept of logical separation in an ASP.NET application. You will look at the benefits of a layered application over the traditional ASP.NET code-behind model.

PART II

The Anatomy of an ASP.NET Application: Learning and Applying Patterns

3

Layering Your Application and Separating Your Concerns

WHAT'S IN THIS CHAPTER?

➤ The benefits of a layered design over the traditional ASP.NET web forms code-behind model

➤ The concepts of logic layering and the separation of your applications concerns

➤ The responsibilities of each distinct layer in an enterprise level ASP.NET application

➤ Example code refactoring from the Smart UI antipattern to a layered approach

This chapter discusses the concept of logical separation in an ASP.NET application. It covers the Smart UI antipattern and its shortcomings when used in enterprise-level ASP.NET applications. It then introduces the benefits of a layered approach to building an ASP.NET application over the code-behind model and what it means to truly separate your concerns. Following that, it looks at the role of each layer and identifies the responsibilities of each of them; the layers which form the content for the remaining chapters of this book.

APPLICATION ARCHITECTURE AND DESIGN

You cannot build a maintainable and scalable application on poor foundations. Planning a good architecture is critical to the success of an application. Before examining a structured approach to designing your application, you must learn why you need to think about the logical structure of your application and the problems you will encounter if you do not start with a good architectural footing.

Antipattern — Smart UI

ASP.NET web forms and Visual Studio make it incredibly easy to create applications simply by dragging and dropping controls onto a HTML designer. Accompanying a page, the code-behind file contains all the event handling, data access, and business logic of the application. The problem with this approach is that all concerns are mingled, causing problems for testing and resulting in a duplication of business logic because it is difficult to reuse logic that is intrinsically tied to a particular view (ASPX page).

Smart UI applications aren't to be avoided at all costs; they are great for prototyping and for throwaway or short-lived applications. The problem, however, is that temporary applications that are successful often are modified and built upon and become mission-critical applications that are hard to maintain.

Seeing, it's said, is believing. To that end, create an example of a Smart UI web application and start to add some business logic to it, and you should see how the concerns and responsibilities are intertwined. Later in the chapter you will rewrite the code and show that, by layering your application, you can adhere to the Separation of Concerns (SoC) principles, thus allowing your application to be far more maintainable and scalable.

To demonstrate the Smart UI antipattern, you will build a page that displays products in a grid similar to what you might typically find in an e-commerce application. The page will list products for sale, displaying their name, recommended retail price (RRP), selling price, discount, and savings percentage. Later you will introduce some business logic by allowing the user to apply a trade discount to the products on sale, but first, the initial display:

1. Fire up Visual Studio and create a new blank solution named `ASPPatterns.Chap3.SmartUI` and add a new web application to it named `ASPPatterns.Chap3.SmartUI.Web`

2. After Visual Studio has built your new web application, add a new SQL express database to the project by right-clicking on the web site and selecting Add ⇨ New Item and selecting a SQL Server Database. Name the database `Shop.mdf`.

3. Now you need to add a table to the database to hold information on the products. Right-click on the newly created database and select Open. When the database explorer opens, right-click on the `tables` folder and select New Table from the context-sensitive menu. Create the table with the schema as shown in Figure 3-1, and name the table `Products`. Ensure you set the `ProductId` to an identity column so that it will automatically generate an ID.

Column Name	Data Type	Allow Nulls
⚷ ProductId	int	☐
ProductName	nvarchar(50)	☐
RRP	smallmoney	☐
SellingPrice	smallmoney	☐
		☐

FIGURE 3-1

4. Add the data in Figure 3-2 to the table.

5. With the table created, you can simply drag and drop it onto the `Default.aspx` page. This automatically creates a `GridView` and adds a `SQLDataSource` control to the page. You should now be able to run the web application and see all the products listed from the database.

ProductId	ProductName	RRP	SellingPrice
1	Drill	109.9900	99.9900
2	Hammer	8.9900	7.9900
3	Shovel	9.9900	9.9900
* NULL	NULL	NULL	NULL

FIGURE 3-2

6. Now add the extra columns that will show any discount and savings. Edit the source file for
`Default.aspx` to include the new template columns and the `OnRowDataBound` property, as
shown in the following listing:

```
<asp:GridView ID="GridView1" runat="server" AutoGenerateColumns="False"
              DataKeyNames="ProductId"
              DataSourceID="SqlDataSource1"
              EmptyDataText="There are no data records to display."
              OnRowDataBound="GridView1_RowDataBound">
    <Columns>
        <asp:BoundField DataField="ProductId"
                        HeaderText="ProductId" ReadOnly="True"
                        SortExpression="ProductId" />
        <asp:BoundField DataField="ProductName" HeaderText="ProductName"
                        SortExpression="ProductName" />
        <asp:BoundField DataField="RRP" HeaderText="RRP"
                        SortExpression="RRP" DataFormatString="{0:C}" />
        <asp:BoundField DataField="SellingPrice" HeaderText="SellingPrice"
                        SortExpression="SellingPrice"
            DataFormatString="{0:C}" />
        <asp:TemplateField HeaderText="Discount">
            <ItemTemplate>
                <asp:Label runat="server" ID="lblDiscount"></asp:Label>
            </ItemTemplate>
        </asp:TemplateField>
        <asp:TemplateField HeaderText="Savings">
            <ItemTemplate>
                <asp:Label runat="server" ID="lblSavings"></asp:Label>
            </ItemTemplate>
        </asp:TemplateField>
    </Columns>
</asp:GridView>
```

7. After that is done, open the code-behind page, `Default.aspx.cs`, and add the following
three methods:

**Available for
download on
Wrox.com**

```
public partial class Default : System.Web.UI.Page
{
    protected void GridView1_RowDataBound(object sender,
                                          GridViewRowEventArgs e)
    {
        if (e.Row.RowType == DataControlRowType.DataRow)
        {
            decimal RRP = decimal.Parse(((
                System.Data.DataRowView)e.Row.DataItem)["RRP"].ToString());
            decimal SellingPrice = decimal.Parse(((
                System.Data.DataRowView)e.Row.DataItem)["SellingPrice"].ToString());

            Label lblSavings =
                (Label)e.Row.FindControl("lblSavings");
            Label lblDiscount =
                (Label)e.Row.FindControl("lblDiscount");

            lblSavings.Text =
              DisplaySavings(RRP, SellingPrice);
```

```
                    lblDiscount.Text = DisplayDiscount(RRP, SellingPrice);
            }
    }

    protected string DisplayDiscount(decimal RRP, decimal SalePrice)
    {
        string discountText = "";

        if (RRP > SalePrice)
            discountText = String.Format("{0:C}", (RRP - SalePrice));

        return discountText;
    }

    protected string DisplaySavings(decimal RRP, decimal SalePrice)
    {
        string savingsTest = "";

        if (RRP > SalePrice)
            savingsTest = (1 - (SalePrice / RRP)).ToString("#%");

        return savingsTest;
    }
}
```

Default.aspx.cs located in the ASPPatterns.Chap3.SmartUI.Web project

The `GridView1_RowDataBound` method is called when each data row is bound to data in the `GridView` control. The method obtains the RRP and selling price and uses `DisplayDiscount` and `DisplaySavings` methods to work out the correct discount. Then it updates the corresponding label server controls. By adding these methods, you are introducing business logic into the user interface (UI) along with the data access. This means that if we wanted to display product prices on a different page, we would need to duplicate the business logic or create some kind of static helper methods.

The page is not only taking the responsibility of the business logic; as it stands, the single ASP.NET web form page is responsible for the data access requirements. Because you used the RAD server controls to provide data access, it will be extremely difficult to test the page and stub out a data access implementation.

Now that the base functionality is in place, you can add the extra business requirements, which will begin to expose the issues you will face when coding to the Smart UI pattern. The business logic that you will be adding will enable a trade discount to be applied to the prices so that they reflect an extra 5 percent of savings. The UI will need a new control: a drop-down list that will enable the users to specify the discount they want to see applied to the products — trade discount or no discount.

Modify the `Default.aspx` page so that there is a new drop-down list control and the selling price is changed to a template field, as can be seen in the following code listing:

```
Display prices with
        <asp:DropDownList ID="ddlDiscountType" runat="server" AutoPostBack="True"
            onselectedindexchanged="ddlDiscountType_SelectedIndexChanged">
            <asp:ListItem Value="0">No Discount</asp:ListItem>
```

```
        <asp:ListItem Value="1">Trade Discount</asp:ListItem>
</asp:DropDownList>

<asp:GridView ID="GridView1" runat="server" AutoGenerateColumns="False"
    DataKeyNames="ProductId" DataSourceID="SqlDataSource1"
    EmptyDataText="There are no data records to display."
    OnRowDataBound="GridView1_RowDataBound">
    <Columns>
        <asp:BoundField DataField="ProductId" HeaderText="ProductId"
                        ReadOnly="True" SortExpression="ProductId" />
        <asp:BoundField DataField="ProductName" HeaderText="ProductName"
                        SortExpression="ProductName" />
        <asp:BoundField DataField="RRP" HeaderText="RRP"
                        SortExpression="RRP" DataFormatString="{0:C}" />
        <asp:TemplateField HeaderText="SellingPrice"
                        SortExpression="SellingPrice">
            <ItemTemplate>
                <asp:Label ID="lblSellingPrice" runat="server"
                    Text='<%# Bind("SellingPrice") %>'></asp:Label>
            </ItemTemplate>
        </asp:TemplateField>
        <asp:TemplateField HeaderText="Discount">
            <ItemTemplate>
                <asp:Label runat="server" ID="lblDiscount"></asp:Label>
            </ItemTemplate>
        </asp:TemplateField>
        <asp:TemplateField HeaderText="Savings">
            <ItemTemplate>
                <asp:Label runat="server" ID="lblSavings"></asp:Label>
            </ItemTemplate>
        </asp:TemplateField>
    </Columns>
</asp:GridView>
```

Default.aspx located in the ASPPatterns.Chap3.SmartUI.Web project

Now update the code-behind so that the logic that will apply the extra trade discount can be added. This can be seen in the bolded code that follows, with the introduction of a new method called ApplyExtraDiscountsTo and the update to the GridView1_RowDataBound event that will set the selling price dependent on the discount strategy applied:

```
public partial class Default : System.Web.UI.Page
{
    protected void GridView1_RowDataBound(object sender, GridViewRowEventArgs e)
    {
        if (e.Row.RowType == DataControlRowType.DataRow)
        {
            decimal RRP = decimal.Parse(((
             System.Data.DataRowView)e.Row.DataItem)["RRP"].ToString());
            decimal SellingPrice = decimal.Parse(((
             System.Data.DataRowView)e.Row.DataItem)["SellingPrice"].ToString());

            Label lblSellingPrice = (Label)e.Row.FindControl("lblSellingPrice");
            Label lblSavings = (Label)e.Row.FindControl("lblSavings");
```

```
            Label lblDiscount = (Label)e.Row.FindControl("lblDiscount");

        lblSavings.Text = DisplaySavings(RRP,
                        ApplyExtraDiscountsTo(SellingPrice));
        lblDiscount.Text = DisplayDiscount(RRP,
                        ApplyExtraDiscountsTo(SellingPrice));
        lblSellingPrice.Text =  String.Format("{0:C}",
                        ApplyExtraDiscountsTo(SellingPrice));
    }
}

protected string DisplayDiscount(decimal RRP, decimal SalePrice)
{
    string discountText = "";

    if (RRP > SalePrice)
        discountText = String.Format("{0:C}", (RRP - SalePrice));

    return discountText;
}

protected string DisplaySavings(decimal RRP, decimal SalePrice)
{
    string savingsTest = "";

    if (RRP > SalePrice)
        savingsTest = (1 - (SalePrice / RRP)).ToString("#%");

    return savingsTest;
}

protected decimal ApplyExtraDiscountsTo(decimal OriginalSalePrice)
{
    decimal price = OriginalSalePrice;

    int discountType = Int16.Parse( this.ddlDiscountType.SelectedValue);

    if (discountType == 1)
    {
        price = price * 0.95M;
    }

    return price;
}

protected void ddlDiscountType_SelectedIndexChanged(object sender, EventArgs e)
{
    GridView1.DataBind();
}

    }
}
```

Default.aspx.cs located in the ASPPatterns.Chap3.SmartUI.Web project

You can now run the application and change discount strategies to see the prices with the trade and no discounts applied to them.

What's wrong with the method you used to display the products and prices? Well, nothing if the application stopped here, but because this is only part of a larger application, the capability to apply discounts will be needed elsewhere, and in its present state the logic is embedded in this single page. This means that the logic will be duplicated when new features are added.

Separating Your Concerns

An antidote to the Smart UI antipattern is the notion of layering your applications. Layering an application is a form of separation of concerns and can be achieved via namespaces, folders, or with separate projects. Figure 3-3 shows the typical architecture of an enterprise-level layered ASP.NET application.

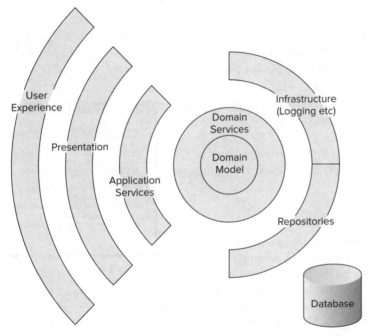

FIGURE 3-3

To demonstrate how you can achieve SoC through layering an ASP.NET application and to look at details of each of the layers, you will reconstruct the small e-commerce page that you built earlier to demonstrate the Smart UI antipattern.

1. Create a new blank solution in Visual Studio and name it `ASPPatterns.Chap3.Layered`.

2. Add a new class library project to the solution by right-clicking the solution name and selecting Add ➪ New Project. Name the new project `ASPPatterns.Chap3.Layered.Repository`.

3. Add a further three class library projects to the solution named:

    ➤ `ASPPatterns.Chap3.Layered.Model`

    ➤ `ASPPatterns.Chap3.Layered.Service`

    ➤ `ASPPatterns.Chap3.Layered.Presentation`

4. Add a new web application to the project by selecting Add ⇨ New Project and selecting the Web Application Project. Name the project `ASPPatterns.Chap3.Layered.WebUI`.

5. Right-click on the `ASPPatterns.Chap3.Layered.Repository` project and add a project reference to the `ASPPatterns.Chap3.Layered.Model` project.

6. Right-click on the `ASPPatterns.Chap3.Layered.Service` project and add a project reference to the `ASPPatterns.Chap3.Layered.Repository` and `ASPPatterns.Chap3.Layered.Model` projects.

7. Right-click on the `ASPPatterns.Chap3.Layered.Presentation` project and add a project reference to the `ASPPatterns.Chap3.Layered.Model` and `ASPPatterns.Chap3.Layered.Service` projects.

8. Right-click on the `ASPPatterns.Chap3.Layered.WebUI` web application and add a project reference to the `ASPPatterns.Chap3.Layered.Model`, `ASPPatterns.Chap3.Layered.Service`, `ASPPatterns.Chap3.Layered.Presentation`, and `ASPPatterns.Chap3.Layered.Repository` projects.

9. Add a solution folder for each of the layers of the application so that your solution resembles Figure 3-4.

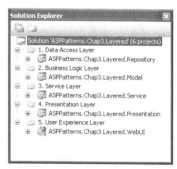

FIGURE 3-4

With your layered project structure complete, you can begin to tackle each of the concerns of the application one at a time, beginning with the business layer.

Business Layer

You're going to start by implementing the business logic for the application. In the Smart UI example, you will remember that the business logic was intermingled with the presentation logic in the code-behind of the ASPX page. With the layered approach, you'll create a domain model to hold all behavior and data related to the business of the simple e-commerce store that we are modeling. You will learn a lot more about the Domain Model pattern in the next chapter, but in a nutshell, think of it as the conceptual model of the system containing all the entities involved and their relationships.

> *The Domain Model pattern is designed to organize complex business logic and relationships. You will look at the Domain Model pattern in more detail in the next chapter.*

Figure 3-5 shows the model you will be using. The `Product` class represents the products of the e-commerce store; the `Price` class will contain the business logic to determine savings and discount; and the discount strategy implementations will contain the logic to apply the trade discount and no discounts, respectively.

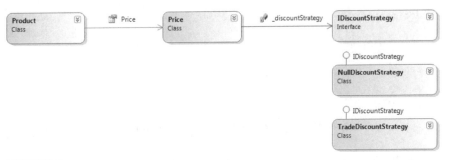

FIGURE 3-5

You will create the domain model in the ASPPatterns.Chap3.Layered.Model project. Add a new interface to the ASPPatterns.Chap3.Layered.Model project named IDiscountStrategy with the following definition:

```
public interface IDiscountStrategy
{
    decimal ApplyExtraDiscountsTo(decimal OriginalSalePrice);
}
```

IDiscountStrategy.cs located in the ASPPatterns.Chap3.Layered.Model project

The purpose of naming the interface IDiscountStrategy is that it actually matches a design pattern named Strategy. You will learn a lot more about the Strategy pattern in Chapter 5; this pattern is being applied here because it enables algorithms to be selected and changed at runtime. The algorithms that will be applied to the Price object are the Discount algorithms. If you look back at the Smart UI example, you will notice that the language I used to describe the process of applying discounts to products used the word *strategy*. When describing a problem, generalize it and focus on the variations. By doing so you will often happen upon the name of a design pattern, and the solution to your problem will present itself without you even looking for it.

 The Strategy pattern enables an algorithm to be encapsulated within a class and switched at runtime to alter an object's behavior. Again, you will examine this pattern in more detail in Chapter 5.

Now that you have the interface, you can add the two implementations of the discount strategy. First, create a new class named TradeDiscountStrategy with the following definition:

```
public class TradeDiscountStrategy : IDiscountStrategy
{
    public decimal ApplyExtraDiscountsTo(decimal originalSalePrice)
    {
```

```
            decimal price = originalSalePrice;

            price = price * 0.95M;

            return price;
        }
    }
```

TradeDiscountStrategy.cs located in the ASPPatterns.Chap3.Layered.Model project

Second, employ the Null Object pattern that was introduced in the previous chapter. Create a new class named `NullDiscountStrategy` with the following definition:

```
public class NullDiscountStrategy : IDiscountStrategy
{
    public decimal ApplyExtraDiscountsTo(decimal OriginalSalePrice)
    {
        return OriginalSalePrice;
    }
}
```

NullDiscountStrategy.cs located in the ASPPatterns.Chap3.Layered.Model project

With the discounts strategies in place, create the `Price` object. Create a new class named `Price` with the following definition:

```
public class Price
{
    private IDiscountStrategy _discountStrategy = new NullDiscountStrategy();
    private decimal _rrp;
    private decimal _sellingPrice;

    public Price(decimal RRP, decimal SellingPrice)
    {
        _rrp = RRP;
        _sellingPrice = SellingPrice;
    }

    public void SetDiscountStrategyTo(IDiscountStrategy DiscountStrategy)
    {
        _discountStrategy = DiscountStrategy;
    }

    public decimal SellingPrice
    {
        get { return _discountStrategy.ApplyExtraDiscountsTo(_sellingPrice); }
    }

    public decimal RRP
    {
        get { return _rrp; }
```

```
        }

        public decimal Discount
        {
            get {
                if (RRP > SellingPrice)
                    return (RRP - SellingPrice);
                else
                    return 0;}
        }

        public decimal Savings
        {
            get{
                if (RRP > SellingPrice)
                    return 1 - (SellingPrice / RRP);
                else
                    return 0;}
        }
    }
```

Price.cs located in the ASPPatterns.Chap3.Layered.Model project

The `Price` object uses the setter flavor of Dependency Injection to enable the discount strategy to be applied to the product's price.

> *Dependency Injection was introduced in the previous chapter, where you used Constructor Injection to supply a cache provider to the product's service. Here you're using another flavor of DI, namely Setter Injection, so you can swap implementations at will after the* `Price` *object is instantiated. DI is covered in greater detail in Chapter 5.*

To complete the model, create the simple `Product` class. Add a new class to the model project named `Product` with the following code listing:

```
public class Product
{
    public int Id {get; set;}
    public string Name { get; set; }
    public Price Price { get; set; }
}
```

Product.cs located in the ASPPatterns.Chap3.Layered.Model project

The business entities are created, but you need a way to hydrate the products from a data store. A service will allow clients to interact with the domain model and retrieve products with a discount applied. To enable the client to specify which discount to apply to the products, you need to create an enumeration that will be used as a service method parameter.

Create a new class named `CustomerType` with the following code listing:

```
public enum CustomerType
{
    Standard = 0,
    Trade = 1
}
```

CustomerType.cs located in the ASPPatterns.Chap3.Layered.Model project

Again, to determine which discount strategy to apply to the price, you need to create a factory class whose sole responsibility will be to return the matching discount strategy for a given `CustomerType`.

Create a new class named `DiscountFactory` with the following definition:

```
public static class DiscountFactory
{
    public static IDiscountStrategy GetDiscountStrategyFor
        (CustomerType customerType)
    {
        switch (customerType)
        {
            case CustomerType.Trade:
                return new TradeDiscountStrategy();
            default:
                return new NullDiscountStrategy();
        }
    }
}
```

DiscountFactory.cs located in the ASPPatterns.Chap3.Layered.Model project

> *The Factory pattern enables a class to delegate the responsibility of creating a valid object. This pattern will be covered in Chapter 5.*

The service layer will interact with a data store to retrieve products. You will use the Repository pattern to achieve this, but you will only specify the interface for the repository because you don't want the model project to be concerned with the specifics of what kind of data store will be used or what kind of technologies will be used to query it. Create a new interface named `IProductRepository` with the single method as shown here:

```
public interface IProductRepository
{
    IList<Product> FindAll();
}
```

IProductRepository.cs located in the ASPPatterns.Chap3.Layered.Model project

> *The Repository pattern acts as an in-memory collection or repository for busi-*
> *ness entities, completely abstracting away the underlying data infrastructure.*
> *This pattern is discussed in more detail in Chapter 7.*

The service class needs to be able to apply a given discount strategy to a collection of products. You could create a custom collection to achieve this, but I prefer the flexibility of extension methods, so create a new class named `ProductListExtensionMethods` with the following definition:

Available for download on Wrox.com

```
public static class ProductListExtensionMethods
{
    public static void Apply(this IList<Product> products,
                                    IDiscountStrategy discountStrategy)
    {
        foreach (Product p in products)
        {
            p.Price.SetDiscountStrategyTo(discountStrategy);
        }
    }
}
```

ProductListExtensionMethods.cs located in the ASPPatterns.Chap3.Layered.Model project

> *The Separated Interface pattern ensures that the client is completely unaware of*
> *the concrete implementations and can help to promote programming to abstrac-*
> *tions rather than implementations and the Dependency Inversion principle.*

You can now create the service class that clients will use to interact with the domain. Create a new class named `ProductService` with the code listing that follows:

Available for download on Wrox.com

```
public class ProductService
{
    private IProductRepository _productRepository;

    public ProductService(IProductRepository productRepository)
    {
        _productRepository = productRepository;
    }

    public IList<Product> GetAllProductsFor(CustomerType customerType)
    {
        IDiscountStrategy discountStrategy =
            DiscountFactory.GetDiscountStrategyFor(customerType);
```

```
        IList<Product> products = _productRepository.FindAll();

        products.Apply(discountStrategy);

        return products;
    }

}
```

ProductService.cs located in the ASPPatterns.Chap3.Layered.Model project

You have now completed all of the business logic that the application will contain. Notice how the business layer is not tied to a particular data store and uses interfaces to program against a repository for all of its persistence needs. The business layer can now be tested in complete isolation from any other part of the application and will also not be affected by changes to other layers. The next layer you will work on is the service layer, which will act as the gateway into the application.

Service Layer

The role of the service layer is to act as an entry point into the application; sometimes this is known as a *facade*. The service layer provides the presentation layer with a strongly typed view model, sometimes called the *presentation model.* A *view model* is a strongly typed class that is optimized for specific views. The view model you will be creating will display the products; again, you will read more about the View Model pattern later in the book.

 The Facade pattern provides a simple interface and controls access to a series of complicated interfaces and subsystems. This pattern is covered in detail in Chapter 6.

 View models are strongly typed classes that are optimized for specific views and contain logic to assist in the presentation of data. This pattern is covered in detail in Chapter 8.

Add a new class to the `ASPPatterns.Chap3.Layered.Service` project named `ProductViewModel` with the following class listing:

```
public class ProductViewModel
{
    Public int ProductId {get; set;}
    public string Name { get; set; }
    public string RRP { get; set; }
    public string SellingPrice { get; set; }
    public string Discount { get; set; }
```

```
        public string Savings { get; set; }
    }
```

ProductViewModel.cs located in the ASPPatterns.Chap3.Layered.Service project

For a client to interact with the service layer, you will be using a Request/Response messaging pattern, covered in detail in Chapter 6. The request part will be supplied by the client and will carry all necessary parameters; in this case, it will contain the `CustomerType` enumeration as defined in the domain model. Create a new class named `ProductListRequest` matching the code that follows:

```
using ASPPatterns.Chap3.Layered.Model;

namespace ASPPatterns.Chap3.Layered.Service
{
    public class ProductListRequest
    {
        public CustomerType CustomerType { get; set; }
    }
}
```

ProductListRequest.cs located in the ASPPatterns.Chap3.Layered.Service project

For the Response object, you will define a few more properties so that the client can check whether the request was completed successfully. There will also be a `Message` property to enable the service to give information to the client if the call was not completed successfully. Create a new class named `ProductListResponse` with the code listing that follows:

```
public class ProductListResponse
{
    public bool Success { get; set; }
    public string Message { get; set; }
    public IList<ProductViewModel> Products { get; set; }
}
```

ProductListResponse.cs located in the ASPPatterns.Chap3.Layered.Service project

To convert the `Product` entity into the `ProductViewModel`, you need a couple of methods: one to convert a single product and one to convert a list. You could add these methods to the `Product` entity in the domain model, but they aren't exactly business logic, so the next best thing is to create them as extension methods so that they can be used as if they were first-class citizens of the `Product` entity.

Create a new class within the Services project named `ProductMapperExtensionMethods`, and add the two methods shown in the following code listing:

```
public static class ProductMapperExtensionMethods
{
    public static IList<ProductViewModel> ConvertToProductListViewModel(
                                    this IList<Model.Product> products)
    {
        IList<ProductViewModel> productViewModels = new List<ProductViewModel>();

        foreach(Model.Product p in products)
```

```
        {
            productViewModels.Add(p.ConvertToProductViewModel());
        }

        return productViewModels;
    }

    public static ProductViewModel ConvertToProductViewModel(
                                        this Model.Product product)
    {
        ProductViewModel productViewModel = new ProductViewModel();
        productViewModel.ProductId = product.Id;
        productViewModel.Name = product.Name;
        productViewModel.RRP = String.Format("{0:C}", product.Price.RRP);
        productViewModel.SellingPrice =
                String.Format("{0:C}", product.Price.SellingPrice);

        if (product.Price.Discount > 0)
            productViewModel.Discount =
                String.Format("{0:C}", product.Price.Discount);

        if (product.Price.Savings < 1 && product.Price.Savings > 0)
            productViewModel.Savings = product.Price.Savings.ToString("#%");

        return productViewModel;
    }
}
```

ProductMapperExtensionMethods.cs located in the ASPPatterns.Chap3.Layered.Service project

Finally, add the ProductService class that will interact with the domain model service to retrieve a list of products and then convert them to a list of ProductViewModels. Add a new class to the service project named ProductService, with the following definition:

```
public class ProductService
{
    private Model.ProductService _productService;

    public ProductService(Model.ProductService ProductService)
    {
        _productService = ProductService;
    }

    public ProductListResponse GetAllProductsFor(
                        ProductListRequest productListRequest)
    {
        ProductListResponse productListResponse = new ProductListResponse();

        try
        {
            IList<Model.Product> productEntities =
              _productService.GetAllProductsFor(productListRequest.CustomerType);

            productListResponse.Products =
```

```
                        productEntities.ConvertToProductListViewModel();
            productListResponse.Success = true;
        }
        catch (Exception ex)
        {
            // Log the exception…
            productListResponse.Success = false;
            // Return a friendly error message
            productListResponse.Message = "An error occurred";
        }
        return productListResponse;
    }
}
```

ProductService.cs located in the ASPPatterns.Chap3.Layered.Service project

The service class catches any errors and returns a friendly message to the client; this is a good place to log errors. By handling any errors here and exposing a success flag, you enable the client to react elegantly if there is a problem with the service layer. This completes the service layer of the application and you can move on to creating the data access layer.

Data Access Layer

As with the Smart UI, you need a database to store the products. Create a database in the WebUI project with the same schema, name, and data that you used in the Smart UI exercise.

For speed, use Linq to SQL as the data access layer, so the first thing to do is create the Linq to SQL data context. Add a new Linq to SQL class to the `ASPPatterns.Chap3.Layered.Repository` project by right-clicking the project name and selecting Add ⇨ New Item. Then select Linq to SQL Classes, and name the class `Shop.dbml`.

With the Server Explorer window open, drag the Products table onto the design surface. Visual Studio creates a Linq to SQL entity named `Product`, as can be seen in Figure 3-6.

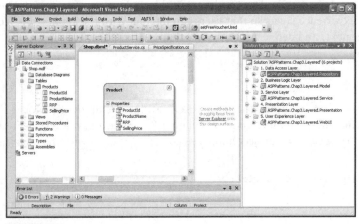

FIGURE 3-6

You can now create a concrete implementation of the `IProductRepository` interface that you created in the model project. Add a new class to the `Repository` project named `ProductRepository` with the following definition.

```
using System;
using System.Collections.Generic;
using System.Linq;
using System.Text;
using ASPPatterns.Chap3.Layered.Model;

namespace ASPPatterns.Chap3.Layered.Repository
{
    public class ProductRepository : IProductRepository
    {
        public IList<Model.Product> FindAll()
        {
            var products = from p in new ShopDataContext().Products
                           select new Model.Product
                           {
                               Id = p.ProductId,
                               Name = p.ProductName,
                               Price = new Model.Price(p.RRP, p.SellingPrice)
                           };

            return products.ToList();
        }

    }
}
```

ProductRepository located in the ASPPatterns.Chap3.Layered.Repository project

In the `FindAll` method, you are querying Linq to SQL to obtain all the products and then creating a list of Product Business entities from the data and returning them.

You have completed the business, data access, and service layers of the application. You now need to create the presentation and user experience layers so that users can interact with the application. You will tackle the presentation layer next, and define a set of views that your application will require before creating the web front end.

Presentation Layer

To separate the presentation logic from the user experience (user interface), employ the Model-View-Presenter pattern, which you will learn more about in Chapter 8. Create a new interface in the `ASPPatterns.Chap3.Layered.Presentation` project named `IProductListView` with the following contract:

```
using ASPPatterns.Chap3.Layered.Service;

public interface IProductListView
{
    void Display(IList<ProductViewModel> Products);
```

```
        Model.CustomerType CustomerType { get; }
        string ErrorMessage { set; }
    }
```

This interface will be implemented by the ASPX web form. By working with interfaces, you can stub out the view when it comes to testing.

Create a new class named `ProductListPresenter` with the following code listing:

```
    ...
    using ASPPatterns.Chap3.Layered.Service;

    namespace ASPPatterns.Chap3.Layered.Presentation
    {
        public class ProductListPresenter
        {
            private IProductListView _productListView;
            private Service.ProductService _productService;

            public ProductListPresenter(IProductListView ProductListView,
                                    Service.ProductService ProductService)
            {
                _productService = ProductService;
                _productListView = ProductListView;
            }

            public void Display()
            {
                ProductListRequest productListRequest = new ProductListRequest();
                productListRequest.CustomerType = _productListView.CustomerType;

                ProductListResponse productResponse =
                            _productService.GetAllProductsFor(productListRequest);

                if (productResponse.Success)
                {
                    _productListView.Display(productResponse.Products);
                }
                else
                {
                    _productListView.ErrorMessage = productResponse.Message;
                }

            }
        }
    }
```

The presenter class is responsible for obtaining data, handling user events, and updating the view via its interface.

This completes the very thin and simple presentation layer. The benefit of having the presentation layer is that it is now easy to test the presentation of the data and interactions between the user and the system without worrying about the difficult-to-unit-test web forms. You can also now add any flavor of user experience on top of your application such as WPF, WINforms, or a web forms application. For now, though, you will stick with web forms and you will tackle this layer next.

User Experience Layer

Finally, you can implement the view so that the products are displayed on the web page. Before getting to work on the HTML, however, you need a way to glue the loosely coupled application together so that concrete implementation of the IProductRepository is created. For this you are going to use StructureMap, an Inversion of Control container. You will learn about Inversion of Control and Inversion of Control Containers in Chapter 8.

Navigate to http://sourceforge.net/projects/structuremap and download the latest version of StructureMap. Once the compressed file has downloaded, unzip it, and extract all files to your desktop. Switch back into Visual Studio, right-click on the solution name, and select Open Folder In Windows Explorer. This will open at the root of your solution. Add a new folder called Lib to the root and copy the StructureMap.dll file from your desktop into the Lib folder. Then add a reference to the StructureMap.dll from within the WebUI project.

Create a new class named BootStrapper in the WebUI project with the following listing:

Available for download on Wrox.com

```
using StructureMap;
using StructureMap.Configuration.DSL;
using ASPPatterns.Chap3.Layered.Repository;
using ASPPatterns.Chap3.Layered.Model;

namespace ASPPatterns.Chap3.Layered.WebUI
{
    public class BootStrapper
    {
        public static void ConfigureStructureMap()
        {
            ObjectFactory.Initialize(x =>
            {
                x.AddRegistry<ProductRegistry>();
            });
        }
    }

    public class ProductRegistry : Registry
    {
        public ProductRegistry()
        {
            ForRequestedType<IProductRepository>()
                .TheDefaultIsConcreteType<ProductRepository>();
        }
    }
}
```

BootStrapper.cs located in the ASPPatterns.Chap3.Layered.WebUI project

The purpose of the `BootStrapper` class is to register all the concrete dependencies with `StructureMap`. When the client code uses `StructureMap` to resolve a class, `StructureMap` inspects the dependencies of that class and automatically injects them based on the selected concrete implements that were specified in the `ProductRegistry`.

The `ConfigureStructureMap` method needs to be run when your application is started so you can add a reference to it in the `global.asax` file. The `global.asax` file won't exist by default, so add it to the root of your WebUI project. Then update the file as can be seen in the following listing:

```
namespace ASPPatterns.Chap3.Layered.WebUI
{
    public class Global : System.Web.HttpApplication
    {
        protected void Application_Start(object sender, EventArgs e)
        {
            BootStrapper.ConfigureStructureMap();
        }
    }
}
```

Global.asax located in the ASPPatterns.Chap3.Layered.WebUI project

Open the `default.aspx` source view and edit the HTML markup so it matches what follows:

```
<asp:DropDownList AutoPostBack="true" ID="ddlCustomerType" runat="server">
    <asp:ListItem Value="0">Standard</asp:ListItem>
    <asp:ListItem Value="1">Trade</asp:ListItem>
</asp:DropDownList>

<asp:Label ID="lblErrorMessage" runat="server" ></asp:Label>

<asp:Repeater ID="rptProducts" runat="server" >
    <HeaderTemplate>
        <table>
            <tr>
                <td>Name</td>
                <td>RRP</td>
                <td>Selling Price</td>
                <td>Discount</td>
                <td>Savings</td>
            </tr>
            <tr>
                <td colspan="5"><hr /></td>
            </tr>
    </HeaderTemplate>
    <ItemTemplate>
            <tr>
                <td><%# Eval("Name") %></td>
                <td><%# Eval("RRP")%></td>
                <td><%# Eval("SellingPrice") %></td>
                <td><%# Eval("Discount") %></td>
                <td><%# Eval("Savings") %></td>
            </tr>
    </ItemTemplate>
    <FooterTemplate>
```

```
                </table>
            </FooterTemplate>
        </asp:Repeater>
```

Default.aspx located in the ASPPatterns.Chap3.Layered.WebUI project

Switch to the code-behind of the page and edit it so that it implements the `IProductListView` interface from the presentation project, as in the code listing that follows:

```csharp
using ASPPatterns.Chap3.Layered.Model;
using ASPPatterns.Chap3.Layered.Repository;
using ASPPatterns.Chap3.Layered.Presentation;
using ASPPatterns.Chap3.Layered.Service;
using StructureMap;

namespace ASPPatterns.Chap3.Layered.WebUI
{
    public partial class _Default : System.Web.UI.Page, IProductListView
    {
        private ProductListPresenter _presenter;

        protected void Page_Init(object sender, EventArgs e)
        {
            _presenter = new ProductListPresenter(this,
                    ObjectFactory.GetInstance<Service.ProductService>());
            this.ddlCustomerType.SelectedIndexChanged +=
                    delegate { _presenter.Display();};
        }

        protected void Page_Load(object sender, EventArgs e)
        {
            if (Page.IsPostBack != true)
                _presenter.Display();
        }

        public void Display(IList<ProductViewModel> products)
        {
            rptProducts.DataSource = products;
            rptProducts.DataBind();
        }

        public CustomerType CustomerType
        {
            get { return (CustomerType)Enum.ToObject(typeof(CustomerType),
                            int.Parse(this.ddlCustomerType.SelectedValue) ); }
        }

        public string ErrorMessage
        {
            set { lblErrorMessage.Text =
                    String.Format("<p><strong>Error</strong><br/>{0}<p/>", value); }
        }
    }
}
```

Default.aspx.cs located in the ASPPatterns.Chap3.Layered.WebUI project

The page simply creates a new instance of the `ProductListPresenter` during the page initiation event and obtains an implementation of the `ProductService` via the `StructureMap`'s `ObjectFactory` `.GetInstance` method. The page then delegates all the other work to the Presenter, simply handling user events and forwarding calls. Again, you will look at `StructureMap` in more detail in Chapter 8, so don't worry that you are flying through the implementation at the moment.

There was a lot more work involved in creating the layered application, but you now have a loosely coupled application that can be tested, is maintainable, and has a strong separation of concerns. Figure 3-7 shows the interactions between the layers and clearly defines the responsibilities of each.

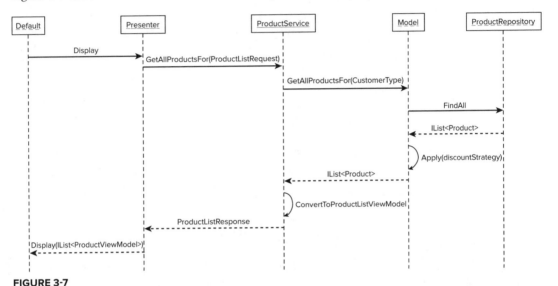

FIGURE 3-7

 This book is not about unit testing or test-driven development; however, you will find a test project full of unit tests and behavior specifications in the code download that accompanies this book. I strongly advise you take a look at it.

SUMMARY

In this chapter you were introduced to the benefit of layering enterprise-level ASP.NET applications. The chapter began with an example of the limitations that the Smart UI antipattern can cause and how all concerns are the responsibility of the specific ASPX page. This leads to an application of logic and a maintenance headache as more and more features are added to the application.

The remedy to this problem is to separate the concerns of the application into distinct layers. The exercise that you tackled chose to separate the layers into projects; however, using folders or namespaces is just as effective. While working through the layer application exercise, you briefly encountered a number of design patterns and principles that you will be examining in greater depth throughout the remainder of this book.

The next six chapters will explore each of the layers in detail before putting all of the patterns and principles into practice with a case study application. The discussion on layering your application continues with patterns to help your organize business logic in the next chapter.

The Business Logic Layer: Organization

WHAT'S IN THIS CHAPTER?

➤ When and how to use the Transaction Script pattern to organize business logic

➤ When and how to use Active Record with the Castle Windsor project to organize business logic

➤ When and how to use the Domain Model pattern with NHibernate to organize business logic

➤ Explanation of the difference between the Anemic Model and the Domain Model patterns to organize business logic

➤ Understanding domain-driven design (DDD) and how to use it to focus your efforts on business logic rather than infrastructure concerns

The business layer is arguably the most import layer within any enterprise application, so it's important to organize your business logic in the most appropriate manner that befits the complexity of your application. In this chapter you will be introduced to four patterns first published in Fowler's *Patterns of Enterprise Application Architecture* book: Transaction Script, Active Record, Anemic Model, and Domain Model. Each of these domain logic patterns has strengths and weaknesses depending on what type of application you are building.

Armed with knowledge of the architectural patterns to organize your domain logic, you will then read about DDD, a design method that can help you understand the business domain that you are modeling more effectively and ensure that the business needs are at the forefront of your mind.

UNDERSTANDING BUSINESS ORGANIZATIONAL PATTERNS

Not all applications are equal, and not all require a complex architecture to encapsulate the business logic of a system. As developers, it's important to understand the strengths and weaknesses of all the domain logic patterns so that you can use the most appropriate one.

Transaction Script

Of the four domain logic patterns you will read about in this chapter, Transaction Script is by far the easiest to understand and get up and running with. The Transaction Script pattern follows a procedural style of development rather than an object-oriented approach. Typically a single procedure is created for each of your business transactions, and it is grouped in some kind of static manager or service class. Each procedure contains all the business logic that is required to complete the business transaction from the workflow, business rules, and validation checks to persistence in the database. Figure 4-1 shows a graphical representation of the Transaction Script pattern.

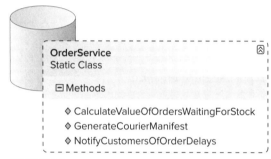

FIGURE 4-1

One of the strengths of the Transaction Script pattern is that it is simple to understand; it can be fast to get new team members up to speed without prior knowledge of the pattern. As new requirements arise, it is easy to add more methods to the class without fear of impacting or breaking existing functionality.

The Transaction Script Pattern is a great for small applications with little or no logic that are not likely to grow in feature set, and for teams with junior developers who are not comfortable with object oriented programming concepts.

The problems with the Transaction Script pattern are revealed when an application grows and the business logic complexities increase. As an application is extended, so is the mass of methods, making for an unhelpful API full of fine-grained methods that overlap in terms of functionality. You can use submethods to avoid repetitive code such as the validation and business rules, but duplication in the workflow cannot be avoided, and the code base can quickly become unwieldy and unmanageable as the application grows.

Because the Transaction Script pattern is simple, you won't be asked to run through an exercise; instead, consider the code snippet that follows, which comes from an HR holiday book application to give you a flavor of how the pattern may look in action.

```
public class HolidayService
    {

        public static bool BookHolidayFor(int employeeId, DateTime From, DateTime To)
        {
            bool booked = false;
            TimeSpan numberOfDaysRequestedForHoliday = To - From;

            if (numberOfDaysRequestedForHoliday.Days > 0)
            {
                if (RequestHolidayDoesNotClashWithExistingHoliday(employeeId, From, To))
                {
                    int holidayAvailable = GetHolidayRemainingFor(employeeId);

                    if (holidayAvailable >=
                                    numberOfDaysRequestedForHoliday.Days)
                    {
                        SubmitHolidayBookingFor(employeeId, From, To);
                        booked = true;
                    }
                }
            }

            return booked;
        }

        private static int GetHolidayRemainingFor(int employeeId)
        {
            // ...
        }

        public static List<EmployeeDTO> GetAllEmployeesOnLeaveBetween(
                                            DateTime From, DateTime To)
        {
            // ...
        }

        public static List<EmployeeDTO> GetAllEmployeesWithHolidayRemaining()
        {
            // ...
        }

    }
```

Code snippet ASPPatterns.Chap4.TransactionScript

As you can see, the entire business case is encapsulated within a single method. The `BookHolidayFor` method is dealing with many responsibilities such as data retrieval and persistence, as well business logic to determine if a holiday can be taken. This style of procedural programming goes against the very nature of object oriented programming, which is fine if logic is kept to the minimum and the application is small and thus easy to manage.

If you have a simple application with minimal business logic, which doesn't warrant a fully object-oriented approach, the Transaction Script pattern can be a good fit. However, if your application will grow, you may need to rethink your business logic structure and look to a more scalable pattern like the Active Record pattern, which is the subject of the next section.

Active Record

The Active Record pattern is a popular pattern that is especially effective when your underlying database model matches your business model. Typically, a business object exists for each table in your database. The business object represents a single row in that table and contains data and behavior as well as a means to persist it and methods to add new instances and find collections of objects. Figure 4-2 shows how `Post` and `Comment` objects from a blogging application relate to their corresponding database tables. The figure also shows that `Post` contains a collection on `Comment` objects.

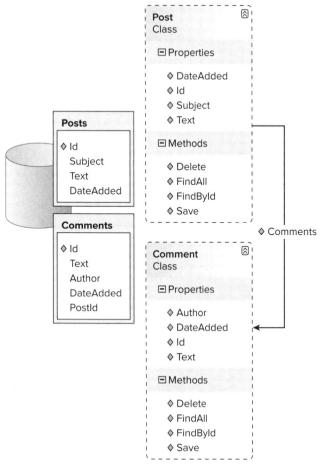

FIGURE 4-2

In the Active Record pattern, each business object is responsible for its own persistence and related business logic.

The Active Record pattern is great for simple applications that have a one-to-one mapping between the data model and the business model, such as with a blogging or a forum engine; it's also a good pattern to use if you have an existing database model or tend to build applications with a "data first" approach. Because the business objects have a one-to-one mapping to the tables in the database and all have the same create, read, update, and delete (CRUD) methods, it's possible to use code generation tools to auto-generate your business model for you. Good code generation tools also build in all the database validation logic to ensure that you are allowing only valid data to be persisted. Automatically generating your business objects and frameworks that use the Active Record pattern is examined in Chapter 7, when how to persist business objects is discussed. As with the Transaction Script pattern, Active Record is similarly straightforward and easy to grasp.

The Active Record pattern is popular with web over database applications, particularly with the Ruby on Rails framework that combines an MVC pattern (Chapter 8) with an Active Record ORM (Chapter 7). In the .NET world, one of the most popular open source Active Record frameworks is the Castle ActiveRecord project that is built upon NHibernate (Chapter 7); that's what you will be using with an ASP.NET MVC application to build a simple blog site. Because a blog contains only a small amount of business logic and there is a good correlation between the business objects and data model, the Active Record pattern is a great match.

Navigate to `www.castleproject.org/castle/download.html` and download the latest release for the ActiveRecord project; at the time of writing this was ActiveRecord 2.1.1 released on January 15, 2010. The download is a simple zip file containing all the assemblies you will need to use the ActiveRecord framework. When the zip file has downloaded, extract all the files to a folder on your desktop.

Now you need to create a new solution for the project. Create a new solution named `ASPPatterns .Chap4.ActiveRecord`. Add a new C# class library to the solution named `ASPPatterns.Chap4 .ActiveRecord.Model` and a new MVC web application named `ASPPatterns.Chap4.Active Record.UI.MVC`.

 The ASP.NET Framework version 2.0 is preinstalled with Visual Studio 2010. However, for Visual Studio 2008 users you will need to navigate to `www.asp.net/ mvc/` *to install the framework.*

Right-click on the solution and select Open Folder in Windows Explorer; within this folder create a new folder named `Lib` and move all the files from the Castle ActiveRecord download into it. Then flip back to the solution and right-click on the `ASPPatterns.Chap4.ActiveRecord.Model` project and click Add Reference, select the Browse tab, and navigate to the new `Lib` folder in the root of your solution and add all the assemblies. Right-click on the `ASPPatterns.Chap4.ActiveRecord.UI.MVC` project and add a reference to the following assemblies:

➤ `Castle.ActiveRecord.dll`

➤ `NHibernate.dll`

Finally, again from the `ASPPatterns.Chap4.ActiveRecord.UI.MVC` project, add a project reference to the `ASPPatterns.Chap4.ActiveRecord.Model` project. Now that your solution is set up, you can create a database to store the blog posts.

Right-click on the `ASPPatterns.Chap4.ActiveRecord.UI.MVC` project and select Add Item. Then select a new database named `Blog.mdf`. Once the database has been created, double-click on it to be taken to the Server Explorer and create two tables with the following definitions.

TABLE 4-1: Posts Table

COLUMN NAME	DATA TYPE	ALLOW NULLS
Id	Int IDENTITY, Primary Key	False
Subject	nvarchar(200)	False
Text	nvarchar(MAX)	False
DateAdded	Datetime	False

TABLE 4-2: Comments Table

COLUMN NAME	DATA TYPE	ALLOW NULLS
Id	Int IDENTITY, Primary Key	False
Text	nvarchar(MAX)	False
Author	nvarchar(50)	False
DateAdded	Datetime	False
PostId	Int	False

Create a new database diagram, add both tables, and create a relationship between them by selecting and dragging the `Posts` table `Id` column to the `Comments` table `PostId` column. After you have made your changes, save the diagram and okay the updates to the tables.

Finally, you can start to create the model that will represent the `Blog Posts` and `Post Comments` entities. Add a new C# class to the `ASPPatterns.Chap4.ActiveRecord.Model` project name `Comment` with the following code listing:

```
using System;
using System.Collections.Generic;
using System.Linq;
using System.Text;
using Castle.ActiveRecord;

namespace ASPPatterns.Chap4.ActiveRecord.Model
{
    [ActiveRecord("Comments")]
    public class Comment : ActiveRecordBase<Comment>
```

```
        {
            [PrimaryKey]
            public int Id { get; set; }

            [BelongsTo("PostID")]
            public Post Post { get; set; }

            [Property]
            public string Text { get; set; }

            [Property]
            public string Author { get; set; }

            [Property]
            public DateTime DateAdded { get; set; }
        }
    }
```

The attributes that decorate the properties of the Comment class inform the framework which properties match database table columns. The Castle ActiveRecord framework then uses this information to automatically persist and retrieve the business entities without the need to write lengthy SQL.

Add a second class to the project named Post with the following definition:

```
using System;
using System.Collections.Generic;
using System.Linq;
using System.Text;
using Castle.ActiveRecord;
using Castle.ActiveRecord.Queries;

namespace ASPPatterns.Chap4.ActiveRecord.Model
{
    [ActiveRecord("Posts")]
    public class Post : ActiveRecordBase<Post>
    {
        [PrimaryKey]
        public int Id { get; set; }

        [Property]
        public string Subject { get; set; }

        [Property]
        public string Text { get; set; }

        public string ShortText
        {
            get {
                if (Text.Length > 20)
                    return Text.Substring(0, 20) + "...";
                else
                    return Text;
            }
```

```
        }

        [HasMany]
        public IList<Comment> Comments { get; set; }

        [Property]
        public DateTime DateAdded { get; set; }

        public static Post FindLatestPost()
        {
            SimpleQuery<Post> q = new SimpleQuery<Post>
                        (@"from Post p order by p.DateAdded desc");

            return (Post)q.Execute()[0];
        }
    }
}
```

And that's all you need to do for the model and data access. Simple, isn't it? This is what the Ruby on Rails guys have been boasting about for so long.

You can now construct the web site to display the posts and comments, but first you need to remove all the files that Visual Studio added for you when you created the project. Go back to the MVC project and remove all the files from the following folders generated for you by Visual Studio:

➤   Content

➤   Controllers

➤   Views

Add a new controller to the `Controllers` folder named `BlogController` with the following code definition:

```
using System;
using System.Collections.Generic;
using System.Linq;
using System.Web;
using System.Web.Mvc;
using System.Web.Mvc.Ajax;
using ASPPatterns.Chap4.ActiveRecord.Model;

namespace ASPPatterns.Chap4.ActiveRecord.UI.MVC.Controllers
{
    public class BlogController : Controller
    {
        // GET: /Blog/
        public ActionResult Index()
        {
            Post[] posts = Post.FindAll();

            if (posts.Count() > 0)
            {
                ViewData["AllPosts"] = posts;
                ViewData["LatestPost"] = Post.FindLatestPost();
                return View();
```

```
            }
            else
                return Create();
        }

        // POST: /Blog/
        [AcceptVerbs(HttpVerbs.Post)]
        public ActionResult CreateComment(string id, FormCollection collection)
        {
            int postId = 0;
            int.TryParse(id, out postId);
            Post post = Post.Find(postId);

            Comment comment = new Comment();
            comment.Post = post;
            comment.Author = Request.Form["Author"];
            comment.DateAdded = DateTime.Now;
            comment.Text = Request.Form["Comment"];

            comment.Save();

            return Detail(post.Id.ToString());
        }

        // GET: /Blog/Detail/1
        public ActionResult Detail(string id)
        {
            ViewData["AllPosts"] = Post.FindAll();

            int postId = 0;
            int.TryParse(id, out postId);

            ViewData["LatestPost"] = Post.Find(postId);

            return View("Index");
        }

        // GET: /Blog/Create
        public ActionResult Create()
        {
            return View("AddPost");
        }

        // POST: /Blog/Create
        [AcceptVerbs(HttpVerbs.Post)]
        public ActionResult Create(FormCollection collection)
        {
            Post post = new Post();
            post.DateAdded = DateTime.Now;
            post.Subject = Request.Form["Subject"];
            post.Text = Request.Form["Content"]; ;
            post.Save();

            return Detail(post.Id.ToString());
        }
    }
}
```

Add two new folders to the `Views` folder: `Blog` and `Shared`. To the `Shared` folder add a new Master page named `BlogMaster.Master`, with the markup seen here:

```
<%@ Master Language="C#" Inherits="System.Web.Mvc.ViewMasterPage" %>

<!DOCTYPE html PUBLIC "-//W3C//DTD XHTML 1.0 Transitional//EN"
            "http://www.w3.org/TR/xhtml1/DTD/xhtml1-transitional.dtd">

<html xmlns="http://www.w3.org/1999/xhtml" >
<head runat="server">
    <link href="../../Content/Site.css" rel="stylesheet" type="text/css" />
    <title><asp:ContentPlaceHolder ID="TitleContent" runat="server" /></title>
</head>
<body>
    <div id="document">
        <div id="header"><h1>My Blog</h1></div>
        <div id="nav"><%= Html.ActionLink("Create Post", "Create") %></div>
        <asp:ContentPlaceHolder ID="MainContent" runat="server">
        </asp:ContentPlaceHolder>
    </div>
</body>
</html>
```

Add a new view within the `Blog` view folder named `Index` with the following markup.

```
<%@ Page Title="" Language="C#" MasterPageFile="~/Views/Shared/BlogMaster.Master"
        Inherits="System.Web.Mvc.ViewPage" %>
<%@ Import Namespace="ASPPatterns.Chap4.ActiveRecord.Model" %>

<asp:Content ID="Content2" ContentPlaceHolderID="MainContent" runat="server">

<div id="content"><h2><%= Html.Encode(((Post)ViewData["LatestPost"]).Subject) %></h2>
        <%= ((Post)ViewData["LatestPost"]).Text.Replace("\n", "<br/>") %>
        <br /><i>posted on
            <%= Html.Encode(((Post)ViewData["LatestPost"])
                                    .DateAdded.ToLongDateString()) %></i>
        <hr />
        Comments<br />
         <% foreach (var item in ((Post)ViewData["LatestPost"]).Comments)
           { %>
                <p><i><%= Html.Encode(item.Author) %>
                said on <%= Html.Encode(item.DateAdded.ToLongDateString()) %>
                at <%= Html.Encode(item.DateAdded.ToShortTimeString()) %>...</i><br />
                <%= Html.Encode(item.Text) %>
                </p>
        <% } %>

        <p>Add a comment</p>
        <% using (Html.BeginForm("CreateComment", "Blog", new {
                    Id = ((Post)ViewData["LatestPost"]).Id }, FormMethod.Post))
        {%>
        <p>
        Your name<br />
        <%= Html.TextBox("Author")%> </p>

        <p>
```

```
          Your comment<br />
          <%= Html.TextArea("Comment")%></p>


          <p>
          <input type="submit" value="Add Comment" />

          </p>
          <%} %>
          </div>
          <div id="rightNav"><h2>All Posts</h2>
          <ul>
          <% foreach (var item in (Post[])ViewData["AllPosts"])
              { %>
                  <li>
                  <%= Html.ActionLink(item.Subject, "Detail",
                                                new { Id=item.Id  })%>
                  <br />
                  <%= Html.Encode(item.ShortText) %>
                  </li>
          <% } %>
          </ul>
          </div>
</asp:Content>
```

Add a second new view named AddPost to the Blog view folder with the following markup:

```
<%@ Page Title="" Language="C#" MasterPageFile="~/Views/Shared/BlogMaster.Master"
       Inherits="System.Web.Mvc.ViewPage" %>

<asp:Content ID="Content2" ContentPlaceHolderID="MainContent" runat="server">
     <% using (Html.BeginForm())
        {%>
        <p>
        Subject<br />
        <%= Html.TextBox("Subject")%> </p>

        <p>
        Content<br />
        <%= Html.TextArea("Content")%></p>

        <p>
        <input type="submit" value="Create" />
        </p>
     <%} %>
  </asp:Content>
```

Open the Global.asax file and update it as shown here:

```
using System;
using System.Collections.Generic;
using System.Linq;
using System.Web;
using System.Web.Mvc;
using System.Web.Routing;
using ASPPatterns.Chap4.ActiveRecord.Model;
using Castle.ActiveRecord.Framework;
```

```
using System.Configuration;

namespace ASPPatterns.Chap4.ActiveRecord.UI.MVC
{
    public class MvcApplication : System.Web.HttpApplication
    {
        public static void RegisterRoutes(RouteCollection routes)
        {
            routes.IgnoreRoute("{resource}.axd/{*pathInfo}");

            routes.MapRoute(
                "Default",
                "{controller}/{action}/{id}",
                new { controller = "Blog", action = "Index", id = "" }
            );

        }

        protected void Application_Start()
        {
            RegisterRoutes(RouteTable.Routes);

            IConfigurationSource source = ConfigurationManager
                                .GetSection("activeRecord") as IConfigurationSource;
            Castle.ActiveRecord.ActiveRecordStarter
                                .Initialize(source, typeof(Post), typeof(Comment));
        }
    }
}
```

The code in the Global.asax file simply tells the Castle ActiveRecord framework to initialize so you can start working with it.

The last thing you need to do to get the Castle ActiveRecord up and running is to amend the web.config file to include the Castle ActiveRecord declarations as displayed in the following configuration snippet:

```
<configuration>
    <configSections>
      <section
        name="activeRecord"
          type="Castle.ActiveRecord.Framework.Config.ActiveRecordSectionHandler,
          Castle.ActiveRecord"/>
      ...
    </configSections>
    <activeRecord isWeb="true">
      <config>
        <add key="hibernate.connection.driver_class"
            value="NHibernate.Driver.SqlClientDriver"/>
        <add key="dialect" value="NHibernate.Dialect.MsSql2005Dialect"/>
        <add key="hibernate.connection.provider"
            value="NHibernate.Connection.DriverConnectionProvider"/>
        <add key="connection.connection_string"
            value="DataSource=.\SQLEXPRESS;AttachDbFilename=|DataDirectory|\Blog.mdf;
```

```
                         Integrated Security=True;User Instance=True"/>
           <add key="proxyfactory.factory_class"
                value="NHibernate.ByteCode.Castle.ProxyFactoryFactory,
                       NHibernate.ByteCode.Castle"/>
           </config>
       </activeRecord>
       ...
     </configuration >
```

To make the blog look pretty, you can add a new style sheet file within the content folder named
`Site.css`:

```
#document{
width:750px;
margin:0 auto;
}

#content {
float:left;
width:500px;
}

#rightNav {
float:right;
width:250px;
}
```

Run the solution, and you will be able to use your blog. Figure 4-3 shows the blog application
running.

FIGURE 4-3

You built the blogging application extremely quickly; this was due in no small measure to the Castle ActiveRecord framework, which was able to automate your data retrieval and access due to the close correlation between your object model and your data model.

The Active Record pattern is no silver bullet. It excels with a good underlying data model that maps to the business model, but when there is a mismatch, sometimes called an *impedance mismatch*, the pattern can struggle to cope. This is the result of complex systems sometimes having a different conceptual business model than the data model. When there is a rich business domain with lots of complex rules, logic, and workflow, the domain model approach is favored. It's the pattern you will be exploring next.

Domain Model

You can think of a domain model as a conceptual layer that represents the domain you are working in. Things exist in this model and have relationships to other things. What do I mean by things? Well, for example, if you were building an e-commerce store, the "things" that would live in the model would represent a Basket, Order, Order Item, and the like. These things have data and, more importantly, they have behavior. Not only would an order have properties that represent a creation date, status, and order number, but it would contain the business logic to apply a voucher to, including all the domain rules that surround it: Is the voucher valid? Can the voucher be used with the products in the basket? Are there any other offers in place that would render the voucher invalid? The closer your domain model represents the real domain the better, as it will be easier for you to understand and replicate the complex business logic, rules, and validation process that exist in an organization. The main difference between the domain model and the Active Record pattern is that the business entities that live in the domain model have no knowledge of how to persist themselves, and there doesn't necessarily need to be a one-to-one mapping between the data model and the business model.

POCO and PI

As mentioned previously, the domain model, unlike the Active Record pattern, has no knowledge of persistence. The term persistence ignorance (PI) has been coined for the plain nature of the plain old common runtime object (POCO) business entities. How then do you persist a business object with the domain model? Typically, the Repository pattern (Chapter 7) is used. When you are employing the Domain Model pattern, it's the responsibility of the Repository object, along with a data mapper (Chapter 7), to map a business entity and its object graph of associated entities to the data model.

Code Example

To demonstrate the Domain Model pattern, you will create a solution to model a banking domain that will involve the creation of accounts and the transferring of funds between them.

Create a new solution named `ASPPatterns.Chap4.DomainModel` and add to it the following class library projects:

➤ `ASPPatterns.Chap4.DomainModel.Model`

➤   `ASPPatterns.Chap4.DomainModel.AppService`

➤   `ASPPatterns.Chap4.DomainModel.Repository`

Also add a new web application named `ASPPatterns.Chap4.DomainModel.UI.Web`. Right-click on the `Repository` project and add a project reference to the `Model` project. Right-click on the `AppService` project and add a project reference to the `Model` and `Repository` projects. Finally, right-click on the `Web` project and add a project reference to the `AppService` project.

Figure 4-4 is a graphical representation of the projects you have created. The responsibilities of each project are listed following the diagram.

➤   **ASPPatterns.Chap4.DomainModel.Model:** The Domain Model project will contain all of the business logic within the application. Domain objects will live in here and will have relationships to other objects to represent the banking domain the application is built around. The project will also define contracts in the form of interfaces for domain object persistence and retrieval; the Repository pattern will be employed for all persistence management needs. (The Repository pattern is discussed in greater detail in Chapter 7.) The Model project will not have a reference to any other project ensuring, it remains free of any infrastructure concerns and focuses squarely on the business domain.

➤   **ASPPatterns.Chap4.DomainModel.Repository:** The Repository project will contain implementations of the repository interfaces defined in the Model project. The Repository has a reference to the Model project in order to hydrate domain objects from the database as well as to persist. The Repository project is concerned only with the responsibility of domain object persistence and retrieval.

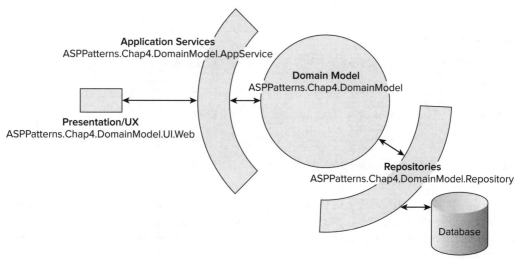

FIGURE 4-4

➤ **ASPPatterns.Chap4.DomainModel.AppService:** The AppService project will act as the gateway into the application—the API if you will. The presentation layer will communicate with the AppService via messages, which are simple data transfer objects. The messaging patterns are covered in detail in Chapter 7. The AppService layer will also define view models, which are flattened views of the domain model used solely for the displaying of data. Chapter 8 covers this topic in greater detail.

➤ **ASPPatterns.Chap4.DomainModel.UI.Web:** The UI.Web project is responsible for the presentation and use experience needs of the application. This project talks only to the AppService and receives strongly typed view models that have been created specifically for the views of the user experience.

With your solution structure in place you can set up the database to store the state of the bank accounts in the domain. Add a new item to the Web project, select new database, and name it BankAccount.mdf. Once the database has been created, double-click on it to be taken to the Server Explorer and create two tables with the following definitions.

TABLE 4-3: BankAccounts Table

COLUMN NAME	DATA TYPE	ALLOW NULLS
BankAccountId	uniqueidentifier, Primary Key	False
Balance	Money	False
CustomerRef	nvarchar(50)	False

TABLE 4-4: Transactions Table

COLUMN NAME	DATA TYPE	ALLOW NULLS
BankAccountId	uniqueidentifier	False
Deposit	money	False
Withdrawal	money	False
Reference	nvarchar(50)	False

Create a new database diagram, add both tables, and create a relationship between them by selecting and dragging the BankAccounts table's BankAccountId column to the Transactions table's BankAccountId column. After you have made your changes, save the diagram and okay the updates to the tables.

With the solution framework and database set up, you can begin the real work of modeling your domain. In this scenario a BankAccount creates a Transaction for every action that occurs. Figure 4-5 shows the class diagram for the simple domain model.

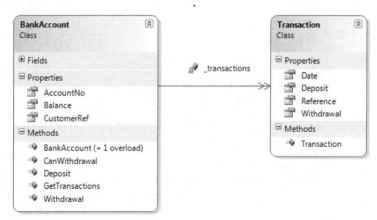

FIGURE 4-5

Create a new class named `Transaction` within the `Model` project with the following code definition:

```
public class Transaction
{
    public Transaction(decimal deposit, decimal withdrawal,
                       string reference, DateTime date)
    {
        this.Deposit = deposit;
        this.Withdrawal = withdrawal;
        this.Reference = reference;
        this.Date = date;
    }

    public decimal Deposit
    { get; internal set; }

    public decimal Withdrawal
    { get; internal set; }

    public string Reference
    { get; internal set; }

    public DateTime Date
    { get; internal set; }
}
```

Note that, for the purposes of this example, the `Transaction` object has no identifier property and that the corresponding data table doesn't have a primary key specified. The `Transaction` object is what is known as a value object, a term used in domain driven design and discussed at the end of this chapter.

Add a second class named `BankAccount` and enter the code listing that follows:

```
public class BankAccount
{
```

```csharp
private decimal _balance;
private Guid _accountNo;
private string _customerRef;
private IList<Transaction> _transactions;

public BankAccount() : this(Guid.NewGuid(), 0,
                            new List<Transaction>(), "")
{
    _transactions.Add(new Transaction(0m, 0m, "account created", DateTime.Now));
}

public BankAccount(Guid Id, decimal balance,
                   IList<Transaction> transactions, string customerRef)
{
    AccountNo = Id;
    _balance = balance;
    _transactions = transactions;
    _customerRef = customerRef;
}

public Guid AccountNo
{
    get { return _accountNo; }
    internal set { _accountNo = value; }
}

public decimal Balance
{
    get { return _balance; }
    internal set { _balance = value; }
}

public string CustomerRef
{
    get { return _customerRef; }
    set { _customerRef = value; }
}

public bool CanWithdraw(decimal amount)
{
    return (Balance >= amount);
}

public void Withdraw(decimal amount, string reference)
{
    if (CanWithdraw(amount))
    {
        Balance -= amount;
        _transactions.Add(new Transaction(0m, amount,
                                          reference, DateTime.Now ));
    }
}

public void Deposit(decimal amount, string reference)
```

```
        {
            Balance += amount;
            _transactions.Add(new Transaction(amount, 0m, reference, DateTime.Now));
        }

        public IEnumerable<Transaction> GetTransactions()
        {
            return _transactions;
        }
    }
```

The BankAccount has three simple methods:

➤ CanWithdraw

➤ Withdraw

➤ Deposit

Because there is a CanWithdraw method, you should expect calling code to use the Test-Doer pattern before trying to withdraw funds from an account like so:

```
If (myBankAccount.CanWithdraw(amountToWithdraw))
{
        myBankAccount.Withdraw(amountToWithdraw);
}
```

If a call to Withdraw is called with insufficient funds without a check, then an exception should be raised. With this in mind, you will require a new custom exception, so add another class to the Model project named InsufficientFundsException with the following code listing:

```
public class InsufficientFundsException : ApplicationException
{
}
```

And amend the Withdraw method on the BankAccount class like so:

```
public void Withdraw(decimal amount, string reference)
{
    if (CanWithdraw(amount))
    {
        Balance -= amount;
        _transactions.Add(new Transaction(0m, amount, reference, DateTime.Now));
    }
    else
    {
        throw new InsufficientFundsException();
    }
}
```

You now need a method to persist the BankAccount and Transactions, but because you don't want to pollute the Domain Model project, you are going to add only the interface for a Repository to define the contract for the entity's persistence and retrieval needs. This is a nod back to what you read about in terms of the PI and POCO, concepts covered earlier in this chapter.

Create a new interface named `IBankAccountRepository` with the following contract:

```
public interface IBankAccountRepository
{
    void Add(BankAccount bankAccount);
    void Save(BankAccount bankAccount);
    IEnumerable<BankAccount> FindAll();
    BankAccount FindBy(Guid AccountId);
}
```

Some actions don't sit well as methods on a domain entity. For cases like these, you can use a domain service. The action of transferring funds between two accounts is a responsibility that belongs on a service class. You will read more about domain services at the end of the chapter.

Add a new class to the Model project named `BankAccountService` with the following code definition:

```
public class BankAccountService
{
    private IBankAccountRepository _bankAccountRepository;

    public BankAccountService(IBankAccountRepository bankAccountRepository)
    {
        _bankAccountRepository = bankAccountRepository;
    }

    public void Transfer(Guid accountNoTo, Guid accountNoFrom,
                                            decimal amount)
    {
        BankAccount bankAccountTo =
                        _bankAccountRepository.FindBy(accountNoTo);
        BankAccount bankAccountFrom = _bankAccountRepository.FindBy(accountNoFrom);

        if (bankAccountFrom.CanWithdraw(amount))
        {
            bankAccountTo.Deposit(amount,
                            "From Acc " + bankAccountFrom.CustomerRef + " ");
            bankAccountFrom.Withdraw(amount,
                        "Transfer To Acc " + bankAccountTo.CustomerRef + " ");

            _bankAccountRepository.Save(bankAccountTo);
            _bankAccountRepository.Save(bankAccountFrom);
        }
        else
        {
            throw new InsufficientFundsException();
        }
    }
}
```

In the current implementation of the `BankAccountService`, any errors that occur between saving the two bank accounts will leave the data in an invalid state. In Chapter 7 you will see how the Unit of Work pattern can ensure that transactions that need to can commit as one atomic action, or rollback in case of an exception.

Now that you have built the domain model, you can get to work on a method to persist the Bank Account and Transaction business objects. From within the Repository project, add a new class named BankAccountRepository. This class will be an implementation of the IBankAccount Repository. My apologies for the length of the code listing that follows. In Chapter 7, you will look at some popular object relational mappers that will cut down on the amount of time you spend writing ADO.NET infrastructure code.

You will need to add a reference to the System.Configuration assembly because the BankAccount Repository needs to obtain a connection string from the application's web.config file.

```
using ASPPatterns.Chap4.DomainModel.Model;
using System.Data.SqlClient;
using System.Data;
using System.Configuration;

namespace ASPPatterns.Chap4.DomainModel.Repository
{
    public class BankAccountRepository : IBankAccountRepository
    {
        private string _connectionString;

        public BankAccountRepository()
        {
            _connectionString = ConfigurationManager
                    .ConnectionStrings["BankAccountConnectionString"].ConnectionString;
        }

        public void Add(BankAccount bankAccount)
        {
            string insertSql = "INSERT INTO BankAccounts " +
                            "(BankAccountID, Balance, CustomerRef) VALUES " +
                            "(@BankAccountID, @Balance, @CustomerRef)";

            using (SqlConnection connection =
                    new SqlConnection(_connectionString))
            {
                SqlCommand command = connection.CreateCommand();
                command.CommandText = insertSql;

                SetCommandParametersForInsertUpdateTo(bankAccount, command);

                connection.Open();

                command.ExecuteNonQuery();
            }

            UpdateTransactionsFor(bankAccount);
        }

        public void Save(BankAccount bankAccount)
        {
            string bankAccoutnUpdateSql =
                    "UPDATE BankAccounts " +
                    "SET Balance = @Balance, CustomerRef= @CustomerRef " +
```

```csharp
            "WHERE BankAccountID = @BankAccountID;";

    using (SqlConnection connection =
            new SqlConnection(_connectionString))
    {
        SqlCommand command = connection.CreateCommand();
        command.CommandText = bankAccoutnUpdateSql;

        SetCommandParametersForInsertUpdateTo(bankAccount, command);

        connection.Open();

        command.ExecuteNonQuery();
    }

    UpdateTransactionsFor(bankAccount);
}

private static void SetCommandParametersForInsertUpdateTo(
                    BankAccount bankAccount, SqlCommand command)
{
   command.Parameters.Add(
        new SqlParameter("@BankAccountID", bankAccount.AccountNo));
    command.Parameters.Add(new SqlParameter("@Balance", bankAccount.Balance));
   command.Parameters.Add(
        new SqlParameter("@CustomerRef", bankAccount.CustomerRef));
}

private void UpdateTransactionsFor(BankAccount bankAccount)
{
    string deleteTransactionSQl =
        "DELETE Transactions WHERE BankAccountId = @BankAccountId;";

    using (SqlConnection connection =
            new SqlConnection(_connectionString))
    {
        SqlCommand command = connection.CreateCommand();
        command.CommandText = deleteTransactionSQl;
        command.Parameters.Add(
            new SqlParameter("@BankAccountID", bankAccount.AccountNo));
        connection.Open();
        command.ExecuteNonQuery();

    }

    string insertTransactionSql =
        "INSERT INTO Transactions " +
            "(BankAccountID, Deposit, Withdraw, Reference, [Date]) VALUES " +
        "(@BankAccountID, @Deposit,  @Withdraw,  @Reference, @Date)";

    foreach (Transaction tran in bankAccount.GetTransactions())
    {
        using (SqlConnection connection =
                new SqlConnection(_connectionString))
        {
            SqlCommand command = connection.CreateCommand();
```

```
            command.CommandText = insertTransactionSql;

            command.Parameters.Add(
                new SqlParameter("@BankAccountID",
                                 bankAccount.AccountNo));
            command.Parameters.Add(new SqlParameter("@Deposit", tran.Deposit));
          command.Parameters.Add(
                new SqlParameter("@Withdraw", tran.Withdrawal));
          command.Parameters.Add(
                new SqlParameter("@Reference", tran.Reference));
          command.Parameters.Add(new SqlParameter("@Date", tran.Date));

            connection.Open();
            command.ExecuteNonQuery();
        }
    }
}

public IEnumerable<BankAccount> FindAll()
{
    IList<BankAccount> accounts = new List<BankAccount>();

    string queryString =
      "SELECT * FROM dbo.Transactions INNER JOIN " +
      "dbo.BankAccounts ON " +
        "dbo.Transactions.BankAccountId = dbo.BankAccounts.BankAccountId " +
      "ORDER BY dbo.BankAccounts.BankAccountId;";

    using (SqlConnection connection =
            new SqlConnection(_connectionString))
    {
            SqlCommand command = connection.CreateCommand();
            command.CommandText = queryString;

            connection.Open();

            using (SqlDataReader reader = command.ExecuteReader())
            {
                accounts = CreateListOfAccountsFrom(reader);
            }
    }

    return accounts;
}

private IList<BankAccount> CreateListOfAccountsFrom(
                                    IDataReader datareader)
{
    IList<BankAccount> accounts = new List<BankAccount>();
    BankAccount bankAccount;
    string id = "";
    IList<Transaction> transactions = new List<Transaction>();

    while (datareader.Read())
    {
        if (id != datareader["BankAccountId"].ToString())
```

```
                {
                    id = datareader["BankAccountId"].ToString();
                    transactions = new List<Transaction>();
                    bankAccount = new BankAccount(
                        new Guid(id), Decimal.Parse(datareader["Balance"].ToString()),
                        transactions, datareader["CustomerRef"].ToString());

                    accounts.Add(bankAccount);
                }
                transactions.Add(CreateTransactionFrom(datareader));
            }

        return accounts;
    }

    private Transaction CreateTransactionFrom(IDataRecord rawData)
    {
        return new Transaction(
                Decimal.Parse(rawData["Deposit"].ToString()),
                Decimal.Parse(rawData["Withdraw"].ToString()),
                rawData["Reference"].ToString(),
                DateTime.Parse(rawData["Date"].ToString()));
    }


    public BankAccount FindBy(Guid accountId)
    {
        BankAccount account;

        string queryString = "SELECT * FROM " +
                            "dbo.Transactions INNER JOIN " +
                            "dbo.BankAccounts ON " +
                            "dbo.Transactions.BankAccountId = " +
                            "dbo.BankAccounts.BankAccountId " +
            "WHERE dbo.BankAccounts.BankAccountId = @BankAccountId;";

        using (SqlConnection connection =
                new SqlConnection(_connectionString))
        {
            SqlCommand command = connection.CreateCommand();
            command.CommandText = queryString;

            SqlParameter Idparam = new SqlParameter("@BankAccountId", accountId);
            command.Parameters.Add(Idparam);

            connection.Open();

            using (SqlDataReader reader = command.ExecuteReader())
            {
                account = CreateListOfAccountsFrom(reader)[0];
            }
        }
        return account;
    }
  }
}
```

Now that you have dealt with the persistence and retrieval needs, you can add a service layer for clients to interact with the system in an easy manner.

Add a new folder to the `AppServices` project named `ViewModel` and add to it a new class named `BankAccountView` and one named `TransactionView` with the following definition:

```
public class TransactionView
{
    public string Deposit { get; set; }
    public string Withdrawal { get; set; }
    public string Reference { get; set; }
    public DateTime Date { get; set; }
}

public class BankAccountView
{
    public Guid AccountNo { get; set; }
    public string Balance { get; set; }
    public string CustomerRef { get; set; }
    public IList<TransactionView> Transactions { get; set; }
}
```

The `BankAccountView` and `TransactionView` offer a flattened view of the domain model for presentation purposes, which is an idea you will examine more closely in Chapter 6. To transform your domain entities into data transfer view models, you will need a mapper class. Again, you will take a closer look at this and a way to automate this process in Chapter 8. Create a new class named `ViewMapper` with the following two static methods:

```
using ASPPatterns.Chap4.DomainModel.Model;

namespace ASPPatterns.Chap4.DomainModel.AppService
{
    public static class ViewMapper
    {
        public static TransactionView CreateTransactionViewFrom(
                                                        Transaction tran)
        {
            return new TransactionView
            {
                Deposit = tran.Deposit.ToString("C"),
                Withdrawal = tran.Withdrawal.ToString("C"),
                Reference = tran.Reference,
                Date = tran.Date
            };
        }

        public static BankAccountView CreateBankAccountViewFrom(
                                                        BankAccount acc)
        {
            return new BankAccountView
            {
                AccountNo = acc.AccountNo,
                Balance = acc.Balance.ToString("C"),
                CustomerRef = acc.CustomerRef,
```

```
                    Transactions = new List<TransactionView>()
            };
        }
    }
}
```

Add a second folder to the `AppServices` project named `Messages`; this folder will contain all the request-reply objects used to communicate with the service layer. Messaging patterns are covered in more detail in Chapter 6. Because all the replies shared a common set of properties, you can create a base class. Add a new class to the `Messages` folder named `ResponseBase`, with the following code listing:

```
namespace ASPPatterns.Chap4.DomainModel.AppService.Messages
{
    public abstract class ResponseBase
    {
        public bool Success { get; set; }
        public string Message { get; set; }
    }
}
```

The `Success` property indicates whether the method called was run successfully, and the `Message` property contains details of the outcome of the method run.

You now need to implement all the request and reply objects; create a new class for each of the class listings displayed next:

```
public class BankAccountCreateRequest
{
    public string CustomerName { get; set; }
}

public class BankAccountCreateResponse : ResponseBase
{
    public Guid BankAccountId { get; set; }
}

public class DepositRequest
{
    public Guid AccountId { get; set; }
    public decimal Amount { get; set; }
}

public class FindAllBankAccountResponse : ResponseBase
{
    public IList<BankAccountView> BankAccountView { get; set; }
}

public class FindBankAccountResponse : ResponseBase
{
    public BankAccountView BankAccount { get; set; }
}

public class TransferRequest
{
```

```
        public Guid AccountIdTo { get; set; }
        public Guid AccountIdFrom { get; set; }
        public decimal Amount { get; set; }
}

public class TransferResponse : ResponseBase
{
}

public class WithdrawalRequest
{
        public Guid AccountId { get; set; }
        public decimal Amount { get; set; }
}
```

With all the messaging objects in place, you can add the service class that coordinates the method calls to the domain entities: service and repository. Add a new class named ApplicationBank AccountService at the root of the AppService project:

```
using ASPPatterns.Chap4.DomainModel.Model;
using ASPPatterns.Chap4.DomainModel.Repository;
using ASPPatterns.Chap4.DomainModel.AppService.Messages;

namespace ASPPatterns.Chap4.DomainModel.AppService
{
    public class ApplicationBankAccountService
    {
        private BankAccountService _bankAccountService;
        private IBankAccountRepository _bankRepository;

        public ApplicationBankAccountService() :
            this (new BankAccountRepository(),
                new BankAccountService(new BankAccountRepository()))
        { }

        public ApplicationBankAccountService(
                        IBankAccountRepository bankRepository,
                        BankAccountService bankAccountService)
        {
            _bankRepository = bankRepository;
            _bankAccountService = bankAccountService;
        }

        public ApplicationBankAccountService(
                        BankAccountService bankAccountService,
                        IBankAccountRepository bankRepository)
        {
            _bankAccountService = bankAccountService;
            _bankRepository = bankRepository;
        }

        public BankAccountCreateResponse CreateBankAccount(
                    BankAccountCreateRequest bankAccountCreateRequest)
        {
            BankAccountCreateResponse bankAccountCreateResponse =
                                    new BankAccountCreateResponse();
```

```
        BankAccount bankAccount = new BankAccount();

        bankAccount.CustomerRef = bankAccountCreateRequest.CustomerName;
        _bankRepository.Add(bankAccount);

        return bankAccountCreateResponse;
    }

    public void Deposit(DepositRequest depositRequest)
    {
        BankAccount bankAccount = _bankRepository.FindBy(depositRequest.AccountId);

        bankAccount.Deposit(depositRequest.Amount, "");

        _bankRepository.Save(bankAccount);
    }

    public void Withdrawal(WithdrawalRequest withdrawalRequest)
    {
        BankAccount bankAccount =
            _bankRepository.FindBy(withdrawalRequest.AccountId);

        bankAccount.Withdraw(withdrawalRequest.Amount, "");

        _bankRepository.Save(bankAccount);
    }

    public TransferResponse Transfer(TransferRequest request)
    {
        TransferResponse response = new TransferResponse();

        try
        {
            _bankAccountService.Transfer(request.AccountIdTo,
                                    request.AccountIdFrom, request.Amount);
            response.Success = true;
        }
        catch (InsufficientFundsException)
        {
            response.Message = "There is not enough funds in account no: " +
                            request.AccountIdFrom.ToString();
            response.Success = false;
        }

        return response;
    }

    public FindAllBankAccountResponse GetAllBankAccounts()
    {
        FindAllBankAccountResponse FindAllBankAccountResponse =
                            new FindAllBankAccountResponse();
        IList<BankAccountView> bankAccountViews =
                            new List<BankAccountView>();
        FindAllBankAccountResponse.BankAccountView = bankAccountViews;

        foreach (BankAccount acc in _bankRepository.FindAll())
```

```
            {
                bankAccountViews.Add(
                        ViewMapper.CreateBankAccountViewFrom(acc));
            }

            return FindAllBankAccountResponse;
        }

        public FindBankAccountResponse GetBankAccountBy(Guid Id)
        {
            FindBankAccountResponse bankAccountResponse = new FindBankAccountResponse();
            BankAccount acc = _bankRepository.FindBy(Id);
            BankAccountView bankAccountView = ViewMapper.CreateBankAccountViewFrom(acc);

            foreach (Transaction tran in acc.GetTransactions())
            {
                bankAccountView.Transactions.Add(
                        ViewMapper.CreateTransactionViewFrom(tran));
            }

            bankAccountResponse.BankAccount = bankAccountView;

            return bankAccountResponse;
        }

    }
}
```

The `BankAccountApplicationService` class coordinates the application activity and delegates all business tasks to the domain model. This layer does not contain business logic and helps to prevent any non-business-related code from polluting the domain model project. The layer also transforms domain entities into data transfer objects that protect the inner workings of the domain and provide an easy API for the presentation layer to work with.

To keep things simple I have elected to use "poor man's dependency injection" and hard coded the default constructor to use the repository domain service implementations that you have coded. In Chapter 8, you will learn about Inversion of Control and Inversion of Control Containers to supply the dependencies of a class.

Your last action is to create a user interface to enable accounts to be created and transactions to take place. Open the `Default.aspx` in source mode from within the `Web` project and edit the markup so it matches the following snippet:

```
...
<form id="form1" runat="server">
<div>

  <fieldset>
     <legend>Create New Account</legend>
  <p>
     Customer Ref:
     <asp:TextBox ID="txtCustomerRef" runat="server" />

     <asp:Button ID="btCreateAccount" runat="server" Text="Create Account"
```

```
            onclick="btCreateAccount_Click" />
</p>
</fieldset>

<fieldset>
    <legend>Account Detail</legend>
    <p>
    <asp:DropDownList AutoPostBack="true"
        ID="ddlBankAccounts" runat="server"
        onselectedindexchanged="ddlBankAccounts_SelectedIndexChanged"/ >
    </p>
    <p>
        Account No:
        <asp:Label ID="lblAccountNo" runat="server" />
    </p>
    <p>
        Customer Ref:
        <asp:Label ID="lblCustomerRef" runat="server" />
    </p>
    <p>
        Balance:
        <asp:Label ID="lblBalance" runat="server" />
    </p>
    <p>
        Amount f<asp:TextBox ID="txtAmount" runat="server" Width="60px"/>
         
        <asp:Button ID="btnWithdrawal" runat="server" Text="Withdrawal"
            onclick="btnWithdrawal_Click" />
         
        <asp:Button ID="btnDeposit" runat="server" Text="Deposit"
            onclick="btnDeposit_Click" />
    </p>
    <p>
        Transfer
        f<asp:TextBox ID="txtAmountToTransfer" runat="server"
                    Width="60px" />

     to
    <asp:DropDownList AutoPostBack="true"
        ID="ddlBankAccountsToTransferTo" runat="server"/>
     
     <asp:Button ID="btnTransfer" runat="server" Text="Commit"
            onclick="btnTransfer_Click" />
    </p>
    <p>
        Transactions</p>
        <asp:Repeater ID="rptTransactions" runat="server">
            <HeaderTemplate>
                <table>
                <tr>
                    <td>deposit</td>
                    <td>withdrawal</td>
                    <td>reference</td>
                </tr>
            </HeaderTemplate>
```

```
                    <ItemTemplate>
                        <tr>
                            <td><%# Eval("Deposit")   %></td>
                            <td><%# Eval("Withdrawal")   %></td>
                            <td><%# Eval("Reference")   %></td>
                            <td><%# Eval("Date")   %></td>
                        </tr>
                    </ItemTemplate>
                    <FooterTemplate>
                        </table>
                    </FooterTemplate>
                </asp:Repeater>
        </fieldset>
        </div>
        </form>
    </body>
</html>
```

Switch to the code behind of the `Default.aspx` page and update to match the following code listing:

```csharp
using System;
using System.Web.UI.WebControls;
using ASPPatterns.Chap4.DomainModel.AppService;
using ASPPatterns.Chap4.DomainModel.AppService.Messages;

namespace ASPPatterns.Chap4.DomainModel.UI.Web
{
    public partial class _Default : System.Web.UI.Page
    {
        protected void Page_Load(object sender, EventArgs e)
        {
            if (!Page.IsPostBack)
                ShowAllAccounts();
        }

        private void ShowAllAccounts()
        {
            ddlBankAccounts.Items.Clear();

            FindAllBankAccountResponse response =
                    new ApplicationBankAccountService().GetAllBankAccounts();
            ddlBankAccounts.Items.Add(new ListItem("Select An Account", ""));

            foreach (BankAccountView accView in response.BankAccountView)
            {
                ddlBankAccounts.Items.Add(
                 new ListItem(accView.CustomerRef, accView.AccountNo.ToString()));
            }
        }

        protected void btCreateAccount_Click(object sender, EventArgs e)
        {
            BankAccountCreateRequest createAccountRequest =
                                        new BankAccountCreateRequest();
            createAccountRequest.CustomerName = this.txtCustomerRef.Text;
```

```
        ApplicationBankAccountService service = new ApplicationBankAccountService();

        service.CreateBankAccount(createAccountRequest);

        ShowAllAccounts();
}

protected void ddlBankAccounts_SelectedIndexChanged(object sender, EventArgs e)
{
    DisplaySelectedAccount();
}

private void DisplaySelectedAccount()
{
    if (ddlBankAccounts.SelectedValue.ToString() != "")
    {
        ApplicationBankAccountService service =
                                    new ApplicationBankAccountService();
        FindBankAccountResponse response =
                service.GetBankAccountBy(
                    new Guid(ddlBankAccounts.SelectedValue.ToString()));
        BankAccountView accView = response.BankAccount;

        this.lblAccountNo.Text = accView.Balance.ToString();
        this.lblBalance.Text = accView.Balance.ToString();
        this.lblCustomerRef.Text = accView.CustomerRef;

        rptTransactions.DataSource = accView.Transactions;
        rptTransactions.DataBind();

        FindAllBankAccountResponse allAccountsResponse =
                                    service.GetAllBankAccounts();

        ddlBankAccountsToTransferTo.Items.Clear();

        foreach (BankAccountView acc in allAccountsResponse.BankAccountView)
        {
            if (acc.AccountNo.ToString() !=
                            ddlBankAccounts.SelectedValue.ToString())
                ddlBankAccountsToTransferTo.Items.Add(
                  new ListItem(acc.CustomerRef, acc.AccountNo.ToString()));
        }
    }
}

protected void btnWithdrawal_Click(object sender, EventArgs e)
{
    ApplicationBankAccountService service = new ApplicationBankAccountService();
    WithdrawalRequest request = new WithdrawalRequest();
    Guid AccId = new Guid(ddlBankAccounts.SelectedValue.ToString());
    request.AccountId = AccId;
    request.Amount = Decimal.Parse(txtAmount.Text);

    service.Withdrawal(request);
    DisplaySelectedAccount();
```

```
        }

        protected void btnDeposit_Click(object sender, EventArgs e)
        {
            ApplicationBankAccountService service = new ApplicationBankAccountService();
            DepositRequest request = new DepositRequest();
            Guid AccId = new Guid(ddlBankAccounts.SelectedValue.ToString());
            request.AccountId = AccId;
            request.Amount = Decimal.Parse(txtAmount.Text);

            service.Deposit(request);
            DisplaySelectedAccount();
        }

        protected void btnTransfer_Click(object sender, EventArgs e)
        {
            ApplicationBankAccountService service = new ApplicationBankAccountService();
            TransferRequest request = new TransferRequest();
            request.AccountIdFrom = new Guid(ddlBankAccounts.SelectedValue.ToString());
            request.AccountIdTo =
                        new Guid(ddlBankAccountsToTransferTo.SelectedValue.ToString());
            request.Amount = Decimal.Parse(txtAmountToTransfer.Text);

            service.Transfer(request);
            DisplaySelectedAccount();
        }
    }
}
```

Finally add the connection string for the database to the web.config file of the web application:

```
<connectionStrings>
    <add name="BankAccountConnectionString"
        connectionString="DataSource=.\SQLEXPRESS;
        AttachDbFilename=|DataDirectory|\BankAccount.mdf;
        Integrated Security=True;User Instance=True"
        providerName="System.Data.SqlClient"/>
</connectionStrings>
```

And that's all there is to it. Launch the application, and you will see a screen that looks similar to the one in Figure 4-6.

Trying to solve complex business problems in software is difficult, but when using the Domain Model pattern, you first create an abstract model of the real business model. With this model in place, you can then model complex logic by following the real domain and recreating the workflow and processing in your domain model. Another advantage that a Domain Model pattern holds over the Transaction Script and the Active Record patterns is that, because it contains no data access code, you can easily unit test it without having to mock and stub out dependencies of such a data access layer. Again, the Domain Model pattern may not always be a great fit for your application needs. One of its great strengths is dealing with complex business logic, but a full-blown domain model is architectural overkill when very little business logic is contained within the application. Another disadvantage of the pattern is the steep learning curve needed to become proficient in it compared to the Active Record and Transaction Script options. Using the pattern effectively takes time and experience and, most importantly, a sound knowledge of the business domain you are trying to model.

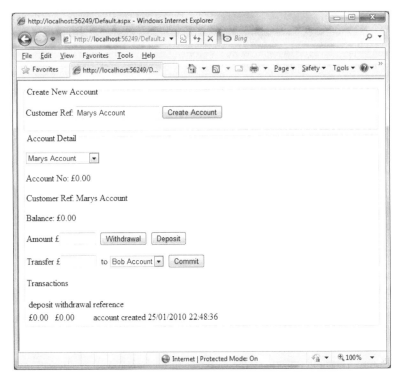

FIGURE 4-6

Anemic Domain Model

The Anemic Domain Model is sometimes referred to as an antipattern. At first glance, the pattern is very similar to the Domain Model in that you will still find domain objects that represent the business domain. Any behavior, however, is not contained within the domain objects. instead, it is found outside of the model, leaving domain objects as simple data transfer classes.

The major disadvantage of this pattern is that the domain services take on the role of a more procedural style of code rather like the Transaction Script pattern that you saw at the beginning of the chapter, which brings along the issues associated with it. One such issue is the violation of the "Tell, Don't Ask" principle which states that objects should tell the client what they can or can't do rather than exposing properties and leaving it up to the client to determine if an object is in a particular state for a given action to take place.

If you consider the example that you used for the Domain Model exercise, the `Transaction` and `BankAccount` domain objects are now stripped of their logic and are simply data containers as can be seen in the following code snippet.

```
public class Transaction
{
```

```
        public Guid Id { get; set; }
        public decimal Deposit { get; set; }
        public decimal Withdraw { get; set; }
        public string Reference { get; set; }
        public DateTime Date { get; set; }
        public Guid BankAccountId { get; set; }
    }

    public class BankAccount
    {
        public BankAccount()
        {
            Transactions = new List<Transaction>();
        }

        public Guid AccountNo { get; set; }
        public decimal Balance { get; set; }
        public string CustomerRef { get; set; }
        public IList<Transaction> Transactions { get; set; }
    }
```

Separate classes are involved to implement logic. The Specification pattern, covered in more detail in Chapter 5, can be used to determine if an account has sufficient funds to make a withdrawal, as shown here:

```
    public class BankAccountHasEnoughFundsToWithdrawSpecification
    {
        private decimal _amountToWithdraw;

        public BankAccountHasEnoughFundsToWithdrawSpecification(
                                        decimal amountToWithdraw)
        {
            _amountToWithdraw = amountToWithdraw;
        }

        public bool IsSatisfiedBy(BankAccount bankAccount)
        {
            return bankAccount.Balance >= _amountToWithdraw;
        }
    }
```

The domain service class that you created in the Domain model will now utilize the specification when coordinating a withdrawal or bank transfer:

```
    public class BankAccountService
    {
        ...

        public void Transfer(Guid accountNoTo, Guid accountNoFrom,
                                            decimal amount)
        {
            BankAccount bankAccountTo =
                    _bankAccountRepository.FindBy(accountNoTo);
            BankAccount bankAccountFrom =
```

```
                    _bankAccountRepository.FindBy(accountNoFrom);

        BankAccountHasEnoughFundsToWithdrawSpecification HasEnoughFunds =
                new BankAccountHasEnoughFundsToWithdrawSpecification(amount);

        if (HasEnoughFunds.IsSatisfiedBy(bankAccountFrom))
        {
            // … make the bank transfer..
        }
        else
        {
            throw new InsufficientFundsException();
        }
    }

    public void Withdraw(Guid accountNo, decimal amount,
                                        string reference)
    {
        BankAccount bankAccount =
                _bankAccountRepository.FindBy(accountNo);

        BankAccountHasEnoughFundsToWithdrawSpecification HasEnoughFunds =
            new BankAccountHasEnoughFundsToWithdrawSpecification(amount);

        if (HasEnoughFunds.IsSatisfiedBy(bankAccount))
        {
            // … make the withdraw …
        }
    }

    ...
}
```

The next section discusses domain-driven design, a popular design methodology that concentrates on business logic over infrastructure concerns, which is a good fit for the Domain Model pattern and the organization of complex business logic.

Domain-Driven Design

The Domain Model pattern is useful when dealing with complex business logic. A popular design methodology that utilizes the Domain Model pattern is known as DDD.

In a nutshell, DDD is a collection of patterns and principles that aid in your efforts to build applications that reflect an understanding of and meet the requirements of your business. Outside of that, it's a whole new way of thinking about your development methodology. DDD is about modeling the real domain by first fully understanding it and placing all the terminology, rules, and logic into an abstract representation within your code, typically in the form of a domain model.

You will take a look at the main aspects of DDD because this is the methodology that is used for the majority of exercises in the remainder of this book.

The Ubiquitous Language

The notion of a ubiquitous language is that it should act as a common vocabulary that is used by developers, domain experts, and anyone else involved in a project to describe the domain. A domain expert is someone with the knowledge and skills in a particular domain who will work closely with you as you develop the domain model to ensure that you fully understand the business model before trying to represent it in code. In the example of a loan application, this could be an underwriter. Through listening to this person, you will build a vocabulary of all terminology used during the process of approving a loan. Your class, methods, and property names should all be based around the same ubiquitous language. This enables you to talk to domain experts about code in a language that they understand; also, new developers working on the code should get a good grounding in what the domain is really all about. It will also enable them to talk to business experts about the smallest details of complex business logic with relative ease. When all parties involved in the development of an application are speaking the same language, problems and solutions can be conveyed easily, making the application quicker and easier to build.

DDD is not a framework, but it does have a set of building blocks or concepts that you can incorporate into your solution. The following sections introduce these concepts one at a time.

Entities

Entities are the things discussed previously in the Domain Model section, such as an order, customer, and product in an e-commerce site and a blog, and post objects in a blogging application. They encompass the data and behavior of the real entity in an abstract manner. Any logic pertaining to an entity should be contained within it. Entities are the things that require an identity, which will remain with it throughout its lifetime. Consider a borrower in terms of a loan application; a borrower has a name, but names can change and can be duplicated, so you need to add a separate identity that will stay with the borrower through its life in the loan application regardless of a name, job, or address change. Typically, a system uses some kind of unique identifier or auto-numbering value for any entities that don't have a natural way to identify them. Sometimes entities do have natural keys, such as a Social Security number or an employee number. Not all the objects in your domain model are unique and require an identity. For some objects, it's the data that is of most importance, not identity; these objects are called *value objects*.

Value Objects

Value objects have no identity; they are of value because of their attributes only. Value objects generally don't live on their own; they are typically, but not always, attributes of an entity. If you cast your mind back to the simple Bank Account application that you worked on in the Domain Model, you remember that the `Transaction` object had no identity because it exists only in terms of the Bank Account that it is associated with; it is a value object because, in this context, it doesn't exist on its own.

Aggregates and Aggregate Roots

Big systems or complex domains can have hundreds of entity and value objects, which have complex relationships. The domain model needs a method of managing these associations; more importantly, logical groups of entities and value objects need to define an interface that lets other entities work with them. Without such a structure, the interaction between groups of objects can be confusing and lead to problems later.

The notion of an aggregation groups logical entities and value objects. From the DDD definition, an *aggregate* is simply "a cluster of associated objects that are treated as a unit for the purpose of data changes." The aggregate root is an entity, which is the only member of the aggregate that any object outside the aggregate is allowed to hold a reference to. The idea of an aggregate exists in DDD to ensure data integrity within the domain model. An aggregate root is a special entity that acts as the logical way into the aggregate. For example, if you take an order in the context of an e-commerce shop, you can regard it as the aggregate root, because you only want to be able to edit an order line or apply a voucher by going through the root of the aggregate—that is, the order entity. This enables complex object graphs to remain consistent and business rules to be adhered to. So, instead of an order just exposing a collection of vouchers issued against it through a simple `List` property, it can have methods with complex rules that enable vouchers to be applied to it and expose the list of vouchers as a read-only collection for display purposes.

Domain Services

As you saw in the Domain Model Pattern Bank Account exercise, the `BankAccountService` class contained the logic to transfer funds between two bank accounts. Methods that don't really fit on a single entity or require access to the repository are contained within domain services. The domain service layer can also contain domain logic of its own and is as much part of the domain model as entities and value objects.

Application Services

The Application service is a thin layer that sits above the domain model and coordinates the application activity. It does not contain business logic and does not hold the state of any entities; however, it can store the state of a business workflow transaction. You use an Application service in the Domain Model Bank Account exercise to provide an API into the domain model using the Request-Reply messaging pattern.

Repository

The Repository pattern, which you will examine in more detail in Chapter 7, acts as an in-memory collection or repository for business entities, completely abstracting away the underlying data infrastructure. This pattern allows you to keep your domain model free of any infrastructure concerns, making it POCO and PI.

Layering

Layering is an important concept in DDD because it helps to enforce the separation of concerns. Figure 4-7 shows a graphical representation of the layers and concepts that make up DDD; however, I should stress that DDD is much more about your mindset when developing complex business applications than how you set up your solution.

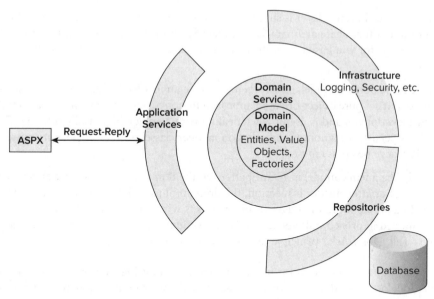

FIGURE 4-7

The Bank Account application you worked on for the domain model exercise was built around the concepts of DDD. Figure 4-8 shows the layers in the Bank Account application and how they relate to the concepts of DDD.

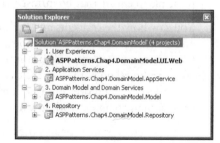

You have only had a brief introduction to DDD in this chapter, although you will revisit it for the case study, where you will also be introduced to user stories for building requirements and understanding the domain you are working in. For a deeper insight into this methodology, I recommend the following books:

FIGURE 4-8

➤ *Domain-Driven Design: Tackling Complexity in the Heart of Software* (Addison-Wesley 2003) by Eric Evans

➤ *Applying Domain-Driven Design and Patterns: Using .Net With Examples in C# and .NET* (Addison-Wesley 2006) by Jimmy Nilsson

SUMMARY

In this chapter you learned about some popular and proven patterns for organizing your business logic. The three main methods were:

➤ **Transaction Script:** If you have a simple application with little or no logic, Transaction Script is a great choice as a straightforward solution that is easily understood by other developers picking up your code down the line.

➤ **Active Record:** If your business layer is simply a thin veil over the top of your database, this is a great pattern to opt for. There are many code-generation tools that can automatically create your business objects for you based on your database schema, and it's not too difficult to create your own.

➤ **Domain Model:** The domain model excels when you have an involved, rich, complex business domain to model. It's a pure object-oriented approach that involves creating an abstract model of the real business domain and is useful when dealing with complex logic and workflow. The domain model is persistence ignorant and relies on mapper classes and the Repository pattern to persist and retrieve business entities.

➤ **Anemic Model:** The anemic model is an antipattern of the domain model. At first glance they appear the same, but after further inspection, the domain objects that represent the domain you are modeling are no more than data transfer objects with no behavior. The logic of the domain is contained in procedural type methods that validate or check the state of an object, violating the "Tell, Don't Ask" principle discussed in Chapter 1.

After learning about the four main methods for organizing your business logic layer, you were introduced to a design methodology named domain-driven design (DDD), which utilizes a domain model to represent complex logic in terms of services, entities, value objects, and aggregates. DDD also encouraged you to focus on the business logic and the domain you are working with and used the POCO or PI principle to ensure that no infrastructure concerns polluted the pure business domain model.

You saw how the concepts and building blocks of DDD were applied to the Bank Account application and how they enabled a clean model of the domain you were working within, free of any infrastructure concerns and an application that spoke the same language as the domain in terms of project, class, and method names. In the case study that you will work on in Chapters 10 and 11, you will see how a larger and more complex domain is used and how, by sticking to the principles of DDD, it is easy to map complex workflow and business transactions.

The next chapter investigates the kinds of patterns and principles that you can use within the business layer of an enterprise application.

5

The Business Logic Layer: Patterns

WHAT'S IN THIS CHAPTER?

➤ How to use the Factory, Decorator, Template, State, Strategy, and Composite GoF patterns in the business layer of an ASP.NET application

➤ Demonstrations of how to utilize the Specification and Layer Supertype enterprise patterns in your ASP.NET code

➤ Improve your code's maintainability and flexibility with Dependency Injection, Interface Segregation, and the Liskov Substitution Principle

The previous chapter introduced the kinds of patterns you can use to organize your applications' middleware. This chapter looks at some specific patterns that you can leverage within the business logic layer. You examine some Gang of Four design patterns, some Enterprise design patterns, and finally some design principles that can help you keep your business logic loosely coupled and highly cohesive. You can use design patterns in any layer of your application. The series of patterns and principles in this chapter is shown in the context of the business layer of an application, but nothing can stop you from applying these patterns in the presentation, infrastructure, or data access layers of your application.

LEVERAGING DESIGN PATTERNS

In this first section, you look at the following design patterns that can assist you in your solution to your application's business problems:

➤ Factory Method pattern

➤ Decorator pattern

➤   Template Method pattern

➤   State pattern

➤   Strategy pattern

Factory Method

The Factory Method pattern belongs to the creational group of the Gang of Four design patterns and handles the issue of creating objects without specifying the exact class of object to be created.

Intent

The main objective of the Factory pattern is to hide the complexities of creating objects. As well, the client doesn't normally specify a particular class to be created. Instead, the client will code against an interface or abstract class and leave the responsibility to the Factory class to create the concrete type. Typically a `Factory` class has a static method that returns an abstract class or interface. The client usually, but not always, supplies some kind of information; using the supplied information the Factory then determines which subclass to create and return.

The ability to abstract away the responsibility of creating subclasses allows your client code to be completely ignorant of how dependent classes are created. This follows the Dependency Inversion principle (DIP) that you will read about later in this chapter. Another benefit of the Factory Method pattern is that you centralize the code for the creation of objects; if a change is required in the way an object is generated, it can be easily located and updated without affecting the code that depends on it.

UML

Figure 5-1 shows the UML representation of the Factory Method pattern.

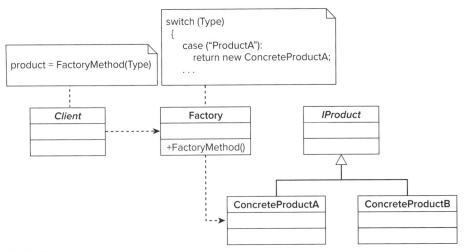

FIGURE 5-1

The classes shown in Figure 5-1 collaborate to form the Factory Method pattern. Their roles are as follows:

➤ The `Client` class obtains an implementation of `IProduct` via a call to the `Factory` class. The `Client` passes some information on the type of subclass but has no idea how to create it.

➤ The `Factory` class is responsible for creating the correct subclass based on information supplied via a parameter.

➤ The `IProduct` is the interface that the `Client` references in its code routine and that is implemented by the `ConcreteProductA` and `ConcreteProductB` classes.

➤ `ConcreteProductA` and `ConcreteProductB` are the subclass implementations of `IProduct`.

Code Example

In this example you employ the Factory Method pattern to obtain the correct shipping courier in a fictional e-commerce application. In this scenario, an `OrderService` class has a single method named `Dispatch` that coordinates the creation of a courier object, which in turn is used to create a consignment identifier for a parcel. Figure 5-2 shows all the classes involved in the solution.

FIGURE 5-2

To build the solution, you need a project, so start by creating a solution named `ASPPatterns.Chap5.FactoryPattern`, and a new C# class library project and naming it `ASPPatterns.Chap5.FactoryPattern.Model`.

First you will build the simple domain model, which consists of an `Order` entity and an `Address` value object, which represent a real order and dispatch address. Add a new class to the project named `Address` with the following code listing:

```
namespace ASPPatterns.Chap5.FactoryPattern.Model
{
    public class Address
    {
        public string CountryCode { get; set; }
    }
}
```

Add a second class to the project named `Order`, with the code listing as defined here:

```
namespace ASPPatterns.Chap5.FactoryPattern.Model
{
    public class Order
    {
        public decimal TotalCost { get; set; }
        public decimal WeightInKG { get; set; }
        public string CourierTrackingId { get; set; }
        public Address DispatchAddress { get; set; }
    }
}
```

Next you need to create the interface for the couriers. Add a new interface to the project named `IShippingCourier`, with the contract as defined here:

```
namespace ASPPatterns.Chap5.FactoryPattern.Model
{
    public interface IShippingCourier
    {
        string GenerateConsignmentLabelFor(Address address);
    }
}
```

The `IShippingCourier` has a single simple method that takes an `Address` parameter as an argument and returns a consignment ID as a string.

Now that you have the contract defined, you can add two implementations of the interface. Add a new class to the project named `DHL` with the following code listing:

```
namespace ASPPatterns.Chap5.FactoryPattern.Model
{
    public class DHL : IShippingCourier
    {
        public string GenerateConsignmentLabelFor(Address address)
        {
            return "DHL-XXXX-XXXX-XXXX";
        }
    }
}
```

Add a second implementation of the interface to the project this time named `RoyalMail`, as shown here:

```
namespace ASPPatterns.Chap5.FactoryPattern.Model
{
    public class RoyalMail : IShippingCourier
    {
        public string GenerateConsignmentLabelFor(Address address)
        {
            return "RMXXXX-XXXX-XXXX"; ;
        }
    }
}
```

To keep the exercise simple, the two courier implementations just return hard-coded string values that represent courier consignment IDs; in reality these classes would integrate with the courier's third-party solution to generate trackable consignment IDs.

The role of the `Factory` class is to determine which courier should be used based on the value and weight of the order. Add a new class to the project named `UKShippingCourierFactory` with the code listing as defined here:

```
namespace ASPPatterns.Chap5.FactoryPattern.Model
{
    public static class UKShippingCourierFactory
    {
        public static IShippingCourier CreateShippingCourier(Order order)
        {
            if ((order.TotalCost > 100) || (order.WeightInKG > 5))
                return new DHL();
            else
                return new RoyalMail();
        }
    }
}
```

The `Factory` class has a single static method named `CreateShippingCourier` that returns a shipping courier implementing the `IShippingCourier` interface. The `Factory` method determines which courier to return based on the total cost and weight of an order.

Finally, add the `OrderService` class. Add a new class to the project named `OrderService` with the code listing here:

```
namespace ASPPatterns.Chap5.FactoryPattern.Model
{
    public class OrderService
    {
        public void Dispatch(Order order)
        {
            IShippingCourier shippingCourier =
                    UKShippingCourierFactory.CreateShippingCourierFor(order);

            order.CourierTrackingId =
                    shippingCourier.GenerateConsignmentLabelFor(order.DispatchAddress);
        }
    }
}
```

As you can see, the `Dispatch` method simply coordinates the obtaining of a valid courier and the creation of a consignment identifier. The role of the `Factory` class in this instance is to be solely responsible for creating a valid shipping courier based on some business logic. By abstracting away business logic to the `Factory` class, you are removing the burden from the `OrderService` class, which can concentrate on its single responsibility of coordinating a task rather than worrying about the low-level details of how this is achieved. If you ever need to introduce a new shipping courier or change the business rules on which courier to use, you can do so by amending the `Factory` class with no impact on the `Service` class; this concept is fundamental to nearly all the patterns and principles found in this book. Keeping your code decoupled from dependent classes enables it to be maintained far more easily, and extensions to it can be made without impacting other modules.

 Please refer to the `ASPPatterns.Chap5.FactoryPattern` *solution that can be downloaded from* www.wrox.com *to see how I have confirmed the behavior of the Factory pattern using unit tests.*

The Factory pattern is a useful one; you will see it used throughout the rest of this chapter and book. For example, in Chapter 8 you will see how the Factory pattern is built into the ASP.NET MVC Framework and how it hides the complexity of creating a correct controller based on a routing match.

The next pattern you will examine deals with the function of adding behavior to a class without changing its structure.

Decorator

The Decorator pattern belongs to the structural patterns group of design patterns and allows new behavior to be added to an existing object on the fly.

Intent

The Decorator pattern enables new behavior to be added to an object dynamically via composition. The pattern achieves this by either inheriting from the same base class or implementing a shared interface in conjunction with injecting an instance of the class to be decorated. In other words, the Decorator pattern is the process of wrapping an existing class with a class that extends the behavior or state. Multiple decorators can be added to a class to combine extended behavior, as you will see in the example later in this section.

UML

Figure 5-3 shows the UML representation of the Decorator pattern.

The classes shown in Figure 5-3 collaborate to form the Decorator pattern. Their roles are as follows:

➤ The `IProduct` defines the interface for a product. The `DefaultProduct` and `ProductDecorator` must implement this interface.

➤ The `DefaultProduct` provides the base functionality of the class that can be decorated.

➤ The `ProductDecorator` implements the `IProduct` interface and is injected with a reference to an `IProduct` instance that enables the inner instance to be wrapped.

➤ `ConcreteDecoratorA` and `ConcreteDecoratorA` inherit from `ProductDecorator` and add state and new behavior to the `IProduct` instance.

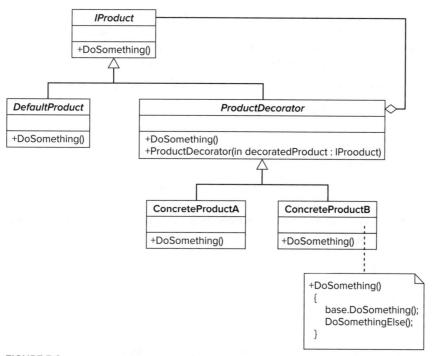

FIGURE 5-3

Code Example

In this example you use the Decorator pattern to apply a discount and a currency multiplier to a list of products that may be used in some kind of product catalog. Again, a `ProductService` class coordinates the retrieval of a list of products and then decorates those products with a discount and currency multiplication. Figure 5-4 shows the classes to be used in this scenario.

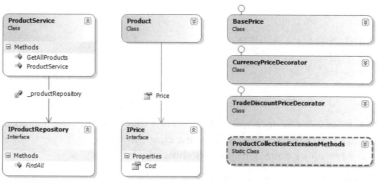

FIGURE 5-4

To build the solution, start by creating a new solution named `ASPPatterns.Chap5.DecoratorPattern` and add a new C# class library project named `ASPPatterns.Chap5.DecoratorPattern.Model`. Again, you begin by creating your simple domain model consisting of the `Product` entity and the `Price` interface, along with two decorator objects that implement the `Price` interface.

Add a new interface to the project named `IPrice` with the following contract:

```
namespace ASPPatterns.Chap5.DecoratorPattern.Model
{
    public interface IPrice
    {
        decimal Cost { get; set; }
    }
}
```

Now add a class that represents the `Product` entity named `Product` and add the following property:

```
namespace ASPPatterns.Chap5.DecoratorPattern.Model
{
    public class Product
    {
        public IPrice Price { get; set; }
    }
}
```

You can add three implementations of the `IPrice` interface. The first implementation is the `BasePrice` class. This gives the default behavior of the product's price and is set by the repository when hydrating a list of products from the data store. Add a new class named `BasePrice` to the project with the following definition:

```
namespace ASPPatterns.Chap5.DecoratorPattern.Model
{
    public class BasePrice : IPrice
    {
        private Decimal _cost;

        public decimal Cost
        {
            get { return _cost; }
            set { _cost = value; }
        }
    }
}
```

The second implementation of the `IPrice` interface you add is the class that decorates the default price behavior with the logic that applies a trade discount. Add a new class named `TradeDiscountPrice Decorator` to the project, with a matching code definition as shown here:

```
namespace ASPPatterns.Chap5.DecoratorPattern.Model
{
    public class TradeDiscountPriceDecorator : IPrice
    {
        private IPrice _basePrice;

        public TradeDiscountPriceDecorator(IPrice price)
```

```
            {
                _basePrice = price;
            }

            public decimal Cost
            {
                get { return _basePrice.Cost * 0.95m; }
                set { _basePrice.Cost = value; }
            }
        }
    }
```

The role of the `TradeDiscountPriceDecorator` class is to wrap an implementation of the `IPrice` interface, supplied via the `TradeDiscountPriceDecorator` constructor, and reduce the cost by a factor of 5 percent. Because the `Product` class is only referencing a price via an interface it, along with any client using it, will be unaware that they are talking to the `TradeDiscountPriceDecorator` class.

The third implementation of the `IPrice` interface is the class that decorates an implementation of `IPrice` with the currency multiplication. Add a new class to the project named `CurrencyPriceDecorator` with the following code listing:

```
namespace ASPPatterns.Chap5.DecoratorPattern.Model
{
    public class CurrencyPriceDecorator : IPrice
    {
        private IPrice _basePrice;
        private decimal _exchangeRate;

        public CurrencyPriceDecorator(IPrice price, decimal exchangeRate)
        {
            _basePrice = price;
            _exchangeRate = exchangeRate;
        }

        public decimal Cost
        {
            get { return _basePrice.Cost * _exchangeRate; }
            set { _basePrice.Cost = value; }
        }
    }
}
```

As with the `TradeDiscountPriceDecorator` class, the `CurrencyPriceDecorator` takes an implementation of `IPrice` as an argument constructor, along with an exchange rate, and applies this exchange rate to the base price — whether that is the actual `BasePrice` class or in fact the `TradeDiscountPrice Decorator` class.

To apply the decorating behavior to the `Product` class, you add a set of extension methods. Add a new class to the project named `ProductCollectionExtensionMethods` with the following code definition:

```
namespace ASPPatterns.Chap5.DecoratorPattern.Model
{
    public static class ProductCollectionExtensionMethods
```

```
    {
        public static void ApplyCurrencyMultiplier(this IEnumerable<Product> products)
        {
            foreach (Product p in products)
                p.Price = new CurrencyPriceDecorator(p.Price, 0.78m);
        }

        public static void ApplyTradeDiscount(this IEnumerable<Product> products)
        {
            foreach (Product p in products)
                p.Price = new TradeDiscountPriceDecorator(p.Price);
        }
    }
}
```

The two methods simply iterate through the collection of products and apply the `CurrencyPrice Decorator` or `TradeDiscountPriceDecorator` depending on which method is called. Typically, a `Factory` class or some other type of configuration is used to obtain the value of the exchange rate for the currency algorithm, but in this exercise I have elected to hard-code the value to keep things simple.

I am using extension methods so that the code in the `ProductService` class is kept to a minimum and so that the `ProductService` class is responsible only for the coordination of a task and not the underlying logic of applying decorating classes. The code is far more fluent when reading with extension methods, as will be shown in the `ProductService` class implementation to follow shortly.

To enable the `ProductService` class to obtain a collection of products, you need to add the product repository interface, so add a new interface to the project named `IProductRepository` with the single `FindAll` method that simply returns a collection of `Product` classes as shown here:

```
namespace ASPPatterns.Chap5.DecoratorPattern.Model
{
    public interface IProductRepository
    {
        IEnumerable<Product> FindAll();
    }
}
```

To complete the solution, you need to add the `ProductService` class that coordinates the retrieval and application of the trade discount and currency multiplication. Add a new class to the project named `ProductService` with the following code listing:

```
namespace ASPPatterns.Chap5.DecoratorPattern.Model
{
    public class ProductService
    {
        private IProductRepository _productRepository;

        public ProductService(IProductRepository productRepository)
        {
            _productRepository = productRepository;
        }
```

```
        public IEnumerable<Product> GetAllProducts()
        {
            IEnumerable<Product> products = _productRepository.FindAll();

            products.ApplyTradeDiscount();

            products.ApplyCurrencyMultiplier();

            return products;
        }
    }
}
```

As you can see, the ProductService class takes an IProductRepository as a constructor argument and has a single method that returns a collection of products decorated with the trade discount and the currency multiplication behavior. As mentioned previously, by using the extension methods, the code in the ProductService method is kept to a minimum, and it's immediately clear what the responsibility of the ProductService class is without getting distracted by how the application of the discount and currency multiplier is achieved.

 Please refer to the ASPPatterns.Chap5.DecoratorPattern *solution available from* www.wrox.com *to see how I have confirmed the behavior of the Decorator pattern using unit tests and specifications.*

The Decorator pattern is extremely useful when you want to add extra functionality to existing classes but you don't want to be tied to a specific implementation. As well as adding new functionality, decorators can restrict functionality; a security decorator can ensure only users with certain privileges can call methods or routines. Decorators are also good for wrapping infrastructure code like logging around method calls without polluting your domain model.

The next pattern defines the skeleton of an algorithm that allows inherited classes to override a number of steps in the workflow.

Template Method

The Template method pattern belongs to the behavioral group of patterns from the Gang of Four and is applied when a skeleton of an algorithm is defined but some steps are deferred to subclasses.

Intent

The Template method defines the skeleton structure of an algorithm but defers certain steps and details to subclasses. The structure and the flow of the algorithm remain static, but the details of the steps are deferred to subclasses.

UML

Figure 5-5 shows the UML representation of the Decorator pattern.

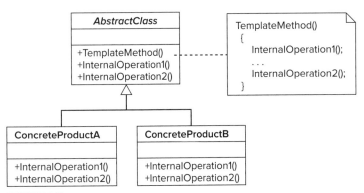

FIGURE 5-5

The classes shown in Figure 5-5 collaborate to form the Template pattern. Their roles are as follows:

➤ The `AbstractClass` defines a skeleton process workflow with abstract steps that `Concrete ClassA` and `ConcreteClassB` override and implement. This enables the details of an algorithm to alter depending on the subclasses but allow the structure to remain consistent.

➤ `ConcreteClassA` and `ConcreteClassB` inherit from the `AbstractClass`, implement the abstract methods, and give the detail to the algorithm.

Code Example

In this example, you apply the Template pattern to a system that handles order returns at an e-commerce site. For each order return, a series of processes occur that differ slightly depending on the type of return that is being processed. At this fictional company, order returns come in two flavors: a no quibbles return and a faulty order return. A no quibbles return enables customers to return goods and receive a full refund minus the price of the original post and packaging; the product is then returned into stock. A faulty return is issued if the customer receives a faulty item and would like a refund, which includes the original post and packaging paid as well as an order for a manufacturer return.

Figure 5-6 shows the classes involved in this exercise.

To get started with this exercise, create a new solution named `ASPPatterns.Chap5.TemplateMethod Pattern` and add a C# class library project to it named `ASPPatterns.Chap5.TemplateMethodPattern .Model`. As before, create the initial domain model. Once this is built you will then implement the skeleton template method before adding the template method subclasses and lastly the `Service` class, which will coordinate the task of returning an order.

Add a new class to the project named `ReturnAction` with the following code listing:

```
namespace ASPPatterns.Chap5.TemplateMethodPattern.Model
{
    public enum ReturnAction
    {
        FaultyReturn = 0,
        NoQuibblesReturn = 1
    }
}
```

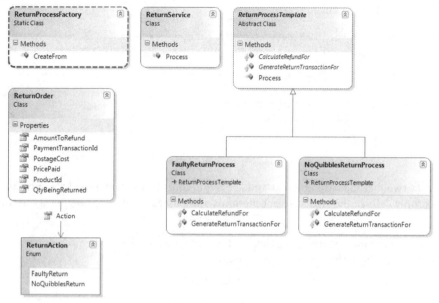

FIGURE 5-6

This enumeration enables you to determine which type of return order is being processed.

Next add the return order entity by adding a new class to the project named `ReturnOrder` with the following definition:

```
namespace ASPPatterns.Chap5.TemplateMethodPattern.Model
{
    public class ReturnOrder
    {
        public ReturnAction Action { get; set; }
        public string PaymentTransactionId { get; set; }
        public decimal PricePaid { get; set; }
        public decimal PostageCost { get; set; }
        public long ProductId { get; set; }
        public decimal AmountToRefund { get; set; }
    }
}
```

The `ReturnOrder` entity represents the customer's order being returned. The `Action` property determines what type of return order it is, the `PaymentTransactionId` refers to the original payment used to purchase the order, and the `PricePaid` and `PostageCost` refer to the order total and shipping costs, respectively. The `ProductId` holds the unique identifier of the product being returned. Finally, the `AmountToRefund` is set; this is the amount to be refunded to the customer.

With the domain model created, you can implement the abstract template method that will be overridden by the specific faulty and no quibbles subclasses. To create the template method, add a new class to the project named `ReturnProcessTemplate` with the following definition:

```
namespace ASPPatterns.Chap5.TemplateMethodPattern.Model
{
```

```
public abstract class ReturnProcessTemplate
{
    protected abstract void GenerateReturnTransactionFor(ReturnOrder returnOrder);
    protected abstract void CalculateRefundFor(ReturnOrder returnOrder);

    public void Process(ReturnOrder returnOrder)
    {
        GenerateReturnTransactionFor(returnOrder);
        CalculateRefundFor(returnOrder);
    }
}
```

The class and the first two methods are abstract and are required to be implemented by a subclass. The third method simply calls in the two abstract methods and passes a `ReturnOrder` entity as an argument.

You can now add the two template method subclasses. First add a new class to the project named `NoQuibblesReturnProcess` with the following code listing:

```
namespace ASPPatterns.Chap5.TemplateMethodPattern.Model
{
    public class NoQuibblesReturnProcess : ReturnProcessTemplate
    {
        protected override void GenerateReturnTransactionFor(ReturnOrder returnOrder)
        {
            // Code to put items back into stock...
        }

        protected override void CalculateRefundFor(ReturnOrder returnOrder)
        {
            ReturnOrder.AmountToRefund = returnOrder.PricePaid;
        }
    }
}
```

As mentioned previously, the `NoQuibblesReturnProcess` returns the item into stock; this logic resides in the override to the `GenerateReturnTransactionFor` method. The code for this has not been included to keep the exercise simple, but you would typically find some code here to add a stock transaction that increased the total stock for the returned product.

The `CalculateRefundFor` overridden method simply sets the `AmountToRefund` property on the return order to the original price of the product. Note that no postage costs are refunded.

The second subclass, which inherits the `ReturnProcessTemplate`, is the `FaultyReturnProcess` class. This class handles the processing of faulty returned items. Add a new class to the project named `FaultyReturnProcess` with the class listing here:

```
namespace ASPPatterns.Chap5.TemplateMethodPattern.Model
{
    public class FaultyReturnProcess : ReturnProcessTemplate
    {
        protected override void GenerateReturnTransactionFor(ReturnOrder returnOrder)
        {
```

```
        // Code to send generate order that sends faulty item back to
        // manufacturer...
    }

    protected override void CalculateRefundFor(ReturnOrder returnOrder)
    {
        ReturnOrder.AmountToRefund = returnOrder.PricePaid +
                                     returnOrder.PostageCost;
    }
  }
}
```

The overridden GenerateReturnTransactionFor method creates a manufacturer return order for sending the faulty item for a refund; again, for clarity, the code for this has not been included. The CalculateRefundFor differs from the NoQuibblesReturnProcess in that the post costs are included in a refund for the customer.

Before you create the Service class that coordinates the process of returning an item, you need a way to obtain the correct processing class based on the type of order being returned. This type of functionality is perfect for the Factory method that you read about previously in this chapter. Create a new class named ReturnProcessFactory that returns the correct processing object as detailed here:

```
namespace ASPPatterns.Chap5.TemplateMethodPattern.Model
{
    public static class ReturnProcessFactory
    {
        public static ReturnProcessTemplate CreateFrom(
                                                ReturnAction returnAction)
        {
            switch (returnAction)
            {
                case (ReturnAction.FaultyReturn):
                    return new FaultyReturnProcess();
                case (ReturnAction.NoQuibblesReturn):
                    return new NoQuibblesReturnProcess();
                default:
                    throw new ApplicationException(
                        "No Process Template defined for Return Action of " +
                                                returnAction.ToString());
            }
        }
    }
}
```

The Factory class hides the complexity (albeit not very complex in this example) from any client and ensures that the logic is contained in one place and is the responsibility of the Factory class.

Finally, you can add the ReturnOrderService class to the project as shown here:

```
namespace ASPPatterns.Chap5.TemplateMethodPattern.Model
{
    public class ReturnService
    {
        public void Process(ReturnOrder returnOrder)
```

```
        {
            ReturnProcessTemplate returnProcess =
                ReturnProcessFactory.CreateFrom(returnOrder.Action);

            returnProcess.Process(returnOrder);

            // Code to refund the money back to the customer...
        }
    }
}
```

The service has one simple `Process` method that takes a `ReturnOrder` as an argument. The service first obtains a `ReturnProcessTemplate` implementation from the factory, passing in the `ReturnOrder` entity, and in turn calls the `Process` method on the `ReturnProcessTemplate`. The call returns the item using the subclass's method and calculates the amount that the customer is entitled to receive. The code to actually refund the customer monies has been left out for brevity.

 Please refer to the `ASPPatterns.Chap5.TemplateMethodPattern` *solution in the code download available from* www.wrox.com *that accompanies this book to see how I have confirmed the behavior of the Template Method pattern using unit tests.*

The Template Method pattern is useful when you want to centralize code common to a series of subclasses. To achieve this, you separate the code that varies from the code that is similar; this enables you to avoid duplication and enables better maintenance of your code base.

The next pattern you will investigate enables the state and behavior of an object to be easily changed at runtime.

State Pattern

The State pattern belongs to the behavioral group of design patterns and is used to represent the state of an object separate from all other behavior.

Intent

The State pattern allows an object to alter its behavior when its internal state changes. This is achieved by swapping internal state objects that implement state-dependent behavior. An object defers all state-based behavior to a dependent state subclass; this alleviates the need for a mass of case statements within methods on the object.

UML

Figure 5-7 shows the UML representation of the State pattern.

The classes shown in Figure 5-7 collaborate to form the State pattern. Their roles are as follows:

➤   The `Context` is the object that has state, which is represented by an instance of the `State` interface. This is the single interface that client code interacts against.

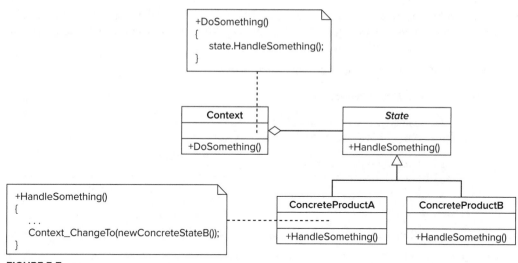

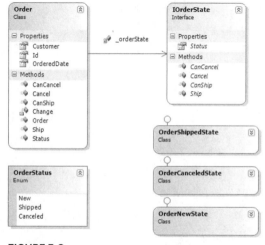

FIGURE 5-7

➤ The `State` represents the interface that defines the behavior dependent on the state of the `Context`.

➤ `ConcreteStateA` and `ConcreteStateB` represent specific states in the lifetime of the `Context`. They implement behavior specific to these states.

Code Example

This example examines how the State pattern can be used to provide the state behavior for an order object. An order is said to be in one of three states at any one time: New, Shipped, or Canceled. A new order can be shipped or cancelled. Shipped and Canceled orders cannot be cancelled or shipped.

Figures 5-8 shows the classes involved in this implementation of the State pattern.

FIGURE 5-8

Create a new solution named ASPPatterns.Chap5.StatePattern and add a new C# library project to it named ASPPatterns.Chap5.StatePattern.Model. With the project created, add a new interface named IOrderState with the following contract:

```csharp
namespace ASPPatterns.Chap5.StatePattern.Model
{
    public interface IOrderState
    {
        bool CanShip(Order order);
        void Ship(Order order);

        bool CanCancel(Order order);
        void Cancel(Order order);
    }
}
```

Next add an enumeration named OrderStatus that will be used to identify which state an order is in:

```csharp
namespace ASPPatterns.Chap5.StatePattern.Model
{
    public enum OrderStatus
    {
        New = 0,
        Shipped = 1,
        Canceled = 2
    }
}
```

Now you can create the actual Order class, add a new class to the project named Order, and add the code that follows:

```csharp
namespace ASPPatterns.Chap5.StatePattern.Model
{
    public class Order
    {
        private IOrderState _orderState;

        public Order(IOrderState baseState)
        {
            _orderState = baseState;
        }

        public int Id { get; set; }

        public string Customer { get; set; }

        public DateTime OrderedDate { get; set; }

        public OrderStatus Status()
        {
            return _orderState.Status;
        }

        public bool CanCancel()
        {
            return _orderState.CanCancel(this);
```

```
            }

            public void Cancel()
            {
                if (CanCancel())
                    _orderState.Cancel(this);
            }

            public bool CanShip()
            {
                return _orderState.CanShip(this);
            }

            public void Ship()
            {
                if (CanShip())
                    _orderState.Ship(this);
            }

            Internal void Change(IOrderState orderState)
            {
                _orderState = orderState;
            }
        }
    }
```

The first state to be created is the canceled order state. When an order is canceled, it cannot be shipped. Add a new class to the project named CanceledOrderState that implements the IOrderState interface with the code listing that follows:

```
namespace ASPPatterns.Chap5.StatePattern.Model
{
    public class OrderCanceledState : IOrderState
    {
        public bool CanShip(Order order)
        {
            return false;
        }

        public void Ship(Order order)
        {
            throw new NotImplementedException(
                            "You can't ship a canceled order!");
        }

        public OrderStatus Status
        {
            get { return OrderStatus.Canceled; }
        }

        public bool CanCancel(Order order)
        {
            return false;
        }

        public void Cancel(Order order)
```

```
            {
                throw new NotImplementedException(
                            "This order is already cancelled!");
            }
        }
    }
```

The next state to implement is the order shipped state. Add another class to implement the
IOrderState interface, and name it OrderShippedState:

```
namespace ASPPatterns.Chap5.StatePattern.Model
{
    public class OrderShippedState : IOrderState
    {
        public bool CanShip(Order order)
        {
            return false;
        }

        public void Ship(Order order)
        {
            throw new NotImplementedException(
                        "You can't ship a shipped order!");
        }

        public OrderStatus Status
        {
            get { return OrderStatus.Shipped; }
        }

        public bool CanCancel(Order Order)
        {
            return false;
        }

        public void Cancel(Order order)
        {
            throw new NotImplementedException(
                        "You can't cancel a shipped order!");
        }
    }
}
```

Finally, add the last order state, which identifies a new order. Add a new class to the project named
OrderNewState, which again implements the IOrderState interface as defined here:

```
namespace ASPPatterns.Chap5.StatePattern.Model
{
    public class OrderNewState : IOrderState
    {
        public bool CanShip(Order order)
        {
            return true;
        }

        public void Ship(Order order)
```

```
        {
            Order.Change(new OrderShippedState());
        }

        public OrderStatus Status
        {
            get { return OrderStatus.New; }
        }

        public bool CanCancel(Order order)
        {
            return true;
        }

        public void Cancel(Order order)
        {
            order.Change(new OrderCanceledState());
        }
    }
}
```

As you can see from this exercise, all state-dependent behavior has been moved into separate sub-classes. This makes it easy to introduce a new state later and to test the state in isolation. By taking advantage of this pattern, you prevent monolithic methods that need to determine the state of the object before implementing behavior; this is typically done through a set of case of nested `if-else` blocks.

> *Please refer to the code in the* `ASPPatterns.Chap5.StatePattern` *solution named which is available from* www.wrox.com *to see how I have confirmed the behavior of the State pattern using unit tests.*

The state is beneficial to use when you have an object that changes behavior depending on its state. It's also a great pattern to refactor toward when you find classes are becoming littered with conditional statements in the form of switch/case or `if` blocks.

The pattern discussed in the next session enables algorithms to be selected at runtime.

Strategy

Chapter 2 briefly covered the Strategy pattern when it was used to enable the discount algorithm to be swapped out depending on the type of customer viewing the products. This section digs deeper into this pattern so you can see how to use it in the business layer of an ASP.NET application.

Intent

The Strategy pattern is the process of disassociating an algorithm from its host and enabling the ability to swap algorithms dynamically at run time. The Strategy pattern encapsulates algorithms as objects. Clients reference them by an abstract or interface, which enables them to be interchangeable.

UML

Figure 5-9 shows the UML representation of the Strategy pattern.

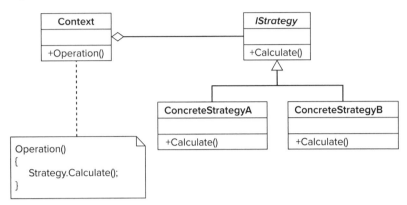

FIGURE 5-9

The classes shown in Figure 5-9 collaborate to form the Strategy pattern. Their roles are as follows:

➤ The `Context` defers all calculations to a `ConcreteStrategy` referenced by its abstract class or interface (`Strategy`); the `Context` may also expose some form of method or property so that the `Strategy` implementation can be changed.

➤ The `Strategy` is an interface for the algorithm. In this instance it contains a single calculate method.

➤ The `ConcreteStrategy` is an implementation of the `Strategy`.

Code Example

To demonstrate the Strategy pattern, you will work through an exercise based on a discount being applied to an e-commerce shopping basket. Figure 5-10 shows the classes involved in this exercise to demonstrate the Strategy pattern.

To get started, create a new solution named `ASPPatterns.Chap5.StrategyPattern` and add a C# class library project named `ASPPatterns.Chap5.StrategyPattern.Model`. Add a new class, named `Basket`, to represent the basket with the following code listing:

```
namespace ASPPatterns.Chap5.StrategyPattern.Model
{
    public class Basket
    {
        public decimal TotalCost { get; set; }
    }
}
```

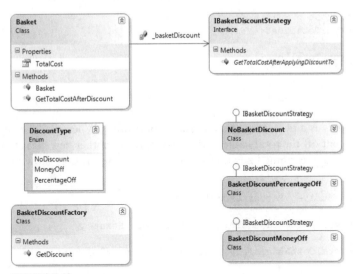

FIGURE 5-10

At the moment there is just a simple property to hold the total cost of the basket. After you have added the discount strategies, return to this class and add a method to obtain the basket total.

To create the discount strategies, first add a new interface named `IBasketDiscountStrategy` with the following simple contract:

```
namespace ASPPatterns.Chap5.StrategyPattern.Model
{
    public interface IBasketDiscountStrategy
    {
        decimal GetTotalCostAfterApplyingDiscountTo(Basket basket);
    }
}
```

The single method takes a basket object. An implementation applies a specific discount and then returns the basket price, including the discount.

The first discount strategy you create enables customers to receive a discount if they meet a certain discount threshold. The thresholds are $10 off basket totals over $100 and $5 off basket totals over $50; if the basket value is $50 or below, no discount is applied. Add a new class named `BasketDiscount MoneyOff` to the project with the following code definition:

```
namespace ASPPatterns.Chap5.StrategyPattern.Model
{
    public class BasketDiscountMoneyOff : IBasketDiscountStrategy
    {
        public decimal GetTotalCostAfterApplyingDiscountTo(Basket basket)
        {
            if (basket.TotalCost > 100)
                return basket.TotalCost - 10m;
```

```
            if (basket.TotalCost > 50)
                return basket.TotalCost - 5m;
            else
                return basket.TotalCost;
        }
    }
}
```

The second discount strategy you apply is a percentage off a basket's total value. When this discount is applied, customers receive 15 percent off the total value of the basket. Add another new class that implements the `IBasketDiscountStrategy` named `BasketDiscountPercentageOff`, as shown in the code that follows:

```
namespace ASPPatterns.Chap5.StrategyPattern.Model
{
    public class BasketDiscountPercentageOff : IBasketDiscountStrategy
    {
        public decimal GetTotalCostAfterApplyingDiscountTo(Basket basket)
        {
            return basket.TotalCost * 0.85m;
        }
    }
}
```

Finally, you need to add a special case discount strategy to be used if no discounts are set. This is an implementation of the Null Object pattern discussed briefly in Chapter 2 and that you will read about later in this chapter. Add a new class to the project named `NoBasketDiscount` that is shown here:

```
namespace ASPPatterns.Chap5.StrategyPattern.Model
{
    public class NoBasketDiscount : IBasketDiscountStrategy
    {
        public decimal GetTotalCostAfterApplyingDiscountTo(Basket basket)
        {
            return basket.TotalCost;
        }
    }
}
```

This discount strategy simply returns the total cost of the basket without applying any kind of discount algorithm.

To determine which strategy algorithm to apply to a basket, you will use the Factory Method pattern discussed earlier in this chapter. To enable the Factory Method pattern to build the correct discount strategy, you need to supply it with some information in the form of an enumeration. Create a new class named `DiscountType` and add it to the project as shown here:

```
namespace ASPPatterns.Chap5.StrategyPattern.Model
{
    public enum DiscountType
    {
        NoDiscount = 0,
        MoneyOff = 1,
```

```
                    PercentageOff = 2
            }
    }
```

With the enumeration in place, you can create the `Factory` class. Add a new class to the project named `BasketDiscountFactory` that contains a single static method to create the implementation of the `IBasketDiscountStrategy` based on the given enumeration as laid out here:

```
namespace ASPPatterns.Chap5.StrategyPattern.Model
{
    public class BasketDiscountFactory
    {
        public static IBasketDiscountStrategy GetDiscount(DiscountType DiscountType)
        {
            switch (DiscountType)
            {
                case DiscountType.MoneyOff:
                    return new BasketDiscountMoneyOff();
                case DiscountType.PercentageOff:
                    return new BasketDiscountPercentageOff();
                default:
                    return new NoBasketDiscount();
            }
        }
    }
}
```

Finally, you can return to the `Basket` class and update it to include a new constructor and method to return the basket to total cost with an applied discount as shown in the following code:

```
namespace ASPPatterns.Chap5.StrategyPattern.Model
{
    public class Basket
    {
        private IBasketDiscountStrategy _basketDiscount;

        public Basket(DiscountType discountType)
        {
            _basketDiscount = BasketDiscountFactory.GetDiscount(discountType);
        }

        public decimal TotalCost { get; set; }

        public decimal GetTotalCostAfterDiscount()
        {
            return _basketDiscount.GetTotalCostAfterApplyingDiscountTo(this);
        }
    }
}
```

The basket is completely unaware of the underlying algorithm that will be used to determine the total price, due to the discount strategy being injected to it and referred to using an interface.

> *Please refer to the* `ASPPatterns.Chap5.StrategyPattern` *solution available from* www.wrox.com *to see how I have confirmed the behavior of the Strategy pattern using unit tests and specifications.*

LEVERAGING ENTERPRISE PATTERNS

Martin Fowler's book, *Patterns of Enterprise Application Architecture*, outlined a number of enterprise patterns that can be used within applications. This section examines the Specification pattern on its own and in conjunction with the Composite Design pattern, and discusses how it can help with business logic criteria. You also look at the Layered Supertype pattern, which removes duplication in commonly used functions.

Specification Pattern

The Specification pattern encapsulates business logic in a boolean algorithm outside of a business entity. These manageable units of logic can then be chained together to form more flexible complex business logic.

Intent

You cannot share or reuse selection criteria logic embedded within business entities. The Specification pattern attempts to address this problem by separating business logic that is used to match an object from the actual object.

Code Example

To demonstrate the Specification pattern, you will be working through an exercise that is based on the domain of an online DVD rental company. In this simple example, you employ the Specification pattern to determine if a customer can rent more DVDs. Figure 5-11 shows the classes involved in the Specification exercise solution.

FIGURE 5-11

Create a new solution named `ASPPatterns.Chap5.Specification` and add a C# class library project for this exercised name `ASPPatterns.Chap5.Specification.Model`. Add a new interface to the project named `ISpecification` to be used as the interface for your specifications, as shown here:

```
namespace ASPPatterns.Chap5.Specification.Model
```

```
{
    public interface ISpecification<T>
    {
        bool IsSatisfiedBy(T candidate);
    }
}
```

Next, create a new implementation of the interface named HasReachedRentalThresholdSpecification that determines if a customer account can rent a DVD. The listing for this class is shown here:

```
namespace ASPPatterns.Chap5.Specification.Model
{
    public class HasReachedRentalThresholdSpecification :
                                    ISpecification<CustomerAccount>
    {
        public bool IsSatisfiedBy(CustomerAccount candidate)
        {
            return candidate.NumberOfRentalsThisMonth >= 5;
        }
    }
}
```

Don't worry that the new class won't build; this is because of the absent CustomerAccount class. To rectify this, add a new class to the project named CustomerAccount with the following code definition:

```
namespace ASPPatterns.Chap5.Specification.Model
{
    public class CustomerAccount
    {
        private ISpecification<CustomerAccount> _hasReachedRentalThreshold;

        public CustomerAccount()
        {
            _hasReachedRentalThreshold = new HasReachedRentalThresholdSpecification();
        }

        public decimal NumberOfRentalsThisMonth { get; set; }

        public bool CanRent()
        {
            return !_hasReachedRentalThreshold.IsSatisfiedBy(this);
        }
    }
}
```

In the preceding exercise, you looked at a simple application of the Specification pattern, but it's simple to chain specifications together to build complex business logic. To achieve this, you can leverage the Composite Design pattern, which is the subject of the next section.

Composite Pattern

The Composite pattern allows a collection of objects to be treated as a single instance of an object.

Intent

In the Composite pattern, objects can be grouped into tree-like or hierarchical collections dynamically and used as if they were a single object. This lets you build up behavior on the fly without the client code needing to understand the complex structure.

UML

Figure 5-12 shows the UML representation of the Composite Design pattern.

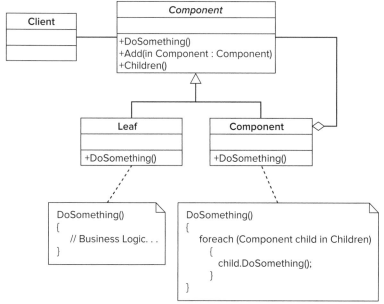

FIGURE 5-12

The classes shown in Figure 5-12 collaborate to form the Composite pattern. Their roles are as follows:

➤   The Component is the abstract base class that provides the means to enable objects to join to create chains of behavior.

➤   The Leaf is a concrete implementation of the Component abstract class that defines specific business logic behavior.

➤   The Composite is also a concrete implementation of the Component that enables related Components to be joined and provides the ability to call recursively into their behavior.

➤   The Client adds objects to and removes objects from the Composite.

Code Example

In this example, you expand on the small exercise you started in the "Specification Pattern" section. The Specification pattern exercise was based on the domain of an online DVD rental site. You built a specification to determine if a customer could rent a DVD based on the number of previous rentals. Now the business logic needs to be altered to consider whether a customer's account is still active and if they have any late fees. You can alter the existing Specification pattern to consider the new requirements, but another way to tackle this quandary is to create a set of small specifications and then chain them together using the Composite pattern; this allows you to reuse the logic in other parts of your system.

Figure 5-13 shows the class diagram from Figure 5-11 with the additional classes needed to create a composite specification.

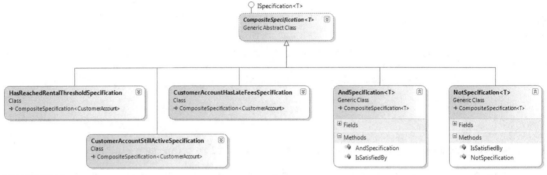

FIGURE 5-13

First expand the `CustomerAccount` class that you created in the Specification pattern. Then add the bolded properties in the code listing that follows:

```
namespace ASPPatterns.Chap5.Specification.Model
{
    public class CustomerAccount
    {
        private ISpecification<CustomerAccount> _hasReachedRentalThreshold;

        public CustomerAccount()
        {
            _hasReachedRentalThreshold = new HasReachedRentalThresholdSpecification();
        }

        public decimal NumberOfRentalsThisMonth { get; set; }

        public bool AccountActive { get; set; }

        public decimal LateFees { get; set; }

        public bool CanRent()
        {
            return !_hasReachedRentalThreshold.IsSatisfiedBy(this);
        }
    }
}
```

The `AccountActive` property shows whether the account is restricted, and the `LateFees` property stores the total fees the customer owes. The new `CanRent` method needs to consider whether the account is active, whether the customer has late fees, and if they have reached their rental threshold.

The first thing you need to do is create the two extra specifications to determine if late fees are owed and whether the account is active. Add a new class to the `ASPPatterns.Chap5.Specification.Model` project you built earlier and name it `CustomerAccountStillActiveSpecification`. Then modify the new class to match the listing that follows:

```
namespace ASPPatterns.Chap5.Specification.Model
{
    public class CustomerAccountStillActiveSpecification :
                                        ISpecification<CustomerAccount>
    {
        public override bool IsSatisfiedBy(CustomerAccount candidate)
        {
            return candidate.AccountActive;
        }
    }
}
```

This specification simply returns whether the `AccountActive` property is equal to `true`.

It's worth mentioning that at present, there doesn't seem to be a whole lot of benefit to using `CustomerAccountStillActiveSpecification`; `myCustomerAccount.AccountActive` would suffice. However, if the rules change, and you need something like the following two lines, a specification suddenly makes a whole lot more sense:

```
return candidate.AccountActive &&
                    candidate.EmailAddressConfirmed;
```

The second specification you add determines if the customer account has late fees. Add a new class to the project named `CustomerAccountHasLateFeesSpecification`, as detailed here:

```
namespace ASPPatterns.Chap5.Specification.Model
{
    public class CustomerAccountHasLateFeesSpecification :
                                    ISpecification<CustomerAccount>
    {
        public override bool IsSatisfiedBy(CustomerAccount candidate)
        {
            return candidate.LateFees > 0;
        }
    }
}
```

Now that you have all three specification classes in place, you can add the necessary classes to enable building of a composite specification. Add a new class to the project named `CompositeSpecification` that matches the code listed here:

```
namespace ASPPatterns.Chap5.Specification.Model
{
    public abstract class CompositeSpecification<T> : ISpecification<T>
    {
```

```
        public abstract bool IsSatisfiedBy(T candidate);

        public ISpecification<T> And(ISpecification<T> other)
        {
            return new AndSpecification<T>(this, other);
        }

        public ISpecification<T> Not()
        {
            return new NotSpecification<T>(this);
        }
    }
}
```

As you can see, this class also implements the ISpecifcation interface so it can be used as if it were a normal specification. You should also be able to see the two new classes: the AndSpecification and the NotSpecification. These two classes provide the chaining functionality to your Composite Specification.

Add a new class named AndSpecification with the following code definition:

```
namespace ASPPatterns.Chap5.Specification.Model
{
    public class AndSpecification<T> : CompositeSpecification<T>
    {
        private ISpecification<T> _leftSpecification;
        private ISpecification<T> _rightSpecification;

        public AndSpecification(ISpecification<T> leftSpecification,
                                ISpecification<T> rightSpecification)
        {
            _leftSpecification = leftSpecification;
            _rightSpecification = rightSpecification;
        }

        public override bool IsSatisfiedBy(T candidate)
        {
            return _leftSpecification.IsSatisfiedBy(candidate) &&
                        _rightSpecification.IsSatisfiedBy(candidate);
        }
    }
}
```

The AndSpecification is a simple class that takes two parameters of type ISpecification and in the IsSatisfiedBy method returns true if both the specifications are satisfied.

Add another new class named NotSpecification with the following definition:

```
namespace ASPPatterns.Chap5.Specification.Model
{
    public class NotSpecification<T> : CompositeSpecification<T>
    {
        private ISpecification<T> _innerSpecification;

        public NotSpecification(ISpecification<T> innerSpecification)
```

```
        {
            _innerSpecification = innerSpecification;
        }

        public override bool IsSatisfiedBy(T candidate)
        {
            return !_innerSpecification.IsSatisfiedBy(candidate);
        }
    }
}
```

As was the case with the `AndSpecification`, the `NotSpecification` is another simple class that, this time, takes a single `ISpecification` as a constructor argument and inverts the result of the inner specification in the `IsSatisfied` method. Notice that both the `AndSpecification` and the `NotSpecification` inherit from the `CompositeSpecification` class, thus inheriting the `And` and `Not` methods. This is what allows you to chain specifications together.

To complete this exercise, you need the three original specifications to inherit from the `Composite Specification` class, as shown in this code snippet:

```
public class HasReachedRentalThresholdSpecification :
            CompositeSpecification<CustomerAccount>
{
    ...
}

public class CustomerAccountStillActiveSpecification :
            CompositeSpecification<CustomerAccount>
{
    ...
}

public class CustomerAccountHasLateFeesSpecification :
            CompositeSpecification<CustomerAccount>
{
    ...
}
```

The last alteration you need to make is to the `ISpecification` interface. It is to include the extra methods added to the composite specification, which enables you to reference specifications via an interface and still have the ability to chain them together.

Update the `ISpecification` interface to include the two bolded method signatures that follow:

```
namespace ASPPatterns.Chap5.Specification.Model
{
    public interface ISpecification<T>
    {
        bool IsSatisfiedBy(T candidate);

        ISpecification<T> And(ISpecification<T> other);

        ISpecification<T> Not();
    }
}
```

Now you can implement the new logic into your `CustomerAccount`'s `CanRent` method, as shown in the code listing that follows:

```
namespace ASPPatterns.Chap5.Specification.Model
{
    public class CustomerAccount
    {
        private ISpecification<CustomerAccount> _hasReachedRentalThreshold;
        private ISpecification<CustomerAccount> _customerAccountIsActive;
        private ISpecification<CustomerAccount> _customerAccountHasLateFees;

        public CustomerAccount()
        {
            _hasReachedRentalThreshold = new HasReachedRentalThresholdSpecification();
            _customerAccountIsActive = new CustomerAccountStillActiveSpecification();
            _customerAccountHasLateFees = new CustomerAccountHasLateFeesSpecification();
        }

        public decimal NumberOfRentalsThisMonth { get; set; }

        public bool AccountActive { get; set; }

        public decimal LateFees { get; set; }

        public bool CanRent()
        {
            ISpecification<CustomerAccount> canRent =
                        _customerAccountIsActive.And(
                            _hasReachedRentalThreshold.Not()).And(
                                _customerAccountHasLateFees.Not());

            return canRent.IsSatisfiedBy(this);
        }
    }
}
```

Download the `ASPPatterns.Chap5.Specification` *solution from* www.wrox.com *to view a set of unit tests that verify the behavior of the specification example.*

Layer Supertype Pattern

The Layer Supertype pattern defines an object that acts as the base class for all types in its layer, and is very much based around inheritance.

Intent

For instances when all objects in your layer share a set of common business logic, you can use the Layer Supertype to remove duplication and centralize logic.

Code Example

To demonstrate the Layer Supertype pattern, you build a class that provides the basic functionality to be used by all entity classes in a business domain model.

You can see the classes used in this exercise in Figure 5-14.

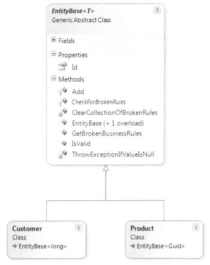

FIGURE 5-14

Start by creating a new solution named `ASPPatterns.Chap5.LayerSuperType` and add a C# class library project to it named `ASPPatterns.Chap5.LayerSuperType.Model`. Add a new abstract class to the project named `EntityBase`; this is the Supertype that all the business entities inherit from. Because all entities need an identifier, the Supertype class can provide the logic to store an ID and ensure it is never changed once set. Another job that the Supertype can perform is providing a simple framework for checking whether the entity class is valid. The code listing that follows shows the abstract base class with the methods for validation and storing the entity's ID:

```
namespace ASPPatterns.Chap5.LayerSuperType.Model
{
    public abstract class EntityBase<T>
    {
        private T _id;
        private IList<string> _brokenRules = new List<string>();
        private bool _idHasBeenSet = false;

        public EntityBase()
        { }

        public EntityBase(T id)
        {
            this.Id = id;
        }

        public T Id
```

```
        {
            get { return _id; }
            set
            {
                if (_idHasBeenSet)
                    ThrowExceptionIfOverwritingAnId()

                _id = value;
                _idHasBeenSet = true;
            }
        }

        private void ThrowExceptionIfOverwritingAnId()
        {
            throw new ApplicationException("You cannot change the id of an entity.");
        }

        public bool IsValid()
        {
            ClearCollectionOfBrokenRules();
            CheckForBrokenRules();
            return _brokenRules.Count() == 0;
        }

        protected abstract void CheckForBrokenRules();

        private void ClearCollectionOfBrokenRules()
        {
            _brokenRules.Clear();
        }

        public IEnumerable<string> GetBrokenBusinessRules()
        {
            return _brokenRules;
        }

        protected void AddBrokenRule(string brokenRule)
        {
            _brokenRules.Add(brokenRule);
        }
    }
}
```

You have used generics in the base class because you can't guarantee that all entities in your model will use the same type for identification.

Now you can add a new entity class that uses this Supertype. Add a new class named `Customer` to your project with the next code listing:

```
namespace ASPPatterns.Chap5.LayerSuperType
{
    public class Customer : EntityBase<long>
    {
        public Customer() { }

        public Customer(long Id)
```

```
                : base(Id)
        { }

        public string FirstName { get; set; }
        public string LastName { get; set; }

        protected override void CheckForBrokenRules()
        {
            if (String.IsNullOrEmpty(FirstName))
                base.AddBrokenRule("You must supply a first name.");

            if (String.IsNullOrEmpty(LastName))
                base.AddBrokenRule("You must supply a last name.");
        }
    }
}
```

The Layer Supertype is a simple pattern purely based around inheritance, but one that can be used to great effect in removing duplication in common logic.

The next section of this chapter details how design principles can be leveraged in an ASP.NET application.

APPLYING DESIGN PRINCIPLES

As with design and enterprise patterns, design principles should be followed throughout your application to enable high cohesion and loose coupling. This section examines the Dependency Inversion and Injection principles as well as the Separated Interface principle.

Dependency Inversion Principle and the Dependency Injection Pattern

The Dependency Inversion principle (DIP) helps to decouple your code by ensuring that you depend on abstractions rather than concrete implementations. This principle, which is paramount to understanding design patterns, has been used throughout this chapter and will be used in the remaining chapters. Dependency Injection (DI) is an implementation of this principle. You will often find the names Dependency Inversion and Dependency Injection used interchangeably, but they both refer to the same process of decoupling your code.

Intent

Robert C. Martin defines the DIP like so:

➤ High-level modules should not depend on low-level modules. Both should depend on abstractions.

➤ Abstractions should not depend on details. Details should depend on abstractions.

By employing the DIP, you can ensure that your high-level modules depend on abstractions rather than concrete implementations of lower-level modules.

The DI pattern is an application of this principle. DI is the act of supplying all classes that a service needs rather that leaving the responsibility to the service to obtain dependent classes.

DI typically comes in three forms:

➤ Constructor Injection

➤ Setter Injection

➤ Method Injection

Code Example

In this example, you refactor a portion of code to introduce the DI principle to completely decouple a `ProductService` class from its underlying dependencies. The example is based on the domain of a product catalogue; a `ProductService` class requires a repository to obtain a set of products and a discount strategy to apply a discount to each product before returning the collection to the caller. Figure 5-15 shows the classes involved in this simple scenario.

FIGURE 5-15

The `Product` class is a simple object that represents a product in the catalog; in this scenario it has a single method named `AdjustPriceWith` that takes the `ChristmasProductDiscount` object as an argument. The `LinqProductRepository` is a simple repository that retrieves a collection of products from an underlying data store. The `ChristmasProductDiscount` represents the type of discount to be applied to the `Product`. The class contains no code and is used merely as a placeholder to demonstrate the principle of DI. Finally, the `ProductService` class is responsible for retrieving the collection of products from the repository and then applying a given discount to them before returning to the calling code.

Before you can refactor this code, you need to build it, so first create a new solution named `ASPPatterns` `.Chap5.DependencyInjection` and add a C# Class Library Project named `ASPPatterns.Chap5` `.DependencyInjection.Model` to it, then add a new class to it named `ChristmasProductDiscount`. The interface is empty, as shown here:

```
namespace ASPPatterns.Chap5.DependencyInjection.Model
{
    public class ChristmasProductDiscount
    {
    }
}
```

Next, you can add a class to represent the `Product`. This contains a single method that has no code but demonstrates the interaction between a `Product` and a `ChristmasProductDiscount`. The code for the `Product` class is shown here:

```
namespace ASPPatterns.Chap5.DependencyInjection.Model
{
    public class Product
    {
        public void AdjustPriceWith(ChristmasProductDiscount discount)
        {

        }
    }
}
```

Add another new class to the project named `LinqProductRepository`. For brevity, the implementation of the `FindAll` method simply returns an empty collection of products, saving you the need to create a real database and LinqToSQL data context. The code for the `LinqProductRepository` is shown here:

```
namespace ASPPatterns.Chap5.DependencyInjection.Model
{
    public class LinqProductRepository
    {
        public IEnumerable<Product> FindAll()
        {
            return new List<Product>();
        }
    }
}
```

To complete the scenario, you need to add the `ProductService` class. Unlike the other classes in this exercise, the `ProductService` class does quite a bit. Add a new class to the project named `ProductService` with the following code definition:

```
namespace ASPPatterns.Chap5.DependencyInjection.Model
{
    public class ProductService
    {
        private LinqProductRepository _productRepository;
        private ChristmasProductDiscount _discountStrategy;

        public ProductService()
        {
            _productRepository = new LinqProductRepository();
            _discountStrategy = new ChristmasProductDiscount();
        }

        public IEnumerable<Product> GetProducts()
        {
            IEnumerable<Product> products = _productRepository.FindAll();

            foreach (Product p in products)
```

```
                    p.AdjustPriceWith(_discountStrategy);

            return products;
        }
    }
}
```

You can see that, in the constructor, the two dependent classes are created. The sole method on the service simply obtains a collection of products from the repository and applies a discount to each one before returning them to the caller.

The problem with the `ProductService` class is that it's tightly coupled to the concrete implementations of the repository and discount offer. This has the negative effect of making the `ProductService` class hard to maintain because it's impossible to test in isolation due to the need to have a valid `Christmas ProductDiscount` class as well as the `LinqProductRepository`. If and when the product discount strategy changes, a change would need to be made to the `Service` class, which breaks the single responsibility principle. To decouple the high-level module (`ProductService`) from the low-level details (`Christmas ProductDiscount` and `LinqProductRepository`), you can refactor the code toward the DIP by introducing two forms of DI.

To begin the process of moving toward the DI pattern, you must ensure that lower-level modules are referenced by abstractions rather than concrete types. Therefore, the first job is to introduce some interfaces for the `ChristmasProductDiscount` and `LinqProductRepository` classes.

Add a new interface to the project named `IProductDiscountStrategy` and ensure that the `Christmas ProductDiscount` implements it. The code for both the `IProductDiscountStrategy` and updated `ChristmasProductDiscount` is shown here:

```
namespace ASPPatterns.Chap5.DependencyInjection.Model
{
    public interface IProductDiscountStrategy
    {
    }
}

namespace ASPPatterns.Chap5.DependencyInjection.Model
{
    public class ChristmasProductDiscount : IProductDiscountStrategy
    {
    }
}
```

Now you need to modify all code that references the `ChristmasProductDiscount` to reference the new interface.

First update the `Product` class as shown here:

```
namespace ASPPatterns.Chap5.DependencyInjection.Model
{
    public class Product
    {
```

```
                public void AdjustPriceWith(IProductDiscountStrategy discount)
                {
                }
        }
}
```

Next, update the `ProductService` class, again as shown here:

```
namespace ASPPatterns.Chap5.DependencyInjection.Model
{
    public class ProductService
    {
        private LinqProductRepository _productRepository;
        private IProductDiscountStrategy _discountStrategy;

        public ProductService()
        {
            _productRepository = new LinqProductRepository();
            _discountStrategy = new ChristmasProductDiscount();
        }

        public IEnumerable<Product> GetProducts()
        {
            IEnumerable<Product> products = _productRepository.FindAll();

            foreach (Product p in products)
                p.AdjustPriceWith(_discountStrategy);

            return products;
        }
    }
}
```

Third, introduce an interface for the `LinqProductRepository`. Because the `LinqProductRepository` has a method defined, you can use a shortcut to create the interface. Open the `LinqProductRepository` class and right-click to bring up the context-sensitive menu and select Refactor ➪ Extract Interface. Name the interface `IProductRepository`, and ensure that the `FindAll` method is checked. Click OK, and the new interface is created with the following definition:

```
using System;
using System.Collections.Generic;

namespace ASPPatterns.Chap5.DependencyInjection.Model
{
    public interface IProductRepository
    {
        IEnumerable<Product> FindAll();
    }
}
```

The `LinqProductRepository` implements the new interface automatically. You can now update the `ProductService` class so that it references this new interface, like so:

```
namespace ASPPatterns.Chap5.DependencyInjection.Model
{
```

```csharp
public class ProductService
{
    private IProductRepository _productRepository;
    private IProductDiscountStrategy _discountStrategy;

    public ProductService()
    {
        _productRepository = new LinqProductRepository();
        _discountStrategy = new ChristmasProductDiscount();
    }

    public IEnumerable<Product> GetProducts()
    {
        IEnumerable<Product> products = _productRepository.FindAll();

        foreach (Product p in products)
            p.AdjustPriceWith(_discountStrategy);

        return products;
    }
}
```

Now that the high-level Service class is referencing all the dependents or lower-level classes by interfaces, you can continue to introduce the DI pattern.

The first flavor of DI to introduce is Constructor Injection. Instead of leaving the responsibility of obtaining an instance of IProductRepository to the ProductService class, you can move it up as a parameter in the constructor, as shown in the code here:

```csharp
namespace ASPPatterns.Chap5.DependencyInjection.Model
{
    public class ProductService
    {
        private IProductRepository _productRepository;
        private IDiscountStrategy _discountStrategy;

        public ProductService(IProductRepository productRepository)
        {
            _productRepository = productRepository;
            _discountStrategy = new ChristmasProductDiscount();
        }

        public IEnumerable<Product> GetProducts()
        {
            IEnumerable<Product> products = _productRepository.FindAll();

            foreach (Product p in products)
                p.AdjustPriceWith(_discountStrategy);

            return products;
        }
    }
}
```

The second flavor of DI you will be refactoring to is known as Method Injection. Currently, if you want to alter the discount offer applied to the products, you are required to alter the ProductService class. This is a code smell, because the ProductService class should be responsible only for coordinating the task of retrieving and applying a discount; this is its single responsibility and its only reason to change. Obtaining the correct discount offer should be of no concern to the Service class. To achieve this, you need to move the instantiation of the discount offer out of the service constructor and onto the parameter list of the GetProducts method, and rename it to GetProductsAndApplyDiscount as shown here:

```
namespace ASPPatterns.Chap5.DependencyInjection.Model
{
    public class ProductService
    {
        private IProductRepository _productRepository;

        public ProductService(IProductRepository productRepository)
        {
            _productRepository = productRepository;
        }

        public IEnumerable<Product> GetProductsAndApplyDiscount(
                                    IProductDiscountStrategy discount)
        {
            IEnumerable<Product> products = _productRepository.FindAll();

            foreach (Product p in products)
                p.AdjustPriceWith(discount);

            return products;
        }
    }
}
```

 A code smell is any symptom in the source code of a program that possibly indicates a deeper problem, such as a reliance on hard coded, so-called magic strings, or a tight coupling to a concrete implementation of a dependent class.

As you may have noticed in the code, you can also rename the method name to something a little more fluent. This refactor has also made the ProductService class open to extension while being closed for modification, because now any type of discount that implements the IProductDiscount Strategy can be applied to the product collection without change to the ProductService class. The Open/Closed principle is another principle that you will read more about in the next chapter.

Figure 5-16 shows the final class diagram for this exercise, after all your refactorings.

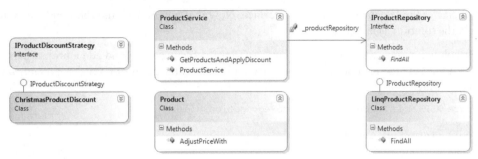

FIGURE 5-16

Interface Segregation Principle

The Interface Segregation principle states that clients should not be forced to depend on interfaces they don't use.

Intent

As interfaces grow, they take on more responsibility. It is crucial that you ensure they aren't trying to be all things to all objects. The Interface Segregation principle is all about separating fat interfaces into small, specific groups of related functionality. This enables subclasses to be created that implement only subsets of behavior instead of classes having to implement a monolithic contract littered with the dreaded `NotImplementedException`.

Code Example

To demonstrate the principle of Interface Segregation, you will work through a small exercise that revolves around the domain of a product catalog. Currently the product catalog is made up of movie products in the form of DVDs and Blu-Ray discs. There is a matching class for each product subtype, as shown in Figure 5-17.

FIGURE 5-17

Both of these classes implement an IProduct interface. Now that you understand the simple domain, you can build the solution as it stands.

Create a new solution named ASPPatterns.Chap5.InterfaceSegregation and add a project named ASPPatterns.Chap5.InterfaceSegregation, then add a new interface to it named IProduct with the following contract:

```
namespace ASPPatterns.Chap5.InterfaceSegregation.Model
{
    public interface IProduct
    {
        decimal Price { get; set; }
        decimal WeightInKg { get; set; }
        int Stock { get; set; }
        int Certification { get; set; }
        int RunningTime { get; set; }
    }
}
```

This interface nicely satisfies the needs of the two products in the catalog. You can add the two other classes to complete the solution as is. Add a new class named DVD and another named BluRayDisc that both implement the IProduct interface:

```
namespace ASPPatterns.Chap5.InterfaceSegregation.Model
{
    public class DVD : IProduct
    {
        public decimal Price { get; set; }

        public decimal WeightInKg { get; set; }

        public int Stock { get; set; }

        public int Certification { get; set; }

        public int RunningTime { get; set; }
    }
}

namespace ASPPatterns.Chap5.InterfaceSegregation.Model
{
    public class BluRayDisc : IProduct
    {
        public decimal Price { get; set; }

        public decimal WeightInKg { get; set; }

        public int Stock { get; set; }

        public int Certification { get; set; }

        public int RunningTime { get; set; }
    }
}
```

All is good with the world. Now introduce a new product type that isn't a movie. Add a new class to the project named TShirt. The TShirt class is a product, so it needs to implement the IProduct interface. Create the following new class:

```
namespace ASPPatterns.Chap5.InterfaceSegregation.Model
{
    public class TShirt : IProduct
    {
        public decimal Price { get; set; }

        public decimal WeightInKg { get; set; }

        public int Stock { get; set; }

        public int Certification { get; set; }

        public int RunningTime { get; set; }
    }
}
```

The problem with the TShirt class implementing the IProduct interface is that the Certification and RunningTime properties mean nothing to a TShirt and don't really belong to it. The answer to this issue is to split what differs between the movie products and the TShirt class and add this to a movie-specific interface.

Add a new interface named IMovie with the following contract:

```
namespace ASPPatterns.Chap5.InterfaceSegregation.Model
{
    public interface IMovie
    {
        int Certification { get; set; }
        int RunningTime { get; set; }
    }
}
```

You can now remove the Certification and RunningTime properties from the IProduct interface. Because the IProduct interface no longer defines these properties in its contract, the TShirt class doesn't need to implement them. So now you can update the TShirt class as shown here:

```
namespace ASPPatterns.Chap5.InterfaceSegregation.Model
{
    public class TShirt : IProduct
    {
        public decimal Price { get; set; }

        public decimal WeightInKg { get; set; }

        public int Stock { get; set; }
    }
}
```

The last action you need to take is to ensure that both the DVD and BluRayDisc class implement the new IMovie interface, as shown in the lines in boldface:

```
namespace ASPPatterns.Chap5.InterfaceSegregation.Model
{
    public class DVD : IProduct, IMovie
    {
        public decimal Price { get; set; }

        public decimal WeightInKg { get; set; }

        public int Stock { get; set; }

        public int Certification { get; set; }

        public int RunningTime { get; set; }
    }
}
namespace ASPPatterns.Chap5.InterfaceSegregation.Model
{
    public class BluRayDisc : IProduct, IMovie
    {
        public decimal Price { get; set; }

        public decimal WeightInKg { get; set; }

        public int Stock { get; set; }

        public int Certification { get; set; }

        public int RunningTime { get; set; }
    }
}
```

Figure 5-18 shows the complete set of classes after the refactors.

FIGURE 5-18

This is the essence of the Interface Segregation principle. It's simple to grasp, but sometimes even the big boys get it wrong. If you have ever written your own custom ASP.NET Membership Provider, you would have had to implement a monster of a contract even if you only wanted to use a subset of the functionality, like the ability to log in and out. By splitting up interfaces, you increase the capability to reuse and understand your code.

Liskov Substitution Principle

The Liskov Substitution principle (LSP) states that subclasses must behave the same as their base class.

Intent

Robert Martin states that subtypes must be substitutable for their base types, meaning that the behavior of a subtype must follow the expected behavior of a base type.

Code Example

To clearly demonstrate the LSP, you'll look at some code that violates it. Then you will refactor the code toward the principle. This exercise should enable you to see the benefit of following the principle and the problems caused if it is ignored.

Figure 5-19 shows the classes involved in this exercise. The domain that this code extract is taken from forms the refund module of an e-commerce company. Specifically, the organization takes and refunds payments using the PayPal and WorldPay payment merchants via their respective web services — in this example, you will simply mock out these web services.

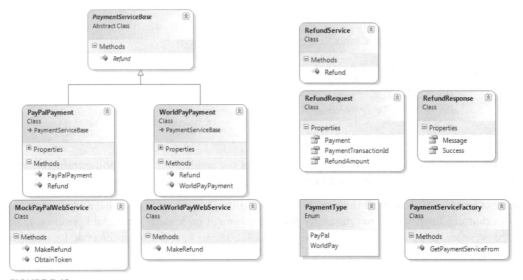

FIGURE 5-19

The RefundService class coordinates the refunding of a RefundRequest by first obtaining the correct payment class (WorldPayPayment or PayPalPayment) via the PaymentServiceFactory. After a refund has been made, the status of the transaction is wrapped within the RefundResponse object and returned to the client.

To get started with this exercise, create a new solution named `ASPPatterns.Chap5.Liskov SubstitutionPrinciple` and add a C# class library named `ASPPatterns.Chap5.LiskovSubstitution Principle`. The first item you can add to the project is the `PaymentType` enumeration. Add the two options as shown in this code listing:

```
namespace ASPPatterns.Chap5.LiskovSubstitutionPrinciple
{
    public enum PaymentType
    {
        PayPal = 1,
        WorldPay = 2
    }
}
```

Next, add two new classes named `RefundRequest` and `RefundResponse` with the following code definitions:

```
namespace ASPPatterns.Chap5.LiskovSubstitutionPrinciple
{
    public class RefundRequest
    {
        public PaymentType Payment { get; set; }
        public string PaymentTransactionId { get; set; }
        public decimal RefundAmount { get; set; }
    }
}

namespace ASPPatterns.Chap5.LiskovSubstitutionPrinciple
{
    public class RefundResponse
    {
        public bool Success { get; set; }
        public string Message { get; set; }
    }
}
```

The `RefundRequest` is sent to the `RefundService` as the single `Refund` method parameter, and `RefundResponse` is returned by the `RefundService` with the status of the refund transaction.

The next two classes represent the live WorldPay and PayPal web services. These are simply mock classes that demonstrate the functionality that the payment merchants offer. Add two new classes named `MockWorldPayWebService` and `MockPayPalWebService`, and update the code for each with the listings shown next:

```
namespace ASPPatterns.Chap5.LiskovSubstitutionPrinciple
{
    // Stub class to act as a PayPal web service
    public class MockPayPalWebService
    {
        public string ObtainToken(string accountName, string password)
        {
            return "xxxxxxxx-xxxxxxxxxxxxxx-xxxxxxxxx";
```

```
                    }

                    public string MakeRefund(decimal amount, string transactionId, string token)
                    {
                        return "Auth:0999";
                    }
                }
            }

namespace ASPPatterns.Chap5.LiskovSubstitutionPrinciple
{
    public class MockWorldPayWebService
    {
        public string MakeRefund(decimal amount, string transactionId,
                                 string username, string password,
                                 string productId)
        {
            return "A_Success-09901";
        }
    }
}
```

As you can see, the API for the payment merchants differs slightly. The return strings are hard-coded to keep the demonstration code simple.

To enable the RefundService to interact with the payment merchants as if they had the same interface, you need to add a PaymentServiceBase class that the WorldPayPayment and PayPalPayment can inherit from and wrap the real web service APIs by using the Adapter pattern. Add a new abstract class to the project named PaymentServiceBase, with the following abstract Refund method shown here:

```
namespace ASPPatterns.Chap5.LiskovSubstitutionPrinciple
{
    public abstract class PaymentServiceBase
    {
        public abstract string Refund(decimal amount, string transactionId);
    }
}
```

The RefundService can interact with the abstract PaymentServiceBase class and be blissfully unaware of which real implementation it is dealing with because they both behave the same — the essence of the LSP.

Now that you have the base class in place, you can create the two merchant adapters. Add a new class to the project named PayPalPayment, which inherits from the PaymentServiceBase class and has the following code definition:

```
namespace ASPPatterns.Chap5.LiskovSubstitutionPrinciple
{
    public class PayPalPayment : PaymentServiceBase
    {
        public string AccountName { get; set; }
        public string Password { get; set; }

        public override string Refund(decimal amount, string transactionId)
```

```
        {
            MockPayPalWebService payPalWebService = new MockPayPalWebService();

            string token = payPalWebService.ObtainToken(AccountName, Password);

            string response = payPalWebService.MakeRefund(amount, transactionId, token);

            return response;
        }
    }
}
```

Because the PayPal web service requires a token with any transaction, you must first log in to obtain a token; therefore, you have to include the two extra properties of AccountName and Password. The Refund method creates a new instance of the web service (a mock object in this example), obtains a transaction token by logging in, and then performs the refund before returning the result to the calling code.

Next, you can add the implementation for the WorldPay merchant adapter. Add a new class to the project named WorldPayPayment, again inheriting from the PaymentServiceBase abstract class with the following code listing:

```
namespace ASPPatterns.Chap5.LiskovSubstitutionPrinciple
{
    public class WorldPayPayment : PaymentServiceBase
    {
        public string AccountId { get; set; }
        public string AccountPassword { get; set; }
        public string ProductId { get; set; }


        public override string Refund(decimal amount, string transactionId)
        {
            MockWorldPayWebService worldPayWebService = new MockWorldPayWebService();

            string response = worldPayWebService.MakeRefund(
                        amount, transactionId, AccountId, AccountPassword, ProductId);

            return response;
        }
    }
}
```

Again, you have had to add two extra properties for logging in and a third to specify the product you are refunding against because the WorldPay merchant allows you to have more than one account when you need to support multiple currencies. The actual Refund method implementation is simpler than that of the PayPalPayment class because you don't have to obtain a token before making a refund.

The last two classes you need to tackle are the RefundService and the PaymentServiceFactory, which is responsible for creating the concrete implementation of the payment adapter. Because the RefundService class depends on the PaymentServiceFactory, you need to build it first. Add a new class to the project named PaymentServiceFactory, and input the following code listing for it:

```
namespace ASPPatterns.Chap5.LiskovSubstitutionPrinciple
```

```
{
    public class PaymentServiceFactory
    {
        public static PaymentServiceBase GetPaymentServiceFrom(PaymentType paymentType)
        {
            switch (paymentType)
            {
                case PaymentType.PayPal:
                    return new PayPalPayment();
                case PaymentType.WorldPay:
                    return new WorldPayPayment();
                default:
                    throw new ApplicationException(
                        "No Payment Service available for " + paymentType.ToString());
            }
        }
    }
}
```

If you read the section on the Factory Method pattern at the start of this chapter, it should be straightforward what is happening in this class. The PaymentType enum is passed, and the matching concrete payment adapter is created and returned to the caller.

Finally, you can add the RefundService class, add a class with the same name, and input the code that follows:

```
namespace ASPPatterns.Chap5.LiskovSubstitutionPrinciple
{
    public class RefundService
    {
        public RefundResponse Refund(RefundRequest refundRequest)
        {
            PaymentServiceBase paymentService = PaymentServiceFactory
                                .GetPaymentServiceFrom(refundRequest.Payment);

            RefundResponse refundResponse = new RefundResponse();

            if ((paymentService as PayPalPayment) != null)
            {
                ((PayPalPayment)paymentService).AccountName = "Scott123-PP";
                ((PayPalPayment)paymentService).Password = "ABCXYZ-PP";
            }

            if ((paymentService as WorldPayPayment) != null)
            {
                ((WorldPayPayment)paymentService)
                                        .AccountId = "Scott123-WP";
                ((WorldPayPayment)paymentService)
                                        .AccountPassword = "ABCXYZ-WP";
                ((WorldPayPayment)paymentService).ProductId = "1";
            }

            string merchantResponse =
                paymentService.Refund(refundRequest.RefundAmount,
```

```
                               refundRequest.PaymentTransactionId);

        refundResponse.Message = merchantResponse;

        if (merchantResponse.Contains("A_Success") ||
                     merchantResponse.Contains("Auth"))
            refundResponse.Success = true;
        else
            refundResponse.Success = false;

        return refundResponse;

    }
  }
}
```

It should be immediately obvious that there is a problem. In its present state, despite your best efforts, it is not possible to substitute the subtype for its base type because each implementation of the payment adapter must be handled differently. You can see this in the code snippet that follows; the downcasting of the base class is another code smell that breaks the LSP:

```
if ((paymentService as PayPalPayment) != null)
    {
        ((PayPalPayment)paymentService)
                     .AccountName = "Scott123-PP";
        ((PayPalPayment)paymentService)
                     .Password = "ABCXYZ-PP";
    }

if ((paymentService as WorldPayPayment) != null)
    {
        ((WorldPayPayment)paymentService)
                     .AccountId = "Scott123-WP";
        ((WorldPayPayment)paymentService)
                     .AccountPassword = "ABCXYZ-WP";
        ((WorldPayPayment)paymentService).ProductId = "1";
    }
```

In a more subtle way, the return code section, shown next, breaks the principle in that you are required to handle all cases for all subtypes; thus, you cannot substitute the subtype without ensuring you have code specific to that subtype; in this example code, check for a PayPal payment refund success and a WorldPay refund success:

```
if (merchantResponse.Contains("A_Success") ||
              merchantResponse.Contains("Auth"))
    refundResponse.Success = true;
else
    refundResponse.Success = false;
```

You can resolve these issues without too much pain. First, tackle the problem of the downcasting. It is clear that without the respective merchants' login credentials, the web services methods cannot be called. Both adapters depend on these values, so it makes sense to move these parameters into the constructor so that neither adapter can be created without them. Update the code in both the WorldPayPayment and PayPalPayment classes so that it matches this:

```
namespace ASPPatterns.Chap5.LiskovSubstitutionPrinciple
{
    public class WorldPayPayment : PaymentServiceBase
    {
        public WorldPayPayment(string accountId, string accountPassword,
                               string productId)
        {
            this.AccountId = accountId;
            this.AccountPassword = accountPassword;
            this.ProductId = productId;
        }

        public string AccountId { get; set; }
        public string AccountPassword { get; set; }
        public string ProductId { get; set; }

        public override string Refund(decimal amount, string transactionId)
        {
            MockWorldPayWebService worldPayWebService = new MockWorldPayWebService();

            string response = worldPayWebService.MakeRefund(
                amount, transactionId, AccountId, AccountPassword, ProductId);

            return response;
        }
    }
}

namespace ASPPatterns.Chap5.LiskovSubstitutionPrinciple
{
    public class PayPalPayment : PaymentServiceBase
    {
        public PayPalPayment(string accountName, string password)
        {
            this.AccountName = accountName;
            this.Password = password;
        }

        public string AccountName { get; set; }
        public string Password { get; set; }

        public override string Refund(decimal amount, string transactionId)
        {
            MockPayPalWebService payPalWebService = new MockPayPalWebService();

            string token = payPalWebService.ObtainToken(AccountName, Password);

            string response = payPalWebService.MakeRefund(amount, transactionId, token);

            return response;
        }
    }
}
```

Because the adapter classes now have constructors, you must update the `PaymentServiceFactory` class as shown in the following bolded lines:

```
namespace ASPPatterns.Chap5.LiskovSubstitutionPrinciple
{
    public class PaymentServiceFactory
    {
        public static PaymentServiceBase GetPaymentServiceFrom(PaymentType paymentType)
        {
            switch (paymentType)
            {
                case PaymentType.PayPal:
                    return new PayPalPayment("Scott123-PP", "ABCXYZ-PP");
                case PaymentType.WorldPay:
                    return new WorldPayPayment("Scott123-WP", "ABCXYZ-WP", "1");
                default:
                    throw new ApplicationException(
                        "No Payment Service available for " + paymentType.ToString());

            }
        }
    }
}
```

In this example, the login credentials are hard-coded strings to keep things simple. In a real application, these would typically be stored in some kind of configuration file. You can now return to the `RefundService` class and remove the downcasting issue.

The second problem with the `RefundService` class as it stands is the refund transaction response. Currently, the `RefundService` class has to inspect the result of the transaction and ensure that it matches the authorization criteria of one of the subtypes, which again breaks the LSP. You can address this by changing the return type from the string to the `RefundResponse` object.

Update the `PaymentServiceBase`, `PayPalPayment`, and `WorldPayPayment` class with the highlighted code modifications as shown here:

```
namespace ASPPatterns.Chap5.LiskovSubstitutionPrinciple
{
    public abstract class PaymentServiceBase
    {
        public abstract RefundResponse Refund(decimal amount, string transactionId);
    }
}

namespace ASPPatterns.Chap5.LiskovSubstitutionPrinciple
{
    public class WorldPayPayment : PaymentServiceBase
    {
        public WorldPayPayment(string accountId, string accountPassword,
                               string productId)
        {
            this.AccountId = accountId;
            this.AccountPassword = accountPassword;
            this.ProductId = productId;
        }
        public string AccountId { get; set; }
```

```
            public string AccountPassword { get; set; }
            public string ProductId { get; set; }

            public override RefundResponse Refund(decimal amount, string transactionId)
            {
                RefundResponse refundResponse = new RefundResponse();
                MockWorldPayWebService worldPayWebService = new MockWorldPayWebService();

                string response = worldPayWebService.MakeRefund
                        (amount, transactionId, AccountId, AccountPassword, ProductId);

                refundResponse.Message = response;

                if (response.Contains("A_Success"))
                    refundResponse.Success = true;
                else
                    refundResponse.Success = false;

                return refundResponse;
            }
        }
    }

namespace ASPPatterns.Chap5.LiskovSubstitutionPrinciple
{
    public class PayPalPayment : PaymentServiceBase
    {
        public PayPalPayment(string accountName, string password)
        {
            this.AccountName = accountName;
            this.Password = password;
        }

        public string AccountName { get; set; }
        public string Password { get; set; }

        public override RefundResponse Refund(decimal amount, string transactionId)
        {
            MockPayPalWebService payPalWebService = new MockPayPalWebService();
            RefundResponse refundResponse = new RefundResponse();

            string token = payPalWebService.ObtainToken(AccountName, Password);

            string response = payPalWebService.MakeRefund(amount, transactionId, token);

            refundResponse.Message = response;

            if (response.Contains("Auth"))
                refundResponse.Success = true;
            else
                refundResponse.Success = false;

            return refundResponse;
        }
    }
}
```

The individual subtypes are now responsible for determining if the refund was successful. They return a simple boolean flag along with the specific transaction response. The RefundService class can now be updated to treat the subtype in the same manner as the base type, with no need to downcast or check for a specific subtype behavior. The updated RefundService class listing is shown here:

```
namespace ASPPatterns.Chap5.LiskovSubstitutionPrinciple
{
    public class RefundService
    {
        public RefundResponse Refund(RefundRequest refundRequest)
        {
            PaymentServiceBase paymentService =
                    PaymentServiceFactory.GetPaymentServiceFrom(refundRequest.Payment);
            RefundResponse refundResponse;

            refundResponse = paymentService.Refund
                (refundRequest.RefundAmount, refundRequest.PaymentTransactionId);

            return refundResponse;
        }
    }
}
```

Figure 5-20 shows the full class diagram after your refactors.

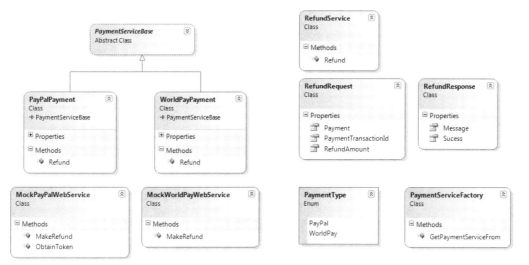

FIGURE 5-20

From working through the exercise, you should understand the subtleness behind the LSP. In a nutshell, it's all about thinking through how your subclasses should act based on the contract of their base classes.

SUMMARY

In this chapter, you learned about patterns and principles that you can use, but not exclusively within the business layer of your application.

You examined the following patterns and principles:

➤ The Factory pattern enables you to encapsulate the creation of objects and remove the responsibility from client code.

➤ The Decorator pattern allows you to add behavior and state to an existing class dynamically.

➤ The Template pattern defines a skeleton algorithm that delegates to subclasses to implement specific steps that could vary.

➤ The State pattern allows you to separate behavior dependent on state from the object itself.

➤ The Strategy pattern permits you to swap algorithms dynamically and separate calculations from data.

➤ The Specification pattern allows selection criteria logic to be separated and reused from business entities.

➤ The Composite pattern enables objects to be combined but act as a single instance to join logic and behavior dynamically.

➤ The Layer Supertype pattern acts as a common base class from all objects in the business layer providing implementation for common logic.

➤ The Dependency Injection principle inverts the responsibility of obtaining dependent classes by allowing them to be injected via a class's constructor, property, or method.

➤ The Interface Segregation principle splits fat interfaces into separate related groups of contracts, making it easier to use and more understandable in your code.

➤ The Liskov Substitution Principle reminds you that subclasses should act as you would expect a base class to be used, without the need to downcast to check for specific subclass behavior.

The next chapter investigates patterns and principles that can be used in the service layer of an enterprise application as well as some SOA (Service Oriented Architecture) patterns that are specific to the service layer.

The Service Layer

WHAT'S IN THIS CHAPTER?

➤ The role of services and the service layer in an enterprise ASP.NET application

➤ Service oriented architecture and why it's needed

➤ The use of the Facade pattern

➤ Messaging patterns such as document message, request-response, reservation, and idempotent

➤ An exercise that utilizes WCF for SOA in addition to well-known messaging patterns

Chapter 4 dealt with the organization of your business middleware, but how do you expose the business logic to your applications in an easy-to-use and consistent manner that maps to your business needs? The answer lies in the service layer.

Sitting between your presentation and business layer, the service layer provides an interface that defines the application's boundaries and the operations available to the client. Behind the façade that the service layer portrays to the client is the encapsulation of business logic, validation, and workflow and the coordination of persistence and retrieval of business entities.

DESCRIBING THE SERVICE LAYER

The role of the service layer is similar to that of the Transaction Script pattern that was introduced in Chapter 4 in that it typically maps to business use cases. Unlike the Transaction pattern, however, the service layer simply coordinates the business use case transaction and delegates work to the business objects for all the lower-level implementation details. The service layer encapsulates the business model and acts as an interface into the application for all parties, rather like a business façade. Another difference between the service layer and the Transaction Script pattern is in the level of granularity; typically, the Transaction Script pattern has fine-grained method calls and offers a chattier interface than a coarse-grained service layer does.

Service Oriented Architecture

Service oriented architecture (SOA) refers to the principles and practices of designing a set of loosely integrated services typically, but not always, for distributed applications. Services are basically core business functions that are used by one or many business applications. You can think of the set of services as a business's API. In the real world, business applications modeling processes need to be dynamic and change often, but the core business rules tend to stay the same. Having these as independent services offers a more flexible architecture and makes it easier to quickly build business applications around the fundamental business procedures.

SOA probably seems very abstract, so before examining it perhaps it's best to see an example of how applying SOA to a legacy application can help improve the architecture and business process reuse. Figure 6-1 shows a typical layout for a medium-sized business.

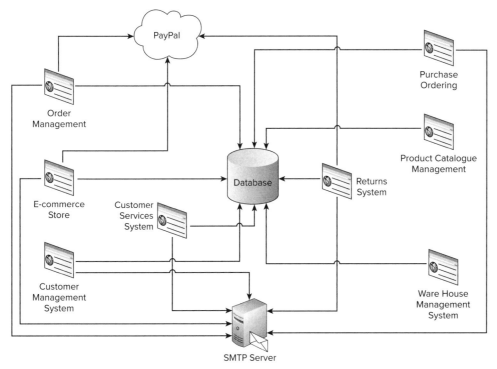

FIGURE 6-1

The systems architecture is for an e-commerce company; all the applications contain a business model, plus logic and rules from their point of view or context. Each application connects directly with the database to persist and retrieve the state of those business objects to the database. All applications send e-mail, so they require a connection to the SMTP server. Many of the systems such as Returns, Order Management, and the E-commerce storefront require a connection to the PayPal web services for the taking and refunding of payments. The purchase ordering department manually confirms orders with suppliers via e-mail.

Over years of working with the current architecture the company has identified some issues that should be addressed:

> ➤ Because each application has its own interpretation of the domain, there is a duplication of business logic so a change to any aspect of the business that requires a logic change to the software needs to be propagated to all the subsystems, which is a maintenance headache.

> ➤ There is a lot of business process duplication because the contexts of each application tend to overlap. For example, the customer service team needs to see orders for a customer, which represents an overlap with the functionality of the Order Management system. Similarly, the Returns system needs to adjust stock during the process of returning an item, which overlaps with the functionality provided by the Warehouse Management system.

> ➤ The applications are closely coupled to the data structure; if a change to the database is required, changes to all applications using the data tables need to be synchronized so they are updated at the same time.

> ➤ Confirming stock availability and purchase orders with suppliers is currently a time-consuming manual process.

> ➤ The business requires lots of highly paid developers to maintain the domain logic within each of the subsystems. New developers to the team often spend a lot of time working through each application to get a handle on the company's business logic.

> ➤ An audit trail and standard logging mechanism are required to be rolled out across all applications so that the customer service department can easily view an order's history, but this has been put off because of the implication cost.

An enterprise SOA approach will seek to address all these issues and restate all business processes as services that communicate with each other and potentially with services outside of the enterprise. The purchase ordering function, for instance, will be converted to a B2B system. All business logic engrained within each of the individual legacy applications will be extracted and exposed as a service so that core business logic can be shared but remain in one central location to assist in logic reusability and maintenance. A Service Bus can then be used to keep the services loosely coupled with each other and to coordinate the flow of information, making it easy to change services as long as the service contract remains the same.

Figure 6-2 shows how the applications within the organization have been restructured to embrace SOA.

All the business core functions have now been turned into service endpoints. The myriad applications are now simply dumb presentation screens with a thin layer of application logic, with all the business logic happening behind the service interface. There is now no logic or code duplication, and business processes can be shared with all the subsystems. The purchase ordering department now communicates with suppliers via a B2B service that enables stock availability to be updated every hour without manual interaction.

With the new SOA in place, the business can now see these benefits:

> ➤ Maintenance is no longer such a big issue; changes to business logic now occur only in one place: behind a service interface. As the company grows, applications can be replaced or rearchitected without affecting the entire system as long as the service contract remains the same. Applications now contain little logic, so junior developers can easily code the thin applications that use the ser-

vices. New developers no longer need to understand the inner workings of the company because they now have an API that exposes all the business functionality from them to work with.

➤ Logging and an audit trail can now be applied to all business transactions because of the existence of a central location.

➤ An API has been defined for the company; this logic can now be shared across all applications, making it fast and almost effortless to deploy small, targeted applications for departments.

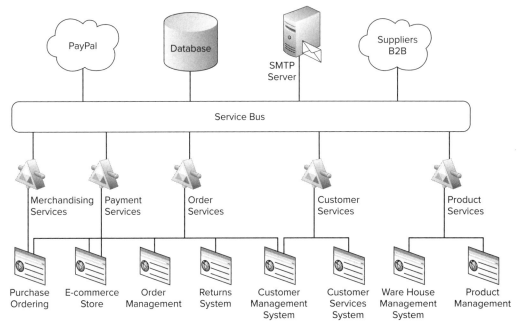

FIGURE 6-2

➤ The data store is now abstracted away behind the service layer. This means that data can be cached from a central location, and any changes required to the data schema need only affect the business logic behind the service layer, not all the applications.

➤ Interaction between the applications and service layer is via a coarse-grained interface, making for a less chatty system and in turn ensuring that the database is no longer a scalability issue.

Hopefully you can see that, by applying a SOA to the organization, you have decreased maintenance complexity and increased the reusability of the code base. This is, of course, just one application of SOA that can be successfully rolled out, but it is by no means the definitive answer to this question: what is SOA?

Four Tenets of SOA

You can adhere to four service principles to ensure better designed services. These are known as the Four Tenets of SOA, and they are explained in the following sections.

Boundaries Are Explicit

A service interface needs to be as clean and simple as possible and have a consistent approach to the exchange of data, often referred to as messages. It is also a good idea to keep a service's API small and clear, favoring coarse-grained methods rather than a host of finer-grained methods. You will see later in the "Leveraging Messaging Patterns" section how a number of patterns can be used to create clean and clear service methods.

Services Are Autonomous

Service methods should be loosely coupled and not rely on other methods to perform a business transaction; a client should not be required to call methods in a particular order to perform a business transaction. A client should be able to invoke a single service and within one atomic action receive a response on the success or failure of that transaction. Service methods should also be stateless and not leave a system in a partially done state before another service is called to complete a request.

Services Share Schema and Contract, Not Class

One of the goals of SOA is interoperability; to this end a service should only expose a contract, not the implementation of the service. Communication is achieved via XML, also known as messages; these are platform neutral and help to achieve interoperability.

Service Compatibility Is Based on Policy

A service should expose a policy on what it can be used for. Clients can then consume a service with good knowledge of how to use it and what to expect in terms of response. Information on what a service does can be exposed using the WS-Policy specification; the WS-Policy represents a set of specifications that describe the capabilities and constraints of the service.

If you are still finding the SOA design methodology a little abstract, there is a large exercise at the end of this chapter that uses WCF to build a SOA. This should help to cement the main points of SOA.

This has only been a brief overview of SOA. For a more in-depth look at SOA, take a look at *SOA Design Patterns* and/or *SOA Principles of Service Design* by the SOA guru Thomas Erl.

In the next section you will learn how one of the Gang of Four patterns can be used in the service layer of an enterprise ASP.NET application.

The Facade Design Pattern

A common pattern used by SOA clients is Facade. The Facade pattern simplifies the interface of a complex subsystem or group of subsystems, giving a client an uncomplicated API to use that is consistent with other APIs that the client may be used to working against.

Intent

The Facade pattern provides a simple interface to a complex API. The Facade pattern can be used in many different scenarios:

➤ It can make a third-party library easier to use by wrapping in an interface consistent with the rest of the application.

➤ It can help to loosely couple code by abstracting away dependencies to other systems and libraries.

➤ It can wrap a complicated subsystem with a simpler interface. This is demonstrated in the UML that follows.

The Facade pattern can be used in the service layer to hide the complexities of talking to remote applications via WCF or web services. You will see an exercise where the Facade pattern is employed to do just this later in the chapter.

UML

Figure 6-3 shows the UML representation of the Facade pattern.

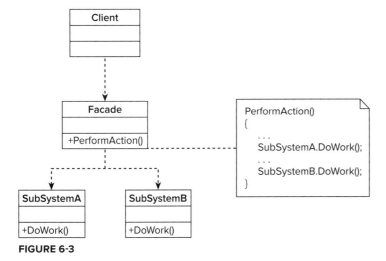

FIGURE 6-3

Figure 6-3 shows all the collaborating roles in the Facade pattern.

➤ The client uses the simple API of the Facade to perform a task. The client remains unaware of what is really needed to achieve the transaction.

➤ The Facade hides the complexities of the system behind its simple API. The Facade then delegates to the subsystems and collates the responses.

➤ SubSystemA and SubSystemB perform the work for the client.

 There is a lengthy code exercise at the end of this chapter that shows how the client of an SOA can use the Facade pattern.

In the next section you will look at patterns found in the communication with services.

LEVERAGING MESSAGING PATTERNS

Design patterns that are associated in the realm of large-scale distributed applications like SOA systems are often referred to as Messaging patterns. Messaging patterns, like Design patterns, provide standard solutions to complex problems. Messaging patterns tackle the sharing of data in a uniform manner among many disconnected systems. In this section you will learn about some common Messaging patterns that you will use in an SOA example with WCF at the end of the chapter. If you are interested in Messaging patterns, pick up the book *Enterprise Integration Patterns: Designing, Building, and Deploying Messaging Solutions* by Gregor Hohpe and Bobby Woolf.

The Document Message and the Request-Response Patterns

The Document Message pattern enables a uniform and flexible approach to communicating with services. Instead of using the typical RPC style of parameterized methods to expose the service API, message objects are employed. Consider this set of RPC-like methods that show why the Document Message pattern has been adopted:

```
Customer[] RetrieveCustomers(string country);
Customer[] RetrieveCustomers (string country, string postalCode);
Customer[] RetrieveCustomers (string country, string postalCode, string street);
```

The preceding service methods enable the client to obtain customer records in three different ways: by supplying a country, by supplying a country and a postal code, and by supplying a street in addition to the country and postal code parameters. As you can see, this type of method approach can fast become a nightmare to maintain and for the client of the API to work with.

The Document Message pattern simplifies the communication by encapsulating all information within the body of the document, leading to a more straightforward and clean service signature, as can be seen here:

```
Customer[] FindBy(CustomerSearchRequest request);
```

The `Document Message` class is shown in the following code:

```
public class CustomerSearchRequest
{
    public string Country { get; set; }
    public string PostalCode { get; set; }
    public string Street { get; set; }
}
```

Messages frequently contain other arbitrary items of information, including service version numbers, a confirmation identifier, and authentication data. These items can be added to a common base class that all requests can inherit. By using the Document Message pattern for all communication, you make it easy for the service method to evolve and include additional parameters without needing to change the signature of the method, as you saw earlier with the RPC example.

The Request-Response pattern ensures that responses as well as requests use the Document Message pattern, so the signature for the `RetrieveCustomers` method now resembles this:

```
CustomerSearchResponse RetrieveCustomers(CustomerSearchRequest request);
```

As with the Request object, the Response can also inherit from a base class, which can provide access to common properties like a generic message and success flag, as well as a Correlation ID. You will learn about Correlation IDs when you look at the Idempotent pattern, coming up shortly.

Figure 6-4 is a graphical representation of the Request-Response pattern utilizing the Document Message pattern.

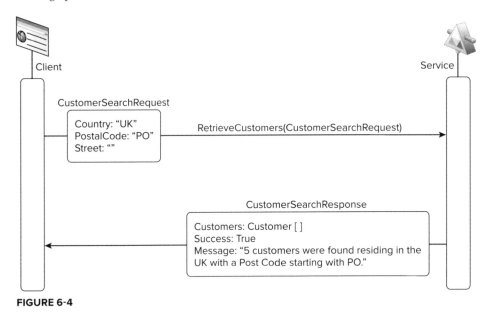

FIGURE 6-4

You can use the Request-Response pattern consistently across all service methods, making for a flexible, simple-to-use API. If you look at PayPal's API by navigating to www.x.com/docs/DOC-1374 and viewing a SOAP operation, you will see that it follows this pattern.

The Reservation Pattern

As you read earlier, one of the four tenets of SOA services is that they should be autonomous. There are times, though, when it is necessary to maintain the state of a long-running process during a complex transaction that requires several messages to be sent to complete a unit of work. For these situations, you can assign a reservation number to the first response. The client can use this reservation number in subsequent requests to allow the service layer to pick up a transaction. Typically, an expiration date is used to allow the reserved state to expire after a given time so it doesn't hold onto resources for an undefined amount of time.

Figure 6-5 shows a simple scenario to demonstrate the Reservation pattern. Note the message exchange within a ticket purchase service.

The client first calls the ReserveTickets service method, supplying data on the event and the number of tickets required. The response from the service layer includes a reservation ID and an expiration date that will guarantee the tickets are held for the client. The client application then performs some logic that may involve taking details from the customer as part of a checkout process. Finally, the client sends the reservation ID in a request via the `PurchaseTicket` service method; the service validates the reservation ID and confirms the purchase of the tickets.

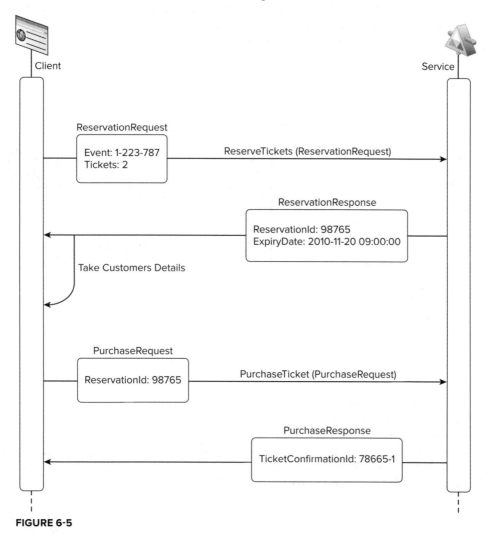

FIGURE 6-5

The Idempotent Pattern

In computing, an *idempotent* operation is one that has no additional effect if it is called more than once with the same input parameters. A service has no control over the clients that use it, so it's important to ensure that repeat calls do not have undesirable effects on the state of a system.

The Idempotent pattern states that any state-altering request should be tagged with a unique identifier. This unique identifier should be checked with some kind of response storage to ensure that it has not been processed before. If the response is found, the result can be returned without affecting the state of the process that was originally called.

Figure 6-6 displays a simple scenario showing the Idempotent pattern in operation. The client sends a request via a service call and specifies a unique identification number. Upon receiving the request, the service checks to see if it has handled it before by searching a local response repository. If the response that matches the unique identifier does not exist, the business transaction can take place. If it does exist, however, the stored response is retrieved and returned to the client.

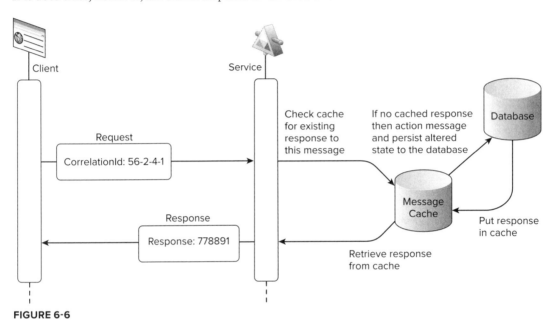

FIGURE 6-6

A further benefit to including a unique identifier with every request can be gained by having the service include the same ID in the response to the client. This allows the client calling the service to verify the response that matches the request; in this case, the unique identifier is known as a *correlation ID*.

AN SOA EXAMPLE

To demonstrate the principles of SOA and messaging patterns in a more practical or hands-on manner, you will work through an exercise that facilitates the reservation and purchasing of tickets. In this domain a central service exposes an API via HTTP, allowing any number of clients to hook up and sell tickets. Figure 6-7 shows the logical diagram for the application you will be building.

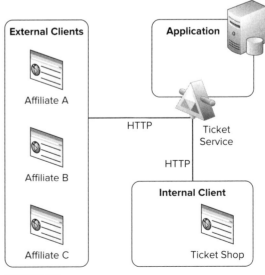

FIGURE 6-7

You will be working on the parts of the system labeled Application and Internal Client using the Reservation pattern to reserve tickets and the Idempotent pattern to ensure that any tickets purchased are purchased only once.

Start by creating a new visual studio solution named `ASPPatterns.Chap6.EventTickets` and adding two solution folders: `service` and `client`.

Domain Model and Repository

The first part of the application you will build is the domain model, which will handle all the application's business logic. For a deeper discussion of the Domain Model pattern, refer to Chapter 4. Figure 6-8 shows the domain model that you will be constructing.

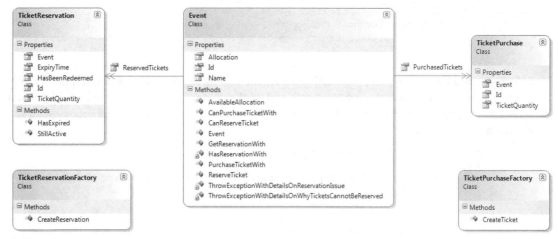

FIGURE 6-8

The `Event` class represents the event that affiliates can purchase tickets for. The `Event` class contains two collections of tickets: the `TicketPurchase` class represents the actual ticket purchase, and the `TicketReservation` class represents the reserved tickets. The two factory classes provide simple interfaces for creating valid `TicketReservation` and `TicketPurchase` instances.

Add a new C# class library to the solution within the `service` solution folder named `ASPPatterns`
`.Chap6.EventTickets.Model`. To this new project add a new class named `TicketReservation`
with the following code listing:

```
public class TicketReservation
{
    public Guid Id { get; set; }
    public Event Event { get; set; }
    public DateTime ExpiryTime { get; set; }
    public int TicketQuantity { get; set; }
    public bool HasBeenRedeemed { get; set; }

    public bool HasExpired()
    {
        return DateTime.Now > ExpiryTime;
```

```
        }

        public bool StillActive()
        {
            return !HasBeenRedeemed && !HasExpired();
        }
    }
```

You will receive a compile-time error because the `Event` class does not yet exist. Don't worry, though; you will get to this in a jiffy. Add a second class to the project named `TicketPurchase` with the code definition as displayed here.

```
    public class TicketPurchase
    {
        public Guid Id { get; set; }
        public Event Event { get; set; }
        public int TicketQuantity { get; set; }
    }
```

Before you add the `Event` class, you need to create the two factory classes that are responsible for creating valid instances of a `TicketPurchase` and `TicketReservation`, respectively. Add two new classes to the project named `TicketPurchaseFactory` and `TicketReservationFactory` with the following code listing:

```
    public class TicketPurchaseFactory
    {
        public static TicketPurchase CreateTicket(Event Event, int tktQty)
        {
            TicketPurchase ticket = new TicketPurchase();

            ticket.Id = Guid.NewGuid();
            ticket.Event = Event;
            ticket.TicketQuantity = tktQty;

            return ticket;
        }
    }

    public class TicketReservationFactory
    {
        public static TicketReservation CreateReservation(Event Event, int tktQty)
        {
            TicketReservation reservation = new TicketReservation();

            reservation.Id = Guid.NewGuid();
            reservation.Event = Event;
            reservation.ExpiryTime = DateTime.Now.AddMinutes(1);
            reservation.TicketQuantity = tktQty;

            return reservation;
        }
    }
```

The two factory classes are fairly straightforward. One point to note, though, is that TicketReservations are constructed with an expiration time of only one minute. In a real application this would be longer, but one minute will enable you to allow the reservation to time out when testing.

With the two ticket classes and factory classes in place, you can add the Event class so that the Model Project can build. Add the new Event class and the following code:

```csharp
public class Event
{
    public Event()
    {
        ReservedTickets = new List<TicketReservation>();
        PurchasedTickets = new List<TicketPurchase>();
    }

    public Guid Id { get; set; }
    public string Name { get; set; }
    public int Allocation { get; set; }
    public List<TicketReservation> ReservedTickets { get; set; }
    public List<TicketPurchase> PurchasedTickets { get; set; }

    public int AvailableAllocation()
    {
        int salesAndReservations = 0;

        PurchasedTickets.ForEach(t => salesAndReservations += t.TicketQuantity);

        ReservedTickets.FindAll(r => r.StillActive())
                        .ForEach(r => salesAndReservations += r.TicketQuantity);

        return Allocation - salesAndReservations;
    }

    public bool CanPurchaseTicketWith(Guid reservationId)
    {
        if (HasReservationWith(reservationId))
            return GetReservationWith(reservationId).StillActive();

        return false;
    }

    public TicketPurchase PurchaseTicketWith(Guid reservationId)
    {
        if (!CanPurchaseTicketWith(reservationId))
            Throw new ApplicationException(
                DetermineWhyATicketCannotbePurchasedWith (reservationId));

        TicketReservation reservation = GetReservationWith(reservationId);

        TicketPurchase ticket =
            TicketPurchaseFactory.CreateTicket(this, reservation.TicketQuantity);

        reservation.HasBeenRedeemed = true;

        PurchasedTickets.Add(ticket);

        return ticket;
```

```
    }

    public TicketReservation GetReservationWith(Guid reservationId)
    {
        if (!HasReservationWith(reservationId))
            throw new ApplicationException(
      String.Format("No reservation ticket with matching id of '{0}'",
                                        reservationId.ToString()));

        return ReservedTickets.FirstOrDefault(t => t.Id == reservationId);
    }

    private bool HasReservationWith(Guid reservationId)
    {
        return ReservedTickets.Exists(t => t.Id == reservationId);
    }

    public string DetermineWhyATicketCannotbePurchasedWith(Guid reservationId)
    {
        string reservationIssue = "";
        if (HasReservationWith(reservationId))
        {
            TicketReservation reservation = GetReservationWith(reservationId);
            if (reservation.HasExpired())
                reservationIssue =
                 String.Format("Ticket reservation '{0}' has expired",
                                                reservationId.ToString());
            else if (reservation.HasBeenRedeemed)
                reservationIssue =
                 String.Format("Ticket reservation '{0}' has already been redeemed",
                                                reservationId.ToString());
        }
        else
            reservationIssue =
                String.Format("There is no ticket reservation with the Id '{0}'",
                                                reservationId.ToString());

        return reservationIssue;
    }

    private void ThrowExceptionWithDetailsOnWhyTicketsCannotBeReserved()
    {
        throw new ApplicationException
            ("There are no tickets available to reserve.");
    }

    public bool CanReserveTicket(int qty)
    {
        return AvailableAllocation() >= qty;
    }

    public TicketReservation ReserveTicket(int tktQty)
    {
        if (!CanReserveTicket(tktQty))
```

```
            ThrowExceptionWithDetailsOnWhyTicketsCannotBeReserved();

        TicketReservation reservation =
            TicketReservationFactory.CreateReservation(this, tktQty);

        ReservedTickets.Add(reservation);

        return reservation;
    }
}
```

code snippet Event.cs in ASPPatterns.Chap6.EventTickets.Model

Before you go any further, take a look at the methods on the Event class:

➤ AvailableAllocation(): This method calculates the number of tickets available to sell based on the initial number of tickets available to an event minus the number of tickets already sold and the number of tickets that are currently reserved.

➤ CanReserveTicket(int qty): This method checks whether there are enough tickets available for reservation.

➤ ReserveTicket(int tktQty): This method creates a new TicketReservation and adds it to the Events collection.

➤ HasReservationWith(Guid reservationId): This method returns a Boolean that determines whether a TicketReservation exists.

➤ GetReservationWith(Guid reservationId): This method returns the TicketReservation that matches the passed in reservation ID.

➤ CanPurchaseTicketWith(Guid reservationId): This method determines if a ticket can be purchased based on the reservation ID.

➤ PurchaseTicketWith(Guid reservationId): This method creates a TicketPurchase that matches the reserved ticket.

➤ DetermineWhyATicketCannotbePurchasedWith(Guid reservationId): This method returns a string detailing why a ticket cannot be purchased based on a reservation ID.

With the domain model built, you need a way to persist and retrieve the Event aggregation. Add a new interface to the model project named IEventRepository with the following contract:

```
public interface IEventRepository
{
    Event FindBy(Guid id);
    void Save(Event eventEntity);
}
```

The interface is simplified in this example to keep the exercise straightforward. In a full application you would expect to see a method to add Events as well. This completes all the code for the domain model. Next you can look at creating the EventRepository implementation.

Add another new C# class library to the solution under the `service` solution folder named `ASPPatterns`
`.Chap6.EventTickets.Repository`, and add a project reference to the Model project:

```csharp
using System.Data.SqlClient;
using System.Data;
using ASPPatterns.Chap6.EventTickets.Model;

namespace ASPPatterns.Chap6.EventTickets.Repository
{
    public class EventRepository : IEventRepository
    {
        private string connectionString =
@"Data Source=.\SQLEXPRESS;AttachDbFilename=|DataDirectory|\EventTickets.mdf;"
+ @"Integrated Security=True;User Instance=True";

        public Event FindBy(Guid id)
        {
            Event Event = default(Event);

            string queryString =
                "SELECT * FROM dbo.Events WHERE Id = @EventId " +
                "SELECT * FROM dbo.PurchasedTickets WHERE EventId = @EventId " +
                "SELECT * FROM dbo.ReservedTickets WHERE EventId = @EventId;";

            using (SqlConnection connection =
                    new SqlConnection(connectionString))
            {
                SqlCommand command = connection.CreateCommand();
                command.CommandText = queryString;

                SqlParameter Idparam = new SqlParameter("@EventId", id.ToString());
                command.Parameters.Add(Idparam);

                connection.Open();

                using (SqlDataReader reader = command.ExecuteReader())
                {
                    if (reader.HasRows)
                    {
                        reader.Read();
                        Event = new Event();
                        Event.PurchasedTickets = new List<TicketPurchase>();
                        Event.ReservedTickets = new List<TicketReservation>();
                        Event.Allocation = int.Parse(reader["Allocation"].ToString());
                        Event.Id = new Guid(reader["Id"].ToString());
                        Event.Name = reader["Name"].ToString();

                        if (reader.NextResult())
                        {
                            if (reader.HasRows)
                            {
                                while (reader.Read())
                                {
                                    TicketPurchase ticketPurchase =
                                            new TicketPurchase();
```

```
                                        ticketPurchase.Id =
                                                  new Guid(reader["Id"].ToString());
                                        ticketPurchase.Event = Event;
                                        ticketPurchase.TicketQuantity =
                                          int.Parse(reader["TicketQuantity"].ToString());
                                        Event.PurchasedTickets.Add(ticketPurchase);
                                    }
                                }
                            }

                            if (reader.NextResult())
                            {
                                if (reader.HasRows)
                                {
                                    while (reader.Read())
                                    {
                                        TicketReservation ticketReservation =
                                                  new TicketReservation();
                                        ticketReservation.Id =
                                                  new Guid(reader["Id"].ToString());
                                        ticketReservation.Event = Event;
                                        ticketReservation.ExpiryTime =
                                          DateTime.Parse(reader["ExpiryTime"].ToString());
                                        ticketReservation.TicketQuantity =
                                          int.Parse(reader["TicketQuantity"].ToString());
                                        ticketReservation.HasBeenRedeemed =
                                          bool.Parse(reader["HasBeenRedeemed"].ToString());
                                        Event.ReservedTickets.Add(ticketReservation);
                                    }
                                }
                            }
                        }
                    }
                }

                return Event;
            }

            public void Save(Event Event)
            {
                // Code to save the Event entity
                // is not required in this scenario

                RemovePurchasedAndReservedTicketsFrom(Event);

                InsertPurchasedTicketsFrom(Event);
                InsertReservedTicketsFrom(Event);

            }

            public void InsertReservedTicketsFrom(Event Event)
            {
                string insertSQL =
                    "INSERT INTO ReservedTickets " +
                    "(Id, EventId, TicketQuantity, ExpiryTime, HasBeenRedeemed) " +
```

```
                "VALUES " +
                "(@Id, @EventId, @TicketQuantity, @ExpiryTime, @HasBeenRedeemed);";

        foreach (TicketReservation ticket in Event.ReservedTickets)
        {
            using (SqlConnection connection =
                     new SqlConnection(connectionString))
            {
                SqlCommand command = connection.CreateCommand();
                command.CommandText = insertSQL;

                SqlParameter Idparam =
                    new SqlParameter("@Id", ticket.Id.ToString());
                command.Parameters.Add(Idparam);

                SqlParameter EventIdparam =
                     new SqlParameter("@EventId", ticket.Event.Id.ToString());
                command.Parameters.Add(EventIdparam);

                SqlParameter TktQtyparam =
                     new SqlParameter("@TicketQuantity", ticket.TicketQuantity);
                command.Parameters.Add(TktQtyparam);

                SqlParameter Expiryparam =
                     new SqlParameter("@ExpiryTime", ticket.ExpiryTime);
                command.Parameters.Add(Expiryparam);

                SqlParameter HasBeenRedeemedparam =
                     new SqlParameter("@HasBeenRedeemed", ticket.HasBeenRedeemed);
                command.Parameters.Add(HasBeenRedeemedparam);

                connection.Open();
                command.ExecuteNonQuery();
            }
        }

    }

    public void InsertPurchasedTicketsFrom(Event Event)
    {
        string insertSQL = "INSERT INTO PurchasedTickets " +
                        "(Id, EventId, TicketQuantity) " +
                        "VALUES " +
                        "(@Id, @EventId, @TicketQuantity);";

        foreach (TicketPurchase ticket in Event.PurchasedTickets)
        {
            using (SqlConnection connection =
                     new SqlConnection(connectionString))
            {
                SqlCommand command = connection.CreateCommand();
```

```
                    command.CommandText = insertSQL;

                    SqlParameter Idparam =
                            new SqlParameter("@Id", ticket.Id.ToString());
                    command.Parameters.Add(Idparam);

                    SqlParameter EventIdparam =
                            new SqlParameter("@EventId", ticket.Event.Id.ToString());
                    command.Parameters.Add(EventIdparam);

                    SqlParameter TktQtyparam =
                            new SqlParameter("@TicketQuantity", ticket.TicketQuantity);
                    command.Parameters.Add(TktQtyparam);

                    connection.Open();
                    command.ExecuteNonQuery();
                }
            }
        }

        public void RemovePurchasedAndReservedTicketsFrom(Event Event)
        {
            string deleteSQL = "DELETE PurchasedTickets WHERE EventId = @EventId; " +
                            "DELETE ReservedTickets WHERE EventId = @EventId;";

            using (SqlConnection connection =
                    new SqlConnection(connectionString))
            {
                SqlCommand command = connection.CreateCommand();
                command.CommandText = deleteSQL;

                SqlParameter Idparam =
                  new SqlParameter("@EventId", Event.Id.ToString());
                command.Parameters.Add(Idparam);

                connection.Open();
                command.ExecuteNonQuery();
            }
        }
    }
}
```

---

code snippet EventRepository.cs in ASPPatterns.Chap6.EventTickets.Repository

There's a lot of ADO.NET code here, but don't dwell on it; it's just a means to an end. You will discover far better ways to persist and retrieve business objects in the next chapter.

Service Layer

With the data access and business logic of the application built, you can decorate it with the service layer. Figure 6-9 shows how the service layer exposes a simple API to the client.

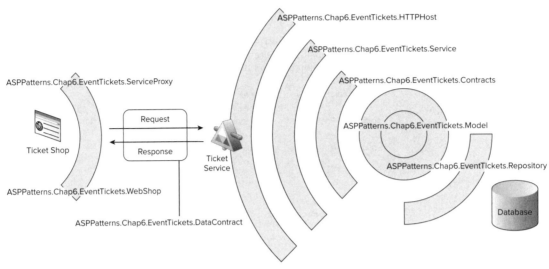

FIGURE 6-9

The service layer consists of four separate projects:

➤ `ASPPatterns.Chap6.EventTickets.Contracts`: This project holds the interface used to define the service contract.

➤ `ASPPatterns.Chap6.EventTickets.Service`: This project contains the implementation of the service contract and coordinates the workflow of business logic and entity persistence/retrieval.

➤ `ASPPatterns.Chap6.EventTickets.DataContract`: This project contains the message's DTOs to pass data via the client; this uses the Document Message messaging pattern to exchange data.

➤ `ASPPatterns.Chap6.EventTickets.HTTPHost`: This project hosts the WCF service.

Separating the interface from the implementation of the service using different assemblies enables the client to be completely unaware of the implementation. This leads to a better design through loose coupling.

You are going to start with the `ASPPatterns.Chap6.EventTickets.DataContract` to hold all the Data Transfer Objects that will be involved in the service workflow. Because you will be using the WCF model to expose your services, you need to add some extra namespaces to the project. Right-click on the project and select Add Reference, select the .NET tab, and add a reference to the following assemblies:

➤ `System.Runtime.Serialization`

➤ `System.ServiceModel`

All the response objects will inherit from a base class that contains some common behavior. Add a new abstract class to the project named Response and add the following code:

```
using System.ServiceModel;
using System.Runtime.Serialization;

namespace ASPPatterns.Chap6.EventTickets.DataContract
{
    [DataContract]
    public abstract class Response
    {
        [DataMember]
        public bool Success { get; set; }

        [DataMember]
        public string Message { get; set; }
    }
}
```

The two response objects that will inherit from the Response base class are PurchaseTicketResponse and ReserveTicketResponse. Add these two classes to the DataContracts project with the following code definitions. The attributes that decorated the properties are key to WCF being able to enable serialization when transporting the request and responses over the wire:

```
using System.ServiceModel;
using System.Runtime.Serialization;

namespace ASPPatterns.Chap6.EventTickets.DataContract
{
    [DataContract]
    public class PurchaseTicketResponse : Response
    {
        [DataMember]
        public string TicketId { get; set; }

        [DataMember]
        public String EventName { get; set; }

        [DataMember]
        public String EventId { get; set; }

        [DataMember]
        public int NoOfTickets { get; set; }
    }
}

using System.ServiceModel;
using System.Runtime.Serialization;

namespace ASPPatterns.Chap6.EventTickets.DataContract
{
    [DataContract]
    public class ReserveTicketResponse : Response
    {
        [DataMember]
```

```
            public string ReservationNumber {get; set;}

            [DataMember]
            public DateTime ExpirationDate { get; set; }

            [DataMember]
            public String EventName { get; set; }

            [DataMember]
            public String EventId { get; set; }

            [DataMember]
            public int NoOfTickets { get; set; }
        }
    }
```

Next, add two classes that will represent the request portion of the messaging data transfer objects. Add two new classes named `PurchaseTicketRequest` and `ReserveTicketRequest`. These data containers are again decorated with the WCF attributes to enable serialization:

```
    using System.ServiceModel;
    using System.Runtime.Serialization;

    namespace ASPPatterns.Chap6.EventTickets.DataContract
    {
        [DataContract]
        public class PurchaseTicketRequest
        {
            [DataMember]
            public string CorrelationId { get; set; }

            [DataMember]
            public string ReservationId { get; set; }

            [DataMember]
            public string EventId { get; set; }
        }
    }

    using System.ServiceModel;
    using System.Runtime.Serialization;

    namespace ASPPatterns.Chap6.EventTickets.DataContract
    {
        [DataContract]
        public class ReserveTicketRequest
        {
            [DataMember]
            public string EventId { get; set; }
            [DataMember]
            public int TicketQuantity { get; set; }
        }
    }
```

The next project you need to add for the construction of the service layer is the ASPPatterns.Chap6 .EventTickets.Contracts project. Again, you will need to add a reference to the following assemblies:

➤ System.Runtime.Serialization

➤ System.ServiceModel

You also need to add a reference to the DataContract project.

This project holds the contract that the service will implement and that the client can work against. Add a new class to the project named ITicketService with the following code contract:

```
using System.ServiceModel;
using ASPPatterns.Chap6.EventTickets.DataContract;

namespace ASPPatterns.Chap6.EventTickets.Contracts
{
    [ServiceContract(Namespace = "ASPPatterns.Chap6.EventTickets/")]
    public interface ITicketService
    {
        [OperationContract()]
        ReserveTicketResponse ReserveTicket(ReserveTicketRequest reserveTicketRequest);

        [OperationContract()]
        PurchaseTicketResponse
            PurchaseTicket(PurchaseTicketRequest PurchaseTicketRequest);
    }
}
```

Add another class library to the service solution folder named ASPPatterns.Chap6.EventTickets .Service. This will hold the concrete implementation of the service as defined in the previous project.

Add the following project references to this project:

➤ ASPPatterns.Chap6.EventTickets.Contracts

➤ ASPPatterns.Chap6.EventTickets.DataContract

➤ ASPPatterns.Chap6.EventTickets.Model

➤ ASPPatterns.Chap6.EventTickets.Repository

Add two new classes named TicketPurchaseExtensionMethods and TicketReservationExtension Methods. These extension method classes enable the service class to convert a TicketReservation and TicketPurchase entity respectively into a message document in a fluent manner, which will become clear when you create the service class:

```
using ASPPatterns.Chap6.EventTickets.DataContract;
using ASPPatterns.Chap6.EventTickets.Model;

namespace ASPPatterns.Chap6.EventTickets.Service
{
    public static class TicketPurchaseExtensionMethods
    {
        public static PurchaseTicketResponse ConvertToPurchaseTicketResponse
```

```
                                            (this TicketPurchase ticketPurchase)
        {
            PurchaseTicketResponse response = new PurchaseTicketResponse();

            response.TicketId = ticketPurchase.Id.ToString();
            response.EventName = ticketPurchase.Event.Name;
            response.EventId = ticketPurchase.Event.Id.ToString();
            response.NoOfTickets = ticketPurchase.TicketQuantity;

            return response;
        }
    }
}

using ASPPatterns.Chap6.EventTickets.DataContract;
using ASPPatterns.Chap6.EventTickets.Model;

namespace ASPPatterns.Chap6.EventTickets.Service
{
    public static class TicketReservationExtensionMethods
    {
        public static ReserveTicketResponse ConvertToReserveTicketResponse
                                    (this TicketReservation ticketReservation)
        {
            ReserveTicketResponse response = new ReserveTicketResponse();

            response.EventId = ticketReservation.Event.Id.ToString();
            response.EventName = ticketReservation.Event.Name;
            response.NoOfTickets = ticketReservation.TicketQuantity;
            response.ExpirationDate = ticketReservation.ExpiryTime;
            response.ReservationNumber = ticketReservation.Id.ToString();

            return response;
        }
    }
}
```

To ensure that unexpected issues don't arise due to problems with a client using the services that you are about to build, you are going to adopt the Idempotent Messaging pattern.

Add a new class to the Services project named MessageResponseHistory with the following code listing:

```
public class MessageResponseHistory<T>
{
    private Dictionary<string, T> _responseHistory;

    public MessageResponseHistory()
    {
        _responseHistory = new Dictionary<string, T>();
    }

    public bool IsAUniqueRequest(string correlationId)
    {
        return !_responseHistory.ContainsKey(correlationId);
```

```
        }

        public void LogResponse(string correlationId, T response)
        {
            if (_responseHistory.ContainsKey(correlationId))
                _responseHistory[correlationId] = response;
            else
                _responseHistory.Add(correlationId, response);
        }

        public T RetrievePreviousResponseFor(string correlationId)
        {
            return _responseHistory[correlationId];
        }
    }
```

This class will hold in memory the result of the service response that is associated with a given correlation identifier. This class could easily be hooked up to some kind of data store to provide out-of-process storage of message responses. It may not be necessary to hold the result of every response, so this class could be made to buffer the last N number of responses to ensure that the business logic is called only once.

Before you create the service class, there is just one more class that you will create to mock handling errors and returning a reference identifier. Add a new class named ErrorLog to the project with the single method detailed here:

```
public class ErrorLog
{
    public static string GenerateErrorRefMessageAndLog(Exception exception)
    {
        // Here you would log the error and the unique reference ID
        return String.Format
            ("If you wish to contact us please quote reference '{0}'",
                                        Guid.NewGuid().ToString());
    }
}
```

Now with all the supporting classes for the service implementation in place, you can create the actual service class. Add a new class to the project named TicketService with the following code listing:

```
using System.ServiceModel.Activation;
using ASPPatterns.Chap6.EventTickets.Contracts;
using ASPPatterns.Chap6.EventTickets;
using ASPPatterns.Chap6.EventTickets.DataContract;
using ASPPatterns.Chap6.EventTickets.Model;
using ASPPatterns.Chap6.EventTickets.Repository;

namespace ASPPatterns.Chap6.EventTickets.Service
{
    [AspNetCompatibilityRequirements(RequirementsMode =
                        AspNetCompatibilityRequirementsMode.Allowed)]
    public class TicketService : ITicketService
    {
        private IEventRepository _eventRepository;
        private static MessageResponseHistory<PurchaseTicketResponse>
```

```
            _reservationResponse =
                new MessageResponseHistory<PurchaseTicketResponse>();

    public TicketService(IEventRepository eventRepository)
    {
        _eventRepository = eventRepository;
    }

    public TicketService() : this (new EventRepository())
    { }

    public ReserveTicketResponse ReserveTicket
                        (ReserveTicketRequest reserveTicketRequest)
    {
        ReserveTicketResponse response = new ReserveTicketResponse();

        try
        {
            Event Event = _eventRepository.FindBy(
                            new Guid(reserveTicketRequest.EventId));
            TicketReservation reservation;

            if (Event.CanReserveTicket(reserveTicketRequest.TicketQuantity)    )
            {
                reservation =
                    Event.ReserveTicket(reserveTicketRequest.TicketQuantity);
                _eventRepository.Save(Event);
                response = reservation.ConvertToReserveTicketResponse();
                response.Success = true;
            }
            else
            {
                response.Success = false;
                response.Message = String.Format(
                                "There are {0} ticket(s) available.",
                                    Event.AvailableAllocation());
            }

        }
        catch (Exception ex)
        {
            // Shield exceptions
            response.Message = ErrorLog.GenerateErrorRefMessageAndLog(ex);
            response.Success = false;
        }
        return response;
    }

    public PurchaseTicketResponse PurchaseTicket
                        (PurchaseTicketRequest purchaseTicketRequest)
    {
        PurchaseTicketResponse response = new PurchaseTicketResponse();

        try
```

```
        {
            // Check for a duplicate transaction using the Idempotent pattern;
            // the Domain Logic could cope but you can't be sure.
            if (_reservationResponse.IsAUniqueRequest
                    (purchaseTicketRequest.CorrelationId))
            {
                TicketPurchase ticket;
                Event Event = _eventRepository.FindBy(
                        new Guid(purchaseTicketRequest.EventId));

                if (Event.CanPurchaseTicketWith
                    (new Guid(purchaseTicketRequest.ReservationId)))
                {
                    ticket = Event.PurchaseTicketWith(
                            new Guid(purchaseTicketRequest.ReservationId));

                    _eventRepository.Save(Event);

                    response = ticket.ConvertToPurchaseTicketResponse();
                    response.Success = true;
                }
                else
                {
                    response.Message =
                        Event.DetermineWhyATicketCannotbePurchasedWith(
                            new Guid(purchaseTicketRequest.ReservationId));
                    response.Success = false;
                }

                _reservationResponse.LogResponse(
                        purchaseTicketRequest.CorrelationId, response);
            }
            else
            {
                response = _reservationResponse.RetrievePreviousResponseFor(
                                purchaseTicketRequest.CorrelationId);
            }
        }
        catch (Exception ex)
        {
            // Shield exceptions
            response.Message = ErrorLog.GenerateErrorRefMessageAndLog(ex);
            response.Success = false;
        }

        return response;
    }
  }
}
```

It's important to explain exactly what this class is doing. First, the TicketService class has a reference to a static instance of a MessageResponseHistory object; this enables all service response messages to be logged against a correlation identifier. When a new message request is received, the service can check the MessageResponseHistory to determine if it has already been processed. You will see this in action when you examine the PurchaseTicket method.

```
private static MessageResponseHistory<PurchaseTicketResponse>
        _reservationResponse =
            new MessageResponseHistory<PurchaseTicketResponse>();
```

The service has two constructors: one that takes no arguments and one that takes an instance of a class that implements the IEventRepository:

```
public TicketService(IEventRepository eventRepository)
{
    _eventRepository = eventRepository;
}

public TicketService() : this (new EventRepository())
{ }
```

To keep things simple, I have opted to hard-code the concrete implementation of the ADO.NET Event Repository. However, later in the book you will be introduced to an Inversion of Control (IoC) container that will enable dependencies to be injected into your code without tying you to a particular implementation.

The ReserveTicket method is invoked by the client using the service. The sole parameter is the ReserveTicketRequest as defined in the DataContract project. The first action of the method is to retrieve the event that is associated with the requests event. Because I wanted to keep the exercise as small as possible, I neglected to add validation of the request to ensure that it contains a valid ReserveTicketRequest; this could be a simple method to ensure the request contains a valid GUID and a nonnegative ticket quantity. Similarly, you could add code to check that an event exists for the given EventId before trying to retrieve it.

If a valid event is found, its CanReserveTicket method is called to determine whether the quantity of tickets requested can in fact be reserved. Refer to the description of the Event methods earlier in this section to see how the Event entity determines whether the reservation request can be satisfied. If the Event entity can reserve the requested number of tickets, a call to the Events ReserveTicket is made; this workflow follows the Tester-Doer pattern. The ReserveTicket method creates a new TicketReservation and adds it to the internal collection of reservations within the Event entity.

The changes to the event are then persisted using the EventRepository, and the TicketReservation invokes the ConvertToReserveTicketResponse extension method to return a ReserveTicketResponse ready to send back to the client:

```
public ReserveTicketResponse ReserveTicket
                        (ReserveTicketRequest reserveTicketRequest)
    {
        ReserveTicketResponse response = new ReserveTicketResponse();

        try
        {
            Event Event = _eventRepository.FindBy(
                            new Guid(reserveTicketRequest.EventId));
            TicketReservation reservation;
```

```
            if (Event.CanReserveTicket(reserveTicketRequest.TicketQuantity)    )
            {
                reservation =
                    Event.ReserveTicket(reserveTicketRequest.TicketQuantity);
                _eventRepository.Save(Event);
                response = reservation.ConvertToReserveTicketResponse();
                response.Success = true;
            }
            else
            {
                response.Success = false;
                response.Message = String.Format(
                                "There are {0} ticket(s) available.",
                                    Event.AvailableAllocation());
            }

        }
        catch (Exception ex)
        {
            // Shield exceptions
            response.Message = ErrorLog.GenerateErrorRefMessageAndLog(ex);
            response.Success = false;
        }
        return response;
    }
```

If the quantity of tickets cannot be reserved, the success flag on the response message is set to false, and a message detailing the remaining ticket allocation is generated. All the logic within the ReserveTicket method is wrapped within a single try catch block to ensure exceptions aren't leaked that could reveal the internal workings of the service. When an exception occurs, the ErrorLog static class is used to log the exception and return a unique reference number the client can use. The unique reference is then added to the response and returned to the client with the success flag set to false, indicating that there was problem when the method was called.

The PurchaseTicket method is set up not too unlike the ReserveTicket method; again, any validation of the Request object has been left out for the sake of brevity:

```
public PurchaseTicketResponse PurchaseTicket
                            (PurchaseTicketRequest purchaseTicketRequest)
    {
        PurchaseTicketResponse response = new PurchaseTicketResponse();

        try
        {
            // Check for a duplicate transaction using the Idempotent pattern;
            // the Domain Logic could cope, but you can't be sure.
            if (_reservationResponse.IsAUniqueRequest
                    (PurchaseTicketRequest.CorrelationId))
            {
                TicketPurchase ticket;
                Event Event = _eventRepository.FindBy(
                            new Guid(purchaseTicketRequest.EventId));

                if (Event.CanPurchaseTicketWith
```

```
                          (new Guid(purchaseTicketRequest.ReservationId)))
                {
                    ticket = Event.PurchaseTicketWith(
                            new Guid(purchaseTicketRequest.ReservationId));

                    _eventRepository.Save(Event);

                    response = ticket.ConvertToPurchaseTicketResponse();
                    response.Success = true;
                }
                else
                {
                    response.Message =
                            Event.DetermineWhyATicketCannotbePurchasedWith(
                                new Guid(purchaseTicketRequest.ReservationId));
                    response.Success = false;
                }

                _reservationResponse.LogResponse(
                            purchaseTicketRequest.CorrelationId, response);
            }
            else
            {
                response = _reservationResponse.RetrievePreviousResponseFor(
                                        purchaseTicketRequest.CorrelationId);
            }
        }
        catch (Exception ex)
        {
            // Shield Exceptions
            response.Message = ErrorLog.GenerateErrorRefMessageAndLog(ex);
            response.Success = false;
        }

        return response;
    }
```

This first action of the PurchaseTicket method is to check to see whether this service call has been completed previously. You use the Idempotent pattern here to determine if there is a matching correlation ID and response. The static MessageResponseHistory object takes care of storing and checking for a matching response. If a match is found, the response is retrieved from the MessageResponseHistory object and returned to the client ensuring that no unexpected problems arise if a client duplicates a call to the service. If the response has not already been called, the workflow is similar to that of the ReserveTicket method. An event is retrieved with a matching event ID, and a check is made to ensure a ticket purchase transaction can continue with the given reservation ID. On success, the ticket is purchased and a response is generated again using the extension method. The response is then logged with the MessageResponseHistory object and returned to the client. If the ticket cannot be purchased using the given reservation ID, a call to the event entity's DetermineWhyATicketCannotbePurchasedWith method returns details on any issues. Again, a single Try Catch block surrounds the method to ensure that any exception thrown will not reveal the internal structure of the service.

The final project required for the service layer solution is the hosting project. Add a new WCF Service application project from the web node of the New Projects dialog box, and call this project `ASPPatterns.Chap6.EventTickets.HTTPHost`. Add a reference to the following two projects:

➤   `ASPPatterns.Chap6.EventTickets.Contracts`

➤   `ASPPatterns.Chap6.EventTickets.Service`

Delete the `Service1.svc` code behind file and the `IService1.svc` interface that are generated by Visual Studio. Rename `Service1.svc` to `TicketService.svc` and update the markup so that it matches the code that follows:

```
<%@ ServiceHost Language="C#"
                Service="ASPPatterns.Chap6.EventTickets.Service.TicketService"  %>
```

Open the `web.config` file so that you can configure the endpoints for the WCF service. You are going to be serving via HTTP, so the binding will be set to `wsHttpBinding`. The contract for the service is defined in a separate assembly `ASPPatterns.Chap6.EventTickets.Contracts.ITicketService`:

```
<configuration>
...
<system.serviceModel>
    <services>
      <service name="ASPPatterns.Chap6.EventTickets.Service.TicketService"
               behaviorConfiguration="metadataBehavior">
        <endpoint address=""
                  binding="wsHttpBinding"
                  contract="ASPPatterns.Chap6.EventTickets.Contracts.ITicketService" />
      </service>
    </services>
    <behaviors>
      <serviceBehaviors>
        <behavior name="metadataBehavior">
          <serviceMetadata httpGetEnabled="true" />
        </behavior>
      </serviceBehaviors>
    </behaviors>
  </system.serviceModel>
</configuration>
```

The one last thing before the service layer is complete is the building of the database that will store the state of the `Event` and `Ticket` entities. Add a new database to the `HTTPHost` project named `EventTickets` and create the following three tables.

TABLE 6-1: Events

COLUMN NAME	DATA TYPE	ALLOW NULLS
ID	Uniqueidentifier, Primary Key	False
Name	nvarchar(50)	False
Allocation	Int	False

TABLE 6-2: PurchasedTickets

COLUMN NAME	DATA TYPE	ALLOW NULLS
ID	Uniqueidentifier, Primary Key	False
TicketQuantity	Int	False
EventID	Uniqueidentifier	False

TABLE 6-3: ReservedTickets

COLUMN NAME	DATA TYPE	ALLOW NULLS
ID	Uniqueidentifier, Primary Key	False
ExpiryTime	Datetime	False
TicketQuantity	Int	False
EventID	Uniqueidentifier	False
HasBeenRedeemed	Bit	False

Run the following SQL to populate the Events table because you haven't added the code to the repository to support adding events:

```
INSERT INTO EVENTS
(Id, Name, Allocation)
VALUES
(NEWID(), 'Portsmouth v Southampton', 50)
```

This completes the service layer. Your solution should resemble Figure 6-10.

With the service layer complete, you can turn to building the client projects that will consume the service.

Client Proxy

To enable the client to use the service, you need to create a proxy. You could have Visual Studio generate one for you by adding a service reference and pointing it at the HTTPHost project's TicketService. However, because you own the client and the service, it makes perfect sense to reuse the data contracts and service contract and create the proxy yourself.

Add a new C# class library project to the client solution folder named ASPPatterns.Chap6. EventTickets.ServiceProxy. Add a project reference to the following projects:

➤   ASPPatterns.Chap6.EventTickets.Contracts

➤   ASPPatterns.Chap6.EventTickets.DataContract

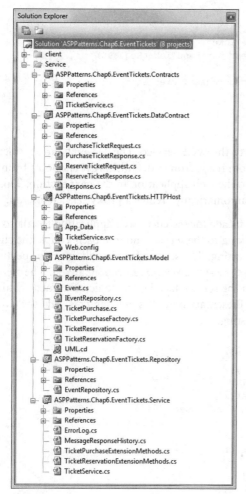

FIGURE 6-10

Add a new class to the `ServiceProxy` project named `TicketServiceClientProxy` with the following definition:

```
using System.ServiceModel;
using ASPPatterns.Chap6.EventTickets.Contracts;
using ASPPatterns.Chap6.EventTickets.DataContract;

namespace ASPPatterns.Chap6.EventTickets.ServiceProxy
{
    public class TicketServiceClientProxy : ClientBase<ITicketService>, ITicketService
    {
        public ReserveTicketResponse ReserveTicket(
                        ReserveTicketRequest reserveTicketRequest)
        {
            return base.Channel.ReserveTicket(reserveTicketRequest);
```

```
            }

    public PurchaseTicketResponse PurchaseTicket(
                    PurchaseTicketRequest purchaseTicketRequest)
    {
        return base.Channel.PurchaseTicket(purchaseTicketRequest);
    }
        }
    }
}
```

This class provides the channel that allows you to talk to the WCF service. The `ClientBase` abstract class that the `TicketServiceClientProxy` inherits from reads from a default target endpoint from the application configuration file, which you will add to the web application in the next section. This is the same base class that is used when Visual Studio automatically creates a proxy service for you.

With the proxy service in place, you can build a service facade for the client web application to talk to. You are creating a facade to hide the complexities of talking to the service and to loosely couple the client application from the service, which will help with testing. The service facade will use two specific Presentation model classes: `TicketPresentation` and `TicketReservationPresentation`. The web application only uses these classes to display data from the service facade; any logic contained within is strictly presentation logic. You will learn more about Presentation models in Chapter 8. Add the two classes, and update them to match the following code listing:

```
public class TicketPresentation
{
    public string TicketId { get; set; }
    public string EventId { get; set; }
    public string Description { get; set; }
    public bool WasAbleToPurchaseTicket { get; set; }
}

public class TicketReservationPresentation
{
    public string EventId { get; set; }
    public string ReservationId {get; set;}
    public string Description { get; set; }
    public DateTime ExpiryDate { get; set; }
    public bool TicketWasSuccessfullyReserved { get; set; }
}
```

With the supporting Presentation model classes in place, you can add the `TicketServiceFacade` class with the following code listing:

```
using ASPPatterns.Chap6.EventTickets.Contracts;
using ASPPatterns.Chap6.EventTickets.DataContract;

namespace ASPPatterns.Chap6.EventTickets.ServiceProxy
{
    public class TicketServiceFacade
    {
        private ITicketService _ticketService;

        public TicketServiceFacade(ITicketService ticketService)
        {
```

```
        _ticketService = ticketService;
}

public TicketReservationPresentation ReserveTicketsFor(
                                    string EventId, int NoOfTkts)
{
    TicketReservationPresentation reservation =
                            new TicketReservationPresentation();
            ReserveTicketRequest request = new ReserveTicketRequest();

    request.EventId = EventId;
    request.TicketQuantity = NoOfTkts;

    ReserveTicketResponse response = _ticketService.ReserveTicket(request);

    if (response.Success)
    {
        reservation.TicketWasSuccessfullyReserved = true;
        reservation.ReservationId = response.ReservationNumber;
        reservation.ExpiryDate = response.ExpirationDate;
        reservation.EventId = response.EventId;
        reservation.Description = String.Format(
                "{0} ticket(s) reserved for {1}.<br/>" +
                "<small>This reservation will expire on {2} at {3}.</small>",
                response.NoOfTickets, response.EventName,
                response.ExpirationDate.ToLongDateString(),
                response.ExpirationDate.ToLongTimeString());
    }
    else
    {
        reservation.TicketWasSuccessfullyReserved = false;
        reservation.Description = response.Message;
    }

    return reservation;
}

public TicketPresentation PurchaseReservedTicket(
                                    string eventId, string reservationId)
{
    TicketPresentation ticket = new TicketPresentation();
    PurchaseTicketResponse response = new PurchaseTicketResponse();
    PurchaseTicketRequest request = new PurchaseTicketRequest();
    request.ReservationId = reservationId;
    request.EventId = eventId;
    request.CorrelationId = reservationId;
    response = _ticketService.PurchaseTicket(request);
    if (response.Success)
    {
        ticket.Description = String.Format(
                "{0} ticket(s) purchased for {1}.<br/>" +
                "<small>Your e-ticket id is {2}.</small>",
                response.NoOfTickets, response.EventName,
                                        response.TicketId);
        ticket.EventId = response.EventId;
        ticket.TicketId = response.TicketId;
```

```
                ticket.WasAbleToPurchaseTicket = true;
        }
        else
        {
                ticket.WasAbleToPurchaseTicket = false;
                ticket.Description = response.Message;
        }

        return ticket;
    }

  }
}
```

---

code snippet TicketServiceFacade.cs in ASPPatterns.Chap6.EventTickets.ServiceProxy

The role of the service facade is to simplify the interaction between the client and the service. The client application does not need to be responsible for knowing about messaging patterns and how to talk with the service proxy. The two methods of the `TicketServiceFacade` should be fairly straightforward because they follow the same workflow.

1. Generate a request.

2. Pass the request to the proxy service (referenced by its interface so that you can test with a mock service).

3. Retrieve the response and build the Presentation model.

With the service proxy constructed you can create a client web application that will use the service proxy to simplify the communication with the real web service.

Client

The last part of the solution consists of creating the web site that will talk to the service facade and in turn to the proxy who talks to the actual service layer.

Add a new web application to the client solution folder named `ASPPatterns.Chap6.EventTickets.WebShop`. Add a reference to the following projects:

➤ `ASPPatterns.Chap6.EventTickets.ServiceProxy`

➤ `ASPPatterns.Chap6.EventTickets.Contracts`

In addition, add a reference to the .NET `System.ServiceModel` assembly.

The first item you will add to the web application project is a `Basket` class that will act as a simple shopping basket for customers to purchase tickets. Add the new `Basket` class with the following listing:

```
using System.Web;
using ASPPatterns.Chap6.EventTickets.ServiceProxy;

namespace ASPPatterns.Chap6.EventTickets.WebShop
{
    public class Basket
```

```
        {
            public Guid Id { get; set;}
            public TicketReservationPresentation Reservation { get; set; }

            public static Basket GetBasket()
            {
                    if (HttpContext.Current.Session["Basket"] == null)
                        HttpContext.Current.Session["Basket"] = new Basket
                                                        { Id = Guid.NewGuid()};

                    return (Basket)HttpContext.Current.Session["Basket"];
            }

            public static void Clear()
            {
                HttpContext.Current.Session["Basket"] = null;
            }
        }
    }
```

This `Basket` class will simply hold onto the current `TicketReservationPresentation`.

The first web page that you will create is the form that will allow customers to input the number of tickets they want to reserve. Amend the `Default.aspx` markup to match the snippet that follows:

```
...
<form id="form1" runat="server">
    <div>
        <h2>Basket</h2>
        I want
        <asp:TextBox ID="txtNoOfTickets" runat="server" Width="43px"/>
        tickets to see
        <asp:DropDownList ID="ddlEvents" runat="server">
            <asp:ListItem Value="2de874d0-00b7-4c86-9925-c7f2c243151c">
            Portsmouth vs Southampton</asp:ListItem>
        </asp:DropDownList>
        <p>
        <asp:Button
            ID="btnReserveTickets" runat="server"
            Text="Reserve & Checkout" onclick="btnReserveTickets_Click" />
        <br />
        <small>"Reserve &amp; Checkout" Reserves the Tickets for you as part
        of the Reservation Pattern.</small>
        </p>
    </div>
</form>
...
```

Ensure that the bolded item in the drop-down list matches the event that you added to the Events table.

Switch to the code behind, and amend it to match the code listing that follows:

```
using ASPPatterns.Chap6.EventTickets.ServiceProxy;
using ASPPatterns.Chap6.EventTickets.Contracts;

namespace ASPPatterns.Chap6.EventTickets.WebShop
```

```
    {
        public partial class _Default : System.Web.UI.Page
        {
            protected void btnReserveTickets_Click(object sender, EventArgs e)
            {
                Basket.Clear();

                TicketServiceFacade ticketService =
                    new TicketServiceFacade(new TicketServiceClientProxy());
                TicketReservationPresentation reservation =
                    ticketService.ReserveTicketsFor(ddlEvents.SelectedValue,
                                                int.Parse(this.txtNoOfTickets.Text));

                if (reservation.TicketWasSuccessfullyReserved)
                {
                    Basket.GetBasket().Reservation = reservation;
                    Response.Redirect("Checkout.aspx");
                }

                Response.Write("Your tickets were unable to be reserved.<br/>" +
                                                reservation.Description);
            }
        }
    }
```

The single method handles the `btnReserveTickets` click event and creates a new `TicketService Facade` passing in an instance of the `TicketServiceClientProxy`. As previously mentioned in Chapter 8, you will look at a better method of supplying your dependencies using an IoC container. Once the `TicketServiceFacade` is created, a call to the `ReserveTicketsFor` method is made, passing in the customer choices. A `TicketReservationPresentation` is returned; based on the `TicketWasSuccessfullyReserved` flag, the customer is forwarded to the checkout page, or a message is displayed explaining why the tickets cannot be allocated.

Now that you can reserve tickets, you need to be able to purchase them. Create a new web form named `Checkout.aspx` and add the following markup:

```
...
<form id="form1" runat="server">
<div>
    <h2>Checkout</h2>
    In your basket you have:
    <p>
    <asp:Label ID="lblBasketContents" runat="server" Text="" />
    </p>
    <asp:Button ID="btnPlaceOrder" runat="server"
                Text="Place Order" onclick="btnPlaceOrder_Click" />
    <br />
    <small>Click the "Place Order" button again and the Ticket Id will
    always return the same due to the use of the Idempotent Pattern.</small>
    <p>
    <asp:Label ID="lblThankYou" runat="server" Text=""></asp:Label>
    <p/>
```

```
    </div>
    </form>
    ...
```

Flip over to the code behind and update it with the following code listing:

```csharp
using ASPPatterns.Chap6.EventTickets.ServiceProxy;
using ASPPatterns.Chap6.EventTickets.Contracts;

namespace ASPPatterns.Chap6.EventTickets.WebShop
{
    public partial class Checkout : System.Web.UI.Page
    {
        protected void Page_Load(object sender, EventArgs e)
        {
            if (!Page.IsPostBack)
                DisplayTicketReservations();
        }

        private void DisplayTicketReservations()
        {
            lblBasketContents.Text = Basket.GetBasket().Reservation.Description;
        }

        protected void btnPlaceOrder_Click(object sender, EventArgs e)
        {
            TicketServiceFacade ticketService =
                        new TicketServiceFacade(new TicketServiceClientProxy());
            TicketPresentation ticket =
                    ticketService.PurchaseReservedTicket(
                        Basket.GetBasket().Reservation.EventId,
                        Basket.GetBasket().Reservation.ReservationId.ToString());

            DisplayTicketReservations();

            if (ticket.WasAbleToPurchaseTicket)
                lblThankYou.Text = "<h2>Thank you for your order.</h2>" +
                                                        ticket.Description;
            else
                lblThankYou.Text = "<h2>Sorry there was a problem with your order.</h2>"
                                                        + ticket.Description;
        }

    }
}
```

The code behind page creates a `TicketServiceFacade` in the same manner as the `Default.aspx` page and calls the `PurchaseReservedTicket` method, passing through the original reservation ID and event ID held within the basket. A `TicketPresentation` is returned from the method call and, depending on the `WasAbleToPurchaseTicket` flag, a message is displayed with the successfully purchased ticket ID or a message detailing why the ticket could not be purchased.

To let the `TicketServiceClientProxy` talk to the WCF service, you have to amend the `web.config` with the binding settings. Open the `web.config` file and enter the following XML:

```
<configuration>
    ...
    <system.serviceModel>
      <client>
        <endpoint
               address="http://localhost:25076/TicketService.svc"
               binding="wsHttpBinding"
               contract="ASPPatterns.Chap6.EventTickets.Contracts.ITicketService"/>
      </client>
    </system.serviceModel>
</configuration>
```

Ensure that the bolded address port number matches the port number that the built-in web server uses to serve the `HTTPHost` project. To obtain this, right-click on the `HTTPHost` project and select Debug ➪ Start New Instance. Make a note of the port number that is displayed on your taskbar, as shown in Figure 6-11.

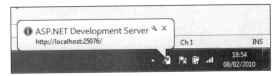

FIGURE 6-11

With the `HTTPPost` project still running, you can right-click on the web application project and select Debug ➪ Start New Instance to launch the web site. You can now test the system. Ensure, however, that the `HTTPPost` project is always running to service the requests.

That completes the SOA exercise; Figure 6-12 shows the solution with the added client projects.

With the service built, other clients can now use the web service, and a host of ticket affiliate agents can use it to reserve and purchase tickets.

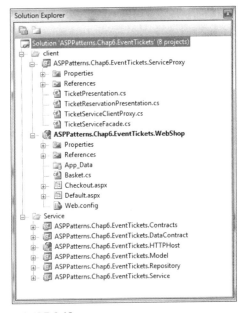

FIGURE 6-12

SUMMARY

In this chapter you looked at the role the service layer plays in an enterprise application. Sitting between the presentation and business layer, the service interface encapsulates the business domain logic, coordinates transactions and responses, and defines an API as a set of coarse-grained methods available to clients. You read about what SOA was and saw how to apply it to an organization to improve maintenance and reusability. SOA has principles in the form of the following tenets:

➤ Boundaries are explicit.

➤ Services are autonomous.

➤ Services share schema and contract, not class.

➤ Service compatibility is based on policy.

The Facade design pattern was introduced to show how a complicated interface can be hidden behind a simplified API that is consistent to your application. Toward the end of the chapter, you used this pattern to abstract the mechanics of communicating with the service endpoints using that messaging pattern, making a simplified interface for the client application.

Messaging patterns were then introduced as a way to create SOAs. You looked at four messaging patterns:

➤ Document Message

➤ Request-Response

➤ Reservation

➤ Idempotent

You finished the chapter with by putting into practice all the information you read about regarding SOA. The exercise used WCF to enable affiliate applications to reserve and purchase tickets via a service interface that encapsulated a domain model.

In the next chapter, you will investigate the various patterns and principles that you can use in the data access layer of an enterprise ASP.NET application.

7

The Data Access Layer

WHAT'S IN THIS CHAPTER?

➤ Two data access strategies to help organize your persistence layer: Repository and Data Access Objects

➤ Data patterns and principles to help you fulfill your data access requirement needs elegantly, including Lazy Loading, Identity Map, Unit of Work, and Query Object

➤ An introduction to object relational mappers and the problems they solve

➤ An enterprise domain-driven exercise with POCO business entities utilizing both NHibernate and the MS Entity Framework

So far, you have read about the business layer of an enterprise ASP.NET application, the patterns used to organize it, and the patterns found within. You then looked at the service layer, which gave an entry point into a system. This chapter focuses on the data access layer (DAL) and covers patterns that allow you to retrieve and persist your business entities, ensuring you leave your data in a valid state.

DESCRIBING THE DAL

The DAL is the layer in your application that is solely responsible for talking to the data store and persisting and retrieving your business objects. (Note the reference to a data store and not a database. You don't always have to have a database; sometimes an XML file is sufficient.) The DAL typically includes all the create, read, update, and delete (CRUD) methods, transaction management, data concurrency, as well as a querying mechanism to enable your business logic layer to retrieve objects for any given criteria.

The DAL should not contain business logic and should be accessed via the business logic layer through interfaces; this adheres to the separation of concerns principle and ensures that the business layer remains unaware of the underlying data access implementation strategy. This is important for both testing and ensuring your business layer is not dependent on a particular data access implementation.

DATA ACCESS STRATEGIES

The choice you make for the organization of your business layer helps shape the architecture of your data access strategy. This section examines three patterns that you can use with the business organization methods as described in Chapter 5. These patterns are Transaction Script, Active Record, and Domain Model.

The Repository Pattern

You have seen examples in previous chapters of the Repository pattern. A Repository acts like an in-memory collection, completely isolating business entities from the underlying data infrastructure, which makes it a great accompaniment for the Domain Model business pattern that utilizes plain old common lanuage runtime object (POCO) and persistence ignorant (PI) objects, as discussed in Chapter 4. When used in projects that support the domain-driven design (DDD) methodology, a Repository typically exists for each aggregate root identified within your domain model. (See Chapter 4 for more information on DDD.)

A typical interface for a Repository is shown here:

```
public interface IRepository<T>
{
    IEnumerable<T> FindAll();
    IEnumerable<T> FindAll(int index, int count);

    IEnumerable<T> FindBy(Query query);
    IEnumerable<T> FindBy(Query query, int index, int count);

    T FindBy(Guid Id);

    void Add(T entity);
    void Save(T entity);
    void Remove(T entity);
}
```

As you can see, the interface provides the standard methods for business entity persistence, but retrieval of business entities is handled slightly differently. A Query Object, which will be discussed later in the chapter, queries the Repository in a data-agnostic manner, thus decoupling the business modules from the underlying data store implementation and the data schema.

With the advent of Language Integrated Query (LINQ) and the delayed execution model, Repositories can now expose an `IQueryable FindAll` method that allows the business layer to query a Repository directly, as in the code snippet that follows:

```
public interface IRepository<T>
```

```
        {
                IQueryable<T> FindAll();

                T FindBy(Guid Id);

                void Add(T entity);
                void Save(T entity);
                void Remove(T entity);
        }
```

An `IQueryable` return type, however, is not universally viewed as such a good way to go when trying to keep persistence concerns out of your domain or business layer, because not all LINQ providers behave in the same manner or offer the same level of features.

You will see examples of the Repository pattern used throughout this chapter.

Data Access Objects Pattern

The Data Access Objects (DAO) pattern is a simple one designed to separate the elements of your DAL from the rest of the application. On the face of it, it seems similar to the Repository pattern. However, the DAO does not hide the fact that behind the interface is a data table, and typically one DAO is created for each table in the database.

The code snippet that follows shows an example of an interface for a DAO:

```
        public interface IProductDAO
        {
                Product Get(int id);

                IEnumerable<Product> FindByCategory(int id);
                IEnumerable<Product> FindByBrand(int id);
                IEnumerable<Product> FindByTopSelling(int count);

                void Add(Product product);
                void Save(Product product);
                void Remove(Product product);
        }
```

Because of their one-to-one match with data tables, DAOs are good matches for both the Active Record and Transaction Script Business patterns. In the end, the DAO and Repository patterns are very similar. The Repository pattern acts at a higher level of abstraction working with aggregations of business entities whereas the DAO objects usually have one-to-one mapping with data tables and entities.

PATTERNS IN DATA ACCESS

The remainder of this chapter focuses on the patterns found behind the interfaces or gateways in the persistence layer offered by both the Repository and DAO interfaces. The patterns cover the fundamentals of any DAL's strategy — namely, transaction management, data integrity, and data querying.

Unit of Work

The Unit of Work pattern is designed to maintain a list of business objects that have been changed by a business transaction, whether by adding, removing, or updating. The Unit of Work then coordinates the persistence of the changes and any concurrency problems flagged. The benefit of utilizing the Unit of Work in your DAL is to ensure data integrity; if an issue arises partway through persisting a series of business objects as part of a transaction, all changes should be rolled back to ensure that the data remains in a valid state.

To demonstrate the Unit of Work pattern, you will be using a simple banking domain to model the transfer of funds between two accounts. Figure 7-1 shows the interaction between the service layer and the repository layer using the Unit of Work pattern to ensure that the transfer commits as one atomic Unit of Work.

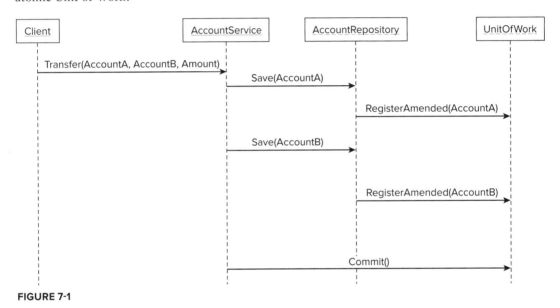

FIGURE 7-1

The Unit of Work structure in this example is based on the framework that Tim McCarthy uses in his book *.NET Domain-Driven Design with C#: Problem-Design-Solution.*

Figure 7-2 shows the classes that you will create in this exercise and exactly how they relate to each other to make unit of work pattern.

Create a new solution named `ASPPatterns.Chap7.UnitOfWork` and add the following class library projects:

➤ `ASPPatterns.Chap7.UnitOfWork.Infrastructure`

➤ `ASPPatterns.Chap7.UnitOfWork.Model`

➤ `ASPPatterns.Chap7.UnitOfWork.Repository`

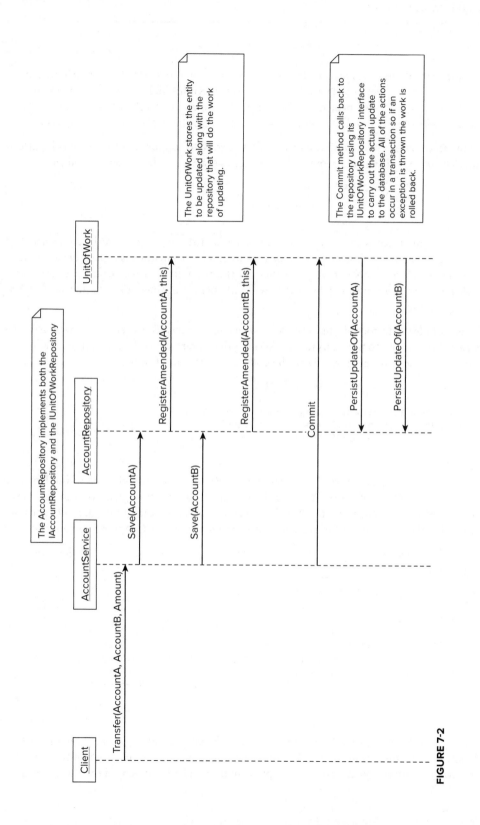

FIGURE 7-2

Right-click on the `ASPPatterns.Chap7.UnitOfWork.Model` and add a project reference to the `ASPPatterns.Chap7.UnitOfWork.Infrastructure` project. Right-click on the `ASPPatterns.Chap7.UnitOfWork.Repository` project and add a project reference to the `ASPPatterns.Chap7.UnitOfWork.Infrastructure` and the `ASPPatterns.Chap7.UnitOfWork.Model` projects.

You will start the solution by creating all the infrastructure code to support the Unit of Work pattern. Add a new interface to the infrastructure named `IAggregateRoot` with the following contract:

```
public interface IAggregateRoot
{
}
```

The `IAggregateRoot` interface is actually a pattern in itself called the marker interface pattern. The interface acts as meta data for a class and methods that interact with instances of that class test for the existence of the interface before carrying out their work. You will see this pattern used later in this chapter when you build a repository layer that will only persist business objects that implement the `IAggregateRoot` interface.

The Unit of Work implementation will use the `IAggregateRoot` interface to reference any business entity that is partaking in an atomic transaction. Add another interface to the `Infrastructure` project named `IUnitOfWorkRepository`, with the contract listing that follows:

```
public interface IUnitOfWorkRepository
{
    void PersistCreationOf(IAggregateRoot entity);
    void PersistUpdateOf(IAggregateRoot entity);
    void PersistDeletionOf(IAggregateRoot entity);
}
```

The `IUnitOfWorkRepository` is a second interface that all Repositories are required to implement if they intend to be used in a Unit of Work. You could have added this contract definition to the model Repository interface that you will add later, but the interfaces are addressing two different types of concerns. This is the definition of the Interface Segregation principle that Chapter 5 introduced.

Finally, add a third interface to the `Infrastructure` project named `IUnitOfWork`, the definition of which you can find here:

```
public interface IUnitOfWork
{
    void RegisterAmended(IAggregateRoot entity,
                    IUnitOfWorkRepository unitofWorkRepository);
    void RegisterNew(IAggregateRoot entity,
                IUnitOfWorkRepository unitofWorkRepository);
    void RegisterRemoved(IAggregateRoot entity,
                    IUnitOfWorkRepository unitofWorkRepository);
    void Commit();
}
```

The `IUnitOfWork` interface requires the `IUnitOfWorkRepository` when registering an amend/addition/deletion so that, on commitment, the Unit of Work can delegate the work of the actual persistence method to the appropriate concrete implementation. The logic behind the `IUnitOfWork` methods will become a lot clearer when you look at a default implementation of the `IUnitOfWork` interface, which is what you are going to do next.

Add a new class to the `Infrastructure` project named `UnitOfWork`, and update the newly created class with the following code:

```csharp
using System.Transactions;

namespace ASPPatterns.Chap7.UnitOfWork.Infrastructure
{
    public class UnitOfWork : IUnitOfWork
    {
        private Dictionary<IAggregateRoot, IUnitOfWorkRepository> addedEntities;
        private Dictionary<IAggregateRoot, IUnitOfWorkRepository> changedEntities;
        private Dictionary<IAggregateRoot, IUnitOfWorkRepository> deletedEntities;

        public UnitOfWork()
        {
            addedEntities =
                new Dictionary<IAggregateRoot, IUnitOfWorkRepository>();
            changedEntities =
                new Dictionary<IAggregateRoot, IUnitOfWorkRepository>();
            deletedEntities =
                new Dictionary<IAggregateRoot, IUnitOfWorkRepository>();
        }

        public void RegisterAmended(IAggregateRoot entity,
                                    IUnitOfWorkRepository unitofWorkRepository)
        {
            if (!changedEntities.ContainsKey(entity))
            {
                changedEntities.Add(entity, unitofWorkRepository);
            }
        }

        public void RegisterNew(IAggregateRoot entity,
                                IUnitOfWorkRepository unitofWorkRepository)
        {
            if (!addedEntities.ContainsKey(entity))
            {
                addedEntities.Add(entity, unitofWorkRepository);
            };
        }

        public void RegisterRemoved(IAggregateRoot entity,
                                    IUnitOfWorkRepository unitofWorkRepository)
        {
            if (!deletedEntities.ContainsKey(entity))
            {
                deletedEntities.Add(entity, unitofWorkRepository);
            }
        }

        public void Commit()
        {
```

```
using (TransactionScope scope = new TransactionScope())
{
    foreach (IAggregateRoot entity in this.addedEntities.Keys)
    {
        this.addedEntities[entity].PersistCreationOf(entity);
    }

    foreach (IAggregateRoot entity in this.changedEntities.Keys)
    {
        this.changedEntities[entity].PersistUpdateOf(entity);
    }

    foreach (IAggregateRoot entity in this.deletedEntities.Keys)
    {
        this.deletedEntities[entity].PersistDeletionOf(entity);
    }

    scope.Complete();
}
```

Code snippet UnitOfWork.cs in the project ASPPatterns.Chap7.UnitOfWork

You are required to add a reference to System.Transactions so you can use the TransactionScope class, which will ensure the persistence will commit in an atomic transaction. The UnitOfWork class uses three dictionaries to track pending changes to business entities. The first dictionary corresponds to entities to be added to the data store. The second dictionary tracks entities to be updated, and the third deals with entity removal. A matching IUnitOfWorkRepository is stored against the entity key in the dictionary and is used in the Commit method to call the Repository, which will contain the code to actually persist an entity. The Commit method loops through each dictionary and calls the appropriate IUnitOfWorkRepository method passing a reference to the entity. The work in the Commit method is wrapped in a TransactionScope using block; this ensures that no work is done until the TransactionScope Complete method is called. If an exception occurs while you are performing work within the IUnitOfWorkRepository, all work is rolled back, and the data store is left in its original state.

To demonstrate the Unit of Work pattern in action, you will build a simple bank account domain to handle transfers between two accounts. Add a new class to the Model project named Account. The Account class represents a bank account and contains a single property to hold the account balance. The code listing for this class is shown here:

```
using ASPPatterns.Chap7.UnitOfWork.Infrastructure;

namespace ASPPatterns.Chap7.UnitOfWork.Model
{
    public class Account : IAggregateRoot
    {
        public decimal balance { get; set; }
    }
}
```

To enable persistence of the `Account`, you will add a cut down version of a Repository interface containing the methods relevant to this example. Create a new interface within the `Model` project named `IAccountRepository` with the following contract:

```
public interface IAccountRepository
{
    void Save(Account account);
    void Add(Account account);
    void Remove(Account account);
}
```

There is no need to add contract definitions for `Account` retrieval, because this demonstration will not use them.

To complete the model, you will create a service class to coordinate the transferring of monies between two accounts. Add a new class named `AccountService` with the following code:

```
using ASPPatterns.Chap7.UnitOfWork.Infrastructure;

namespace ASPPatterns.Chap7.UnitOfWork.Model
{
    public class AccountService
    {
        private IAccountRepository _accountRepository;
        private IUnitOfWork _unitOfWork;

        public AccountService(IAccountRepository accountRepository,
                              IUnitOfWork unitOfWork)
        {
            _accountRepository = accountRepository;
            _unitOfWork = unitOfWork;
        }

        public void Transfer(Account from, Account to, decimal amount)
        {
            if (from.balance >= amount)
            {
                from.balance -= amount;
                to.balance += amount;

                _accountRepository.Save(from);
                _accountRepository.Save(to);
                _unitOfWork.Commit();
            }
        }
    }
}
```

The `AccountService` requires an implementation of the `IAccountRepository` and `IUnitOfWork` via its constructor. (See Chapter 5, which covers Dependency Injection.) The `Transfer` method checks that the transfer of funds can take place before adjusting the balances of each account. It then calls the account Repository to save both accounts. Finally, it calls the `Commit` method of the Unit of Work instance to ensure that the transaction is completed as an atomic Unit of Work. So how do the Repository and Unit of Work interact? Well, you'll stub out an implementation of the `Account` Repository to find out.

Add a new class named `AccountRepository` to the `Repository` project and update it with the following code listing:

```
using ASPPatterns.Chap7.UnitOfWork.Model;
using ASPPatterns.Chap7.UnitOfWork.Infrastructure;

namespace ASPPatterns.Chap7.UnitOfWork.Repository
{
    public class AccountRepository : IAccountRepository, IUnitOfWorkRepository
    {
        private IUnitOfWork _unitOfWork;

        public AccountRepository(IUnitOfWork unitOfWork)
        {
            _unitOfWork = unitOfWork;
        }

        public void Save(Account account)
        {
            _unitOfWork.RegisterAmended(account, this);
        }

        public void Add(Account account)
        {
            _unitOfWork.RegisterNew(account, this);
        }

        public void Remove(Account account)
        {
            _unitOfWork.RegisterRemoved(account, this);
        }

        public void PersistUpdateOf(IAggregateRoot entity)
        {
            // ADO.NET code to update the entity...
        }

        public void PersistCreationOf(IAggregateRoot entity)
        {
            // ADO.NET code to add the entity...
        }

        public void PersistDeletionOf(IAggregateRoot entity)
        {
            // ADO.NET code to delete the entity...
        }
    }
}
```

The `AccountRepository` implements both the `Model.IAccountRepository` and the `Infrastructre.IUnitOfWorkRepository` interfaces. The implementation of the `IAccountRepository` methods simply delegates work to the Unit of Work, passing the entity to be persisted along with a reference to the Repository, which of course implements the `IUnitOfWorkRepository`. As seen previously when the Unit of Work's `Commit` method is called, the Unit of Work refers to the Repository's implementation of the `IUnitOfWorkRepository` contract to perform the real persistence requirements.

For brevity, and to keep the example simple and easy to follow, the ADO.NET code to persist the Account entity has been omitted. Note that the Unit of Work implementation is injected into the Repository via its constructor. This allows many Repositories to share the Unit of Work, because some transactions will span more than one Repository.

Data Concurrency Control

Data Concurrency Control is the system of handling multiple modifications to business objects being persisted at the same time. When multiple users change the state of a business object and try to concurrently persist it to the database, a mechanism needs to be in place to ensure that one user's modification does not negatively affect the state of the transaction from other concurrent users.

There are two forms of concurrency control: optimistic and pessimistic. The optimistic concurrency option assumes that there are no issues with multiple users making changes simultaneously to the state of business objects, also known as *last change wins*. For some systems, this is perfectly reasonable behavior; however, when the state of your business objects needs to be consistent with the state when retrieved from the database, pessimistic concurrency is required.

Pessimistic concurrency can come in many flavors, from locking the data table when a record is retrieved to keeping a copy of the original contents of a business object and comparing that to the version in the data store before an update is made to ensure there have been no changes to a record during a transaction. In this section, you will use a version number to check whether a business entity has been amended since being retrieved from the database. Upon an update, the version number of the business entity will be compared to the version number residing in the database before committing a change. This ensures that the business entity has not been modified since being retrieved.

To demonstrate the pessimistic concurrency pattern, you will build a simple application to save details and ensure that data integrity is maintained between the retrieval and update of an entity.

Create a new solution named `ASPPatterns.Chap7.Concurrency` and add the following class library projects:

➤   `ASPPatterns.Chap7.Concurrency.Model`

➤   `ASPPatterns.Chap7.Concurrency.Repository`

Right-click on the `Repository` project and add a reference to the `Model` project. Add a new class to the `Model` project named `Person`. Update the class with the following code listing:

```
public class Person
{
    public Guid Id { get; set; }

    public string FirstName { get; set; }

    public string LastName { get; set; }

    public int Version { get; set; }
}
```

The `Version` property will be set when the `Person` entity is retrieved from the data store. If you feel uncomfortable with the `Version` property being on the `Person` entity because in the domain that you are modeling a version isn't an attribute of a `Person`, you could use an Entity Layer Supertype class as shown in the following code snippet (see also Chapter 5) or return a Proxy version of the Person entity and include the version ID within. You will examine the Proxy design pattern later in this chapter.

```
public abstract class EntityBase
{
    private int Version { get; set; }
}

public class Person : EntityBase
{
```

To complete the simple domain model, add a new interface to the Model project named IPerson Repository with the following cut-down contract definition:

```
public interface IPersonRepository
{
    void Add(Person person);
    void Save(Person person);
    Person FindBy(Guid Id);
}
```

With the Model complete, you can turn your attention to the implementation of the Person Repository. Add a new class to the Repository project named PersonRepository that implements Model.IPerson Repository. With this example, I have included the relevant ADO.NET code to show how concurrency checking with versions works:

```
using ASPPatterns.Chap7.Concurrency.Model;
using System.Data.SqlClient;

namespace ASPPatterns.Chap7.Concurrency.Repository
{
    public class PersonRepository : IPersonRepository
    {
        private string _connectionString;
        private string _findByIdSQL =
            "SELECT * FROM People WHERE PersonId = @PersonId";
        private string _insertSQL =
            "INSERT People (FirstName, LastName, PersonId, Version) VALUES " +
            "(@FirstName, @LastName, @PersonId, @Version)";
        private string _updateSQL =
            "UPDATE People SET FirstName = "
                + "@FirstName, LastName = @LastName, Version = " +
            "@Version + 1 WHERE PersonId = @PersonId AND Version = @Version;";

        public PersonRepository(string connectionString)
        {
            _connectionString = connectionString;
        }

        public void Add(Person person)
        {
            using (SqlConnection connection =
                    new SqlConnection(_connectionString))
            {
                SqlCommand command = connection.CreateCommand();
```

```csharp
            command.CommandText = _insertSQL;

            command.Parameters.Add
                  (new SqlParameter("@PersonId", person.Id));
            command.Parameters.Add
                  (new SqlParameter("@Version", person.Version));
            command.Parameters.Add
                  (new SqlParameter("@FirstName", person.FirstName));
            command.Parameters.Add
                  (new SqlParameter("@LastName", person.LastName));

            connection.Open();
            command.ExecuteNonQuery();
        }
    }

    public void Save(Person person)
    {
        int numberOfRecordsAffected = 0;

        using (SqlConnection connection =
                  new SqlConnection(_connectionString))
        {
            SqlCommand command = connection.CreateCommand();
            command.CommandText = _updateSQL;

            command.Parameters.Add
                  (new SqlParameter("@PersonId", person.Id));
            command.Parameters.Add
                  (new SqlParameter("@Version", person.Version));
            command.Parameters.Add
                  (new SqlParameter("@FirstName", person.FirstName));
            command.Parameters.Add
                  (new SqlParameter("@LastName", person.LastName));

            connection.Open();
            numberOfRecordsAffected = command.ExecuteNonQuery();
        }

        if (numberOfRecordsAffected == 0)
         throw new ApplicationException(
           @"No changes were made to Person Id (" + person.Id + "), this was "
              + "due to another process updating the data.");
        else
            person.Version++;
    }

    public Person FindBy(Guid Id)
    {
        Person person = default(Person);

        using (SqlConnection connection = new SqlConnection(_connectionString))
        {
            SqlCommand command = connection.CreateCommand();
```

```
                command.CommandText = _findByIdSQL;
                command.Parameters.Add(new SqlParameter("@PersonId", Id));
                connection.Open();

                using (SqlDataReader reader = command.ExecuteReader())
                {
                    if (reader.Read())
                    {
                        person = new Person
                        {
                            FirstName = reader["FirstName"].ToString(),
                            LastName = reader["LastName"].ToString(),
                            Id = new Guid(reader["PersonId"].ToString()),
                            Version = int.Parse(reader["Version"].ToString())
                        };
                    }
                }

            return person;
            }
        }
    }
```

Code snippet PersonRepository.cs in the project ASPPatterns.Chap7.Concurrency

The `FindBy` and `Add` methods are straightforward enough with ADO.NET code to populate a single `Person` entity from a select query and ADO.NET to insert a new `Person` entity into the database. The `Save` method contains the logic that controls data integrity of the `Person` entity. When a `Person` entity is being saved to the database, the version of the changed entity is included in the `where` clause. If the versions do not match, no update occurs, and the `ExecuteNonQuery` method returns a zero records affected count. At this point, some kind of stale entity exception could be thrown to alert the user that the `Person` entity has changed or been deleted since the original retrieval and the update has failed.

If you download the source code for this exercise, you will find accompanying unit tests that verify the behavior of the pessimistic concurrency pattern.

Lazy Loading and the Proxy Pattern

Lazy Loading is an enterprise design pattern that defers the loading of a resource until you need it. Martin Fowler defined it as "an object that doesn't contain all of the data you need but knows how to get it" in *Patterns of Enterprise Application Architecture*. If you take the canonical customer and order example, when retrieving a customer from the database, you may not want to pull back his entire order history if you need only part of it. By deferring the execution of retrieving the customer's orders, you can increase the speed at which the customer info is returned and decrease the load on the database server. If the customer `Orders` collection is required, you can pull it from the database directly from the `Orders` collection property. Shortly, you will see an example of the Lazy Loading pattern, which utilizes the Proxy pattern.

The Proxy pattern acts as a surrogate for another object, enabling the proxy to control access to it and allowing it to add extra logic related to the operation.

Intent

Because the Proxy pattern controls access to other objects' properties, it is extremely useful for scenarios that sometimes need access to expensive resources, such as these:

➤ A virtual proxy is a placeholder for resource-intensive objects. The real object or methods on that object are called only when they are needed.

➤ A remote proxy provides a local representative for an object that resides in a different address space; you saw an application of this in the previous chapter in the WCF example. In fact, a proxy is created when you add a reference to a service via Visual Studio.

UML

Figure 7-3 shows the UML representation of the Proxy pattern and all the collaborating roles.

➤ The Client depends on the abstract Customer. Both the RealCustomer and the ProxyCustomer implement the same interface, so the client is unaware of which she is using.

➤ The ProxyCustomer has a reference to the RealCustomer and controls the access to the RealCustomer properties. The ProxyCustomer can perform extra logic before calling on the RealCustomer properties.

➤ The Customer defines the interface that the Client will program against and that the RealCustomer and ProxyCustomer will implement.

➤ The RealCustomer defines the default behavior for the Customer interface.

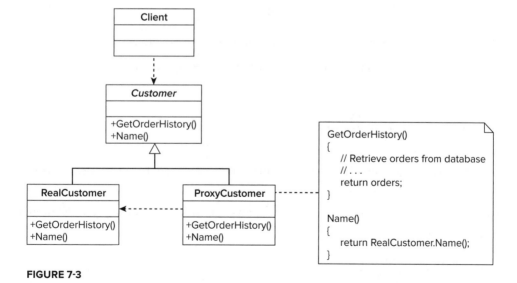

FIGURE 7-3

Code Example

For the code example, you will be working in the domain of Customers and Orders. A Customer Repository enables you to retrieve customers who have a deferred loading on their Orders collection. Figure 7-4 shows the sequence of code that you will be writing for the Lazy Loading pattern using the Proxy pattern.

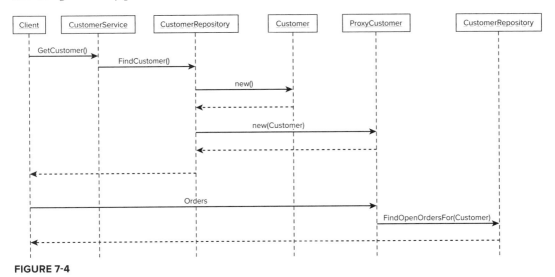

FIGURE 7-4

Create a new solution named `ASPPatterns.Chap7.ProxyPattern` and add the following class libraries:

➤   `ASPPatterns.Chap7.ProxyPattern.Model`

➤   `ASPPatterns.Chap7.ProxyPattern.Repository`

Right-click on the `Repository` project and add a reference to the `Model` project.

Add a new class to the `Model` project named `Order` with the following definition:

```
public class Order
{
    public Guid Id { get; set; }
    public DateTime OrderDate { get; set; }
}
```

The `Order` class represents a customer's order. The attributes of an `Order` have been deliberately kept to a minimum to simplify the example.

Next, add a second class to the `Model` project named `Customer` with the following code definition:

```
public class Customer
{
    public Guid Id { get; set; }
    public string Name { get; set; }
    public virtual IEnumerable<Order> Orders { get; set; }
}
```

Again, as with the `Order` class, I have included minimal properties to represent a `Customer`. To enable the retrieval of a customer, you need a Repository contract defined in the `Model` project, so add a new interface named `ICustomerRepository` with the following contract:

```
public interface ICustomerRepository
{
    Customer FindBy(Guid id);
}
```

In this example, you are only interested in retrieving a `Customer` by his `Id`. No other methods that you would normally find on a Repository interface are applicable for this demonstration of the Lazy Loading and Proxy pattern.

You will also require a Repository to retrieve all of a customer's orders, so add a second interface to the `Model` project named `IOrderRepository`:

```
public interface IOrderRepository
{
    IEnumerable<Order> FindAllBy(Guid customerId);
}
```

Again, you are only interested in the `Orders` of a specific `Customer`, so this is the only method signature that appears on the interface.

Now that you have created the model, you can turn your attention to creating the implementations of the Repositories in the `Repository` project.

Add a new class named `OrderRepository` to the `Repository` project. Have it implement the `IOrder Repository` from the `Model` project and update the class so that it matches the following listing:

```
using ASPPatterns.Chap7.ProxyPattern.Model;

namespace ASPPatterns.Chap7.ProxyPattern.Repository
{
    public class OrderRepository : IOrderRepository
    {
        public IEnumerable<Order> FindAllBy(Guid customerId)
        {
            IEnumerable<Order> customerOrders = new List<Order>();

            // Code to connect to the database and populate the collection
            // of customers' orders...

            return customerOrders;
        }
    }
}
```

Your next step is to create the `CustomerProxy` class. This class will inherit from the `Customer` class as defined in the `Model` project and act as the `Customer` unbeknownst to the client code. The code that follows shows the implementation for the `CustomerProxy` class:

```
using ASPPatterns.Chap7.ProxyPattern.Model;

namespace ASPPatterns.Chap7.ProxyPattern.Repository
```

```
    {
        public class CustomerProxy : Customer
        {
            private bool _haveLoadedOrders = false;
            private IEnumerable<Order> _orders;

            public IOrderRepository OrderRepository { get; set; }

            public bool HaveLoadedOrders()
            {
                return _haveLoadedOrders;
            }

            public override IEnumerable<Order> Orders
            {
                get
                {
                    if (!HaveLoadedOrders())
                    {
                        RetrieveOrders();
                        _haveLoadedOrders = true;
                    }

                    return _orders;
                }
                set
                {
                    base.Orders = value;
                }
            }

            private void RetrieveOrders()
            {
                _orders = OrderRepository.FindAllBy(base.Id);
            }
        }
    }
```

When calling the get method of the Orders property, a check is made on a flag that identifies whether the Orders collection has been loaded from the Repository. If the Orders collection has not been loaded, a call is made to the OrderRepository property to populate the Orders collection, the flag is updated, and the Orders are returned.

The final class to implement for this exercise is the implementation of the ICustomerRepository as defined in the Model project. Create a new class named CustomerRepository and have it implement the ICustomerRepository. The full listing for this class is as follows:

```
using ASPPatterns.Chap7.ProxyPattern.Model;

namespace ASPPatterns.Chap7.ProxyPattern.Repository
{
    public class CustomerRepository : ICustomerRepository
    {
        private IOrderRepository _orderRepository;

        public CustomerRepository(IOrderRepository orderRepository)
```

```
        {
            _orderRepository = orderRepository;
        }

        public Customer FindBy(Guid id)
        {

            Customer customer = new CustomerProxy();

            // Code to connect to the database and retrieve a customer…

            ((CustomerProxy)customer).OrderRepository = _orderRepository;

            return customer;
        }
    }
}
```

In the `FindBy` method, a `CustomerProxy` is created, and its properties are populated from the call to the database. An instance of an `OrderRepository`, injected via the `CustomerRepository` constructor, is set on the `CustomerProxy` object before being returned to the calling code.

If you download the source code for this exercise, you will find accompanying unit tests that verify the behavior of the proxy customer and the Lazy Loading of the `Orders` collection.

Identity Map

From the description from Martin Fowler's *Patterns of Enterprise Application Architecture*, an Identity Map "ensures that each object gets loaded only once by keeping every loaded object in a map" and "looks up objects using the map when referring to them." When dealing with data concurrency, it is important to have a strategy for multiple users affecting the same business entity, but it is just as important for a single user to use a consistent version of a business entity through a long-running or complex transaction. An Identity Map provides this functionality by keeping a version of all business objects used in a transaction; if the same `Employee` entity is requested twice, the same instance is returned.

Typically, an Identity Map is used per business transaction. This ensures that if an entity is retrieved twice in the same transaction, it will be unique and include any modifications that the transaction made.

To demonstrate this pattern, you will walk through a simple coding exercise that creates an Identity Map for use with the retrieval of simple `Employee` business objects from a Repository. Create a new solution named `ASPPatterns.Chap7.IdentityMap` and add the following new class library projects:

➤   `ASPPatterns.Chap7.IdentityMap.Model`

➤   `ASPPatterns.Chap7.IdentityMap.Repository`

Right-click on the `Repository` project and add a reference to the `Model` project.

Add a new class to the `Model` project named `Employee` with the following code listing:

```
        public class Employee
        {
```

```
        public Guid Id { get; set; }
        public string FirstName { get; set; }
        public string LastName { get; set; }
    }
```

The only other class in the `Model` project is a Repository with a single method definition that allows the retrieval of `Employees` by their `Id`. Create a new interface and name it `IEmployeeRepository`. Then add the `FindBy` method signature as shown here:

```
    public interface IEmployeeRepository
    {
        Employee FindBy(Guid Id);
    }
```

With the `Model` in place, you can switch your attention to the `Repository` project. Add a new class to this project named `IdentityMap`. This class will use generics to provide a type safe Identity Map implementation for supplying unique `Employee` entities during a business transaction. The code for the `IdentityMap` class is shown here:

```
    public class IdentityMap<T>
    {
        Hashtable entities = new Hashtable();

        public T GetById(Guid Id)
        {
            if (entities.ContainsKey(Id))
                return (T)entities[Id];
            else
                return default(T);
        }

        public void Store(T entity, Guid key)
        {
            if (!entities.Contains(key))
                entities.Add(key, entity);
        }
    }
```

The `IdentityMap` contains a hash table to store the business entities that are being used in a transaction and provides a simple interface to store and retrieve an entity.

You will use the `IdentityMap` within an implementation of the `IEmployeeRepository`. Add a new class to the `Repository` project named `EmployeeRepository`, and have it implement the `IEmployee Repository` interface contained within the `Model` project. The listing for this class is displayed here:

```
    using ASPPatterns.Chap7.IdentityMap.Model;

    namespace ASPPatterns.Chap7.IdentityMap.Repository
    {
        public class EmployeeRepository : IEmployeeRepository
        {
            private IdentityMap<Employee> _employeeMap;

            public EmployeeRepository)
            {
```

```
            _employeeMap = new IdentityMap<Employee>();
        }

        public Employee FindBy(Guid Id)
        {
            Employee employee = _employeeMap.GetById(Id);

            if (employee == null)
            {
                employee = DatastoreFindBy(Id);
                if (employee != null)
                    _employeeMap.Store(employee, employee.Id);
            }

            return employee;
        }

        private Employee DatastoreFindBy(Guid Id)
        {
            Employee employee = default(Employee);

            // Code to hydrate employee from datastore...

            return employee;
        }
    }
}
```

When the `FindBy` method is called, the Employee `Repository` first checks the `IdentityMap` to determine if the `Employee` entity has been retrieved before. If it has, it is returned to the caller. If not, the data store is queried for the `Employee` instance using its identity and then is added to the `IdentityMap` ready to be retrieved if the same `Employee` entity is needed from the `Employee` `Repository` again.

As with all the code examples in this book, if you download the source code for this exercise, you will find accompanying unit tests that verify the behavior of the Identity Map pattern.

The next pattern you will look at deals with querying the data access layer.

Query Object Pattern

You saw at the beginning of this chapter that the interface for a Repository defined a method that took a Query Object. The Query Object represented a query written in the language of the domain and was an implementation of the Query Object pattern. The Query Object pattern as described by Fowler is "an object that represents a database query." Without some mechanism of querying, the Repository would be awash with myriad retrieval methods such as can be seen in this code snippet:

```
public interface ICustomerRepository
{
    IEnumerable<Customer> FindAll();
    IEnumerable<Customer> FindAllVIPCustomers();
    IEnumerable<Customer> FindByOrder(Guid ID);
    IEnumerable<Customer> FindAllCustomersThatHaveOutstandingOrders();
    …
}
```

Instead, the Query Object enables any query to be constructed and then sent to the Repository to be satisfied. The major benefit of the Query Object pattern is that it completely abstracts away the underlying database querying language and thus keeps the infrastructure concerns of data persistence and retrieval out of the business layer. At some point, however, the raw querying language of the database needs to be created; this is achieved using a database-specific `QueryTranslator` that takes the Query Objects and converts them into the language of the database.

You will now create an implementation of the Query Object pattern. Create a solution named `ASPPatterns.Chap7.QueryObject` and add the following class libraries to the solution:

➤ `ASPPatterns.Chap7.QueryObject.Infrastructure`

➤ `ASPPatterns.Chap7.QueryObject.Model`

➤ `ASPPatterns.Chap7.QueryObject.Repository`

Right-click on the `Model` project and add a reference to the `Infrastructure` project. Right-click also on the `Repository` project and add a reference to the `Model` and `Infrastructure` project.

You will start with defining the model for the Query Object pattern. Figure 7-5 shows the class diagram.

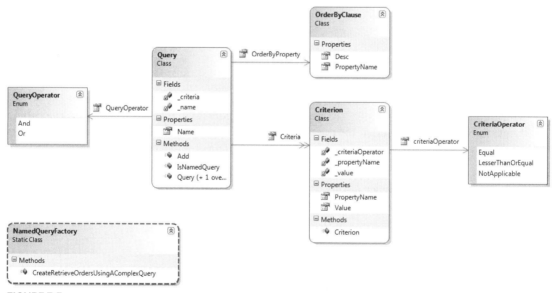

FIGURE 7-5

Add a new folder to the `Infrastructure` project named `Query` and add a new enumeration named `CriteriaOperator`. The enumeration class is shown here:

```
public enum CriteriaOperator
{
    Equal,
    LessThanOrEqual,
    NotApplicable
}
```

In this example, you will require only the three criteria operations shown in the preceding listing. For a full implementation, you would add the remaining operations.

Next, add a class to represent the criterion named `Criterion`. The `Criterion` represents part of the filter that forms the query, specifying an entity property, a value to compare it to, and the way it should be compared. The code for the `Criterion` class is displayed here:

```
public class Criterion
{
    private string _propertyName;
    private object _value;
    private CriteriaOperator _criteriaOperator;

    public Criterion(string propertyName, object value,
                     CriteriaOperator criteriaOperator)
    {
        _propertyName = propertyName;
        _value = value;
        _criteriaOperator = criteriaOperator;
    }

    public string PropertyName
    {
        get { return _propertyName; }
    }

    public object Value
    {
        get { return _value; }
    }

    public CriteriaOperator criteriaOperator
    {
        get { return _criteriaOperator; }
    }
}
```

The next class to create will represent the ordering property to be used on the query. Create a new class named `OrderByClause` with the following code listing:

```
public class OrderByClause
{
    public string PropertyName { get; set; }
    public bool Desc { get; set; }
}
```

You use a second enumeration to determine how the `Criterion` objects will be evaluated together. Add a new enumeration named `QueryOperator` with the following syntax:

```
public enum QueryOperator
{
    And,
    Or
}
```

Sometimes complex queries are difficult to create. In these cases, you can use a named query that points to a view or stored procedure in the database. These named queries are added as an enumeration. Add a new class named `QueryName` to store this list of queries with the following code listing:

```
public enum QueryName
{
    Dynamic = 0,
    RetrieveOrdersUsingAComplexQuery = 1
}
```

Included in the list is the `Dynamic` value. This value will be used if the query is not named and is instead created by the business layer.

The class that brings the Query Object pattern together is the `Query` class. Add a new class to the project named `Query`, and update it with the following code definition:

```
public class Query
{
    private QueryName _name;
    private IList<Criterion> _criteria;

    public Query()
        : this(QueryName.Dynamic, new List<Criterion>())
    { }

    public Query(QueryName name, IList<Criterion> criteria)
    {
        _name = name;
        _criteria = criteria;
    }

    public QueryName Name
    {
        get { return _name; }
    }

    public bool IsNamedQuery()
    {
        return Name != QueryName.Dynamic;
    }

    public IEnumerable<Criterion> Criteria
    {
        get {return _criteria ;}
    }

    public void Add(Criterion criterion)
    {
        if (!IsNamedQuery())
            _criteria.Add(criterion);
        else
            throw new ApplicationException(
                "You cannot add additional criteria to named queries");
```

```
        }

        public QueryOperator QueryOperator { get; set; }

        public OrderByClause OrderByProperty { get; set; }
    }
```

The class contains a collection of `Criterion` objects, an `OrderByClause`, and an `Operator` value. The `Query` class also contains an `IsNamedQuery` method that flags if the query has been dynamically generated or relates to a precreated query in the Repository.

The last class you need to create is the `NamedQueryFactory` class. Add this to the project and update as follows:

```
    public static class NamedQueryFactory
    {
        public static Query CreateRetrieveOrdersUsingAComplexQuery(Guid CustomerId)
        {
            IList<Criterion> criteria = new List<Criterion>();
            Query query =
                new Query(QueryName.RetrieveOrdersUsingAComplexQuery, criteria);

            criteria.Add(new Criterion ("CustomerId", CustomerId,
                                            CriteriaOperator.NotApplicable));

            return query;
        }
    }
```

This class simply creates a Query Object for a named query. The `QueryTranslator` can inspect the Query Object to determine if it's a named query and use the `Criterions` as values for a stored database query. This completes the Query Object pattern implementation. Please note that there is no notion of a subquery in the Query Object pattern that you have created. To provide subqueries, you simply need to add a collection of Query Objects to the Query Object. However, if you need to use subqueries or anything other than simple querying, it is often better to use a stored query in the Repository or database.

 You will build upon the Query Object framework you have built here to include subqueries in the case study part at the end of this book.

You will now create a simple domain model to demonstrate using the Query Object implementation that you have created. Add a new class to the `Model` project named `Order`:

```
    public class Order
    {
        public Guid Id { get; set; }
        public bool HasShipped { get; set; }
        public DateTime OrderDate { get; set; }
        public Guid CustomerId { get; set; }
    }
```

You also need to create an interface for an order Repository within the Model project. Because you are only interested in the functions of the Query Object pattern, you only need to include the single method relating to obtaining Order entities from the Repository using a Query Object. With this in mind, add a new interface to the Model project named IOrderRepository with the contract shown in the code listing that follows:

```
using ASPPatterns.Chap7.QueryObject.Infrastructure.Query;

namespace ASPPatterns.Chap7.QueryObject.Model
{
    public interface IOrderRepository
    {
        IEnumerable<Order> FindBy(Query query);
    }
}
```

The final class to add to the Model project is the domain service class, which will use the Query Object implementation to query the Repository.

Add a new class named OrderService, and update it with the code that follows:

```
using ASPPatterns.Chap7.QueryObject.Infrastructure.Query;

namespace ASPPatterns.Chap7.QueryObject.Model
{
    public class OrderService
    {
        private IOrderRepository _orderRepository;

        public OrderService(IOrderRepository orderRepository)
        {
            _orderRepository = orderRepository;
        }

        public IEnumerable<Order> FindAllCustomersOrdersBy(Guid customerId)
        {
            IEnumerable<Order> customerOrders = new List<Order>();

            Query query = new Query();
            query.Add
              (new Criterion("CustomerId", customerId, CriteriaOperator.Equal));
            query.OrderByProperty = new OrderByClause
                                    { PropertyName = "CustomerId", Desc = true };

            customerOrders = _orderRepository.FindBy(query);

            return customerOrders;
        }

        public IEnumerable<Order> FindAllCustomersOrdersWithInOrderDateBy(
                                    Guid customerId, DateTime orderDate)
        {
            IEnumerable<Order> customerOrders = new List<Order>();

            Query query = new Query();
```

```
        query.Add
          (new Criterion("CustomerId", customerId, CriteriaOperator.Equal));
        query.QueryOperator = QueryOperator.And;
        query.Add(new Criterion
                ("OrderDate", orderDate, CriteriaOperator.LessThanOrEqual));
        query.OrderByProperty = new OrderByClause
                                  { PropertyName = "OrderDate", Desc = true };

        customerOrders = _orderRepository.FindBy(query);

        return customerOrders;
    }

    public IEnumerable<Order> FindAllCustomersOrdersUsingAComplexQueryWith(
                                                    Guid customerId)
    {
        IEnumerable<Order> customerOrders = new List<Order>();

        Query query =
         NamedQueryFactory.CreateRetrieveOrdersUsingAComplexQuery(customerId);

        customerOrders = _orderRepository.FindBy(query);

        return customerOrders;
    }
  }
}
```

Code snippet OrderService.cs in the project ASPPatterns.Chap7.QueryObject

The `OrderService` class contains three methods that create queries that are then passed to the
Repository. The `FindAllCustomersOrdersBy` and `FindAllCustomersOrdersWithInOrderDateBy`
methods create a dynamic query by adding `Criterions` and an `OrderByClause`. The last method,
`FindAllCustomersOrdersUsingAComplexQueryWith`, is a named query that uses the `NameQuery`
`Factory` to create the Query Object to be passed to the Repository.

With the domain model and service layer complete, you can now implement the `IOrderRepository`
and create a `QueryTranslator` to convert the Query Object into a language that your database can
understand.

Add a new class to the Repository project named `OrderQueryTranslator`. This class will contain
an extension method that gives the Query Object the ability to convert itself into an SQL command
ready to be run against the database.

```
using ASPPatterns.Chap7.QueryObject.Infrastructure.Query;
using System.Data.SqlClient;
using System.Data;

namespace ASPPatterns.Chap7.QueryObject.Repository
{
    public static class OrderQueryTranslator
    {
        private static string baseSelectQuery = "SELECT * FROM Orders ";

        public static void TranslateInto(this Query query, SqlCommand command)
```

```
    {
        if (query.IsNamedQuery())
        {
            command.CommandType = CommandType.StoredProcedure;
            command.CommandText = query.Name.ToString();

            foreach (Criterion criterion in query.Criteria)
            {
                command.Parameters.Add(
                    new SqlParameter("@" + criterion.PropertyName,
                                                criterion.Value));
            }
        }
        else
        {
            StringBuilder sqlQuery = new StringBuilder();
            sqlQuery.Append(baseSelectQuery);

            bool _isNotfirstFilterClause = false;

            if (query.Criteria.Count() > 0)
                sqlQuery.Append("WHERE ");

            foreach (Criterion criterion in query.Criteria)
            {
                if (_isNotfirstFilterClause)
                    sqlQuery.Append(GetQueryOperator(query));

                sqlQuery.Append(AddFilterClauseFrom(criterion));

                command.Parameters.Add(
                    new SqlParameter("@" + criterion.PropertyName,
                                                criterion.Value));

                _isNotfirstFilterClause = true;
            }

            sqlQuery.Append(GenerateOrderByClauseFrom(query.OrderByProperty));

            command.CommandType = CommandType.Text;
            command.CommandText = sqlQuery.ToString();
        }
    }

    private static string GenerateOrderByClauseFrom
                                        (OrderByClause orderByClause)
    {

        return String.Format("ORDER BY {0} {1}",
            FindTableColumnFor(orderByClause.PropertyName),
            orderByClause.Desc ? "DESC" : "ASC");
    }

    private static string GetQueryOperator(Query query)
    {
```

```
        if (query.QueryOperator == QueryOperator.And)
            return "AND ";
        else
            return "OR ";
    }

    private static string AddFilterClauseFrom(Criterion criterion)
    {
        return string.Format("{0} {1} @{2} ",
                             FindTableColumnFor(criterion.PropertyName),
                             FindSQLOperatorFor(criterion.criteriaOperator),
                             criterion.PropertyName);
    }

    private static string FindSQLOperatorFor(CriteriaOperator criteriaOperator)
    {
        switch (criteriaOperator)
        {
            case CriteriaOperator.Equal:
                return "=";
            case CriteriaOperator.LessThanOrEqual:
                return "<=";
            default:
                throw new ApplicationException("No operator defined.");
        }
    }

    private static string FindTableColumnFor(string propertyName)
    {
        switch (propertyName)
        {
            case "CustomerId":
                return "CustomerId";
            case "OrderDate":
                return "OrderDate";
            default:
                throw new ApplicationException(
                        "No column defined for this property.");
        }
    }
  }
}
```

Code snippet OrderQueryTranslator.cs in the project ASPPatterns.Chap7.QueryObject

The `TranslateInto` method takes an ADO.NET command and populates it with a database query. The first thing that the `TranslateInto` method does is identify whether the Query Object is a named query. If it is, the command is set to expect a stored procedure, the name of which is the query enumeration name. The stored procedure exists in the database within the unit tests project that can be found in the code download that accompanies this book. The `Criterions` of the `Query` then provide any parameters that the stored procedure expects.

If the `Query` has been dynamically created, the translator loops through each of the `Criterions` and builds up a SQL statement, using methods to convert the property name of the `Order` entity into the column name of the `Order` table. You may be wondering why the `FindTableColumnFor` method exists. At the moment there is a one-to-one mapping between the data table column and entity property but this may not always be the case — especially as the domain model evolves over time. The second and final class that you need in the `Repository` project is the implementation of the `IOrderRepository` as defined in the `Model` project. Add a new class to the `Repository` project named `OrderRepository` and update the class with this code:

```
using ASPPatterns.Chap7.QueryObject.Infrastructure.Query;
using ASPPatterns.Chap7.QueryObject.Model;
using System.Data.SqlClient;

namespace ASPPatterns.Chap7.QueryObject.Repository
{
    public class OrderRepository : IOrderRepository
    {
        private string _connectionString;

        public OrderRepository(string connectionString)
        {
            _connectionString = connectionString;
        }

        public IEnumerable<Order> FindBy(Query query)
        {
            IList<Order> orders = new List<Order>();

            using (SqlConnection connection =
                    new SqlConnection(_connectionString))
            {
                SqlCommand command = connection.CreateCommand();
                query.TranslateInto(command);
                connection.Open();

                using (SqlDataReader reader = command.ExecuteReader())
                {
                    while (reader.Read())
                    {
                        orders.Add(new Order
                        {
                            CustomerId = new Guid(reader["CustomerId"].ToString()),
                            OrderDate = DateTime.Parse(
                                        reader["OrderDate"].ToString()),
                            Id = new Guid(reader["Id"].ToString())
                        });

                    }
                }
            }

            return orders;
        }

    }
}
```

Code snippet OrderRepository.cs in the project ASPPatterns.Chap7.QueryObject

The `OrderRepository` calls the `TranslateInto` extension method on the Query Object to populate an ADO.NET command object. When the command object is populated with the SQL statement, the command is executed and a collection of orders is generated and returned to the caller.

Those of you with a keen eye have probably noticed the similarity between the Query Object pattern and LINQ. The `System.Linq.Expressions` namespace is an implementation of a Query Object pattern, and under the covers LINQ to SQL works in a very similar manner to the framework you have created.

To see the code working, you need to download the source code that accompanies this book. It contains a host of unit tests that verify the behavior of the Query Object implementation.

USING AN OBJECT RELATIONAL MAPPER

Traditional Microsoft developers have built their own DAL by hand to map the business objects to their corresponding database tables. There's nothing inherently bad about this; it's just that it can be a little, dare I say, boring? Not only that, but hand-rolling your own DAL can be error prone, because ADO.NET is not type safe, and it can be difficult to maintain when changes are needed in the schema of the application as similar code is duplicated. With large projects, the amount of plumbing code needed can quickly engulf the project, and developers can lose sight of the end goal — that is, getting the business processes and logic right — because of hours spent writing stored procedures and low-level ADO.NET objects.

The role of an object relational mapper (ORM) is to bridge the gap between the relational model (the database) and the object-oriented model. This problem is often referred to as the *impedance mismatch*. Using mapping files or attributes on a business object, you can use an ORM framework to persist business objects to the database and retrieve them simply via the ORM framework's API with no or little SQL needed.

You will now look at two of the popular ORMs for the .NET framework.

NHibernate

NHibernate is a port of the popular open source Hibernate framework for Java. Hibernate has been around for years, and it's a proven and robust piece of software. ORM has had a slow take-up in the .NET world, but with the release of LINQ to SQL and the beta of the Entity Framework, many developers are starting to see the benefit of automating their DAL. One of the best features of NHibernate is the support for persistence ignorance; this means that your business objects don't have to inherit from base classes or implement framework interfaces. NHibernate uses an instance of an ISession as its DataContext; it is similar to the DataContexts of LINQ to SQL and the Entity Framework in that it acts as your persistence manager and gateway into the database, allowing you to query against it, as well as saving, deleting, and adding entities. There are a number of ways to map business objects to database tables in NHibernate. One of the most popular is via an XML configuration file (shown in Figure 7-6), but attributes and a fluent code mapping option are also available.

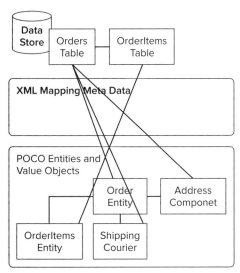

FIGURE 7-6

For a more in-depth introduction to NHibernate, read the book titled *NHibernate in Action* by Pierre Kuate et al., or my Wrox Blox, "NHibernate with ASP.NET Problem Design Solution."

MS Entity Framework

The Entity Framework is Microsoft's enterprise-level ORM. It differs from NHibernate in that it maps business entities to far more complex or unusual relational data models. This is because of the three layers of mapping, which you will learn about as you step through a simple exercise in a moment. The Entity Framework's strength lies in the mapping of relational data models that don't have a one-to-one mapping to the business model, as shown in Figure 7-7.

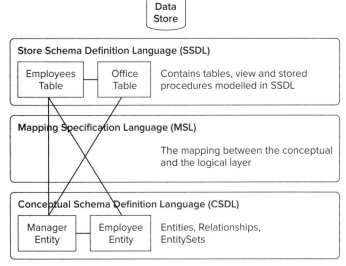

FIGURE 7-7

For a more in-depth look at the MS Entity Framework, read *Programming Entity Framework* by Julia Lerman.

ORM Code Example

To demonstrate the amount of work an ORM can save you, you will build a simple application that utilizes both NHibernate and Entity Framework as part of a Repository layer. The business code will be able to use either Repository without needing to alter any code. Furthermore, a pure ADO. NET version of the Repository supporting all the patterns you have looked at will be included in the code download that accompanies this book so that you can evaluate the amount of work required to build your own ORM rather than use an existing framework.

The application you will be building is based on the domain of a library. Figure 7-8 shows the actors and the use cases that the system will satisfy.

Within the system, members can be added, books can be added, and members can loan and return books. The only business rule is that a book cannot be loaned out to more than one member at any one time. This domain model and the related business rules have been kept simple so that you can focus on how to use NHibernate and Entity Framework as a Repository within your enterprise ASP.NET application.

Library Domain Model

For this coding exercise, you need to use Visual Studio 2010 because it supports Entity Framework 4, which at the time of writing was in its beta state.

Create a new solution named `ASPPatterns.Chap7 .Library` and add the following C# class libraries:

➤ `ASPPatterns.Chap7.Library .Infrastructure`

➤ `ASPPatterns.Chap7.Library.Model`

➤ `ASPPatterns.Chap7.Library .Repository.EF`

➤ `ASPPatterns.Chap7.Library .Repository.NHibernate`

➤ `ASPPatterns.Chap7.Library.Services`

Add a new web application project to the solution named `ASPPatterns.Chap7.Library.UI.Web`.

You need to add the following references to each of the projects:

➤ Right-click on the `ASPPatterns.Chap7 .Library.Model` project and add a reference to the `Infrastructure` project.

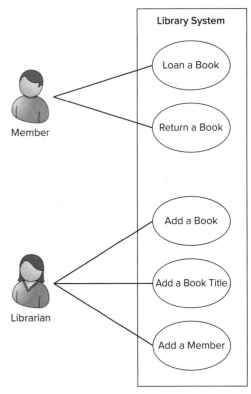

FIGURE 7-8

➤ Right-click on the `ASPPatterns.Chap7.Library.Repository.EF` project and add a reference to the `Infrastructure` project and the `Model` project.

➤ Right-click on the `ASPPatterns.Chap7.Library.Repository.NHibernate` project and add a reference to the `Infrastructure` project and the `Model` project.

➤ Right-click on the `ASPPatterns.Chap7.Library.Services` project and add a reference to the `Infrastructure` project and the `Model` project.

➤ Right-click on the `ASPPatterns.Chap7.Library.UI.Web` project and add a reference to all the class library projects in the solution.

Before you begin to design the domain model that will represent the library domain, you need to set up the infrastructure concerns. Luckily, you can reuse the set of classes you created for the Query Object pattern and the Unit of Work pattern exercises earlier in the chapter. Copy the `Query` folder from within the `ASPPatterns.Chap7.QueryObject` `.Infrastructure` project and add it to the `ASPPatterns` `.Chap7.Library.Infrastructure` projects. Next, create a `UnitOfWork` folder within the `ASPPatterns.Chap7` `.Library.Infrastructure` project and copy all the files from `ASPPatterns.Chap7.UnitOfWork.Infrastructure`. You need to update the namespaces so they start with `ASPPatterns.Chap7.Library` instead of `ASPPatterns` `.Chap7.QueryObject/UnitOfWork`. Your solution should now resemble Figure 7-9.

I have moved the `IAggregateRoot` interface into the root of the `Infrastructure` project because it's not intrinsically tied with the Unit of Work operations.

FIGURE 7-9

With the infrastructure concerns taken care of, you can work on the domain model for the library system. Figure 7-10 shows the class diagram for the library domain model.

There will be a matching Repository for each of the aggregate roots (the classes that implement the `IAggregateRoot` interface.

The first class you need to create is `BookTitle`. Add this class to the `Model` project with the code listing that follows:

```
using ASPPatterns.Chap7.Library.Infrastructure;

namespace ASPPatterns.Chap7.Library.Model
{
    public class BookTitle : IAggregateRoot
    {
        public string ISBN { get; set; }

        public string Title { get; set; }
    }
}
```

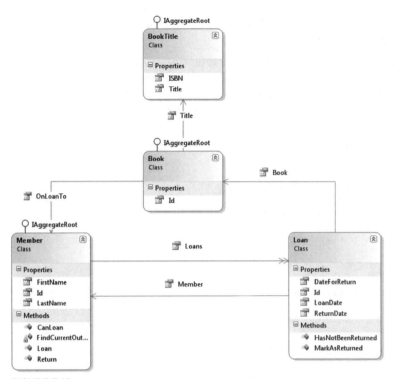

FIGURE 7-10

The `BookTitle` represents the title information for a book, such as the `ISBN` and `Title`. If you wanted to expand on this model, you could add an `Author` attribute to the `BookTitle`.

The entity that will represent the book that a member can loan out is the `Book` class. Add this to the `Model` project with the code as displayed here:

```
using ASPPatterns.Chap7.Library.Infrastructure;

namespace ASPPatterns.Chap7.Library.Model
{
    public class Book : IAggregateRoot
    {
        public Guid Id { get; set; }

        public virtual BookTitle Title { get; set; }

        public virtual Member OnLoanTo { get; set; }

    }
}
```

The `OnLoanTo` property is `null` if it is not currently on loan; otherwise, it contains the `Member` that the book is on loan to at the current time. Notice that the `BookTitle` and `Member` properties of the `Book` class have been marked as virtual to allow Entity Framework and NHibernate to create proxies for these properties to support Lazy Loading. The Lazy Loading and Proxy patterns were discussed earlier in this chapter.

The next class to create is the `Member` class. This class represents the `Member` entity and contains some logic to enable the loaning and returning of books. It is a valid argument to state that a member doesn't loan a book herself and that a librarian would perform a loan transaction; however, to keep the sample simple, leave this functionality associated with a member.

```
using System;
using System.Collections.Generic;
using System.Linq;
using System.Text;
using ASPPatterns.Chap7.Library.Infrastructure;

namespace ASPPatterns.Chap7.Library.Model
{
    public class Member : IAggregateRoot
    {
        public Guid Id { get; set; }

        public string LastName { get; set; }

        public string FirstName { get; set; }

        public virtual IList<Loan> Loans { get; set; }

        public void Return(Book book)
        {
            Loan loan = FindCurrentOutstandingLoanFor(book);

            if (loan != null)
            {
                loan.MarkAsReturned();
                book.OnLoanTo = null;
            }
            else
                throw new ApplicationException(String.Format(
                "Cannot return book '{0}'. Member '{1}'"
                        + " does not have this book on loan.",
                book.Id.ToString(), this.Id.ToString()));
        }

        private Loan FindCurrentOutstandingLoanFor(Book book)
        {
            return Loans.FirstOrDefault
                    (l => (l.Book.Id == book.Id && l.HasNotBeenReturned()));
        }

        public bool CanLoan(Book book)
        {
            return book.OnLoanTo == null;
        }

        public Loan Loan(Book book)
        {
```

```
                Loan loan = default(Loan);
                if (CanLoan(book))
                {
                    loan = LoanFactory.CreateLoanFrom(book, this);
                    Loans.Add(loan);
                }
                else
                    throw new ApplicationException(String.Format(
                        "Cannot loan book '{0}'. Book is on loan to member '{1}'",
                        book.Id.ToString(), book.OnLoanTo.Id.ToString()));

                return loan;
            }
        }
    }
```

Here's a rundown of each of the methods of the `Member` class that contains business logic:

➤   `CanLoan`: This is a simple method that establishes whether the `Book` attempting to be loaned is in fact on loan to a `Member` already.

➤   `Loan`: This method first establishes that a `Book` can be loaned. If all is well, a `Loan` is created using the `LoanFactory`. You will create both the `Loan` and the `LoanFactory` shortly. If the `Loan` is already out with another member, an exception is thrown.

➤   `FindCurrentOutstandingLoanFor`: This method returns the outstanding `Loan` for a given `Book`.

➤   `Return`: This method first obtains the `Loan` that relates to the `Book` trying to be returned. If a `Loan` exists, it is marked as returned, and the `OnLoanTo` property of the `Book` is set to `null`. If the `Book` cannot be returned, an exception is thrown because this is an exceptional event.

The next class to create is the `Loan` class, which the `Member` class referenced already. Create the `Loan` class and update it with the following code listing:

```
using ASPPatterns.Chap7.Library.Infrastructure;

namespace ASPPatterns.Chap7.Library.Model
{
    public class Loan
    {
        public Guid Id { get; set; }

        public DateTime LoanDate { get; set; }

        public DateTime DateForReturn { get; set; }

        public DateTime? ReturnDate { get; set; }

        public virtual Book Book { get; set; }

        public Member Member { get; set; }

        public bool HasNotBeenReturned()
```

```
        {
            return ReturnDate == null;
        }

        public void MarkAsReturned()
        {
            ReturnDate = DateTime.Now;
        }
    }
}
```

The `Loan` class is simple. Again, the `Book` property has the virtual attribute defined to enable Lazy Loading:

```
public static class LoanFactory
    {
        public static Loan CreateLoanFrom(Book book, Member member)
        {
            Loan loan = new Loan();
            loan.Book = book;
            loan.Member = member;
            loan.LoanDate = DateTime.Now;
            loan.DateForReturn = DateTime.Now.AddDays(7);
            return loan;
        }
    }
```

In this implementation of the library domain model, there are no business rules or validation checking on the domain entities. This functionality has been left out to keep the sample as simple as possible. For information on how to add validation to your domain entities, please check the case study which starts on Chapter 10.

The next three classes define the Repository interfaces for each of the aggregate roots. Add three interfaces to the `Model` project named `IBookRepository`, `IBookTitleRepository`, and `IMemberRepository`. The code for these Repositories matches the contract defined for a Repository that the beginning of this chapter introduced:

```
using ASPPatterns.Chap7.Library.Infrastructure;
using ASPPatterns.Chap7.Library.Infrastructure.Query;

namespace ASPPatterns.Chap7.Library.Model
{
    public interface IBookRepository
    {
        void Add(Book book);
        void Remove(Book book);
        void Save(Book book);

        Book FindBy(Guid Id);

        IEnumerable<Book> FindAll();
        IEnumerable<Book> FindAll(int index, int count);

        IEnumerable<Book> FindBy(Query query);
```

```csharp
        IEnumerable<Book> FindBy(Query query, int index, int count);
    }
}

using ASPPatterns.Chap7.Library.Infrastructure;
using ASPPatterns.Chap7.Library.Infrastructure.Query;

namespace ASPPatterns.Chap7.Library.Model
{
    public interface IBookTitleRepository
    {
        void Add(BookTitle book);
        void Remove(BookTitle book);
        void Save(BookTitle book);

        BookTitle FindBy(string ISBN);

        IEnumerable<BookTitle> FindAll();
        IEnumerable<BookTitle> FindAll(int index, int count);

        IEnumerable<BookTitle> FindBy(Query query);
        IEnumerable<BookTitle> FindBy(Query query, int index, int count);
    }
}

using ASPPatterns.Chap7.Library.Infrastructure;
using ASPPatterns.Chap7.Library.Infrastructure.Query;

namespace ASPPatterns.Chap7.Library.Model
{
    public interface IMemberRepository
    {
        void Add(Member member);
        void Remove(Member member);
        void Save(Member member);

        Member FindBy(Guid Id);

        IEnumerable<Member> FindAll();
        IEnumerable<Member> FindAll(int index, int count);

        IEnumerable<Member> FindBy(Query query);
        IEnumerable<Member> FindBy(Query query, int index, int count);
    }
}
```

With the model and Repository interfaces in place, you can now turn your attention to the domain services. The only service that is required is a LoanService. Add the LoanService class to the Model project and update it with the following code listing:

```csharp
using System;
using System.Collections.Generic;
using System.Linq;
using System.Text;
```

```
using ASPPatterns.Chap7.Library.Infrastructure;
using ASPPatterns.Chap7.Library.Infrastructure.UnitOfWork;

namespace ASPPatterns.Chap7.Library.Model
{
    public class LoanService
    {
        private IMemberRepository _memberRepository;
        private IBookRepository _bookRepository;
        private IUnitOfWork _unitOfWork;

        public LoanService(IBookRepository bookRepository,
                           IMemberRepository memberRepository,
                           IUnitOfWork unitOfWork)
        {
            _bookRepository = bookRepository;
            _memberRepository = memberRepository;
            _unitOfWork = unitOfWork;
        }

        public Loan Loan(Guid memberId, Guid bookId)
        {
            Loan loan = default(Loan);
            Book book = _bookRepository.FindBy(bookId);
            Member member = _memberRepository.FindBy(memberId);

            if (member.CanLoan(book))
            {
                member.Loan(book);
                book.OnLoanTo = member;
                _memberRepository.Save(member);
                _bookRepository.Save(book);
                _unitOfWork.Commit();
            }

            return loan;
        }

        public void Return(Guid bookId)
        {
            Book book = _bookRepository.FindBy(bookId);
            Member member = book.OnLoanTo;

            member.Return(book);

            _memberRepository.Save(member);
            _bookRepository.Save(book);
            _unitOfWork.Commit();
        }
    }
}
```

The `LoanService` has two methods:

➤ `Loan`: Coordinates the loaning of a `Book`

➤ `Return`: Coordinates the returning of a `Book`

The `LoanService` is injected with an instance of an `IBookRepository`, an `IMemberRepository`, and an `IUnitOfWork` via its constructor.

The `Model` project now resembles Figure 7-11.

This completes all the code for the business logic relating to the domain of a lending library. In the next section, you will add a service layer that will expose an interface that will act as an entry point into the system.

The Service Layer

The service layer as discussed in the previous chapter acts as a facade or entry point into the system. The service layer you will build in this section will use some of messaging patterns discussed in Chapter 6, so refer to that chapter as you progress through this section.

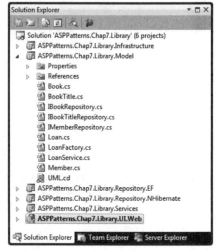

FIGURE 7-11

Create a new folder within the `Services` project named `Views`, and add a new class named `BookTitleView`. This class, like all views in this section, is a data transfer object that will act as a specific view of the domain. The `BookTitle` is a simple view; you can find the code for it in the following code listing:

```
public class BookTitleView
{
    public string ISBN { get; set; }
    public string Title { get; set; }
}
```

Add another three classes to the `Views` folder: `BookView`, `LoanView`, and `MemberView`. These are views of the domain model that are required for this application. The code for the three classes is shown here:

```
public class BookView
{
    public string Id { get; set; }
    public string ISBN { get; set; }
    public string Title { get; set; }
    public string OnLoanTo { get; set; }
}

public class LoanView
{
    public string BookTitle { get; set; }
    public string CopyId { get; set; }
    public string LoanId { get; set; }
```

```
            public string LoanDate { get; set; }
            public string ReturnDate { get; set; }
            public string DateForReturn { get; set; }
            public string MemberName { get; set; }
            public string MemberId { get; set; }
            public bool StillOutOnLoan { get; set; }
        }

        public class MemberView
        {
            public string MemberId { get; set; }
            public string FullName { get; set; }
            public IList<LoanView> Loans { get; set; }
        }
```

Add another new folder to the root of the `Services` project named `Mappers`. The `Mappers` folder contains all the extension methods to convert domain entities into view data transfer objects.

Four classes provide extension methods to each of the domain entities and enable them to be converted to their corresponding views. Add four new classes to the `Mappers` folder named `LoanExtension Methods`, `MemberExtensionMethods`, `BookTitleExtensionMethods`, and `BookExtensionMethods`.

```
    using ASPPatterns.Chap7.Library.Services.Views;
    using ASPPatterns.Chap7.Library.Model;

    namespace ASPPatterns.Chap7.Library.Services.Mappers
    {
        public static class LoanExtensionMethods
        {
            public static LoanView ConvertToLoanView(this Loan loan)
            {
                return new LoanView
                {
                    BookTitle = loan.Book.Title.Title,
                    CopyId = loan.Book.Id.ToString(),
                    LoanId = loan.Id.ToString(),
                    MemberId = loan.Member.Id.ToString(),
                    MemberName = loan.Member.FirstName + ' ' + loan.Member.LastName,
                    LoanDate = loan.LoanDate.ToString(),
                    ReturnDate = loan.ReturnDate.ToString(),
                    DateForReturn  = loan.DateForReturn.ToString(),
                    StillOutOnLoan = loan.HasNotBeenReturned()
                };
            }

            public static IList<LoanView> ConvertToLoanViews
                                    (this IEnumerable<Loan> loans)
            {
                IList<LoanView> loanViews = new List<LoanView>();
                foreach (Loan loan in loans)
                {
                    loanViews.Add(loan.ConvertToLoanView());
                }

                return loanViews;
```

```csharp
            }
        }
}



using ASPPatterns.Chap7.Library.Services.Views;
using ASPPatterns.Chap7.Library.Model;

namespace ASPPatterns.Chap7.Library.Services.Mappers
{
    public static class MemberExtensionMethods
    {
        public static MemberView ConvertToMemberView(this Member member)
        {
            return new MemberView
            {
                FullName = member.FirstName + ' ' + member.LastName,
                MemberId = member.Id.ToString(),
                Loans = GenerateLoanViewsFrom(member.Loans)
            };
        }

        private static IList<LoanView> GenerateLoanViewsFrom
                                        (IEnumerable<Loan> loans)
        {
            if (loans == null)
                return new List<LoanView>();
            else
                return loans.ConvertToLoanViews();
        }

        public static IList<MemberView> ConvertToMemberViews(
                                        this IEnumerable<Member> members)
        {
            IList<MemberView> memberViews = new List<MemberView>();
            foreach (Member member in members)
            {
                memberViews.Add(member.ConvertToMemberView());
            }

            return memberViews;
        }
    }
}



using ASPPatterns.Chap7.Library.Services.Views;
using ASPPatterns.Chap7.Library.Model;

namespace ASPPatterns.Chap7.Library.Services.Mappers
{
    public static class BookTitleExtensionMethods
```

```
        {
            public static BookTitleView ConvertToBookTitleView
                                        (this BookTitle bookTitle)
            {
                return new BookTitleView
                {
                    ISBN = bookTitle.ISBN,
                    Title = bookTitle.Title
                };
            }

            public static IList<BookTitleView> ConvertToBookTitleViews
                                (this IEnumerable<BookTitle> bookTitles)
            {
                IList<BookTitleView> bookViews = new List<BookTitleView>();
                foreach (BookTitle bookTitle in bookTitles)
                {
                    bookViews.Add(bookTitle.ConvertToBookTitleView());
                }

                return bookViews;
            }
        }
    }
}


using ASPPatterns.Chap7.Library.Services.Views;
using ASPPatterns.Chap7.Library.Model;

namespace ASPPatterns.Chap7.Library.Services.Mappers
{
    public static class BookExtensionMethods
    {
        public static BookView ConvertToBookView(this Book book)
        {
            return new BookView
            {
                Id = book.Id.ToString(),
                ISBN = book.Title.ISBN,
                Title = book.Title.Title ,
                OnLoanTo = FormatMemberNameFrom(book.OnLoanTo)
            };
        }

        private static string FormatMemberNameFrom(Member member)
        {
            if (member != null)
                return String.Format("{0} {1}", member.FirstName, member.LastName);
            else
                return "";
        }

        public static IList<BookView> ConvertToBookViews
                                    (this IEnumerable<Book> books)
        {
```

```
                IList<BookView> bookViews = new List<BookView>();
                foreach (Book book in books)
                {
                    bookViews.Add(book.ConvertToBookView());
                }

                return bookViews;
            }
        }
    }
```

Add a third folder to the root of the `Services` project named `Messages`. This folder will contain the message objects that are exchanged between the client and the service layer. The message and request-response pattern are covered in Chapter 6.

All response messages inherit from a common base class named `ResponseBase` that provides common behavior. This behavior is in the form of a Boolean flag property named `Success` that lets clients know if their request was handled without error. The `Message` property contains information on the state of the response. If there was an error while processing a request, the `Message` would contain details on the error (not the exception details). If the request was successfully processed, the `Message` could be empty or contain some kind of confirmation message.

```
namespace ASPPatterns.Chap7.Library.Services.Messages
{
    public abstract class ResponseBase
    {
        public bool Success { get; set; }
        public string Message { get; set; }
    }
}
```

Each business use case is exposed as a method on the service class, and each business use case has a corresponding request and reply object. These objects are simple data transfer objects that make interacting with the service layer from the client simple and consistent. All data required for a business use case is contained within the request object via properties. The response objects inherit from the `ResponseBase` and contain extra properties if the client expects a return value.

For the business case of adding a book, create a pair of request-response classes within the `Messages` folder named `AddBookRequest` and `AddBookResponse`, as seen here:

```
namespace ASPPatterns.Chap7.Library.Services.Messages
{
    public class AddBookRequest
    {
        public string ISBN { get; set; }
    }
}

namespace ASPPatterns.Chap7.Library.Services.Messages
{
public class AddBookResponse : ResponseBase
    {
    }
}
```

For the business case of adding a book title, create a pair of request-response classes within the Messages folder named AddBookTitleRequest and AddBookTitleResponse, like this:

```
namespace ASPPatterns.Chap7.Library.Services.Messages
{
    public class AddBookTitleRequest
    {
        public string ISBN { get; set; }
        public string Title { get; set; }
    }
}

namespace ASPPatterns.Chap7.Library.Services.Messages
{
    public class AddBookTitleResponse : ResponseBase
    {
    }
}
```

For the business case of adding a member, create a pair of request-response classes within the Messages folder named AddMemberRequest and AddMemberResponse, as shown here:

```
namespace ASPPatterns.Chap7.Library.Services.Messages
{
    public class AddMemberRequest
    {
        public string FirstName { get; set; }
        public string LastName { get; set; }
    }
}

namespace ASPPatterns.Chap7.Library.Services.Messages
{
    public class AddMemberResponse : ResponseBase
    {
    }
}
```

For the business case of finding a book or books, create a pair of request-response classes within the Messages folder named FindBooksRequest and FindBooksResponse, like so:

```
namespace ASPPatterns.Chap7.Library.Services.Messages
{
    public class FindBooksRequest
    {
        public string Id { get; set; }
        public string ISBN { get; set; }
        public bool All { get; set; }
    }
}

using ASPPatterns.Chap7.Library.Services.Views;

namespace ASPPatterns.Chap7.Library.Services.Messages
{
    public class FindBooksResponse : ResponseBase
```

```
    {
        public IEnumerable<BookView> Books { get; set; }
    }
}
```

For the business case of finding a book title or titles, create a pair of request-response classes within the Messages folder named FindBookTitlesRequest and FindBookTitlesResponse:

```
namespace ASPPatterns.Chap7.Library.Services.Messages
{
    public class FindBookTitlesRequest
    {
        public string ISBN { get; set; }
        public bool All { get; set; }
    }
}

using ASPPatterns.Chap7.Library.Services.Views;

namespace ASPPatterns.Chap7.Library.Services.Messages
{
    public class FindBookTitlesResponse : ResponseBase
    {
        public IEnumerable<BookTitleView> BookTitles { get; set; }
    }
}
```

For the business case of finding a member, create a pair of request-response classes within the Messages folder named FindMemberRequest and FindMemberResponse:

```
namespace ASPPatterns.Chap7.Library.Services.Messages
{
    public class FindMemberRequest
    {
        public string MemberId { get; set; }
        public bool All { get; set; }
    }
}

using ASPPatterns.Chap7.Library.Services.Views;

namespace ASPPatterns.Chap7.Library.Services.Messages
{
    public class FindMembersResponse : ResponseBase
    {
        public IEnumerable<MemberView> MembersFound { get; set; }
    }
}
```

For the business case of loaning a book, create a pair of request-response classes within the Messages folder named LoanBookRequest and LoanBookResponse:

```
namespace ASPPatterns.Chap7.Library.Services.Messages
{
    public class LoanBookRequest
    {
```

```
            public string MemberId { get; set; }
            public string CopyId { get; set; }
        }
    }

    using ASPPatterns.Chap7.Library.Services.Views;

    namespace ASPPatterns.Chap7.Library.Services.Messages
    {
        public class LoanBookResponse : ResponseBase
        {
            public LoanView loan { get; set; }
        }
    }
```

For the business case of returning a book, create a pair of request-response classes within the
`Messages` folder named `ReturnBookRequest` and `ReturnBookResponse`:

```
    namespace ASPPatterns.Chap7.Library.Services.Messages
    {
        public class ReturnBookRequest
        {
            public string CopyId { get; set; }
        }
    }

    namespace ASPPatterns.Chap7.Library.Services.Messages
    {
        public class ReturnBookResponse : ResponseBase
        {
        }
    }
```

The final class to create within the `Services` project is the `LibraryService` class. Because you can
perform only a handful of operations at this library, it makes sense to group them into one library
service class. Add a new class to the root of the `Services` project named `LibraryService`, and
update it with the code listing shown here:

```
    using ASPPatterns.Chap7.Library.Services.Messages;
    using ASPPatterns.Chap7.Library.Services.Mappers;
    using ASPPatterns.Chap7.Library.Services.Views;
    using ASPPatterns.Chap7.Library.Model;
    using ASPPatterns.Chap7.Library.Infrastructure.UnitOfWork;

    namespace ASPPatterns.Chap7.Library.Services
    {
        public class LibraryService
        {
            private IUnitOfWork _uow;
            private IBookRepository _bookRepository;
            private IBookTitleRepository _bookTitleRepository;
            private IMemberRepository _memberRepository;
            private LoanService _loanService;

            public LibraryService(IBookTitleRepository bookTitleRepository,
```

```csharp
                        IBookRepository bookRepository,
                        IMemberRepository memberRepository,
                        IUnitOfWork unitOfWork)
{
    _uow = unitOfWork;
    _memberRepository = memberRepository;
    _bookTitleRepository = bookTitleRepository;
    _bookRepository = bookRepository;
    _loanService =
            new LoanService(_bookRepository, _memberRepository, _uow);
}

public AddBookResponse AddBook(AddBookRequest request)
{
    AddBookResponse response = new AddBookResponse();

    BookTitle bookTitle = _bookTitleRepository.FindBy( request.ISBN);
    Book book = new Book();
    book.Title = bookTitle;
    book.Id = Guid.NewGuid();
    _bookRepository.Add(book);
    _uow.Commit();

    response.Success = true;

    return response;
}

public AddBookTitleResponse AddBookTitle(AddBookTitleRequest request)
{
    AddBookTitleResponse response = new AddBookTitleResponse();

    BookTitle bookTitle = new BookTitle();
    bookTitle.ISBN = request.ISBN;
    bookTitle.Title = request.Title;

    _bookTitleRepository.Add(bookTitle);
    _uow.Commit();

    response.Success = true;

    return response;
}


public FindBooksResponse FindBooks(FindBooksRequest request)
{
    FindBooksResponse response = new FindBooksResponse();

    IEnumerable<Book> books = _bookRepository.FindAll();
    IEnumerable<BookView> bookViews = books.ConvertToBookViews();

    response.Books = bookViews;

    return response;
```

```
    }

    public FindBookTitlesResponse FindBookTitles(FindBookTitlesRequest request)
    {
        FindBookTitlesResponse response = new FindBookTitlesResponse();

        IList<BookTitleView> bookTitles = new List<BookTitleView>();

        if (request.All)
        {
            bookTitles =
                _bookTitleRepository.FindAll().ConvertToBookTitleViews();
        }
        else
        {
            BookTitle bookTitle = _bookTitleRepository.FindBy(request.ISBN);
            bookTitles.Add(bookTitle.ConvertToBookTitleView());
        }

        response.BookTitles = bookTitles;
        response.Success = true;

        return response;
    }

    public LoanBookResponse LoanBook(LoanBookRequest request)
    {
        LoanBookResponse response = new LoanBookResponse();

        Loan loan = _loanService.Loan(
                new Guid(request.MemberId), new Guid(request.CopyId));

        if (loan != null)
        {
            response.loan = loan.ConvertToLoanView();
            response.Success = true;
        }
        else
        {
            response.Success = false;
        }

        return response;
    }

    public ReturnBookResponse ReturnBook(ReturnBookRequest request)
    {
        ReturnBookResponse response = new ReturnBookResponse();

        _loanService.Return(new Guid(request.CopyId));

        return response;
```

```
        }

        public AddMemberResponse AddMember(AddMemberRequest request)
        {
            AddMemberResponse response = new AddMemberResponse();

            Member member = new Member();
            member.FirstName = request.FirstName;
            member.LastName = request.LastName;
            member.Id = Guid.NewGuid();

            _memberRepository.Add(member);
            _uow.Commit();

            return response;
        }

        public FindMembersResponse FindMembers(FindMemberRequest request)
        {
            FindMembersResponse response = new FindMembersResponse();
            IList<MemberView> members = new List<MemberView>();

            if (request.All)
            {
                members = _memberRepository.FindAll().ConvertToMemberViews();
            }
            else
            {
                Member member =
                    _memberRepository.FindBy(new Guid(request.MemberId));
                members.Add(member.ConvertToMemberView());
            }

            response.MembersFound = members;
            response.Success = true;

            return response;
        }
    }
}
```

Code snippet LibraryService.cs in the project ASPPatterns.Chap7.Library.Services

The LibraryService class contains eight methods that map to the eight business cases related to the Library domain. All eight methods are straightforward and coordinate the retrieval or persistence of an entity to the corresponding Repository. The LoanBook and ReturnBook methods are slightly different in that they use a LoanService, which is a domain service to coordinate the returning or loaning of a book. The coordination of this activity is a domain concern.

All dependencies in the form of Repositories and the Unit of Work implementation are injected into the service class via its constructor. This is a form of Dependency Injection, which Chapter 5 covered.

Again, there is no validation of the request messages; this has been omitted to keep the sample concise. In a real-world application, you should validate all requests.

The `Services` project now resembles Figure 7-12.

FIGURE 7-12

With the Domain Model, supporting infrastructure code (Unit of Work pattern and Query Object pattern), and service layer in place, you can work on the persistence concerns, starting with the database and continuing with the NHibernate and Entity Framework Repository implementations.

Database

From within the `UI.Web` web application project, right-click and select Add ➪ New Item from the pop-up menu. Then select the Data tab and choose SQL Server Database. Name the database `Library.mdf`.

Construct the library database schema as shown in Figure 7-13.

FIGURE 7-13

NHibernate Repository

To work with NHibernate, you need the framework. Navigate to www.nhibernate.org and click on the latest release; at the time of writing, this is version 2.0.1.GA. You are redirected to SourceForge. Once there, click Download to display all the downloads for this release. Select the project named, at the time of this writing, NHibernate-2.1.0.Beta2-bin.zip. When this download has completed, extract all the containing folders and files into a new folder named lib that you should create within the root of the solution folder. When all files have been extracted, switch back to Visual Studio, and from the NHibernateRepository project, add a reference to the following files from the lib folder:

➤ Iesi.Collections

➤ LinFu.DynamicProxy

➤ log4net

➤ NHibernate

➤ NHibernate.ByteCode.LinFu

The first task is to create files that map the database tables and columns to your domain entities and properties, as defined in the Model project.

Add a new folder named MappingFiles, and add to it a new XML file named BookTitle.hbm.xml. The XML file is meta data whose purpose is to inform the NHibernate framework how your domain model and the data model relate to each other. There are two other ways to add meta data: one is via a fluent interface in code, and the other is via attributes in the entity class. For this example, you will be using an XML mapping file.

The listing that follows shows the meta data for the BookTitle.hbm.xml file:

```xml
<?xml version="1.0" encoding="utf-8" ?>
<hibernate-mapping xmlns="urn:nhibernate-mapping-2.2"
    namespace="ASPPatterns.Chap7.Library.Model"
```

```
            assembly="ASPPatterns.Chap7.Library.Model">

  <class name="ASPPatterns.Chap7.Library.Model.BookTitle"
                              table="t_Books" lazy="false" >

    <id  name="ISBN" column="ISBN" type="String">
      <generator class="assigned" />
    </id>

    <property name="Title">
      <column name="Title" sql-type="nvarchar(50)" not-null="true" />
    </property>

  </class>

</hibernate-mapping>
```

After you have updated the BookTitle.hbm.xml file to match the preceding listing, you need to change the build action for the file. Right-click on the class to bring up its properties from the context-sensitive menu. Once the Properties dialog is displayed, change the build action to Embedded Resource. This ensures that the XML data is embedded when the assembly is built. All the mapping files need to have their build actions changed to Embedded Resource.

The next mapping file is for the Book entity. Add a new XML file to the MappingFiles folder named Book.hbm.xml, and update it with the following markup:

```
<?xml version="1.0" encoding="utf-8" ?>
<hibernate-mapping xmlns="urn:nhibernate-mapping-2.2"
    namespace="ASPPatterns.Chap7.Library.Model"
        assembly="ASPPatterns.Chap7.Library.Model">

  <class name="ASPPatterns.Chap7.Library.Model.Book" table="t_Copies" lazy="false">

    <id name="Id" column="Id" type="guid">
      <generator class="guid" />
    </id>

    <many-to-one name="Title"
                 class="BookTitle"
                 column="BookISBN"
                 not-null="true"/>

    <many-to-one name="OnLoanTo"
                 class="Member"
                 column="MemberId"/>

  </class>

</hibernate-mapping>
```

Add a third XML file for the Loan entity named Loan.hbm.xml with the markup displayed here:

```
<?xml version="1.0" encoding="utf-8" ?>
<hibernate-mapping xmlns="urn:nhibernate-mapping-2.2"
    namespace="ASPPatterns.Chap7.Library.Model"
```

```xml
            assembly="ASPPatterns.Chap7.Library.Model">

  <class name="ASPPatterns.Chap7.Library.Model.Loan"
                                table="t_Loans" lazy="false" >

    <id name="Id" column="Id" type="guid">
      <generator class="guid" />
    </id>

    <many-to-one name="Book"
                 class="Book"
                 column="CopyId" />

    <property name="LoanDate">
      <column name="LoanDate" sql-type="datetime" not-null="true" />
    </property>

    <property name="DateForReturn">
      <column name="DateForReturn" sql-type="datetime" not-null="true" />
    </property>

    <property name="ReturnDate">
      <column name="ReturnDate" sql-type="datetime" not-null="false" />
    </property>

    <many-to-one name="Member"
                 class="Member"
                 column="MemberId" not-null="false" />
  </class>
</hibernate-mapping>
```

Finally, add an XML file for the Member entity with the name Member.hbm.xml and the following markup:

```xml
<?xml version="1.0" encoding="utf-8" ?>
<hibernate-mapping xmlns="urn:nhibernate-mapping-2.2"
    namespace="ASPPatterns.Chap7.Library.Model"
        assembly="ASPPatterns.Chap7.Library.Model">

  <class name="ASPPatterns.Chap7.Library.Model.Member"
         table="t_Members" lazy="false">

  <id name="Id" column="Id" type="guid">
    <generator class="guid" />
  </id>

  <property name="FirstName">
    <column name="FirstName" sql-type="nvarchar(50)" not-null="true" />
  </property>

  <property name="LastName">
    <column name="LastName" sql-type="nvarchar(50)" not-null="true" />
  </property>

  <bag name="Loans" inverse="true" cascade="all" lazy="true" >
    <key column="MemberId"/>
```

```
    <one-to-many class="Loan"></one-to-many>
  </bag>

  </class>

</hibernate-mapping>
```

Again, ensure you have changed each of the file's build action to Embedded Resource so that the NHibernate framework can find the mapping meta data.

I won't go into detail about the syntax of these files because this is not a book on using NHibernate, but it should be easy to work out how NHibernate maps columns and tables to business entities and properties. For a deeper insight into the world of NHibernate, check out the many online resources or the book *NHibernate in Action*.

Now that you have configured how your business entities map to your data tables, you can begin programming the NHibernate Repository. Create a folder within the root of the NHibernateRepository project named SessionStorage; this contains all the code necessary to store a Unit of Work, also known as a *session* in NHibernate. You will store instances of a session differently depending on whether you are working within a web application or a Windows smart client; for this reason, you will create an interface to communication with a session container. Create a new interface named ISessionStorageContainer with the following contract:

```
using NHibernate;

namespace ASPPatterns.Chap7.Library.Repository.NHibernate.SessionStorage
{
    public interface ISessionStorageContainer
    {
        ISession GetCurrentSession();
        void Store(ISession session);
    }
}
```

Because you will be working within a web environment that has an HTTP context, you require a session container that utilizes the HTTP item's collection to store NHibernate sessions. Add a new class that implements the ISessionStorageContainer interface named HttpSessionContainer with the following code listing:

```
using global::NHibernate;
using System.Web;

namespace ASPPatterns.Chap7.Library.Repository.NHibernate.SessionStorage
{
    public class HttpSessionContainer : ISessionStorageContainer
    {
        private string _sessionKey = "NHSession";

        public ISession GetCurrentSession()
        {
            ISession nhSession = null;

            if (HttpContext.Current.Items.Contains(_sessionKey))
```

```
                nhSession = (ISession)HttpContext.Current.Items[_sessionKey];

            return nhSession;
        }

        public void Store(ISession session)
        {
            if (HttpContext.Current.Items.Contains(_sessionKey))
                HttpContext.Current.Items[_sessionKey] = session;
            else
                HttpContext.Current.Items.Add(_sessionKey, session);
        }
    }
}
```

This class stores and retrieves NHibernate sessions from the HTTP items collection. For completeness, you can create a smart client version for use in non-web scenarios. Add a new class to the Session Storage folder named ThreadSessionStorageContainer that also implements the ISessionStorage Container. The code for this class is shown here:

```
using global::NHibernate;
using System.Collections;
using System.Threading;

namespace ASPPatterns.Chap7.Library.Repository.NHibernate.SessionStorage
{
    public class ThreadSessionStorageContainer : ISessionStorageContainer
    {
        private static readonly Hashtable _nhSessions = new Hashtable();

        public ISession GetCurrentSession()
        {
            ISession nhSession = null;

            if (_nhSessions.Contains(GetThreadName()))
                nhSession = (ISession)_nhSessions[GetThreadName()];

            return nhSession;
        }

        public void Store(ISession session)
        {
            if (_nhSessions.Contains(GetThreadName()))
                _nhSessions[GetThreadName()] = session;
            else
                _nhSessions.Add(GetThreadName(), session);
        }

        private static string GetThreadName()
        {
            return Thread.CurrentThread.Name;
        }
    }
}
```

This class retains sessions within a hash table using the current thread name as a key.

To obtain the best session container for your application, you will add a factory class that will be responsible for creating and supplying a valid session container. Add a new class to the `SessionStorage` folder named `SessionStorageFactory` with the following listing:

```
using System.Web;

namespace ASPPatterns.Chap7.Library.Repository.NHibernate.SessionStorage
{
    public static class SessionStorageFactory
    {
        public static ISessionStorageContainer _nhSessionStorageContainer;

        public static ISessionStorageContainer GetStorageContainer()
        {
            if (_nhSessionStorageContainer == null)
            {
                if (HttpContext.Current == null)
                    _nhSessionStorageContainer =
                                new ThreadSessionStorageContainer();
                else
                    _nhSessionStorageContainer = new HttpSessionContainer();
            }

            return _nhSessionStorageContainer;
        }
    }
}
```

This `SessionStorageFactory` determines if an HTTP context exists. If so, an `HttpSessionContainer` is created; otherwise, a `ThreadSessionStorageContainer` is used. Once the concrete implementation of the `ISessionStorageContainer` interface is created, it is stored in a static variable named `_nhSessionStorageContainer`.

With the ability to store sessions taken care of, you now need a way to create them so that you can use NHibernate to persist and retrieve your business entities. Add a new class to the root of the `NHibernate` project and name it `SessionFactory`. The code for this class follows:

```
using NHibernate;
using NHibernate.Cfg;
using System.Web;
using ASPPatterns.Chap7.Library.Repository.NHibernate.SessionStorage;

namespace ASPPatterns.Chap7.Library.Repository.NHibernate
{
    public class SessionFactory
    {
        private static ISessionFactory _SessionFactory;

        private static void Init()
        {
```

```
            Configuration config = new Configuration();
            config.AddAssembly("ASPPatterns.Chap7.Library.Repository.NHibernate");

            log4net.Config.XmlConfigurator.Configure();

            config.Configure();

            _SessionFactory = config.BuildSessionFactory();
        }

        private static ISessionFactory GetSessionFactory()
        {
            if (_SessionFactory == null)
                Init();

            return _SessionFactory;
        }

        private static ISession GetNewSession()
        {
            return GetSessionFactory().OpenSession();
        }

        public static ISession GetCurrentSession()
        {
            ISessionStorageContainer _sessionStorageContainer =
                                SessionStorageFactory.GetStorageContainer();

            ISession currentSession = _sessionStorageContainer.GetCurrentSession();

            if (currentSession == null)
            {
                currentSession = GetNewSession();
                _sessionStorageContainer.Store(currentSession);
            }

            return currentSession;
        }
    }
}
```

Here's a look at each method of this class.

➤ Init: This method is called from the GetSessionFactory method only once. Within the Init, you create an instance of NHibernate's configuration class, called the configure method. It configures NHibernate based on the application configuration file that you will define later in the web.config file. You then add the assembly that contains the embedded mapping meta data. Finally, you ask the configuration to build an instance of the ISessionFactory.

➤ ISessionFactory: An ISessionFactory is typically created as a singleton object because of the relatively expensive operation of creating it. One of the jobs of the SessionFactory is to provide ISession instances. As mentioned before, the ISession is the main interface that persists and retrieves business entities. Think of the `ISession` as your gateway to the database. The NHibernate site defines it as the "persistence manager."

➤ `GetSessionFactory`: The `GetSessionFactory` method is called and invokes the `Init` method if it has not already done so.

➤ `GetNewSession`: The `GetNewSession` private method uses the `GetSessionFactory` to create a new session to work with.

➤ `GetCurrentSession`: The `GetCurrentSession` method, which you will be using with the implementations of the Repositories, creates a new session and stores it in the appropriate session container, obtained from the `SessionStorageFactory`.

Now that you have configured NHibernate, you can start to use it. Add a new class to the root of the `NHibernate` project named `NHUnitOfWork`. This is NHibernate's implementation of the Unit of Work pattern that you defined in the `Infrastructure` project. The code for this class can be seen here:

```
using ASPPatterns.Chap7.Library.Infrastructure;
using NHibernate;
using ASPPatterns.Chap7.Library.Infrastructure.UnitOfWork;

namespace ASPPatterns.Chap7.Library.Repository.NHibernate
{
    public class NHUnitOfWork : IUnitOfWork
    {
        public void RegisterAmended(IAggregateRoot entity,
                                IUnitOfWorkRepository unitofWorkRepository)
        {
            SessionProvider.GetCurrentSession().SaveOrUpdate(entity);
        }

        public void RegisterNew(IAggregateRoot entity,
                                IUnitOfWorkRepository unitofWorkRepository)
        {
            SessionProvider.GetCurrentSession().Save(entity);
        }

        public void RegisterRemoved(IAggregateRoot entity,
                                IUnitOfWorkRepository unitofWorkRepository)
        {
            SessionProvider.GetCurrentSession().Delete(entity);
        }

        public void Commit()
        {
            using (ITransaction transaction =
                        SessionProvider.GetCurrentSession().BeginTransaction())
            {
                try
                { transaction.Commit(); }
                catch (Exception ex)
                {
                    transaction.Rollback();
```

```
                    throw;
                }
            }
        }
    }
}
```

As the `ISession` interface implements the Unit of Work pattern discussed earlier in this chapter, no changes will occur until a transaction is committed. Another pattern built into NHibernate is Identity Map, which maintains a single instance of a business entity in the `ISession` no matter how many times you retrieve it.

The Repository implementations are easy to create thanks to generics. You can create a base `Repository` class using generics to provide all the functionality for all the Repositories. Create a new folder named `Repositories` and add a new class to it named `Repository`, with the code listing shown here:

```
using NHibernate;
using ASPPatterns.Chap7.Library.Infrastructure.UnitOfWork;
using ASPPatterns.Chap7.Library.Infrastructure;
using ASPPatterns.Chap7.Library.Infrastructure.Query;

namespace ASPPatterns.Chap7.Library.Repository.NHibernate.Repositories
{
    public abstract class Repository<T, EntityKey> where T : IAggregateRoot
    {
        private IUnitOfWork _uow;

        public Repository(IUnitOfWork uow)
        {
            _uow = uow;
        }

        public void Add(T entity)
        {
            _uow.RegisterNew(entity, null);
        }

        public void Remove(T entity)
        {
            _uow.RegisterRemoved(entity, null);
        }

        public void Save(T entity)
        {
            _uow.RegisterAmended(entity, null);
        }

        public T FindBy(EntityKey Id)
        {
            return SessionProvider.GetCurrentSession().Get<T>(Id);
        }

        public IEnumerable<T> FindAll()
```

```
        {
            ICriteria CriteriaQuery =
                    SessionProvider.GetCurrentSession().CreateCriteria(typeof(T));

            return (List<T>)CriteriaQuery.List<T>();
        }

        public IEnumerable<T> FindAll(int index, int count)
        {
            ICriteria CriteriaQuery =
                    SessionProvider.GetCurrentSession().CreateCriteria(typeof(T));

            return (List<T>)CriteriaQuery.SetFetchSize(count)
                                            .SetFirstResult(index).List<T>();
        }

        public IEnumerable<T> FindBy(Query query)
        {
            ICriteria nhQuery = query.TranslateIntoNHQuery<T>();

            return nhQuery.List<T>();
        }

        public IEnumerable<T> FindBy(Query query, int index, int count)
        {
            ICriteria nhQuery = query.TranslateIntoNHQuery<T>();

            return nhQuery.SetFetchSize(count).SetFirstResult(index).List<T>();
        }
    }
}
```

You will build the `QueryTranslator` classes a little later, so don't worry that your class can't compile at this stage. With the generic `Repository` base class in place, you can add the implementations.

Create three new classes within the `Repositories` folder named `BookRepository`, `BookTitle Repository`, and `MemberRepository`: one for each of the interfaces defined in the `Models` project. The code listing for these classes is shown here:

```
using ASPPatterns.Chap7.Library.Model;
using ASPPatterns.Chap7.Library.Infrastructure;
using ASPPatterns.Chap7.Library.Infrastructure.UnitOfWork;

namespace ASPPatterns.Chap7.Library.Repository.NHibernate.Repositories
{
    public class BookRepository : Repository<Book, Guid>, IBookRepository
    {
        public BookRepository(IUnitOfWork unitOfWork) : base(unitOfWork)
        { }
    }
}

using ASPPatterns.Chap7.Library.Model;
using ASPPatterns.Chap7.Library.Infrastructure;
```

```
using ASPPatterns.Chap7.Library.Infrastructure.UnitOfWork;

namespace ASPPatterns.Chap7.Library.Repository.NHibernate.Repositories
{
    public class BookTitleRepository : Repository<BookTitle, string>,
                                                        IBookTitleRepository
    {
        public BookTitleRepository(IUnitOfWork unitOfWork) : base(unitOfWork)
        { }
    }
}

using ASPPatterns.Chap7.Library.Model;
using ASPPatterns.Chap7.Library.Infrastructure;
using ASPPatterns.Chap7.Library.Infrastructure.UnitOfWork;

namespace ASPPatterns.Chap7.Library.Repository.NHibernate.Repositories
{
    public class MemberRepository : Repository<Member, Guid>, IMemberRepository
    {
        public MemberRepository(IUnitOfWork unitOfWork) : base(unitOfWork)
        { }
    }
}
```

The final class to create to complete the NHibernate Repository is the `QueryTranslator`. This class provides an extension method for the Query Object as defined in the `Infrastructure` project. Add a new class for the `QueryTranslator`, and update it with the code listing that follows:

```
using ASPPatterns.Chap7.Library.Infrastructure.Query;
using ASPPatterns.Chap7.Library.Model;
using NHibernate;
using NHibernate.Criterion;

namespace ASPPatterns.Chap7.Library.Repository.NHibernate.Repositories
{
    public static class QueryTranslator
    {
        public static ICriteria TranslateIntoNHQuery<T>(this Query query)
        {
            ICriteria criteria;

            if (query.IsNamedQuery())
            {
                criteria = FindNHQueryFor(query);
            }
            else
            {
                criteria =
                    SessionProvider.GetCurrentSession().CreateCriteria(typeof(T));

                foreach (Criterion c in query.Criteria)
                {
```

```
            global::NHibernate.Criterion.ICriterion criterion;

            switch (c.criteriaOperator)
            {
                case CriteriaOperator.Equal:
                    criterion = Expression.Eq(c.PropertyName, c.Value);
                    break;
                case CriteriaOperator.LesserThanOrEqual:
                    criterion = Expression.Le(c.PropertyName, c.Value);
                    break;
                default:
                    throw new ApplicationException("No operator defined");
            }

            if (query.QueryOperator == QueryOperator.And)
                criteria.Add(Expression.Conjunction().Add(criterion));
            else
                criteria.Add(Expression.Disjunction().Add(criterion));
        }

        criteria.AddOrder(new Order(
                query.OrderByProperty.PropertyName,
                        !query.OrderByProperty.Desc));
    }
    return criteria;
}

private static ICriteria FindNHQueryFor(Query query)
{
    // No complex queries have been defined in this sample.
    throw new NotImplementedException();
}
    }
}
```

NHibernate has two interfaces for querying: `IQuery` and `ICriteria`. The `IQuery` interface supports NHibernate's own brand of SQL — HQL that queries using object syntax (that is, classes and properties instead of SQL syntax tables and columns). The `ICriteria` interface enables the querying of entities in an object-oriented manner as well as querying by example. The `QueryTranslator` class simply converts your query into an `ICriteria` instance ready for use with NHibernate. NHibernate also supports native SQL for retrieving entities, so if you have a particularly complex query, you can create a stored procedure or run the raw SQL from within NHibernate. These queries would then be defined as Named Queries in the Query Object pattern so that the `Query Translator` could use the `FindNHQueryFor` method to obtain an `ICriteria` instance.

To finish the NHibernate Repository, you need to update the `Web.config` file from within the `UI.Web` web application project to include NHibernate configuration meta data. You can see this in the code snippet that follows:

```
<configuration>
 <configSections>
 <! -- NHibernate Section -- >
 <section name="hibernate-configuration"
 type="NHibernate.Cfg.ConfigurationSectionHandler, NHibernate"/>
```

```
<! -- NHibernate Section End -- >
</configSections >

....

<hibernate-configuration xmlns="urn:nhibernate-configuration-2.2">
<session-factory name="NHibernate.Test">
<property name="connection.driver_class">
NHibernate.Driver.SqlClientDriver</property>
<property name="connection.connection_string">
Data Source=.\SQLEXPRESS;
AttachDbFilename=|DataDirectory|Library.mdf;
Integrated Security=True;User Instance=True
</property>
<property name="adonet.batch_size">10</property>
<property name="show_sql">true</property>
<property name="dialect">
 NHibernate.Dialect.MsSql2005Dialect</property>
<property name="use_outer_join">true</property>
<property name="command_timeout">60</property>
<property name="query.substitutions">
true 1, false 0, yes 'Y', no 'N'</property>
<property name="proxyfactory.factory_class">
NHibernate.ByteCode.LinFu.ProxyFactoryFactory,
 NHibernate.ByteCode.LinFu</property>
</session-factory>
</hibernate-configuration>

....

</configuration>
```

The `Repository.NHibernate` project now resembles Figure 7-14.

You will now create a version of the Repository using Microsoft's Entity Framework.

Entity Framework Repository

Unlike NHibernate, Microsoft's Entity Framework has a built-in graphical designer and wizard step-by-step menu for configuring the model and database mapping. Other than that, NHibernate and Entity Framework are similar, as you will see after you have built an Entity Framework repository layer implementation in this section.

Create a new ADO.NET Entity Model by right-clicking on the `Repository.EF` project, selecting Add New Item, and choosing the ADO.NET Entity Data Model item from the data submenu. Name the model `Library.edmx` and click Add. To create your Entity Data Model, you are taken through a series of steps from the Entity Data Model Wizard. The first step is to determine how you want to create your model. Because you have already set up a database, you can select Generate from Database, as shown in Figure 7-15.

The second step asks you to confirm the location of the database, as shown in Figure 7-16. By default, the wizard should pick up the local database you created within the `UI.Web` web application project. Leave the default settings and the name of the connection string, and click Next.

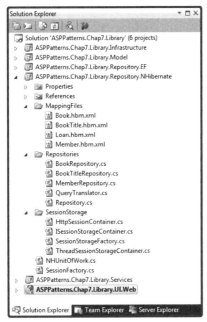

FIGURE 7-14

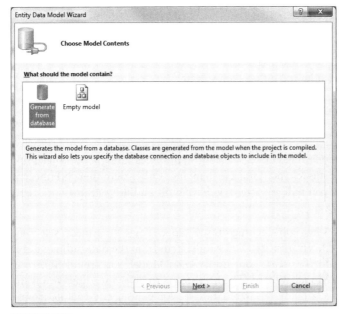

FIGURE 7-15

FIGURE 7-16

The Entity Framework then prompts you to copy the database to the `Repository.EF` project, as shown in Figure 7-17. Click No.

FIGURE 7-17

The wizard generates a list of database objects that you can include in your model. Select the items as shown in Figure 7-18, and deselect the option to include foreign keys in the model. Then click Finish.

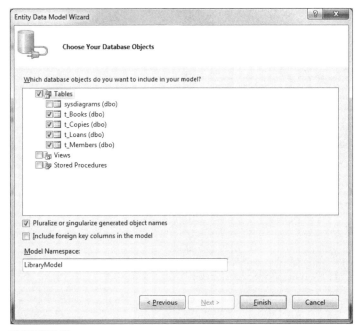

FIGURE 7-18

The Entity Data Model Wizard now generates a model for you. You need to modify the default model so that you can use it with the domain model you created in the Model project. Perform the following refinements to the model generated by Visual Studio:

➤ Rename the t_Members entity to Member

➤ Remove the navigation property t_Copies

➤ Rename the t_Loans navigation property to Loans

➤ Rename the t_Copies entity to Book

➤ Remove the t_Loans navigation property

➤ Rename the t_Books navigation property to Title

➤ Rename the t_Members navigation property to OnLoanTo

➤ Rename the t_Loans entity to Loan

➤ Rename the t_Copies navigation property to Book

➤ Rename the t_Members navigation property to Member

➤ Rename the t_Books entity to BookTitle

➤ Remove the t_Copies navigation property

After you have updated your model, it should resemble Figure 7-19.

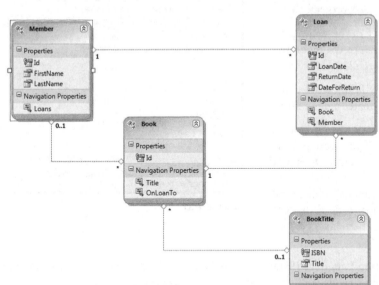

FIGURE 7-19

There are just a few more changes you need to make before you start to create the Repository implementations. Right-click on the `Library.edmx` file and select Properties. Then delete the `EntityModel CodeGenerator` from the Custom Tool property box.

You created your business entities in the `Model` project earlier, so there is no need to let Entity Framework generate the model classes for you.

Right-click anywhere within the Entity Framework diagram and select Properties. Then change the namespace of the project to `ASPPatterns.Chap7.Library.Model`, as shown in Figure 7-20.

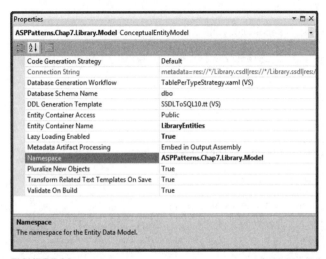

FIGURE 7-20

The Entity Framework now uses the business entities that you defined in the `Model` project.

Right-click on the `Id` property of the `Loan` entity
and change the `StoredGenerationPattern` to
`Identity`, as shown in Figure 7-21.

This is required so that Entity Framework can
create an identity for newly created `Loan` entities.

Even though you have been using the designer to
configure the mapping layer, if you were to right-
click on the `Library.edmx` file, select Open With,
and choose the XML (Text) Editor, you would
find the XML mapping meta data similar to the
NHibernate mapping files. Following is the XML
meta data that represents the three layers of the
Entity Framework.

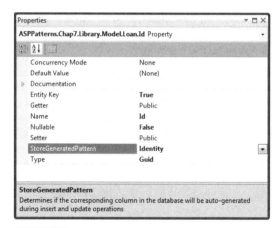

FIGURE 7-21

➤ **Store Schema Definition Language (SSDL):** The SSDL maps the database structure, including
   tables and relationships, views, and stored procedures. This is your logic layer.

➤ **Conceptual Schema Definition Language (CSDL):** The CSDL maps the conceptual view
   detailing your entities and their relationships. This is the conceptual layer.

➤ **Mapping Specification Language (MSL):** The MSL maps the logical layer to the conceptual
   layer. It maps your business entities to the underlying database.

With the domain model and data model mapped, you can start to build the Entity Framework
Repository. Create a new file in the root of the `Repository.EF` project named `LibraryDataContext`
with the following listing:

```
using System.Data.Objects;
using System.Data;
using ASPPatterns.Chap7.Library.Model;

namespace ASPPatterns.Chap7.Library.Repository.EF
{
    public class LibraryDataContext : ObjectContext
    {
        private ObjectSet<Member> _members;
        private ObjectSet<Book> _books;
        private ObjectSet<BookTitle> _bookTitles;

        public LibraryDataContext()
            : base("name=LibraryEntities", "LibraryEntities")
        {
            _members = CreateObjectSet<Member>();
            _books = CreateObjectSet<Book>();
            _bookTitles = CreateObjectSet<BookTitle>();
            base.ContextOptions.LazyLoadingEnabled = true;
        }

        public ObjectSet<Member> Members
```

```
    {
        get { return _members; }
    }

    public ObjectSet<Book> Books
    {
        get { return _books; }
    }

    public ObjectSet<BookTitle> BookTitles
    {
        get { return _bookTitles; }
    }
    }
}
```

This class is similar to the NHibernate's `Session` class in that it provides the gateway to the persistence management and retrieval of business entities using Entity Framework.

Just as with NHibernate, you need to create a set of classes to store current `DataContext` (`Session` in the case of NHibernate). These classes are set up in the same manner as was used with NHibernate. Add a new folder to the `Repository.EF` project named `DataContextStorage`, and add an interface for the storage container named `IDataContextStorageContainer` whose contract can be found here:

```
    public interface IDataContextStorageContainer
    {
        LibraryDataContext GetDataContext();
        void Store(LibraryDataContext libraryDataContext);
    }
```

Next, create an implementation for use within a web scenario named `HttpDataContextStorage Container`:

```
    using System.Web;

    namespace ASPPatterns.Chap7.Library.Repository.EF.DataContextStorage
    {
        public class HttpDataContextStorageContainer : IDataContextStorageContainer
        {
            private string _dataContextKey = "DataContext";

            public LibraryDataContext GetDataContext()
            {
                LibraryDataContext objectContext = null;
                if (HttpContext.Current.Items.Contains(_dataContextKey))
                    objectContext =
                        (LibraryDataContext)HttpContext.Current.Items[_dataContextKey];

                return objectContext;
            }

            public void Store(LibraryDataContext libraryDataContext)
            {
                if (HttpContext.Current.Items.Contains(_dataContextKey))
                    HttpContext.Current.Items[_dataContextKey] = libraryDataContext;
```

```
        else
            HttpContext.Current.Items.Add(_dataContextKey, libraryDataContext);
    }

}
}
```

Also, create an implementation for use within a non-web scenario named `ThreadDataContext StorageContainer` with the following code:

```
using System.Threading;

namespace ASPPatterns.Chap7.Library.Repository.EF.DataContextStorage
{
    public class ThreadDataContextStorageContainer : IDataContextStorageContainer
    {
        private static readonly Hashtable _libraryDataContexts = new Hashtable();

        public LibraryDataContext GetDataContext()
        {
            LibraryDataContext libraryDataContext = null;

            if (_libraryDataContexts.Contains(GetThreadName()))
                libraryDataContext =
                    (LibraryDataContext)_libraryDataContexts[GetThreadName()];

            return libraryDataContext;
        }

        public void Store(LibraryDataContext libraryDataContext)
        {
            if (_libraryDataContexts.Contains(GetThreadName()))
                _libraryDataContexts[GetThreadName()] = libraryDataContext;
            else
                _libraryDataContexts.Add(GetThreadName(), libraryDataContext);
        }

        private static string GetThreadName()
        {
            return Thread.CurrentThread.Name;
        }
    }
}
```

As was the case with NHibernate, to determine which storage container to use, you will use a factory class. Create a new class within the root of the project named `DataContextStorageFactory` with the following code listing:

```
    public class DataContextStorageFactory
    {
        public static IDataContextStorageContainer _dataContextStorageContainer;

        public static IDataContextStorageContainer CreateStorageContainer()
        {
            if (_dataContectStorageContainer == null)
```

```
            {
                if (HttpContext.Current == null)
                    _dataContextStorageContainer =
                        new ThreadDataContextStorageContainer();
                else
                    _dataContextStorageContainer =
                                new HttpDataContextStorageContainer();
            }

            return _dataContextStorageContainer;
        }
    }
```

As with NHibernate's `GetCurrentSession`, you need a way to obtain the current Entity Framework `DataContext`. You can achieve this by using a `DataContext` factory. Add a new class to the root of the `Repository.EF` project named `DataContextFactory` with the following code listing:

```
using ASPPatterns.Chap7.Library.Repository.EF.DataContextStorage;

namespace ASPPatterns.Chap7.Library.Repository.EF
{
    public class DataContextFactory
    {
        public static LibraryDataContext GetDataContext()
        {
            IDataContextStorageContainer _dataContextStorageContainer =
                            DataContextStorageFactory.CreateStorageContainer();

            LibraryDataContext libraryDataContext =
                            _dataContextStorageContainer.GetDataContext();
            if (libraryDataContext == null)
            {
                libraryDataContext = new LibraryDataContext();
                _dataContextStorageContainer.Store(libraryDataContext);
            }

            return libraryDataContext;
        }
    }
}
```

The next class you will create is Entity Framework's implementation of the `IUnitOfWork` interface, as defined in the `Infrastructure` project. Add a new class named `EFUnitOfWork` and update with the code shown here:

```
using ASPPatterns.Chap7.Library.Infrastructure;
using ASPPatterns.Chap7.Library.Infrastructure.UnitOfWork;

namespace ASPPatterns.Chap7.Library.Repository.EF
{
    public class EFUnitOfWork : IUnitOfWork
    {
        public void Commit()
        {
            DataContextFactory.GetDataContext().SaveChanges();
```

```
        }

        public void RegisterAmended(IAggregateRoot entity,
                                    IUnitOfWorkRepository unitofWorkRepository)
        {
            unitofWorkRepository.PersistUpdateOf(entity);
        }

        public void RegisterNew(IAggregateRoot entity,
                                IUnitOfWorkRepository unitofWorkRepository)
        {
            unitofWorkRepository.PersistCreationOf(entity);
        }

        public void RegisterRemoved(IAggregateRoot entity,
                                    IUnitOfWorkRepository unitofWorkRepository)
        {
            unitofWorkRepository.PersistDeletionOf(entity);
        }
    }
}
```

The `EFUnitOfWork` class delegates all work persistence back to the `IUnitOfWorkRepository` but does commit the change to the database via the `DataContextFactory` that you looked at previously.

Querying within Entity Framework is achieved using LINQ to Entities, which is similar to the LINQ to SQL querying mechanism, using strongly typed objects or the literal-based Entity SQL. You will use the literal-based Entity SQL to convert the generic Query Object to language that Entity Framework understands.

Add a new folder named `QueryTranslators` to the `Repository.EF` project, and add a class that each of the Repositories will inherit from. This will be named `QueryTranslator` and will offer a method to produce an Entity SQL String builder along with a list of Object Parameters from the Query Object.

```
using System.Data.Objects;
using ASPPatterns.Chap7.Library.Infrastructure.Query;

namespace ASPPatterns.Chap7.Library.Repository.EF.QueryTranslators
{
    public abstract class QueryTranslator
    {
        public void CreateQueryAndObjectParameters(Query query,
                                                   StringBuilder queryBuilder,
                                                   IList<ObjectParameter> paraColl)
        {
            foreach (Criterion criterion in query.Criteria)
            {
                switch (criterion.criteriaOperator)
                {
                    case CriteriaOperator.Equal:
                        queryBuilder.Append(
                            String.Format("it.{0} = @{0}",
                                    criterion.PropertyName));
                        break;
```

```
                        case CriteriaOperator.LesserThanOrEqual:
                            queryBuilder.Append(
                                String.Format("it.{0} <= @{0}",
                                            criterion.PropertyName));
                            break;
                        default:
                            throw new ApplicationException("No operator defined");
                    }

                    paraColl.Add(
                        new ObjectParameter(criterion.PropertyName, criterion.Value));
                }
            }
        }
    }
```

Do this for each of the Repositories defined in the Model project — BookQueryTranslator, BookTitle QueryTranslator, and MemberQueryTranslator. The code for each of these classes is shown here:

```csharp
using System.Data.Objects;

using ASPPatterns.Chap7.Library.Infrastructure.Query;
using ASPPatterns.Chap7.Library.Model;

namespace ASPPatterns.Chap7.Library.Repository.EF.QueryTranslators
{
    public class BookQueryTranslator : QueryTranslator
    {
        public ObjectQuery<Book> Translate(Query query)
        {
            ObjectQuery<Book> bookQuery;

            if (query.IsNamedQuery())
            {
                bookQuery = FindEFQueryFor(query);
            }
            else
            {
                StringBuilder queryBuilder = new StringBuilder();
                IList<ObjectParameter> paraColl = new List<ObjectParameter>();
                CreateQueryAndObjectParameters(query, queryBuilder, paraColl);

                bookQuery =
                    DataContextFactory.GetDataContext().Books.Include("Title")
                            .Where(queryBuilder.ToString(), paraColl.ToArray())
                            .OrderBy(
                        String.Format("it.{0} desc",
                                    query.OrderByProperty.PropertyName));
            }

            return bookQuery;
        }

        private ObjectQuery<Book> FindEFQueryFor(Query query)
        {
```

```
                // No complex queries have been defined in this sample.
                throw new NotImplementedException();
            }
        }
    }


using System.Data.Objects;
using ASPPatterns.Chap7.Library.Infrastructure.Query;
using ASPPatterns.Chap7.Library.Model;

namespace ASPPatterns.Chap7.Library.Repository.EF.QueryTranslators
{
    public class BookTitleQueryTranslator : QueryTranslator
    {
        public ObjectQuery<BookTitle> Translate(Query query)
        {
            ObjectQuery<BookTitle> bookTitleQuery;

            if (query.IsNamedQuery())
            {
                bookTitleQuery = FindEFQueryFor(query);
            }
            else
            {
                StringBuilder queryBuilder = new StringBuilder();
                IList<ObjectParameter> paraColl = new List<ObjectParameter>();
                CreateQueryAndObjectParameters(query, queryBuilder, paraColl);

                bookTitleQuery = DataContextFactory.GetDataContext().BookTitles
                  .Where(queryBuilder.ToString(), paraColl.ToArray())
                  .OrderBy(
                   String.Format("it.{0} desc", query.OrderByProperty.PropertyName));

            }

            return bookTitleQuery;
        }

        private ObjectQuery<BookTitle> FindEFQueryFor(Query query)
        {
            // No complex queries have been defined in this sample.
            throw new NotImplementedException();
        }
    }
}


using System.Data.Objects;
using ASPPatterns.Chap7.Library.Infrastructure.Query;
using ASPPatterns.Chap7.Library.Model;

namespace ASPPatterns.Chap7.Library.Repository.EF.QueryTranslators
```

```
    {
        public class MemberQueryTranslator : QueryTranslator
        {
            public ObjectQuery<Member> Translate(Query query)
            {
                ObjectQuery<Member> memberQuery;

                if (query.IsNamedQuery())
                {
                    memberQuery = FindEFQueryFor(query);
                }
                else
                {
                    StringBuilder queryBuilder = new StringBuilder();
                    IList<ObjectParameter> paraColl = new List<ObjectParameter>();
                    CreateQueryAndObjectParameters(query, queryBuilder, paraColl);

                    memberQuery = DataContextFactory.GetDataContext().Members
                      .Where(queryBuilder.ToString(), paraColl.ToArray())
                      .OrderBy(
                       String.Format("it.{0} desc", query.OrderByProperty.PropertyName));
                }

                return memberQuery;
            }

            private ObjectQuery<Member> FindEFQueryFor(Query query)
            {
                // No complex queries have been defined in this sample.
                throw new NotImplementedException();
            }
        }
    }
}
```

Each of the translator classes first establishes if the query is for a named query or if it is to be built dynamically. If it's to be built dynamically, a call to the base method `CreateQueryAndObject Parameters` is made a string builder, and a collection of object parameters is populated from the query. Once returned, the query is built and the order property is added.

It is now time to build the Repository implementations. Add a new folder to the root of the `Repository.EF` project named `Repositories`. Add a new class that will act as a base class for all Repositories, named `Repository`. You can see the code for this file here:

```
using ASPPatterns.Chap7.Library.Infrastructure;
using ASPPatterns.Chap7.Library.Infrastructure.UnitOfWork;
using ASPPatterns.Chap7.Library.Infrastructure.Query;
using ASPPatterns.Chap7.Library.Repository.EF.QueryTranslators;
using System.Data.Objects;

namespace ASPPatterns.Chap7.Library.Repository.EF.Repositories
{
    public abstract class Repository<T, EntityKey>
                : IUnitOfWorkRepository where T : IAggregateRoot
    {
```

```
private IUnitOfWork _uow;

public Repository(IUnitOfWork uow)
{
    _uow = uow;
}

public void Add(T entity)
{
    _uow.RegisterNew(entity, this);
}

public void Remove(T entity)
{
    _uow.RegisterRemoved(entity, this);
}

public void Save(T entity)
{
    // Do nothing as EF tracks changes
}

public abstract IQueryable<T> GetObjectSet();

public abstract string GetEntitySetName();

public abstract T FindBy(EntityKey Id);

public abstract ObjectQuery<T> TranslateIntoObjectQueryFrom(Query query);

public IEnumerable<T> FindAll()
{
    return GetObjectSet().ToList<T>();
}

public IEnumerable<T> FindAll(int index, int count)
{
    return GetObjectSet().Skip(index).Take(count).ToList<T>();
}

public IEnumerable<T> FindBy(Query query)
{
    ObjectQuery<T> efQuery = TranslateIntoObjectQueryFrom(query);

    return efQuery.ToList<T>();
}

public IEnumerable<T> FindBy(Query query, int index, int count)
{
    ObjectQuery<T> efQuery = TranslateIntoObjectQueryFrom(query);

    return efQuery.Skip(index).Take(count).ToList<T>();
}

public void PersistCreationOf(IAggregateRoot entity)
```

```
        {
            DataContextFactory.GetDataContext().AddObject(GetEntitySetName(),
                                                          entity);
        }

        public void PersistUpdateOf(IAggregateRoot entity)
        {
            // Do nothing as EF tracks changes
        }

        public void PersistDeletionOf(IAggregateRoot entity)
        {
            DataContextFactory.GetDataContext().DeleteObject(entity);
        }
    }
}
```

Code snippet Repository.cs in the project ASPPatterns.Chap7.Library.Repository.EF

The three Repository implementations that will inherit from the `Repository` base class are `BookRepository`, `BookTitleRepository`, and `MemberRepository`. The code for each of these Repositories is shown here:

```
using System.Data.Objects;
using ASPPatterns.Chap7.Library.Model;
using ASPPatterns.Chap7.Library.Infrastructure;
using ASPPatterns.Chap7.Library.Infrastructure.Query;
using ASPPatterns.Chap7.Library.Infrastructure.UnitOfWork;
using ASPPatterns.Chap7.Library.Repository.EF.QueryTranslators;

namespace ASPPatterns.Chap7.Library.Repository.EF.Repositories
{
    public class BookRepository : Repository<Book, Guid>, IBookRepository
    {
        public BookRepository(IUnitOfWork uow) : base(uow)
        {    }

        public override Book FindBy(Guid Id)
        {
            return GetObjectSet().FirstOrDefault<Book>(b => b.Id == Id);
        }

        public override IQueryable<Book> GetObjectSet()
        {
            return DataContextFactory.GetDataContext().CreateObjectSet<Book>();
        }

        public override string GetEntitySetName()
        {
            return "Books";
        }

        public override ObjectQuery<Book> TranslateIntoObjectQueryFrom(Query query)
        {
```

```csharp
                return new BookQueryTranslator().Translate(query);
        }
    }
}




using System.Data.Objects;
using System.Data;
using ASPPatterns.Chap7.Library.Model;
using ASPPatterns.Chap7.Library.Infrastructure;
using ASPPatterns.Chap7.Library.Infrastructure.UnitOfWork;
using ASPPatterns.Chap7.Library.Infrastructure.Query;

namespace ASPPatterns.Chap7.Library.Repository.EF.Repositories
{
    public class BookTitleRepository
            : Repository<BookTitle, string>, IBookTitleRepository
    {
        public BookTitleRepository(IUnitOfWork uow)
            : base(uow)
        { }

        public override BookTitle FindBy(string Id)
        {
            return GetObjectSet().FirstOrDefault<BookTitle>(b => b.ISBN == Id);
        }

        public override IQueryable<BookTitle> GetObjectSet()
        {
            return DataContextFactory.GetDataContext().CreateObjectSet<BookTitle>();
        }

        public override string GetEntitySetName()
        {
            return "BookTitles";
        }

        public override ObjectQuery<BookTitle> TranslateIntoObjectQueryFrom
                                                            (Query query)
        {
            throw new NotImplementedException();
        }
    }
}




using System.Data.Objects;
using ASPPatterns.Chap7.Library.Model;
using ASPPatterns.Chap7.Library.Infrastructure;
```

```
using ASPPatterns.Chap7.Library.Infrastructure.UnitOfWork;
using ASPPatterns.Chap7.Library.Repository.EF.QueryTranslators;

namespace ASPPatterns.Chap7.Library.Repository.EF.Repositories
{
    public class MemberRepository : Repository<Member, Guid>, IMemberRepository
    {
        public MemberRepository(IUnitOfWork uow) : base(uow)
        { }

        public override Member FindBy(Guid Id)
        {
            return GetObjectSet().FirstOrDefault<Member>(m => m.Id == Id);
        }

        public override IQueryable<Member> GetObjectSet()
        {
            return DataContextFactory.GetDataContext().CreateObjectSet<Member>();
        }

        public override string GetEntitySetName()
        {
            return "Members";
        }

        public override ObjectQuery<Member>
                    TranslateIntoObjectQueryFrom(Infrastructure.Query.Query query)
        {
            return new MemberQueryTranslator().Translate(query);
        }
    }
}
```

The last task to complete the Entity Framework Repository implementation is adding some configuration data to the `Web.config` file, which you can find within the `UI.Web` web application project. The data you need to add is the Entity Framework connection string. This connection string is located in the `App.config` file found within the `Repository.EF`. You can see the `Web.config` file code snippet here:

```
...
    <connectionStrings>
      <add name="LibraryEntities"
           providerName="System.Data.EntityClient"
connectionString=
"metadata=res://*/Library.csdl|res://*/Library.ssdl|res://*/Library.msl;
provider=System.Data.SqlClient;
provider connection string='Data Source=.\SQLEXPRESS;AttachDbFilename=&quot;
|DataDirectory|Library.mdf&quot;
;Integrated Security=True;User Instance=True;MultipleActiveResultSets=True'"/>
    </connectionStrings>
...
```

The `Repository.EF` project now resembles Figure 7-22.

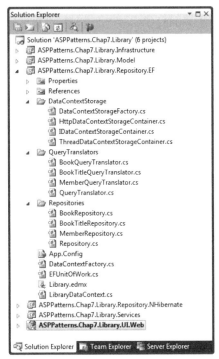

FIGURE 7-22

It's now time to bring the whole solution together and create the presentation layer that will use all the projects you have built.

Presentation

You will build a basic presentation layer using ASP.NET web forms so that you can see the full application working. To allow switching between the NHibernate and Entity Framework Repository implementations, you will add a setting to the `Web.config` file. Open the `Web.config` file and add the following code snippet:

```
...
<appSettings>
    <! --
       NH - NHibernate Repository
       EF - Entity Framework Repository
    -- >
    <add key="PersistenceStrategy" value="NH"/>
</appSettings>
...
```

A service factory enables you to easily switch between the two Repositories and provides a valid instance of the `LibraryService` class with all dependencies. Add a new class to the `UI.Web` web application named `ServiceFactory`, and update it to match the code listing that follows:

```
using ASPPatterns.Chap7.Library.Services;
using ASPPatterns.Chap7.Library.Model;
using ASPPatterns.Chap7.Library.Infrastructure;
using ASPPatterns.Chap7.Library;
using ASPPatterns.Chap7.Library.Infrastructure.UnitOfWork;
using System.Configuration;

namespace ASPPatterns.Chap7.Library.UI.Web
{
    /// <summary>
    /// For a better solution, look at Chapter 8,
    /// which uses an IoC Container to inject the concrete implementations
    /// </summary>
    public static class ServiceFactory
    {
        public static LibraryService CreateLibraryService()
        {
            IUnitOfWork uow;
            IBookRepository bookRepository;
            IBookTitleRepository bookTitleRepository;
            IMemberRepository memberRepository;

            string persistenceStrategy =
                    ConfigurationManager.AppSettings["PersistenceStrategy"];

            if (persistenceStrategy == "EF")
            {
                uow = new Repository.EF.EFUnitOfWork();
                bookRepository =
                    new Repository.EF.Repositories.BookRepository(uow);
                bookTitleRepository =
                        new Repository.EF.Repositories.BookTitleRepository(uow);
                memberRepository =
                        new Repository.EF.Repositories.MemberRepository(uow);
            }
            else
            {
                uow = new Repository.NHibernate.NHUnitOfWork();
                bookRepository =
                        new Repository.NHibernate.Repositories.BookRepository(uow);
                bookTitleRepository =
                        new Repository.NHibernate.Repositories
                                                    .BookTitleRepository(uow);
                memberRepository =
                        new Repository.NHibernate.Repositories.MemberRepository(uow);
            }

            return new LibraryService(
```

```
                          bookTitleRepository, bookRepository, memberRepository, uow);
                }
        }
}
```

The `ServiceFactory` has a single method named `CreateLibraryService` that returns an instance of the `LibraryService` configured to use the Repository defined in the `Web.config` file.

Now for the presentation needs. Open the `Default.aspx` file in the source code version and update the markup to match what follows:

```aspx
<%@ Page Language="C#" AutoEventWireup="true" CodeBehind="Default.aspx.cs"
        Inherits="ASPPatterns.Chap7.Library.UI.Web.Default" %>

<!DOCTYPE html PUBLIC "-//W3C//DTD XHTML 1.0 Transitional//EN"
        "http://www.w3.org/TR/xhtml1/DTD/xhtml1-transitional.dtd">

<html xmlns="http://www.w3.org/1999/xhtml">
<head id="Head1" runat="server">
    <title></title>
</head>
<body>
    <form id="form1" runat="server">
    <div>
        <h1>Library System</h1>
        <h2>Members</h2>
        Add new member:<br />
        First Name <asp:TextBox ID="txtFirstName" runat="server" /><br />
        Last Name <asp:TextBox ID="txtLastName" runat="server" /><br />
        <asp:Button ID="btnCreateMember" runat="server"
                    Text="Add Member" onclick="btnCreateMember_Click" />

    </div>
    <p>
        All Members
        <asp:Repeater ID="rptMembers" runat="server">
         <HeaderTemplate>
            <ul>
         </HeaderTemplate>
         <ItemTemplate>
           <li><%# Eval("FullName")%>
           (<a href="MemberDetail.aspx?Id=<%# Eval("MemberId")%>">view details</a>)
           </li>
           </ItemTemplate>
           <FooterTemplate>
               </ul>
           </FooterTemplate>
        </asp:Repeater>
    </p>
    <h2>Books</h2>
    Add a Book<br />
    Title <asp:DropDownList ID="ddlBookTitles" runat="server" /> 
```

```
            <asp:Button ID="btnAddBook" runat="server"
                    onclick="btnAddBook_Click" Text="Add Book" />
    <p>
        All Books
        <asp:Repeater ID="rptBooks" runat="server">
            <HeaderTemplate>
                <ul>
            </HeaderTemplate>
            <ItemTemplate>
                    <li><%# Eval("Title")%></li>
            </ItemTemplate>
            <FooterTemplate>
                </ul>
            </FooterTemplate>
        </asp:Repeater>
    </p>

    <p>
        Add
        Book Title<br />
        <br />
        ISBN<asp:TextBox ID="txtBookISBN" runat="server" /><br />
        Title<asp:TextBox ID="txtBookTitle" runat="server" /></p>
    <p>
        <asp:Button ID="btnAddTitle" runat="server"
                    onclick="btnAddTitle_Click" Text="Add Title" /></p>
    <p>
        All Book titles<asp:Repeater ID="rptBookTitles" runat="server">
            <HeaderTemplate>
                <ul>
            </HeaderTemplate>
            <ItemTemplate>
                    <li><%# Eval("Title")%><br />
                        <small>ISBN: <%# Eval("ISBN")%></small></li>
            </ItemTemplate>
            <FooterTemplate>
                </ul>
            </FooterTemplate>
        </asp:Repeater>
    </p>
    </form>
</body>
</html>
```

Code snippet Default.aspx in the project ASPPatterns.Chap7.Library.UI.Web

The Default.aspx page lists all Members, Books, and BookTitles and lets you add new Members, Books, and BookTitles.

The code behind for the Default.aspx is shown here:

```
using ASPPatterns.Chap7.Library.Model;
using ASPPatterns.Chap7.Library.Infrastructure;
```

```csharp
using ASPPatterns.Chap7.Library.Services.Views;
using ASPPatterns.Chap7.Library.Services.Messages;
using ASPPatterns.Chap7.Library.Services;
using ASPPatterns.Chap7.Library.Infrastructure.Query;

namespace ASPPatterns.Chap7.Library.UI.Web
{
    public partial class Default : System.Web.UI.Page
    {
        protected void Page_Load(object sender, EventArgs e)
        {
            if (!Page.IsPostBack)
            {
                DisplayCustomers();
                DisplayBooks();
            }
        }

        private void DisplayCustomers()
        {
            FindMemberRequest request = new FindMemberRequest();
            LibraryService service = ServiceFactory.CreateLibraryService();
            request.All = true;
            FindMembersResponse response = service.FindMembers(request);

            rptMembers.DataSource = response.MembersFound;
            rptMembers.DataBind();
        }

        protected void btnCreateMember_Click(object sender, EventArgs e)
        {
            LibraryService service = ServiceFactory.CreateLibraryService();
            AddMemberRequest request = new AddMemberRequest();
            request.FirstName = txtFirstName.Text;
            request.LastName = txtLastName.Text;

            service.AddMember(request);

            DisplayCustomers();
        }

        protected void btnAddBook_Click(object sender, EventArgs e)
        {
            LibraryService service = ServiceFactory.CreateLibraryService();
            AddBookRequest request = new AddBookRequest();
            request.ISBN = ddlBookTitles.SelectedValue;

            service.AddBook(request);
            DisplayBooks();
        }

        private void DisplayBooks()
        {
```

```csharp
            LibraryService service = ServiceFactory.CreateLibraryService();
            FindBooksRequest request = new FindBooksRequest();
            request.All = true;
            FindBooksResponse response = service.FindBooks(request);

            rptBooks.DataSource = response.Books;
            rptBooks.DataBind();

            FindBookTitlesRequest bookTitleRequest = new FindBookTitlesRequest();
            bookTitleRequest.All = true;
            FindBookTitlesResponse bookTitlesResponse =
                                        service.FindBookTitles(bookTitleRequest);


            ddlBookTitles.DataSource = bookTitlesResponse.BookTitles;
            ddlBookTitles.DataTextField = "Title";
            ddlBookTitles.DataValueField = "ISBN";
            ddlBookTitles.DataBind();

            rptBookTitles.DataSource = bookTitlesResponse.BookTitles;
            rptBookTitles.DataBind();
        }

        protected void btnAddTitle_Click(object sender, EventArgs e)
        {
            AddBookTitleRequest request = new AddBookTitleRequest();
            request.ISBN = txtBookISBN.Text;
            request.Title = txtBookTitle.Text;

            LibraryService service = ServiceFactory.CreateLibraryService();

            service.AddBookTitle(request);
            DisplayBooks();
        }
    }
}
```

There isn't anything exciting going on in the code behind apart from the building of messages and their sending and receiving between the client and the service layer.

The second page you will create is used to loan books to Members. You access this page by clicking on a Member from the Default.aspx page. Add a new ASP.NET web form to the web application named MemberDetail.aspx and update the markup with the code listing that follows:

```aspx
<%@ Import Namespace="ASPPatterns.Chap7.Library.Services.Views" %>
<%@ Page Language="C#" AutoEventWireup="true" CodeBehind="MemberDetail.aspx.cs"
 Inherits="ASPPatterns.Chap7.Library.UI.Web.MemberDetail" %>

<!DOCTYPE html PUBLIC "-//W3C//DTD XHTML 1.0 Transitional//EN"
 "http://www.w3.org/TR/xhtml1/DTD/xhtml1-transitional.dtd">

<html xmlns="http://www.w3.org/1999/xhtml">
<head runat="server">
```

```
    <title></title>
</head>
<body>
    <form id="form1" runat="server">
    <div>
    <h1>Library System</h1>
        <a href="default.aspx">Library System Home</a>
        <h2><asp:Literal ID="litName" runat="server" /></h2>
    <p>
        Books on Loan
        <asp:Repeater ID="rptLoans" runat="server">
            <HeaderTemplate>
                <ul>
            </HeaderTemplate>
            <ItemTemplate>
             <li><%# Eval("BookTitle")%><br />
             <small>
              <%# DisplayLoanStatus((LoanView)Container.DataItem) %></small>
                </li>
            </ItemTemplate>
            <FooterTemplate>
                </ul>
            </FooterTemplate>
        </asp:Repeater>

    </p>

        Select a book to loan out:<br />
        <br />
        <asp:Repeater ID="rptBooks" runat="server">
            <HeaderTemplate>
                <ul>
            </HeaderTemplate>
            <ItemTemplate>
                <li><%# Eval("Title")%>
                    <%# LoanStatus((BookView)Container.DataItem)%></li>
            </ItemTemplate>
            <FooterTemplate>
                </ul>
            </FooterTemplate>
        </asp:Repeater>
    </div>
    </form>
</body>
</html>
```

The `MemberDetail.aspx` page lists a history of loans for the given `Member` and a list of all available books to loan. The code behind for this page follows:

```
using ASPPatterns.Chap7.Library.Repository.EF;
using ASPPatterns.Chap7.Library.Services.Messages;
using ASPPatterns.Chap7.Library.Services.Views;
```

```
using ASPPatterns.Chap7.Library.Services;

using ASPPatterns.Chap7.Library.Model;

namespace ASPPatterns.Chap7.Library.UI.Web
{
    public partial class MemberDetail : System.Web.UI.Page
    {
        protected void Page_Load(object sender, EventArgs e)
        {
            if (!Page.IsPostBack)
            {
                string memberId = Request.QueryString["Id"];
                string copyToReturnId = "";
                string copyToLoanId=  "";

                if (Request.QueryString.AllKeys
                        .FirstOrDefault(s => s == "CopyIdToReturn") != null)
                    copyToReturnId = Request.QueryString["CopyIdToReturn"];

                if (Request.QueryString.AllKeys
                        .FirstOrDefault(s => s == "CopyToLoanId") != null)
                    copyToLoanId = Request.QueryString["CopyToLoanId"];

                if (copyToLoanId != "")
                    LoanBook(new Guid(copyToLoanId));

                if (copyToReturnId != "")
                    ReturnBook(new Guid(copyToReturnId));

                DisplayMember(new Guid(memberId));
                DisplayBooks();
            }
        }

        private void LoanBook(Guid copyId)
        {
            LibraryService service = ServiceFactory.CreateLibraryService();
            LoanBookRequest request = new LoanBookRequest();
            LoanBookResponse response;
            request.CopyId = copyId.ToString() ;
            request.MemberId = Request.QueryString["Id"];

            response = service.LoanBook(request);
        }

        private void ReturnBook(Guid copyId)
        {
            LibraryService service = ServiceFactory.CreateLibraryService();
            ReturnBookRequest request = new ReturnBookRequest();

            request.CopyId = copyId.ToString();

            service.ReturnBook(request);
```

```
        }

        private void DisplayMember(Guid Id)
        {
            LibraryService service = ServiceFactory.CreateLibraryService();
            FindMemberRequest request =
                        new FindMemberRequest { MemberId = Id.ToString() };
            FindMembersResponse response = service.FindMembers(request);

            if (response.Success)
            {
                litName.Text = response.MembersFound.First().FullName;
                rptLoans.DataSource = response.MembersFound
                                        .First().Loans.OrderBy(l => l.LoanDate);
                rptLoans.DataBind();
            }
        }


        private void DisplayBooks()
        {
            LibraryService service = ServiceFactory.CreateLibraryService();
            FindBooksRequest request = new FindBooksRequest();
            request.All = true;
            FindBooksResponse response = service.FindBooks(request);

            this.rptBooks.DataSource = response.Books;
            rptBooks.DataBind();

        }

        public string DisplayLoanStatus(LoanView loan)
        {
            if (loan.StillOutOnLoan)
                return String.Format(
    @"due back on {0} <a href=""Memberdetail.aspx? "
 + @"CopyIdToReturn={1}&Id={2}"">return?</a>",
        loan.DateForReturn, loan.CopyId, loan.MemberId);
            else
                return "returned on " + loan.ReturnDate;

        }

        public string LoanStatus(BookView book)
        {
            if (!String.IsNullOrEmpty(book.OnLoanTo))
                return "On loan to " + book.OnLoanTo;
            else
              return String.Format(
                @"<a href=""MemberDetail.aspx?Id={0}&CopyToLoanId={1}"">Loan?</a>",
                                        Request.QueryString["Id"], book.Id);
        }
    }
}
```

Again, the code behind is straightforward, and logic is relevant only to presentation needs. Figure 7-23 shows the complete UI.Web web application project.

Set the web application as your start-up project, and press F5 to run the application. Figures 7-24 and 7-25 show you the application in use.

After you have run through the application and used all the functions, change the Repository setting from within the web.config to test the other Repository.

Raw ADO.NET Repository

If you want to see a raw ADO.NET Repository implementation using all the patterns discussed in the first half of this chapter, download this book's source code from www. wrox.com.

FIGURE 7-23

As you can see, several options are available when it comes to implementing your repository layer. Both the NHibernate and Entity Framework products are powerful but do require some initial upfront investment in terms of time to learn the syntax and API. However, the cost of investment is low compared to building your own Repository that supports all the patterns discussed in this chapter.

SUMMARY

This chapter introduced the following patterns that you can apply to the DAL of an enterprise ASP. NET application:

➤ **Repository:** The Repository pattern is used mostly with logical collections of objects, or aggregates as they are better known. The CRUD methods take an instance of the aggregate root and persist and retrieve all the associated objects in the object graph. This works well if you are taking a domain-driven design approach to development. It is also a good fit with the domain model business pattern and the POCO/PI business models.

➤ **DAO:** This simple pattern is designed to separate the elements of your DAL from the rest of the application. Typically, a DAO exists for each table and contains all the CRUD methods, which makes it an ideal DAL pattern for the Transaction Script and Active Record business patterns.

➤ **Unit of Work:** The Unit of Work pattern maintains all the entities that a business transaction adds, updates, and removes and commits the changes as one atomic action. This ensures that, if an exception were to occur, all changes would be rolled back and the data would be left in a valid state.

➤ **Data Concurrency:** Data concurrency is vital in any enterprise application. You looked at using version IDs to ensure that another user hadn't modified a business entity during a business transaction. This again ensured that your data remained valid at all times.

➤ **Lazy Loading and Proxy:** Lazy Loading is the process of deferring the loading of an expensive resource until you need it. The proxy pattern provides acts as a surrogate to another object. You saw how the proxy pattern returned a `ProxyCustomer` instead of a real customer. The `ProxyCustomer` was then able to only load the collection of orders when needed.

➤ **Identity Map:** An Identity Map pattern ensures that each business entity retrieved from the DAL is loaded only once by storing that business entity into a map and loading it from there for subsequent calls for the duration of a business transaction.

➤ **Query Object:** The Query Object pattern provides a data provider–agnostic manner in which to query a Repository for a business entities.

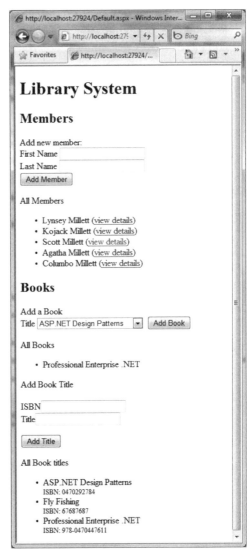

FIGURE 7-24

You then looked at two popular ORMs:

➤ **NHibernate:** NHibernate is a port of the popular Hibernate open source ORM for Java. NHibernate has been around for years, and it's a proven and robust piece of software with a large active community working on the product.

➤ **Entity Framework:** Entity Framework is Microsoft's enterprise-level ORM. Much criticized when it launched, it's now in version 4 and has support for POCO and PI, which makes it a great product for your persistence needs.

It should now be clear that there is a lot to do to ensure your enterprise-level ASP.NET application has a solid and well-thought-out persistence layer. Whether you are going to opt for an ORM or roll your own, it's important that you understand the patterns and principles involved so that you can be best placed to build a solution for your data access needs.

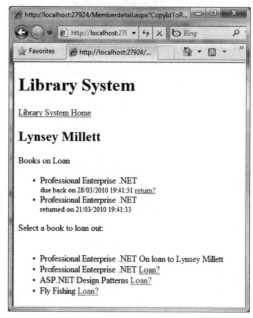

FIGURE 7-25

In the next chapter, you will look at patterns that can be used to separate concerns at the presentation level of your ASP.NET applications.

The Presentation Layer

WHAT'S IN THIS CHAPTER?

➤ Tying your loosely coupled code with StructureMap and Inversion of Control container

➤ Letting the view be in charge with the Model-View-Presenter pattern and ASP.NET web forms

➤ FrontController - Command pattern and Chain of Responsibility pattern

➤ Model-View-Controller pattern with ASP.NET MVC and Castle Monorail

➤ PageController pattern with ASP.NET web forms

➤ The ViewModel pattern and how to automate domain entities to ViewModel mapping with AutoMapper

This chapter deals with the needs of the presentation of an ASP.NET enterprise application and discusses a number of patterns at your disposal to organize your presentation code. The chapter starts with a discussion of how you can tie together your loosely coupled code so that a concrete implementation can be consumed from the presentation layer via the use of an Inversion of Control (IoC) container. The chapter then moves onto the patterns that promote separation of concerns, including the Model-View-Presenter pattern, the Front Controller pattern, the Model-View-Controller pattern, and the Page Controller pattern. Various frameworks and open source products are discussed to assist you in the organization of your presentation concerns, and a number of coding exercises are presented to help you understand the patterns concepts.

INVERSION OF CONTROL

Throughout this book, you have read about the benefits and principles behind loosely coupling your code. In Chapter 3, you were introduced to the Dependency Inversion (sometimes known as Dependency Injection) principle from the S.O.L.I.D. design principles, which taught you to depend on abstractions rather than implementations, thereby inverting the relationship of a dependent to its dependencies. However, at some point, you need to create concrete implementations. This typically occurs at the presentation or service layer, so you are now left with the unenviable task of creating those dependencies without coupling your code to a specific implementation. Luckily, a number of patterns can help you with this task, which you will look at now.

Factory Design Pattern

Many of the exercises up to this point have utilized the Factory Design pattern (see Chapter 5) to create all the concrete implementations. You have typically seen code similar to the snippet shown here:

```
public static class OrderServiceFactory
{
    public static OrderService CreateOrderService()
    {
        ICourier courier = new FedExCourier();
        IDispatchService DispatchService = new DispatchService(courier);

        IPaymentMerchant paymentMerchant = new StreamLinePaymentMerchant();
        IPaymentGateway paymentGateway =
                    new PaymentGateway(StreamLinePaymentMerchant);

        return new OrderService(DispatchService, paymentGateway);
    }
}
```

The OrderServiceFactory completely removes the responsibility from the client code and provides a simple method to obtain a complex service, the OrderService. However, the Factory pattern has its drawbacks: when you introduce more dependencies and thus more ways to create the service, the number of methods on the class increases to accommodate all the different OrderService dependency permutations, as you see in the following code snippet:

```
public static class OrderServiceFactory
{
    public static OrderService CreateFedExOrderService()
    {
        ICourier courier = new FedExCourier();
        IDispatchService DispatchService = new DispatchService(courier);

        IPaymentMerchant paymentMerchant = new StreamLinePaymentMerchant();
        IPaymentGateway paymentGateway =
                    new PaymentGateway(StreamLinePaymentMerchant);

        return new OrderService(DispatchService, paymentGateway);
    }

    public static OrderService CreateDHLOrderService()
    {
        ICourier courier = new DHLCourier();
        IDispatchService DispatchService = DispatchService(courier);

        IPaymentMerchant paymentMerchant = new StreamLinePaymentMerchant();
```

```
            IPaymentGateway paymentGateway =
                    new PaymentGateway(StreamLinePaymentMerchant);

            return new OrderService(DispatchService, paymentGateway);
        }

        public static OrderService CreateTNTOrderService()
        {
            ICourier courier = new TNTCourier();
            IDispatchService DispatchService = DispatchService(courier);

            IPaymentMerchant paymentMerchant = new StreamLinePaymentMerchant();
            IPaymentGateway paymentGateway =
                    new PaymentGateway(StreamLinePaymentMerchant);

            return new OrderService(DispatchService, paymentGateway);
        }
    }
```

The downside is that a client using the factory is tightly coupled to a single implementation of the OrderService, and variations to the type of OrderService class needed by the client require a change in the factory class method being called.

The next pattern to solve the issue of creating concrete types is the Service Locator pattern.

Service Locator

The role of the Service Locator is to act as a central service repository with a simple interface that knows how to get hold of any service required by the application. A Service Locator provides methods to register services and usually takes a literal name value of a service or an object type to resolve them.

Think of a Service Locator as a kind of beefed-up factory. Instead of having a mass of different factory methods for variants of your service, you have a single Resolve method that will allow you to obtain any service for a given key. Like the Factory pattern, the Service Locator pattern hides the complexities of wiring up a service with its required dependent objects, except that the service locator can be reused in many applications and is a lot more abstract than the Factory Design pattern.

```
OrderService orderService =
        serviceLocator.Locate<OrderService>("OrderServiceWithFedExCourier");
```

Typically, the code to register the service would reside in a startup class, ideally in the global.asax file's Application_Start event. The Service Locator is a far easier model to work with and does not need lots of explicitly named methods to provide implementations of the OrderService.

The code snippet that follows shows how a simple ServiceLocator would look.

```
        public class ServiceLocator
        {
          private IDictionary<string, Object> registeredTypes =
                        new Dictionary<string, Object>();
          public void Register<T>(string ServiceName, T obj)
          {
                registeredTypes.Add(ServiceName, obj);
```

```
        }

        public T Locate<T>(string ServiceName)
        {
                return (T)registeredTypes[ServiceName];
        }
    }
}
```

For a more in-depth look at the Service Locator pattern, read my previous book, *Professional Enterprise .NET*, published by Wrox.

The third pattern you will look at to resolve dependencies is the IoC container.

IoC Containers

All the options you have looked at so far have one thing in common: the client code is responsible for obtaining or fetching a service and all its dependencies. The Factory and Service Locator patterns remove the need to know how to construct the service but still place the burden on the client code to specify which service implementation is required. What an IoC container does is completely invert this relationship by injecting the service into the client, thus pushing rather than pulling, if you will. The term Inversion of Control describes the act of the client relinquishing control to the IoC container, that is the Inversion of Control from client to container. There is another name for this pattern that is a lot more descriptive: the Hollywood principle of "Don't call us, we'll call you." Essentially, IoC is all about taking the traditional flow of control — the client code creating the service — and inverting it using the IoC container to inject the service into the client code.

When you use an IoC container, the client code can simply depend on an interface or abstract class and not have a care in the world as to what is providing it with the concrete implementation at runtime.

There are numerous open source IoC containers out there, such as Castle Windsor, Spring.Net, Ninject, and PicoContainer.NET, as well as Microsoft's Unity, but you will be using StructureMap by Jeremy D. Miller in the next exercise and for the rest of the exercises in this chapter.

StructureMap

To demonstrate the power of an IoC container, you will work through an exercise based on the code snippets shown in the discussion on the Factory and Service Locator patterns. The exercise revolves around the domain of an order payment and dispatch service. The domain model you will create will contain no code, but it will demonstrate how an IoC container can resolve nested dependencies.

To get started with StructureMap, the first thing you need to do is download the framework. Navigate to http://sourceforge.net/projects/structuremap and download the latest version of StructureMap. Once the compressed file has downloaded, unzip it, and extract all files to a folder on your desktop ready to be included with the solution.

Create a new solution named ASPPatterns.Chap8.IoC, and to it add a class library project named ASPPatterns.Chap8.IoC.Model and a web application project named ASPPatterns.Chap8.IoC .UI.Web. Right-click on the UI.Web web application and a reference to the Model project.

Add two folders within the `Model` project named `Dispatch` and `Payment`. Also, add two new interfaces to the `Dispatch` folder named `IDispatchService` and `ICourier` with the following code contracts:

```
public interface IDispatchService
{
}

public interface ICourier
{
}
```

Add a class to the `Dispatch` folder named `DispatchService` that implements the `IDispatchService` interface, and update the class with the code as displayed here:

```
public class DispatchService : IDispatchService
{
    private ICourier _courier;

    public DispatchService(ICourier courier)
    {
        _courier = courier;
    }

    public override string ToString()
    {
        return _courier.ToString();
    }
}
```

Next, add a second class named `FedExCourier` that implements the `ICourier` interface as shown here:

```
public class FedExCourier : ICourier
{
}
```

Add two new interfaces to the `Payment` folder named `IPaymentGateway` and `IPaymentMerchant` with the contracts defined here:

```
public interface IPaymentGateway
{
}

public interface IPaymentMerchant
{
}
```

Add a class to the `Payment` folder named `StreamLinePaymentMerchant` that implements the `IPayment Merchant` interface as shown in the code listing that follows:

```
public class StreamLinePaymentMerchant : IPaymentMerchant
{
}
```

Add a class to the `Payment` folder named `PaymentGateway` that implements the `IPaymentGateway` interface as shown here:

```
public class PaymentGateway : IPaymentGateway
{
    IPaymentMerchant _paymentMerchant;

    public PaymentGateway(IPaymentMerchant paymentMerchant)
    {
        _paymentMerchant = paymentMerchant;
    }

    public override string ToString()
    {
        return _paymentMerchant.ToString();
    }
}
```

Finally, to finish the `Model` project, add a new class named `OrderService` to the root of the project with the following code definition:

```
using ASPPatterns.Chap8.IoC.Model.Payment;
using ASPPatterns.Chap8.IoC.Model.Dispatch;

namespace ASPPatterns.Chap8.IoC.Model
{
    public class OrderService
    {
        private IPaymentGateway _paymentGateway;
        private IDispatchService _DispatchService;

        public OrderService(IPaymentGateway paymentGateway,
                            IDispatchService DispatchService)
        {
            _paymentGateway = paymentGateway;
            _DispatchService = DispatchService;
        }

        public override string ToString()
        {
            return String.Format("Payment Gateway: {0}, Dispatch Service: {1}",
                        _paymentGateway.ToString(), _DispatchService.ToString());
        }
    }
}
```

The `ToString` method override enables you to ascertain that the IoC container correctly resolved all dependencies, which will become clearer later.

The next step is to add a reference to the `StructureMap.dll` that you downloaded earlier. Right-click on the `UI.Web` web application project and add a reference to `StructureMap.dll`. Next, add a new class to the `UI.Web` project named `BootStrapper` with the following code listing:

```
using StructureMap;
using StructureMap.Configuration.DSL;
```

```
using ASPPatterns.Chap8.IoC.Model.Payment;
using ASPPatterns.Chap8.IoC.Model.Dispatch;

namespace ASPPatterns.Chap8.IoC.UI.Web
{
    public class BootStrapper
    {
        public static void ConfigureStructureMap()
        {
            ObjectFactory.Initialize(x =>
            {
                x.AddRegistry<ModelRegistry>();

            });
        }

        public class ModelRegistry : Registry
        {
            public ModelRegistry()
            {
                ForRequestedType<IPaymentGateway>()
                    .TheDefault.Is.OfConcreteType<PaymentGateway>();

                ForRequestedType<IPaymentMerchant>()
                    .TheDefault.Is.OfConcreteType<StreamLinePaymentMerchant>();

                ForRequestedType<IDispatchService>()
                    .TheDefault.Is.OfConcreteType<DispatchService>();

                ForRequestedType<ICourier>()
                    .TheDefault.Is.OfConcreteType<FedExCourier>();
            }

        }

    }
}
```

The `ModelRegistry` class is simply setting up the concrete implementations to return when a specific type is asked for. The `Registry` is then initialized with the StructureMap framework within the `ConfigureStructureMap` method. There are a couple of different ways to configure your concrete dependencies via attributes and xml files that are detailed on the StructureMap project page `http://structuremap.github.com/structuremap/`.

Typically, you will want to configure your dependencies at startup, so add a `global.asax` to your UI.Web project if one does not exist, and then add the code to call the `ConfigureStructureMap` method during the `Application_Start` event, as can be seen here:

```
public class Global : System.Web.HttpApplication
{
    protected void Application_Start(object sender, EventArgs e)
    {
        BootStrapper.ConfigureStructureMap();
    }
}
```

Finally, you can use StructureMap to obtain an instance of the `OrderService` with all dependencies resolved. Switch to the code behind view of the `Default.aspx` page and add the following lines within the `Page_Load` event:

```
using ASPPatterns.Chap8.IoC.Model;
using ASPPatterns.Chap8.IoC.Model.Payment;
using ASPPatterns.Chap8.IoC.Model.Dispatch;
using StructureMap;


namespace ASPPatterns.Chap8.IoC.UI.Web
{
    public partial class _Default : System.Web.UI.Page
    {
        protected void Page_Load(object sender, EventArgs e)
        {
            OrderService orderService =
                    ObjectFactory.GetInstance<OrderService>();

            Response.Write(orderService.ToString());
        }
    }
}
```

When you run the page, it displays the names of both of the nested dependencies. You may have noticed that you didn't explicitly register the `OrderService` type with StructureMap even though it was able to resolve it. This happens because StructureMap auto-wires the dependencies based on what it already has in its container. Auto-wiring your dependencies gives you the maximum benefit of using any type of container. Your client code can remain blissfully unaware of the concrete dependencies defined.

You will be utilizing StructureMap with the remaining exercises in this chapter.

The remainder of this book covers patterns design to organize your presentation logic and to separate it from your business and data access layer. The first pattern you will look at is the Model-View-Presenter.

MODEL-VIEW-PRESENTER

The Model-View-Presenter (MVP) pattern places the emphasis on the view to control the flow of logic throughout the presentation layer. Three distinct parts make up the MVP pattern:

➤ The model represents the business data that is to be displayed by or modified by the view.

➤ The view displays the model data obtained via the presenter and delegates user input to the presenter.

➤ The presenter is called from the view to display data pulled from the model and to handle user input.

Figure 8-1 shows how these three parts work together.

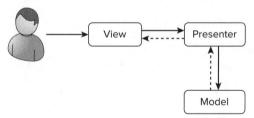

FIGURE 8-1

As shown in the diagram, a user requests a view. The view in turn delegates the request to the associated presenter and typically passes a reference to itself upon construction of the presenter. The presenter then talks to the model to retrieve the business data applicable to the view. Once obtained, the presenter updates the reference of the view with model data.

A framework has been built to enable the MVP pattern to be used with ASP.NET web forms. You can find more information by navigating to http://webformsmvp.com. You will create an implementation of the MVP pattern using web forms without the need of a framework.

ASP.NET Web Forms with MVP

The domain model that you will build for this exercise will be used for the presentation patterns in the remainder of this chapter. The solution revolves around the domain of an online shop — specifically, the displaying of the product catalog.

Create a new solution named ASPPatterns.Chap8.MVP and add the following three class library projects:

➤ ASPPatterns.Chap8.MVP.Model

➤ ASPPatterns.Chap8.MVP.Presentation

➤ ASPPatterns.Chap8.MVP.StubRepository

Next, add a web application project named ASPPatterns.Chap8.MVP.UI.Web. To set up the project dependencies, right-click on the StubRepository project and add a reference to the Model project. Next, right-click on the Presentation project and a reference to both the Model project and the StubRepository project. Finally, right-click on the UI.Web project and add a reference to the Model, StubRepository, and Presentation projects.

With the solution set up, you can begin to flesh out the domain model. Add a new class to the Model project named Category with the following code listing:

```
public class Category
{
    public int Id { get; set; }
    public string Name { get; set; }
}
```

Add a second class to the `Model` project named `Product`, and update it to match the code shown here:

```
public class Product
{
    public int Id { get; set; }
    public Category Category { get; set; }
    public string Name { get; set; }
    public decimal Price { get; set; }
    public string Description { get; set; }
}
```

Next, add two interfaces that will define a contract for the `Product` and `Category` repositories. Name the two interfaces `ICategoryRepository` and `IProductRepository`, respectively. Update the interfaces to match the code contracts that follow:

```
public interface ICategoryRepository
{
    IEnumerable<Category> FindAll();
    Category FindBy(int Id);
}

public interface IProductRepository
{
    IEnumerable<Product> FindAll();
    Product FindBy(int Id);
}
```

Finally, add a domain service class named `ProductService` that coordinates the retrieval of `Products` and `Categories` using the repository contracts. The code for the `ProductService` class is shown here:

```
public class ProductService
{
    private ICategoryRepository _categoryRepository;
    private IProductRepository _productRepository;

    public ProductService(ICategoryRepository categoryRepository,
                          IProductRepository productRepository)
    {
        _categoryRepository = categoryRepository;
        _productRepository = productRepository;
    }

    public Product GetProductBy(int id)
    {
        return _productRepository.FindBy(id);
    }

    public IEnumerable<Product> GetAllProductsIn(int categoryId)
    {
        return _productRepository.FindAll()
                .Where(cat => cat.Category.Id == categoryId);
    }

    public Category GetCategoryBy(int id)
```

```
    {
        return _categoryRepository.FindBy(id);
    }

    public IEnumerable<Category> GetAllCategories()
    {
        return _categoryRepository.FindAll();
    }

    public IEnumerable<Product> GetBestSellingProducts()
    {
        return _productRepository.FindAll().Take(4);
    }
}
```

The domain model has purposely been kept simple so it wouldn't detract from the presentation patterns. With the model in place, you can create a stub repository implementation. You are creating a stub because there is no real need to create a fully database-driven solution.

Add a new class to the `StubRespository` project named `DataContext`, which will provide the data for your repositories. You can see the code for this class here:

```
using ASPPatterns.Chap8.MVP.Model;

namespace ASPPatterns.Chap8.MVP.StubRepository
{
    public class DataContext
    {
        private List<Product> _products;
        private List<Category> _categories;

        public DataContext()
        {
            _categories = new List<Category>();

            Category hatCategory = new Category { Id = 1, Name = "Hats" };
            Category gloveCategory = new Category { Id = 2, Name = "Gloves" };
            Category scarfCategory = new Category { Id = 3, Name = "Scarfs" };

            _categories.Add(hatCategory);
            _categories.Add(gloveCategory);
            _categories.Add(scarfCategory);

            _products = new List<Product>();
            _products.Add(new Product
                { Id = 1, Name = "BaseBall Cap", Price = 9.99m, Category = hatCategory });
            _products.Add(new Product
                { Id = 2, Name = "Flat Cap", Price = 5.99m, Category = hatCategory });
            _products.Add(new Product
                { Id = 3, Name = "Top Hat", Price = 6.99m, Category = hatCategory });

            _products.Add(new Product
                { Id = 4, Name = "Mitten", Price = 10.99m, Category = gloveCategory });
            _products.Add(new Product
```

```
                    { Id = 5, Name = "Fingerless Glove", Price = 13.99m,
                     Category = gloveCategory });
                _products.Add(new Product
                    { Id = 6, Name = "Leather Glove", Price = 7.99m,
                     Category = gloveCategory });

                _products.Add(new Product
                    { Id = 7, Name = "Silk Scarf",
                     Price = 23.99m, Category = scarfCategory });
                _products.Add(new Product
                    { Id = 8, Name = "Woolen", Price = 14.99m, Category = scarfCategory });
            }

            public List<Product> Products
            {
                get { return _products; }
            }

            public List<Category> Categories
            {
                get { return _categories; }
            }
        }
    }
```

Code snippet DataContext.cs in project ASPPatterns.Chap8.MVP.StubRepository

The DataContext simply defines a collection of Products and Categories that you can work against. With your data in place, you can create implementations of the repository contracts defined in the Model project. Add a new class to the StubRepository project named IProductRepository, and update it to match this listing:

```
using ASPPatterns.Chap8.MVP.Model;

namespace ASPPatterns.Chap8.MVP.StubRepository
{
    public class ProductRepository : IProductRepository
    {
        public IEnumerable<Product> FindAll()
        {
            return new DataContext().Products;
        }

        public Product FindBy(int Id)
        {
            Product productFound = new DataContext()
                    .Products.FirstOrDefault(prod => prod.Id == Id);

            if (productFound != null)
            {
                productFound.Description =
                    "orem ipsum dolor sit amet, consectetur adipiscing elit." +
                   "Praesent est libero, imperdiet eget dapibus vel, tempus." +
                    "Nullam eu metus justo." +
                    "Curabitur sit amet lectus lorem, a tempus felis. " +
                    "Phasellus consectetur eleifend est, euismod cursus tellus.";
```

```
                    }

                    return productFound;
                }
            }
        }
```

The `FindBy` method adds some descriptive text to the found product for use on the product detail page that you will see later in this exercise.

The second and last class required for the `StubRepository` project is the implementation of the `ICategoryRepository` interface defined in the `Model` project. Add a new class named `Category Repository`, and again update it to match the code that follows:

```
using ASPPatterns.Chap8.MVP.Model;

namespace ASPPatterns.Chap8.MVP.StubRepository
{
    public class CategoryRepository : ICategoryRepository
    {
        public IEnumerable<Category> FindAll()
        {
            return new DataContext().Categories;
        }

        public Category FindBy(int Id)
        {
            return new DataContext().Categories.FirstOrDefault(cat => cat.Id == Id);
        }
    }
}
```

This completes the `StubRepository` project. You will use the `Model` and `StubRepository` projects throughout this chapter to demonstrate the various presentation patterns.

Now switch to the `Presentation` project and add a new interface named `IHomeView` with the following contract definition:

```
public interface IHomeView
{
    IEnumerable<Product> TopSellingProduct { set; }
    IEnumerable<Category> CategoryList {set; }
}
```

This interface defines the view for the home page of the e-commerce shop. On the home page are categories of products and a selection of the top-selling products.

Create a new class to act as the presenter associated with this view, name the class `HomePagePresenter`, and update it to match the code listing that follows:

```
using ASPPatterns.Chap8.MVP.Model;

namespace ASPPatterns.Chap8.MVP.Presentation
{
    public class HomePagePresenter : IHomePagePresenter
    {
```

```
        private IHomeView _view;
        private ProductService _productService;

        public HomePagePresenter(IHomeView view, ProductService productService)
        {
            _productService = productService;
            _view = view;
        }

        public void Display()
        {
            _view.TopSellingProduct = _productService.GetBestSellingProducts();
            _view.CategoryList = _productService.GetAllCategories();
        }
    }
}
```

The presenter is lightweight and simply populates the properties of the view with Products and Categories retrieved from the ProductService. You will notice that the presenter implements an IHomePagePresenter interface; I have defined this to loosely couple the code and to aid testing. Please add this to the project with the following contract:

```
        public interface IHomePagePresenter
        {
            void Display();
        }
```

Next is the view that contains all products within a category. Create a new interface for this view named ICategoryProductsView, and update it to match the contract displayed here:

```
        using ASPPatterns.Chap8.MVP.Model;

        namespace ASPPatterns.Chap8.MVP.Presentation
        {
            public interface ICategoryProductsView
            {
                Category Category { set; }
                int CategoryId { get;}
                IEnumerable<Product> CategoryProductList { set; }
                IEnumerable<Category> CategoryList { set; }
            }
        }
```

The ICategoryProductsView again displays a list of categories but also all the products within a category specified by the CategoryId property. The CategoryId property has been marked as get only, so the view will specify this information. The remaining property is the Category property, which will be filled with the category matching the CategoryId. The category can then be used to display a title for the page using its Name property.

Create a presenter that works with the view named CategoryProductsPresenter, and update it to match the code listing shown here:

```
        using ASPPatterns.Chap8.MVP.Model;

        namespace ASPPatterns.Chap8.MVP.Presentation
```

```
    {
        public class CategoryProductsPresenter : ICategoryProductsPresenter
        {
            private ICategoryProductsView _view;
            private ProductService _productService;

            public CategoryProductsPresenter(ICategoryProductsView view,
                                             ProductService productService)
            {
                _productService = productService;
                _view = view;
            }

            public void Display()
            {
                _view.CategoryProductList =
                                _productService.GetAllProductsIn(_view.CategoryId);
                _view.Category = _productService.GetCategoryBy(_view.CategoryId);
                _view.CategoryList = _productService.GetAllCategories();
            }
        }
    }
```

The CategoryProductsPresenter is similar to the HomePagePresenter in that it updates the view with categories and products obtained from the ProductService. It differs slightly, however, in that it asks the view to supply the CategoryId. As you will see later, the view supplies the CategoryId from the value of the query string parameter passed to the page. Again, I have defined an interface for the presenter named ICategoryProductsPresenter, seen here:

```
    public interface ICategoryProductsPresenter
    {
        void Display();
    }
```

The next view that you create represents the product detail view. This view displays details on a specific product and enables customers to add the product to a basket. It requires a number of supporting classes that you need to create before the view itself.

Add a new folder to the Presentation project named Basket and add a new interface to it named IBasket. You can see the contract for this interface here:

```
    using ASPPatterns.Chap8.MVP.Model;

    namespace ASPPatterns.Chap8.MVP.Presentation.Basket
    {
        public interface IBasket
        {
            IEnumerable<Product> Items { get; }
            void Add(Product product);
        }
    }
```

The interface defines a contract for a simple basket that stores products added from the product detail view.

Add a new class to the `Basket` folder named `WebBasket` that implements the `IBasket` interface. You need to add a reference to the `System.Web` assembly because you will be referencing the `HttpContext`. You can see the code for the `WebBasket` class here:

```
using System.Collections.Generic;
using System.Web;
using ASPPatterns.Chap8.MVP.Model;
namespace ASPPatterns.Chap8.MVP.Presentation.Basket
{
   public class WebBasket : IBasket
   {
         public IEnumerable<Product> Items
         {
             get { return GetBasketProducts(); }
         }
         public void Add(Product product)
         {
             IList<Product> products = GetBasketProducts();
             products.Add(product);
         }

         private IList<Product> GetBasketProducts()
         {
            IList<Product> products =
                    HttpContext.Current.Session["Basket"] as IList<Product>;

            if (products == null)
            {
                products = new List<Product>();
                HttpContext.Current.Session["Basket"] = products;
            }

            return products;
         }
      }
   }
}
```

The `WebBasket` class simply uses the current session to store and retrieve a collection of products.

The second supporting set of classes required for the product detail view is to enable the navigation to the basket page after the Add to Basket button is clicked from the product detail view. Create a second folder within the `Presentation` project named `Navigation`. To this folder add a new enumeration class shown here:

```
public enum PageDirectory
{
    Basket
}
```

Next, add an interface named `IPageNavigator` and update it to match the code listing that follows:

```
public interface IPageNavigator
{
    void NaviagteTo(PageDirectory page);
}
```

Finally, you can create an implementation of the `IPageNavigator` interface. Add a new class named `PageNavigator` and update it with the following code definition:

```
public class PageNavigator : IPageNavigator
{
    public void NaviagteTo(PageDirectory page)
    {
        switch (page)
        {
            case PageDirectory.Basket:
                HttpContext.Current.Response.Redirect("/Views/Basket/Basket.aspx");
                break;
            default:
                throw new ApplicationException(
                                "Cannot navigate to " + page.ToString() );
        }
    }
}
```

The `PageNavigator` simply registers an HTTP redirect for the matching `PageDirectory` enumeration.

With the supporting classes in place, you can create the product detail view. First, create an interface at the root of the `Presentation` project named `IProductDetailView` with the contract that follows:

```
using ASPPatterns.Chap8.MVP.Model;

namespace ASPPatterns.Chap8.MVP.Presentation
{
    public interface IProductDetailView
    {
        int ProductId {get;}
        string Name {set;}
        decimal Price { set; }
        string Description { set; }
        IEnumerable<Category> CategoryList { set; }
    }
}
```

Next, add a corresponding `Presenter` class named `ProductDetailPresenter`, seen here:

```
using ASPPatterns.Chap8.MVP.Model;
using ASPPatterns.Chap8.MVP.Presentation.Basket;
using ASPPatterns.Chap8.MVP.Presentation.Navigation;

namespace ASPPatterns.Chap8.MVP.Presentation
{
    public class ProductDetailPresenter : IProductDetailPresenter
    {
        private IProductDetailView _view;
        private ProductService _productService;
        private IBasket _basket;
        private IPageNavigator _pageNavigator;

        public ProductDetailPresenter(IProductDetailView view,
                                    ProductService productService,
```

```
                                    IBasket basket, IPageNavigator pageNavigator)
    {
        _productService = productService;
        _view = view;
        _basket = basket;
        _pageNavigator = pageNavigator;
    }

    public void Display()
    {
        Product product = _productService.GetProductBy(_view.ProductId);
        _view.Name = product.Name;
        _view.Description = product.Description;
        _view.Price = product.Price;
        _view.CategoryList = _productService.GetAllCategories();
    }

    public void AddProductToBasketAndShowBasketPage()
    {
        Product product = _productService.GetProductBy(_view.ProductId);

        _basket.Add(product);

        _pageNavigator.NaviagteTo(PageDirectory.Basket);
    }
    }
}
```

Code snippet ProductDetailPresenter.cs in project ASPPatterns.Chap8.MVP.Presentation

---

The `ProductDetailPresenter` class takes an `IBasket` and `IPageNavigator` instance along with the `IProductDetailView` and `ProductService`. The `Display` method is similar to what you have seen before, but the `AddProductToBasketAndShowBasketPage` method uses the `IBasket` and `IPageNavigator` to store the current product and navigate to the basket page view.

Again, the `ProductDetailPresenter` implements an interface named `IProductDetailPresenter` that can be added to the project, the code for which can be seen here:

```
public interface IProductDetailPresenter
{
    void Display();
    void AddProductToBasketAndShowBasketPage();
}
```

The last view to create is the view of the basket. Create a new interface named `IBasketView` with the following code contract:

```
using ASPPatterns.Chap8.MVP.Model;

namespace ASPPatterns.Chap8.MVP.Presentation
{
    public interface IBasketView
    {
```

```
        IEnumerable<Category> CategoryList { set; }
        IEnumerable<Product> BasketItems { set; }
    }
}
```

The `IBasketView` interface displays all products in the customer's basket along with a list of product categories for the catalog navigation.

Next, create a new Presenter class to accompany the `IBasketView` named `BasketPresenter`, and update it to match the following code listing:

```
using ASPPatterns.Chap8.MVP.Model;
using ASPPatterns.Chap8.MVP.Presentation.Basket;

namespace ASPPatterns.Chap8.MVP.Presentation
{
    public class BasketPresenter : IBasketPresenter
    {
        private IBasketView _view;
        private ProductService _productService;
        private IBasket _basket;

        public BasketPresenter(IBasketView view, ProductService productService,
                               IBasket basket)
        {
            _productService = productService;
            _view = view;
            _basket = basket;
        }

        public void Display()
        {
            _view.BasketItems = _basket.Items;
            _view.CategoryList = _productService.GetAllCategories();
        }
    }
}
```

The `BasketPresenter` is as straightforward as the previous presenters except that it utilizes the `IBasket` as well as the `ProductService` to provide data to the view.

Again, the `BasketPresenter` implements an interface called `IBasketPresenter`, seen here:

```
public interface IBasketPresenter
{
    void Display();
}
```

This completes the `Presentation` project, so now you can concentrate on the view implementation.

Create a new folder within the `UI.Web` web application named `Views`, and within this folder add four folders named `Basket`, `Home`, `Product`, and `Shared`. This folder contains your ASPX pages that implement the view interfaces as defined in the `Presentation` project. You also need to add a reference to the `StructureMap.dll`, because you will be using it as an IoC container, as discussed at the beginning of this chapter.

Each of the views shares a number of characteristics — namely, the displaying of a list of categories and the displaying of products. Because of this, you will create two user controls or partial views that can be shared. Add a new user control to the `Shared` folder named `CategoryList.ascx` with the following markup:

```
<%@ Control Language="C#" AutoEventWireup="true"
        CodeBehind="CategoryList.ascx.cs"
        Inherits="ASPPatterns.Chap8.MVP.UI.Web.Views.Shared.CategoryList" %>

<asp:Repeater ID="rptCategoryList" runat="server">
    <HeaderTemplate>
        <ul>
    </HeaderTemplate>
    <ItemTemplate>
       <li>
       <a href="/Views/Product/CategoryProducts.aspx?CategoryId=<%# Eval("Id")%>">
       <%# Eval("Name")%></a>
       </li>
    </ItemTemplate>
    <FooterTemplate>
        </ul>
    </FooterTemplate>
</asp:Repeater>
```

Switch to the code behind view and add the following method, which allows the setting of the `Category` collection source:

```
using ASPPatterns.Chap8.MVP.Model;

namespace ASPPatterns.Chap8.MVP.UI.Web.Views.Shared
{
    public partial class CategoryList : System.Web.UI.UserControl
    {
        public void SetCategoriesToDisplay(IEnumerable<Category> categories)
        {
            this.rptCategoryList.DataSource = categories;
            this.rptCategoryList.DataBind();
        }
    }
}
```

The second partial view you will create is for the displaying of products. Add a user control named `ProductList.ascx` to the `Shared` folder with the markup as displayed here:

```
<%@ Control Language="C#" AutoEventWireup="true"
            CodeBehind="ProductList.ascx.cs"
            Inherits="ASPPatterns.Chap8.MVP.UI.Web.Views.Shared.ProductList" %>
<%@ Import Namespace="System.Collections.Generic"%>
<%@ Import Namespace="ASPPatterns.Chap8.MVP.Model"%>

<asp:Repeater ID="rptProducts" runat="server">
    <ItemTemplate>
```

```
        <%# Eval("Name") %> only <%#Eval("Price", "{0:C}")%><br />
      <a href="/Views/Product/ProductDetail.aspx?ProductId=<%# Eval("Id") %>">
       more information</a>
      <hr />
    </ItemTemplate>
</asp:Repeater>
```

Again, switch to the code behind view and add the following method this time to set the `Product` collection source:

```
using ASPPatterns.Chap8.MVP.Model;

namespace ASPPatterns.Chap8.MVP.UI.Web.Views.Shared
{
    public partial class ProductList : System.Web.UI.UserControl
    {
        public void SetProductsToDisplay(IEnumerable<Product> products)
        {
            this.rptProducts.DataSource = products;
            this.rptProducts.DataBind();
        }
    }
}
```

To ensure the view has a consistent look and feel, use a master page to set the page layout. Add a new master page to the `Shared` folder named `Shop.master` with the markup as displayed here:

```
<%@ Master Language="C#" AutoEventWireup="true"
         CodeBehind="Shop.master.cs"
         Inherits="ASPPatterns.Chap8.MVP.UI.Web.Views.Shared.Shop" %>
<%@ Register src="~/Views/Shared/CategoryList.ascx"
          tagname="CategoryList" tagprefix="uc1" %>

<!DOCTYPE html PUBLIC "-//W3C//DTD XHTML 1.0 Transitional//EN"
"http://www.w3.org/TR/xhtml1/DTD/xhtml1-transitional.dtd">

<html xmlns="http://www.w3.org/1999/xhtml" >
<head runat="server">
    <title></title>
</head>
<body>
    <form id="form1" runat="server">
    <div>
      <table width="70%">
          <tr>
             <td colspan="2">
             <h2><a href="/Views/Home/Index.aspx">Scotts Shop</a></h2><hr /></td>
          </tr>
          <tr>
             <td valign="top" width="15%">
                 <uc1:CategoryList ID="CategoryList1" runat="server" />
             </td>
             <td valign="top" width="85%">
               <asp:ContentPlaceHolder ID="ContentPlaceHolder1" runat="server"/>
             </td>
          </tr>
```

```
                </table>
            </div>
            </form>
        </body>
    </html>
```

Switch to the code behind view and add the following property:

```
        public partial class Shop : System.Web.UI.MasterPage
        {
            public CategoryList CategoryListControl
            {
                get { return this.CategoryList1; }
            }
        }
```

This makes it easier when working with the master page to set the `CategoryList` control's data source.

Now with the layout and display controls created, you can start to implement the views defined in the `Model` project.

Add a new web form to the `Home` folder named `Index.aspx` with the following markup:

```
    <%@ Page Title="" Language="C#" MasterPageFile="~/Views/Shared/Shop.Master"
            AutoEventWireup="true" CodeBehind="Index.aspx.cs"
            Inherits="ASPPatterns.Chap8.MVP.UI.Web.Views.Home.Index" %>
    <%@ Register src="~/Views/Shared/ProductList.ascx" tagname="ProductList"
        tagprefix="uc1" %>

    <asp:Content ID="Content1" ContentPlaceHolderID="ContentPlaceHolder1" runat="server">
        <h2>Today's Top Products</h2>
        <uc1:ProductList ID="plBestSellingProducts" runat="server" />
    </asp:Content>
```

Switch to the code behind and amend the class so that it implements the `IHomeView`, and update the class so that it matches the code listing that follows:

```
    ...
    using ASPPatterns.Chap8.MVP.Presentation;
    using ASPPatterns.Chap8.MVP.Model;
    using ASPPatterns.Chap8.MVP.StubRepository;
    using ASPPatterns.Chap8.MVP.UI.Web.Views.Shared;
    using StructureMap;

    namespace ASPPatterns.Chap8.MVP.UI.Web.Views.Home
    {
        public partial class Index : System.Web.UI.Page, IHomeView
        {
            private IHomePagePresenter _presenter;

            protected void Page_Init(object sender, EventArgs e)
            {
                _presenter =
                    new HomePagePresenter(this, ObjectFactory
```

```
                                              .GetInstance<ProductService>());
        }

        protected void Page_Load(object sender, EventArgs e)
        {
            _presenter.Display();
        }

        public IEnumerable<Model.Product> TopSellingProduct
        {
            set { plBestSellingProducts.SetProductsToDisplay(value); }
        }

        public IEnumerable<Category> CategoryList
        {
            set {
                Shop shopMasterPage = (Shop)Page.Master;
                shopMasterPage.CategoryListControl.SetCategoriesToDisplay(value);
            }
        }
    }
}
```

Here's a rundown of what's happening in the code behind: In the `Page_Init` event, the presenter is created first, passing a reference to the page itself using the `this` keyword and then using the StructureMap object factory to resolve the `ProductService` dependencies. During the `Page_Load` event, the `Display` method is called, which sets both the `TopSellingProduct` and `CategoryList` properties. The view then uses the data to populate the display controls `plBestSellingProducts` and `CategoryListControl` contained on the `MasterPage`.

The next view to implement is the `ICategoryProductsView` defined in the `Model` project. Create a new web form named `CategoryProducts.aspx` within the `Product` folder and update the markup to match the code that follows:

```
<%@ Page Title="" Language="C#" MasterPageFile="~/Views/Shared/Shop.Master"
        AutoEventWireup="true" CodeBehind="CategoryProducts.aspx.cs"
        Inherits="ASPPatterns.Chap8.MVP.UI.Web.Views.Product.CategoryProducts" %>
<%@ Register src="~/Views/Shared/ProductList.ascx" tagname="ProductList"
    tagprefix="uc1" %>

<asp:Content ID="Content1" ContentPlaceHolderID="ContentPlaceHolder1" runat="server">
    <h2>All <asp:Literal ID="litCategoryName" runat="server" /></h2>
    <uc1:ProductList ID="plCategoryProducts" runat="server" />
</asp:Content>
```

Switch to the code behind view and update the class. Have it implement the `ICategoryProductsView` so that it matches the code listing shown here:

```
...
using ASPPatterns.Chap8.MVP.Presentation;
using ASPPatterns.Chap8.MVP.Model;
using ASPPatterns.Chap8.MVP.UI.Web.Views.Shared;
using StructureMap;

namespace ASPPatterns.Chap8.MVP.UI.Web.Views.Product
```

```
{
    public partial class CategoryProducts : System.Web.UI.Page, ICategoryProductsView
    {
        private ICategoryProductsPresenter _presenter;

        protected void Page_Init(object sender, EventArgs e)
        {
            _presenter = new CategoryProductsPresenter(this,
                                ObjectFactory.GetInstance<ProductService>());
        }

        protected void Page_Load(object sender, EventArgs e)
        {
            _presenter.Display();
        }

        public int CategoryId
        {
            get { return int.Parse(Request.QueryString["CategoryId"]); }
        }

        public Category Category
        {
            set { litCategoryName.Text = value.Name; }
        }

        public IEnumerable<Model.Product> CategoryProductList
        {
            set { this.plCategoryProducts.SetProductsToDisplay(value); }
        }

        public IEnumerable<Category> CategoryList
        {
            set
            {
                Shop shopMasterPage = (Shop)Page.Master;
                shopMasterPage.CategoryListControl.SetCategoriesToDisplay(value);
            }
        }

    }
}
```

The class is similar to the code behind for the `Index.aspx` page you created earlier. The main difference is that the view sets the category in question via the query string parameter passed to the page, which can be seen in the `CategoryId` property setter.

Next, add another web form to the `Product` folder named `ProductDetail.aspx`, which implements the `IProductDetailView` as defined within the `Model` project. Update the markup of this page to match the HTML listing here:

```
<%@ Page Title="" Language="C#" MasterPageFile="~/Views/Shared/Shop.Master"
        AutoEventWireup="true" CodeBehind="ProductDetail.aspx.cs"
```

```
                Inherits="ASPPatterns.Chap8.MVP.UI.Web.Views.Product.ProductDetail" %>

<asp:Content ID="Content1" ContentPlaceHolderID="ContentPlaceHolder1" runat="server">
<h2><asp:Literal ID="litName" runat="server"/></h2>
<p>pay: <asp:Literal ID="litPrice" runat="server"/></p>
<p><asp:Literal ID="litDescription" runat="server"/></p>
<p><asp:Button ID="btnAddToBasket" runat="server" Text="Add to Basket"
                onclick="btnAddToBasket_Click"/></p>
</asp:Content>
```

Again, switch to the code behind view and update the code listing so that it implements the IProductDetailView, as shown next:

```
...
using ASPPatterns.Chap8.MVP.Presentation;
using ASPPatterns.Chap8.MVP.Model;
using ASPPatterns.Chap8.MVP.Presentation.Basket;
using ASPPatterns.Chap8.MVP.Presentation.Navigation;
using ASPPatterns.Chap8.MVP.UI.Web.Views.Shared;
using StructureMap;

namespace ASPPatterns.Chap8.MVP.UI.Web.Views.Product
{
    public partial class ProductDetail : System.Web.UI.Page, IProductDetailView
    {
        private IProductDetailPresenter _presenter;

        protected void Page_Init(object sender, EventArgs e)
        {
            _presenter = new ProductDetailPresenter(this,
                            ObjectFactory.GetInstance<ProductService>(),
                            ObjectFactory.GetInstance<IBasket>(),
                            ObjectFactory.GetInstance<IPageNavigator>());
        }

        protected void Page_Load(object sender, EventArgs e)
        {
            _presenter.Display();
        }

        public int ProductId
        {
            get { return int.Parse(Request.QueryString["ProductId"]); }
        }

        public string Name
        {
            set { this.litName.Text = value; }
        }

        public decimal Price
        {
            set { this.litPrice.Text = String.Format("{0:C}", value); }
```

```
        }

        public string Description
        {
            set { this.litDescription.Text = value; }
        }

        public IEnumerable<Category> CategoryList
        {
            set
            {
                Shop shopMasterPage = (Shop)Page.Master;
                shopMasterPage.CategoryListControl.SetCategoriesToDisplay(value);
            }
        }

        protected void btnAddToBasket_Click(object sender, EventArgs e)
        {
            _presenter.AddProductToBasketAndShowBasketPage();
        }
    }
}
```

Again, this view implementation is similar to the ones you have created thus far. The one change is the call to the presenter's `AddProductToBasketAndShowBasketPage` method during the `btnAddTo Basket_Click` event firing. This method adds the product to a session basket and then redirects the page to the basket display page.

The final view to implement is the basket view. Add a new web form to the `Basket` folder named `Basket.aspx` and update the HTML markup view to match the listing that follows:

```
<%@ Page Title="" Language="C#" MasterPageFile="~/Views/Shared/Shop.Master"
        AutoEventWireup="true" CodeBehind="Basket.aspx.cs"
        Inherits="ASPPatterns.Chap8.MVP.UI.Web.Views.Basket.Basket" %>

<asp:Content ID="Content1" ContentPlaceHolderID="ContentPlaceHolder1" runat="server">
<h2>Your Basket</h2>
<ul>
<asp:Repeater ID="rptBasket" runat="server">
    <ItemTemplate>
    <li>1 x <a href="/Views/Product/ProductDetail.aspx?ProductId=<%# Eval("Id") %>">
            <%# Eval("Name") %></a> for <%#Eval("Price", "{0:C}")%></li>
    </ItemTemplate>
</asp:Repeater>
</ul>
</asp:Content>
```

Switch to the code behind and amend the class, as you have done before, to implement the `IBasketView`; then update it to match the listing that follows:

```
using ASPPatterns.Chap8.MVP.Presentation;
using ASPPatterns.Chap8.MVP.StubRepository;
using ASPPatterns.Chap8.MVP.Model;
```

```
using ASPPatterns.Chap8.MVP.Presentation.Basket;
using ASPPatterns.Chap8.MVP.UI.Web.Views.Shared;
using StructureMap;

namespace ASPPatterns.Chap8.MVP.UI.Web.Views.Basket
{
    public partial class Basket : System.Web.UI.Page, IBasketView
    {
        private IBasketPresenter _presenter;

        protected void Page_Init(object sender, EventArgs e)
        {
            _presenter = new BasketPresenter(this,
                                    ObjectFactory.GetInstance<ProductService>(),
                                    ObjectFactory.GetInstance<IBasket>());
        }

        protected void Page_Load(object sender, EventArgs e)
        {
            _presenter.Display();
        }

        public IEnumerable<Category> CategoryList
        {
            set
            {
                Shop shopMasterPage = (Shop)Page.Master;
                shopMasterPage.CategoryListControl.SetCategoriesToDisplay(value);
            }
        }

        public IEnumerable<Model.Product> BasketItems
        {
            set {
                rptBasket.DataSource = value;
                rptBasket.DataBind();
            }
        }
    }
}
```

The view implementation is straightforward and matches the other views that you have created up to this point.

With all the views created, you now need to configure StructureMap to register all the dependences of the presenters. Add a new class to the UI.Web project named BootStrapper and update it to match the code listing that follows:

```
...
using StructureMap;
using StructureMap.Configuration.DSL;
using ASPPatterns.Chap8.MVP.Model;
using ASPPatterns.Chap8.MVP.Presentation.Navigation;
```

```
using ASPPatterns.Chap8.MVP.StubRepository;
using ASPPatterns.Chap8.MVP.Presentation;
using ASPPatterns.Chap8.MVP.Presentation.Basket;

namespace ASPPatterns.Chap8.MVP.UI.Web
{
    public class BootStrapper
    {
        public static void ConfigureDependencies()
        {
            // Initialize the registry
            ObjectFactory.Initialize(x =>
            {
                x.AddRegistry<ControllerRegistry>();

            });
        }

        public class ControllerRegistry : Registry
        {
            public ControllerRegistry()
            {
                ForRequestedType<ICategoryRepository>()
                    .TheDefault.Is.OfConcreteType<CategoryRepository>();
                ForRequestedType<IProductRepository>()
                    .TheDefault.Is.OfConcreteType<ProductRepository>();
                ForRequestedType<IPageNavigator>()
                    .TheDefault.Is.OfConcreteType<PageNavigator>();
                ForRequestedType<IBasket>()
                    .TheDefault.Is.OfConcreteType<WebBasket>();
            }
        }
    }
}
```

The class defines the concrete types to be used when creating the `ProductService`.

`ConfigureDependencies` is called when the application starts for the first time, so it makes sense to call it within the `Application_Start` event. Add a `Global.asax` file if one does not already exist, and add the following method call to the `Application_Start` event.

```
public class Global : System.Web.HttpApplication
{
    protected void Application_Start(object sender, EventArgs e)
    {
        BootStrapper.ConfigureDependencies();
    }
}
```

The final task is to update the code behind of the `Default.aspx` page created by Visual Studio so that it redirects to the `Index.aspx` page within the `Home` folder, as can be seen here:

```
public partial class _Default : System.Web.UI.Page
{
```

```
        protected void Page_Load(object sender, EventArgs e)
        {
            Response.Redirect("/Views/Home/Index.aspx");
        }
    }
```

Your solution should now resemble Figure 8-2.

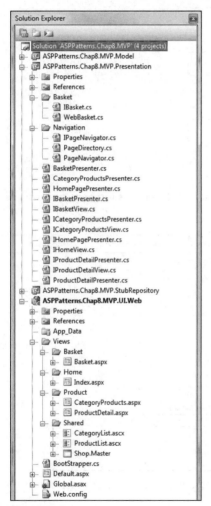

FIGURE 8-2

With the solution complete, you can now set the `UI.Web` project as the startup project and press F5 or run the debugger to browse the product catalog.

Figure 8-3 shows an updated version of the Model-View-Presenter diagram that you saw at the beginning of this section so that you can see how the classes involved in the displaying of the product detail view relate to the Model-View-Presenter concepts.

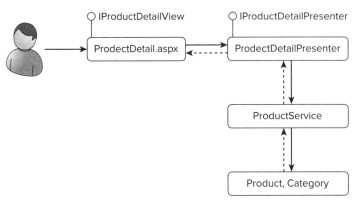

FIGURE 8-3

Figure 8-4 shows a sequence in the MVP pattern and how each of the classes interacts to form the pattern.

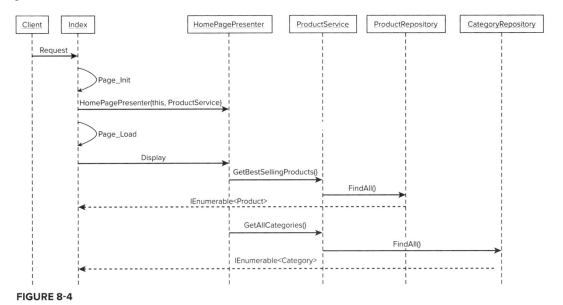

FIGURE 8-4

The Model-View-Presenter is a great pattern if you are sticking with the web forms model for ASP.NET development. You can typically find it within stateful windows client applications so it works well with the state full view generated by ASP.NET web forms.

The next pattern you will look at for your presentation needs is the Front Controller, which is at the heart of the Model-View-Controller pattern.

FRONT CONTROLLER

The Front Controller acts as the initial point of contact for requests, centralizing all business functions and supporting infrastructure concerns such as authorization, security, and the rendering of views. The view in the Front Controller pattern is completely passive and is rendered by the command that handles the request. This ensures that little if any logic is contained within the views and certainly helps to avoid the code behind model supported out of the box by the web forms framework, which can lead to a muddle of concerns between your view and controller. Having a central controller detached from the views also helps to promote code reuse and the sharing of business logic. With presentation logic in one place, it becomes easy to change the actions of a request.

Figure 8-5 shows the chain of events in the life of the request when employing the Front Controller pattern. The request is sent to an `HttpHandler` which then forwards it to the Front Controller. The Front Controller has a registry of web commands and searches for one that matches the request. When the `WebCommand` is found, it processes the request and performs any business logic required before navigating to the view that the client renders.

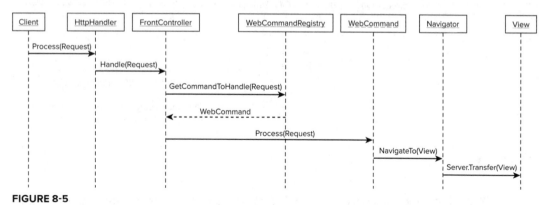

FIGURE 8-5

In this section, you walk through an exercise that creates a Front Controller first using the Command pattern and then an alternative version using the Chain of Responsibility pattern.

Command Pattern

The Command pattern defines an object that represents a method, encapsulating all the information needed to call it at a later time.

Intent

The Command pattern is most useful when dealing with a request that you have no prior knowledge of what operation to perform in response to it. There are four parts to the Command pattern: the client, the invoker, the receiver, and of course the command.

The client instantiates the command object and provides it with a receiver object to handle a request. An invoker then obtains the command, referencing it via its interface, and invokes its execute method, which in turn calls into the receiver's specific method to handle the request.

UML

Figure 8-6 shows the UML representation of the Command pattern and all the collaborating roles based on the Front Controller pattern that you will be creating next.

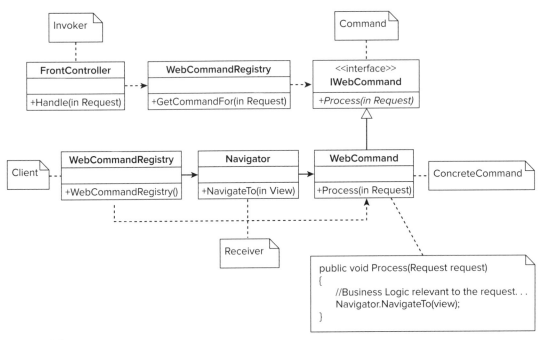

FIGURE 8-6

➤ The `IWebCommand` interface (command) declares an interface for executing an operation.

➤ The `WebCommand` (ConcreteCommand) is an implementation of the `IWebCommand` interface. The `WebCommand` requires a `Navigator` object (receiver), to which it will invoke the corresponding operation(s) on the receiver.

➤ The `Navigator` (receiver) object knows how to handle the request — in this instance, which view to create.

➤ The `WebCommandRegistry` (client) creates a collection of `WebCommand` objects and provides the receiver at creation time.

➤ The `FrontController` (invoker) uses the `WebCommandRegistry` to obtain a `WebCommand` to process the request and in turn asks the `WebCommand` to carry out the request by invoking the `Process` method.

Code Example

The exercise you will now work through is based on an implementation that J.P. Boodhoo (http://www.jpboodhoo.com/) showed me on his excellent .NET boot camp. If you have the opportunity, take the course. You will build the set of classes as shown in figure 8-5 that was featured at the start of this section.

Create a new solution named `ASPPatterns.Chap8.FrontController` and add to it the following class library projects:

➤   `ASPPatterns.Chap8.FrontController.Controller`

➤   `ASPPatterns.Chap8.FrontController.Model`

➤   `ASPPatterns.Chap8.FrontController.StubRepository`

Next, add a web application project named `ASPPatterns.Chap8.FrontController.UI.Web`. With the solution projects in place, you can now set up the project dependencies. Right-click on the `Controller` project and add a reference to the `Model` and `StubRepository` project. Also add a reference to the `System.Web` assembly. Right-click on the `StubRepository` and add a reference to the `Model` project. Finally, right-click on the `UI.Web` project and add a reference to the `Model` and `Controller` projects. You also need to add a reference to the `StructureMap.dll` for the `Controller` project.

You can copy all the code from the `Model` and `StubRepository` projects that you created for the Model-View-Presenter exercise earlier in the chapter, because this exercise uses the same domain mode.

From the `Controller` project, create the following folders: `ActionCommands`, `Navigation`, `Request`, `Routing`, `Storage`, and `WebCommands`.

The first set of classes you will create will deal with the storage of data generated from the Front Controller and to be used on the view. Create a new interface named `IViewStorage` within the `Storage` folder with the following contract:

```
public interface IViewStorage
{
    void Add(ViewStorageKeys key, object value);

    object Get(ViewStorageKeys key);
}
```

Create a default implementation of this interface named `ViewStorage` with the following code listing:

```
...
using System.Web;

public class ViewStorage : IViewStorage
{
    public void Add(ViewStorageKeys key, object value)
    {
        HttpContext.Current.Items.Add(key.ToString(), value);
```

```
            }

        public object Get(ViewStorageKeys key)
        {
            return HttpContext.Current.Items[key.ToString()];
        }
    }
```

The controller will use this `ViewStorage` class to store the `Model` data pulled from the `ProductService`, and the view will use it via a factory class that you will build next to populate the `.aspx` and `.ascx` pages.

Create the `ViewStorageFactory` class that the views will use, and update it to match the code definition that follows:

```
    public class ViewStorageFactory
    {
        public static IViewStorage GetStorage()
        {
            return new ViewStorage();
        }
    }
```

The last class to support the storage of `Model` data is the `ViewStorageKeys` enumeration class. Create the enumeration and amend it to match the code listing shown here:

```
    public enum ViewStorageKeys
    {
        Categories,
        Category,
        Products,
        Product
    }
```

The enumeration ensures that your code isn't littered with magic strings that can be misspelled and cause run-time errors.

The view storage framework will be used to pass data to the .ASPX view as shown in the following code snippet.

```
    <% Product product = (Product)ViewStorageFactory.GetStorage()
                                   .Get(ViewStorageKeys.Product); %>

    <h2><%=product.Name %></h2>
    <p>pay: <%=String.Format("{0:C}", product.Price)%></p>
    <p><%=product.Description %></p>
```

The next section of code to create deals with navigation. The enumeration of available pages will be catered for first. Add a new class to the `Navigation` folder named `PageDirectory`, as shown here:

```
    public enum PageDirectory
    {
        Home,
        CategoryProducts,
        ProductDetail,
```

```
        MissingPage
    }
```

Add a new interface to the `Navigation` folder named `IPageNavigator`, as shown next. You will use the `IPageNavigator` to navigate to the view after the controller handles the request.

```
public interface IPageNavigator
{
    void NavigateTo(PageDirectory page);
}
```

Next, add an implementation of the `IPageNavigator` named `PageNavigator` with the following definition:

```
...
using System.Web;

namespace ASPPatterns.Chap8.FrontController.Controller.Navigation
{
    public class PageNavigator : ASPPatterns.Chap8.FrontController
                                .Controller.Navigation.IPageNavigator
    {
        public void NavigateTo(PageDirectory page)
        {
            switch (page)
            {
                case PageDirectory.Home:
                    HttpContext.Current.Server.Transfer("~/views/Home/Index.aspx");
                    break;
                case PageDirectory.ProductDetail:
                    HttpContext.Current
                        .Server.Transfer("~/views/Product/ProductDetail.aspx");
                    break;
                case PageDirectory.CategoryProducts:
                    HttpContext.Current
                        .Server.Transfer("~/views/Product/CategoryProducts.aspx");
                    break;
                case PageDirectory.MissingPage:
                    HttpContext.Current.Server.Transfer("~/views/Shared/404.aspx");
                    break;
            }
        }
    }
}
```

The `PageNavigator` serves the ASPX view that corresponds to the `PageDirectory` enumeration.

The third set of classes you will create deals with the function of creating requests from the HTTP context. Add a new class to the `Request` folder named `Argument`. This class will represent the query string parameter passed to the view:

```
...
using System.Collections.Specialized;

namespace ASPPatterns.Chap8.FrontController.Controller.Request
```

```
{
    public class Argument<T>
    {
        private string _key;

        public Argument(string key)
        {
            _key = key;
        }

        public string Key
        {
            get { return _key; }
        }

        public T ExtractFrom(NameValueCollection queryArguments)
        {
            try
            {
                return (T)Convert.ChangeType(queryArguments[_key], typeof(T));
            }
            catch
            {
                return default(T);
            }
        }
    }
}
```

You use the ExtractFrom method to obtain the value of the key from the queryArguments NameValue Collection. This collection is populated from the Request.QueryString NameValueCollection, which you will see later.

Add a second class named ActionArguments to the Request folder to act as a read-only collection of available arguments for the controller to process.

```
public class ActionArguments
{
    public static readonly Argument<int> CategoryId =
                            new Argument<int>("categoryId");
    public static readonly Argument<int> ProductId =
                            new Argument<int>("productId");
}
```

The next class to add represents the request itself. Add a new class named WebRequest to the Request folder with the following definition:

```
...
using System.Collections.Specialized;

namespace ASPPatterns.Chap8.FrontController.Controller.Request
{
    public class WebRequest
    {
        public string RequestedURL { get; set; }
```

```
                    public NameValueCollection QueryArguments { get; set; }
        }
}
```

The `WebRequest` class contains a `RequestedURL` property that can hold the URL and a `NameValue` `Collection` of query arguments to be populated by the query string parameters.

A factory will convert the HttpContext URL into a `WebRequest`. Before you add the class, you need to create the interface. Add a new interface named `IWebRequestFactory` with the following code contract:

```
...
using System.Web;

namespace ASPPatterns.Chap8.FrontController.Controller.Request
{
    public interface IWebRequestFactory
    {
        WebRequest CreateFrom(HttpContext context);
    }
}
```

Now add a class to implement the `IWebRequestFactory` named `WebRequestFactory`, as shown here:

```
...
using System.Web;

namespace ASPPatterns.Chap8.FrontController.Controller.Request
{
    public class WebRequestFactory : IWebRequestFactory
    {
        public WebRequest CreateFrom(HttpContext context)
        {
            WebRequest webrequest = new WebRequest();
            webrequest.RequestedURL = context.Request.Url.ToString();
            webrequest.QueryArguments = context.Request.QueryString;

            return webrequest;
        }
    }
}
```

The `WebRequestFactory` creates a new `WebRequest` and populates its properties with the content of the current HTTP context.

This completes the `Requests` section of code. Now you can turn your attention to routing requests to the correct command. Add a new class in the `Routing` folder named `Route`, and update it to match the code listing shown here:

```
...
using ASPPatterns.Chap8.FrontController.Controller.Request;

namespace ASPPatterns.Chap8.FrontController.Controller.Routing
{
    public class Route
```

```
    {
        private string _route;

        public Route(string route)
        {
            _route = route;
        }

        public bool Matches(WebRequest request)
        {
            return request.RequestedURL.ToLower().Contains(_route.ToLower());
        }

        public string URL
        {
            get { return _route; }
        }
    }
}
```

The `Route` class takes a string route in the constructor and uses it within the `Matches` method to compare to a `WebRequest` to check. A command will use the `Route` class to determine whether it should handle the request.

The second class to add to the `Routing` folder is named `Routes`, and it will hold a read-only collection of valid routes. The code for this class follows:

```
    ...
    public class Routes
    {
        public static readonly Route Home = new Route("/Home.catalog");
        public static readonly Route CategoryProducts = new Route("/Products.catalog");
        public static readonly Route ProductDetail = new Route("/Product.catalog");
    }
```

With all the framework code created, you can start to add the commands that will perform the actions dependent on the view you requested. As with all the classes in this solution, you will start with an interface. Add a new interface to the `ActionCommands` folder named `IActionCommand`, with the contract as detailed here:

```
    ...
    using ASPPatterns.Chap8.FrontController.Controller.Request;

    namespace ASPPatterns.Chap8.FrontController.Controller.ActionCommands
    {
        public interface IActionCommand
        {
            void Process(WebRequest webRequest);
        }
    }
```

You will use the `IActionCommand` interface to create discrete actions that web commands can utilize to build the data for a view.

The first concrete action you will create is for populating the view storage with the best-selling products. Add a new class named GetTopSellingProductsCommand to the ActionCommands folder and have it implement the IActionCommand, as can be seen in the code that follows:

```
...
using ASPPatterns.Chap8.FrontController.Controller.Storage;
using ASPPatterns.Chap8.FrontController.Model;
using ASPPatterns.Chap8.FrontController.Controller.Request;

namespace ASPPatterns.Chap8.FrontController.Controller.ActionCommands
{
    public class GetTopSellingProductsCommand : IActionCommand
    {
        private IViewStorage _storage;
        private ProductService _productService;

        public GetTopSellingProductsCommand(IViewStorage storage,
                                        ProductService productService)
        {
            _storage = storage;
            _productService = productService;
        }

        public void Process(WebRequest webRequest)
        {
            _storage.Add(ViewStorageKeys.Products,
                            _productService.GetBestSellingProducts());
        }
    }
}
```

The sole responsibility of the GetTopSellingProductsCommand is to populate the ViewStorage with a list of best-selling products via the ProductService.

The next ActionCommand to create is obtaining a category via its ID. Add a new class to the Action Commands folder named GetCategoryCommand, and update it to match the code listing shown here:

```
...
using ASPPatterns.Chap8.FrontController.Controller.Storage;
using ASPPatterns.Chap8.FrontController.Model;
using ASPPatterns.Chap8.FrontController.Controller.Request;

namespace ASPPatterns.Chap8.FrontController.Controller.ActionCommands
{
    public class GetCategoryCommand : IActionCommand
    {
        private IViewStorage _storage;
        private ProductService _productService;

        public GetCategoryCommand(IViewStorage storage, ProductService productService)
        {
            _storage = storage;
            _productService = productService;
        }
```

```
                }

                public void Process(WebRequest webRequest)
                {
                    int categoryId =
                        ActionArguments.CategoryId.ExtractFrom(webRequest.QueryArguments);

                    Category category = _productService.GetCategoryBy(categoryId);

                    _storage.Add(ViewStorageKeys.Category, category);
                }

            }
        }
```

The GetCategoryCommand class uses the CategoryId ActionArgument to convert the CategoryId within the QueryArguments into an integer for use with the ProductService's GetCategoryBy method to obtain the corresponding Category before adding it to the ViewStorage.

The third command to create is the GetCategoryListCommand, which is responsible for obtaining and storing a list of categories. You can view the code to this class here:

```
...
using ASPPatterns.Chap8.FrontController.Model;
using ASPPatterns.Chap8.FrontController.Controller.Storage;
using ASPPatterns.Chap8.FrontController.Controller.Request;

namespace ASPPatterns.Chap8.FrontController.Controller.ActionCommands
{
    public class GetCategoryListCommand : IActionCommand
    {
        private IViewStorage _storage;
        private ProductService _productService;

        public GetCategoryListCommand(IViewStorage storage,
                                      ProductService productService)
        {
            _storage = storage;
            _productService = productService;
        }

        public void Process(WebRequest webRequest)
        {
            _storage.Add(ViewStorageKeys.Categories,
                    _productService.GetAllCategories());
        }
    }
}
```

The fourth ActionCommand deals with obtaining the collection of products relating to a specific category. Create a new class for this ActionCommand named GetCategoryProductsCommand and modify it to match the code listing that follows:

```
...
using ASPPatterns.Chap8.FrontController.Model;
```

```
using ASPPatterns.Chap8.FrontController.Controller.Storage;
using ASPPatterns.Chap8.FrontController.Controller.Request;

namespace ASPPatterns.Chap8.FrontController.Controller.ActionCommands
{
    public class GetCategoryProductsCommand : IActionCommand
    {
        private IViewStorage _storage;
        private ProductService _productService;

        public GetCategoryProductsCommand(IViewStorage storage,
                                          ProductService productService)
        {
            _storage = storage;
            _productService = productService;
        }

        public void Process(WebRequest webRequest)
        {
            int categoryId =
                    ActionArguments.CategoryId.ExtractFrom(webRequest.QueryArguments);

            _storage.Add(ViewStorageKeys.Products,
                        _productService.GetAllProductsIn(categoryId));
        }
    }
}
```

The final `ActionCommand` is responsible for obtaining and storing a `Product` with a given `ProductId`. Add a new class named `GetProductDetailCommand`, and update it to match the code listing that follows:

```
...
using ASPPatterns.Chap8.FrontController.Controller.Storage;
using ASPPatterns.Chap8.FrontController.Model;
using ASPPatterns.Chap8.FrontController.Controller.Request;

namespace ASPPatterns.Chap8.FrontController.Controller.ActionCommands
{
    public class GetProductDetailCommand : IActionCommand
    {
        private IViewStorage _storage;
        private ProductService _productService;

        public GetProductDetailCommand(IViewStorage storage,
                                       ProductService productService)
        {
            _storage = storage;
            _productService = productService;
        }

        public void Process(WebRequest webRequest)
        {
            int productId =
```

```
                            ActionArguments.ProductId.ExtractFrom(webRequest.QueryArguments);

                    _storage.Add(ViewStorageKeys.Product,
                                _productService.GetProductBy(productId));
                }
            }
        }
```

Now that you have defined all the discrete ActionCommands, you need to define a web command that brings together the routes and a collection of ActionCommands that will be used to handle requests. The WebCommand implements an interface named IWebCommand. Create the IWebCommand interface within the WebCommands folder, and amend the contract to match the following code listing:

```
...
using ASPPatterns.Chap8.FrontController.Controller.Request;

namespace ASPPatterns.Chap8.FrontController.Controller.WebCommands
{
    public interface IWebCommand
    {
        Boolean CanHandle(WebRequest webRequest);
        void Process(WebRequest webRequest);
    }
}
```

With the contract defined, you can now create an implementation. Add a new class to the WebCommands folder named WebCommand, and update it to match the code definition found here:

```
...
using ASPPatterns.Chap8.FrontController.Controller.ActionCommands;
using ASPPatterns.Chap8.FrontController.Controller.Storage;
using ASPPatterns.Chap8.FrontController.Model;
using ASPPatterns.Chap8.FrontController.Controller.Navigation;
using ASPPatterns.Chap8.FrontController.Controller.Routing;
using ASPPatterns.Chap8.FrontController.Controller.Request;

namespace ASPPatterns.Chap8.FrontController.Controller.WebCommands
{
    public class WebCommand : IWebCommand
    {
        private IPageNavigator _navigator;
        private List<IActionCommand> _actionCommands;
        private Route _route;
        private PageDirectory _page;

        public WebCommand(IPageNavigator navigator,
                        List<IActionCommand> actionCommands,
                        Route route, PageDirectory page)
        {
            _navigator = navigator;
            _actionCommands = actionCommands;
            _route = route;
            _page = page;
```

```
        }

        public bool CanHandle(WebRequest webRequest)
        {
            return _route.Matches(webRequest);
        }

        public void Process(WebRequest webRequest)
        {
            _actionCommands.ForEach(cmd => cmd.Process(webRequest));
            _navigator.NavigateTo(_page);
        }
    }
}
```

The `WebCommand` takes an instance of an `IPageNavigator`, a collection of `IActionCommands`, a `Route`, and a `PageDirectory` enumeration. The `WebCommand` utilizes the route to determine if it can handle the request; if so, it executes all the `IActionCommands` and then navigates to the correct page to display.

To create the list of `WebCommands`, you need to use a command registry. Add a new interface to the `WebCommands` folder named `IWebCommandRegistry`, and update it to match the interface shown here:

```
...
using ASPPatterns.Chap8.FrontController.Controller.Request;

namespace ASPPatterns.Chap8.FrontController.Controller.WebCommands
{
    public interface IWebCommandRegistry
    {
        IWebCommand GetCommandFor(WebRequest webRequest);
    }
}
```

Next, create an implementation of the `IWebCommandRegistry` named `WebCommandRegistry`, as shown in the code listing that follows:

```
...
using ASPPatterns.Chap8.FrontController.Model;
using ASPPatterns.Chap8.FrontController.Controller.Request;
using ASPPatterns.Chap8.FrontController.Controller.Navigation;
using ASPPatterns.Chap8.FrontController.Controller.ActionCommands;
using StructureMap;
using ASPPatterns.Chap8.FrontController.Controller.Routing;

namespace ASPPatterns.Chap8.FrontController.Controller.WebCommands
{
    public class WebCommandRegistry : IWebCommandRegistry
    {
        private IList<IWebCommand> _webCommands = new List<IWebCommand>();

        public WebCommandRegistry()
        {
            _webCommands.Add(CreateGetCategoryProductsCommand());
```

```
        _webCommands.Add(CreateGetHomePageCommand());
        _webCommands.Add(CreateGetProductDetailCommand());
}

public IWebCommand GetCommandFor(WebRequest webRequest)
{
        return _webCommands.FirstOrDefault(wc => wc.CanHandle(webRequest)) ??
            new Display404PageCommand(
                    ObjectFactory.GetInstance<IPageNavigator>());
}

public IWebCommand CreateGetCategoryProductsCommand()
{
        List<IActionCommand> _categoryProductsActionCommands =
                                    new List<IActionCommand>();
        _categoryProductsActionCommands.Add(
                ObjectFactory.GetInstance<GetCategoryListCommand>());
        _categoryProductsActionCommands.Add(
                ObjectFactory.GetInstance<GetCategoryProductsCommand>());
        _categoryProductsActionCommands.Add(
                ObjectFactory.GetInstance<GetCategoryCommand>());

        return new WebCommand(
                ObjectFactory.GetInstance<IPageNavigator>(),
                _categoryProductsActionCommands,
                Routes.CategoryProducts,
                PageDirectory.CategoryProducts);
}

public IWebCommand CreateGetHomePageCommand()
{
    List<IActionCommand> _homePageActionCommands = new List<IActionCommand>();
     _homePageActionCommands.Add(
                ObjectFactory.GetInstance<GetCategoryListCommand>());
     _homePageActionCommands.Add(
                ObjectFactory.GetInstance<GetTopSellingProductsCommand>());

        return new WebCommand(
              ObjectFactory.GetInstance<IPageNavigator>(),
              _homePageActionCommands,
              Routes.Home,
              PageDirectory.Home);
}

public IWebCommand CreateGetProductDetailCommand()
{
        List<IActionCommand> _productDetailActionCommands =
                                    new List<IActionCommand>();
        _productDetailActionCommands.Add(
                ObjectFactory.GetInstance<GetCategoryListCommand>());
        _productDetailActionCommands.Add(
                ObjectFactory.GetInstance<GetProductDetailCommand>());

        return new WebCommand(
              ObjectFactory.GetInstance<IPageNavigator>(),
```

```
                           _productDetailActionCommands,
                           Routes.ProductDetail,
                           PageDirectory.ProductDetail);
                  }
          }
  }
```

Code snippet WebCommandRegistry.cs in project ASPPatterns.Chap8.FrontController.Controller

---

Here's a breakdown of what the `WebCommandRegistry` is doing. Within the constructor, the various commands to handle each request of the product browsing catalog are created. If you take `CreateGet CategoryProductsCommand` as an example first, a list of discrete `IActionCommands` is created that are relevant to the `WebCommand`. Then the `WebCommand` is created with the correct corresponding `Route` and `PageDirectory`, and the `StructureMap ObjectFactory` is used to resolve dependencies of the `WebCommand`. The `GetCommandFor` method searches for a `WebCommand` that can satisfy the `WebRequest`. If it cannot find one, a default `Display404PageCommand` is returned, which is the class that you will create next.

The role of `Display404PageCommand` is to redirect the customer to an error page in the event of a matching `WebCommand` not being found to handle the `WebRequest`. Add a new class to the `WebCommands` folder named `Display404PageCommand`, and update it with the code listing that follows:

```
...
using ASPPatterns.Chap8.FrontController.Controller.Navigation;
using ASPPatterns.Chap8.FrontController.Controller.Request;

namespace ASPPatterns.Chap8.FrontController.Controller.WebCommands
{
    public class Display404PageCommand : IWebCommand
    {
        private IPageNavigator _navigator;

        public Display404PageCommand(IPageNavigator navigator)
        {
            _navigator = navigator;
        }

        public bool CanHandle(WebRequest webRequest)
        {
            return true;
        }

        public void Process(WebRequest webRequest)
        {
            _navigator.NavigateTo(PageDirectory.MissingPage);
        }
    }
}
```

You can now create the Front Controller. Add a new class to the root of the `Controllers` project named `FrontController` with the following code definition:

```
...
using ASPPatterns.Chap8.FrontController.Controller.WebCommands;
```

```
using ASPPatterns.Chap8.FrontController.Controller.Request;

namespace ASPPatterns.Chap8.FrontController.Controller
{
    public class FrontController
    {
        IWebCommandRegistry _webCommandRegistry;

        public FrontController(IWebCommandRegistry webCommandRegistry)
        {
            _webCommandRegistry = webCommandRegistry;
        }

        public void handle(WebRequest request)
        {
            _webCommandRegistry.GetCommandFor(request).Process(request);
        }
    }
}
```

The `FrontController` is a simple class that takes an instance of an `IWebCommandRegistry` and uses it to search for an `IWebCommand` to process the `WebRequest`.

The last major class to create is the custom implementation of the `IHttpHandler`. Add a new class to the root of the `Controller` project named `CustomHttpHandler`, with the following code listing:

```
...
using System.Web;
using ASPPatterns.Chap8.FrontController.Controller.Request;
using StructureMap;

namespace ASPPatterns.Chap8.FrontController.Controller
{
    public class CustomHTTPHandler : IHttpHandler
    {
        public void ProcessRequest(HttpContext context)
        {
            ObjectFactory.GetInstance<FrontController>()
                .handle(ObjectFactory.GetInstance<IWebRequestFactory>()
                .CreateFrom(context));
        }

        public bool IsReusable
        {
            get { return true; }
        }
    }
}
```

`StructureMaps ObjectFactory` is used within the `ProcessRequest` method to obtain an instance of the `FrontController`, which is used in turn to handle a `WebRequest` created by an implementation of an `IWebRequestFactory`, which again is resolved by `StructureMaps ObjectFactory`.

You will need a couple of supporting classes to create within the `Controller` project. The first is the dependencies set up to configure `StructureMap`. Add a new class to the root of the `Controller` project named `BootStrapper` with the following code definition:

```
...
using ASPPatterns.Chap8.FrontController.Controller.ActionCommands;
using ASPPatterns.Chap8.FrontController.Controller.Storage;
using ASPPatterns.Chap8.FrontController.StubRepository;
using ASPPatterns.Chap8.FrontController.Model;
using ASPPatterns.Chap8.FrontController.Controller.WebCommands;
using ASPPatterns.Chap8.FrontController.Controller.Navigation;
using ASPPatterns.Chap8.FrontController.Controller.Routing;
using StructureMap;
using StructureMap.Configuration.DSL;
using ASPPatterns.Chap8.FrontController.Controller.Request;

namespace ASPPatterns.Chap8.FrontController.Controller
{
    public class BootStrapper
    {
        public static void ConfigureDependencies()
        {
            ObjectFactory.Initialize(x =>
            {
                x.AddRegistry<ControllerRegistry>();

            });
        }

        public class ControllerRegistry : Registry
        {
            public ControllerRegistry()
            {
                ForRequestedType<ICategoryRepository>()
                    .TheDefault.Is.OfConcreteType<CategoryRepository>();
                ForRequestedType<IProductRepository>()
                    .TheDefault.Is.OfConcreteType<ProductRepository>();
                ForRequestedType<IViewStorage>()
                    .TheDefault.Is.OfConcreteType<ViewStorage>();
                ForRequestedType<IPageNavigator>()
                    .TheDefault.Is.OfConcreteType<PageNavigator>();
                ForRequestedType<IWebCommandRegistry>()
                    .TheDefault.Is.OfConcreteType<WebCommandRegistry>();
                ForRequestedType<IWebRequestFactory>()
                    .TheDefault.Is.OfConcreteType<WebRequestFactory>();
            }
        }
    }
}
```

The `BootStrapper` class just hooks up the dependencies of the solution, as you have seen before in other exercises within this chapter.

The second supporting class to create is assisting in the creation of URLs for the views. Add a new class to the root of the `Controller` project named `URLHelper` with the following code listing:

```
...
using ASPPatterns.Chap8.FrontController.Model;
using ASPPatterns.Chap8.FrontController.Controller.Routing;
using ASPPatterns.Chap8.FrontController.Controller.Request;

namespace ASPPatterns.Chap8.FrontController.Controller
{
    public static class UrlHelper
    {
        public static string BuildHomePageLink()
        {
            return Routes.Home.URL;
        }

        public static string BuildProductDetailLinkFor(Product product)
        {
            return Routes.ProductDetail.URL + "?" +
                        ActionArguments.ProductId.Key + "=" + product.Id;
        }

        public static string BuildProductCategoryLinkFor(Category category)
        {
            return Routes.CategoryProducts.URL + "?" +
                        ActionArguments.CategoryId.Key + "=" + category.Id;
        }
    }
}
```

This completes the `Controller` project. Your project should now resemble the solution in Figure 8-7.

To complete this exercise, turn your attention to the `UI.Web` project. Create a folder within the `UI.Web` project named `Views`, and add three folders to this folder named `Home`, `Product`, and `Shared`.

Add a new user control to the `Shared` folder named `CategoryList.ascx` with the following markup:

```
<%@ Control Language="C#" AutoEventWireup="true" CodeBehind="CategoryList.ascx.cs"
    Inherits="ASPPatterns.Chap8.FrontController.UI.Web.Views.Shared.CategoryList"
%>
<%@ Import Namespace="System.Collections.Generic"%>
<%@ Import Namespace="ASPPatterns.Chap8.FrontController.Model"%>
<%@ Import Namespace="ASPPatterns.Chap8.FrontController.Controller"%>
<%@ Import Namespace="ASPPatterns.Chap8.FrontController.Controller.Storage"%>

    <ul>
    <% foreach (Category cat in (IEnumerable<Category>)
                    ViewStorageFactory.GetStorage().Get(ViewStorageKeys.Categories))
    {%>
        <li>
        <a href="<%=UrlHelper.BuildProductCategoryLinkFor(cat)%>"><%=cat.Name%></a>
        </li>
    <%} %>
    </ul>
```

FIGURE 8-7

As you can see, the `CategoryList.ascx` control uses the `ViewStorageFactory` class defined in the `Controllers` project to retrieve the data for it to display. This pattern is used for all the ASPX/ASCX views in the `UI.Web` project.

Add a second user control to the `Shared` folder named `ProductList.ascx`. Again, modify the markup to match the code that follows:

```
<%@ Control Language="C#" AutoEventWireup="true" CodeBehind="ProductList.ascx.cs"
         Inherits="ASPPatterns.Chap8.FrontController.UI.Web.Views.Shared.ProductList"
%>
<%@ Import Namespace="System.Collections.Generic"%>
<%@ Import Namespace="ASPPatterns.Chap8.FrontController.Model"%>
<%@ Import Namespace="ASPPatterns.Chap8.FrontController.Controller"%>
<%@ Import Namespace="ASPPatterns.Chap8.FrontController.Controller.Storage"%>


    <% foreach (Product prod in (IEnumerable<Product>)
```

```
                            ViewStorageFactory.GetStorage().Get(ViewStorageKeys.Products))
    {%>
      <%=prod.Name%> only <%=String.Format("{0:C}", prod.Price)%><br />
      <a href="<%=UrlHelper.BuildProductDetailLinkFor(prod) %>">more information</a>
      <hr />
    <%} %>
```

Next, add a `MasterPage` to the `Shared` folder named `Shop.Master` with the markup displayed here:

```
<%@ Master Language="C#" AutoEventWireup="true" CodeBehind="Shop.master.cs"
        Inherits="ASPPatterns.Chap8.FrontController.UI.Web.Views.Shared.Shop" %>
<%@ Register src="CategoryList.ascx" tagname="CategoryList" tagprefix="uc1" %>
<%@ Import Namespace="ASPPatterns.Chap8.FrontController.Controller"%>

<!DOCTYPE html PUBLIC "-//W3C//DTD XHTML 1.0 Transitional//EN"
"http://www.w3.org/TR/xhtml1/DTD/xhtml1-transitional.dtd">

<html xmlns="http://www.w3.org/1999/xhtml" >
<head runat="server">
    <title></title>
</head>
<body>
    <form id="form1" runat="server">
    <div>
        <table width="70%">
            <tr>
                <td colspan="2">
                <h2><a href="<%=UrlHelper.BuildHomePageLink() %>">Scotts Shop</a></h2>
                <hr /></td>
            </tr>
            <tr>
                <td valign="top" width="15%">
                    <uc1:CategoryList ID="CategoryList1" runat="server" /></td>
                <td valign="top" width="85%">
                 <asp:ContentPlaceHolder ID="ContentPlaceHolder1" runat="server" />
                </td>
            </tr>
        </table>
    </div>
    </form>
</body>
</html>
```

Then add a page to be displayed if a `WebCommand` cannot be found to handle the `WebRequest`. Name it `404.aspx`, and update the markup with the code definition shown here:

```
<%@ Page Language="C#" AutoEventWireup="true" CodeBehind="404.aspx.cs"
        Inherits="ASPPatterns.Chap8.FrontController.UI.Web.Views.Shared._04" %>
<%@ Import Namespace="ASPPatterns.Chap8.FrontController.Controller"%>

<!DOCTYPE html PUBLIC "-//W3C//DTD XHTML 1.0 Transitional//EN"
"http://www.w3.org/TR/xhtml1/DTD/xhtml1-transitional.dtd">

<html xmlns="http://www.w3.org/1999/xhtml" >
<head runat="server">
```

```
        <title></title>
    </head>
    <body>
        <form id="form1" runat="server">
        <div>
        <h2>Sorry</h2>
        We couldn't find the page you were after, please navigate back to the
        <a href="<%=UrlHelper.BuildHomePageLink() %>">home page</a>.
        </div>
        </form>
    </body>
    </html>
```

For the home page view, add a new web form named Index.aspx to the Home folder, and amend the markup to match that shown here:

```
<%@ Page Title="" Language="C#" MasterPageFile="~/views/Shared/Shop.Master"
        AutoEventWireup="true" CodeBehind="Index.aspx.cs"
        Inherits="ASPPatterns.Chap8.FrontController.UI.Web.Views.Home.Index" %>
<%@ Register src="~/views/Shared/ProductList.ascx" tagname="ProductList"
    tagprefix="uc1" %>

<asp:Content ID="Content2" ContentPlaceHolderID="ContentPlaceHolder1" runat="server">
    <h2>Today's Top Products</h2>
    <uc1:ProductList ID="ProductList1" runat="server" />
</asp:Content>
```

For the category products view, add a new web form named CategoryProducts.aspx to the Product folder with the markup displayed here:

```
<%@ Page Title="" Language="C#" MasterPageFile="~/Views/Shared/Shop.Master"
        AutoEventWireup="true" CodeBehind="CategoryProducts.aspx.cs"
        Inherits="ASPPatterns.Chap8.FrontController.UI.Web.Views.Product.CategoryProducts"
%>
<%@ Register src="~/Views/Shared/ProductList.ascx" tagname="ProductList"
    tagprefix="uc1" %>
<%@ Import Namespace="ASPPatterns.Chap8.FrontController.Controller.Storage"%>
<%@ Import Namespace="ASPPatterns.Chap8.FrontController.Model"%>

<asp:Content ID="Content2" ContentPlaceHolderID="ContentPlaceHolder1" runat="server">
    <h2>All <%=((Category)ViewStorageFactory.GetStorage()
                        .Get(ViewStorageKeys.Category)).Name%></h2>
    <uc1:ProductList ID="ProductList1" runat="server" />
</asp:Content>
```

Lastly, for the detailed view of the product, add a new web form named ProductDetail.aspx to the Product folder, and update the markup to match that shown here:

```
<%@ Page Title="" Language="C#" MasterPageFile="~/Views/Shared/Shop.Master"
        AutoEventWireup="true" CodeBehind="ProductDetail.aspx.cs"
        Inherits="ASPPatterns.Chap8.FrontController.UI.Web.Views.Product.ProductDetail"
%>
<%@ Import Namespace="System.Collections.Generic"%>
<%@ Import Namespace="ASPPatterns.Chap8.FrontController.Model"%>
<%@ Import Namespace="ASPPatterns.Chap8.FrontController.Controller"%>
```

```
<%@ Import Namespace="ASPPatterns.Chap8.FrontController.Controller.Storage"%>

<asp:Content ID="Content2" ContentPlaceHolderID="ContentPlaceHolder1" runat="server">

<% Product product = (Product)ViewStorageFactory
                .GetStorage().Get(ViewStorageKeys.Product); %>

<h2><%=product.Name %></h2>
<p>pay: <%=String.Format("{0:C}", product.Price)%></p>
<p><%=product.Description %></p>

</asp:Content>
```

Switch to the code behind view of the Default.aspx page created by Visual Studio, and amend the Page_Load event to redirect the browser to the Home.Catalog page, as can be seen here:

```
public partial class Default : System.Web.UI.Page
{
    protected void Page_Load(object sender, EventArgs e)
    {
        Response.Redirect("Home.catalog");
    }
}
```

You also need to add a Global.asax file to the UI.Web project if one does not already exist to call the BootStrapper class on the Application_Start event. See the code that follows:

```
...
using ASPPatterns.Chap8.FrontController.Controller;

namespace ASPPatterns.Chap8.FrontController.UI.Web
{
    public class Global : System.Web.HttpApplication
    {
        protected void Application_Start(object sender, EventArgs e)
        {
            BootStrapper.ConfigureDependencies();
        }
    }
}
```

The last change you need to make to the UI.Web project is to register the CustomerHttpHandler you defined in the Controllers project within the Web.Config file. Open the Web.config file and amend it to include the next line:

```
...
<httpHandlers>
    <remove verb="*" path="*.asmx"/>

    <add verb="*" path="*.catalog" validate="false"
        type="ASPPatterns.Chap8.FrontController.Controller.CustomHTTPHandler,
                        ASPPatterns.Chap8.FrontController.Controller"/>

    ...
</httpHandlers>
...
```

You can now run the solution and browse the product catalog.

Chain of Responsibility Pattern

Another design pattern that you can use to handle a web request within the Front Controller is the Chain of Responsibility pattern.

Intent

The intent of the Change of Responsibility pattern is to avoid coupling the sender of a request to its receiver by giving more than one object a chance to handle the request. This is achieved by chaining together receiving objects and passing the request along the chain until an object is found that can handle it.

UML

Figure 8-8 shows the UML representation of the Change of Responsibility pattern and all the collaborating roles.

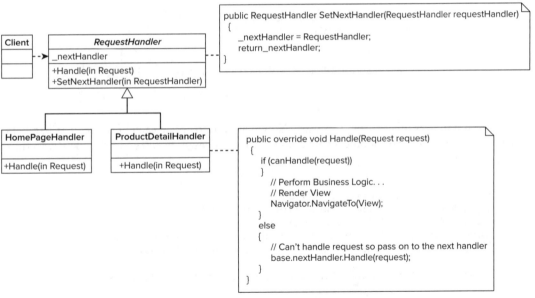

FIGURE 8-8

➤ The abstract class `RequestHandler` defines the interface for handling requests and provides a method named `SetNextHandler` to chain `RequestHandler`s.

➤ The `Client` invokes the `Handle` method referenced by the abstract `RequestHandler` class, and a concrete handler on the chain will handle the request.

➤ The `HomePageHandler` and `ProductDetailHandler` check if they can handle the request. If they can, they perform any action required; otherwise, the request is forwarded to the next `RequestHandler` down the chain.

Code Example

In this exercise, you modify the solution created in the previous section. In the code download, however, the solution to this section has been created under the solution `ASPPatterns.Chap8.CoR`.

To start this exercise, create a copy of the entire `ASPPatterns.Chap8.FrontController` project that you built in the previous section and add a new folder to the `Controller` project named `Handlers`.

Add a new abstract class to the `Handlers` folder named `RequestHandler` with the code listing as displayed here:

```
...
using ASPPatterns.Chap8.FrontController.Controller.Request;

namespace ASPPatterns.Chap8.FrontController.Controller.Handlers
{
    public abstract class RequestHandler
    {
        protected RequestHandler _nextHandler;

        public RequestHandler SetNextHandler(RequestHandler requestHandler)
        {
            _nextHandler = requestHandler;
            return _nextHandler;
        }

        public abstract void Handle(WebRequest request);
    }
}
```

All request handlers inherit from this class. Now you need to create each of the request handlers for each of the views. Start by adding a new class named `CategoryProductsPageHandler` with the code listing shown here:

```
...
using ASPPatterns.Chap8.FrontController.Model;
using ASPPatterns.Chap8.FrontController.Controller.Storage;
using ASPPatterns.Chap8.FrontController.Controller.Routing;
using ASPPatterns.Chap8.FrontController.Controller.Navigation;
using ASPPatterns.Chap8.FrontController.Controller.Request;

namespace ASPPatterns.Chap8.FrontController.Controller.Handlers
{
    public class CategoryProductsPageHandler : RequestHandler
    {
        private Route _route;
        private ProductService _productService;
        private IViewStorage _viewStorage;
        private IPageNavigator _pageNavigator;

        public CategoryProductsPageHandler(Route route, ProductService productService,
                                IViewStorage viewStorage,
                                IPageNavigator pageNavigator)
        {
            _route = route;
```

```
            _productService = productService;
            _viewStorage = viewStorage;
            _pageNavigator = pageNavigator;
        }

        public override void Handle(WebRequest request)
        {
            if (_route.Matches(request))
            {
                int categoryId =
                    ActionArguments.CategoryId.ExtractFrom(request.QueryArguments);

                IEnumerable<Category> categories = _productService.GetAllCategories();
                _viewStorage.Add(ViewStorageKeys.Categories, categories);

                Category category = _productService.GetCategoryBy(categoryId);
                _viewStorage.Add(ViewStorageKeys.Category, category);

                IEnumerable<Product> products =
                            _productService.GetAllProductsIn(categoryId);
                _viewStorage.Add(ViewStorageKeys.Products, products);

                _pageNavigator.NavigateTo(PageDirectory.CategoryProducts);
            }
            else
                base._nextHandler.Handle(request);
        }
    }
}
```

If the `Route` matches the `WebRequest`, the handler handles this request; otherwise, the `WebRequest` is passed on to the next handler for processing. Other than that, the code within the `Handle` method is the same as was contained in the various `IActionCommands` of the Command pattern example you created in the previous section.

You now need to create the remaining `RequestHandlers` for each of the views. Add another new class to the `Handlers` folder named `HomePageHandler` with the code definition that follows:

```
...
using ASPPatterns.Chap8.FrontController.Model;
using ASPPatterns.Chap8.FrontController.Controller.Storage;
using ASPPatterns.Chap8.FrontController.Controller.Routing;
using ASPPatterns.Chap8.FrontController.Controller.Navigation;
using ASPPatterns.Chap8.FrontController.Controller.Request;

namespace ASPPatterns.Chap8.FrontController.Controller.Handlers
{
    public class HomePageHandler : RequestHandler
    {
        private Route _route;
        private ProductService _productService;
        private IViewStorage _viewStorage;
        private IPageNavigator _pageNavigator;

        public HomePageHandler(Route route, ProductService productService,
```

```
                            IViewStorage viewStorage, IPageNavigator pageNavigator)
{
    _route = route;
    _productService = productService;
    _viewStorage = viewStorage;
    _pageNavigator = pageNavigator;
}

public override void Handle(WebRequest request)
{
    if (_route.Matches(request))
    {
        IEnumerable<Category> categories = _productService.GetAllCategories();
        _viewStorage.Add(ViewStorageKeys.Categories, categories);

        IEnumerable<Product> products =
                            _productService.GetBestSellingProducts();
        _viewStorage.Add(ViewStorageKeys.Products, products);

        _pageNavigator.NavigateTo(PageDirectory.Home);
    }
    else
        base._nextHandler.Handle(request);
    }
  }
}
```

Add another `RequestHandler` to the `Handlers` folder, this time to handle requests for the product detail view named `ProductDetailHandler` with the code as shown here:

```
...
using ASPPatterns.Chap8.FrontController.Model;
using ASPPatterns.Chap8.FrontController.Controller.Storage;
using ASPPatterns.Chap8.FrontController.Controller.Routing;
using ASPPatterns.Chap8.FrontController.Controller.Navigation;
using ASPPatterns.Chap8.FrontController.Controller.Request;

namespace ASPPatterns.Chap8.FrontController.Controller.Handlers
{
    public class ProductDetailPageHandler : RequestHandler
    {
        private Route _route;
        private ProductService _productService;
        private IViewStorage _viewStorage;
        private IPageNavigator _pageNavigator;

        public ProductDetailPageHandler(Route route, ProductService productService,
                                IViewStorage viewStorage,
                                IPageNavigator pageNavigator)
        {
            _route = route;
            _productService = productService;
            _viewStorage = viewStorage;
            _pageNavigator = pageNavigator;
```

```
        }

        public override void Handle(WebRequest request)
        {
            if (_route.Matches(request))
            {
                int productId =
                    ActionArguments.ProductId.ExtractFrom(request.QueryArguments);

                IEnumerable<Category> categories = _productService.GetAllCategories();
                _viewStorage.Add(ViewStorageKeys.Categories, categories);

                Product product = _productService.GetProductBy(productId);
                _viewStorage.Add(ViewStorageKeys.Product, product);

                _pageNavigator.NavigateTo(PageDirectory.ProductDetail);
            }
            else
                base._nextHandler.Handle(request);
        }
    }
}
```

Finally, add a `RequestHandler` that will catch requests not handled by a `RequestHandler`, name this class `PageNotFoundHandler`, and update it to match the code shown here:

```
...
using ASPPatterns.Chap8.FrontController.Model;
using ASPPatterns.Chap8.FrontController.Controller.Storage;
using ASPPatterns.Chap8.FrontController.Controller.Navigation;
using ASPPatterns.Chap8.FrontController.Controller.Request;

namespace ASPPatterns.Chap8.FrontController.Controller.Handlers
{
    public class PageNotFoundHandler : RequestHandler
    {
        private ProductService _productService;
        private IViewStorage _viewStorage;
        private IPageNavigator _pageNavigator;

        public PageNotFoundHandler(ProductService productService,
                                   IViewStorage viewStorage,
                                   IPageNavigator pageNavigator)
        {
            _productService = productService;
            _viewStorage = viewStorage;
            _pageNavigator = pageNavigator;
        }

        public override void Handle(WebRequest request)
        {
            _pageNavigator.NavigateTo(PageDirectory.MissingPage);
        }
    }
}
```

To build the Chain of Responsibility using the `RequestHandlers`, you require a factory class. First, define a contract for this class within the `Handlers` folder named `IHandlerFactory`, and amend the contract to match the interface listed next:

```
namespace ASPPatterns.Chap8.FrontController.Controller.Handlers
{
    public interface IHandlerFactory
    {
        RequestHandler GetHandlers();
    }
}
```

Now you can create the implementation of the `IHandlerFactory`. Add a new class to the `Handlers` folder named `HandlerFactory`, and amend the code to match the listing shown here:

```
...
using StructureMap;
using ASPPatterns.Chap8.FrontController.Controller.Routing;
using ASPPatterns.Chap8.FrontController.Model;
using ASPPatterns.Chap8.FrontController.Controller.Storage;
using ASPPatterns.Chap8.FrontController.Controller.Navigation;

namespace ASPPatterns.Chap8.FrontController.Controller.Handlers
{
    public class HandlerFactory : IHandlerFactory
    {
        public RequestHandler GetHandlers()
        {
            RequestHandler handler = GetHomePageHandler();

            handler
                .SetNextHandler(GetCategoryProductsPageHandler())
                .SetNextHandler(GetProductDetailPageHandler())
                .SetNextHandler(GetPageNotFoundHandler());

            return handler;
        }

        private RequestHandler GetPageNotFoundHandler()
        {
            return new PageNotFoundHandler(
                    ObjectFactory.GetInstance<ProductService>(),
                    ObjectFactory.GetInstance<IViewStorage>(),
                    ObjectFactory.GetInstance<IPageNavigator>());
        }

        private RequestHandler GetProductDetailPageHandler()
        {
            return new ProductDetailPageHandler(
                    Routes.ProductDetail,
                    ObjectFactory.GetInstance<ProductService>(),
                    ObjectFactory.GetInstance<IViewStorage>(),
                    ObjectFactory.GetInstance<IPageNavigator>());
```

```
        }

        private RequestHandler GetCategoryProductsPageHandler()
        {
            return new CategoryProductsPageHandler(
                        Routes.CategoryProducts,
                        ObjectFactory.GetInstance<ProductService>(),
                        ObjectFactory.GetInstance<IViewStorage>(),
                        ObjectFactory.GetInstance<IPageNavigator>());
        }

        private RequestHandler GetHomePageHandler()
        {
            return new HomePageHandler(
                        Routes.Home,
                        ObjectFactory.GetInstance<ProductService>(),
                        ObjectFactory.GetInstance<IViewStorage>(),
                        ObjectFactory.GetInstance<IPageNavigator>());
        }
    }

}
```

Code snippet HandlerFactory.cs in project ASPPatterns.Chap8.FrontController.Controller

The GetHandlers method constructs the chain of responsibility. Pay particular attention to the ordering of the handlers, ensuring that PageNotFoundHandler is added last because this handler always returns true for matching the request and simply navigates to the 404 page.

One of the last things that needs to be done is to amend the FrontController class to accept an instance of the IHandlerFactory rather than the IWebCommandRegistry, as was used in the previous section. The updated code for the FrontController class can be seen here:

```
...
using ASPPatterns.Chap8.FrontController.Controller.Handlers;
using ASPPatterns.Chap8.FrontController.Controller.Request;

namespace ASPPatterns.Chap8.FrontController.Controller
{
    public class FrontController
    {
        RequestHandler _requestHandler;

        public FrontController(IHandlerFactory handlerFactory)
        {
            _requestHandler = handlerFactory.GetHandlers();
        }

        public void handle(WebRequest request)
        {
            _requestHandler.Handle(request);
        }
    }
}
```

To complete the change toward using the Chain of Responsibility pattern rather than the Command pattern, you need to update the `BootStrapper`'s class to register a default instance of the `IHandlerFactory`, as here within the `ControllerRegistery` subclass.

```
public class ControllerRegistry : Registry
{
    public ControllerRegistry()
    {
        ForRequestedType<ICategoryRepository>()
            .TheDefault.Is.OfConcreteType<CategoryRepository>();
        ForRequestedType<IProductRepository>()
            .TheDefault.Is.OfConcreteType<ProductRepository>();
        ForRequestedType<IViewStorage>()
            .TheDefault.Is.OfConcreteType<ViewStorage>();
        ForRequestedType<IPageNavigator>()
            .TheDefault.Is.OfConcreteType<PageNavigator>();
        ForRequestedType<IWebRequestFactory>()
            .TheDefault.Is.OfConcreteType<WebRequestFactory>();
        ForRequestedType<IHandlerFactory>()
            .TheDefault.Is.OfConcreteType<HandlerFactory>();
    }
}
```

The modified solution now looks like Figure 8-9.

Figure 8-9 shows the solution structure from the downloadable project with the `ASPPatterns.Chap8 .CoR` namespace. This is identical to the modified `ASPPatterns.Chap8.FrontController` project, as discussed in the earlier exercise.

You can now run the solution by pressing F5 or by running the debugger.

FIGURE 8-9

MODEL-VIEW-CONTROLLER

The Model-View-Controller (MVC) pattern, like the Model-View-Presenter pattern, separates an application into three main components: the model, the view, and the controller.

➤ The model represents the business data that the view is to display or modify.

➤ The controller can be an implementation of the FrontController pattern. It is the initial contact for a request handling all user interaction. It interacts with the model based on the request and selects the appropriate view to render.

➤ The view is passive and has no knowledge of the controller. It simply displays the model data supplied from the controller.

Figure 8-10 shows the three components and how they relate to form the MVC pattern.

As shown in the diagram, a user makes a request that, in the first instance, the controller handles. The controller interacts with the model based on the requirements of the request. It renders the appropriate view and supplies it with the necessary data to display.

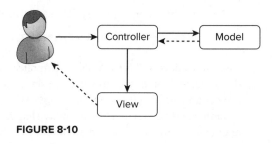

FIGURE 8-10

ViewModel Pattern

In the MVC pattern, views typically map to domain model entities; however, for scenarios in which the view requires data from many entities, a ViewModel can be used. A ViewModel is a class optimized for use with a specific view template; it provides a flattened view of the domain, potentially exposing properties that do not exist within the domain model. A ViewModel also helps to detach the view from the underlying domain model and can be a lot more flexible than using real domain entities.

Figure 8-11 shows a graphical view of how a ViewModel maps to a series of domain entities.

The `CustomerView` class exposes two properties: one that is mapped to a concatenation of the `Customer` entity's `FirstName` and `LastName` properties and the other that is a count of the number of orders the customer has.

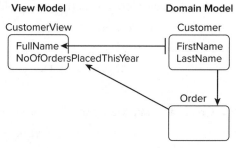

FIGURE 8-11

You will now work through two examples of the MVC pattern. First, you'll use Microsoft's ASP.NET MVC framework, which will employ the ViewModel pattern discussed earlier. Then you'll use the Castle project's MonoRail framework. You will also look at a product called `AutoMapper`, which will assist you when mapping your domain entities to ViewModel classes.

The ASP.NET MVC Framework

The ASP.NET MVC framework is Microsoft's implementation of the MVC pattern, giving an alternative method for creating ASP.NET sites. The framework is available as a separate install from `http://www.asp.net/mvc/`, and version ASP.NET MVC 2.0 is included with Visual Studio 2010.

In the following exercise, you create a solution to the product catalog browsing site that has formed the domain for all the exercises in this chapter.

Create a new solution named `ASPPatterns.Chap8.ASPNETMVC`, and add to it the following class library projects:

➤ `ASPPatterns.Chap8.ASPNETMVC.Model`

➤ `ASPPatterns.Chap8.ASPNETMVC.StubRepository`

➤   `ASPPatterns.Chap8.ASPNETMVC.Controllers`

➤   `ASPPatterns.Chap8.ASPNETMVC.AppService`

Also, add a new ASP.NET MVC web application named `ASPPatterns.Chap8.ASPNETMVC.UI.Web`. With the projects created, you now need to set up the project dependencies. Right-click on the `Controllers` project and add a reference to the `AppService` project as well as a reference to the `System.Web.MVC` assembly and `StructureMap` assembly that you downloaded earlier in the chapter. Right-click on the `AppService` project, and add a reference to the `Model` and `StubRepository` project. Right-click on the `StubRepository` and add a reference to the `Model` project. Finally, right-click on the `UI.Web` project and add a reference to the `AppService` project.

You can copy all the code from the `Model` and `StubRepository` projects that you created for the Model-View-Presenter exercise earlier in the chapter because this exercise uses the same domain model.

With the solution framework in place, you can start to create your application. First, add two folders to the `AppService` project named `Mapping` and `Views`. The Views folder will contain all of the ViewModel objects as defined in the previous section.

Create a new view within the `Views` folder named `CategoryView`.

```
public class CategoryView
{
    public int Id { get; set; }
    public string Name { get; set; }
}
```

Create a second view named `ProductView`, as shown in the listing that follows:

```
public class ProductView
{
    public string Name { get; set; }
    public string Price { get; set; }
    public string Id { get; set; }
}
```

Next, create a view of a product with extra detail named `ProductDetailView`, as shown in the listing that follows:

```
public class ProductDetailView : ProductView
{
    public string Description { get; set; }
}
```

The three classes that you have created form the view on the domain model. You will now create the views specifically for the views being displayed to the user. Create a new base view class that all the views will inherit from named `BaseView`, as can be seen here:

```
public abstract class BaseView
{
    public IEnumerable<CategoryView> Categories { get; set; }
}
```

Next, create the three classes that will provide the ViewModel for the views that the user will interact with — namely, the `CategoryProductsView`, the `ProductDetailView`, and the `HomeView`. These classes are shown here:

```
public class CategoryProductsPageView : BaseView
{
    public IEnumerable<ProductView> Products { get; set; }
    public CategoryView Category { get; set; }
}

public class ProductDetailPageView : BaseView
{
    public ProductDetailView Product { get; set; }
}

public class HomeView : BaseView
{
    public IEnumerable<ProductView> BestSellingProducts { get; set; }
}
```

Now that you have the ViewModels defined, you need a method of converting the domain entities into the ViewModels. Add a new class to the `Mapping` folder named `ProductMapperExtensionMethods` with the code definition displayed here:

```
...
using ASPPatterns.Chap8.ASPNETMVC.AppService.Views;
using ASPPatterns.Chap8.ASPNETMVC.Model;

namespace ASPPatterns.Chap8.ASPNETMVC.AppService.Mapping
{
    public static class ProductMapperExtensionMethods
    {
        public static IEnumerable<ProductView> ConvertToProductViewList
                                       (this IEnumerable<Product> products)
        {
            IList<ProductView> productViews = new List<ProductView>();

            foreach (Product p in products)
            {
                productViews.Add(p.ConvertToProductView());
            }

            return productViews;
        }

        public static ProductView ConvertToProductView(this Product product)
        {
            ProductView productView = new ProductView();
            productView.Name = product.Name;
            productView.Id = product.Id.ToString();
            productView.Price = String.Format("{0:c}", product.Price);

            return productView;
```

```
        }

        public static ProductDetailView ConvertToProductDetailView(this Product product)
        {
            ProductDetailView productView = new ProductDetailView();
            productView.Name = product.Name;
            productView.Id = product.Id.ToString();
            productView.Price = String.Format("{0:c}", product.Price);
            productView.Description = product.Description;

            return productView;
        }
    }
}
```

This class provides method extensions to the product and collections of product domain entities. This makes it trivial and fluent to convert your `Product` entities into ViewModels. Add a second class to the `Mappings` folder that will do the same for the `Category` domain entities, and name this class `Category MapperExtensionMethods`. You can see the code for this class here:

```
...
using ASPPatterns.Chap8.ASPNETMVC.AppService.Views;
using ASPPatterns.Chap8.ASPNETMVC.Model;

namespace ASPPatterns.Chap8.ASPNETMVC.AppService.Mapping
{
    public static class CategoryMapperExtensionMethods
    {
        public static IEnumerable<CategoryView> ConvertToCategoryViewList
                                    (this IEnumerable<Category> categories)
        {
            IList<CategoryView> categoryViews = new List<CategoryView>();

            foreach (Category c in categories)
            {
                categoryViews.Add(c.ConvertToCategoryView());
            }

            return categoryViews;
        }

        public static CategoryView ConvertToCategoryView(this Category category)
        {
            CategoryView categoryView = new CategoryView();
            categoryView.Name = category.Name;
            categoryView.Id = category.Id;

            return categoryView;
        }
    }
}
```

Again, this class provides a simple way to convert the `Category` domain entity into the `CategoryView`.

The final class for the `AppService` project is the `ShopService` class, which is responsible for coordinating the retrieval of entities and converting them into ViewModels. You can see the code for this class here:

```
...
using ASPPatterns.Chap8.ASPNETMVC.Model;
using ASPPatterns.Chap8.ASPNETMVC.AppService.Views;
using ASPPatterns.Chap8.ASPNETMVC.AppService.Mapping;

namespace ASPPatterns.Chap8.ASPNETMVC.AppService
{
    public class ShopService
    {
        private ProductService _productService;

        public ShopService(ProductService productService)
        {
            _productService = productService;
        }

        public HomeView GetHomePageView()
        {
            IEnumerable<ProductView> products =
                    _productService.GetBestSellingProducts().ConvertToProductViewList();
            IEnumerable<CategoryView> categories =
                    _productService.GetAllCategories().ConvertToCategoryViewList();

            HomeView productViewModel =
                new HomeView { BestSellingProducts = products,
                               Categories = categories };

            return productViewModel;
        }

        public ProductDetailPageView GetProductDetailPageViewFor(int ProductId)
        {
            ProductDetailView product =
                    _productService.GetProductBy(ProductId)
                    .ConvertToProductDetailView();
            IEnumerable<CategoryView> categories =
                    _productService.GetAllCategories().ConvertToCategoryViewList();

            ProductDetailPageView productDetailPageViewModel =
                new ProductDetailPageView { Product = product,
                                            Categories = categories};

            return productDetailPageViewModel;
        }

        public CategoryProductsPageView GetCategoryProductPageViewFor(int categoryId)
        {
            IEnumerable<ProductView> products =
                _productService.GetAllProductsIn(categoryId)
                .ConvertToProductViewList();
            CategoryView category =
```

```
                    _productService.GetCategoryBy(categoryId).ConvertToCategoryView();
            IEnumerable<CategoryView> categories =
                    _productService.GetAllCategories().ConvertToCategoryViewList();

            CategoryProductsPageView categoryProductsPageView =
                    new CategoryProductsPageView {
                                                 Category = category,
                                                 Products = products,
                                                 Categories = categories };

            return categoryProductsPageView;
        }
    }
}
```

Code snippet ShopService.cs in project ASPPatterns.Chap8.ASPNETMVC.AppService

The ShopService uses the ProductService to obtain the domain entities and then converts them into ViewModels via the extension methods.

With the AppService project complete and the ViewModels defined, you can start to create your controllers. Add a new class to the Controllers project named HomeController, and update it to match the listing that follows:

```
...
using System.Web.Mvc;
using ASPPatterns.Chap8.ASPNETMVC.AppService;
using ASPPatterns.Chap8.ASPNETMVC.AppService.Views;

namespace ASPPatterns.Chap8.ASPNETMVC.Controllers
{
    public class HomeController : Controller
    {
        private ShopService _shopService;

        public HomeController(ShopService shopService)
        {
            _shopService = shopService;
        }

        public ActionResult Index()
        {
            HomeView viewModel = _shopService.GetHomePageView();
            ViewData["categories"] = viewModel.Categories;

            return View(viewModel);
        }
    }
}
```

The HomeController inherits from a Controller base class that is part of the System.Web.Mvc assembly. The single method on the HomeController is Index, which will map to the Home/Index URL. The method returns an abstract ActionResult base class that is again part of the System.Web.Mvc assembly. The actual ActionResult returned from this method is a ViewResult, which renders a view to the response that is achieved using the View method and passing the ViewModel as an argument.

The `ViewData` is a `ViewDataDictionary` used to store data ready for the view similar to the `ViewStorage` that you created in the `FrontController` project earlier in this chapter. You will see how to use this when you create the views for this project.

The second controller you will create will handle requests for the `ProductDetail` and `ProductCategory` views. Create a new class named `ProductController`, and update it to match the code that follows:

```
...
using System.Web.Mvc;
using ASPPatterns.Chap8.ASPNETMVC.AppService;
using ASPPatterns.Chap8.ASPNETMVC.AppService.Views;

namespace ASPPatterns.Chap8.ASPNETMVC.Controllers
{
    public class ProductController : Controller
    {
        private ShopService _shopService;

        public ProductController(ShopService shopService)
        {
            _shopService = shopService;
        }

        public ActionResult CategoryProducts(int categoryId)
        {
            CategoryProductsPageView viewModel =
                _shopService.GetCategoryProductPageViewFor(categoryId);

            ViewData["categories"] = viewModel.Categories;

            return View(viewModel);
        }

        public ActionResult Detail(string Id)
        {
            ProductDetailPageView viewModel =
                _shopService.GetProductDetailPageViewFor(int.Parse(Id));

            ViewData["categories"] = viewModel.Categories;

            return View("ProductDetail", viewModel);
        }
    }
}
```

This `ProductController` is similar to the `HomeController` but has methods to display the `CategoryProducts` and `ProductDetail` view. By convention, the call to the `View` method will return a view with a name matching that method. As you can see in the `Detail` method, the view does not match, so you have specified the `ProductDetail` name as an argument in the overloaded constructor `View` base method.

For the controllers you have created to handle a request, the frameworks routing engine that you will look at later will pick apart the requested URL to find the controller type. Once found, the framework will pass it to an `MvcHandler` whose job it is to instantiate the controller using a `ControllerFactory`.

The default `ControllerFactory` can only instantiate a controller if it has a parameterless constructor. This is obviously a problem, because your controllers require an instance of the `ShopService` to work. To overcome this limitation, you can create your own `ControllerFactory` that will use `StructureMap` to resolve dependencies.

Create a new class within the `Controllers` project named `IoCControllerFactory`, and have it inherit from the `DefaultControllerFactory` class, as can be seen here:

```
...
using System.Web.Mvc;
using StructureMap;

namespace ASPPatterns.Chap8.ASPNETMVC.Controllers
{
    public class IoCControllerFactory : DefaultControllerFactory
    {
        protected override IController GetControllerInstance(Type controllerType)
        {
            return ObjectFactory.GetInstance(controllerType) as IController;
        }
    }
}
```

StructureMap's `ObjectFactory` will then be able to resolve any dependencies that the controllers require.

The last class to create within the `Controllers` project is the `BootStrapper` class, which will be used to register the concrete implementations with `StructureMap`. Create the `BootStrapper` class and update it to match the following listing:

```
...
using ASPPatterns.Chap8.ASPNETMVC.Model;
using ASPPatterns.Chap8.ASPNETMVC.StubRepository;
using StructureMap;
using StructureMap.Configuration.DSL;

namespace ASPPatterns.Chap8.ASPNETMVC.Controllers
{
    public class BootStrapper
    {
        public static void ConfigureDependencies()
        {
            ObjectFactory.Initialize(x =>
            {
                x.AddRegistry<ControllerRegistry>();

            });
        }

        public class ControllerRegistry : Registry
        {
            public ControllerRegistry()
            {
                ForRequestedType<ICategoryRepository>()
```

```
                .TheDefault.Is.OfConcreteType<CategoryRepository>();
            ForRequestedType<IProductRepository>()
                .TheDefault.Is.OfConcreteType<ProductRepository>();
        }
    }
  }
}
```

Your solution will resemble Figure 8-12.

Now it's time to switch your attention to creating the views. Visual Studio has already created a whole host of classes for you, but you want to start with a clean palette, so delete all the files within the UI.Web application project except for the following files:

➤ Global.asax

➤ Web.Config

➤ Default.aspx

➤ Views/Web.Config

Now add the following folders within the Views folder:

➤ Home

➤ Product

➤ Shared

FIGURE 8-12

Add a new partial view to the Shared folder by right-clicking and selecting View from the context-sensitive menu. When the dialog box appears, check the Create a Partial View (.ascx) and Create a Strongly-Typed View check boxes and select ASPPatterns.Chap8 .ASPNETMVC.AppService.Views.CategoryView from the drop-down list. Name the partial view Categories and click the Add button.

Because the view will deal with collections of CategoryViews, amend the Inherits keyword to be strongly typed to an IList of CategoryView, as can be seen in the code listing that follows:

```
<%@ Control Language="C#"
    Inherits="System.Web.Mvc.ViewUserControl<IList<CategoryView>>"
%>
<%@ Import Namespace="ASPPatterns.Chap8.ASPNETMVC.AppService.Views"%>

<ul>
 <% foreach (var item in Model) { %>
    <li><%= Html.ActionLink(item.Name,
                       "CategoryProducts",
                       "Product", new { CategoryId = item.Id }, null)%>
    </li>
<% } %>
</ul>
```

Because the page inherits from the System.Web.Mvc.ViewUserControl class, you get the HTML link helper class to build your links. Also, because the class is strongly typed, you have full intellisense on the ViewData via the Model property.

Add a second partial view to the Shared folder named Products.ascx, and strongly type it to the ASPPatterns.Chap8.ASPNETMVC.AppService.Views.ProductView class. Update the markup to match the code listing that follows, remembering to change the ProductView to an IList<ProductView>.

```
<%@ Control Language="C#"
        Inherits="System.Web.Mvc.ViewUserControl<List< ProductView>>" %>

<%@ Import Namespace="ASPPatterns.Chap8.ASPNETMVC.AppService.Views"%>

 <% foreach (var item in Model) { %>
   <%=item.Name%> only <%=String.Format("{0:C}", item.Price)%><br />
       <%= Html.ActionLink("More Information", "Detail",
                       "Product", new { Id = item.Id }, null)%>
        <hr />
<% } %>
```

The final file to add to the Shared folder is an MVC View Master Page. Right-click on the Shared folder and select Add New Item. You can find the MVC View Master Page from the MVC tab beneath the Web tab when the Add New Item dialog box appears. Name the master page Shop.Master, and update the markup to match the code shown here:

```
<%@ Master Language="C#" Inherits="System.Web.Mvc.ViewMasterPage" %>
<%@ Import Namespace="ASPPatterns.Chap8.ASPNETMVC.AppService.Views"%>
<!DOCTYPE html PUBLIC "-//W3C//DTD XHTML 1.0 Strict//EN"
"http://www.w3.org/TR/xhtml1/DTD/xhtml1-strict.dtd">
<html xmlns="http://www.w3.org/1999/xhtml">
<head runat="server">
</head>

<body>
    <table width="70%">
        <tr>
            <td colspan="2">
              <h2><%= Html.ActionLink("Scotts Shop", "Index", "Home") %></h2><hr /></td>
        </tr>
        <tr>
            <td valign="top" width="15%">
            <% Html.RenderPartial("~/Views/Shared/Categories.ascx",
            (IList< CategoryView>)ViewData["categories"]); %></td>
            <td valign="top" width="85%">
               <asp:ContentPlaceHolder ID="MainContent" runat="server" /></td>
        </tr>
    </table>
</body>
</html>
```

Next, add a new view to the Home folder strongly typed to AppService.Views.HomeView, and name it Index.aspx. The markup for this view can be seen here:

```
<%@ Page Language="C#" MasterPageFile="~/Views/Shared/Site.Master"
        Inherits="System.Web.Mvc.ViewPage<HomeView>" %>
```

```
<%@ Import Namespace="ASPPatterns.Chap8.ASPNETMVC.AppService.Views"%>

<asp:Content ID="indexContent" ContentPlaceHolderID="MainContent" runat="server">
    <h2>Today's Top Products</h2>
    <% Html.RenderPartial("~/Views/Shared/Products.ascx", Model.BestSellingProducts); %>
</asp:Content>
```

The view uses the `Products.ascx` partial view and loads it using the base HTML helper methods. It also passes it the view model data required.

Add another view to the `Product` folder, this time strongly typed to the `AppService.Views.Category View`, and name it `CategoryProducts.aspx`. The markup for this view is displayed here:

```
<%@ Page Title="" Language="C#" MasterPageFile="~/Views/Shared/Site.Master"
    Inherits="System.Web.Mvc.ViewPage<CategoryProductsPageView>" %>
<%@ Import Namespace="ASPPatterns.Chap8.ASPNETMVC.AppService.Views"%>

<asp:Content ID="Content1" ContentPlaceHolderID="MainContent" runat="server">
    <h2>All <%=Model.Category.Name %></h2>
    <% Html.RenderPartial("~/Views/Shared/Products.ascx", Model.Products); %>
</asp:Content>
```

To complete the view requirements, add a second view to the `Product` folder named `Product Detail.aspx` and strongly type it to the `AppService.Views.ProductDetailPageView` class. Again, the markup for this view is displayed here:

```
<%@ Page Title="" Language="C#" MasterPageFile="~/Views/Shared/Site.Master"
    Inherits="System.Web.Mvc.ViewPage<ProductDetailPageView>" %>

<%@ Import Namespace="ASPPatterns.Chap8.ASPNETMVC.AppService.Views"%>

<asp:Content ID="Content1" ContentPlaceHolderID="MainContent" runat="server">

    <% ProductDetailView productModel = Model.Product;  %>

    <h2><%=productModel.Name%></h2>
    <p>pay: <%=productModel.Price%></p>
    <p><%=productModel.Description%></p>

</asp:Content>
```

You now need to configure the `IoCControllerFactory` that you created in the `Controllers` project and call the `BootStrapper.ConfigureDependencies` method to register all dependencies with `StructureMap`. Open the `Global.asax` file and update it to include the two new calls, as shown in the code listing that follows:

```
...
using ASPPatterns.Chap8.ASPNETMVC.Controllers;

namespace ASPPatterns.Chap8.ASPNETMVC.UI.Web
{
    public class MvcApplication : System.Web.HttpApplication
    {
        public static void RegisterRoutes(RouteCollection routes)
        {
```

```
        routes.IgnoreRoute("{resource}.axd/{*pathInfo}");
        routes.IgnoreRoute("{*favicon}", new
                             { favicon = @"(.*/)?favicon.ico(/.*)?" });

        routes.MapRoute(
            "Default",                           // Route name
            "{controller}/{action}/{id}",        // URL with parameters
            new { controller = "Home",
                  action = "Index", id = "" } // Parameter defaults
        );
    }

    protected void Application_Start()
    {
        RegisterRoutes(RouteTable.Routes);

        BootStrapper.ConfigureDependencies();

        ControllerBuilder.Current.SetControllerFactory(new IoCControllerFactory());
    }
  }
}
```

The other interesting thing that is happening in this class is the mapping of routes to controllers. The RegisterRoutes method adds a new URL template pattern that, if matched by the requested URL, is passed onto an MvcHandler, which in turn obtains a controller from the IoCControllerFactory to handle the request. Note also that you will need to include an IgnoreRoute declaration to ignore requests for faviocon.ico that is requested by default by some browsers.

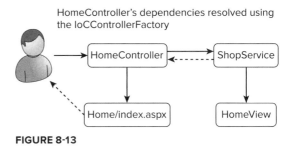

FIGURE 8-13

Figure 8-13 is an update to the MVC diagram first shown at the beginning of this section to relate the actual classes to the concepts discussed earlier.

The solution is now complete, and you will be able to press F5 or run the debugger to browse through the product catalog.

Mapping ViewModels with AutoMapper

The mapping of domain entities to ViewModels is a tedious task of left to right object-to-object mapping. AutoMapper is an open source product that can automate this mapping using a fluent configuration API. You can find more information on AutoMapper via the project home page at http://automapper.codeplex.com.

To demonstrate the power and features of AutoMapper, you will use a different domain model than you have used up to now to show how AutoMapper can be used to automate the mapping between your domain entities and the ViewModels. The domain model is based on a Customer/Order model that is typically seen in an e-commerce store.

Create a new solution named `ASPPatterns.Chap8.AutoMapper` and add the following class libraries:

➤ `ASPPatterns.Chap8.AutoMapper.Model`

➤ `ASPPatterns.Chap8.AutoMapper.AppService`

➤ `ASPPatterns.Chap8.AutoMapper.StubRepository`

Finally, add a web application project named `ASPPatterns.Chap8.AutoMapper.UI.Web`. Before you go any further, you need to download the `AutoMapper` assembly. Navigate to the project's home page at `http://automapper.codeplex.com/` and click the download link. `AutoMapper` is just a single dll. To keep things organized, create a folder named `Lib` via Windows Explorer at the root of your solution and save the `AutoMapper.dll` there.

Now that you have all the projects in place, you need to set up the dependencies. Right-click on the `StubRepository` and add a reference to the `Model` project. Right-click on the `AppService` project and add a reference to the `Model` and `StubRepository` projects as well as the `AutoMapper.dll`. Finally right-click on the `UI.Web` application and add a reference to the `AppService` project.

You are going to create a simple domain model to demonstrate the power of `AutoMapper`. Add four new classes to the `Model` project named `Customer`, `Product`, `Item`, and `Order`, with the following code listing:

```
public class Customer
{
    public string Name { get; set; }
}

public class Product
{
    public string Name { get; set; }
}

public class Item
{
    public Product Product { get; set; }
    public int Qty { get; set; }
}

public class Order
{
    public Customer Customer { get; set; }
    public DateTime OrderDate { get; set; }
    public IList<Item> Items { get; set; }
}
```

These classes form the simple domain model that you will program against. To retrieve an order, you will create a repository interface that will be implemented in the `StubRepository` project. Add a new interface to the `Model` project named `IOrderRepository`, and update it to match the contract that follows:

```
public interface IOrderRepository
{
    Order FindBy(int Id);
}
```

Switch to the `StubRepository` project and add a new class that implements the newly created `IOrderRepository`. Name this class `OrderRepository`, and update it to match the listing that follows:

```
...
using ASPPatterns.Chap8.AutoMapper.Model;

namespace ASPPatterns.Chap8.AutoMapper.StubRepository
{
    public class OrderRepository : IOrderRepository
    {
        public Order FindBy(int Id)
        {
            Order order = new Order();
            order.OrderDate = DateTime.Now;
            order.Customer = new Customer { Name = "Scott Millett" };
            order.Items = new List<Item>();
            order.Items.Add(new Item { Qty = 1,
                                      Product = new Product { Name = "Hat" } });

            return order;
        }
    }
}
```

The `OrderRepository` lives only to provide some dummy data to work against.

Next, add a new folder to the `AppService` project named `Views`, and add two new classes within this folder named `ItemView` and `OrderView`. The code for these classes is shown here:

```
public class ItemView
{
    public string ProductName { get; set; }
    public int Qty { get; set; }
}

public class OrderView
{
    public string CustomerName { get; set; }
    public DateTime OrderDate { get; set; }
    public IList<ItemView> Items { get; set; }
}
```

Now, usually you would create a series of classes to convert the domain entities into views — basically, a lot of object-to-object mapping. What `AutoMapper` brings to the table is the ability to map your domain entities into view models for you. Create a `BootStrapper` class to set up the entity to view model mapping contracts and add the following code:

```
...
using AutoMapper;
using ASPPatterns.Chap8.AutoMapper.Model;
using ASPPatterns.Chap8.AutoMapper.AppService.Views;

namespace ASPPatterns.Chap8.AutoMapper.AppService
{
```

```
public class BootStrapper
{
    public static void ConfigureAutoMapper()
    {
        Mapper.CreateMap<Order, OrderView>();
        Mapper.CreateMap<Item, ItemView>();
    }
}
```

The ConfigureAutoMapper method simply tells AutoMapper to create a mapping between the domain entities and the view models. It is able to perform this flattening of the domain model due to the naming of the view model properties. The Order entity has a Customer entity property, and the Customer entity has a property named Name. AutoMapper is able to deduce that the OrderView property CustomerName is from the Customer's Name property and thus map it accordingly. The rest of the mapping within the ItemView is performed in the same way. For more complex mapping, please refer to the AutoMapper project home page http://automapper.codeplex.com/. You will also use some more advanced features of AutoMapper in the case study that starts in Chapter 10.

You are now able to add an extension method to the Views folder named OrderExtensionMethods that calls AutoMapper to perform the conversion for you:

```
...
using ASPPatterns.Chap8.AutoMapper.Model;
using AutoMapper;

namespace ASPPatterns.Chap8.AutoMapper.AppService.Views
{
    public static class OrderExtensionMethods
    {
        public static OrderView ConvertToOrderView(this Order order)
        {
            return Mapper.Map<Order, OrderView>(order);
        }
    }
}
```

The final class to complete the AppService project is the OrderService class. Add a new class to the root of the project named OrderService, and update it to match the following code listing:

```
...
using AutoMapper;
using ASPPatterns.Chap8.AutoMapper.Model;
using ASPPatterns.Chap8.AutoMapper.StubRepository;
using ASPPatterns.Chap8.AutoMapper.AppService.Views;

namespace ASPPatterns.Chap8.AutoMapper.AppService
{
    public class OrderService
    {
        private IOrderRepository _orderRepository;

        public OrderService()
            : this(new OrderRepository())
```

```
            { }

            public OrderService(IOrderRepository orderRepository)
            {
                _orderRepository = orderRepository;
            }

            public OrderView GetOrder(int orderId)
            {
                OrderView orderView;
                Order order = _orderRepository.FindBy(orderId);

                orderView = order.ConvertToOrderView();

                return orderView;
            }
        }
    }
```

I have added some poor man's dependency injection by adding a parameterless constructor that creates a concrete version of the OrderRepository to keep the solution simple.

The GetOrder method obtains an Order entity and then calls the extension method to convert it to an OrderView with a little help from AutoMapper.

You can create a call to the OrderService from the Default.aspx code behind in the UI.Web application to complete the exercise. Add the following code to the code behind view of the Default.aspx page:

```
...
using ASPPatterns.Chap8.AutoMapper.AppService;
using ASPPatterns.Chap8.AutoMapper.AppService.Views;

namespace ASPPatterns.Chap8.AutoMapper.UI.Web
{
    public partial class _Default : System.Web.UI.Page
    {
        protected void Page_Load(object sender, EventArgs e)
        {
            OrderView order = new OrderService().GetOrder(1);

            Response.Write(String.Format("CustomerName: {0}<br/>", order.CustomerName));
            Response.Write(String.Format("OrderDate: {0}<br/>", order.OrderDate));

            foreach (ItemView item in order.Items)
            {
                Response.Write(String.Format
                    ("Qty: {0}, Product: {1}<br/>", item.Qty, item.ProductName ));
            }
        }
    }
}
```

Lastly, you need to call into the `BootStrapper` class on the application start event, so add a `Global.asax` file if one does not already exist, and update the code behind to include a call to the `BootStrapper.ConfigureAutoMapper` method as shown next:

```
...
using ASPPatterns.Chap8.AutoMapper.AppService;

namespace ASPPatterns.Chap8.AutoMapper.UI.Web
{
    public class Global : System.Web.HttpApplication
    {
        protected void Application_Start(object sender, EventArgs e)
        {
            BootStrapper.ConfigureAutoMapper();
        }
    }
}
```

You can now run the project and see that the `AutoMapper` generates the ViewModel.

You have only touched the surface on the functionality that `AutoMapper` can bring to help your domain model to view model mapping needs. Please consult the project's home page for more information on the advanced features of `AutoMapper`.

Castle MonoRail

Castle MonoRail is an open source web application framework built on top of the ASP.NET platform reminiscent of the Rails framework for Ruby. MonoRail follows the MVC pattern and can be used with the Castle ActiveRecord framework, as discussed in Chapter 4 for the ActiveRecord exercise. You can find more information on the Castle MonoRail project at the project's homepage at `www.castleproject.org/monorail/`.

To demonstrate the MonoRail framework you will be using the same domain model that you have used throughout this chapter and will construct the same product catalog browsing site as in the ASP.NET MVC exercise to enable you to compare frameworks.

Create a new solution named `ASPPatterns.Chap8.CastleMonoRail`, and add the following class libraries to it:

➤ `ASPPatterns.Chap8.CastleMonoRail.Model`

➤ `ASPPatterns.Chap8.CastleMonoRail.StubRepository`

➤ `ASPPatterns.Chap8.CastleMonoRail.Controllers`

Add a web application project to the solution named `ASPPatterns.Chap8.CastleMonoRail.UI.NVelocity`.

NVelocity is a template engine written in C# for .Net that is a port of the popular Java project Velocity; you can find out more on it from its project home page `http://nvelocity.sourceforge.net`. You will be using NVelocity to generate your `Html` views.

You need to download the Castle MonoRail framework to use MonoRail, so navigate to www.castle project.org/castle/download.html and download the assemblies; at the time of writing, this was version 2.0. Once it's downloaded, create a folder named Lib via Windows Explorer in the root of the Solution folder and extract all the Castle MonoRail files into it. Once it's extracted, right-click on the Controllers project and add a reference to the Castle.MonoRail.Framework.dll. Next, right-click on the UI.NVelocity project and add a reference to the following assemblies:

➤ Castle.Components.DictionaryAdapter

➤ Castle.Core

➤ Castle.MonoRail.Framework

➤ Castle.MonoRail.Framework.Views.NVelocity

➤ NVelocity

To finish setting the project's dependencies, right-click on the StubRepository project and add a reference to the Model project. Right-click on the Controllers project and add a reference to the Model and Controllers project as well as the StructureMap.dll you downloaded at the beginning of this chapter. Lastly, right-click on the UI.NVelocity project and add a reference to the Model and Controllers projects.

You can copy all the code from the Model and StubRepository projects that you created for the Model-View-Presenter exercise earlier in the chapter because this exercise uses the same domain model.

The first class you need to create is the HomeController class within the Controllers project. Add the class, and update it to match the listing that follows:

```
...
using Castle.MonoRail.Framework;
using ASPPatterns.Chap8.CastleMonoRail.Model;
using ASPPatterns.Chap8.CastleMonoRail.StubRepository;
using StructureMap;

namespace ASPPatterns.Chap8.CastleMonoRail.UI.Web.Controllers
{
    [Layout("default")]
    public class HomeController : SmartDispatcherController
    {
        private ProductService _productService;

        public HomeController()
        {
            _productService = ObjectFactory.GetInstance<ProductService>();
        }

        public void Index()
        {
            PropertyBag["products"] = _productService.GetBestSellingProducts();
            PropertyBag["categories"] = _productService.GetAllCategories();
        }
    }
}
```

The HomeController inherits from the SmartDispatcherController base controller, which is part of the MonoRail framework. The layout attribute that decorates the class simply lets the framework know which layout template to use when rendering the view, which you will create a little later. The layout attribute basically works like an ASPX master page. The constructor uses StructureMap to obtain an instance of the ProductService with all dependencies resolved. The single Index method obtains the data needed for the view and stores it within a property bag. By convention, there is no need to call a method to show the view, because a view matching the name of the Index method name is displayed by default. In contrast, ASP.MVC works in the same way except a call to View() must be made, but if no argument is passed the view that matches the name of the action is rendered.

Add a second class to the project named ProductController, and update it to match the code listing that follows:

```
...
using Castle.MonoRail.Framework;
using ASPPatterns.Chap8.CastleMonoRail.Model;
using ASPPatterns.Chap8.CastleMonoRail.StubRepository;
using StructureMap;

namespace ASPPatterns.Chap8.CastleMonoRail.UI.Web.Controllers
{
    [Layout("default")]
    public class ProductController : SmartDispatcherController
    {
        private ProductService _productService;

        public ProductController()
        {
            _productService = ObjectFactory.GetInstance<ProductService>();
        }

        public void ProductDetail()
        {
            int productId;
            int.TryParse(Request.QueryString["ProductId"], out productId);

            Product product = _productService.GetProductBy(productId);

            if (product != null)
            {
                PropertyBag["product"] = _productService.GetProductBy(productId);
                PropertyBag["categories"] = _productService.GetAllCategories();
            }
            else
            {
                // The view name is passed here
                // as it does not match the method name
                RenderView("productnotfound");
            }
        }

        public void CategoryProducts()
        {
```

```
          int categoryId = int.Parse(Request.QueryString["CategoryId"]);

          PropertyBag["products"] = _productService.GetAllProductsIn(categoryId);
          PropertyBag["categories"] = _productService.GetAllCategories();
          PropertyBag["category"] = _productService.GetCategoryBy(categoryId);


       }
     }
   }
```

The `ProductController` is nearly identical to the `HomeController`. It differs only in that it displays an alternative view if a product cannot be found that relates to the product ID obtained from the query string, as can be seen in the `ProductDetail` method.

To register the dependencies, you again create a `BootStrapper` class, seen here:

```
...
using StructureMap.Configuration.DSL;
using StructureMap;
using ASPPatterns.Chap8.CastleMonoRail.Model;
using ASPPatterns.Chap8.CastleMonoRail.StubRepository;

namespace ASPPatterns.Chap8.CastleMonoRail.Controllers
{
    public class BootStrapper
    {
        public static void ConfigureDependencies()
        {
            ObjectFactory.Initialize(x =>
            {
                x.AddRegistry<ControllerRegistry>();

            });
        }

        public class ControllerRegistry : Registry
        {
            public ControllerRegistry()
            {
                ForRequestedType<ICategoryRepository>()
                    .TheDefault.Is.OfConcreteType<CategoryRepository>();
                ForRequestedType<IProductRepository>()
                    .TheDefault.Is.OfConcreteType<ProductRepository>();
            }
        }
    }
}
```

This completes the `Controllers` project. You are now going to use a view engine called `NVelocity` to build the views. You could have also used a number of other view engines, such as AspView, Brail, StringTemplate, and indeed the ASPX web forms engine. Add a new `Views` folder, and within it add the following four folders:

➤   Home

➤   Product

➤   Layout

➤   Shared

Add a new partial view to the Shared folder named categories.vm with the following markup:

```
<ul>
  #foreach($category in $categories)

  <li>$UrlHelper.Link($category.Name, "%{controller='Product',
                  action='CategoryProducts',
                  querystring='CategoryId=$category.Id'}")</li>

  #end
</ul>
```

Because Visual Studio won't have an item type for the extension .vm, create a text file and amend the extension to *.vm. The call to the $categories references the view model that you added via the PropertyBag property within the Controllers project. URLHelper is a class that helps you to create links based on your controller methods. For more information on the NVelocity syntax refer to the projects home page at http://nvelocity.sourceforge.net.

Create another partial view in the Shared folder named products.vm, and update it to match the markup shown here:

```
#foreach($product in $products)

$product.Name only $product.Price
<br />

$UrlHelper.Link("more information", "%{controller='Product',
              action='ProductDetail', querystring='ProductId=$product.Id'}")
<hr />

#end
```

This view is nearly identical to the categories.vm view.

The next file to create is the layout template that you decorated your controller classes with back in the Controllers project. Add a new file to the Layout folder named default.vm, and update it to match the markup shown here:

```
<!DOCTYPE html PUBLIC "-//W3C//DTD XHTML 1.0 Transitional//EN"
                    "http://www.w3.org/TR/xhtml1/DTD/xhtml1-transitional.dtd">

<html xmlns="http://www.w3.org/1999/xhtml" >
<head runat="server">
    <title></title>
</head>
<body>
    <div>
        <table width="70%">
            <tr>
                <td colspan="2"><h2>
                $UrlHelper.Link("Scotts Shop", "%{controller='Home', action='Index'}")
```

```
            </h2><hr /></td>
        </tr>
        <tr>
            <td valign="top" width="15%">#parse("Shared/categories.vm")</td>
            <td valign="top" width="85%">$childContent</td>
        </tr>
    </table>
</div>
</body>
</html>
```

The `default.vm` layout template includes the `categories.vm` partial view by using the `#parse` method. The layout also defines a content area named `$childContent` that will be populated by the concrete view that the controller generates.

Create a new view for the product catalog home page within the `Home` folder named `index.vm`, and update it with the following markup:

```
<p>
  <h2>Today's Top Products</h2>
  #parse("Shared/products.vm")
</p>
```

Again, this view uses the shared `products.vm` partial view to render the best selling products.

Create another view for the displaying of products within a specific category in the `Product` folder named `categoryproducts.vm`. Again, update it to match the markup that follows:

```
<h2>All $category.Name</h2>
#parse("Shared/products.vm")
```

Add another view to the `Product` folder named `productdetail.vm` that renders the details of a product, as shown here:

```
<h2>$product.Name</h2>
<p>pay: $product.Price</p>
<p>$product.Description</p>
```

The final view to create is displayed if a product cannot be found. Name this view `productnotfound.vm`, and add it again to the `Product` folder.

```
Sorry the product you were looking for could not be found.
<br/><br/>
Please return to the $UrlHelper.Link("home page", "%{controller='Home',
                                    action='Index'}") and try again.
```

This completes all the views. You now need to change to the `Web.Config` file so that you can hook up the MonoRail `HttpHandler` and configure the location of your controllers. Open the `Web.config` file and add the following sections:

```
<configuration>

<configSections>
    <section name="monorail"
        type="Castle.MonoRail.Framework.Configuration.MonoRailSectionHandler,
```

```
                        Castle.MonoRail.Framework"/>
        …
    </configSections>

    <monorail>
        <controllers>
            <assembly>ASPPatterns.Chap8.CastleMonoRail.Controllers</assembly>
        </controllers>
        <viewEngines viewPathRoot="Views">
     <add type="Castle.MonoRail.Framework.Views.NVelocity.NVelocityViewEngine,
                Castle.MonoRail.Framework.Views.NVelocity"/>
        </viewEngines>
    </monorail>

    …

    <httpHandlers>
        <remove verb="*" path="*.asmx"/>
        <add verb="*" path="*.catalog"
           type="Castle.MonoRail.Framework.MonoRailHttpHandlerFactory,
                Castle.MonoRail.Framework"/>
            …
    </httpHandlers>

    …

    </configuration>
```

You also need to redirect all calls to Default.aspx to redirect to the default home controller, as can be seen here:

```
…
public partial class _Default : System.Web.UI.Page
    {
        protected void Page_Load(object sender, EventArgs e)
        {
            Response.Redirect("home/index.catalog");
        }
    }
```

Lastly, add a Global.asax file and add a call to the BootStrapper.ConfigureDependencies method within the Application_Start event, as can be seen here:

```
…
using ASPPatterns.Chap8.CastleMonoRail.Controllers;

namespace ASPPatterns.Chap8.CastleMonoRail.UI.NVelocity
{
    public class Global : System.Web.HttpApplication
    {
        protected void Application_Start(object sender, EventArgs e)
        {
            BootStrapper.ConfigureDependencies();
        }
    }
}
```

The completed solution resembles Figure 8-14.

You can now press F5 or run the debugger to navigate the product catalog.

PAGE CONTROLLER

The Page Controller is a simple pattern that has one controller for each view of the web application. That controller may be the page itself, as was the case in classic ASP, or it can follow the code behind model and live in a separate object that corresponds to the page. The Page Controller pattern is built in to the ASP.NET Web Forms framework and uses a separate code behind class to separate the view from the Page Controller. This can be seen by the way the ASP.NET page is divided into two distinct parts: the .aspx, which forms the view, and the .aspx.cs code behind file, forming the Page Controller. The code behind updates the view with the data from the model and coordinates the rendering of other views via redirection.

Figure 8-15 shows a graphical representation of the Page Controller pattern classes involved in the Page Controller pattern.

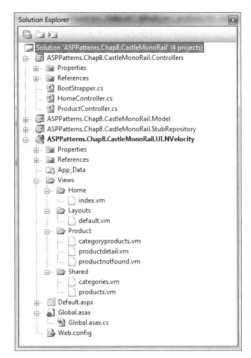

FIGURE 8-14

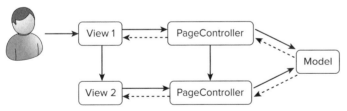

FIGURE 8-15

I won't include a coding exercise for this pattern as you have already been using it if you have used web forms.

SUMMARY

This chapter started with a look at how you can tie up your loosely coupled code by using an Inversion of Control container within your presentation layer to obtain concrete implementations of services simply by referencing an interface, thus leaving your code loosely coupled and not tied to a particular implementation of a service. The container you looked at was the popular open source StructureMap.

You then went on to look at the following patterns, which help organize your presentation logic:

➤ **Model-View-Presenter:** The Model-View-Presenter pattern splits an application into three distinct sections: the model representing a view of the business domain to be displayed or interacted with; the view that displays the model data; and the presenter that mediates between the model and the view by persisting data changed by the view and retrieved data from the model for displaying on the view. The view is the gateway to the pattern and all actions are routed through it and delegated to the presenter. The MVP pattern is particularly suited to ASP.NET web forms because it provides a stateful view of the web.

➤ **Front Controller:** The Front Controller acts as the initial point of contact for handling a request. The controller manages the handling of the request and delegates it to the appropriate handler, which in turn handles any model retrieval or persistence and renders the corresponding view. The view is completely passive in this pattern and rarely if ever follows the code behind model.

➤ **Model-View-Controller:** Like the MVP pattern, the Model-View-Controller pattern has three distinct parts: the model, which as in MVP represents a view of the business domain to be displayed or interacted with; the view that is rendered by the controller; and the controller itself that is based on the Front Controller pattern and is the initial point of contact for a request. After a request is made, the controller delegates to an appropriate command to handle the request and renders the view, passing any model data required as part of the process.

➤ **ViewModel:** The ViewModel pattern defines strongly typed classes that are created for the sole purpose of satisfying a particular view. They are Data Transfer Objects and usually have a one-to-one relationship with the view template. The ViewModels are typically but not always flattened views of a particular subset of the Domain entity's object graph. ViewModels can be used with all the presentation patterns discussed in this chapter.

➤ **Page Controller:** The Page Controller pattern defines one controller for each view in the application. The Page Controller pattern is an easy-to-grasp pattern especially for people coming from a web forms background because this is the pattern built into the framework.

In the next chapter, you look at the patterns that appear in the user experience portion of an enterprise-level application — specifically AJAX design patterns.

The User Experience Layer

➤ An explanation of what AJAX is

➤ Using JavaScript libraries to simplify your scripting needs

➤ The AJAX Periodic Refresh and Timeout patterns

➤ Maintaining history with the Unique URL pattern

➤ Client-side data binding with jTemplate

➤ The AJAX Predictive Fetch pattern

This chapter starts with a description of what AJAX is and what JavaScript libraries are available to make it easier to write AJAX applications. The chapter ends with common AJAX patterns that make up the user experience layer, with full exercises to see how these patterns are implemented.

WHAT IS AJAX?

AJAX (Asynchronous JavaScript and XML) is a way of programming to make asynchronous client callbacks from the browser to the server. Traditionally, data that the server returns is serialized into XML; however, more often JSON (JavaScript Object Notation) is used, because JSON is lightweight and therefore faster than XML.

The underlying technology used for AJAX is the XMLHttpRequest object. The XMLHttpRequest object allows client-side JavaScript code to send HTTP requests and handle responses. The ability to request data from a server asynchronously is half of the AJAX story, because now you need to update the browser page to show the new information. You can achieve this by using the Document Object Model (DOM). The DOM enables the page to be updated with the new data retrieved from the XMLHttpRequest object. These two pieces of technology are what make AJAX possible.

However, you will rarely use these objects directly, because many powerful and free JavaScript libraries make using AJAX simple and hide the complexities of cross-browser DOM implementation. The next section discusses these.

USING JAVASCRIPT LIBRARIES

A JavaScript library is a library of prewritten JavaScript controls and helper methods that facilitate the ease of cross-browser development. A number of libraries have been developed to ease JavaScript programming, such as Script.aculo.us, Dojo Toolkit, and Google Web Toolkit. Microsoft has even created its own AJAX JavaScript library for use with the AJAX control kit: a drag-and-drop method of developing AJAX applications with no requirements to hand-code JavaScript. Microsoft, however, has shifted its focus from the client-side JavaScript library to the more server-side AJAX control toolkit and has opted to support jQuery as its JavaScript library of choice. jQuery is included with the ASP.NET MVC project template that you used in Chapter 8. In Visual Studio 2010, jQuery 1.4.1 is included with both ASP.NET Web Forms and MVC 2. jQuery is the library you will be using for the remainder of this chapter, so the next section takes a closer look at it.

jQuery is the most popular JavaScript library in use today, so much so that even Microsoft has started shipping it with Visual Studio 2010. It has fast become the developers' choice due to its animation functionalities as well as its AJAX and event-handling features. You can download the library free from http://jquery.com/; you will use the jQuery library for the exercise to demonstrate the AJAX patterns.

This chapter will not go into detail on using jQuery, so I suggest a dedicated book on the subject, such as the Wrox Blox *jQuery for ASP.NET Developers* by Joe Brinkman or *jQuery in Action* by Bear Bibeault and Yehuda Katz.

UNDERSTANDING AJAX PATTERNS

Just as with server-side code and the Gang of Four patterns, patterns have started to emerge for client-side code and AJAX technologies to help with best practices. You will examine the following patterns in this section:

- ➤ Periodic Refresh and Timeout
- ➤ Unique URL
- ➤ Data binding with JavaScript Templates
- ➤ Predictive Fetch

Periodic Refresh and Timeout

As the name suggests, the Periodic Refresh pattern sees the browser periodically issuing an XMLHttpRequest call to retrieve new or updated information and update the display. The BBC's goal flashes and major incidents text commentary ticker that provides all the action at the football matches (soccer) use the Periodic Refresh pattern. Figures 9-1 through 9-3 show how the page updates periodically to demonstrate major events of games being played.

FIGURE 9-1

FIGURE 9-2

FIGURE 9-3

The pattern is also used for online chat programs and social networking applications to update the messages or status of users. Another popular use of the pattern is for web-based e-mail accounts. Once a user logs in, the browser automatically checks for new e-mails periodically; there's no need for the page to post back or the user to manually refresh it.

The problem that comes with the Periodic Refresh pattern is that users typically leave a browser open without interacting with it, meaning that the application happily polls for hours or even days. This could cause a lot of extra load on web servers. To solve this issue, you can use the Timeout pattern.

The Timeout pattern is another well-named pattern that times out the browser after a specified period of user inactivity; the browser can then either alert the server that the user has left or in the case of the Periodic Refresh pattern stop the updates to the page until the user resumes activity.

Periodic Refresh and Timeout Pattern Code Example

In this example, you will re-create the BBC's goal flashes and major incidents text commentary ticker to automatically keep the browser up-to-date with a football (soccer) match. However, to save server resources, you need to pause the periodic refresh after a specified period of user inactivity. If the user resumes interaction with the page, the page should in turn resume polling the server for updates.

This example uses lots of complex jQuery routines, so it is suggested that you download the source code for reference; however, the full code listing with step-by-step instructions is included if you want to follow along.

Create a new empty Visual Studio solution named `ASPPatterns.Chap9.PeriodicRefresh`, and add the following projects to the solution:

➤ A class library named `ASPPatterns.Chap9.PeriodicRefresh.Model`

➤ A class library named `ASPPatterns.Chap9.PeriodicRefresh.Repository`

➤ A web application project named `ASPPatterns.Chap9.PeriodicRefresh.UI.Web`

With your projects created, you now need to set up the project dependencies. Right-click on the Repository project and add a reference to the Model project. Lastly, right-click on the web application and add a reference to the Model and Repository projects.

Add a new class to the Model project named Event with the code definition that follows:

```
public class Event
{
    public int Id { get; set; }
    public string Time { get; set; }
    public DateTime RealTime { get; set; }
    public string Text { get; set; }
}
```

The Event class holds information pertaining to an event that has occurred in a football match. The RealTime property simulates events occurring during a match.

To retrieve a list of events, you need to define an interface for an Event repository. Add a new interface named IEventRepository to the Model project, as shown here:

```
public interface IEventRepository
{
    IEnumerable<Event> FindAllSince(int eventId);
}
```

For the implementation of the IEventRepository, you will use an in-memory collection of events to keep the project simple. Create a new class within the Repository project named EventRepository, and update it to match the code listing that follows:

```
...
using ASPPatterns.Chap9.PeriodicRefresh.Model;

namespace ASPPatterns.Chap9.PeriodicRefresh.Repository
{
    public class EventRepository : IEventRepository
    {
        private DateTime _startTime = DateTime.Now;

        public IEnumerable<Event> FindAllSince(int eventId)
        {
            return GetAllEvents()
                .FindAll(e => (e.Id > eventId) && (e.RealTime < DateTime.Now));
        }

        private List<Event> GetAllEvents()
        {
```

```
                    List<Event> events = new List<Event>();

                    events.Add(new Event { Id = 1,
                        Text = "Corner taken left-footed by Jamie Hara" +
                            " from the right by-line…",
                         RealTime = _startTime,
                         Time = _startTime.ToShortTimeString() });

                    events.Add(new Event { Id = 2,
                        Text = "Quincy Owusu-Abeyie fires in a goal from deep inside…",
                        RealTime = _startTime.AddSeconds(10),
                        Time = _startTime.ToShortTimeString() });

                    events.Add(new Event { Id = 3,
                        Text = "Dean Hammond takes a shot. Save made by David James.",
                        RealTime = _startTime.AddSeconds(12),
                        Time = _startTime.ToShortTimeString() });

                    …

                    events.Add(new Event { Id = 31,
                        Text = "The final whistle is blown by the referee.",
                        RealTime = _startTime.AddSeconds(130),
                        Time = _startTime.AddMinutes(23).ToShortTimeString() });

                    return events;
                }
            }
        }
```

The EventRepository implements the single method on the IEventRepository interface as well as a second method that returns a collection of events. Only a portion of the full collection of events is shown to give you an idea of how the collection is created. The FindAllSince method retrieves all events that have occurred up to the current time or after the Event ID passed as the method parameter. Note that the EventRepository has a private _startTime member that determines whether the event has occurred. In a real commentary application, there would be some kind of administration portal for reporters to enter updates on a sporting event in real time.

To enable the browser and client-side JavaScript to periodically check for new events within the football match, you need to create a web service. Add a new web service to the UI.Web web application project named LiveScoreSummary.asmx, and update it to match the listing that follows:

```
using System.Collections.Generic;
using System.Web.Services;
using ASPPatterns.Chap9.PeriodicRefresh.Model;
using ASPPatterns.Chap9.PeriodicRefresh.Repository;

namespace ASPPatterns.Chap9.PeriodicRefresh.UI.Web
{
    /// <summary>
    /// Summary description for LiveScoreSummary
    /// </summary>
    [WebService(Namespace = "http://tempuri.org/")]
    [WebServiceBinding(ConformsTo = WsiProfiles.BasicProfile1_1)]
    [System.ComponentModel.ToolboxItem(false)]
```

```csharp
// To allow this web service to be called from script,
// using ASP.NET AJAX, uncomment the following line.
[System.Web.Script.Services.ScriptService]
public class LiveScoreSummary : System.Web.Services.WebService
{
    private static IEventRepository _eventRepository;

    public static void SetUpEventData()
    {
        _eventRepository = new EventRepository();
    }

    [WebMethod]
    public IEnumerable<Event> GetEventsThatHaveOccuredSince(int eventId)
    {
        return _ eventRepository.FindAllSince(eventId);
    }
}
```

Pay particular attention to the un-commenting of the `[System.Web.Script.Services.ScriptService]` attribute that decorates the class. This allows the service to be called from JavaScript.

The web service has a single method that calls into the repository and returns a collection of events that have occurred since the Event ID passed. The second method on the class creates a new `EventRepository` to work with. This is important because the dummy data is time dependent.

To ensure that a new `EventRepository` is created, you can invoke the `LiveScoreSummary` `SetUpEventData` method on the `Page_Load` event. Doing so resets the data every time you refresh the page so that you can test the behavior of the client-side JavaScript:

```csharp
public partial class _Default : System.Web.UI.Page
{
    protected void Page_Load(object sender, EventArgs e)
    {
        LiveScoreSummary.SetUpEventData();
    }
}
```

Before you implement the script that will be the implementation of the Periodic Refresh and Timeout patterns, you need to add some supporting content files. Add a new folder to the `UI.Web` web project named `Content`, and to it add a file named `Site.CSS`, as displayed here:

```css
.Loading
{
    background: #CCC;
    text-align: center;
    display: none;
    position : absolute;
    z-index:1;
    font-family : verdana,helvetica,arial,sans-serif;
    font-size : 13px;
}

#Paused
```

```css
{
    background: #FFFF00;
    display: none;
    font-weight : bold;
    font-family : verdana,helvetica,arial,sans-serif;
    font-size : 13px;
    text-align: center;
}

.LoadingBlock
{
    background: #CCC;
    display: none;
}

p
{
    font-family : verdana,helvetica,arial,sans-serif;
    font-size : 13px;
}

.EventItem
{
    line-height:1.3em;
    font-family : verdana,helvetica,arial,sans-serif;
    font-size : 13px;
}


#Events
{
    width: 500px;
}

#wrap{
    width:500px;
    margin:0 auto;
    text-align:left;
}

#main-content{
    float:left;
}
```

Also, add an image file named `ajax-loader.gif` to the `Content` folder, which you can find in the code download.

Next, add a second folder named `Scripts`, and add the `jQuery-1.3.2.js` JavaScript library to the folder. You can download `jQuery` from `http://docs.jquery.com/Downloading_jQuery`. The latest version at the time of writing is 1.4.2, which also works, but 1.3.2 was the version that shipped with the ASP.NET MVC Framework module.

The final code for this project is the client-side JavaScript routines that reside within the markup of the `Default.aspx` page. For simplicity, I have embedded the JavaScript within the page; however, in a production, it makes sense to move the functions into a JavaScript library file. There is a lot going on in the `Default.aspx` page. Look at the source code that follows, which is included for completeness. You'll then see what is happening function by function:

```
<%@ Page Language="C#" AutoEventWireup="true" CodeBehind="Default.aspx.cs"
        Inherits="ASPPatterns.Chap9.PeriodicRefresh.UI.Web._Default" %>
<!DOCTYPE html PUBLIC "-//W3C//DTD XHTML 1.0 Transitional//EN"
        "http://www.w3.org/TR/xhtml1/DTD/xhtml1-transitional.dtd">

<html xmlns="http://www.w3.org/1999/xhtml" >
<head runat="server">
    <title></title>
    <script type="text/javascript" src="/Scripts/jquery-1.3.2.js"></script>
    <link href="/Content/Site.css" type="text/css" rel="stylesheet" />
    <script type="text/javascript">

        var pollforupdates = true;
        var mostRecentEvent = 0;
        var timer;

        $(document).ready(function() {
            // Periodic Refresh Pattern Implementation
            // When the document has fully loaded, start the polling for data
            getLatestEvents();

            // Timeout Pattern Implementation
            // Set up a timer to monitor user inactivity
            setupTimerToCheckForInactivity();
            // Hook up event handlers to actions that prove
            // the user is still using the page
            hookUpEventHandlersToDetermineActivity();
        });

        function getLatestEvents() {

            // This method performs an asynchronous POST to
            // retrieve any new events since the last event was displayed
            dto = { 'eventId': mostRecentEvent };
            varType = "POST";
            varUrl = "LiveScoreSummary.asmx/GetEventsThatHaveOccuredSince";
            varContentType = "application/json; charset=utf-8";
            varDataType = "json";
            varData = JSON.stringify(dto);

            $.ajaxSetup({ cache: false });

            $.ajax({
                type: varType, //GET or POST or PUT or DELETE verb
                url: varUrl, // Location of the service
                data: varData, //Data sent to server
                contentType: varContentType, // content type sent to server
                dataType: varDataType, // expected data format from server
                success: serviceSuccessful, // on successful service, call the
                                            // serviceSuccessful method
```

```
                    error: serviceFailed // on unsuccessful service, call
                                         // the serviceFailed method
        });
}

function setupTimerToCheckForInactivity() {

    // This method sets up a timer to pause the
    // polling of events after a given time.
    // In this example, a user is inactive if he hasn't
    // interacted with the screen for more than 5 seconds.
    timer = setTimeout(
        function() {
            pauseUpdates()
        }, 5000);
}

function hookUpEventHandlersToDetermineActivity() {

    // This method sets up event handlers that
    // reset the inactivity timer

    // This hooks into the mouse move event
    $(document).mousemove(function(event) {
        resetInactivityTimeCounter();
    });

    // This hooks into the window focus event
    $(window).bind("focus", function() {
        resetInactivityTimeCounter();
    });

}

function pauseUpdates() {
    pollforupdates = false;
}

function displayPauseMessage() {
    $("#Paused").slideDown("slow");
}

function resetInactivityTimeCounter() {

    // If the viewer had timed out, the
    // polling for events would need to resume
    if (pollforupdates == false) {
        pollforupdates = true;
        getLatestEvents();
    }

    $("#Paused").hide();
    // Stop the timer
    clearTimeout(timer);
    // Restart the timer
```

```
        setupTimerToCheckForInactivity()
}

function serviceFailed(result) {
    alert('Service call failed: ' + result.status + '' + result.statusText);
}

function serviceSuccessful(resultObject) {
    // On a successful AJAX POST, the JSON array result
    // is passed to the displayEvents method
    displayEvents(resultObject.d, 0);
}

function displayEvents(events, indexOfEventToAdd) {

    if (events.length > indexOfEventToAdd)
    {
        var event = events[indexOfEventToAdd];
        var eventId = "#Event_" + event.Id;

        if (eventDoesNotExistOnPage(eventId)) {

            // Update the most recent event
            mostRecentEvent = event.Id

            addEventDivAndShowLoadingDiv(event, eventId);

            // Wait 2 seconds and then hide the loading divs
            // and show the event
            setTimeout(function() {

                hideLoadingDivAndShowEventDiv(eventId);

                // Wait 2 seconds and then display
                // the next event returned from
                // the call to the service recursively calling
                // this function
                 setTimeout(function() {
                     displayEvents(events, indexOfEventToAdd + 1)
                 }, 2000);

            }, 2000);
        }
        else {
            // The event already exists on the page, so
            // check the next event by recursively calling this function
            displayEvents(events, indexOfEventToAdd + 1)
        }
    }
    else {

        // Check to see if you should call the AJAX method
        // i.e. if the user is still active
        if (pollforupdates == true) {
            pauseThenCheckForNewEvents()
```

```
            }
            else
                displayPauseMessage();
        }
    }

    function hideLoadingDivAndShowEventDiv(eventId) {
        $("#LoadingBlock").hide();
        $(eventId).show();
        $("#Loading").fadeOut('slow');
    }

    function addEventDivAndShowLoadingDiv(event, eventId) {

        // Prepend the new event to the event div
        $("#Event").prepend("<div id='Event_" +
            event.Id + "' class='EventItem'><b>" +
            event.Time + " :</b> " + event.Text + "<br/><br/></div>");

        // Get the position of the new event div
        var pos = $(eventId).offset();
        var width = $("#Event").width();
        var height = $(eventId).height();

        // Hide the new event div because you want to show a loading
        // screen to alert the user of a new event
        $(eventId).hide();

        // Show the waiting loading div directly over the newly added event
        $("#Loading").css({ "width": width + "px",
                            "left": pos.left + "px",
                            "top": pos.top + "px",
                            "height": height + "px" });
        $("#LoadingBlock").css({ "height": height + "px" });
        $("#Loading").slideDown("slow");
        $("#LoadingBlock").slideDown("slow");
    }

    function pauseThenCheckForNewEvents() {
        // Wait 3 seconds and then call the AJAX method to
        // retrieve new events
        setTimeout(
                    function() {
                        getLatestEvents()
                    }, 3000);
    }

    function eventDoesNotExistOnPage(eventId) {
        // This checks to see if there is a div
        // for the given event
        return ($(eventId).length == 0);
    }

</script>
```

```
    </head>
    <body>
        <form id="form1" runat="server">
        <div id="wrap">
            <h1>The Periodic Refresh Pattern</h1>
                <p>
                All the action as it happens from today's football games<br />
                by your man in the stand Steve Mills
                </p>
            <hr />
            <div id="main-content">
                <div id="Paused">Paused due to inactivity.</div>
                <div id="Events">
                    <div id="LoadingBlock" class="LoadingBlock"></div>
                    <div id="Event"></div>
                </div>
                <div id="Loading" class="Loading">Updating...
                        <img src='Content/ajax-loader.gif' /></div>
            </div>
        </div>
        </form>
    </body>
    </html>
```

Code snippet Default.aspx in project ASPPatterns.Chap9.PeriodicRefresh.UI.Web

The script contains implementations for both the Periodic Refresh and Timeout patterns, both of which are started when the document is fully loaded.

```
$(document).ready(function() {
        // Periodic Refresh Pattern Implementation
        // When the document has fully loaded, start the polling for data
        getLatestEvents();

        // Timeout Pattern Implementation
        // Set up a timer to monitor user inactivity
        setupTimerToCheckForInactivity();
        // hook up event handlers to actions that prove the user is still using
        // the page
        hookUpEventHandlersToDetermineActivity();
    });
```

The next sections look at both of these pattern implementations in detail.

Periodic Refresh Implementation Script

The displaying of events forms the Periodic Refresh AJAX pattern. The first method, `getLatest Events`, calls into the web service passing the last event ID displayed (initially 0) and receives a JSON array of event objects from the server.

```
function getLatestEvents() {

        // This method performs an asynchronous POST to
        // retrieve any new events since the last event was displayed
```

```
dto = { 'eventId': mostRecentEvent };

varType = "POST";
varUrl = "LiveScoreSummary.asmx/GetEventsThatHaveOccuredSince";
varContentType = "application/json; charset=utf-8";
varDataType = "json";
varData = JSON.stringify(dto);

$.ajaxSetup({ cache: false });

$.ajax({
    type: varType, //GET or POST or PUT or DELETE verb
    url: varUrl, // Location of the service
    data: varData, //Data sent to server
    contentType: varContentType, // content type sent to server
    dataType: varDataType, // expected data format from server
    success: serviceSuccessful, // on successful service, call the
                                    // serviceSuccessful method
    error: serviceFailed // on unsuccessful service, call
                            // the serviceFailed method
});
}
```

If the call is successful, the serviceSuccessful method is called, which simply passes the JSON array to the displayEvents method:

```
function serviceSuccessful(resultObject) {
    // On a successful AJAX POST, the JSON array result
    // is passed to the displayEvents method
    displayEvents(resultObject.d, 0);
}
```

The indexOfEventToAdd parameter tells the displayEvents method the index of which Event to display. The displayEvents method is then called recursively until all events within the JSON array have been displayed.

 If you are wondering what the d attribute is that wraps the array of Json events, it is basically a security feature and ensures that the Json array returned from the web service call is not valid JavaScript. The reason for wanting to return invalid JavaScript is to prevent cross-site scripting attacks. For more information on this security measure, visit www.asp.net/ajaxlibrary/Using%20JSON%20 Syntax%20with%20Ajax.ashx.

The displayEvents method first determines whether there is an event at the index specified; if there's not, the logic checks to see if the method should continue to poll (pauseThenCheckForNewEvents) or simply display a message letting users know that they have become inactive (displayPauseMessage).

If there is an event at the specified index, a check is made to see if it has already been added to the page (eventDoesNotExistOnPage). If it has been added, the next event in the array is processed by recursively calling the method and increasing the index by 1. If the event does not already appear on the page, it is added, and a loading div is displayed (addEventDivAndShowLoadingDiv). The loading div is removed after 2 seconds to give the user the chance to be alerted to an updated event message (hideLoadingDivAndShowEventDiv). After a further 2 seconds, the next event in the array is processed by recursively calling the method and increasing the index by 1.

```
function displayEvents(events, indexOfEventToAdd) {

    if (events.length > indexOfEventToAdd)
    {
        var event = events[indexOfEventToAdd];
        var eventId = "#Event_" + event.Id;

        if (eventDoesNotExistOnPage(eventId)) {

            // Update most recent event
            mostRecentEvent = event.Id

            addEventDivAndShowLoadingDiv(event, eventId);

            // Wait 2 seconds and then hide the loading divs
            // and show the event
            setTimeout(function() {

                hideLoadingDivAndShowEventDiv(eventId);

                // Wait 2 seconds and then display the
                // next event returned from
                // the call to the service recursively
                // calling this function
                 setTimeout(function() {
                     displayEvents(events, indexOfEventToAdd + 1)
                 }, 2000);

            }, 2000);
        }
        else {
            // The event already exists on the page, so
            // check the next event by recursively calling this function
            displayEvents(events, indexOfEventToAdd + 1);
        }
    }
    else {

        // Check to see if we should call the AJAX method
        // i.e. if the user is still active
        if (pollforupdates == true) {
            pauseThenCheckForNewEvents();
        }
        else
            displayPauseMessage();
    }
}
```

The script contained within the methods `addEventDivAndShowLoadingDiv` and `hideLoadingDivAnd
ShowEventDiv` uses `jQuery`'s animation functions. The details of using the `jQuery` animation func-
tions are beyond the scope of this book, but a dedicated `jQuery` reference is recommended. The `jQuery`
scripts should be easy to understand.

You will now see how the Timeout pattern is implemented in the script.

Timeout Pattern Implementation Script

When the `setupTimerToCheckForInactivity` method is called, it sets a 5-second timer. When trig-
gered, this timer calls a method named `pauseUpdates`, which in turn sets a flag named `pollforupdates`
to `false`. This flag is used with the `displayEvents` to determine whether polling should continue. In a
production application, the time to determine a user's inactivity would be longer; however, keeping it to a
low number helps you view the behavior of the Timeout pattern after you moved focus from the browser
window.

```
function setupTimerToCheckForInactivity() {

    // This method sets up a timer to pause the
    // polling of events after a given time.
    // In this example, a user is inactive if he hasn't
    // interacted with the screen for more than 5 seconds.
    timer = setTimeout(
        function() {
            pauseUpdates()
        }, 5000);
}

function pauseUpdates() {
    pollforupdates = false;
}
```

However, if the user is active, you don't want the polling of events to stop. You avoid this by calling
the `hookUpEventHandlersToDetermineActivity` method when the document is fully loaded and
setting up two event handlers:

```
function hookUpEventHandlersToDetermineActivity() {

    // This method sets up event handlers that
    // reset the inactivity timer

    // This hooks into the mouse move event
    $(document).mousemove(function(event) {
        resetInactivityTimeCounter();
    });

    // This hooks into the window focus event
    $(window).bind("focus", function() {
        resetInactivityTimeCounter();
    });
}
```

The event handlers trigger the resetInactivityTimeCounter method if the mouse is moved or the window is put in focus. The resetInactivityTimeCounter resets the check for user inactivity.

The resetInactivityTimeCounter method also kicks the polling for events back on if it has been stopped due to user inactivity:

```
function resetInactivityTimeCounter() {

    // If the viewer had timed out, the
    // polling for events needs to resume
    if (pollforupdates == false) {
        pollforupdates = true;
        getLatestEvents();
    }

    $("#Paused").hide();
    // Stop the timer
    clearTimeout(timer);
    // Restart the timer
    setupTimerToCheckForInactivity()
}
```

With the solution complete, you can now run the project and see the events update as if you were watching the commentary on a live football match. Figure 9-4 shows the browser updating with a new event, and Figure 9-5 shows the pause message displayed due to user inactivity.

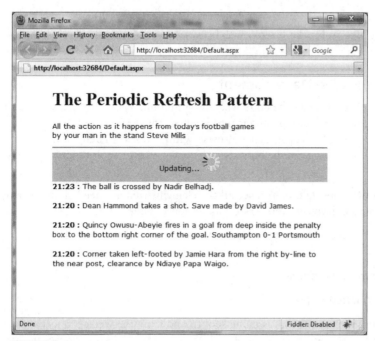

FIGURE 9-4

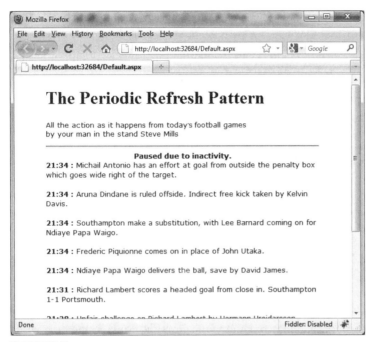

FIGURE 9-5

You will now install a popular plug-in for the Firefox web browser so you can see what is happening for each request.

Using Firefox and Firebug for Web Development

If you really want to see what's going on under the hood when programming with AJAX, download the Firefox browser from `www.mozilla.com/firefox` and install Firebug from `http://getfirebug.com/`. Now you can right-click on the `Default.aspx` page, click Browse With, and select Firefox. Open Firebug by clicking on the bug icon in the right corner of the browser or by navigating to Tools ➪ Firebug ➪ Open Firebug.

When the page loads, click on the Console tab. You see all the elements that are needed for the page being downloaded. You then see a call to the web service, as shown in Figure 9-6.

By expanding on the POST call, you can inspect the headers, post data, and response. In Figure 9-6, you are posting an event ID of 5.

Figure 9-7 shows the response from the server.

Figure 9-8 shows the JSON-formatted response.

Using Firebug is a great way to understand what is being sent to and from the web server. It's also a great tool to use when debugging. You will use this tool with the other two AJAX exercises in this chapter.

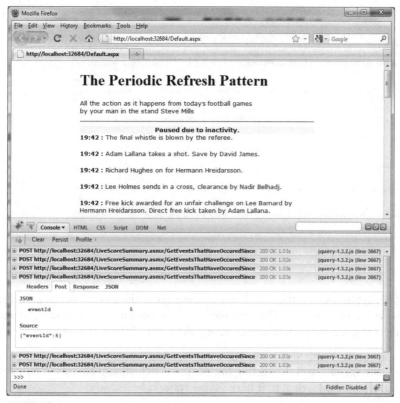

FIGURE 9-6

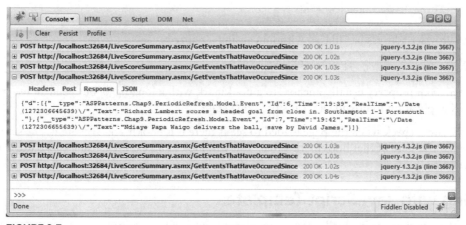

FIGURE 9-7

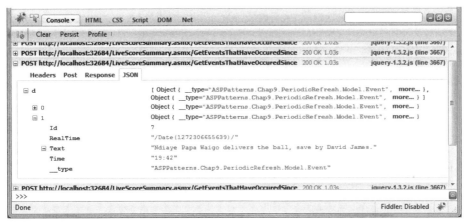

FIGURE 9-8

Unique URL

One of the issues with AJAX applications is the fact that, because calls to the server happen asynchronously, the URL of the browser never changes. Thus, it's impossible to bookmark a state in an application, such as when filtering through a list of products or saving the order of the sorted products.

To get around this issue, you need to provide unique URLs for the various states of an application. When a user filters a product page or alters the sorting options, the URL should alter as well, allowing the user to bookmark the page and return to it in the same state.

To accomplish this, you can set the `window.location.hash` value, as can be seen in the code snippet that follows:

```
window.location.hash = newStateInformation;
```

Updating the browser address bar like so without causing a redirect:

```
http://www.mysite.co.uk/mypage.aspx#OpenState
```

The `location.hash` property usually anchors to a bookmark with a long page, but you can use it with an AJAX application to provide a means of saving state.

To retrieve the state, check when the page loaded to see if there is a bookmark. If there is, the script should return to the state of that bookmark value. You will look at an example using this pattern in the next section.

Databinding with JavaScript Templates

`jTemplates` is a template engine for JavaScript available from `http://jtemplates.tpython.com` that helps to display large lists of information without the need to write masses of JavaScript code.

The page that follows is an example of the template in action. You need to download `jTemplates` from `http://jtemplates.tpython.com` and reference the `jQuery` library that you used in the last exercise to see this demo working.

```xml
<?xml version="1.0" encoding="UTF-8"?>
<!DOCTYPE html PUBLIC "-//W3C//DTD XHTML 1.1//EN"
                    "http://www.w3.org/TR/xhtml11/DTD/xhtml11.dtd">
<html xmlns="http://www.w3.org/1999/xhtml" xml:lang="en">
<head>
    <script type="text/javascript" src="jquery-1.3.2.js"></script>
    <script type="text/javascript" src="jquery-jtemplates.js"></script>

    <script type="text/javascript">
        // data - JSON array
        $(document).ready(function() {
            var data = {
                items: [
                            { Id: 1, Name: 'Scott', Age: 32 },
                            { Id: 2, Name: 'Lynsey', Age: 31 },
                            { Id: 3, Name: 'Agatha', Age: 3 },
                            { Id: 4, Name: 'Kojack', Age: 2 },
                            ]
             };

            // Attach the template to the output div
            $("#userList").setTemplate($("#userListTemplate").html());
            // Process the template by feeding in the JSON array
            $("#userList").processTemplate(data);
        });
    </script>
    <title></title>
</head>

<body>
    <! -- template -- >
    <script type="text/html" id="userListTemplate">
        <table>
        {#foreach $T.items as record}
        <tr>
            <td>{$T.record.Name}</td>
            <td>{$T.record.Age}</td>
                <td>
                  <a href="Detail.aspx?Id={$T.record.Id}">view details</a>
                </td>
            </tr>
        {#/for}
        </table>
    </script>

        <! -- results output div -- >
    <div id="userList"></div>
</body>
</html>
```

The template is defined within a script tag so that it is not shown when the page loads:

```
<script type="text/html" id="userListTemplate">
 <table>
 {#foreach $T.items as record}
 <tr>
     <td>{$T.record.Name}</td>
     <td>{$T.record.Age}</td>
         <td>
           <a href="Detail.aspx?Id={$T.record.Id}">view details</a>
         </td>
     </tr>
 {#/for}
 </table>
</script>
```

Then when the document is ready and fully loaded, a set of dummy JSON objects is created, the template is set against the output div called `userlist`, the template is processed, and the JSON array is fed in.

```
$(document).ready(function() {
    var data = {
        items: [
          { Id: 1, Name: 'Scott', Age: 32 },
          { Id: 2, Name: 'Lynsey', Age: 31 },
          { Id: 3, Name: 'Agatha', Age: 3 },
          { Id: 4, Name: 'Kojack', Age: 2 }
          ]
    };

    // Attach the template to the output div
    $("#userList").setTemplate($("#userListTemplate").html());
    // Process the template by feeding in the JSON array
    $("#userList").processTemplate(data);
});
```

You can see the output of the sample page in Figure 9-9.

Many features of `jTemplate` are beyond the scope of this book, but you can find more information on them at the project's home page at `http://jtemplates.tpython.com`.

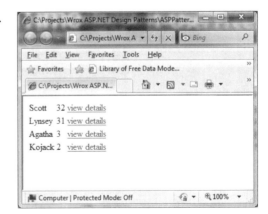

FIGURE 9-9

History and Templates Code Example

To demonstrate the data-binding capabilities with `jTemplate` and the unique URL pattern, you will build upon the solution you created in the previous chapter: a product catalog browsing site. This site will be written using the ASP.NET MVC framework and will allow customers to refine their category browsing by brand using an asynchronous callback to the server.

Create a new Visual Studio solution named ASPPatterns.Chap9.AjaxTemplates, and add the following class library projects to it:

➤   ASPPatterns.Chap9.AjaxTemplates.Controllers

➤   ASPPatterns.Chap9.AjaxTemplates.Model

➤   ASPPatterns.Chap9.AjaxTemplates.StubRepository

Lastly, add a new ASP.NET MVC application to the solution named ASPPatterns.Chap9.Ajax Templates.UI.Web.

Now you'll set the references between the projects. Right-click on the Controllers project and add a reference to the Model and the StubRepository project; also add a reference to System.Web.Mvc. Right-click on the StubRepository project and add a reference to the Model project. Finally, right-click on the UI.Web project and add a reference to the Controllers and Model projects.

The model for the project is based on the same model that you used for the sample applications in the previous chapter. Figure 9-10 shows the objects that form the domain model of the application.

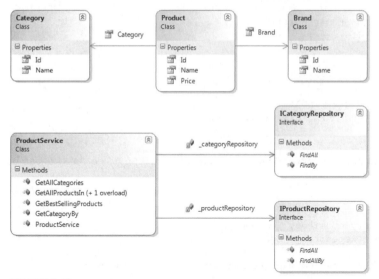

FIGURE 9-10

From within the model project create a new class that represents product brands named Brand:

```
public class Brand
{
    public int Id { get; set; }
    public string Name { get; set; }
}
```

Add a class that represents product categories named Category:

```
public class Category
```

```
    {
        public int Id { get; set; }
        public string Name { get; set; }
    }
```

Next, add the class that represents the product itself:

```
public class Product
{
    public Brand Brand { get; set; }
    public Category Category { get; set; }
    public string Name { get; set; }
    public decimal Price { get; set; }
    public int Id { get; set; }
}
```

To retrieve products and categories, create the two repository contracts named
`ICategoryRepository` and `IProductRepository`:

```
public interface ICategoryRepository
{
    IEnumerable<Category> FindAll();
    Category FindBy(int Id);
}

public interface IProductRepository
{
    IEnumerable<Product> FindAll();
    IEnumerable<Product> FindAllBy(int categoryId);
}
```

To coordinate the retrieving of products and categories, create a `ProductService` class, as can be
seen here:

```
public class ProductService
{
    private ICategoryRepository _categoryRepository;
    private IProductRepository _productRepository;

    public ProductService(ICategoryRepository categoryRepository,
                          IProductRepository productRepository)
    {
        _categoryRepository = categoryRepository;
        _productRepository = productRepository;
    }

    public IEnumerable<Product> GetAllProductsIn(int categoryId)
    {
        return _productRepository.FindAllBy(categoryId);
    }

    public IEnumerable<Product> GetAllProductsIn(int categoryId, int brandId)
    {
        return _productRepository.FindAllBy(categoryId)
                                 .Where(prod => prod.Brand.Id == brandId);
```

```
        }

        public Category GetCategoryBy(int id)
        {
            return _categoryRepository.FindBy(id);
        }

        public IEnumerable<Category> GetAllCategories()
        {
            return _categoryRepository.FindAll();
        }

        public IEnumerable<Product> GetBestSellingProducts()
        {
            return _productRepository.FindAll().Take(4);
        }
    }
}
```

Your Model project is now complete.

Switch your attention to the StubRepository project, because you are now going to create the repository implements as defined in the Model project by the interfaces ICategoryRepository and IProductRepository. To keep the solution simple, you will use an in-memory collection of products that a data context will generate. Add a new class named DataContext to the StubRepository project, and update it to match the code listing that follows:

```
using System.Collections.Generic;
using ASPPatterns.Chap9.AjaxTemplates.Model;

namespace ASPPatterns.Chap9.AjaxTemplates.StubRepository
{
    public class DataContext
    {
        private List<Product> _products;
        private List<Category> _categories;

        public DataContext()
        {
            Brand brandX = new Brand { Id = 1, Name = "Brand X" };
            Brand brandY = new Brand { Id = 2, Name = "Brand Y" };

            _categories = new List<Category>();

            Category hatCategory = new Category { Id = 1, Name = "Hats" };
            Category gloveCategory = new Category { Id = 2, Name = "Gloves" };
            Category scarfCategory = new Category { Id = 3, Name = "Scarfs" };

            _categories.Add(hatCategory);
            _categories.Add(gloveCategory);
            _categories.Add(scarfCategory);

            _products = new List<Product>();

            _products.Add(new Product { Id = 1, Name = "BaseBall Cap",
                                        Price = 9.99m,
```

```
                                    Category = hatCategory, Brand = brandX });
            _products.Add(new Product { Id = 2, Name = "Flat Cap", Price = 5.99m,
                                    Category = hatCategory, Brand = brandX });
            _products.Add(new Product { Id = 3, Name = "Top Hat", Price = 6.99m,
                                    Category = hatCategory, Brand = brandY });

            _products.Add(new Product { Id = 4, Name = "Mitten",
                                    Price = 10.99m,
                                    Category = gloveCategory,
                                    Brand = brandY });
            _products.Add(new Product { Id = 5, Name = "Fingerless Glove",
                                    Price = 13.99m, Category = gloveCategory,
                                    Brand = brandY });
            _products.Add(new Product { Id = 6, Name = "Leather Glove",
                                    Price = 7.99m,
                                    Category = gloveCategory,
                                    Brand = brandX });

            _products.Add(new Product { Id = 7, Name = "Silk Scarf",
                                    Price = 23.99m,
                                    Category = scarfCategory,
                                    Brand = brandY });
            _products.Add(new Product { Id = 8, Name = "Woolen",
                                    Price = 14.99m,
                                    Category = scarfCategory,
                                    Brand = brandX });
        }

        public List<Product> Products
        {
            get { return _products; }
        }

        public List<Category> Categories
        {
            get { return _categories; }
        }
    }
}
```

Code snippet DataContext.cs in project ASPPatterns.Chap9.AjaxTemplates.StubRepository

With the `DataContext` in place, you can now create the implementations of the `ICategoryRepository` and `IProductRepository` contracts. Add two new classes to the `StubRepository` project named `CategoryRepository` and `ProductRepository`, as shown here:

```
using System.Collections.Generic;
using System.Linq;
using ASPPatterns.Chap9.AjaxTemplates.Model;

namespace ASPPatterns.Chap9.AjaxTemplates.StubRepository
{
    public class CategoryRepository : ICategoryRepository
    {
```

```
            public IEnumerable<Category> FindAll()
            {
                return new DataContext().Categories;
            }

            public Category FindBy(int Id)
            {
                return new DataContext().Categories
                            .FirstOrDefault(cat => cat.Id == Id);
            }
        }
    }

    using System.Collections.Generic;
    using ASPPatterns.Chap9.AjaxTemplates.Model;

    namespace ASPPatterns.Chap9.AjaxTemplates.StubRepository
    {
        public class ProductRepository : IProductRepository
        {
            public IEnumerable<Product> FindAll()
            {
                return new DataContext().Products;
            }

            public IEnumerable<Product> FindAllBy(int categoryId)
            {
                return new DataContext().Products
                        .FindAll(prod => prod.Category.Id == categoryId);
            }
        }
    }
```

With the data retrieval concerns covered, you can turn your attention to the Controllers project. Add a new class to the Controllers project named CategoryBrandView, as defined here:

```
    using System.Collections.Generic;
    using ASPPatterns.Chap9.AjaxTemplates.Model;

    namespace ASPPatterns.Chap9.AjaxTemplates.Controllers
    {
        public class CategoryBrandView
        {
            public int Id { get; set; }
            public string Name { get; set; }
            public IEnumerable<Brand>  Brands { get; set; }
        }
    }
```

The CategoryBrandView class provides a view of the domain model specifically for refining products browsing by brand. To create a CategoryBrandView, you need to invent a mapping class that takes real domain entities and converts them into the view model. Add a new class named CategoryBrand ViewMapper to the Controllers project, and update it to match the listing that follows:

```
    using System.Collections.Generic;
```

```
using System.Linq;
using ASPPatterns.Chap9.AjaxTemplates.Model;

namespace ASPPatterns.Chap9.AjaxTemplates.Controllers
{
    public class CategoryBrandViewMapper
    {
        public static List<CategoryBrandView> GetCategoryBrandViews(
                                        IEnumerable<Category> categories)
        {
            return GetCategoryBrandViews(0, categories, null);
        }

        public static  List<CategoryBrandView> GetCategoryBrandViews(
                                        int categoryId,
                                      IEnumerable<Category> categories,
                                      IEnumerable<Product> products)
        {
            List<CategoryBrandView> categoryBrandViews =
                                        new List<CategoryBrandView>();

            foreach (Category cat in categories)
            {
                CategoryBrandView categoryBrandView =
                                        new CategoryBrandView
                    { Name = cat.Name, CategoryId = cat.Id,
                                    Brands = new List<Brand>() };

                if (cat.Id == categoryId)
                    categoryBrandView.Brands = (from p in products
                                            group p by p.Brand into b
                                        select b.Key as Brand)
                                        .ToList<Brand>();

                categoryBrandViews.Add(categoryBrandView);
            }
            return categoryBrandViews;
        }
    }
}
```

The CategoryBrandViewMapper has an overloaded method named GetCategoryBrandViews that converts a list of categories into CategoryBrandViews. The overloaded method takes a specific category ID and a list of products within that category as optional parameters. When supplied with these extra parameters, the method populates the category matching the categoryId with a collection of distinct brands that belong to products within that category. This displays the refine-by listings that you will see later.

Next, create a new MVC controller named HomeController, and update it to match the code listing that follows. To keep the solution simple, I used a form of poor man's dependency injection (see Chapter 5 for more information on dependency injection) by creating an overloaded constructor and hard-coded a default set of dependencies:

```
using System.Collections.Generic;
using System.Web.Mvc;
using ASPPatterns.Chap9.AjaxTemplates.Model;
using ASPPatterns.Chap9.AjaxTemplates.StubRepository;

namespace ASPPatterns.Chap9.AjaxTemplates.Controllers
{
    public class HomeController : Controller
    {
        private ProductService _productService;

        public HomeController()
            : this(new ProductService(new CategoryRepository(),
                                      new ProductRepository()))
        { }

        public HomeController(ProductService productService)
        {
            _productService = productService;
        }

        public ActionResult Index()
        {
            IEnumerable<Category> categories = _productService.GetAllCategories();
            IList<CategoryBrandView> categoryBrandViews =
                    CategoryBrandViewMapper.GetCategoryBrandViews(categories);

            ViewData["categories"] = categoryBrandViews;

            return View();
        }
    }
}
```

The HomeController has a single action, Index, that refers to the home page of the product catalog browsing site. This site simply lists the categories of products. You will create the view for this action a little later.

The next class to create is the ProductController:

```
using System.Collections.Generic;
using System.Web.Mvc;
using ASPPatterns.Chap9.AjaxTemplates.Model;
using ASPPatterns.Chap9.AjaxTemplates.StubRepository;

namespace ASPPatterns.Chap9.AjaxTemplates.Controllers
{
    public class ProductController : Controller
    {
        private ProductService _productService;

        public ProductController()
            : this(new ProductService(new CategoryRepository(),
                                      new ProductRepository()))
```

```
{ }

public ProductController(ProductService productService)
{
    _productService = productService;
}

public ActionResult CategoryProducts(int categoryId)
{
    IEnumerable<Category> categories = _productService.GetAllCategories();
    IEnumerable<Product> products = _productService
                                    .GetAllProductsIn(categoryId);
    List<CategoryBrandView> categoryBrandViews =
                    CategoryBrandViewMapper
                        .GetCategoryBrandViews(categoryId,
                                            categories,
                                            products);

    ViewData["categories"] = categoryBrandViews;

    return View(products);
}


public JsonResult GetProductsIn(string categoryId, string brandId)
{
    IEnumerable<Product> products = _productService
            .GetAllProductsIn(int.Parse(categoryId), int.Parse(brandId));

    // To simulate a long-running task
    System.Threading.Thread.Sleep(1000);

    return Json(products);
}
    }
}
```

If you are using MVC 2 you will need to update the GetProductsIn method to allow the Json object to be returned as shown in bold in the following code:

```
public JsonResult GetProductsIn(string categoryId, string brandId)
        {
                IEnumerable<Product> products = _productService
                    .GetAllProductsIn(int.Parse(categoryId),
                                        int.Parse(brandId));

            System.Threading.Thread.Sleep(1000);

            return Json(products, JsonRequestBehavior.AllowGet);
        }
```

The `ProductController` has an action to display the products in a given category called `Category Products`, and it has a method that returns a `JsonResult` called `GetProductsIn` that returns a JSON array of products that have a matching category and brand ID.

Now that the project is all set up, all that is left is to create the user experience. Switch your attention to the `UI.Web` ASP.NET MVC project, and delete the `Controllers` folder because you already defined your controllers in a separate project. Next, delete the `Views/Account` folder and all files under the `Home` and `Shared` folders.

Next, navigate to the `Views/Shared` folder and add a new partial view to the folder named `Categories.ascx` with the following markup:

```
<%@ Control Language="C#" Inherits="System.Web.Mvc.ViewUserControl" %>
<%@ Import Namespace="ASPPatterns.Chap9.AjaxTemplates.Model" %>
<%@ Import Namespace="ASPPatterns.Chap9.AjaxTemplates.Controllers" %>
<ul>
<% foreach (CategoryBrandView categoryBrandView in
                       (IEnumerable<CategoryBrandView>)ViewData["categories"])
    {%>
        <li><%= Html.ActionLink(categoryBrandView.Name,
                    "CategoryProducts",
                    "Product",
                  new { CategoryId = categoryBrandView.CategoryId }, null)%>
            <% if (categoryBrandView.Brands.Count() > 0) {%>
            <p>
            refine by brand:
            <br />
            <% foreach (Brand brand in categoryBrandView.Brands)
                { %>
            <a href="JavaScript:filterProductsBy(<%=brand.Id %>,
                                    <%=categoryBrandView.CategoryId %>);">
                            <%=brand.Name%></a><br />
            <% } %>
            </p>
            <% } %>
        </li>
<%} %>
</ul>
```

The `Categories.ascx` partial view displays the list of `CategoryBrandViews` held within the view data. If the `CategoryBrandView` has a list of brands, each brand is displayed below the category name; this allows the user to refine the category search by brand.

To keep a consistent look and feel, create a master template again within the `Shared` folder named `Shop.Master`. You can see the markup for the `Shop.Master` page here:

```
<%@ Master Language="C#" Inherits="System.Web.Mvc.ViewMasterPage" %>
<%@ Register src="Categories.ascx" tagname="Categories" tagprefix="uc1" %>

<!DOCTYPE html PUBLIC "-//W3C//DTD XHTML 1.0 Transitional//EN"
        "http://www.w3.org/TR/xhtml1/DTD/xhtml1-transitional.dtd">

<html xmlns="http://www.w3.org/1999/xhtml" >
```

```
<head runat="server">
    <script type="text/javascript" src="/Scripts/jquery-1.3.2.js"></script>
    <script type="text/javascript" src="/Scripts/jquery-jtemplates.js"></script>
    <link href="/Content/Site.css" type="text/css" rel="stylesheet" />
</head>
<body>
    <form id="form1" runat="server">
    <div id="wrap">
      <h1>The DataBinding and History Pattern</h1><hr />
      <div id="main-content">
        <asp:ContentPlaceHolder ID="MainContent" runat="server" />
      </div>
      <div id="sub-content">
        <uc1:Categories ID="Categories1" runat="server" />
      </div>
    </div>
    </form>
</body>
</html>
```

Create a new view named `Index.aspx`, and select `Shop.Master` for its master template; then update the file to match the markup that follows:

```
<%@ Page Title="" Language="C#" MasterPageFile="~/Views/Shared/Shop.Master"
    Inherits="System.Web.Mvc.ViewPage" %>

<asp:Content ID="Content1" ContentPlaceHolderID="MainContent" runat="server">
      Welcome to my shop. Please browse the product categories.
</asp:Content>
```

The last view to create is the category products view; this view displays all products within a specific category and allows the user to refine the results by filtering by product brand.

Create a new view named `CategoryProducts.aspx`, and strongly type it to an `IEnumerable<Model .Product>` collection. Again, to keep the project simple, I have added the JavaScript in line with the page. Look at the markup that follows, and then I will step through what is happening:

```
<%@ Page Title="" Language="C#" MasterPageFile="~/Views/Shared/Shop.Master"
Inherits="System.Web.Mvc.ViewPage<IEnumerable<Product>>" %>
<%@ Import Namespace="ASPPatterns.Chap9.AjaxTemplates.Model" %>
<asp:Content ID="Content1" ContentPlaceHolderID="MainContent" runat="server">

<script type="text/javascript">

    $(document).ready(function() {
        initializeStateFromURL();
    });

    function initializeStateFromURL() {

        figuresRE = /#([0-9])/;
        figuresSpec = window.location.hash;
        if (!figuresRE.test(figuresSpec)) {
            return; // Ignore URL if invalid
```

```
    }

    var brandId = figuresSpec.replace(figuresRE, "$1");
    var categoryId = $("#categoryId").val();

    filterProductsBy(brandId, categoryId);
}

function filterProductsBy(brandId, categoryId) {

    showOverlay();

    window.location.hash = brandId;

    $.getJSON('/Product/GetProductsIn?brandId=' + brandId +
                        '&categoryId=' + categoryId,
            function(data) {

                var mydata = {
                    items: data
                };

                $("#items").setTemplate($("#productItemTemplate").html());
                $("#items").processTemplate(mydata);

                hideOverlay();
            }
            );

}

function hideOverlay() {

    $("#overlay").animate({ opacity: "hide" }, "slow");
}

function showOverlay() {

  //Get the position of the placeholder element
  var pos = $("#products").offset();
  var width = $("#products").width();
  var height = $("#products").height();
  //Show the waiting overlay directly over the products
  $("#overlay").css({ "width": width + "px",
                      "left": pos.left + "px",
                      "top": pos.top + "px",
                      "height": height + "px" });
  $("#overlay").show();

  $("#overlay").animate
        (
            { opacity: 0.7 },
            1,
```

```
                function() { }
              );
    }

</script>

<script type="text/html" id="productItemTemplate">
{#foreach $T.items as record}
  {$T.record.Brand.Name} {$T.record.Name} only {$T.record.Price}<br />
    <a href="#">more information</a><hr />
{#/for}
</script>

<h2>Category Products</h2>

<div id="products">
    <div id="overlay" class="overlay"></div>
    <div id="items">
    <% foreach (Product product in Model)
       {%>
     <%=product.Brand.Name %> <%=product.Name %> only <%=product.Price %><br />
        <a href="#">more information</a><hr />
    <%} %>
    </div>
</div>

<input type="hidden" id="categoryId" name="categoryId"
       value="<%=Request.QueryString["categoryId"] %>" />

</asp:Content>
```

Code snippet CategoryProducts.aspx in project ASPPatterns.Chap9.AjaxTemplates.UI.Web

When a user clicks to refine by a brand, the `filterProductsBy` method is called. It displays the loading overlay div by calling the `showOverlay` method. Then the current URL is set to include the brand ID being refined; this enables the page to be bookmarked and linked to. Next, the JSON array is retrieved via a call to the `GetProductsIn` action, and the `jTemplate` library processes the response and updates the view. Finally, the loading div is hidden by calling the `hideOverlay` method:

```
function filterProductsBy(brandId, categoryId) {

        showOverlay();

        window.location.hash = brandId;

        $.getJSON('/Product/GetProductsIn?brandId=' + brandId +
                             '&categoryId=' + categoryId,
                  function(data) {

                        var mydata = {
                            items: data
                        };

                        $("#items").setTemplate($("#productItemTemplate").html());
```

```
                    $("#items").processTemplate(mydata);

                    hideOverlay();
                }
            );
    }
```

The `jTemplate` library picks up the template as defined in the script tags and replaces the placeholders with a list of products:

```
        <script type="text/html" id="productItemTemplate">
          {#foreach $T.items as record}
          {$T.record.Brand.Name} {$T.record.Name} only {$T.record.Price}<br />
          <a href="#">more information</a><hr />
      {#/for}
        </script>
```

If a user bookmarks the page or arrives at the page by following a link upon the page being fully loaded, there is a check to see if the brand refinement ID has been set:

```
    $(document).ready(function() {
        initializeStateFromURL();
    });

    function initializeStateFromURL() {

        figuresRE = /#([0-9])/;
        figuresSpec = window.location.hash;
        if (!figuresRE.test(figuresSpec)) {
            return; // Ignore URL if invalid
        }

        var brandId = figuresSpec.replace(figuresRE, "$1");
        var categoryId = $("#categoryId").val();

        filterProductsBy(brandId, categoryId);

    }
```

If the URL contains a brand ID, the call to filter the products is made automatically. To make it easier, pick up the category ID from a hidden text box on the page, which is set server side.

Before running the project, you need to update the `Content/Site.css` file to match what follows:

```
    #overlay{
        background: #ccc url(/content/ajax-loader.gif) no-repeat 50% 150px;
        display: none;
        position: absolute;
        text-align: center;
        z-index:1;
        border:1px dashed #CCC;
    }

    #products{
```

```
        border:1px dashed #CCC;
        height: 300px;
    }

    #wrap{
        width:770px;
        margin:0 auto;
        text-align:left;
    }

    #main-content{
        width:400px;
        float:left;
        margin-left:185px;
    }

    #sub-content{
        width:175px;
        float:left;
        margin-left:-585px;
    }
```

Now you can run the solution, and you can see the brand filtering without a post back. Notice that the URL changes to include the brand ID, as evident in Figures 9-11 and 9-12.

If you want to look at the JSON that the server is returning, switch to Firefox and open Firebug, as you can see in Figure 9-13.

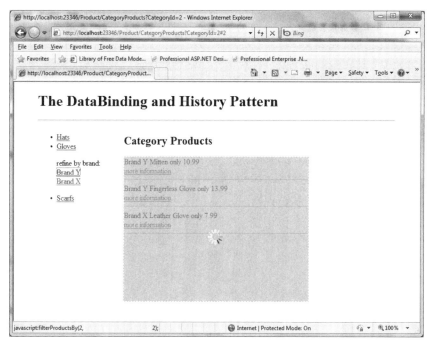

FIGURE 9-11

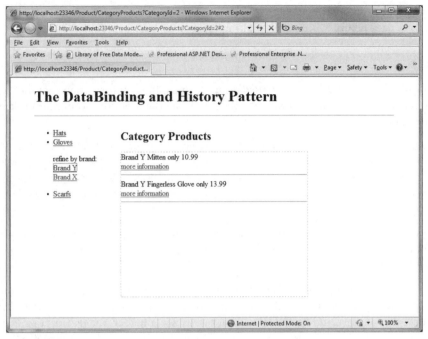

FIGURE 9-12

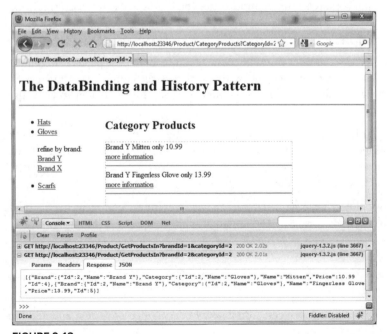

FIGURE 9-13

In the next section you will examine the predictive fetch pattern, which anticipates a user's action and proactively retrieves data before it is needed, making for a faster user experience.

Predictive Fetch

The Predictive Fetch pattern does what it says by predicting the most likely information that the user will require and fetching it asynchronously before he needs it. When the user does want that information, it is available instantly.

For the pattern to work effectively, you must know the next likely action of your user. In some applications, this can be easy to determine, such as a user reading a long article that spans several pages. If the user is on the page for more than 20 seconds, you can assume that he is reading the page and is likely to want to read the next page, so it makes sense to download the data for the reader while he is reading.

Incorrectly implemented, the Predictive Fetch pattern can be counterproductive in that you will spend server time and resources downloading data that the user will never see. You must understand your users to make optimal use of this pattern.

A progression of the predictive fetch pattern (also known as the on demand pattern) can be seen on Amazon.com in the form of scrolling-based fetching. If you navigate to www.amazon.com/Beginning-ASP-NET-4-C-VB/dp/0470502215/ and scroll down, you briefly see a loader image, the customer discussions section, a recommendations section, and so on. These sections are added to the DOM on demand just before the user needs them.

You will now walk through a small exercise that demonstrates the Predictive Fetch pattern.

Predictive Fetch Code Example

To demonstrate the Predictive Fetch example, you will create a simple blog post page that contains comments from previous readers. By default, the page will not display the comments. However, after 5 seconds, the page will asynchronously download the comments ready for the reader to view after he has read the blog post.

Create a new Visual Studio solution named ASPPatterns.Chap9.PredictiveFetch. Add a new C# class library project to the solution named ASPPatterns.Chap9.PredictiveFetch.Model. Next, add a web application project named ASPPatterns.Chap9.PredictiveFetch.UI.Web. Right-click on the UI.Web project and add a reference to the Model project.

The Model project contains one simple class named Comment to represent the comment from a reader. Add the new Comment class to the Model project, and update it with a single Text property:

```
public class Comment
{
    public string Text { get; set; }
}
```

Next, switch your attention to the UI.Web project. Add a new folder named Scripts, and add the jquery-1.3.2.js JavaScript library to the folder. You can download jQuery from http://docs.jquery.com/Downloading_jQuery. The latest version at the time of writing is 1.4.2, which also works, but 1.3.2 was the version that shipped with the ASP.NET MVC Framework module. Also, download the `jTemplate` script file from `http://jtemplates.tpython.com/` that you used in the previous exercise, and add it to the `Scripts` folder.

Add a second folder to the `UI.Web` project named `Content`. Then add a CSS file named `Site.css` to the folder and update it to match the listing that follows:

```
#Loading
{
    text-align: center;
    display: none;
    font-family : verdana,helvetica,arial,sans-serif;
    font-size : 13px;
}
```

You also need to add a loading GIF to the `Content` folder. If you download the code, you will find a file named `ajax-loader.gif` that you can use.

Right-click and select Add New Item. Then select AJAX-Enabled WCF Service, and name it `BlogService`. This service enables the web page to obtain the comments for the blog post while the user is reading the blog post:

```
using System.ServiceModel;
using System.ServiceModel.Activation;
using ASPPatterns.Chap9.PredictiveFetch.Model;
using System.Collections.Generic;

namespace ASPPatterns.Chap9.PredictiveFetch.UI.Web
{
    [ServiceContract(Namespace = "")]
    [AspNetCompatibilityRequirements
        (RequirementsMode = AspNetCompatibilityRequirementsMode.Allowed)]
    public class BlogService
    {
        // Add [WebGet] attribute to use HTTP GET
        [OperationContract]
        public List<Comment> GetCommentsFor(long postId)
        {
            // Simulates a long-running task
            System.Threading.Thread.Sleep(3000);

            List<Comment> posts = new List<Comment>();

            posts.Add(new Comment { Text = "Lorem ipsum ..." });
            posts.Add(new Comment { Text = "Suspendisse ut faucibus mi..."});
            posts.Add(new Comment { Text = "Lorem ipsum dolor sit amet, ... " });
            posts.Add(new Comment { Text = "Lorem ipsum dolor sit amet..." });

            return posts;
        }
    }
}
```

To simulate the long-running task of obtaining comments, there is a call for the current thread to sleep for 3 seconds before returning the collection of comments. Other than that, the class is straightforward.

The final step for the solution is to add the script that predictively fetches the comments for the blog post. Open the `Default.aspx` file that Visual Studio created for you, and update the markup to match the following code. Then I'll walk you through what is going on.

```
<%@ Page Language="C#" AutoEventWireup="true" CodeBehind="Default.aspx.cs"
    Inherits="ASPPatterns.Chap9.PredictiveFetch.UI.Web._Default" %>

<!DOCTYPE html PUBLIC "-//W3C//DTD XHTML 1.0 Transitional//EN"
          "http://www.w3.org/TR/xhtml1/DTD/xhtml1-transitional.dtd">

<html xmlns="http://www.w3.org/1999/xhtml" >
<head runat="server">
    <title></title>
    <script type="text/javascript" src="/Scripts/jquery-1.3.2.js"></script>
    <script type="text/javascript" src="/Scripts/jquery-jtemplates.js"></script>
    <link href="/Content/Site.css" type="text/css" rel="stylesheet" />
    <script type="text/javascript">

        var showCommentsAfterLoad = false;
        var timerToShowComments;
        var blogComments;

        $.ajaxSetup({
            type: "post",
            contentType: "application/json; charset=utf-8",
            dataType: "json"
        })

        $(document).ready(function() {

            timerToShowComments = setTimeout(function() {
                    getComments()
                }, 5000);
        });

        function storeComments(comments)
        {
            blogComments = comments;
            if (showCommentsAfterLoad == true)
                showComments(blogComments);
        }

        function showComments(comments) {
            $("#comments").setTemplate($("#productItemTemplate").html());
            $("#comments").processTemplate(comments);
            $("#Loading").hide();
        }

        function getComments()
        {
            // The post ID parameter is for illustration only
```

```
            var dto = { postId: 100 };
            $.ajax(
            {
                url: "/BlogService.svc/GetCommentsFor",
                data: JSON.stringify(dto),
                success: storeComments
             });
        }

        function displayComments() {

            if (blogComments != null)
            {
                showComments(blogComments);
            }
            else
            {
                showCommentsAfterLoad = true;
                clearTimeout(timerToShowComments);
                getComments();
                $("#Loading").show();
            }
        }

    </script>

</head>
<body>
    <form id="form1" runat="server">
    <script type="text/html" id="productItemTemplate">
    {#foreach $T.d as record}
     {$T.record.Text}<br /><hr />
        {#/for}
    </script>
    <div>
        <h1>
            Post Title
        </h1>
        <p>
            Lorem ipsum dolor sit amet, consectetur adipiscing elit.
            Donec justo nisl,
            ...
        </p>
        <p>
            <i>Posted by Scott Millett on 17 March 2010.</i></p>
        <p>
            <a href="JavaScript:displayComments();">Read comments on this post</a>.
        </p>
         <div id="comments"></div>
         <div id="Loading">Updating... <img src='Content/ajax-loader.gif' /></div>
    </div>
    </form>
</body>
</html>
```

Code snippet Default.aspx in project ASPPatterns.Chap9.PredictiveFetch.UI.Web

When the document is fully loaded, a timer is set for 5 seconds to call a `getComments` function that fetches the collection of comments:

```
$(document).ready(function() {

    timerToShowComments = setTimeout(function() {
            getComments()
        }, 5000);
});
```

The `getComments` method calls the web service. On success, it calls into the `storeComments` method:

```
function getComments()
{
    // The post ID parameter is for illustration only
    var dto = { postId: 100 };
    $.ajax(
    {
        url: "/BlogService.svc/GetCommentsFor",
        data: JSON.stringify(dto),
        success: storeComments
    });
}
```

The `storeComments` method saves the comments to a variable named `blogComments`; then a check is made to ascertain if the user had requested to see the comments. If so, the comments are displayed using the `showComments` method:

```
function storeComments(comments)
{
    blogComments = comments;
    if (showCommentsAfterLoad == true)
        showComments(blogComments);
}
```

The `showComments` method uses the `jTemplate` script library to display the collection of comments:

```
function showComments(comments) {
    $("#comments").setTemplate($("#productItemTemplate").html());
    $("#comments").processTemplate(comments);
    $("#Loading").hide();
}
```

The link that the users can click when they want to view comments calls into the `displayComments` method. This method checks whether the comments have already been downloaded as part of the predictive fetch; if not, the timer to automatically retrieve the comments is cleared, and the comments are pulled down immediately. The loading div is shown to the user; the call to retrieve the comments will take 3 seconds:

```
function displayComments() {

    if (blogComments != null)
    {
        showComments(blogComments);
    }
```

```
        else
        {
            showCommentsAfterLoad = true;
            clearTimeout(timerToShowComments);
            getComments();
            $("#Loading").show();
        }
    }
```

Build the solution and then right-click on the `Default.aspx` file. Select Browse With, and select the Firefox web browser. You will be able to see the AJAX call using Firebug, as shown in Figure 9-14.

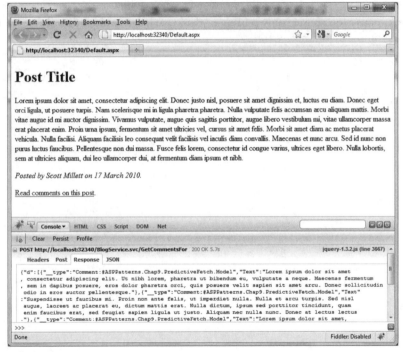

FIGURE 9-14

SUMMARY

This chapter introduced you to AJAX and how it fits in with the user experience layer. You read about the two technologies that enable AJAX to happen: the XMLHttpRequest object and the Document Object Model. You then looked at a popular JavaScript library named `jQuery` that can help you deal with the complexities of JavaScript and cross-browser interpretation.

With an understanding of AJAX and JavaScript libraries, you looked a number of AJAX patterns:

➤ **Periodic Refresh and Timeout:** The Periodic Refresh pattern concerns the updating of a page at given intervals, typically used for chat programs, web-based e-mail, and sporting events commentary. The Timeout pattern ensures that the periodic refresh occurs only while the user is still active and times out the user by setting a timer that fires after a period of inactivity.

➤ **Client-side data binding with `jTemplate`:** Templates like `jTemplate` make it easy to bind JSON data arrays to a client-side template without having to write masses of JavaScript code.

➤ **Unique URL:** The Unique URL pattern enables you to bookmark AJAX applications and restore them to a given application state by using the URL bookmark hash.

➤ **Predictive Fetch:** The Predictive Fetch pattern guesses at what the most likely action of the user will be and then asynchronously downloads the data related to the action to offer a better user experience.

The final part of this book focuses on a case study pulling in the knowledge gained from the previous chapters to form a working online e-commerce store.

PART III
Case Study: The Online E-Commerce Store

10

Requirements and Infrastructure

WHAT'S IN THIS CHAPTER?

➤ Introduction to Agatha's e-commerce store, which will form the case study putting into practice all the patterns and principles you have learned up to this point

➤ Building the `Infrastructure` project to support the application

➤ Using the design patterns and principles that you have learned to keep the code base loosely coupled and easy to maintain

The final five chapters in this book form a case study that puts into practice all the design patterns and principles you have learned throughout the previous nine chapters. The case study is based on an e-commerce site built for a fictional clothes retailer named Agatha's. In this chapter, you are given a set of requirements for the e-commerce site so you can build the infrastructure to support the site's construction in the next four chapters.

AGATHA'S CLOTHING STORE REQUIREMENTS

Figure 10-1 shows the layout of the website you will build. It has three main sections:

➤ **Product Catalog:** Customers will be able to view a selection of "top" products from the home page of the site. A full list of product categories will be displayed on all Product Catalog pages, enabling customers to view all products within a given category. A page to display the full details of a product will also be included in the product catalog browsing functionality. Finally, the Product Catalog will include the ability to add products to a basket ready for checkout.

➤ **Customer Account:** This is where customers can check on the status of orders and view a complete order history. Customers can also update their details and manage a delivery address book. Customers need to register and log in prior to being able to access this area.

➤ **Checkout and Payment:** The checkout area enables customers to create orders and pay for them using a third-party pay merchant. Customers need to register and log in prior to accessing this area.

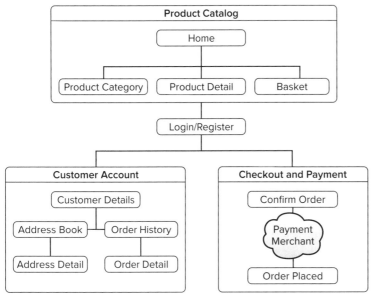

FIGURE 10-1

You will now examine each of the three sections in more detail with screen shots so you can see the look and feel of each page and information on the requirements of each of the sections.

Product Catalog and Basket Screens

Figure 10-2 shows the layout for the home page to the site.

The home page contains a list of product categories in the top-left corner, a list of top products in the main content area of the page, and a summary of items in the basket along with options to log in or register in the top right. The basket summary and account options are featured on all the Product Catalog pages. One of the requirements of the site is that all pages are fast to load and don't make unnecessary calls to the database. With this in mind, you will store the basket summary information in a cookie and update the cookie every time the basket contents change.

Figure 10-3 shows the Product Category page. This page displays all products within a given category and allows customers to refine their search by selecting only products in a combination of brands, colors, and sizes.

FIGURE 10-2

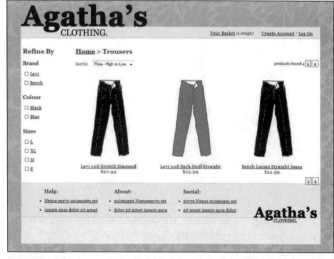

FIGURE 10-3

Another requirement of the site is to give the customers a rich experience so the feature that allows the user to refine the list of displayed products in a given category will be achieved using Ajax calls.

Figure 10-4 shows the Product Detail page. From here, customers can select the size of a product and add it to their basket.

FIGURE 10-4

As with the requirement for product category refinements, you can add an item to a basket via an Ajax call. The summary refreshes to indicate to the user that his selection is now in the basket.

Figure 10-5 shows the Basket Detail page. From here, customers can remove products, adjust the quantity of the product required, and select the delivery option. Again, all this functionality is achieved via Ajax calls without needing the entire page to post back to the server.

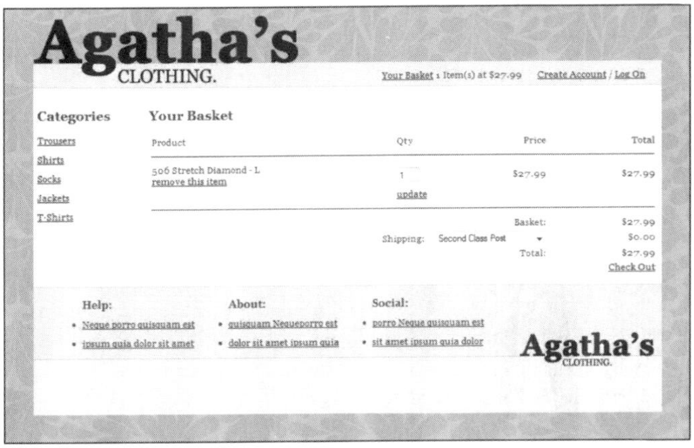

FIGURE 10-5

The look, feel, and layout of the product catalog pages is replicated throughout the site with different options for the left-side navigation being displayed at the various sections.

You will now look at the screens and the requirements for the Customer Account section.

Customer Account Screens

Figure 10-6 shows the Login page. Notice that this page gives customers two options to log in. The first is authentication using the site's own customer membership functionality, and the second authenticates by using a third-party Internet account such as Google, Twitter, or OpenID. A third-party tool that you will set up in Chapter 13 supplies the functionality of authentication through Internet sites.

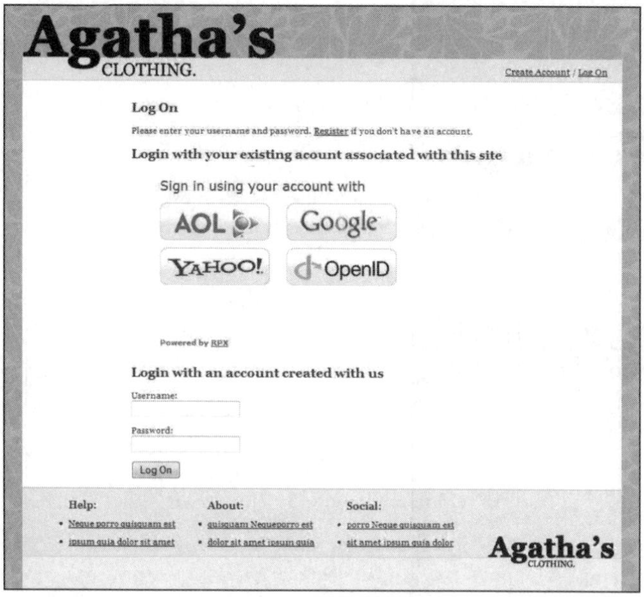

FIGURE 10-6

Figure 10-7 shows the User Details Management page. From here, a user can update her name and address details. Notice how the top-right navigation option changes from Create Account / Log On to View Your Account / Log Off. Also, notice that the left-hand navigation is in context with the customer account section and shows the options available in this section.

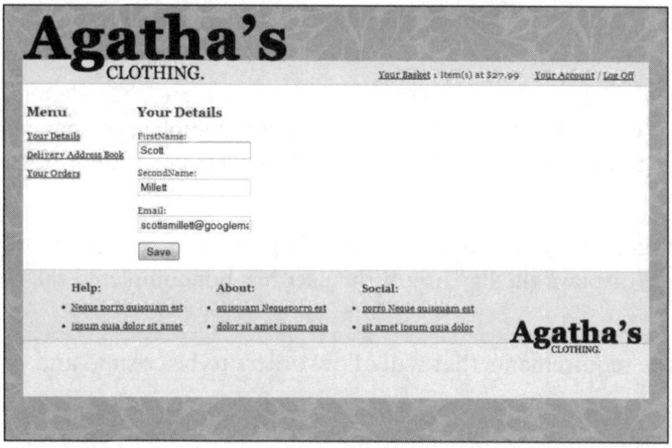

FIGURE 10-7

Figure 10-8 shows the Delivery Address Management page. From here, a user can add new delivery addresses and update existing ones. Figure 10-9 shows the Add New / Edit Existing Delivery Address Details page.

FIGURE 10-8

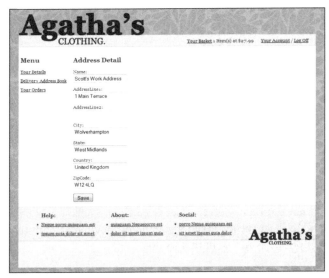

FIGURE 10-9

Figure 10-10 displays all the orders that the user has placed. If a user cannot complete the payment for an order, she can navigate to this page and pay later. The next section covers creating orders and taking payments.

Figure 10-11 shows the Order Detail page, which displays all the details pertaining to a given order. Similar to the All Orders page, this page displays the Pay link if the user has not completed the payment for the order.

You will now look at the screens and the requirements that will allow orders to be created and payments taken.

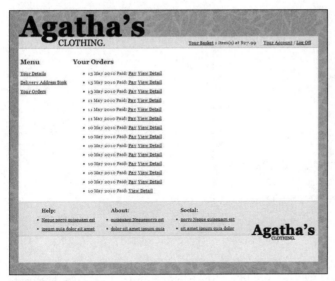

FIGURE 10-10

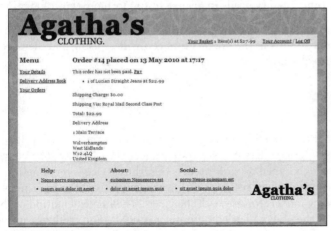

FIGURE 10-11

Checkout Screens

Figure 10-12 shows the Order Confirmation page, which allows the user to select an address or create a new one before placing the order.

After the order is created, the user is be redirected via an HTTP Post call to a third-party payment merchant that you will look at in more detail in Chapter 14. A requirement of taking payments is being be able to handle any payment merchants that use HTTP Post to check out.

FIGURE 10-12

Caching and Logging

The site needs to be fast and responsive, so you should use the caching of product data. The caching mechanism should be easy to change to support any type of storage (that is, distrusted or in memory). As with the caching, the logging functionality needs to be able to support any type of logging framework.

With the requirements gathered, it's time to look at the architecture you will be using and then fire up Visual Studio and start to create the solution.

ARCHITECTURE

Figure 10-13 shows the architecture that the site will be using. The front end of the site will utilize the ASP.NET MVC framework, with the controllers in a separate project class library. The views within the ASP.NET MVC site are strongly typed to view models that the service layer supplies. When called from the controllers, the service layer retrieves business entities from the repository layer and converts them into custom view models for use with the views. The implementation of the repository layer utilizes NHibernate as the object relational wrapper (ORM). For product catalog views, the controller talks to the cached service layer, which returns cached results if they exist. If cached results do not exist, the cached service layer speaks to the real service layer and updates its cache before returning to the controller.

Now that you understand the requirements and the architecture of the site, you can begin working on the solution. In the remainder of this section, you will build the solution structure and parts of the supporting infrastructure projects.

You can use either ASP.NET MVC 1 in Visual Studio 2005 or ASP.NET MVC 2 in Visual Studio 2010 to create this solution; any breaking changes between the two are highlighted in the text.

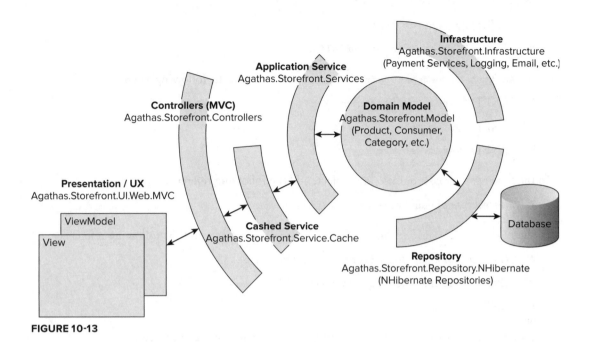

FIGURE 10-13

Create a new solution named `Agathas.Storefront` and add the following class library projects to it:

➤ `Agathas.Storefront.Controllers`

➤ `Agathas.Storefront.Infrastructure`

➤ `Agathas.Storefront.Model`

➤ `Agathas.Storefront.Repository.NHibernate`

➤ `Agathas.Storefront.Services`

➤ `Agathas.Storefront.Services.Cache`

You can delete the `Class1.cs` class that Visual Studio helpfully creates for you in all of the projects. Next add an MVC application project to the solution named `Agathas.Storefront.UI.Web.MVC`.

With the solution skeleton in place, you can set up all the dependencies between the projects and .NET assemblies.

To the `Agathas.Storefront.Controllers project`, add the following references:

➤ (Project) `Agathas.Storefront.Infrastructure`

➤ (Project) `Agathas.Storefront.Model`

➤ (Project) `Agathas.Storefront.Services`

➤ (.NET) `System.Web.Mvc`

➤ (.NET) `System.ServiceModel.Web`

➤ (.NET) `System.Web.Abstractions`

➤ (.NET) `System.Runtime.Serialization`

To the `Agathas.Storefront.Infrastructure` project, add the following references:

➤ (.NET) `System.Configuration`

➤ (.NET) `System.Web`

➤ (.NET) `System.Web.Mvc`

To the `Agathas.Storefront.Model` project, add the following references:

➤ (Project) `Agathas.Storefront.Infrastructure`

To the `Agathas.Storefront.Repository.NHibernate` project, add the following references

➤ (Project) `Agathas.Storefront.Infrastructure`

➤ (Project) `Agathas.Storefront.Model`

➤ (.NET) `System.Web`

To the `Agathas.Storefront.Services` project, add the following references:

➤ (Project) `Agathas.Storefront.Infrastructure`

➤ (Project) `Agathas.Storefront.Model`

To the `Agathas.Storefront.Services.Cache` project, add the following references:

➤ (Project) `Agathas.Storefront.Infrastructure`

➤ (Project) `Agathas.Storefront.Services`

➤ (Project) `Agathas.Storefront.Model`

➤ (.NET) `System.Web`

Finally to the `Agathas.Storefront.UI.Web.MVC` project, add the following references:

➤ (Project) `Agathas.Storefront.Infrastructure`

➤ (Project) `Agathas.Storefront.Services`

➤ (Project) `Agathas.Storefront.Services.Cache`

➤ (Project) `Agathas.Storefront.Model`

➤ (Project) `Agathas.Storefront.Controllers`

➤ (Project) `Agathas.Storefront.Repository.NHibernate`

You have now set up the foundations for your solution. Before you start to work on the product catalog feature, however, you must add the supporting infrastructure code.

Setting Up the Supporting Infrastructure

Before you begin working on the solution for Agatha's store, it makes sense to set up your supporting infrastructure so that you can then fully concentrate on meeting each of the business requirements.

You will be using StructureMap as your Inversion of Control (IoC) container. Chapter 8 covered StructureMap and Inversion Control in detail. To get a copy of StructureMap, navigate to http:// sourceforge.net/projects/structuremap and download the latest version. Extract all files into a new folder named Lib that you can create at the root of your solution via Windows Explorer. After you have downloaded StructureMap, switch back to the Visual Studio solution and add a StructureMap.dll reference to the Controllers, Infrastructure, and Web.MVC projects.

As mentioned before, you will be using the NHibernate ORM framework for your data persistence and retrieval requirements. NHibernate and patterns for the data access layer were covered in detail in Chapter 7. To work with NHibernate, you first need the framework, so navigate to www .nhibernate.org and click on the latest release; at the time of writing, this was version 2.0.1.GA. You will be redirected to SourceForge. Once there, click Download to display all the downloads for this release. Select the project named; at the time of this writing, it was NHibernate-2.1.0.Beta2 -bin.zip. When the download has completed, extract all the containing folders and files into the folder named Lib that you created earlier within the root of the solution folder. When all files have been extracted, switch back to Visual Studio and from the NHibernate project add a reference to the following files from the Lib folder:

➤ Iesi.Collections

➤ LinFu.DynamicProxy

➤ log4net

➤ NHibernate

➤ NHibernate.ByteCode.LinFu

log4net is an open source logging framework that ships with NHibernate, so it makes sense to use it for your logging requirements. Add a log4net.dll reference to the Infrastructure project.

The last open source framework you will use is AutoMapper. AutoMapper is a domain model to view the model mapping framework that removes the need to write repetitive left-to-right code when you are converting your domain objects into view model objects. For a more detailed discussion on AutoMapper, refer to Chapter 8. To get the framework, navigate to the project's home page at http://automapper.codeplex.com/ and click the Download link. AutoMapper is just a single dll. Save it to the Lib folder at the root of your solution, and then add a reference to it from the Services and the Controller projects.

With the third-party assemblies in place, you now need to set up your Infrastructure project. Create a series of new folders within the Infrastructure project that match the folders in Figure 10-14.

All of the code that you will create within the Infrastructure *project is not specific to the Agatha's store application. This means that the* Infrastructure *project is reusable for any other solution you may have. Outside of the scope of this case study it makes sense to rename the project to something like* Agathas .Core *and have it as a separate dependency that you import to all new solutions.*

You will now add the functionality for the following:

➤   Domain Layer supertype

➤   Unit of Work pattern

➤   Query Object pattern

➤   Application configuration settings

➤   Logging

➤   E-mail service

➤   Helper classes

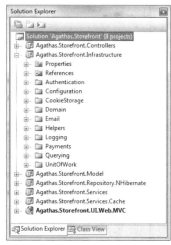

FIGURE 10-14

Domain Layer Supertype

To the Domain folder, add an interface named IAggregateRoot that will identify domain entities that will act as an aggregate root:

```
namespace Agathas.Storefront.Infrastructure.Domain
{
    public interface IAggregateRoot
    {
    }
}
```

The *aggregate root* is a term used in domain-driven design (DDD) to define the entry point into a logical aggregation of related domain entities. The job of the aggregate root is to ensure that the aggregation remains in a consistent and valid state. The entity acting as the aggregate root will also have a corresponding repository to enable data persistence and retrieval. Aggregate roots and DDD are covered in more detail in Chapter 4.

To check the validity of a domain entity prior to persistence, you will create a simple business rule class to store a rule and related entity property. The class will populate a collection of broken rules before saving an entity. Name the new class BusinessRule and update it so that it matches the following code listing:

```
namespace Agathas.Storefront.Infrastructure.Domain
{
    public class BusinessRule
    {
        private string _property;
```

```
            private string _rule;

            public BusinessRule(string property, string rule)
            {
                this._property = property;
                this._rule = rule;
            }

            public string Property
            {
                get { return _property; }
                set { _property = value; }
            }

            public string Rule
            {
                get { return _rule; }
                set { _rule = value; }
            }
        }
    }
```

Because all entities will share the same validation mechanism, you will create a Layer Supertype (as discussed in Chapter 5) that all your domain entities will inherit from and that will provide the infrastructure for checking domain validity. You can see the code for the EntityBase class that will contain the logic for validating an entity in the following listing:

```
namespace Agathas.Storefront.Infrastructure.Domain
{
    public abstract class EntityBase<TId>
    {
        private List<BusinessRule> _brokenRules = new List<BusinessRule>();

        public TId Id { get; set; }

        protected abstract void Validate();

        public IEnumerable<BusinessRule> GetBrokenRules()
        {
            _brokenRules.Clear();
            Validate();
            return _brokenRules;
        }

        protected void AddBrokenRule(BusinessRule businessRule)
        {
            _brokenRules.Add(businessRule);
        }

        public override bool Equals(object entity)
        {
            return entity != null
                && entity is EntityBase<TId>
                && this == (EntityBase<TId>)entity;
```

```
        }

        public override int GetHashCode()
        {
            return this.Id.GetHashCode();
        }

        public static bool operator ==(EntityBase<TId> entity1,
            EntityBase<TId> entity2)
        {
            if ((object)entity1 == null && (object)entity2 == null)
            {
                return true;
            }

            if ((object)entity1 == null || (object)entity2 == null)
            {
                return false;
            }

            if (entity1.Id.ToString() == entity2.Id.ToString())
            {
                return true;
            }

            return false;
        }

        public static bool operator !=(EntityBase<TId> entity1,
            EntityBase<TId> entity2)
        {
            return (!(entity1 == entity2));
        }
    }
}
```

Before persisting an entity, you will call its `GetBrokenRules` method and check for a count of 0. The `GetBrokenRules` method clears the last collection of `BusinessRules` before calling the `Validate` method, which the business entity will implement. The `Validate` method adds `BusinessRules` to the inner collection using the `AddBrokenRule` helper method.

Not all objects in the domain model will be modeled as entities. As discussed in Chapter 4, value objects are objects that do not have an identity and should be immutable. Value objects will inherit from a separate base type named `ValueObjectBase`. Because value objects are immutable and cannot be changed, they will need to be created in a valid state. If a value object is not created in a valid state, an exception will be thrown. Add a new class to the `Domain` folder named `ValueObjectIsInvalidException` with the following code listing:

```
using System;

namespace Agathas.Storefront.Infrastructure.Domain
{
```

```
        public class ValueObjectIsInvalidException : Exception
        {
            public ValueObjectIsInvalidException(string message)
                : base(message)
            {

            }
        }
    }
```

The `ValueObjectBase` class, as shown in the following listing, is very similar to the `EntityBase` class; expect that an exception will be thrown if it is invalid. The `ThrowExceptionIfInvalid` will be called from the subclasses constructor.

```
using System.Collections.Generic;
using System.Linq;
using System.Text;

namespace Agathas.Storefront.Infrastructure.Domain
{
    public abstract class ValueObjectBase
    {
        private List<BusinessRule> _brokenRules = new List<BusinessRule>();

        public ValueObjectBase()
        {
        }

        protected abstract void Validate();

        public void ThrowExceptionIfInvalid()
        {
            _brokenRules.Clear();
            Validate();
            if (_brokenRules.Count() > 0)
            {
                StringBuilder issues = new StringBuilder();
                foreach (BusinessRule businessRule in _brokenRules)
                    issues.AppendLine(businessRule.Rule);

                throw new ValueObjectIsInvalidException(issues.ToString());
            }
        }

        protected void AddBrokenRule(BusinessRule businessRule)
        {
            _brokenRules.Add(businessRule);
        }
    }
}
```

There will be two sets of aggregations in Agatha's store: namely, groups of entities that can be retrieved and persisted and groups of entities that can be retrieved only. To support this behavior, you will create two base interfaces that will define the interface for the repositories. Refer back to Chapter 7 for a more in depth look at the repository pattern.

Create two new interfaces in the Domain folder named IReadOnlyRepository and IRepository, with the following contracts:

```
using System.Collections.Generic;
using Agathas.Storefront.Infrastructure.Querying;

namespace Agathas.Storefront.Infrastructure.Domain
{
    public interface IReadOnlyRepository<T, TId> where T : IAggregateRoot
    {
        T FindBy(TId id);
        IEnumerable<T> FindAll();
        IEnumerable<T> FindBy(Query query);
        IEnumerable<T> FindBy(Query query, int index, int count);
    }
}

namespace Agathas.Storefront.Infrastructure.Domain
{
    public interface IRepository<T, TId> : IReadOnlyRepository<T, TId>
                                    where T : IAggregateRoot
    {
        void Save(T entity);
        void Add(T entity);
        void Remove(T entity);
    }
}
```

All the repository implementations in the domain model will use these two repository contracts. Notice that there is a clause for the repository stating that a repository can be defined only for an aggregate root, reinforcing the concepts of DDD that you looked at in Chapter 4. Note that the IRepository interface inherits from the IReadOnlyRepository, giving it a contract that supports both read and write methods.

The next infrastructure section you will work on is the code to provide a contract for the unit of work pattern.

Unit of Work Pattern

The Unit of Work pattern (covered in Chapter 7) enables the change tracking of multiple aggregations of domain entities and the persistence of them in one atomic operation, ensuring a valid business domain. Each repository within the solution is required to implement the IUnitOfWork Repository, as shown in the listing that follows:

```
using Agathas.Storefront.Infrastructure.Domain;

namespace Agathas.Storefront.Infrastructure.UnitOfWork
{
    public interface IUnitOfWorkRepository
```

```
    {
        void PersistCreationOf(IAggregateRoot entity);
        void PersistUpdateOf(IAggregateRoot entity);
        void PersistDeletionOf(IAggregateRoot entity);
    }
}
```

The Unit of Work contract is kept outside the repository project because the concrete implementation is of no concern to the domain services that will use it. It will be trivial to change data layer implementations at a later date; stub implementations of the Unit of Work pattern can be created for your unit tests. The contract for the Unit of Work pattern is shown in the following code listing:

```
using Agathas.Storefront.Infrastructure.Domain;

namespace Agathas.Storefront.Infrastructure.UnitOfWork
{
    public interface IUnitOfWork
    {
        void RegisterAmended(IAggregateRoot entity,
                             IUnitOfWorkRepository unitofWorkRepository);
        void RegisterNew(IAggregateRoot entity,
                         IUnitOfWorkRepository unitofWorkRepository);
        void RegisterRemoved(IAggregateRoot entity,
                             IUnitOfWorkRepository unitofWorkRepository);
        void Commit();
    }
}
```

The next piece of infrastructure code supports the querying of the repository from the server layer.

Query Object Pattern

Chapter 7 introduced the query object pattern. A *query object* represents a query written in the language of the domain. The query can be constructed within the domain service layer and then passed to the repository to be satisfied, with some kind of query translator to convert the object query into a query that the underlying database persistence framework understands. The query object you will create for this project needs to deal with subqueries, so it will build upon your knowledge gained from Chapter 7. Figure 10-15 shows the class diagram for the Query Object pattern you will create.

Add a new enumeration named CriteriaOperator to the Querying folder. The enumeration class is shown here:

```
namespace Agathas.Storefront.Infrastructure.Querying
{
    public enum CriteriaOperator
    {
        Equal,
        LesserThanOrEqual,
        NotApplicable
    }
}
```

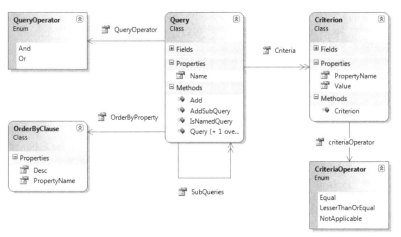

FIGURE 10-15

In this case study, you require only the three criteria operations shown in the preceding listing. As the solution grows, you would add the other operators as necessary, or better still, you would create a separate project with a full query object pattern solution and simply include it whenever you start a new project.

Next, add a class to represent the criterion named `Criterion`. The `Criterion` represents part of the filter that forms the query, specifying an entity's property value to compare it to and the way it should be compared. The code for the `Criterion` class is displayed here:

```
namespace Agathas.Storefront.Infrastructure.Querying
{
    public class Criterion
    {
        private string _propertyName;
        private object _value;
        private CriteriaOperator _criteriaOperator;

        public Criterion(string propertyName, object value,
                         CriteriaOperator criteriaOperator)
        {
            _propertyName = propertyName;
            _value = value;
            _criteriaOperator = criteriaOperator;
        }

        public string PropertyName
        {
            get { return _propertyName; }
        }

        public object Value
        {
            get { return _value; }
```

```
        }

        public CriteriaOperator criteriaOperator
        {
            get { return _criteriaOperator; }
        }
    }
}
```

The next class to create represents the ordering property to be used on the query. Create a new class named OrderByClause with the following code listing:

```
namespace Agathas.Storefront.Infrastructure.Querying
{
    public class OrderByClause
    {
        public string PropertyName { get; set; }
        public bool Desc { get; set; }
    }
}
```

A second enumeration determines how the Criterion objects will be evaluated together. Add a new enumeration named QueryOperator with the following syntax:

```
namespace Agathas.Storefront.Infrastructure.Querying
{
    public enum QueryOperator
    {
        And,
        Or
    }
}
```

The class that brings the Query Object pattern together is Query. Add a new class to the project named Query, and update it with the following code definition:

```
using System.Collections.Generic;

namespace Agathas.Storefront.Infrastructure.Querying
{
    public class Query
    {
        private IList<Query> _subQueries = new List<Query>();
        private IList<Criterion> _criteria = new List<Criterion>();

        public IEnumerable<Criterion> Criteria
        {
            get {return _criteria ;}
        }

        public IEnumerable<Query> SubQueries
        {
            get { return _subQueries;}
```

```
            }

            public void AddSubQuery(Query subQuery)
            {
                _subQueries.Add(subQuery);
            }

            public void Add(Criterion criterion)
            {
                _criteria.Add(criterion);
            }

            public QueryOperator QueryOperator { get; set; }

            public OrderByClause OrderByProperty { get; set; }
        }
    }
```

The class contains a collection of `Criterion` objects, an `OrderByClause`, a `QueryOperator` value, and a collection of sub queries. Later, you will create an NHibernate query translator to convert the `Query` object into a language it can understand.

To avoid the dreaded magic strings when building queries, you will create a helper method that allows you to use an expression parameter. This means your properties will be type safe and can be renamed via a refactoring tool:

```
using System;
using System.Linq.Expressions;

namespace Agathas.Storefront.Infrastructure.Querying
{
    public static class PropertyNameHelper
    {
        public static string ResolvePropertyName<T>(
                        Expression<Func<T, object>> expression)
        {
            var expr = expression.Body as MemberExpression;
            if (expr == null)
            {
                var u = expression.Body as UnaryExpression;
                expr = u.Operand as MemberExpression;
            }
            return expr.ToString().Substring(expr.ToString().IndexOf(".") + 1);
        }
    }
}
```

This allows you to add a new criterion to a query, like so

```
aQuery.Add(new Criterion(PropertyNameHelper
    .ResolvePropertyName<Product>(p => p.Colour.Id), id, CriteriaOperator.Equal));
```

instead of using magic strings, as shown in the code snippet that follows:

```
aQuery.Add(new Criterion("Colour.Id", id, CriteriaOperator.Equal));
```

However, that's still a bit of a mouthful, so to make it even easier to create Criterion objects, update the Criterion class to include a helper method as shown in bold in the following listing:

```
using System;
using System.Linq.Expressions;

namespace Agathas.Storefront.Infrastructure.Querying
{
    public class Criterion
    {
        private string _propertyName;
        private object _value;
        private CriteriaOperator _criteriaOperator;

        public Criterion(string propertyName, object value,
                         CriteriaOperator criteriaOperator)
        {
            _propertyName = propertyName;
            _value = value;
            _criteriaOperator = criteriaOperator;
        }

        public string PropertyName
        {
            get { return _propertyName; }
        }

        public object Value
        {
            get { return _value; }
        }

        public CriteriaOperator criteriaOperator
        {
            get { return _criteriaOperator; }
        }

        public static Criterion Create<T>(Expression<Func<T, object>> expression,
                                          object value,
                                          CriteriaOperator criteriaOperator)
        {
            string propertyName = PropertyNameHelper
                                    .ResolvePropertyName<T>(expression);
            Criterion myCriterion = new Criterion(propertyName, value,
                                                  criteriaOperator);
            return myCriterion;
        }
    }
}
```

This helper method will allow users to create Criterion objects like so:

```
aQuery.Add(Criterion.Create<Product>(p => p.Colour.Id, id,
                                CriteriaOperator.Equal));
```

The next piece of functionality that you will add to the `Infrastructure` project is the ability to obtain configuration settings, such as the number of products to appear on a page or the details used for a payment merchant.

Application Configuration Settings

The store that you will be building will use various configuration settings. These will initially be stored in the `Web.config` of the `Web.MVC` project but could change, so create a component that abstracts away from the actual implementation of where configuration settings are placed.

Add a new interface to the `Configuration` folder named `IApplicationSettings`:

```
namespace Agathas.Storefront.Infrastructure.Configuration
{
    public interface IApplicationSettings
    {
        string LoggerName { get; }
    }
}
```

The interface contains a single property getter named `LoggerName` that will be used for the logging mechanism you will create next. As you progress through this chapter and the next, you will add more settings to the interface.

Create a factory class that will be used to obtain a logger named `ApplicationSettingsFactory`:

```
namespace Agathas.Storefront.Infrastructure.Configuration
{
    public class ApplicationSettingsFactory
    {
        private static IApplicationSettings _applicationSettings;

        public static void InitializeApplicationSettingsFactory(
                               IApplicationSettings applicationSettings)
        {
            _applicationSettings = applicationSettings;
        }

        public static IApplicationSettings GetApplicationSettings()
        {
            return _applicationSettings;
        }
    }
}
```

This class uses method injection to inject a valid `IApplicationSettings` instance and has a single static `GetApplicationSettings`. The reason for the static method and the method injection over constructor injection is to allow your services and other classes to use the `ApplicationSettings Factory` without having to add it to the class's constructor. This keeps the infrastructure concerns out of your service layer.

The implementation of the `IApplicationSettings` will be a class that uses the `Web.config` to store application settings. Add a new class to the `Configuration` folder named `WebConfigApplication Settings`, with the following code listing:

```
using System.Configuration;

namespace Agathas.Storefront.Infrastructure.Configuration
{
    public class WebConfigApplicationSettings : IApplicationSettings
    {
        public string LoggerName
        {
            get { return ConfigurationManager.AppSettings["LoggerName"]; }
        }

    }
}
```

Switch to the `Web.config` within the `Web.MVC` project, and add the `AppSetting` key as shown here:

```
<appSettings>
    <add key="LoggerName" value="AgathaLogger"/>
</appSettings >
```

You will now add logging concerns to the `Infrastructure` project.

Logging

The logging mechanism works in the exact same way as the application setting functionality. Start by adding an interface named `ILogger` to the `Logging` folder:

```
namespace Agathas.Storefront.Infrastructure.Logging
{
    public interface ILogger
    {
        void Log(string message);
    }
}
```

Then, as with the application settings code, add a `LoggingFactory` class, as shown in the following code definition:

```
namespace Agathas.Storefront.Infrastructure.Logging
{
    public class LoggingFactory
    {
        private static ILogger _logger;

        public static void InitializeLogFactory(ILogger logger)
        {
            _logger = logger;
        }

        public static ILogger GetLogger()
```

```
            {
                return _logger;
            }
        }
    }
```

Next, add an implementation of the ILogger named Log4NetAdapter that will use log4net to log events:

```
using Agathas.Storefront.Infrastructure.Configuration;
using log4net;
using log4net.Config;

namespace Agathas.Storefront.Infrastructure.Logging
{
    public class Log4NetAdapter : ILogger
    {
        private readonly log4net.ILog _log;

        public Log4NetAdapter()
        {
            XmlConfigurator.Configure();
            _log = LogManager
              .GetLogger(ApplicationSettingsFactory.GetApplicationSettings()
                                                    .LoggerName);
        }

        public void Log(string message)
        {
            _log.Info(message);
        }
    }
}
```

The Log4NetAdapter is an implementation of the Adapter pattern. Refer Chapter 2 for a full explanation of the Adapter pattern.

As you can see, the Log4NetAdapter class uses the ApplicationSettingsFactory to obtain the logger name, which determines the logging strategy that log4net will use.

The logging strategy itself is configured in the Web.config of the Web.MVC project, as can be seen in the following code snippet:

```
<configuration>
  <configSections>
      <section name="log4net"
               type="log4net.Config.Log4NetConfigurationSectionHandler,log4net"/>
    ...

  </configSections>

  <log4net>
    <logger name="AgathaLogger">
        <level value="INFO"/>
```

```
            <appender-ref ref="RollingLogFileAppender" />
        </logger>

    <appender name="RollingLogFileAppender"
                type="log4net.Appender.RollingFileAppender">
        <file value="C:/logs.txt" />
        <appendToFile value="true" />
        <rollingStyle value="Size" />
        <maxSizeRollBackups value="10" />
        <maximumFileSize value="10MB" />
        <staticLogFileName value="true" />
        <layout type="log4net.Layout.PatternLayout">
            <conversionPattern value="%-5p %d %5rms %-22.22c{1} %-18.18M - %m%n" />
        </layout>
    </appender>
    </log4net>

    ...

</configuration>
```

The configuration is set to log files into a text file named Logs.txt, located at the root of the C drive. For more information on configuring log4net, check out its project home page at http://logging .apache.org/log4net/.

The next infrastructure concern you will deal with will be the e-mail service.

E-Mail Service

The e-mail service functionality will be delivered in the same manner as the logging and application settings implementations. Add a new interface named IEmailService to the Email folder:

```
namespace Agathas.Storefront.Infrastructure.Email
{
    public interface IEmailService
    {
        void SendMail(string from, string to, string subject, string body);
    }
}
```

Create a factory class named EmailServiceFactory with a static method to retrieve an implementation of the IEmailService:

```
namespace Agathas.Storefront.Infrastructure.Email
{
    public class EmailServiceFactory
    {
        private static IEmailService _emailService;

        public static void InitializeEmailServiceFactory(
                                        IEmailService emailService)
        {
            _emailService = emailService;
```

```
        }

        public static IEmailService GetEmailService()
        {
            return _emailService;
        }
    }
}
```

The .NET framework has a built-in e-mail support within the `System.Net.Mail` code namespace. Create a new class named `SMTPService` that utilizes this to send e-mails:

```
using System.Net.Mail;

namespace Agathas.Storefront.Infrastructure.Email
{
    public class SMTPService : IEmailService
    {
        public void SendMail(string from, string to, string subject, string body)
        {
            MailMessage message = new MailMessage();

            message.Subject = subject;
            message.Body = body;

            SmtpClient smtp = new SmtpClient();

            smtp.Send(message);
        }
    }
}
```

A corresponding `Web.config` application setting is needed to give details of your SMTP server:

```
<system.net>
  <mailSettings>
    <smtp>
      <network host="yoursmtpserver" port="25"
               userName="username" password="password"
               defaultCredentials="true" />
    </smtp>
  </mailSettings>
</system.net>
```

If you don't have an SMTP server and you don't like a local one in IIS, you can always create an implementation of the `IEmailService` to save the contents of the e-mail to send it to a text file. To accomplish this, create a new class named `TextLoggingEmailService` with the following code:

```
using System;
using System.Text;
using Agathas.Storefront.Infrastructure.Logging;

namespace Agathas.Storefront.Infrastructure.Email
{
```

```
public class TextLoggingEmailService : IEmailService
{
    public void SendMail(string from, string to, string subject, string body)
    {
        StringBuilder email = new StringBuilder();

        email.AppendLine(String.Format("To: {0}", to));
        email.AppendLine(String.Format("From: {0}", from));
        email.AppendLine(String.Format("Subject: {0}", subject));
        email.AppendLine(String.Format("Body: {0}", body));

        LoggingFactory.GetLogger().Log(email.ToString());
    }
}
```

Better yet, you can configure `system.net` to drop the complete e-mails as text messages on disk, as shown in the following snippet from the `web.config`:

```
<system.net>
  <mailSettings>
    <smtp deliveryMethod="SpecifiedPickupDirectory" >
      <network host="yoursmtpserver" port="25"
               userName="username" password="password"
               defaultCredentials="true" />
        <specifiedPickupDirectory pickupDirectoryLocation="C:\MyEmails"/>
    </smtp>
  </mailSettings>
</system.net>
```

Next, you will create helper classes that will be used to format money variables and resolve URLs.

Helper Classes

All product, order, and basket prices will be displayed in U.S. dollars and will be formatted in the same manner. To accomplish this, add a new class named `PriceHelper` to the `Helpers` folder with the following code definition:

```
namespace Agathas.Storefront.Infrastructure.Helpers
{
    public static class PriceHelper
    {
        public static string FormatMoney(this decimal price)
        {
            return String.Format("${0}", price);
        }
    }
}
```

The `FormatMoney` method is an extension method to a `decimal` variable, meaning that any variable of type `decimal` will have access to this method and will be able to generate a string with the U.S. dollar currency symbol.

The second helper class you will create is named `UrlHelper`, and its role is to produce a fully resolved URL for a resource. You can see the code for this class in the following listing:

```
using System.Web;

namespace Agathas.Storefront.Infrastructure.Helpers
{
    public static class UrlHelper
    {
        public static string Resolve(string resource)
        {
            return string.Format("{0}://{1}{2}{3}",
                HttpContext.Current.Request.Url.Scheme,
                HttpContext.Current.Request.ServerVariables["HTTP_HOST"],
                (HttpContext.Current.Request.ApplicationPath.Equals("/")) ?
                    string.Empty : HttpContext.Current.Request.ApplicationPath,
                resource);
        }
    }
}
```

This completes the initial requirements for the `Infrastructure` project, but as you work through the features of the case study, you will return to this project and add supporting frameworks for payment services, authentication, and cookie storage.

SUMMARY

In the first of five chapters in which you will create an e-commerce store, you looked at the requirements for Agatha's store and were taken through each of the sections you will create. You then created a solution for and built the infrastructure to support the site in a loosely coupled fashion, allowing any module to be updated without affecting the site. This included an e-mail service, logging mechanism, application setting functionality, and a querying engine.

In the next chapter, you tackle the requirement of displaying the store's product catalog, and allowing customers to filter categories of products.

11

Creating The Product Catalog

WHAT'S IN THIS CHAPTER?

➤ Requirements for the product catalog browsing experience

➤ Creating the product domain model

➤ Building the repository infrastructure with NHibernate

➤ Using AutoMapper to provide object-to-object mapping in the service layer to create view models

➤ Utilizing JavaScript Object Notation (JSON) to communicate between the controllers and the ASPX views to provide Asynchronous JavaScript and XML (AJAX) functionality

In the previous chapter, you were introduced to the requirements for Agatha's store, and you built the project structure for the solution. You also began to lay the foundations of the infrastructure that will support the site's development. In this chapter, you will build the product catalog browsing functionality that will enable customers to browse for products while utilizing AJAX and adopting a web 2.0 feel throughout.

CREATING THE PRODUCT CATALOG

Figure 11-1 shows the pages involved in displaying the product catalog for customers to browse. In this section, you will build all the code to enable customers to browse for products, and in the next section, you will build the basket functionality.

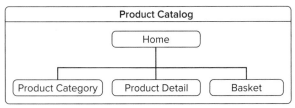

FIGURE 11-1

Product Catalog Model

Figure 11-2 shows the classes that form the product catalog model. The product catalog part of the domain model is fairly anemic, with little business logic. A `ProductTitle` represents the name of a product, and a product has a number of attributes, such as a `Brand`, `ProductColor`, and `Category`. A `Product` represents the physical `Product` a user can add to her basket and includes a `ProductSize` as well as a reference to its `ProductTitle` and some helper methods to quickly obtain access to the other attributes.

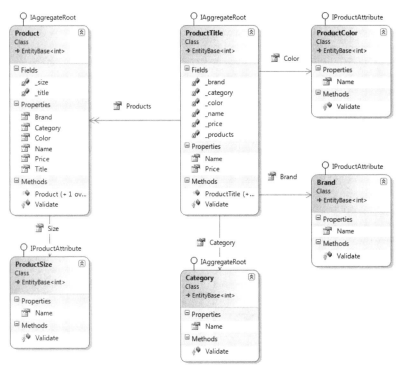

FIGURE 11-2

You will start to create the product catalog model by adding the following folders to the `Model` project to help organize the aggregates:

➤   `Categories`

➤   `Products`

Because the user will be able to refine a list of categories by attributes, you will create an `IProductAttribute` interface for all product attributes to implement:

```
namespace Agathas.Storefront.Model.Products
{
    public interface IProductAttribute
    {
        int Id { get; set; }
        string Name { get; set; }
    }
}
```

The first attribute of a product is a brand. Add a new class named `Brand` to the `Products` folder within the `Model` project:

```
namespace Agathas.Storefront.Model.Products
{
    public class Brand : EntityBase<int>, IProductAttribute
    {
        public string Name { get; set; }

        protected override void Validate()
        {
            throw new NotImplementedException();
        }
    }
}
```

In the context of this application, you will not be including an administration section to edit, add, and remove products, brands, and categories, so you will not implement the Validate method.

The second attribute is a products category. Add a new class named `Category` to the `Categories` folder with the following code definition:

```
using Agathas.Storefront.Infrastructure.Domain;
using Agathas.Storefront.Model.Products;

namespace Agathas.Storefront.Model.Categories
{
    public class Category : EntityBase<int>, IAggregateRoot, IProductAttribute
    {
        public string Name { get; set; }

        protected override void Validate()
        {
            throw new NotImplementedException();
        }
    }
}
```

Because `Category` is an aggregate root and you need to obtain a list of all categories for navigation outside the `Product` aggregate, you will create an `ICategoryRepository` interface:

```
using Agathas.Storefront.Infrastructure.Domain;

namespace Agathas.Storefront.Model.Categories
```

```
    {
        public interface ICategoryRepository : IReadOnlyRepository<Category,int>
        {
        }
    }
```

You didn't create a repository interface for the `Brand` entity simply because there is no requirement to obtain a `Brand` entity outside of a `Product`, unlike the `Category` entity. If you were looking at a `Brand` entity from a different context, such as a product merchandiser whose job it was to add product brands to the site, then the `Brand` would become an aggregate root, but in this context, you have no need to obtain `Brands` independently of `Products`.

The next attribute is size; create a new class within the `Products` folder named `ProductSize`. As with the `Brand`, this entity has not been marked as its own aggregate root because product sizes in this context cannot be obtained outside the product aggregation.

```
using Agathas.Storefront.Infrastructure.Domain;
using System;
namespace Agathas.Storefront.Model.Products
{
    public class ProductSize : EntityBase<int>, IProductAttribute
    {
        public string Name { get; set; }

        protected override void Validate()
        {
            throw new NotImplementedException();
        }
    }
}
```

The last attribute is the product's color. Create a new class named `ProductColor` within the `Products` folder, with the following code definition. Again, regarding the aggregate root, the same reasons apply as with the `ProductColor` class:

```
using System;
using Agathas.Storefront.Infrastructure.Domain;

namespace Agathas.Storefront.Model.Products
{
    public class ProductColor : EntityBase<int>, IProductAttribute
    {
        public string Name { get; set; }

        protected override void Validate()
        {
            throw new NotImplementedException();
        }
    }
}
```

The next class to create is the `Product` entity. Add a new class to the `Products` folder named `Product`, with the following listing:

```
using System;
using Agathas.Storefront.Infrastructure.Domain;
using Agathas.Storefront.Model.Brands;
using Agathas.Storefront.Model.Categories;

namespace Agathas.Storefront.Model.Products
{
    public class Product : EntityBase<int>, IAggregateRoot
    {
        public ProductSize Size { get; set; }

        public ProductTitle Title { get; set; }

        public string Name
        {
            get { return Title.Name; }
        }

        public Decimal Price
        {
            get { return Title.Price; }
        }

        public Brand Brand
        {
            get { return Title.Brand; }
        }

        public ProductColor Color
        {
            get { return Title.Color; }
        }

        public Category Category
        {
            get { return Title.Category; }
        }

        protected override void Validate()
        {
            throw new NotImplementedException();
        }
    }
}
```

The last class to create is the `ProductTitle` entity, shown next. This class again resides within the `Products` folder:

```
using System;
using Agathas.Storefront.Infrastructure.Domain;
```

```
using Agathas.Storefront.Model.Brands;
using Agathas.Storefront.Model.Categories;

namespace Agathas.Storefront.Model.Products
{
    public class ProductTitle : EntityBase<int>, IAggregateRoot
    {
        public string Name { get; set; }
        public decimal Price { get; set; }
        public Brand Brand { get; set; }
        public Category Category { get; set; }
        public ProductColor Color { get; set; }
        public IEnumerable<Product> Products { get; set; }

        protected override void Validate()
        {
            throw new NotImplementedException();
        }

    }
}
```

Both the `Product` and `ProductTitle` classes require a read-only repository, so create a repository interface for each entity named `IProductTitleRepository` and `IProductRepository` respectively in the `Products` folder with the following code definition:

```
using Agathas.Storefront.Infrastructure.Domain;

namespace Agathas.Storefront.Model.Products
{
    public interface IProductTitleRepository :
                        IReadOnlyRepository<ProductTitle, int>
    {
    }
}

using Agathas.Storefront.Infrastructure.Domain;

namespace Agathas.Storefront.Model.Products
{
    public interface IProductRepository : IReadOnlyRepository<Product, int>
    {
    }
}
```

This completes the simple product catalog model. You will now create the database tables to store instances of products and their attributes.

Product Catalog Data Tables

Within the `Web.MVC` project, create a new database within the `App_Data` folder named `Shop.mdf`. Once you've done that, add the tables shown in Figure 11-3. Ensure that you set all the primary key fields as identity fields; this will mean that the database is in charge of creating the entity's identity.

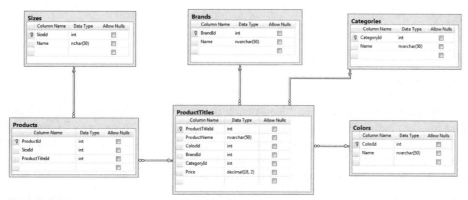

FIGURE 11-3

After the data model is created, you need to set up the mapping files so NHibernate can retrieve the products.

Product Catalog Repositories

With the data model and the business model built, you can build the repositories that enable you to retrieve products to display to the customers. You will be using NHibernate, an object relational mapper (ORM) that has many enterprise patterns built in. The first task to set up the repositories is to create files that map the database tables and columns to your domain entities and properties, as defined in the Model project.

> *Refer to Chapter 7 for more detail data access the patterns and the NHibernate framework.*

Add a new folder named Mapping to the NHibernate project, and to it add a new XML file named Brand.hbm.xml. The XML file is metadata that enables the NHibernate framework to know how your business entity within the domain model and the data table within the data model relate to each other.

The listing that follows shows the metadata for the Brand.hbm.xml file:

```xml
<?xml version="1.0" encoding="utf-8" ?>
<hibernate-mapping xmlns="urn:nhibernate-mapping-2.2"
    namespace="Agathas.Storefront.Model.Products"
        assembly="Agathas.Storefront.Model">

  <class name="Brand" table="Brands" lazy="false" >

    <id  name="Id" column="BrandId"  type="int" unsaved-value="0">
      <generator class="native" />
    </id>

    <property name="Name">
```

```
        <column name="Name" sql-type="nvarchar(50)" not-null="true" />
      </property>

   </class>

</hibernate-mapping>
```

After you have updated the `Brand.hbm.xml` file to match the preceding listing, you need to change the build action for the file. Right-click on the XML file and bring up its properties from the context-sensitive menu. Once the properties dialog is displayed, change the build action to Embedded Resource. This ensures that the XML data is embedded when the assembly is built. All the mapping files need to have their build actions changed to Embedded Resource.

The next mapping file is for the `Category` entity. Add a new XML file to the `Mapping` folder named `Category.hbm.xml`, and update it with the following markup. Again, change the build action property of the XML file to Embedded Resource.

```
<?xml version="1.0" encoding="utf-8" ?>
<hibernate-mapping xmlns="urn:nhibernate-mapping-2.2"
    namespace="Agathas.Storefront.Model.Categories"
        assembly="Agathas.Storefront.Model">

  <class name="Category" table="Categories" lazy="false" >

    <id  name="Id" column="CategoryId"  type="int" unsaved-value="0">
      <generator class="native" />
    </id>

    <property name="Name">
      <column name="Name" sql-type="nvarchar(50)" not-null="true" />
    </property>

  </class>

</hibernate-mapping>
```

Add a third XML file for the `Product` entity named `Product.hbm.xml`, with the markup displayed here:

```
<?xml version="1.0" encoding="utf-8" ?>
<hibernate-mapping xmlns="urn:nhibernate-mapping-2.2"
    namespace="Agathas.Storefront.Model.Products"
        assembly="Agathas.Storefront.Model">

  <class name="Product" table="Products" lazy="false" >

    <id  name="Id" column="ProductId" unsaved-value="0">
      <generator class="native" />
    </id>

    <many-to-one name="Size"
                 class="ProductSize"
                 column="SizeId"
```

```
                              not-null="true"/>

        <many-to-one name="Title"
                     class="ProductTitle"
                     column="ProductTitleId"
                     not-null="true"
                     lazy="false"/>
    </class>

</hibernate-mapping>
```

Add the mapping files in the same manner for the ProductColor, ProductSize, and ProductTitle entities.

The following listing is the mapping file for the ProductColor named ProductColor.hbm.xml.

```
<?xml version="1.0" encoding="utf-8" ?>
<hibernate-mapping xmlns="urn:nhibernate-mapping-2.2"
    namespace="Agathas.Storefront.Model.Products"
        assembly="Agathas.Storefront.Model">

  <class name="ProductColor" table="Colors" lazy="false" >

    <id  name="Id" column="ColorId"  type="int" unsaved-value="0">
      <generator class="native" />
    </id>

    <property name="Name">
      <column name="Name" sql-type="nvarchar(50)" not-null="true" />
    </property>

  </class>

</hibernate-mapping>
```

The following listing is the mapping file for the ProductSize class named ProductSize.hbm.xml.

```
<?xml version="1.0" encoding="utf-8" ?>
<hibernate-mapping xmlns="urn:nhibernate-mapping-2.2"
    namespace="Agathas.Storefront.Model.Products"
        assembly="Agathas.Storefront.Model">

  <class name="ProductSize" table="Sizes" lazy="false" >

    <id  name="Id" column="SizeId"  type="int" unsaved-value="0">
      <generator class="native" />
    </id>

    <property name="Name">
      <column name="Name" sql-type="nvarchar(50)" not-null="true" />
    </property>

  </class>

</hibernate-mapping>
```

The following listing is for the `ProductTitle` class named `ProductTitle.hbm.xml`.

```xml
<?xml version="1.0" encoding="utf-8" ?>
<hibernate-mapping xmlns="urn:nhibernate-mapping-2.2"
    namespace="Agathas.Storefront.Model.Products"
        assembly="Agathas.Storefront.Model">

  <class name="ProductTitle" table="ProductTitles" lazy="false" >

    <id name="Id" column="ProductTitleId"  type="int" unsaved-value="0">
      <generator class="native" />
    </id>

    <property name="Price">
      <column name="Price" sql-type="decimal(18, 2)" not-null="true" />
    </property>

    <property name="Name">
      <column name="ProductName" sql-type="nvarchar(50)" not-null="true" />
    </property>

    <many-to-one name="Color"
                 class="ProductColor"
                 column="ColorId"
                 not-null="true"/>

    <many-to-one name="Brand"
                 class="Brand"
                 column="BrandId"
                 not-null="true"/>

    <many-to-one name="Category"
                 class="Agathas.Storefront.Model.Categories.Category"
                 column="CategoryId"
                 not-null="true"
                 lazy="false"/>

    <bag name="Products" inverse="true" cascade="all" lazy="false" fetch="join"  >
      <key column="ProductTitleId"/>
      <one-to-many class="Product"></one-to-many>
    </bag>

  </class>

</hibernate-mapping>
```

Again, ensure that you have changed each of the file's build actions to Embedded Resource so that the NHibernate framework can find the mapping metadata.

Now that you have configured how your business entities map to your data tables, you can begin programming the NHibernate Repository. Create a folder within the root of the NHibernate project named `SessionStorage`. This will contain all the code necessary to store a unit of work, also known as a *session* in NHibernate. You will typically store instances of a session differently depending on whether you are working within a web application or a Windows smart client. For this reason, you will create an interface to communicate with a session container. Create a new interface named ISessionStorageContainer with the following contract:

```
using NHibernate;

namespace Agathas.Storefront.Repository.NHibernate.SessionStorage
{
    public interface ISessionStorageContainer
    {
        ISession GetCurrentSession();
        void Store(ISession session);
    }
}
```

Because you will be working within a web environment that has an HTTP context, you need a session container that utilizes the HTTP items collection to store sessions. Add a new class that implements the ISessionStorageContainer interface named HttpSessionContainer with the following code listing. Note that you have to make a reference to the System.Web assembly in the NHibernate project:

```
using NHibernate;
using System.Web;

namespace Agathas.Storefront.Repository.NHibernate.SessionStorage
{
    public class HttpSessionContainer : ISessionStorageContainer
    {
        private string _sessionKey = "NHSession";

        public ISession GetCurrentSession()
        {
            ISession nhSession = null;

            if (HttpContext.Current.Items.Contains(_sessionKey))
                nhSession = (ISession)HttpContext.Current.Items[_sessionKey];

            return nhSession;
        }

        public void Store(ISession session)
        {
            if (HttpContext.Current.Items.Contains(_sessionKey))
                HttpContext.Current.Items[_sessionKey] = session;
            else
                HttpContext.Current.Items.Add(_sessionKey, session);
        }
    }
}
```

This class simply stores and retrieves NHibernate sessions from the HTTP items collection. For completeness, you can create a smart client version for use in nonweb scenarios. Add a new class to the `SessionStorage` folder named `ThreadSessionStorageContainer` that also implements the `ISessionStorageContainer`. The code for this class is shown here:

```
using global::NHibernate;
using System.Collections;
using System.Threading;

namespace Agathas.Storefront.Repository.NHibernate.SessionStorage
{
    public class ThreadSessionStorageContainer : ISessionStorageContainer
    {
        private static readonly Hashtable _nhSessions = new Hashtable();

        public ISession GetCurrentSession()
        {
            ISession nhSession = null;

            if (_nhSessions.Contains(GetThreadName()))
                nhSession = (ISession)_nhSessions[GetThreadName()];

            return nhSession;
        }

        public void Store(ISession session)
        {
            if (_nhSessions.Contains(GetThreadName()))
                _nhSessions[GetThreadName()] = session;
            else
                _nhSessions.Add(GetThreadName(), session);
        }

        private static string GetThreadName()
        {
            return Thread.CurrentThread.Name;
        }
    }
}
```

This class simply retains sessions within a hash table using the current thread name as a key.

To obtain the best session container for your application, add a factory class that will be responsible for creating and supplying a valid session container. Add a new class to the `SessionStorage` folder named `SessionStorageFactory` with the following listing:

```
using System.Web;

namespace Agathas.Storefront.Repository.NHibernate.SessionStorage
{
    public static class SessionStorageFactory
    {
        private static ISessionStorageContainer _nhSessionStorageContainer;

        public static ISessionStorageContainer GetStorageContainer()
        {
            if (_nhSessionStorageContainer == null)
```

```
                {
                    if (HttpContext.Current == null)
                        _nhSessionStorageContainer =
                                new ThreadSessionStorageContainer();
                    else
                        _nhSessionStorageContainer = new HttpSessionContainer();
                }

                return _nhSessionStorageContainer;
            }
        }
    }
```

This `SessionStorageFactory` determines whether an HTTP context exists. If it does, an `HttpSession Container` is created; otherwise, a `ThreadSessionStorageContainer` is used. Once the concrete implementation of the `ISessionStorageContainer` interface is created, it is stored in a static variable.

With the ability to store sessions taken care of, you need a way to create them so that you can use NHibernate to persist and retrieve your business entities. Add a new class to the root of the NHibernate project, and name it `SessionFactory`. The code for this class follows:

```
using NHibernate;
using NHibernate.Cfg;
using System.Web;
using Agathas.Storefront.Repository.NHibernate.SessionStorage;

namespace Agathas.Storefront.Repository.NHibernate
{
    public class SessionFactory
    {
        private static ISessionFactory _sessionFactory;

        private static void Init()
        {
            Configuration config = new Configuration();
            config.AddAssembly("Agathas.Storefront.Repository.NHibernate");

            log4net.Config.XmlConfigurator.Configure();

            config.Configure();

            _sessionFactory = config.BuildSessionFactory();
        }

        private static ISessionFactory GetSessionFactory()
        {
            if (_sessionFactory == null)
                Init();

            return _sessionFactory;
        }

        private static ISession GetNewSession()
        {
```

```
            return GetSessionFactory().OpenSession();
        }

        public static ISession GetCurrentSession()
        {
            ISessionStorageContainer sessionStorageContainer =
                                SessionStorageFactory.GetStorageContainer();

            ISession currentSession = sessionStorageContainer.GetCurrentSession();

            if (currentSession == null)
            {
                currentSession = GetNewSession();
                sessionStorageContainer.Store(currentSession);
            }

            return currentSession;
        }
    }
}
```

 Please refer to Chapter 7 for a detailed discussion on the SessionFactory *class.*

Now that you have configured NHibernate, you can start to use it. Add a new class to the root of the NHibernate project named NHUnitOfWork. This will be NHibernate's implementation of the Unit of Work pattern that you defined in the infrastructure project. The code for this class follows:

```
using System;
using Agathas.Storefront.Infrastructure.Domain;
using Agathas.Storefront.Infrastructure.UnitOfWork;
using Agathas.Storefront.Repository.NHibernate.SessionStorage;
using NHibernate;

namespace Agathas.Storefront.Repository.NHibernate
{
    public class NHUnitOfWork : IUnitOfWork
    {
        public void RegisterAmended(IAggregateRoot entity,
                                IUnitOfWorkRepository unitofWorkRepository)
        {
            SessionFactory.GetCurrentSession().SaveOrUpdate(entity);
        }

        public void RegisterNew(IAggregateRoot entity,
                                IUnitOfWorkRepository unitofWorkRepository)
        {
            SessionFactory.GetCurrentSession().Save(entity);
        }

        public void RegisterRemoved(IAggregateRoot entity,
```

```
                                        IUnitOfWorkRepository unitofWorkRepository)
    {
        SessionFactory.GetCurrentSession().Delete(entity);
    }

    public void Commit()
    {
        using (ITransaction transaction =
                        SessionFactory.GetCurrentSession().BeginTransaction())
        {
            try
            { transaction.Commit(); }
            catch (Exception ex)
            {
                transaction.Rollback();
                throw;
            }
        }
    }
}
}
```

Because the ISession interface implements the Unit of Work pattern discussed earlier in this chapter, no changes will occur until a transaction is committed. Another pattern built into NHibernate is Identity Map (see Chapter 7), which maintains a single instance of a business entity in the ISession no matter how many times you retrieve it.

The repository implementations are easy to create thanks to generics. You can create a base repository class using generics to provide all the functionality for all the repositories. Create a new folder named Repositories, and add a new class to it named Repository, with the code listing shown here:

```
using System.Collections.Generic;
using Agathas.Storefront.Infrastructure.Domain;
using Agathas.Storefront.Infrastructure.Querying;
using Agathas.Storefront.Infrastructure.UnitOfWork;
using Agathas.Storefront.Repository.NHibernate.SessionStorage;
using NHibernate;

namespace Agathas.Storefront.Repository.NHibernate.Repositories
{
    public abstract class Repository<T, TEntityKey> where T : IAggregateRoot
    {
        private IUnitOfWork _uow;

        public Repository(IUnitOfWork uow)
        {
            _uow = uow;
        }

        public void Add(T entity)
        {
            SessionFactory.GetCurrentSession().Save(entity);
        }
```

```
public void Remove(T entity)
{
    SessionFactory.GetCurrentSession().Delete(entity);
}

public void Save(T entity)
{
    SessionFactory.GetCurrentSession().SaveOrUpdate(entity);
}

public T FindBy(TEntityKey id)
{
    return SessionFactory.GetCurrentSession().Get<T>(id);
}

public IEnumerable<T> FindAll()
{
    ICriteria criteriaQuery =
            SessionFactory.GetCurrentSession().CreateCriteria(typeof(T));

    return (List<T>)criteriaQuery.List<T>();
}

public IEnumerable<T> FindAll(int index, int count)
{
    ICriteria criteriaQuery =
            SessionFactory.GetCurrentSession().CreateCriteria(typeof(T));

    return (List<T>)criteriaQuery.SetFetchSize(count)
                        .SetFirstResult(index).List<T>();
}

public IEnumerable<T> FindBy(Query query)
{
    ICriteria criteriaQuery =
            SessionFactory.GetCurrentSession().CreateCriteria(typeof(T));

    AppendCriteria(criteriaQuery);

    query.TranslateIntoNHQuery<T>(criteriaQuery);

    return criteriaQuery.List<T>();
}

public IEnumerable<T> FindBy(Query query, int index, int count)
{
    ICriteria criteriaQuery =
            SessionFactory.GetCurrentSession().CreateCriteria(typeof(T));

    AppendCriteria(criteriaQuery);

    query.TranslateIntoNHQuery<T>(criteriaQuery);

    return criteriaQuery.SetFetchSize(count)
```

```
                              .SetFirstResult(index).List<T>();
        }

        public virtual void AppendCriteria(ICriteria criteria)
        {

        }
    }
}
```

Code snippet Repository.cs in project Agathas.Storefront.Repository.NHibernate

After you have created the `Repository` class, you will get a compile time error due to the nonexistent `TranslateIntoNHQuery` extension method. However, you can fix this by creating the class now. Add a new class named `QueryTranslator` to the `Repositories` folder with the following code listing. This class simply converts the data access technology agnostic query object that you created in the `Infrastructure` project into a query that NHibernate understands:

```csharp
using System;
using System.Collections.Generic;
using Agathas.Storefront.Infrastructure.Querying;
using NHibernate;
using NHibernate.Criterion;

namespace Agathas.Storefront.Repository.NHibernate.Repositories
{
    public static class QueryTranslator
    {
        public static ICriteria TranslateIntoNHQuery<T>(this Query query,
                                                        ICriteria criteria)
        {
            BuildQueryFrom(query, criteria);

            if(query.OrderByProperty != null)
                criteria.AddOrder(new Order(query.OrderByProperty.PropertyName,
                                            !query.OrderByProperty.Desc));

            return criteria;
        }

        private static void BuildQueryFrom(Query query, ICriteria criteria)
        {
            IList<ICriterion> criterions = new List<ICriterion>();

            if (query.Criteria != null)
            {
                foreach (Criterion c in query.Criteria)
                {
                    ICriterion criterion;

                    switch (c.criteriaOperator)
                    {
                        case CriteriaOperator.Equal:
                            criterion = Expression.Eq(c.PropertyName, c.Value);
```

```
                                    break;
                            case CriteriaOperator.LesserThanOrEqual:
                                criterion = Expression.Le(c.PropertyName, c.Value);
                                break;
                            default:
                                throw new ApplicationException("No operator defined");
                        }

                        criterions.Add(criterion);
                    }

                    if (query.QueryOperator == QueryOperator.And)
                    {
                        Conjunction andSubQuery = Expression.Conjunction();
                        foreach (ICriterion criterion in criterions)
                        {
                            andSubQuery.Add(criterion);
                        }

                        criteria.Add(andSubQuery);
                    }
                    else
                    {
                        Disjunction orSubQuery = Expression.Disjunction();
                        foreach (ICriterion criterion in criterions)
                        {
                            orSubQuery.Add(criterion);
                        }
                        criteria.Add(orSubQuery);
                    }

                    foreach (Query sub in query.SubQueries)
                    {
                        BuildQueryFrom(sub, criteria);
                    }
                }
            }
        }
    }
```

Code snippet QueryTranslator.cs in project Agathas.Storefront.Repository.NHibernate

All the repository implementations for the product catalog are similar, so create three repository implements named `CategoryRepository`, `ProductTitleRepository`, and `ProductRepository` with the following code definition:

```
using Agathas.Storefront.Infrastructure.UnitOfWork;
using Agathas.Storefront.Model.Categories;

namespace Agathas.Storefront.Repository.NHibernate.Repositories
{
    public class CategoryRepository : Repository<Category, int>,
                                      ICategoryRepository
    {
```

```
            public CategoryRepository(IUnitOfWork uow) : base(uow)
            {
            }
        }
    }


using Agathas.Storefront.Infrastructure.UnitOfWork;
using Agathas.Storefront.Model.Products;

namespace Agathas.Storefront.Repository.NHibernate.Repositories
{
    public class ProductTitleRepository : Repository<ProductTitle, int>,
                                          IProductTitleRepository
    {
        public ProductTitleRepository(IUnitOfWork uow) : base(uow)
        {
        }
    }
}


using Agathas.Storefront.Infrastructure.UnitOfWork;
using Agathas.Storefront.Model.Products;
using NHibernate;

namespace Agathas.Storefront.Repository.NHibernate.Repositories
{
    public class ProductRepository : Repository<Product, int>, IProductRepository
    {
        public ProductRepository(IUnitOfWork uow)
            : base(uow)
        {
        }

        public override void AppendCriteria(ICriteria criteria)
        {
            criteria.CreateAlias("Title", "ProductTitle");
            criteria.CreateAlias("ProductTitle.Category", "Category");
            criteria.CreateAlias("ProductTitle.Brand", "Brand");
            criteria.CreateAlias("ProductTitle.Color", "Color");
        }
    }
}
```

Notice that the `ProductRepository` implementation is slightly different because there is a need to create some aliases. An alias helps NHibernate resolve relationships. Without an alias, NHibernate wouldn't be able to resolve `"Category.Id"` or `"Brand.Id"` as a query from the `Product` entity because NHibernate would assume that you're referring to an explicit property name and would be unclear about how the object model should be traversed. Using `CreateAlias` lets NHibernate know how to resolve the relationship; this way when you are building a query in the service, you can happily refer to the `Product` properties.

The last task to complete the repository implementation is to add the following code to the `Web.config` in the `Web.MVC` file, which configures NHibernate:

```
<configuration>

  <configSections>
    <section name="hibernate-configuration"
             type="NHibernate.Cfg.ConfigurationSectionHandler, NHibernate"/>
    …
  </configSections>

  …

  <hibernate-configuration xmlns="urn:nhibernate-configuration-2.2">
    <session-factory name="NHibernate.Test">
      <property name="connection.driver_class">
              NHibernate.Driver.SqlClientDriver</property>
      <property name="connection.connection_string">
        Data Source=.\SQLEXPRESS;AttachDbFilename=|DataDirectory|Shop.mdf;
                    Integrated Security=True;User Instance=True
      </property>
      <property name="adonet.batch_size">10</property>
      <property name="show_sql">true</property>
      <property name="dialect">NHibernate.Dialect.MsSql2005Dialect</property>
      <property name="use_outer_join">true</property>
      <property name="command_timeout">60</property>
      <property name="query.substitutions">
          true 1, false 0, yes 'Y', no 'N'</property>
      <property name="proxyfactory.factory_class">
        NHibernate.ByteCode.LinFu.ProxyFactoryFactory, NHibernate.ByteCode.LinFu
      </property>
    </session-factory>
  </hibernate-configuration>
  …
</configuration>
```

With the model and repositories now built, you can turn your attention to the service layer, the API for the application.

Product Services

The role of the service layer in the Agatha solution is to coordinate the retrieval and persistence of business entities. A service receives requests from the controllers for updates to the domain model as well as a specific view of the domain. All the views (ASPX pages) are based on a strongly typed view model. Figure 11-4 shows the flow of data after a controller handles a request.

 Refer to Chapter 8 for a detailed description of view models.

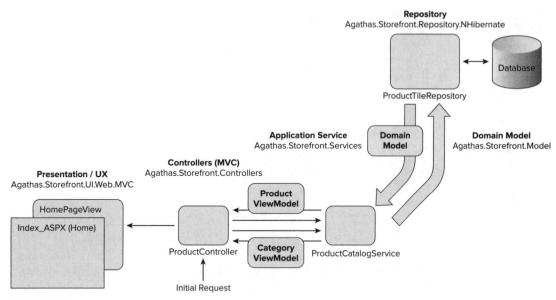

FIGURE 11-4

The controller receives the initial request and calls the appropriate service method(s). In this example, the request is for the site's homepage. The service in turn contacts the repository to obtain a collection of `Product` domain entities. It then converts them into a collection of `ProductViews`, which it returns to the controller. The controller receives the collection of `ProductViews` and any other necessary information to be displayed on the web page, such as a basket summary or customer name. It does this before creating a `HomePageView`, which is strongly typed to the .ASPX view, and sending it to the view for display. All the views in the solution have a dedicated view model for displaying purposes.

You will now create all the views required for the product catalog functionality before creating the service methods. The views are simple data transfer objects that represent a view of the domain model from a particular context.

Product Views

Figure 11-5 shows all the product views that will be created in this section.

Create a new folder in the `Services` project named `ViewModels`, and add to it a new class named `ProductSizeOption` with the following code listing:

```
namespace Agathas.Storefront.Services.ViewModels
{
    public class ProductSizeOption
    {
        public int Id { get; set; }
        public string SizeName { get; set; }
    }
}
```

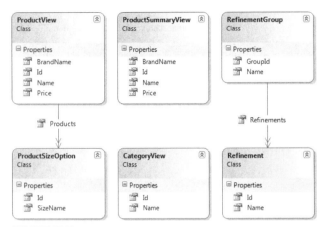

FIGURE 11-5

This view represents the physical product that you can buy. The next view to create is `ProductView`, which has a collection of `ProductSizeOptions` that which will be used to display the details of a product:

```
using System.Collections.Generic;

namespace Agathas.Storefront.Services.ViewModels
{
    public class ProductView
    {
        public int Id { get; set; }
        public string BrandName { get; set; }
        public string Name { get; set; }
        public string Price { get; set; }
        public IEnumerable<ProductSizeOption> Products { get; set; }
    }
}
```

The `ProductSummaryView` is used when listing groups of products:

```
namespace Agathas.Storefront.Services.ViewModels
{
    public class ProductSummaryView
    {
        public int Id { get; set; }
        public string BrandName { get; set; }
        public string Name { get; set; }
        public string Price { get; set; }
    }
}
```

The `CategoryView` is responsible for representing a view of all `Product Category` objects and is used for the category navigation:

```
namespace Agathas.Storefront.Services.ViewModels
{
```

```
        public class CategoryView
        {
            public int Id { get; set; }
            public string Name { get; set; }
        }
    }
```

The next three views — `RefinementGroupings`, `Refinement`, and `RefinementGroup` — are utilized in the product category refinement function, which allows customers to refine the results of viewing all products within a particular category:

```
namespace Agathas.Storefront.Services.ViewModels
{
    public enum RefinementGroupings
    {
        brand = 1,
        size = 2,
        color = 3
    }
}

namespace Agathas.Storefront.Services.ViewModels
{
    public class Refinement
    {
        public int Id { get; set; }
        public string Name { get; set; }
    }
}

using System.Collections.Generic;

namespace Agathas.Storefront.Services.ViewModels
{
    public class RefinementGroup
    {
        public string Name { get; set; }
        public int GroupId { get; set; }
        public IEnumerable<Refinement> Refinements { get; set; }
    }
}
```

That completes the view models that are required for the product catalog pages. You will now create the `ProductCatalogService` class that the controllers will use to obtain the view models to power the product catalog browsing experience.

ProductCatalogService

The `ProductCatalogService` forms the facade or entry point into the application for matters pertaining to the displaying of products. The `ProductCatalogService` includes methods to perform the following operations:

➤ Retrieve a collection of products for a given category and a given set of refinement criteria that the customer supplies

➤ Retrieve a selection of products for display on the site's homepage

➤ Retrieve a product and all its detail

➤ Retrieve all product categories

The controllers will communicate with the service layer using the Request and Reply message pattern, as discussed in Chapter 6. You'll start with the method that allows customers to refine a collection of products within a category. As part of the refinement process, customers can sort products within a category by descending and ascending price. A message is sent to the service, which includes an enumeration defining how the customer wants matching product records to be ordered. Add a new folder to the `Services` project named `Messaging`, and then add another folder inside it named `ProductCatalogService`. After that, add a new enumeration named `ProductsSortBy`, as shown in the following listing:

```
namespace Agathas.Storefront.Services.Messaging.ProductCatalogService
{
    public enum ProductsSortBy
    {
        PriceHighToLow = 1,
        PriceLowToHigh = 2
    }
}
```

The message that will be sent to the service with the full set of customer refinement criteria is `ProductSearchRequest`, which is shown here:

```
namespace Agathas.Storefront.Services.Messaging.ProductCatalogService
{
    public class GetProductsByCategoryRequest
    {
        public GetProductsByCategoryRequest()
        {
            ColorIds = new int[0];
            BrandIds = new int[0];
            SizeIds = new int[0];
        }
        public int CategoryId { get; set; }

        public int[] ColorIds { get; set; }
        public int[] BrandIds { get; set; }
        public int[] SizeIds { get; set; }

        public ProductsSortBy SortBy { get; set; }
        public int Index { get; set; }
        public int NumberOfResultsPerPage { get; set; }
    }
}
```

This class contains integer arrays for color, brand, and size IDs. The idea is that customers should be able to refine their search for a product by filtering for products in specific colors, brands, and sizes. The `ProductSearchRequest` also contains properties named `Index` and `NumberOfResultsPerPage` to assist with the paging of data.

The response that the service class returns is the `GetProductsByCategoryResponse` class shown next, which gives details on the refinements available to the resulting product collection result:

```
using System.Collections.Generic;
using Agathas.Storefront.Services.ViewModels;

namespace Agathas.Storefront.Services.Messaging.ProductCatalogService
{
    public class GetProductsByCategoryResponse
    {
        public string SelectedCategoryName { get; set; }
        public int SelectedCategory { get; set; }

        public IEnumerable<RefinementGroup> RefinementGroups { get; set; }

        public int NumberOfTitlesFound { get; set; }
        public int TotalNumberOfPages { get; set; }
        public int CurrentPage { get; set; }

        public IEnumerable<ProductSummaryView> Products { get; set; }
    }
}
```

For the controller to obtain the detail for a specific product, two more classes are required. `GetProduct Request` is sent to the service layer, and `GetProductResponse` is the response:

```
namespace Agathas.Storefront.Services.Messaging.ProductCatalogService
{
    public class GetProductRequest
    {
        public int ProductId { get; set; }
    }
}

using Agathas.Storefront.Services.ViewModels;

namespace Agathas.Storefront.Services.Messaging.ProductCatalogService
{
    public class GetProductResponse
    {
        public ProductView Product { get; set; }
    }
}
```

To obtain the featured set of products that appear on the front page, no request object is necessary because no information is required to retrieve the collection of featured products. You need to create only the `GetFeaturedProductsResponse` class:

```
using System.Collections.Generic;
using Agathas.Storefront.Services.ViewModels;

namespace Agathas.Storefront.Services.Messaging.ProductCatalogService
{
    public class GetFeaturedProductsResponse
```

```
    {
        public IEnumerable<ProductSummaryView> Products { get; set; }
    }
}
```

As with retrieving products for the front page, the category listing service function requires no request object — only the `GetAllCategoriesResponse`, as shown in the following listing:

```
using System.Collections.Generic;
using Agathas.Storefront.Services.ViewModels;

namespace Agathas.Storefront.Services.Messaging.ProductCatalogService
{
    public class GetAllCategoriesResponse
    {
        public IEnumerable<CategoryView> Categories { get; set; }
    }
}
```

With the messaging objects complete, you can now create the service contract and then create an implementation. You can see the interface for the `ProductCatalogService` next. Create a new folder named `Interfaces` within the `Service` project, and add a new interface named `IProductCatalogService` with the code listing that follows:

```
using Agathas.Storefront.Services.Messaging.ProductCatalogService;

namespace Agathas.Storefront.Services.Interfaces
{
    public interface IProductCatalogService
    {
        GetFeaturedProductsResponse GetFeaturedProducts();
        GetProductsByCategoryResponse GetProductsByCategory(
                                    GetProductsByCategoryRequest request);
        GetProductResponse GetProduct(GetProductRequest request);

        GetAllCategoriesResponse GetAllCategories();
    }
}
```

All the service methods return response objects that contain view models. To automate the process of mapping domain entities into view models, use AutoMapper.

Create a new class named `AutoMapperBootStrapper` at the root of the `Services` project. This class defines the mapping between the domain entities and the view models that you created earlier. Also contained within this class is an implementation of AutoMapper's `IValueFormatter` that will be used when mapping properties. If a property of type `decimal` is found, the call to the extension method formats the value to include the U.S. dollar currency symbol. This helper method was created in the previous chapter and resides in the `Infrastructure` project:

```
...
using AutoMapper;
using Agathas.Storefront.Model.Brands;
using Agathas.Storefront.Model.Categories;
```

```
using Agathas.Storefront.Model.Products;
using Agathas.Storefront.Services.ViewModels;
using Agathas.Storefront.Infrastructure.Helpers;

namespace Agathas.Storefront.Services
{
    public class AutoMapperBootStrapper
    {
        public static void ConfigureAutoMapper()
        {
            // Product Title and Product
            Mapper.CreateMap<ProductTitle, ProductSummaryView>();
            Mapper.CreateMap<ProductTitle, ProductView>();
            Mapper.CreateMap<Product, ProductSummaryView>();
            Mapper.CreateMap<Product, ProductSizeOption>();

            // Category
            Mapper.CreateMap<Category, CategoryView>();

            // IProductAttribute
            Mapper.CreateMap<IProductAttribute, Refinement>();

            // Global Money Formatter
            Mapper.AddFormatter<MoneyFormatter>();

        }
    }

    public class MoneyFormatter : IValueFormatter
    {
        public string FormatValue(ResolutionContext context)
        {
            if (context.SourceValue is decimal)
            {
                decimal money = (decimal)context.SourceValue;

                return money.FormatMoney();
            }

            return context.SourceValue.ToString();
        }
    }
}
```

The `ConfigureAutoMapper` method is called from within the `Web.MVC` project's `Global.asax` `Application_Start` event, which you will configure a little later.

For the mapping between the domain entities and the view models to take place, create a series of domain entity extension methods that call into AutoMapper to perform the conversion. Create a new folder within the `Services` project named `Mapping`, and add the first mapping class named `ProductTitleMapper`:

```
using System.Collections.Generic;
using Agathas.Storefront.Model.Products;
```

```
using Agathas.Storefront.Services.ViewModels;
using AutoMapper;

namespace Agathas.Storefront.Services.Mapping
{
    public static class ProductTitleMapper
    {
        public static IEnumerable<ProductSummaryView> ConvertToProductViews(
                    this IEnumerable<ProductTitle> products)
        {
            return Mapper.Map<IEnumerable<ProductTitle>,
                    IEnumerable<ProductSummaryView>>(products);
        }

        public static ProductView ConvertToProductDetailView
                    (this ProductTitle product)
        {
            return Mapper.Map<ProductTitle, ProductView>(product);
        }
    }
}
```

The `ProductTitleMapper` class is simply an extension method of the `ProductTitle` domain entity. It enables easy conversion from the entity into the view model, which you will see used in the `IProduct CatalogService` in just a moment.

The next mapper class is `IProductAttributeMapper`, shown next. This class does a little bit extra and takes `RefinementGrouping`'s enumeration type to add to the `RefinementGroup` generated from the `IProductAttribute`:

```
using Agathas.Storefront.Model.Products;
using AutoMapper;
using Agathas.Storefront.Services.ViewModels;

namespace Agathas.Storefront.Services.Mapping
{
    public static class IProductAttributeMapper
    {
        public static RefinementGroup ConvertToRefinementGroup(
                    this IEnumerable<IProductAttribute> productAttributes,
                    RefinementGroupings refinementGroupType)
        {
            RefinementGroup refinementGroup = new RefinementGroup()
                    { Name = refinementGroupType.ToString(),
                      GroupId = (int)refinementGroupType };

            refinementGroup.Refinements =
                    Mapper.Map<IEnumerable<IProductAttribute>,
                                IEnumerable<Refinement>> (productAttributes);

            return refinementGroup;
        }
    }
}
```

The `CategoryMapper` shown in the following listing generates `CategoryView` objects from `Category` domain entities:

```
using System.Collections.Generic;
using Agathas.Storefront.Model.Categories;
using Agathas.Storefront.Services.ViewModels;
using AutoMapper;

namespace Agathas.Storefront.Services.Mapping
{
    public static class CategoryMapper
    {
        public static IEnumerable<CategoryView> ConvertToCategoryViews(
                                     this IEnumerable<Category> categories)
        {
            return Mapper.Map<IEnumerable<Category>,
                           IEnumerable<CategoryView>>(categories);
        }
    }
}
```

The final mapping extension class that you will create is a little more complex than the previous ones. This extension method takes `GetProductsByCategoryRequest` and a collection of products that match the request and converts it into a `GetProductsByCategoryResponse`. You can view the code for the `ProductMapper` class here:

```
using System.Collections.Generic;
using System.Linq;
using Agathas.Storefront.Model.Products;
using Agathas.Storefront.Services.Messaging.ProductCatalogService;
using Agathas.Storefront.Services.ViewModels;

namespace Agathas.Storefront.Services.Mapping
{
    public static class ProductMapper
    {
        public static GetProductsByCategoryResponse CreateProductSearchResultFrom(
                            this IEnumerable<Product> productsMatchingRefinement,
                                        GetProductsByCategoryRequest request)
        {
            GetProductsByCategoryResponse productSearchResultView =
                                    new GetProductsByCategoryResponse();

            IEnumerable<ProductTitle> productsFound =
                        productsMatchingRefinement.Select(p => p.Title).Distinct();

            productSearchResultView.SelectedCategory = request.CategoryId;

            productSearchResultView.NumberOfTitlesFound = productsFound.Count();

            productSearchResultView.TotalNumberOfPages =
                    NoOfResultPagesGiven(request.NumberOfResultsPerPage,
                                    productSearchResultView.NumberOfTitlesFound);

            productSearchResultView.RefinementGroups =
```

```
                        GenerateAvailableProductRefinementsFrom(productsFound);

    productSearchResultView.Products =
                        CropProductListToSatisfyGivenIndex(request.Index,
                            request.NumberOfResultsPerPage, productsFound);

    return productSearchResultView;
}

private static IEnumerable<ProductSummaryView>
    CropProductListToSatisfyGivenIndex(int pageIndex,
                                int numberOfResultsPerPage,
                                IEnumerable<ProductTitle> productsFound)
{
    if (pageIndex > 1)
    {
        int numToSkip = (pageIndex - 1) * numberOfResultsPerPage;
        return productsFound.Skip(numToSkip)
                .Take(numberOfResultsPerPage).ConvertToProductViews();
    }
    else
        return productsFound
                .Take(numberOfResultsPerPage).ConvertToProductViews();
}

private static int NoOfResultPagesGiven(int numberOfResultsPerPage,
                                    int numberOfTitlesFound)
{
    if (numberOfTitlesFound < numberOfResultsPerPage)
        return 1;
    else
    {
        return (numberOfTitlesFound / numberOfResultsPerPage) +
            (numberOfTitlesFound % numberOfResultsPerPage);
    }
}

private static IList<RefinementGroup>
    GenerateAvailableProductRefinementsFrom(
                            IEnumerable<ProductTitle> productsFound)
{
    var brandsRefinementGroup = productsFound
                .Select(p => p.Brand).Distinct().ToList()
                .ConvertAll<IProductAttribute>(b => (IProductAttribute)b)
                .ConvertToRefinementGroup(RefinementGroupings.brand);

    var colorsRefinementGroup = productsFound
                .Select(p => p.Color).Distinct().ToList()
                .ConvertAll<IProductAttribute>(c => (IProductAttribute)c)
                .ConvertToRefinementGroup(RefinementGroupings.color);

    var sizesRefinementGroup = (from p in productsFound
                            from si in p.Products
                            select si.Size).Distinct().ToList()
                .ConvertAll<IProductAttribute>(s => (IProductAttribute)s)
```

```
                    .ConvertToRefinementGroup(RefinementGroupings.size);

            IList<RefinementGroup> refinementGroups = new List<RefinementGroup>();

            refinementGroups.Add(brandsRefinementGroup);
            refinementGroups.Add(colorsRefinementGroup);
            refinementGroups.Add(sizesRefinementGroup);
            return refinementGroups;
        }
    }
}
```

Code snippet ProductMapper.cs in project Agathas.Storefront.Services

The method takes a `GetProductsByCategoryRequest` and an `IEnumerable<Product>`, which contains all products matching the search. A distinct collection of `ProductTitles` is generated from the found `Products`. From this collection, the detail needed to set the properties used for paging is completed via a call to the `NoOfResultPagesGiven` method. Next, the refinement groups are generated via the `Generate AvailableProductRefinementsFrom` method and then appended to the `ProductSearchResultView`. Finally, the `ProductTitles` are added to the `GetProductsByCategoryResponse` based on the page index that the user is viewing, which is the responsibility of the `CropProductListToSatisfyGiven Index` method.

To convert the `GetProductsByCategoryRequest` into a query, you need to create a query generator class. Add a new folder named `Implementations`, and add to it a new class named `ProductSearch RequestQueryGenerator` with the following definition:

```
using System.Linq;
using Agathas.Storefront.Infrastructure.Querying;
using Agathas.Storefront.Model.Products;
using Agathas.Storefront.Services.Messaging.ProductCatalogService;

namespace Agathas.Storefront.Services.Implementations
{
    public class ProductSearchRequestQueryGenerator
    {
        public static Query CreateQueryFor(
                    GetProductsByCategoryRequest getProductsByCategoryRequest)
        {
            Query productQuery = new Query();
            Query colorQuery = new Query();
            Query brandQuery = new Query();
            Query sizeQuery = new Query();

            colorQuery.QueryOperator = QueryOperator.Or;
            foreach (int id in getProductsByCategoryRequest.ColorIds)
              colorQuery.Add(Criterion.Create<Product>(p => p.Color.Id, id,
                                                CriteriaOperator.Equal));

            if (colorQuery.Criteria.Count() > 0)
                productQuery.AddSubQuery(colorQuery);

            brandQuery.QueryOperator = QueryOperator.Or;
```

```
        foreach (int id in getProductsByCategoryRequest.BrandIds)
            brandQuery.Add(Criterion.Create<Product>(p => p.Brand.Id, id,
                                               CriteriaOperator.Equal));

        if (brandQuery.Criteria.Count() > 0)
            productQuery.AddSubQuery(brandQuery);

        sizeQuery.QueryOperator = QueryOperator.Or;
        foreach (int id in getProductsByCategoryRequest.SizeIds)
            sizeQuery.Add(Criterion.Create<Product>(p => p.Size.Id, id,
                                               CriteriaOperator.Equal));

        if (sizeQuery.Criteria.Count() > 0)
            productQuery.AddSubQuery(sizeQuery);

        productQuery.Add(Criterion.Create<Product>(p => p.Category.Id,
                getProductsByCategoryRequest.CategoryId, CriteriaOperator.Equal));

        return productQuery;
    }
  }
}
```

The role of the `ProductSearchRequestQueryGenerator` class is to convert the `GetProductsBy` `CategoryRequest` into a `Query` object so that the repository can satisfy it. Each of the filtering criteria the customer selects is turned into a subquery and then added to the main query, which contains a `Category` equality `Criterion`.

The implementation of the `IProductCatalogService` is named `ProductCatalogService` and can be seen in the following code listing. A description of the code follows the listing:

```
using System.Collections.Generic;
using System.Linq;
using Agathas.Storefront.Infrastructure.Querying;
using Agathas.Storefront.Model.Categories;
using Agathas.Storefront.Model.Products;
using Agathas.Storefront.Services.Interfaces;
using Agathas.Storefront.Services.Mapping;
using Agathas.Storefront.Services.Messaging.ProductCatalogService;

namespace Agathas.Storefront.Services.Implementations
{
    public class ProductCatalogService : IProductCatalogService
    {
        private readonly IProductTitleRepository _productTitleRepository;
        private readonly IProductRepository _productRepository;
        private readonly ICategoryRepository _categoryRepository;

        public ProductCatalogService(IProductTitleRepository productTitleRepository,
                                     IProductRepository productRepository,
                                     ICategoryRepository categoryRepository)
        {
            _productTitleRepository = productTitleRepository;
            _productRepository = productRepository;
            _categoryRepository = categoryRepository;
```

```
    }

    private IEnumerable<Product> GetAllProductsMatchingQueryAndSort(
                                GetProductsByCategoryRequest request,
                                                Query productQuery)
    {
        IEnumerable<Product> productsMatchingRefinement =
                                    _productRepository.FindBy(productQuery);

        switch (request.SortBy)
        {
            case ProductsSortBy.PriceLowToHigh:
                productsMatchingRefinement = productsMatchingRefinement
                                        .OrderBy(p => p.Price);
                break;
            case ProductsSortBy.PriceHighToLow:
                productsMatchingRefinement = productsMatchingRefinement
                                        .OrderByDescending(p => p.Price);
                break;
        }
        return productsMatchingRefinement;
    }

    public GetFeaturedProductsResponse GetFeaturedProducts()
    {
        GetFeaturedProductsResponse response =
                            new GetFeaturedProductsResponse();

        Query productQuery = new Query();

        productQuery.OrderByProperty = new OrderByClause()
            { Desc = true,
              PropertyName = PropertyNameHelper
                    .ResolvePropertyName<ProductTitle>(pt => pt.Price) };

        response.Products = _productTitleRepository
                        .FindBy(productQuery, 0, 6).ConvertToProductViews();

        return response;
    }

    public GetProductsByCategoryResponse GetProductsByCategory(
                                    GetProductsByCategoryRequest request)
    {
        GetProductsByCategoryResponse response;

        Query productQuery =
                ProductSearchRequestQueryGenerator.CreateQueryFor(request);

        IEnumerable<Product> productsMatchingRefinement =
                    GetAllProductsMatchingQueryAndSort(request, productQuery);

        response = productsMatchingRefinement
                        .CreateProductSearchResultFrom(request);

        response.SelectedCategoryName =
```

```
                    _categoryRepository.FindBy(request.CategoryId).Name;

            return response;
        }

        public GetProductResponse GetProduct(GetProductRequest request)
        {
            GetProductResponse response = new GetProductResponse();

            ProductTitle productTitle =
                            _productTitleRepository.FindBy(request.ProductId);

            response.Product = productTitle.ConvertToProductDetailView();

            return response;
        }

        public GetAllCategoriesResponse GetAllCategories()
        {
            GetAllCategoriesResponse response = new GetAllCategoriesResponse();
            IEnumerable<Category> categories = _categoryRepository.FindAll();
            response.Categories = categories.ConvertToCategoryViews();

            return response;
        }
    }
}
```

Code snippet ProductCatalogService.cs in project Agathas.Storefront.Services

The `ProductCatalogService` class uses constructor injection to obtain a reference to the necessary repositories that it requires. The `GetFeaturedProducts` method in lieu of any real business logic simply creates a query that obtains six products in order of price, descending. This method is used to obtain products for display on the site's homepage.

The `GetProductsByCategory` method takes a `GetProductsByCategoryRequest` and retrieves products that satisfy the customers' filter criteria by delegating the responsibility of creating a Query to the `ProductSearchRequestQueryGenerator`. When the Query is generated, it is sent to the `GetAll ProductsMatchingQueryAndSort` private method to be satisfied by the `ProductRepository`. When the matching products are returned, the resulting collection is ordered by the sorting enumeration the customer chooses. The `GetProductsByCategory` method then coordinates the collection of products being turned into a `GetProductsByCategoryResponse` by using the `CreateProductSearch ResultFrom` extension method. Finally, the name of the selected category is retrieved and added to the `GetProductsByCategoryResponse` before being returned to the caller.

The `GetProduct` method is straightforward. It obtains a `ProductTitle` by ID and then converts it to a `ProductDetailView` before wrapping it in a response object.

The last method on the `ProductCatalogService` class is another straightforward method named `GetAllCategories`. It simply returns a list of all product categories.

You have now completed the product service layer that will fulfill the needs of the MVC controllers when customers are browsing the products available on the site. In the next section, you build the controllers that use the service, along with the views that display the view models.

Controllers

Figure 11-6 shows all the view models that are strongly typed to the corresponding .ASPX views.

FIGURE 11-6

All the view models inherit from a common `BaseProductCatalogPageView` because all the views related to the product catalog also display a full list of categories.

Create a new folder within the `Controllers` project named `ViewModels`, and add another folder within it named `ProductCatalog`.

The `BaseProductCatalogPageView` is an abstract class that contains a single property exposing a full list of product categories:

```
using System.Collections.Generic;
using Agathas.Storefront.Services.ViewModels;

namespace Agathas.Storefront.Controllers.ViewModels.ProductCatalog
{
    public abstract class BaseProductCatalogPageView
    {
        public IEnumerable<CategoryView> Categories { get; set;}
    }
}
```

The `HomePageView` that is strongly typed to the site's homepage .ASPX view displays a list of top products for sale along with a full list of categories and a summary of the customer's basket:

```
using System.Collections.Generic;
using Agathas.Storefront.Services.ViewModels;

namespace Agathas.Storefront.Controllers.ViewModels.ProductCatalog
```

```
{
    public class HomePageView : BaseProductCatalogPageView
    {
        public IEnumerable<ProductSummaryView> Products { get; set;}
    }
}
```

The product detail .ASPX view that you create later in this section is strongly typed to the Product DetailView view model to display the details of a product. ProductDetailView inherits from BaseProductCatalogPageView because the product detail page also displays the full list of product categories available in the store:

```
using Agathas.Storefront.Services.ViewModels;

namespace Agathas.Storefront.Controllers.ViewModels.ProductCatalog
{
    public class ProductDetailView : BaseProductCatalogPageView
    {
        public ProductView Product { get; set; }
    }
}
```

The ProductSearchResultView also inherits from the BaseProductCatalogPageView and is strongly typed to the ProductSearchResultView.ASPX view:

```
using System.Collections.Generic;
using Agathas.Storefront.Services.ViewModels;

namespace Agathas.Storefront.Controllers.ViewModels.ProductCatalog
{
    public class ProductSearchResultView : BaseProductCatalogPageView
    {
        public ProductSearchResultView()
        {
            RefinementGroups = new List<RefinementGroup>();
        }

        public string SelectedCategoryName { get; set; }
        public int SelectedCategory { get; set; }

        public IEnumerable<RefinementGroup> RefinementGroups { get; set; }

        public int NumberOfTitlesFound { get; set; }
        public int TotalNumberOfPages { get; set; }
        public int CurrentPage { get; set; }

        public IEnumerable<ProductSummaryView> Products { get; set; }
    }
}
```

This completes the view models. You can now start to work on the controllers.

The two controllers responsible for displaying the product catalog inherit from a base Product CatalogBaseController, as shown in Figure 11-7.

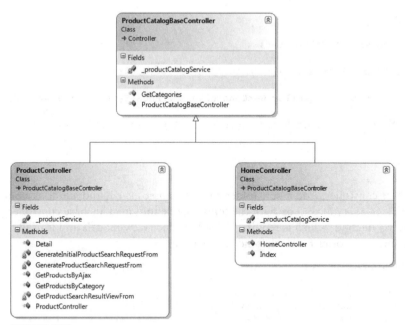

FIGURE 11-7

The services that the controllers use are referenced by interfaces and injected via the controllers' constructors. Because a controller is automatically selected for a URL from the controller factory, you need to create your own controller factory to replace the default one, which uses StructureMap to resolve the dependencies. Add a new class to the Controllers project named IoCControllerFactory with the following code definition:

```
Using System;
using System.Web.Mvc;
using StructureMap;
using System.Web.Routing;

namespace Agathas.Storefront.Controllers
{
    public class IoCControllerFactory : DefaultControllerFactory
    {
        protected override IController GetControllerInstance(
                RequestContext requestContext, Type controllerType)
        {
          return ObjectFactory.GetInstance(controllerType) as IController;
        }
    }
}
```

If you're using the MVC 1.0 framework, you will need to change the signature of the GetControllerInstance method as shown in bold in the following code listing:

```
using System;
using System.Web.Mvc;
```

```
using StructureMap;

namespace Agathas.Storefront.Controllers
{
    public class IoCControllerFactory : DefaultControllerFactory
    {
        protected override IController GetControllerInstance(Type controllerType)
        {
            return ObjectFactory.GetInstance(controllerType) as IController;
        }
    }
}
```

You can now create the base controller. Add a new folder named `Controllers`, and add to it a new class named `ProductCatalogBaseController` with the following definition. This base controller contains the `GetCategories` method, which is required for all product view models and is used to display the full list of product categories for the left-side navigation:

```
using System.Collections.Generic;
using System.Web.Mvc;
using Agathas.Storefront.Services.Interfaces;
using Agathas.Storefront.Services.Messaging.ProductCatalogService;
using Agathas.Storefront.Services.ViewModels;

namespace Agathas.Storefront.Controllers.Controllers
{
    public class ProductCatalogBaseController : Controller
    {
        private readonly IProductCatalogService _productCatalogService;

        public ProductCatalogBaseController(
                        IProductCatalogService productCatalogService)
        {
            _productCatalogService = productCatalogService;
        }

        public IEnumerable<CategoryView> GetCategories()
        {
            GetAllCategoriesResponse response =
                        _productCatalogService.GetAllCategories();

            return response.Categories;
        }
    }
}
```

The `HomeController` inherits from the `ProductCatalogBaseController` class and has a single method to handle the homepage request:

```
using System.Web.Mvc;
using Agathas.Storefront.Controllers.ViewModels.ProductCatalog;
using Agathas.Storefront.Services.Interfaces;
using Agathas.Storefront.Services.Messaging.ProductCatalogService;

namespace Agathas.Storefront.Controllers.Controllers
```

```
{
    public class HomeController : ProductCatalogBaseController
    {
        private readonly IProductCatalogService _productCatalogService;

        public HomeController(IProductCatalogService productCatalogService)
            : base(productCatalogService)
        {
            _productCatalogService = productCatalogService;
        }

        public ActionResult Index()
        {
            HomePageView homePageView = new HomePageView();
            homePageView.Categories = base.GetCategories();

            GetFeaturedProductsResponse response =
                        _productCatalogService.GetFeaturedProducts();
            homePageView.Products = response.Products;

            return View(homePageView);
        }
    }
}
```

A customer wanting to refine product category pages using AJAX needs to send requests with complex data containing the refinement filters. You use JSON objects to accomplish this requirement. To enable the JSON objects to be converted automatically into .NET objects, you need an implementation of the MVC ModelBinder.

The default ModelBinder maps HTTP parameters to action method parameters. To work with JSON objects, you need to create your own JsonModelBinder. Add a new folder named JsonDTOs to the Controllers project, and add a new class named JsonModelBinder to it, with the following code listing:

```
using System.IO;
using System.Linq;
using System.Text;
using System.Runtime.Serialization.Json;
using System.Web.Mvc;
using System.Web.Script.Serialization;

namespace Agathas.Storefront.Controllers.JsonDTOs
{
    public class JsonModelBinder : IModelBinder
    {
        public object BindModel(ControllerContext controllerContext,
                                ModelBindingContext bindingContext)
        {
            if (controllerContext == null)
                throw new ArgumentNullException("controllerContext");
            if (bindingContext == null)
                throw new ArgumentNullException("bindingContext");

            var serializer = new DataContractJsonSerializer(
```

```
                                              bindingContext.ModelType);
            return serializer
                .ReadObject(controllerContext.HttpContext.Request.InputStream);
        }
    }
}
```

The classes that the JSON objects are converted to are JsonRefinementGroup and JsonProduct SearchRequest. Create these two classes within the JsonDTOs folder with the following code listings:

```
using System.Runtime.Serialization;
using System.Web.Mvc;

namespace Agathas.Storefront.Controllers.JsonDTOs
{
    [DataContract]
    [ModelBinder(typeof(JsonModelBinder))]
    public class JsonRefinementGroup
    {
        [DataMember]
        public int GroupId { get; set; }

        [DataMember]
        public int[] SelectedRefinements { get; set; }
    }
}

using System.Collections.Generic;
using System.Runtime.Serialization;
using System.Web.Mvc;
using Agathas.Storefront.Services.Messaging.ProductCatalogService;

namespace Agathas.Storefront.Controllers.JsonDTOs
{
    [DataContract]
    [ModelBinder(typeof(JsonModelBinder))]
    public class JsonProductSearchRequest
    {
        [DataMember]
        public int CategoryId { get; set; }
        [DataMember]
        public int[] ColorIds { get; set; }
        [DataMember]
        public int[] SizeIds { get; set; }
        [DataMember]
        public int[] BrandIds { get; set; }
        [DataMember]
        public ProductsSortBy SortBy { get; set; }
        [DataMember]
        public IEnumerable<JsonRefinementGroup> RefinementGroups { get; set; }
        [DataMember]
        public int Index { get; set; }
    }
}
```

As you can see, each of the classes is decorated with a `ModelBinder` attribute to indicate that the `JsonModelBinder` should deserialize it

The last class to create is `ProductController`. This class uses the `IApplicationSettings` instance that you created in the infrastructure project to obtain the number of products to display on a page.

Switch back to the `IApplicationSettings` interface in the `Configuration` folder of the `Infrastructure` project, and update the interface to include a new property named `NumberOfResultsPerPage`, as shown here:

```
namespace Agathas.Storefront.Infrastructure.Configuration
{
    public interface IApplicationSettings
    {
        string LoggerName { get; }
        string NumberOfResultsPerPage { get; }


    }
}
```

You also need to update the `WebConfigApplicationSettings` implementation:

```
using System.Configuration;

namespace Agathas.Storefront.Infrastructure.Configuration
{
    public class WebConfigApplicationSettings : IApplicationSettings
    {
        public string LoggerName
        {
            get { return ConfigurationManager.AppSettings["LoggerName"]; }
        }

        public string NumberOfResultsPerPage
        {
            get { return ConfigurationManager
                        .AppSettings["NumberOfResultsPerPage"]; }
        }
    }
}
```

Lastly, you need to add the application setting key and value to the `Web.Config` that lives within the `Web.MVC` project.

```
<appSettings>
    <add key="LoggerName" value="AgathaLogger"/>
    <add key="NumberOfResultsPerPage" value="6"/>
</appSettings >
```

With the application settings updated, you can create the `ProductController` class. This class is large, so add it first. Then I will walk you through the methods:

```
using System.Collections.Generic;
using System.Web.Mvc;
using Agathas.Storefront.Controllers.JsonDTOs;
```

```
using Agathas.Storefront.Controllers.ViewModels.ProductCatalog;
using Agathas.Storefront.Infrastructure.Configuration;
using Agathas.Storefront.Services.Interfaces;
using Agathas.Storefront.Services.Messaging.ProductCatalogService;
using Agathas.Storefront.Services.ViewModels;

namespace Agathas.Storefront.Controllers.Controllers
{
    public class ProductController : ProductCatalogBaseController
    {
        private readonly IProductCatalogService _productService;

        public ProductController(IProductCatalogService productService)
            : base(productService)
        {
            _productService = productService;
        }

        public ActionResult GetProductsByCategory(int categoryId)
        {
            GetProductsByCategoryRequest productSearchRequest =
                    GenerateInitialProductSearchRequestFrom(categoryId);

            GetProductsByCategoryResponse response =
                    _productService.GetProductsByCategory(productSearchRequest);

            ProductSearchResultView productSearchResultView =
                    GetProductSearchResultViewFrom(response);

            return View("ProductSearchResults", productSearchResultView);
        }

        private ProductSearchResultView GetProductSearchResultViewFrom(
                                    GetProductsByCategoryResponse response)
        {
            ProductSearchResultView productSearchResultView =
                                        new ProductSearchResultView();

            productSearchResultView.Categories = base.GetCategories();
            productSearchResultView.CurrentPage = response.CurrentPage;
            productSearchResultView.NumberOfTitlesFound =
                                response.NumberOfTitlesFound;
            productSearchResultView.Products = response.Products;
            productSearchResultView.RefinementGroups = response.RefinementGroups;
            productSearchResultView.SelectedCategory = response.SelectedCategory;
            productSearchResultView.SelectedCategoryName =
                                response.SelectedCategoryName;
            productSearchResultView.TotalNumberOfPages =
                                response.TotalNumberOfPages;
            return productSearchResultView;
        }

        private static GetProductsByCategoryRequest
                        GenerateInitialProductSearchRequestFrom(int categoryId)
        {
```

```csharp
        GetProductsByCategoryRequest productSearchRequest =
                            new GetProductsByCategoryRequest();

        productSearchRequest.NumberOfResultsPerPage =  int.Parse(
                    ApplicationSettingsFactory
                    .GetApplicationSettings().NumberOfResultsPerPage);

        productSearchRequest.CategoryId = categoryId;
        productSearchRequest.Index = 1;
        productSearchRequest.SortBy = ProductsSortBy.PriceHighToLow;
        return productSearchRequest;
}

[AcceptVerbs(HttpVerbs.Post)]
public JsonResult GetProductsByAjax(
                        JsonProductSearchRequest jsonProductSearchRequest)
{
    GetProductsByCategoryRequest productSearchRequest =
            GenerateProductSearchRequestFrom(jsonProductSearchRequest);
    GetProductsByCategoryResponse response =
            _productService.GetProductsByCategory(productSearchRequest);

    ProductSearchResultView productSearchResultView =
                GetProductSearchResultViewFrom(response);

    return Json(productSearchResultView);
}

private static GetProductsByCategoryRequest
    GenerateProductSearchRequestFrom(
                    JsonProductSearchRequest jsonProductSearchRequest)
{
    GetProductsByCategoryRequest productSearchRequest =
                                    new GetProductsByCategoryRequest();

    productSearchRequest.NumberOfResultsPerPage = int.Parse(
                    ApplicationSettingsFactory
                    .GetApplicationSettings().NumberOfResultsPerPage);

    productSearchRequest.Index = jsonProductSearchRequest.Index;
    productSearchRequest.CategoryId = jsonProductSearchRequest.CategoryId;
    productSearchRequest.SortBy = jsonProductSearchRequest.SortBy;

    List<RefinementGroup> refinementGroups = new List<RefinementGroup>();
    RefinementGroup refinementGroup;

    foreach (JsonRefinementGroup jsonRefinementGroup in
                            jsonProductSearchRequest.RefinementGroups)
    {
        switch ((RefinementGroupings)jsonRefinementGroup.GroupId)
        {
            case RefinementGroupings.brand:
                productSearchRequest.BrandIds =
                            jsonRefinementGroup.SelectedRefinements;
                break;
```

```
                case RefinementGroupings.color:
                    productSearchRequest.ColorIds =
                                jsonRefinementGroup.SelectedRefinements;
                    break;
                case RefinementGroupings.size:
                    productSearchRequest.SizeIds =
                                jsonRefinementGroup.SelectedRefinements;
                    break;
                default:
                    break;
            }
        }
        return productSearchRequest;
    }

    public ActionResult Detail(int id)
    {
        ProductDetailView productDetailView = new ProductDetailView();
        GetProductRequest request = new GetProductRequest() {ProductId = id};
        GetProductResponse response = _productService.GetProduct(request);

        ProductView productView = response.Product;

        productDetailView.Product = productView;
        productDetailView.Categories = base.GetCategories();

        return View(productDetailView);
    }
  }
}
```

Code snippet ProductController.cs in project Agathas.Storefront.Controllers

The GetProductsByCategory method handles the request for the product category view with no refinements set by the customer. The method creates a GetProductsByCategoryRequest by delegating the work to the GenerateInitialProductSearchRequestFrom method and supplying the categoryId of the chosen category. The method then sends the request to the product service, where a GetProductsByCategoryResponse is returned. The GetProductsByCategory method then calls the internal method GetProductSearchResultViewFrom to convert the GetProductsByCategoryResponse into a ProductSearchResultView, which is passed to the view.

The GetProductsByAjax method is similar to GetProductsByCategory. However, GetProductsByAjax takes a JsonProductSearchRequest converted from a JSON object, which contains the refinements the customer made. The GetProductsByAjax method delegates the work of converting the JsonProductSearchRequest into a GetProductsByCategoryRequest using the GenerateProductSearchRequestFrom and sends it to the product service. The returned GetProductsByCategoryResponse is converted into a ProductSearchResultView and then returned to the caller as JSON.

The last method on the controller is Detail. This method is simple and returns a ProductDetailView for the corresponding given product ID.

With the controllers created, you can work on the views that will display the data.

Product Catalog Views

Each of the views in the product catalog browsing collection is strongly typed to a view model class. Each of the views also has a common master page, which in turn has its own site layout master page. Figure 11-8 shows the relationships between the views and the view models.

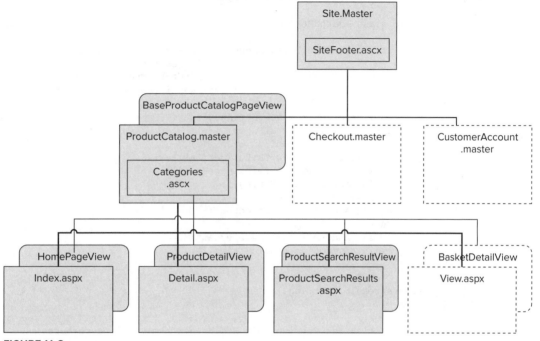

FIGURE 11-8

Before you start to create the views to support browsing the product catalog, you need to tidy up the MVC project that Visual Studio auto-generated for you. Delete the following files and folders from the Web.MVC project:

➤ Controllers folder

➤ Models folder

➤ Content/Site.css file

➤ Views/Account/ChangePassword.aspx file

➤ Views/Account/ChangePasswordSuccess.aspx file

➤ Views/Home/About.aspx file

➤ Views/Shared/LogOnUserControl.ascx file

Before you create your first view, add a new folder to the Web.MVC project named Helpers. Then add a new class to the folder named AgathaHtmlHelper. This class provides a couple of extension methods to the MVC `HtmlHelper` class that enable you to build a list of pages for paging product results and fully resolve a resource:

```csharp
using System;
using System.Text;
using System.Web.Mvc;
namespace Agathas.Storefront.UI.Web.MVC.Helpers
{
    public static class AgathaHtmlHelper
    {
        public static string BuildPageLinksFrom(this HtmlHelper html,
                                        int currentPage,
                                        int totalPages,
                                        Func<int, string> pageUrl)
        {
            StringBuilder result = new StringBuilder();
            for (int i = 1; i <= totalPages; i++)
            {
                TagBuilder tag = new TagBuilder("a");
                tag.MergeAttribute("href", pageUrl(i));
                tag.InnerHtml = i.ToString();
                if (i == currentPage)
                    tag.AddCssClass("selected");
                else
                    tag.AddCssClass("notselected");
                result.AppendLine(tag.ToString());
            }

            return result.ToString();
        }

        public static string Resolve(this HtmlHelper html, string resource)
        {
            return Agathas.Storefront.Infrastructure.Helpers
                            .UrlHelper.Resolve(resource);
        }
    }
}
```

Notice that the `Resolve` method calls into the `Infrastructure` project's `UrlHelper` class that you created earlier in the chapter. This method is in the `Infrastructure` project because it will be used elsewhere in the solution in the next chapter.

You can now finally start to create the views. Add an MVC user control named `SiteFooter.ascx` to the `Views/Shared` folder with the following markup:

```
<%@ Control Language="C#" Inherits="System.Web.Mvc.ViewUserControl" %>
<%@ Import Namespace="Agathas.Storefront.UI.Web.MVC.Helpers" %>

<div id="prefooter">
    <span style="float: left; margin-left: 20px;">
        <table>
            <tr>
                <td>
```

```
                            <ul>
                                <li class="footer-list-header">Help:</li>
                                <li><a href="#">Neque porro quisquam est</a></li>
                                <li><a href="#">ipsum quia dolor sit amet</a></li>
                            </ul>
                        </td>
                        <td>
                            <ul>
                                <li class="footer-list-header">About:</li>
                                <li><a href="#">quisquam Nequeporro est</a></li>
                                <li><a href="#">dolor sit amet ipsum quia </a></li>
                            </ul>
                        </td>
                        <td>
                            <ul>
                                <li class="footer-list-header">Social:</li>
                                <li><a href="#">porro Neque quisquam est</a></li>
                                <li><a href="#">sit amet ipsum quia dolor</a></li>
                            </ul>
                        </td>
                    </tr>
                </table>
            </span>
            <span style="float: right; margin-top: 60px; margin-right: 10px;">
                <a href="<%=Html.Resolve("") %>">
                <img alt="Agatha's Clothing Store"
                    src="<%=Html.Resolve("/Content/Images/Structure/sm_logo.png")%>"
                    border="0" /></a>
            </span>
        </div>
        <div id="footer">

        </div>
```

The `SiteFooter.ascx` control is used on the site's master page and does little more than help with layout. At the moment, it is more of a placeholder, but this is where you would add link information on the sites, such as contact forms and return information.

Next, open the `Site.Master` file, found within the `Views/Shared` folder, and update the markup to match the markup that follows:

```
<%@ Master Language="C#" Inherits="System.Web.Mvc.ViewMasterPage"  %>
<%@ Import Namespace="Agathas.Storefront.UI.Web.MVC.Helpers" %>
<!DOCTYPE html PUBLIC "-//W3C//DTD XHTML 1.0 Strict//EN"
                "http://www.w3.org/TR/xhtml1/DTD/xhtml1-strict.dtd">
<html xmlns="http://www.w3.org/1999/xhtml">

<head id="Head1" runat="server">
    <title><asp:ContentPlaceHolder ID="TitleContent" runat="server" /></title>
    <link href="<%=Html.Resolve("/Content/Site.css") %>"
          rel="stylesheet" type="text/css" />
    <script type="text/javascript"
        src="<%=Html.Resolve("/Scripts/jquery-1.4.2.min.js") %>"></script>
    <script type="text/javascript"
```

```
            src="<%=Html.Resolve("/Scripts/jquery-ui-1.8.1.custom.min.js") %>">
        </script>
    <script type="text/javascript"
        src="<%=Html.Resolve("/Scripts/jquery-jtemplates.js") %>"></script>
    <script type="text/javascript"
        src="<%=Html.Resolve("/Scripts/json2.js") %>"></script>
    <script type="text/javascript"
         src="<%=Html.Resolve("/Scripts/agatha-common-scripts.js") %>"></script>
</head>

<body>
<div id="main">
    <div id="header">
        <span><a href="<%=Html.Resolve("") %>">
        <img alt="Agatha's Clothing Store"
            src="<%=Html.Resolve("/Content/Images/Structure/lg_logo.png") %>"
            border="0" /></a></span>
    </div>

    <div id="headerSummary">
        <asp:ContentPlaceHolder ID="headerBasketSummary" runat="server">
        </asp:ContentPlaceHolder>
    </div>
    <div class="topBarContainer">
        <div id="background">
            <div id="navigation">
                <asp:ContentPlaceHolder ID="MenuContent" runat="server">
                </asp:ContentPlaceHolder>
            </div>
            <div id="content">
                <asp:ContentPlaceHolder ID="MainContent" runat="server" />
            </div>
            <div style="clear: both;" />
        </div>
    </div>
    <% Html.RenderPartial("~/Views/Shared/SiteFooter.ascx"); %>
</div>
</body>
</html>
```

The `Site.Master` file defines the store's layout and serves as the base master page for the more specific master pages. Notice that the `Site.Master` references numerous CSS and JavaScript files.

Create the following folder structure within the `Content` folder to store the images used on the site:

➤   `Content\Images\Products`

➤   `Content\Images\Structure`

> *You can find all the images used within the case study contained within the `Agathas.Storefront` solution, downloadable from Wrox.com.*

Create a new file named `Site.css` within the `Content` folder with the following style rules. This is a long listing, so it may be worth downloading the project and copying the `Site.css` file. `Site.css` is listed for completeness:

```css
/* Site Layout */
html { height: 100%;  margin-bottom: 1px; }

body {
    background:url("images/Structure/retro_background.gif")
        repeat fixed 50% 0 #EFEFEF;
    height: 100%; margin: 0 auto; color:#333333;
    font-family:Georgia,"Times New Roman",Times,serif; font-size:70%; }

#main { margin: 0px auto; padding: 0px; border:0; width: 840px; }
#background { background-position: left top;
            background: url(images/Structure/background.gif) repeat left top; }
#header { margin-top : 10px; height: 60px; }

#headerSummary{
    background:none repeat scroll 0 0 #EEEEEE;
    border-bottom:1px solid #CCCCCC; clear:both; display:block; margin:auto;
    overflow:auto; width:840px; height: 30px; }

#navigation {
    float: left; width: 158px; margin-left:5px; padding-top:1em;
    margin-bottom:50px;
    height : 100%;}

#content {
    margin: 0; float: left; width: 665px; margin-left:5px; margin-right:5px;
    padding-top:1em;}

.navigation-items{ padding:10px; margin:10px; }

#basketSummary{ width: 300px; float: right; }

#footer {
   clear: both; text-align : center; background:none repeat scroll 0 0 #FFF2D9;
   padding: 20px 0 0px 0px; height: 50px; margin:auto; width:840px;
   font-family:Georgia,"Times New Roman",Times,serif; font-size:1.4em; }

#prefooter {
    height: 90px; width: 840px; float: right;
    background:none repeat scroll 0 0 #EEEEEE;
    border-top:1px solid #CCCCCC; border-bottom:1px solid #CCCCCC;}

.footer-list-header {list-style-type: none; font-weight : bold;
                    font-size:1.2em; }

/* Loading Overlay */
#overlay {
    background: #ccc url(images/Structure/ajax-loader.gif) no-repeat 50% 50%;
    display: none; position: absolute; text-align: center; z-index:1;
```

```
        border:1px dashed #CCC;}

#smoverlay {
    background: #ccc url(images/Structure/sm-ajax-loader.gif) no-repeat 50% 50%;
    display: none; position: absolute; text-align: center; z-index:1;
    border:1px dashed #CCC; }

 /* Model Popup Dialog */
.ui-widget-overlay {
    background:url("images/Structure/modal-background.png") repeat #AAAAAA;
    opacity: 0.5; left:0; position:absolute; top:0; }

.ui-widget-content { background: #F4F0EC; border:1px solid #E0CFC2;
                     color:#1E1B1D; }

/* Category Refinement */
.refine-attributes { list-style-type: none; padding:0px;  margin:0px; }

.refinement-box{
    border:1px solid #CCCCCC; height: 100px; overflow: auto; margin-right : 10px; }

li { background-repeat: no-repeat; background-position: 0px 0px;
      padding-bottom: 2px; }

li a.selectedItem {
    background-image: url(images/Structure/refinement-selected.gif);
    background-repeat: no-repeat; background-position: 2px 2px; padding-left: 16px;
    cursor: pointer; }

li a.selecteddisabledItem {
    background-image: url(images/Structure/refinement-selecteddisabled.gif);
    background-repeat: no-repeat; background-position: 2px 2px; padding-left: 16px;
    cursor: pointer; color:#DDDDDD; }

li a.disabledItem {
    background-image: url(images/Structure/refinement-disabled.gif);
    background-repeat: no-repeat; background-position: 2px 2px;
    padding-left: 16px; cursor:default; color:#DDDDDD; }

li a.availableItem {
    background-image: url(images/Structure/refinement-available.gif);
    background-repeat: no-repeat; background-position: 2px 2px;
    padding-left: 16px; cursor: pointer; }

/* Product Listing */
ul li.item-detail { float: left; width: 17em;
                    border:1px solid #D1D1D1;
                    margin-right : 2em; margin-bottom : 2em; }
ul.items-list { width: 60em;list-style-type: none; padding:0px; margin:0px; }
.item-productimage { border: medium none; height: 230px; width: 180px;
                     text-decoration: none; }
.item-productimage-link { border-style: none; text-decoration: none;
                          width: 180px; }
.item-productname { text-align:center; width: 180px; }
.item-price {text-align:center; width: 180px; }
```

```
.item-sortdropdown { font-size:1em; height:17px; margin:0 0 0 10px; }
.item-displayoptions-sort { float:left; font-size:0.9em;  position:relative; }
.item-displayoptions-pages { float:right; font-size:0.9em; position:relative; }

a.selected { background-color:#EDEDED; border:1px solid #666666; padding:2px 5px; }
a.notselected { background-color:#FFFFFF; border:1px solid #666666;
                padding:2px 5px; }

/* Basket Display */
.basket-details { margin-top : 10px; margin-right : 20px; float: right;
                  text-align :right; }
.itemQtyBox { font-size:0.9em; height:12px; width:25px; }

/* Product Detail */
.productsTitle {border-bottom:1px solid #D1D1D1; margin-bottom : 10px; }
```

Code snippet Site.css in project Agathas.Storefront.UI.Web.MVC

The other files that are included with the `Site.Master` page are:

➤   `json2.js`

➤   `jquery-1.4.2.min.js`

➤   `jquery-ui-1.8.1.custom.min.js`

➤   `jquery-jtemplates.js`

You can download the `json2.js` file from `http://www.json.org/json2.js` and save it to the `Scripts` folder within the `Web.MVC` project. The `json2.js` file is used to parse JSON-formatted data before sending it to the service for AJAX-related functionality. After you have downloaded `json2.js`, ensure that you remove the dialog box, which is the first line in the script library. The `jquery-1.4.2.min.js` is the latest version of the core `jQuery` library, which you can obtain from `http://jquery.com/`. The `jquery-ui-1.8.1.custom.min.js` file is a subset of the `jQuery` UI library, which includes the scripts necessary to provide the `jQuery` model dialog functionality used later in this chapter. The file is available from `http://jqueryui.com/download`. At the download page, deselect all components and scroll to the Widgets section. Check the dialog box, click Download, extract the contents of the zipped archive, and copy the `jquery-ui-1.8.1.custom.min.js` file into the `Scripts` folder. Finally, you can download the `JTemplates.js` library from `http://jtemplates.tpython.com`. All the JavaScript library versions were correct at the time of writing. If the versions are different, you can either download the JavaScript files from the solution from `www.wrox.com` or use the new files and update the `Site.Master`'s include files to reflect the updated version names.

The next control to add is responsible for displaying all the product categories available on the site. Add a new MVC user control named `Categories.ascx` to the `Views/Shared` folder with the following markup:

```
<%@ Control Language="C#"
            Inherits="System.Web.Mvc.ViewUserControl<IEnumerable<CategoryView>>" %>
<%@ Import Namespace="Agathas.Storefront.Services.ViewModels" %>

<h2>Categories</h2>
```

```
<ul class="refine-attributes">
<% foreach (CategoryView categoryView in Model)
   { %>
   <li><%= Html.ActionLink(categoryView.Name, "GetProductsByCategory", "Product",
                           new { categoryId = categoryView.Id }, null)%></li>
<% } %>
</ul>
```

Next, create the `ProductCatalog.Master` page that handles the layout of all pages within the product catalog:

```
<%@ Master Language="C#" MasterPageFile="Site.Master"
       Inherits="System.Web.Mvc.ViewMasterPage<BaseProductCatalogPageView>" %>
<%@ Import
       Namespace="Agathas.Storefront.Controllers.ViewModels.ProductCatalog" %>


<asp:Content ID="TitleContent" ContentPlaceHolderID="TitleContent" runat="server">
   <asp:ContentPlaceHolder ID="TitleContent" runat="server">
   </asp:ContentPlaceHolder>
</asp:Content>

<asp:Content ID="MainContent" ContentPlaceHolderID="MainContent" runat="server">
   <asp:ContentPlaceHolder ID="MainContent" runat="server">

   </asp:ContentPlaceHolder>
</asp:Content>

<asp:Content ID="headerBasketSummary"
             ContentPlaceHolderID="headerBasketSummary" runat="server">
</asp:Content>

<asp:Content ID="MenuContent" ContentPlaceHolderID="MenuContent" runat="server">
   <asp:ContentPlaceHolder ID="MenuContent" runat="server">
      <% Html.RenderPartial("~/Views/Shared/Categories.ascx",
                            ((BaseProductCatalogPageView)Model).Categories); %>
   </asp:ContentPlaceHolder>
</asp:Content>
```

Within the folder `Views/Home`, update the `Index.aspx` view with the following markup:

```
<%@ Page Language="C#" MasterPageFile="~/Views/Shared/ProductCatalog.Master"
   Inherits="System.Web.Mvc.ViewPage<HomePageView>" %>

<%@ Import
   Namespace="Agathas.Storefront.Controllers.ViewModels.ProductCatalog" %>
<%@ Import Namespace="Agathas.Storefront.Services.ViewModels" %>
<%@ Import Namespace="Agathas.Storefront.UI.Web.MVC.Helpers" %>

<asp:Content ID="indexTitle" ContentPlaceHolderID="TitleContent" runat="server">
   Home Page
</asp:Content>
<asp:Content ID="indexContent" ContentPlaceHolderID="MainContent" runat="server">
   <img width="559" height="297"
        src="<%=Html.Resolve("/Content/Images/Products/product-lifestyle.jpg")%>"
        style="border-width: 0px; padding: 0px; margin: 0px" />
```

```
    <div style="clear: both;"></div>
    <h2>Top Products</h2>
    <div id="items" style="border-width: 1px; padding: 0px; margin: 0px">
        <ul class="items-list">
            <% foreach (ProductSummaryView product in Model.Products)
               {%>
            <li class="item-detail">
             <a class="item-productimage-link"
                href="<%=Url.Action("Detail", "Product",
                                    new { id = product.Id }, null) %>">
          <img class="item-productimage"
              src="<%=Html.Resolve("/Content/Images/Products/" +
                                   product.Id.ToString() +".jpg")%>" /></a>
                <div class="item-productname">
                    <%= Html.ActionLink(product.BrandName + " " + product.Name,
                            "Detail", "Product", new { id = product.Id }, null)%>
                </div>
                <div class="item-price">
                    <%= Html.Encode(product.Price)%></div>
            </li>
            <%}%>
        </ul>
    </div>
</asp:Content>
```

Note in the bolded section of the Index.aspx markup that products' images are named by the product ID and stored in the Content/Images/Products folder for simplicity.

Create a new folder in Views named Product, and add the next view for the product catalog browsing functionality named Detail.aspx with the following markup:

```
<%@ Page Title="" Language="C#"
        MasterPageFile="~/Views/Shared/ProductCatalog.Master"
        Inherits="System.Web.Mvc.ViewPage<ProductDetailView>" %>

<%@ Import Namespace="Agathas.Storefront.Services.ViewModels" %>
<%@ Import Namespace="Agathas.Storefront.Controllers.ViewModels.ProductCatalog" %>
<%@ Import Namespace="Agathas.Storefront.UI.Web.MVC.Helpers" %>

<asp:Content ID="Content1" ContentPlaceHolderID="TitleContent" runat="server">
        <%=Model.Product.BrandName %> <%=Model.Product.Name %>
        for only  <%=Model.Product.Price %>
</asp:Content>

<asp:Content ID="Content2" ContentPlaceHolderID="MainContent" runat="server">

    <h2><%=Model.Product.BrandName %> <%=Model.Product.Name %></h2>

    <div>
        <span style="float : left">
        <img src="<%=Html.Resolve("/Content/Images/Products/"
                                  + Model.Product.Id.ToString() + ".jpg") %>" />
        </span>
        <div>
            <%=Model.Product.Price %><br />
```

```
                <%=Model.Product.BrandName %> <%=Model.Product.Name %><br />
                <p>

                <select id="productsizes">
                <% foreach (ProductSizeOption option in Model.Product.Products)
                    {%>
                        <option value="<%=option.Id %>"><%=option.SizeName %></option>
                <%
                    }%>
                </select>
                <input type="button" value="+ Add to cart" />
                </p>
                <p>
                * - Rutrum mattis nulla sodales<br />
                * - Duis sodales tempor felis ac<br />
                * - Ut porta metus a metus<br />
                </p>
            </div>
        </div>
        <div style="clear: both;" />

        <h3>Returns / Delivery / Info</h3>
        <p>Pellentesque magna lorem, faucibus quis feugiat non, aliquet in libero.
            Integer sit amet gravida erat. Duis sodales tempor felis ac adipiscing.
            Suspendisse nonlectus enim.
            Vestibulum aliquet imperdiet posuere. Suspendisse ac diam odio.
            Ut porta metus a
            metus rutrum mattis. Nulla sodales, arcu ut mollis vehicula, tellus ante
            ultricies mauris, ultricies porttitor nunc purus a nisi.</p>
        <p>
            Nulla ipsum urna, cursus sed consectetur nec, varius quis diam.
            Morbi consequat sapien ut leo placerat ornare.</p>

    </asp:Content>
```

The last view that will complete the product browsing experience requires JavaScript and will be used by other views within the site. To this end, create a new JavaScript file within the Scripts folder named agatha-common-scripts.js.

```
function hideOverlay(overlayId) {

    $("#" + overlayId).animate({ opacity: "hide" });
}

function showOverlay(overlayId, idOfDivToOverlay) {

    heightAdditionOfOverlay = 0;

    var pos = $("#" + idOfDivToOverlay).offset();
    var width = $("#" + idOfDivToOverlay).width();
    var height = $("#" + idOfDivToOverlay).height();
    $("#" + overlayId).css({ "width": width + "px",
                            "left": pos.left + "px",
                            "top": pos.top + "px",
```

```
                                    "height": height + heightAdditionOfOverlay + "px" });
    $("#" + overlayId).show();

    $("#" + overlayId).animate
            (
            { opacity: 0.7 },
            1,
                        function() { }
            );
    }
```

This JavaScript file allows an overlay and loading GIF to appear when the page is updating via an AJAX request.

The `ProductSearchResults.aspx` that should be created within the `Views/Product` folder has the following markup defined for the `MenuContent` placeholder, which is defined in the `ProductCatalog` `.Master` page:

```
<%@ Page Title="" Language="C#"
        MasterPageFile="~/Views/Shared/ProductCatalog.Master"
        Inherits="System.Web.Mvc.ViewPage<ProductSearchResultView>" %>
<%@ Import Namespace="Agathas.Storefront.Controllers.ViewModels.ProductCatalog" %>
<%@ Import Namespace="Agathas.Storefront.Services.ViewModels" %>
<%@ Import Namespace="Agathas.Storefront.UI.Web.MVC.Helpers" %>

<asp:Content ID="Content1" ContentPlaceHolderID="TitleContent" runat="server">
        Products
</asp:Content>

<asp:Content ID="Content2" ContentPlaceHolderID="MenuContent" runat="server">

  <div class="productsTitle">
  <h2>Refine By</h2>
    </div>
    <% foreach (RefinementGroup refinementGroup in Model.RefinementGroups)
      {
        <h3><%=Html.Encode(refinementGroup.Name) %></h3>
        <div class="refinement-box">
        <ul class="refine-attributes">
        <% foreach (Refinement refinement in refinementGroup.Refinements)
          { %>
          <li>
            <a class="availableItem"
                id="RefGrp-<%=Html.Encode(
                                refinementGroup.GroupId.ToString() + '-' +
                                refinement.Id.ToString())%>"
              href="JavaScript:refineSearch(
                                <%=Html.Encode(refinementGroup.GroupId)%>,
                                <%=Html.Encode(refinement.Id.ToString())%>)">
            <%=Html.Encode(refinement.Name)%>
          </a>
        </li>
      <% }%>
      </ul>
    </div>
```

```
   <% } %>

</asp:Content>

<asp:Content ID="Content3" ContentPlaceHolderID="MainContent" runat="server">

...

</asp:Content>
```

This section of the page displays all the refinement groups that are available to be filtered within the collection of products in a given category.

The next part of the `ProductSearchResults.aspx` markup is views main contents, as can be seen in the following listing:

```
<asp:Content ID="Content3" ContentPlaceHolderID="MainContent" runat="server">

<script type="text/javascript">

    ...

</script>

<div id="productResults">
<div class="productsTitle">
<h2><%= Html.ActionLink("Home", "Index", "Home")%> >
    <%=Html.Encode(Model.SelectedCategoryName) %></h2>
</div>

<div style="margin-bottom: 41px;">
   <span class="item-displayoptions-sort">Sort by
   <select class="item-sortdropdown" id="ddlSortBy">
        <option value="1">Price - High to Low</option>
        <option value="2">Price - Low to High</option>
   </select>
   </span>
   <span class="item-displayoptions-pages">products found
   <span id="numberOfProductsFound"><%=Html.Encode(Model.NumberOfTitlesFound) %>
   </span>
   <span id="pageLinksTop">
   <%=Html.BuildPageLinksFrom(Model.CurrentPage,
                       Model.TotalNumberOfPages,
                       x => "JavaScript:displayPage("+ x +")")%></span>
</span>
</div>

<div style="clear: both;"></div>

<div id="overlay" class="overlay"></div>
<div id="items">
   <ul class="items-list">
   <% foreach (ProductSummaryView product in Model.Products){ %>
      <li class="item-detail">
      <a class="item-productimage-link"
         href="<%=Url.Action("Detail", "Product",
```

```
                                new { id = product.Id }, null) %>">
      <img class="item-productimage"
          src="<%=Html.Resolve("/Content/images/Products/" +
                              product.Id.ToString() + ".jpg") %>" /></a>
        <div class="item-productname">
          <%= Html.ActionLink(Html.Encode(product.BrandName) + " " +
              Html.Encode(product.Name), "Detail",
                              "Product",
                              new { id = product.Id }, null)%></div>
                      <div class="item-price"><%=product.Price %></div>
      </li>
  <% } %>
  </ul>
</div>

<div style="clear: both;"></div>

<span class="item-displayoptions-pages">
  <span id="pageLinksBottom">
    <%=Html.BuildPageLinksFrom(Model.CurrentPage,
                              Model.TotalNumberOfPages,
                              x => "JavaScript:displayPage("+ x +")")%></span>
</span>

<p> </p>

<script type="text/html" id="productItemTemplate">
    <ul class="items-list">
        {#foreach $T.items as record}
        <li class="item-detail">
          <a class="item-productimage-link"
            href="<%=Html.Resolve("/Product/Detail/") %>{$T.record.Id}">
          <img class="item-productimage"
          src="<%=Html.Resolve("/Content/images/Products/{$T.record.Id}.jpg") %>"
          /></a>

          <div class="item-productname">
            <a href="<%=Html.Resolve("/Product/Detail/") %>
                {$T.record.Id}">{$T.record.BrandName} {$T.record.Name}</a>
          </div>

          <div class="item-price">{$T.record.Price}</div>
        </li>
        {#/for}
    </ul>
</script>

<%=Html.Hidden("categoryId", Html.Encode(Model.SelectedCategory.ToString()))%>
</div>

<div id="dialog-noproducts" title="No products found matching your refinement">
  <p>Your selection caused no results to be returned -
    please widen your search  criteria.</p>
</div>
</asp:Content>
```

Code snippet ProductSearchResults.aspx in project Agathas.Storefront.UI.Web.MVC

Bolded in the listing are calls to the `BuildPageLinksFrom` helper method that you created earlier in the section to produce the paging links. The second highlighted section simply generates the list of products on the page. The third highlighted section uses the `JTemplate` library, as discussed in Chapter 9, to data bind a JSON array. The fourth highlight is the modal dialog box, which is displayed if a customer refines her selections and no results are produced.

To get a better idea of how the refinements behave, look at Figure 11-9.

Figure 11-9 shows that a customer has selected the Trousers category and then refined the results to only display black Levi's trousers. All other selections have been disabled that don't correspond to the first two criteria that the customer has specified. Figures 11-10 through 11-13 show all the states of the filter criteria that are achieved by changing the CSS class associated with the element.

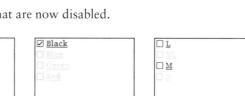

FIGURE 11-9

Figure 11-10 shows what is available for selection.

Figure 11-11 shows the color black selected.

Figure 11-12 shows some filter criteria disabled.

Figure 11-13 shows selected criteria that are now disabled.

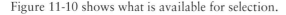

| FIGURE 11-10 | FIGURE 11-11 | FIGURE 11-12 | FIGURE 11-13 |

There is a lot of JavaScript code to support the product attribute refinements' functionality, so I will present the entire JavaScript code that sits on the `ProductSearchResults.aspx` page before discussing what is happening:

```
<asp:Content ID="Content3" ContentPlaceHolderID="MainContent" runat="server">

<script type="text/javascript">

    // Array to store the refinement selections made by a user.
    var refinementSelections = [];
    // Flag to stop user who is selecting from doing anything while the page
    // is being reloaded.
    var disallowUpdates = false;
    // Vars to store data on the last refinement selection.
    var lastSelectedRefinementItemId;
    var lastSelectedRefinementGroupId;
```

```
// Flag to show if last action was a narrowing or criteria widening selection.
var lastActionWasToNarrowProductRefinement = false;

// OnPage Load function; run when DOM is fully loaded.
// ==================================================================
$().ready(function() {

    $('#ddlSortBy').change(function() {
        if (disallowUpdates == false)
            displayPage(1);
    });

    jQuery("#dialog-noproducts").dialog({
        bgiframe: true, autoOpen: false, height: 100, modal: true
    });

});

// Method called to determine the sort ordering and the current category.
// =====================================================================
function displayPage(index) {

    if (disallowUpdates == false) {

        var categoryId = $('#categoryId').val();
        var sortBy = $('#ddlSortBy').val();

        getProducts(index, categoryId, sortBy);
    }
}

// Method called when a refinement is clicked; this changes the image displayed
// and stores the selection before calling displayPage to update the view.
// =====================================================================
function refineSearch(refinementGroupId, refinementItemId) {

    if (disallowUpdates == false) {
        itemRefinementElementId =
            buildRefinementItemElementIdForm(refinementGroupId,
                                             refinementItemId);

        lastSelectedRefinementItemId = refinementItemId;
        lastSelectedRefinementGroupId = refinementGroupId;

        if (!isDisabled(itemRefinementElementId)) {
            if (isAvailable(itemRefinementElementId)) {
                setAsSelected(itemRefinementElementId);
                saveRefinementToFilterSelection(refinementGroupId,
                                                refinementItemId);
                lastActionWasToNarrowProductRefinement = true;
                displayPage(1);
            }
            else if (isSelectedButDisabled(itemRefinementElementId)) {
                setAsDisabled(itemRefinementElementId);
                removeRefinementFromFilterSelection(refinementGroupId,
```

```
                                                            refinementItemId);
                }
                else {
                    setAsAvailable(itemRefinementElementId);
                    removeRefinementFromFilterSelection(refinementGroupId,
                                                    refinementItemId);
                    lastActionWasToNarrowProductRefinement = false;
                    displayPage(1);
                }
            }
        }
    }
}

// This function sends a post request to obtain the new view model after a
// customer has changed his refinement criteria, changed page,
// or changed the product result ordering.
// ================================================================
function getProducts(index, categoryId, sortBy) {

    if (disallowUpdates == false) {
        disallowUpdates = true;

        showOverlay("overlay", "main", 10);

        var jsonData = JSON.stringify(
            { "CategoryId": categoryId,
              "Index": index,
              "SortBy": sortBy,
              "RefinementGroups": refinementSelections
            });

        $.ajax({
            url: '<%=Html.Resolve("/Product/GetProductsByAjax") %>',
            type: 'POST',
            dataType: 'json',
            data: jsonData,
            contentType: 'application/json; charset=utf-8',
            success: function(data) {

                var mydata = { items: data.Products };

                if (data.Products.length == 0) {

                    showNoProductsFoundDialogBoxAndRevertSelection();
                }
                else {

                    $("#items").setTemplate(
                                $("#productItemTemplate").html());
                    $("#items").processTemplate(mydata);

                    $('#numberOfProductsFound').text(
                                data.NumberOfTitlesFound);

                    buildPageLinksFor("#pageLinksTop",
```

```
                                data.CurrentPage, data.TotalNumberOfPages);
                        buildPageLinksFor("#pageLinksBottom",
                                data.CurrentPage, data.TotalNumberOfPages);

                        for (var i = data.RefinementGroups.length - 1;
                                                    i >= 0;  -- i) {
                            filterOutRefinements(
                                    data.RefinementGroups[i].GroupId,
                                    data.RefinementGroups[i].Refinements);
                        }
                    }

                    hideOverlay("overlay");

                    disallowUpdates = false;
                }
            });
    }
}

// Method used to work out which refinements to mark as
// available/disabled/selected based on the list of products that matched the
// customer's last selection.
// ================================================================
function filterOutRefinements(refinementGroupId, availableProductRefinements) {

    $("[id^='" + buildGroupRefinementElementIdForm(refinementGroupId) +
                                            "']").each(function() {

        itemRefinementElementId = $(this).attr('id');

        var refinementItemId = findRefinementItemIdFrom(
                            itemRefinementElementId);

        var refinementItemIdMatched =
                refinementItemIdIsInProductAvailableRefinements
                (availableProductRefinements, refinementItemId);

        if (!lastSelectionWasMadeIn(refinementGroupId)) {

            if (lastActionWasToNarrowProductRefinement == true) {

                if ((isSelected(itemRefinementElementId) ||
                      isSelectedButDisabled(itemRefinementElementId)) &&
                      !refinementItemIdMatched) {
                    setAsSelectedButDisabled(itemRefinementElementId);
                }
                else if (!refinementItemIdMatched) {
                    setAsDisabled(itemRefinementElementId);
                }
                else if (isDisabled(itemRefinementElementId) &&
                        refinementItemIdMatched) {
                    setAsAvailable(itemRefinementElementId);
                }
                else if (isSelectedButDisabled(itemRefinementElementId) &&
```

```
                        refinementItemIdMatched) {
                    setAsSelected(itemRefinementElementId);
                }
            }
            else {

                if ((isSelected(itemRefinementElementId) ||
                    isSelectedButDisabled(itemRefinementElementId)) &&
                    !refinementItemIdMatched) {
                    setAsSelectedButDisabled(itemRefinementElementId);
                }
                else if ((isSelected(itemRefinementElementId) ||
                        isSelectedButDisabled(itemRefinementElementId)) &&
                        refinementItemIdMatched) {
                    setAsSelected(itemRefinementElementId);
                }
                else if (isDisabled(itemRefinementElementId) &&
                        refinementItemIdMatched) {
                    setAsAvailable(itemRefinementElementId);
                }
                else if (isDisabled(itemRefinementElementId) &&
                    !refinementItemIdMatched &&
                    !otherRefinementSelectionsExistApartFrom(refinementGroupId))
                {
                    setAsAvailable(itemRefinementElementId);
                }
                else if (isAvailable(itemRefinementElementId) &&
                        !refinementItemIdMatched) {
                    setAsDisabled(itemRefinementElementId);
                }
            }
        }
        else if (lastActionWasToNarrowProductRefinement == false) {

            if (isSelected(itemRefinementElementId)) {
                setAsSelected(itemRefinementElementId);
            }
            else if (!otherRefinementSelectionsExistApartFrom(
                                            refinementGroupId)) {
                setAsAvailable(itemRefinementElementId);
            }
        }
        else if (isDisabled(itemRefinementElementId) &&
                                refinementItemIdMatched) {
            setAsAvailable(itemRefinementElementId);
        }
    });
}

// Method called to show a dialog box and revert selection if
// a customer makes a selection that produces no results.
// ===============================================================
function showNoProductsFoundDialogBoxAndRevertSelection() {

    itemRefinementElementId = buildRefinementItemElementIdForm
```

```
                    (lastSelectedRefinementGroupId, lastSelectedRefinementItemId);

        setAsSelected(itemRefinementElementId);

        saveRefinementToFilterSelection(lastSelectedRefinementGroupId,
                                        lastSelectedRefinementItemId);

        $("#dialog-noproducts").dialog('open');
    }

    // Method used to get the refinement item ID from the element name.
    // ================================================================
    function findRefinementItemIdFrom(itemRefinementElementId) {

        var refinementItemId = 0;

        refinementItemId = itemRefinementElementId.substring
        (itemRefinementElementId.lastIndexOf("-")+1,
                            itemRefinementElementId.length);

        return refinementItemId;
    }

    // Method used to determine if the given refinement group ID is of the same
    // group that the last selection was made.
    // ================================================================
    function lastSelectionWasMadeIn(refinementGroupId)
    {
        return lastSelectedRefinementGroupId == refinementGroupId;
    }

    // Method used to determine if the user has selected other refinements in other
    // groups than the given refinement group ID.
    // ================================================================
    function otherRefinementSelectionsExistApartFrom(refinementGroupId) {

        var refinementSelectionsCount = 0;

        for (var i = refinementSelections.length - 1; i >= 0;  -- i) {

            if (refinementSelections[i].GroupId != refinementGroupId) {
                refinementSelectionsCount +=
                    refinementSelections[i].SelectedRefinements.length;
            }
        }

        return refinementSelectionsCount > 0;
    }

    // Method to determine if the given refinement item is in the list of matches
    // for the last
    // ================================================================
    function refinementItemIdIsInProductAvailableRefinements(
                        availableProductRefinements,refinementItemId) {

        for (var i = availableProductRefinements.length - 1; i >= 0;  -- i) {
```

```
        if (availableProductRefinements[i].Id == refinementItemId)
            return true;
    }
    return false;
}

// Helper methods
// ===========================================================
function buildGroupRefinementElementIdForm(refinementGroupId) {
    return 'RefGrp-' + refinementGroupId;
}

function buildRefinementItemElementIdForm(refinementGroupId,
                                          refinementItemId) {
    return 'RefGrp-' + refinementGroupId + '-' + refinementItemId;
}

function serviceFailed(result) {
    alert('Service call failed: ' + result.status + '' + result.statusText);
}

// Methods to store, retrieve, and update the refinement selections
// ===========================================================
function removeRefinementFromFilterSelection(refinementGroupId,
                                             refinementItemId) {

    var refinementSelectionGroup;

    for (var i = refinementSelections.length - 1; i >= 0;  -- i) {

        if (refinementSelections[i].GroupId == refinementGroupId) {
            refinementSelectionGroup = refinementSelections[i];
        }
    }

    refinementSelectionGroup.SelectedRefinements.splice(
            findIndexOf(refinementSelectionGroup.SelectedRefinements,
                    refinementItemId), 1);

}

function findIndexOf(refinementGroupId, refinementItemId) {

    for (var i = refinementGroupId.length - 1; i >= 0;  -- i) {
        if (refinementGroupId[i] == refinementItemId)
            return i;
    }
    return -1;
}

function saveRefinementToFilterSelection(refinementGroupId, refinementItemId) {

    var refinementSelectionGroup = new Object();
    var foundExistingGroup = false;

    if (refinementSelections.length == 0) {
```

```
             refinementSelectionGroup.GroupId = refinementGroupId;
             refinementSelections[0] = refinementSelectionGroup;
             refinementSelectionGroup.SelectedRefinements = [];
        }
        else {

          for (var i = refinementSelections.length - 1; i >= 0;  -- i) {

              if (refinementSelections[i].GroupId == refinementGroupId) {
                  refinementSelectionGroup = refinementSelections[i];
                  foundExistingGroup = true;
              }

          }
          if (foundExistingGroup == false) {
              refinementSelectionGroup.GroupId = refinementGroupId;
              refinementSelections[refinementSelections.length] =
                                             refinementSelectionGroup;
              refinementSelectionGroup.SelectedRefinements = [];
          }
      }

      refinementSelectionGroup.
        SelectedRefinements[refinementSelectionGroup.SelectedRefinements.length] =
                                                 refinementItemId
    }

    // Method to build the paging links after a refine selection.
    // ==================================================================
    function buildPageLinksFor(spanId, index, totalPages) {

        var i = 1;
        var html = '';
        for (i = 1; i <= totalPages; i++) {

            if (i == index)
                html = html + "<a class='selected'
                                href='JavaScript:displayPage(" + i +
                                        ")'>" + i + "</a> ";
            else
                html = html + "<a class='notselected'
                                href='JavaScript:displayPage(" + i
                                + ")'>" + i + "</a> ";
        }

        $(spanId).html(html);
    }

    // Helper methods to determine the state of a refinement.
    // ==================================================================
    function setAsSelectedButDisabled(elementName) {
        $('#' + elementName).removeClass().addClass('selecteddisabledItem');
    }

    function setAsSelected(elementName) {
```

```
        $('#' + elementName).removeClass().addClass('selectedItem');
    }

    function setAsAvailable(elementName) {
        $('#' + elementName).removeClass().addClass('availableItem');
    }

    function setAsDisabled(elementName) {
        $('#' + elementName).removeClass().addClass('disabledItem');
    }

    function isSelected(elementName) {
        return ($('#' + elementName).attr("class") == "selectedItem");
    }

    function isAvailable(elementName) {
        return ($('#' + elementName).attr("class") == "availableItem");
    }

    function isDisabled(elementName) {
        return ($('#' + elementName).attr("class") == "disabledItem");
    }

    function isSelectedButDisabled(elementName) {
        return ($('#' + elementName).attr("class") == "selecteddisabledItem");
    }

</script>
...

</asp:Content>
```

Code snippet ProductSearchResults.aspx in project Agathas.Storefront.UI.Web.MVC

When you click a refinement, a call to `refineSearch(refinementGroupId, refinementItemId)` is made, and the following steps occur:

1. A check is made to determine if a refinement can take — that is, if it's not partway through handling the last refinement.

2. The class of the refinement is changed to reflect the change in state.

3. The selection is added or removed to an internal array to register what was selected or deselected. The `saveRefinementToFilterSelection` method handles this.

4. A call to `displayPage` is made.

The `displayPage` method then obtains the order to sort the results and the category that this page refers to before calling `getProducts`, which is the method that makes the AJAX call.

The `getProducts` method performs several steps:

1. The overlay div is shown to display a loading GIF to the customer via the `showOverlay` method.

2. The customer's selections held within the internal array are turned into a JSON array, and an HTTP POST is made to the controller.

3. If no products are returned, the modal box is shown via the `showNoProductsFoundDialog BoxAndRevertSelection` method.

4. If products are found, the collection is data bound using the `jTemplate` library, and then each of the refinement groups is updated using the `filterOutRefinements` method.

This gives a high-level overview of what the JavaScript code is doing. I highly recommend downloading the source code for this case study and studying it from within Visual Studio for a better understanding of the logic.

The product functionality is now complete. Your last task is to wire up all the loosely coupled code.

Setting Up IoC

Switch to the `Web.MVC` project and add a new class named `BootStrapper`, which uses StructureMap to configure your dependencies:

```
using Agathas.Storefront.Infrastructure.Logging;
using Agathas.Storefront.Infrastructure.UnitOfWork;
using Agathas.Storefront.Infrastructure.Configuration;
using Agathas.Storefront.Model.Categories;
using Agathas.Storefront.Model.Products;
using Agathas.Storefront.Services.Implementations;
using Agathas.Storefront.Services.Interfaces;
using StructureMap;
using StructureMap.Configuration.DSL;
using Agathas.Storefront.Infrastructure.Email;

namespace Agathas.Storefront.UI.Web.MVC
{
    public class BootStrapper
    {
        public static void ConfigureDependencies()
        {
            ObjectFactory.Initialize(x =>
            {
                x.AddRegistry<ControllerRegistry>();

            });
        }

        public class ControllerRegistry : Registry
        {
            public ControllerRegistry()
            {
                // Repositories
                ForRequestedType<ICategoryRepository>()
                    .TheDefault.Is.OfConcreteType
                    <Repository.NHibernate.Repositories.CategoryRepository>();
                ForRequestedType<IProductTitleRepository>()
                    .TheDefault.Is.OfConcreteType
                    <Repository.NHibernate.Repositories.ProductTitleRepository>();
                ForRequestedType<IProductRepository>().TheDefault.Is.OfConcreteType
                    <Repository.NHibernate.Repositories.ProductRepository>();
```

```
                    ForRequestedType<IUnitOfWork>().TheDefault.Is.OfConcreteType
                        <Repository.NHibernate.NHUnitOfWork>();

                    // Product Catalogue
                    ForRequestedType<IProductCatalogService>()
                        .TheDefault.Is.OfConcreteType
                        <ProductCatalogService>();

                    // Application Settings
                    ForRequestedType<IApplicationSettings>()
                        .TheDefault.Is.OfConcreteType
                        <WebConfigApplicationSettings>();

                    // Logger
                    ForRequestedType<ILogger>().TheDefault.Is.OfConcreteType
                        <Log4NetAdapter>();

                    // E-Mail Service
                    ForRequestedType<IEmailService>().TheDefault.Is.OfConcreteType
                        <TextLoggingEmailService>();
                }
            }
        }
    }
```

Refer to Chapter 8 for the details of wiring up dependencies with StructureMap.

Switch to the code view of `Global.asax`, and update it so that the StructureMap `BootStrapper` and `AutoMapperBootStrapper` are called and the `ApplicationSettingsFactory`, `LoggingFactory`, and `EmailServiceFactory` are initialized.

Also add a second route to ignore browsers that request a favorite icon for the website:

```
using System.Web.Mvc;
using System.Web.Routing;
using Agathas.Storefront.Controllers;
using Agathas.Storefront.Infrastructure.Configuration;
using Agathas.Storefront.Infrastructure.Email;
using Agathas.Storefront.Infrastructure.Logging;
using StructureMap;

namespace Agathas.Storefront.UI.Web.MVC
{

        public static void RegisterRoutes(RouteCollection routes)
        {
            routes.IgnoreRoute("{resource}.axd/{*pathInfo}");
            routes.IgnoreRoute("{*favicon}",
                        new { favicon = @"(.*/)?favicon.ico(/.*)?"});

            ...

        }

        protected void Application_Start()
```

```
                    {
                        RegisterRoutes(RouteTable.Routes);

                        BootStrapper.ConfigureDependencies();

                        Services.AutoMapperBootStrapper.ConfigureAutoMapper();

                        ApplicationSettingsFactory.InitializeApplicationSettingsFactory
                                (ObjectFactory.GetInstance<IApplicationSettings>());

                        LoggingFactory.InitializeLogFactory(ObjectFactory.GetInstance<ILogger>());

                        EmailServiceFactory.InitializeEmailServiceFactory
                                (ObjectFactory.GetInstance<IEmailService>());

                        ControllerBuilder.Current
                                .SetControllerFactory(new IoCControllerFactory());

                        LoggingFactory.GetLogger().Log("Application Started");
                    }
                }
            }
```

If you add some product information to the database, or if you download the code for this chapter from www.wrox.com and copy the Shop.mdf database, you will be able to browse the product catalog, as can be seen in Figure 11-14. Just set Web.MVC as the start-up project, select Default.aspx as the start-up page, and press F5 or run the debugger.

FIGURE 11-14

SUMMARY

This was a lengthy chapter that achieved a lot. Here's a recap:

➤   You started by designing a domain model for the product catalog. The model was fairly ane-mic because it contained no behavior. After building the domain model, you created a data-base and built the data model that would store the state of the product catalogue.

➤   To retrieve the product catalog entities, you utilized NHibernate as your data access strat-egy. Your first job was to map the product catalog domain model to the data model via the XML mapping files. Your second job was to build the repository structure to retrieve the entities. The base repository structure you build will be used throughout the rest of the site construction.

➤   To expose the entities to a consumer, you built a service layer. You started by creating view models that reflected a view on the domain model and utilized AutoMapper for the object-to-object mapping requirements. You then created the services and used the Request Reply Messaging pattern for communication.

➤   The consumer of the service layer was the controllers project. Within the controllers product, you added the actions of the site that would communicate with the service layer to obtain the product catalog views. You also enabled Ajax communication from the UX layer by exposing JSON actions for which you had to add a model binder that would enable JSON objects to be mapped to .NET data transfer objects.

➤   Lastly, you built the views of the product catalog. You built these views on a consistent lay-out that will be used for the entire site and were strongly typed to view models supplied by the controllers containing view models supplied by the service layer. The product category .ASPX view contained a large amount of JavaScript to perform Ajax filtering of products.

In the next chapter, you will build the basket functionality for the store.

12

Implementing the Shopping Basket

WHAT'S IN THIS CHAPTER?

➤ Adding products to a basket via AJAX

➤ Using the client's cookie to store a summary of the basket contents

➤ Utilizing AJAX for the basket detail page when modifying the basket or shipping options

In Chapter 11, you enabled a customer to browse for products; this chapter addresses the needs of a customer to store the items they would like to order in a basket.

IMPLEMENTING THE BASKET

The basket implementation should use AJAX in all of its functionality, in keeping with the rich web 2.0 theme of the product browsing pages. Therefore, you will use AJAX to add, amend, and remove items from a basket, as well as select the dispatch options. A summary of the basket will appear on all product browsing pages, which will be stored in the client's cookie to enable faster page generation

Basket Domain Model

Figure 12-1 shows the domain model of the entities involved with the basket functionality.

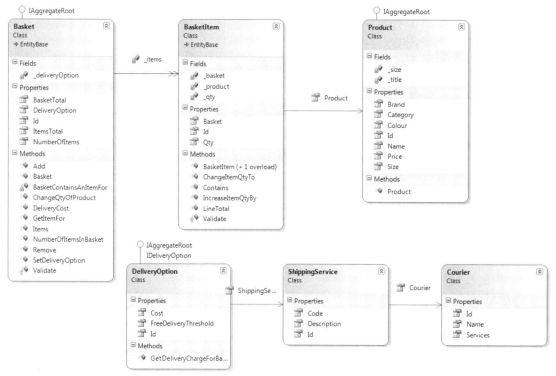

FIGURE 12-1

Create a new folder within the `Model` project named `Shipping`, and add to it a new class named `Courier` that inherits from the `EntityBase` class that you created in the `Infrastructure` project.

```
using System.Collections.Generic;
using Agathas.Storefront.Infrastructure.Domain;

namespace Agathas.Storefront.Model.Shipping
{
    public class Courier : EntityBase<int>
    {
        private readonly string _name;
        private readonly IEnumerable<ShippingService> _services;

        public Courier()
        {
        }

        public Courier(string name, IEnumerable<ShippingService> services)
        {
            _name = name;
            _services = services;
        }

        public string Name
        {
```

```
            get { return _name; }
        }

        public IEnumerable<ShippingService> Services
        {
            get { return _services; }
        }

        protected override void Validate()
        {
            throw new NotImplementedException();
        }
    }
}
```

The `Courier` class represents the shipping courier that will deliver the customer's order. A courier has a collection of shipping services that it can provide, so create a new class named `ShippingService` within the `Shipping` folder:

```
using Agathas.Storefront.Infrastructure.Domain;

namespace Agathas.Storefront.Model.Shipping
{
    public class ShippingService : EntityBase<int>
    {
        private readonly string _code;
        private readonly string _description;
        private readonly Courier _courier;

        public ShippingService()
        {    }

        public ShippingService(string code, string description, Courier courier)
        {
            _code = code;
            _description = description;
            _courier = courier;
        }

        public string Code
        {
            get { return _code;}
        }

        public string Description
        {
            get { return _description; }
        }

        public Courier Courier
        {
            get { return _courier; }
        }

        protected override void Validate()
```

```
        {
            throw new NotImplementedException();
        }
    }
}
```

A customer can select a delivery option from her basket. A delivery option consists of a `shipping service` and a delivery charge to the customer. A delivery option also contains a free delivery threshold that allows the customer to receive free delivery if her basket total exceeds a given amount.

Create an interface contract in the `Shipping` folder for the delivery option named `IDeliveryOption` matching the following code listing:

```
namespace Agathas.Storefront.Model.Shipping
{
    public interface IDeliveryOption
    {
        int Id { get; set; }
        decimal FreeDeliveryThreshold { get; }
        decimal Cost { get;   }
        ShippingService ShippingService { get;}
        decimal GetDeliveryChargeForBasketTotalOf(decimal total);
    }
}
```

Next, create a default implementation of the `IDeliveryOption` named `DeliveryOption`, as shown in the following listing:

```
using Agathas.Storefront.Infrastructure.Domain;

namespace Agathas.Storefront.Model.Shipping
{
    public class DeliveryOption : EntityBase<int>, IAggregateRoot, IDeliveryOption
    {
        private readonly decimal _freeDeliveryThreshold;
        private readonly decimal _cost;
        private readonly ShippingService _shippingService;

        public DeliveryOption()
        {
        }

        public DeliveryOption(decimal freeDeliveryThreshold, decimal cost,
                              ShippingService shippingService)
        {
            _freeDeliveryThreshold = freeDeliveryThreshold;
            _cost = cost;
            _shippingService = shippingService;
        }

        public decimal GetDeliveryChargeForBasketTotalOf(decimal total)
        {
            if (total > FreeDeliveryThreshold)
```

```
            return 0;

        return Cost;
    }

    public decimal FreeDeliveryThreshold
    {
        get { return _freeDeliveryThreshold; }
    }

    public decimal Cost
    {
        get { return _cost;}
    }

    public ShippingService ShippingService
    {
        get { return _shippingService; }
    }

    protected override void Validate()
    {
        throw new NotImplementedException();
    }
        }
    }
```

Before a customer has selected a delivery option, a `NullDeliveryOption` is used to calculate the basket costs. More information on the Null Object pattern can be found in Chapter 2. Add the new `NullDeliveryOption` class to the `Shipping` folder matching the code definition that follows:

```
using System;

namespace Agathas.Storefront.Model.Shipping
{
    public class NullDeliveryOption : IDeliveryOption
    {
        public int Id { get; set; }

        public decimal FreeDeliveryThreshold
        {
            get { return 0; }
        }

        public decimal Cost
        {
            get { return 0; }
        }

        public ShippingService ShippingService
        {
            get { throw new NotImplementedException(); }
            set { throw new NotImplementedException(); }
```

```
        }

        public decimal GetDeliveryChargeForBasketTotalOf(decimal total)
        {
            return 0;
        }
    }
}
```

In the context of the store, there is no requirement to obtain the courier or the shipping service outside of a delivery option. With this in mind, you need only to create an interface for the delivery options repository named IDeliveryOptionRepository:

```
using Agathas.Storefront.Infrastructure.Domain;

namespace Agathas.Storefront.Model.Shipping
{
    public interface IDeliveryOptionRepository :
                            IReadOnlyRepository<DeliveryOption, int>
    {
    }
}
```

With the courier and delivery options sorted, you can turn your attention to the basket domain.

Unlike the product entities, baskets are created and not just retrieved from the database; therefore, validation must occur before you try to persist a transient basket. Create a folder within the Models project named Basket. Add two new classes named BasketBusinessRules and BasketItem BusinessRules, which will contain all the business rules that relate to a customer's basket:

```
using Agathas.Storefront.Infrastructure.Domain;

namespace Agathas.Storefront.Model.Basket
{
    public class BasketBusinessRules
    {
        public static readonly BusinessRule DeliveryOptionRequired =
                new BusinessRule("DeliveryOption",
                            "A basket must have a valid delivery option.");
        public static readonly BusinessRule ItemInvalid =
                new BusinessRule("Item",
                            "A basket cannot have any invalid items.");
    }
}

using Agathas.Storefront.Infrastructure.Domain;

namespace Agathas.Storefront.Model.Basket
{
    public class BasketItemBusinessRules
    {
        public static readonly BusinessRule BasketRequired =
            new BusinessRule("Basket",
                            "A basket item must be related to a basket.");
```

```
        public static readonly BusinessRule ProductRequired =
            new BusinessRule("Product",
                             "A basket item must be related to a product.");
        public static readonly BusinessRule QtyInvalid =
            new BusinessRule("Qty",
                             "The quantity of a basket item cannot be negative.");
    }
}
```

Add a class named `BasketItem` to the `Basket` folder with the following code listing:

```
using Agathas.Storefront.Infrastructure.Domain;
using Agathas.Storefront.Model.Products;

namespace Agathas.Storefront.Model.Basket
{
    public class BasketItem : EntityBase<int>
    {
        private int _qty;
        private Product _product;
        private Basket _basket;

        public BasketItem()
        {
        }

        public BasketItem(Product product, Basket basket, int qty)
        {
            _product = product;
            _basket = basket;
            _qty = qty;
        }

        public decimal LineTotal()
        {
            return Product.Price*Qty;
        }

        public int Qty { get { return _qty; } }

        public Product Product { get { return _product; } }

        public Basket Basket { get { return _basket; } }

        public bool Contains(Product product)
        {
            return Product == product;
        }

        public void IncreaseItemQtyBy(int qty)
        {
            _qty += qty;
        }

        public void ChangeItemQtyTo(int qty)
```

```
        {
            _qty = qty;
        }

        protected override void Validate()
        {
            if (Qty < 0)
                base.AddBrokenRule(BasketItemBusinessRules.QtyInvalid);

            if (Product == null)
                base.AddBrokenRule(BasketItemBusinessRules.ProductRequired);

            if (Basket == null)
                base.AddBrokenRule(BasketItemBusinessRules.BasketRequired);
        }
    }
}
```

The `BasketItem` class simply represents each item in a customer's basket. To create a basket item, add a `BasketItemFactory`, as shown in the following listing:

```
using Agathas.Storefront.Model.Products;

namespace Agathas.Storefront.Model.Basket
{
    public static class BasketItemFactory
    {
        public static BasketItem CreateItemFor(Product product, Basket basket)
        {
            return new BasketItem(product, basket, 1);
        }
    }
}
```

With the business rules and basket items created, you can create the `Basket` entity:

```
using System;
using System.Collections.Generic;
using System.Linq;
using Agathas.Storefront.Infrastructure.Domain;
using Agathas.Storefront.Model.Shipping;
using Agathas.Storefront.Model.Products;

namespace Agathas.Storefront.Model.Basket
{
    public class Basket : EntityBase<Guid>, IAggregateRoot
    {
        private IList<BasketItem> _items;
        private IDeliveryOption _deliveryOption;

        public Basket()
        {
            _items = new List<BasketItem>();
            _deliveryOption = new NullDeliveryOption();
```

```
    }

    public Guid Id { get; set; }

    public int NumberOfItems
    {
        get { return _items.Sum(i => i.Qty);  }
    }

    public decimal BasketTotal
    {
        get { return ItemsTotal + DeliveryCost(); }
    }

    public decimal ItemsTotal
    {
        get { return _items.Sum(i => i.Qty * i.Product.Price); }
    }

    public void Add(Product product)
    {
        if (BasketContainsAnItemFor(product))
            GetItemFor(product).IncreaseItemQtyBy(1);
        else
            _items.Add(BasketItemFactory.CreateItemFor(product, this));
    }

    public BasketItem GetItemFor(Product product)
    {
        return _items.Where(i => i.Contains(product)).FirstOrDefault();
    }

    private bool BasketContainsAnItemFor(Product product)
    {
        return _items.Any(i => i.Contains(product));
    }

    public void Remove(Product product)
    {
        if (BasketContainsAnItemFor(product))
        {
            _items.Remove(GetItemFor(product));
        }
    }

    public void ChangeQtyOfProduct(int qty, Product product)
    {
        if (BasketContainsAnItemFor(product))
        {
            GetItemFor(product).ChangeItemQtyTo(qty);
        }
    }

    public int NumberOfItemsInBasket()
```

```
        {
            return _items.Sum(i => i.Qty);
        }

        public IEnumerable<BasketItem> Items()
        {
            return _items;
        }

        public decimal DeliveryCost()
        {
            return DeliveryOption.GetDeliveryChargeForBasketTotalOf(ItemsTotal);
        }

        public IDeliveryOption DeliveryOption
        {
            get { return _deliveryOption; }
        }

        public void SetDeliveryOption(IDeliveryOption deliveryOption)
        {
            _deliveryOption = deliveryOption;
        }

        protected override void Validate()
        {
            if (DeliveryOption == null)
                base.AddBrokenRule(BasketBusinessRules.DeliveryOptionRequired);

            foreach (BasketItem item in this.Items())
            {
                if (item.GetBrokenRules().Count() > 0)
                    base.AddBrokenRule(BasketBusinessRules.ItemInvalid);
            }
        }
    }
}
```

The `Basket` class consists of methods to add, remove, and modify the items in its collection as well as the ability to set a `DeliveryOption`.

To retrieve and persist baskets, you need to define a contract for a basket repository. Add a new interface named `IBasketRepository` to the `Basket` folder with the following listing:

```
using System;
using Agathas.Storefront.Infrastructure.Domain;

namespace Agathas.Storefront.Model.Basket
{
    public interface IBasketRepository : IRepository<Basket, Guid>
    {
    }
}
```

Now that the basket model is complete, you can update the database to add the new tables required to hold the state of the basket aggregation as well as information pertaining to shipping and delivery options.

Create the Basket Tables

You will now create the data tables to store the basket and shipping details. Open the `Shop.mdf` database within the `Web.MVC` project and add the following tables, as shown in Figure 12-2. (The `Products` table already exists, because you created this in Chapter 11.) Ensure that you set all the primary key fields as identity fields. Apart from the `Baskets` table, this means that the database is in charge of creating the entity's identity.

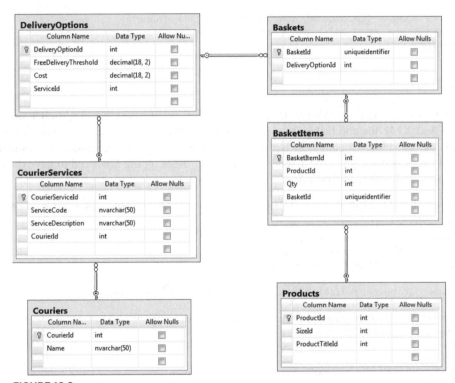

FIGURE 12-2

After the data model is created, you need to set up the mapping files so that NHibernate can retrieve and persist customers' baskets.

NHibernate Mapping

As with the Product entities, you will create a set of mapping files so that NHibernate knows how to map between the data model and the domain model.

The mapping file for the Courier class is Courier.hbm.xml, and the markup follows. Add the XML file to the NHibernate Mapping folder:

```xml
<?xml version="1.0" encoding="utf-8" ?>
<hibernate-mapping xmlns="urn:nhibernate-mapping-2.2"
    namespace="Agathas.Storefront.Model.Shipping"
        assembly="Agathas.Storefront.Model">

  <class name="Courier" table="Couriers" lazy="false" >

    <id name="Id" column="CourierId" type="int" unsaved-value="0">
      <generator class="native" />
    </id>

    <property access="field.camelcase-underscore" name="Name">
      <column name="Name" sql-type="nvarchar(50)" not-null="true" />
    </property>

  </class>
</hibernate-mapping>
```

Remember that you need to change the build action for the Courier.hbm.xml file. Right-click on the Courier.hbm.xml XML file and bring up its properties from the context-sensitive menu. Once the Properties dialog is displayed, change the build action to Embedded Resource. Doing so ensures that the XML data is embedded when the assembly is built. All the mapping files need to have their build actions changed to Embedded Resource.

The mapping file for the ShippingService class is ShippingService.hbm.xml and is shown next:

```xml
<?xml version="1.0" encoding="utf-8" ?>
<hibernate-mapping xmlns="urn:nhibernate-mapping-2.2"
    namespace="Agathas.Storefront.Model.Shipping"
        assembly="Agathas.Storefront.Model">

  <class name="ShippingService" table="CourierServices" lazy="false" >

    <id name="Id" column="CourierServiceId" type="int" unsaved-value="0">
      <generator class="native" />
    </id>

    <property access="field.camelcase-underscore" name="Code">
      <column name="ServiceCode" sql-type="nvarchar(50)" not-null="true" />
    </property>

    <property access="field.camelcase-underscore" name="Description">
      <column name="ServiceDescription" sql-type="nvarchar(50)" not-null="true" />
    </property>

    <many-to-one access="field.camelcase-underscore"  name="Courier"
                 class="Courier"
                 column="CourierId"
                 not-null="true"
                 lazy="false"/>
  </class>
</hibernate-mapping>
```

The mapping file for the `Basket` entity is `Basket.hbm.xml`:

```xml
<?xml version="1.0" encoding="utf-8" ?>
<hibernate-mapping xmlns="urn:nhibernate-mapping-2.2"
    namespace="Agathas.Storefront.Model.Basket"
        assembly="Agathas.Storefront.Model">

  <class name="Basket" table="Baskets" lazy="false" >

    <id name="Id" column="BasketId" type="guid">
      <generator class="guid" />
    </id>

    <bag name="Items" access="field.camelcase-underscore" inverse="true"
        cascade="all-delete-orphan" lazy="true" >
      <key column="BasketId"/>
      <one-to-many class="BasketItem"></one-to-many>
    </bag>

    <many-to-one access="field.camelcase-underscore" name="DeliveryOption"
                class="Agathas.Storefront.Model.Shipping.DeliveryOption"
                column="DeliveryOptionId"
                not-null="true"/>
  </class>

</hibernate-mapping>
```

The mapping file for the `BasketItem` entity is `BasketItem.hbm.xml`:

```xml
<?xml version="1.0" encoding="utf-8" ?>
<hibernate-mapping xmlns="urn:nhibernate-mapping-2.2"
    namespace="Agathas.Storefront.Model.Basket"
        assembly="Agathas.Storefront.Model">

  <class name="BasketItem" table="BasketItems" lazy="false" >

    <id  name="Id" column="BasketItemId" unsaved-value="0">
      <generator class="native" />
    </id>

    <property access="field.camelcase-underscore" name="Qty">
      <column name="Qty" sql-type="int" not-null="true" />
    </property>

    <many-to-one access="field.camelcase-underscore" name="Product"
                class="Agathas.Storefront.Model.Products.Product"
                column="ProductId"
                cascade="none"
                not-null="true"/>

    <many-to-one access="field.camelcase-underscore" name="Basket"
                class="Basket"
                column="BasketId"
                not-null="true"/>
  </class>
</hibernate-mapping>
```

The mapping file for the `DeliveryOption` entity is `DeliveryOption.hbm.xml`:

```xml
<?xml version="1.0" encoding="utf-8" ?>
<hibernate-mapping xmlns="urn:nhibernate-mapping-2.2"
    namespace="Agathas.Storefront.Model.Shipping"
        assembly="Agathas.Storefront.Model">

  <class name="DeliveryOption" table="DeliveryOptions" lazy="false" >

    <id name="Id" column="DeliveryOptionId" type="int" unsaved-value="0">
      <generator class="native" />
    </id>

    <property access="field.camelcase-underscore" name="FreeDeliveryThreshold">
      <column name="FreeDeliveryThreshold"
              sql-type="decimal(18, 2)"
              not-null="true" />
    </property>

    <property access="field.camelcase-underscore"  name="Cost">
      <column name="Cost" sql-type="decimal(18, 2))" not-null="true" />
    </property>

    <many-to-one access="field.camelcase-underscore" name="ShippingService"
                 class="ShippingService"
                 column="ServiceId"
                 not-null="true"
                 lazy="false"/>
  </class>
</hibernate-mapping>
```

Because the framework for the `NHibernate` repository was built in the previous chapter, there is nothing else to do other than add a concrete implementation of the `BasketRepository` and the `DeliveryOptionRepository` to the `Repositories` folder and let the NHibernate base repository handle retrieval and persistence of `Baskets` and `DeliveryOptions`:

```csharp
using System;
using Agathas.Storefront.Infrastructure.UnitOfWork;
using Agathas.Storefront.Model.Basket;

namespace Agathas.Storefront.Repository.NHibernate.Repositories
{
    public class BasketRepository : Repository<Basket, Guid>, IBasketRepository
    {
        public BasketRepository(IUnitOfWork uow)
            : base(uow)
        {
        }
    }
}

using Agathas.Storefront.Infrastructure.UnitOfWork;
using Agathas.Storefront.Model.Shipping;

namespace Agathas.Storefront.Repository.NHibernate.Repositories
```

```
    {
        public class DeliveryOptionRepository : Repository<DeliveryOption, int>,
                                                        IDeliveryOptionRepository
        {
            public DeliveryOptionRepository(IUnitOfWork uow)
                : base(uow)
            {
            }
        }
    }
```

With the data access layer taken care of, you will now look at creating the service layer to allow clients to use the basket logic.

Basket Service

Figure 12-3 shows the views that are required for the BasketService.

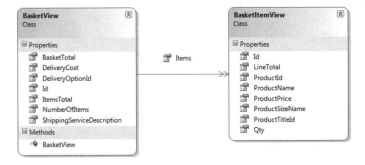

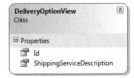

FIGURE 12-3

The DeliveryOptionView is a simple summary of the delivery options available to the customer. Create the DeliveryOptionView class in the ViewModels folder of the Service project:

```
namespace Agathas.Storefront.Services.ViewModels
{
    public class DeliveryOptionView
    {
        public int Id { get; set; }
        public string ShippingServiceDescription { get; set; }
    }
}
```

The `BasketItemView` is a flattened view of the `BasketItem` entity and is used to display items in a basket:

```
namespace Agathas.Storefront.Services.ViewModels
{
    public class BasketItemView
    {
        public int Id { get; set; }
        public int ProductId { get; set; }
        public string ProductName { get; set; }
        public string ProductSizeName { get; set; }
        public int ProductTitleId { get; set; }
        public int Qty { get; set; }
        public string ProductPrice { get; set; }
        public string LineTotal { get; set; }
    }
}
```

The `BasketView` is a flattened view of the `Basket` entity:

```
using System;
using System.Collections.Generic;

namespace Agathas.Storefront.Services.ViewModels
{
    public class BasketView
    {
        public BasketView()
        {
            Items = new List<BasketItemView>();
        }
        public Guid Id { get; set; }
        public string ItemsTotal { get; set; }
        public int NumberOfItems { get; set; }
        public IEnumerable<BasketItemView> Items { get; set; }
        public string BasketTotal { get; set; }
        public string DeliveryCost { get; set; }
        public string ShippingServiceDescription { get; set; }
        public int DeliveryOptionId { get; set; }
    }
}
```

For the `BasketService` to convert the `Basket` entity into a `BasketView`, you need to wire up `AutoMappper`, as you did in the previous chapter for the `Product` entities and view models.

Open the `AutoMapperBootStrapper` class within the root of the `Service` project, and amend it to include mapping configuration for the `Basket` and `DeliveryOption` entities, as highlighted next:

```
...
using Agathas.Storefront.Model.Basket;
using Agathas.Storefront.Model.Shipping;

namespace Agathas.Storefront.Services
{
    public class AutoMapperBootStrapper
    {
```

```
public static void ConfigureAutoMapper()
{
    …

    // Basket
    Mapper.CreateMap<DeliveryOption, DeliveryOptionView>();
    Mapper.CreateMap<BasketItem, BasketItemView>();
    Mapper.CreateMap<Basket, BasketView>();

    …

}
}

…
}
```

For a Basket entity to be converted to a view model, you will add an extension method that returns a BasketView. Add a new class named BasketMapper to the Mapping folder of the Services project:

```
using Agathas.Storefront.Model.Basket;
using Agathas.Storefront.Services.ViewModels;
using AutoMapper;

namespace Agathas.Storefront.Services.Mapping
{
    public static class BasketMapper
    {
        public static BasketView ConvertToBasketView(this Basket basket)
        {
            return Mapper.Map<Basket, BasketView>(basket);
        }
    }
}
```

You need to create a similar extension class for the DeliveryOption entities. Add a new class to the Mapping folder of the Services project named DeliveryOptionMapper with the following code definition:

```
using System.Collections.Generic;
using Agathas.Storefront.Model.Shipping;
using Agathas.Storefront.Services.ViewModels;
using AutoMapper;

namespace Agathas.Storefront.Services.Mapping
{
    public static class DeliveryOptionMapper
    {
        public static IEnumerable<DeliveryOptionView> ConvertToDeliveryOptionViews
                            (this IEnumerable<DeliveryOption> deliveryOptions)
        {
            return Mapper.Map<IEnumerable<DeliveryOption>,
                        IEnumerable<DeliveryOptionView>>(deliveryOptions);
        }
    }
}
```

To communicate with the `BasketService`, you will be using the request and reply messaging pattern. More details of this pattern can be found in Chapter 6. To create a `Basket`, add a pair of request and reply classes within the folder `Messaging/ProductCatalogService` named `CreateBasketRequest` and `CreateBasketResponse`:

```
using System.Collections.Generic;

namespace Agathas.Storefront.Services.Messaging.ProductCatalogService
{
    public class CreateBasketRequest
    {
        public CreateBasketRequest()
        {
            ProductsToAdd = new List<int>();
        }
        public IList<int> ProductsToAdd { get; set; }
    }
}

using Agathas.Storefront.Services.ViewModels;

namespace Agathas.Storefront.Services.Messaging.ProductCatalogService
{
    public class CreateBasketResponse
    {
        public BasketView Basket { get; set; }
    }
}
```

Note that the `CreateBasketRequest` can be given a list of product IDs to add to the newly created `Basket`, alleviating the need for a separate call.

Create a pair of request and reply classes for the task of retrieving a `Basket`. Name these classes `GetBasketRequest` and `GetBasketResponse`.

```
using System;

namespace Agathas.Storefront.Services.Messaging.ProductCatalogService
{
    public class GetBasketRequest
    {
        public Guid BasketId { get; set; }
    }
}

using Agathas.Storefront.Services.ViewModels;

namespace Agathas.Storefront.Services.Messaging.ProductCatalogService
{
    public class GetBasketResponse
    {
        public BasketView Basket { get; set; }
    }
}
```

For a customer to update the quantities of products ordered, she has to submit a `ModifyBasketRequest`, which contains a collection of `ProductQtyUpdateRequests` containing information on the changes to the `BasketItems`:

```
namespace Agathas.Storefront.Services.Messaging.ProductCatalogService
{
    public class ProductQtyUpdateRequest
    {
        public int ProductId { get; set; }
        public int NewQty { get; set; }
    }
}
```

The `ModifyBasketRequest` contains a collection of `BasketItemUpdateRequests`, a list of items to remove and products to add, as well as a way to update the shipping service. The `ModifyBasket Request` and `ModifyBasketResponse` classes are shown in the following listings:

```
using System;
using System.Collections.Generic;

namespace Agathas.Storefront.Services.Messaging.ProductCatalogService
{
    public class ModifyBasketRequest
    {
        public ModifyBasketRequest()
        {
            ItemsToRemove = new List<int>();
            ProductsToAdd = new List<int>();
            ItemsToUpdate = new List<ProductQtyUpdateRequest>();
        }

        public Guid BasketId { get; set; }
        public IList<int> ItemsToRemove { get; set; }
        public IList<ProductQtyUpdateRequest> ItemsToUpdate { get; set; }
        public int SetShippingServiceIdTo {get; set;}
        public IList<int> ProductsToAdd { get; set; }
    }
}

using Agathas.Storefront.Services.ViewModels;

namespace Agathas.Storefront.Services.Messaging.ProductCatalogService
{
    public class ModifyBasketResponse
    {
        public BasketView Basket { get; set; }
    }
}
```

No request object is required to retrieve a collection of `DeliveryOptionViews` — only a `GetAllDispatch OptionsResponse` as shown here:

```
using System.Collections.Generic;
using Agathas.Storefront.Services.ViewModels;

namespace Agathas.Storefront.Services.Messaging.ProductCatalogService
```

```
{
    public class GetAllDispatchOptionsResponse
    {
        public IEnumerable<DeliveryOptionView> DeliveryOptions { get; set; }
    }
}
```

With all the messaging and view models in place, you can work on the BasketService. Define the BasketService contract by adding a new interface named IBasketService to the Interfaces folder of the Services project:

```
using Agathas.Storefront.Services.Messaging.ProductCatalogService;

namespace Agathas.Storefront.Services.Interfaces
{
    public interface IBasketService
    {
        GetBasketResponse GetBasket(GetBasketRequest basketRequest);
        CreateBasketResponse CreateBasket(CreateBasketRequest basketRequest);
        ModifyBasketResponse ModifyBasket(ModifyBasketRequest request);
        GetAllDispatchOptionsResponse GetAllDispatchOptions();
    }
}
```

If a request is sent to retrieve or modify a basket that does not exist, an exception of type BasketDoesNotExistException is thrown, as can be seen next. The controller can then catch this exception and call the BasketService to create a new basket:

```
using System;

namespace Agathas.Storefront.Services.Implementations
{
    public class BasketDoesNotExistException : Exception
    {
    }
}
```

The concrete implementation of the IBasketService is BasketService, and should be created within the Implementations folder of the Services project:

Available for download on Wrox.com

```
using System;
using System.Collections.Generic;
using System.Linq;
using System.Text;
using Agathas.Storefront.Infrastructure.Domain;
using Agathas.Storefront.Infrastructure.UnitOfWork;
using Agathas.Storefront.Model.Basket;
using Agathas.Storefront.Model.Shipping;
using Agathas.Storefront.Model.Products;
using Agathas.Storefront.Services.Interfaces;
using Agathas.Storefront.Services.Mapping;
using Agathas.Storefront.Services.Messaging.ProductCatalogService;
using Agathas.Storefront.Services.ViewModels;

namespace Agathas.Storefront.Services.Implementations
```

```csharp
{
    public class BasketService : IBasketService
    {
        private readonly IBasketRepository _basketRepository;
        private readonly IProductRepository _productRepository;
        private readonly IDeliveryOptionRepository _deliveryOptionRepository;
        private readonly IUnitOfWork _uow;

        public BasketService(IBasketRepository basketRepository,
                             IProductRepository productRepository,
                             IDeliveryOptionRepository deliveryOptionRepository,
                             IUnitOfWork uow)
        {
            _basketRepository = basketRepository;
            _productRepository = productRepository;
            _deliveryOptionRepository = deliveryOptionRepository;
            _uow = uow;
        }

        public GetBasketResponse GetBasket(GetBasketRequest request)
        {
            GetBasketResponse response = new GetBasketResponse();

            Basket basket = _basketRepository.FindBy(request.BasketId);
            BasketView basketView;

            if (basket != null)
                basketView = basket.ConvertToBasketView();
            else
                basketView = new BasketView();

            response.Basket = basketView;

            return response;
        }

        public CreateBasketResponse CreateBasket(CreateBasketRequest request)
        {
            CreateBasketResponse response = new CreateBasketResponse();

            Basket basket = new Basket();

            basket.SetDeliveryOption(GetCheapestDeliveryOption());

            AddProductsToBasket(request.ProductsToAdd, basket);

            ThrowExceptionIfBasketIsInvalid(basket);

            _basketRepository.Save(basket);
            _uow.Commit();

            response.Basket = basket.ConvertToBasketView();

            return response;
```

```
    }

    private DeliveryOption GetCheapestDeliveryOption()
    {
        return _deliveryOptionRepository.FindAll()
                        .OrderBy(d => d.Cost).FirstOrDefault();
    }

    private void ThrowExceptionIfBasketIsInvalid(Basket basket)
    {
        if (basket.GetBrokenRules().Count() > 0)
        {
            StringBuilder brokenRules = new StringBuilder();
            brokenRules.AppendLine("There were problems saving the Basket:");
            foreach (BusinessRule businessRule in basket.GetBrokenRules())
            {
                brokenRules.AppendLine(businessRule.Rule);
            }

            throw new ApplicationException(brokenRules.ToString());

        }
    }

    public ModifyBasketResponse ModifyBasket(ModifyBasketRequest request)
    {
        ModifyBasketResponse response = new ModifyBasketResponse();
        Basket basket = _basketRepository.FindBy(request.BasketId);

        if (basket == null)
            throw new BasketDoesNotExistException();

        AddProductsToBasket(request.ProductsToAdd, basket);

        UpdateLineQtys(request.ItemsToUpdate, basket);

        RemoveItemsFromBasket(request.ItemsToRemove, basket);

        if (request.SetShippingServiceIdTo != 0)
        {
            DeliveryOption deliveryOption =
              _deliveryOptionRepository.FindBy(request.SetShippingServiceIdTo);
            basket.SetDeliveryOption(deliveryOption);
        }

        ThrowExceptionIfBasketIsInvalid(basket);

        _basketRepository.Save(basket);
        _uow.Commit();

        response.Basket = basket.ConvertToBasketView();

        return response;
    }

    private void RemoveItemsFromBasket(IList<int> productsToRemove,
```

```
                                      Basket basket)
    {
        foreach (int productId in productsToRemove)
        {
            Product product = _productRepository.FindBy(productId);
            if (product != null)
                basket.Remove(product);
        }
    }

    private void UpdateLineQtys(
            IList<ProductQtyUpdateRequest> productQtyUpdateRequests,
            Basket basket)
    {
        foreach (ProductQtyUpdateRequest productQtyUpdateRequest in
                                        productQtyUpdateRequests)
        {
            Product product = _productRepository
                            .FindBy(productQtyUpdateRequest.ProductId);

            if (product != null)
                basket.ChangeQtyOfProduct(productQtyUpdateRequest.NewQty,
                                        product);
        }
    }

    private void AddProductsToBasket(IList<int> productsToAdd, Basket basket)
    {
        Product product;

        if (productsToAdd.Count() > 0)
            foreach (int productId in productsToAdd)
            {
                product = _productRepository.FindBy(productId);
                basket.Add(product);
            }
    }

    public GetAllDispatchOptionsResponse GetAllDispatchOptions()
    {
        GetAllDispatchOptionsResponse response =
                    new GetAllDispatchOptionsResponse();
        response.DeliveryOptions = _deliveryOptionRepository.FindAll()
                    .OrderBy(d => d.Cost).ConvertToDeliveryOptionViews();

        return response;
    }
  }
}
```

Code snippet BasketService.cs in project Agathas.Storefront.Services

The BasketService class is straightforward and simply handles requests for obtaining, creating, or modifying a basket. A check is made to the basket prior to its being saved. If the basket has more than zero broken business rules, an exception is thrown detailing the issues.

With the `BasketService` in place, you can construct the basket controller that will consume the `BasketService` layer.

Basket Controller and Basket Views

Figure 12-4 shows how the `BasketSummary.ascx` control fits into the `ProductCatalog.Master` control.

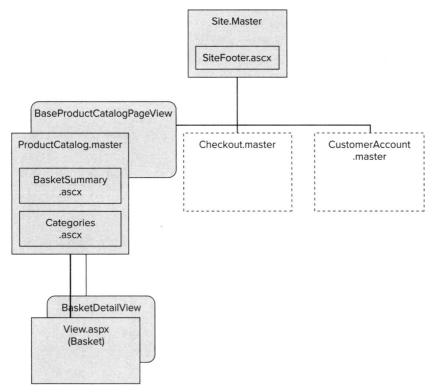

FIGURE 12-4

All product catalog views must supply a basket summary. Figure 12-5 shows the updated view model inheritance tree to include the `BasketSummary` class, which is used on the `BasketSummary.ascx` control.

Create a new view named `BasketSummaryView` at the root of the `ViewModels` folder in the `Controllers` project:

```
namespace Agathas.Storefront.Controllers.ViewModels
{
    public class BasketSummaryView
    {
        public int NumberOfItems { get; set; }
        public string BasketTotal { get; set; }
    }
}
```

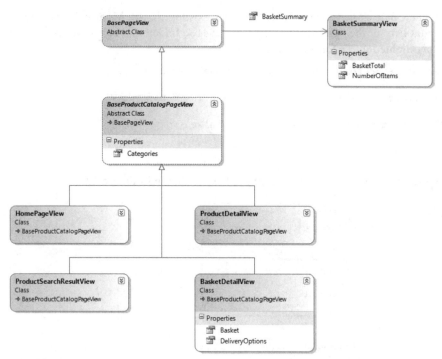

FIGURE 12-5

Create another view named `BasketDetailView` within the `ViewModels/ProductCatalog` folder that will be strongly typed to the `basket` .ASPX view:

```
using System.Collections.Generic;
using Agathas.Storefront.Services.ViewModels;

namespace Agathas.Storefront.Controllers.ViewModels.ProductCatalog
{
    public class BasketDetailView : BaseProductCatalogPageView
    {
        public BasketView Basket { get; set; }
        public IEnumerable<DeliveryOptionView> DeliveryOptions { get; set; }
    }
}
```

Next, create the `BasePageView` class in the root of the `ViewModels` folder. The `BaseProductCatalog PageView` created in the previous chapter now inherits from the `BasePageView` class to provide access to the `BasketSummaryView`:

```
namespace Agathas.Storefront.Controllers.ViewModels
{
    public abstract class BasePageView
    {
        public BasketSummaryView BasketSummary { get; set; }
    }
}
```

Now that you have a new base class, you need to update some existing classes. Modify the `BaseProduct`
`CatalogPageView` that lives in the `ViewModels/ProductCatalog` folder so that it inherits from the
`BasePageView`, as highlighted in the following listing:

```
namespace Agathas.Storefront.Controllers.ViewModels.ProductCatalog
{
    public abstract class BaseProductCatalogPageView : BasePageView
    {
        public IEnumerable<CategoryView> Categories { get; set;}
    }
}
```

The `controllers` also inherit from a new `BaseController`, as shown in Figure 12-6.

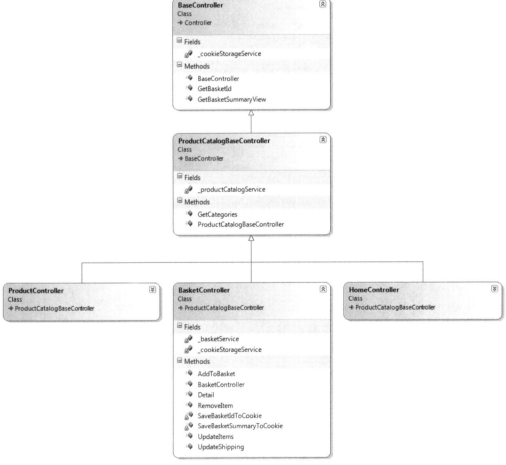

FIGURE 12-6

The `BaseController` exposes methods to obtain a `BasketSummary` object based on data from a cookie
as well as a basket ID from the cookie. To work with cookie storage in a loosely coupled manner, first

define an `ICookieStorageService`. Add the new interface to the folder named `CookieStorage`, found within the `Infrastructure` project:

```
using System;

namespace Agathas.Storefront.Infrastructure.CookieStorage
{
    public interface ICookieStorageService
    {
        void Save(string key, string value, DateTime expires);
        string Retrieve(string key);
    }
}
```

The next class to create again within the `CookieStorage` folder of the `Infrastructure` project is the implementation of the `ICookieStorageService`, named `CookieStorageService`:

```
using System;
using System.Web;

namespace Agathas.Storefront.Infrastructure.CookieStorage
{
    public class CookieStorageService : ICookieStorageService
    {
        public void Save(string key, string value, DateTime expires)
        {
            HttpContext.Current.Response.Cookies[key].Value = value;
            HttpContext.Current.Response.Cookies[key].Expires = expires;
        }

        public string Retrieve(string key)
        {
            HttpCookie cookie = HttpContext.Current.Request.Cookies[key];
            if (cookie != null)
                return cookie.Value;
            return "";
        }
    }
}
```

To obtain and set specific keys, define an enumeration to avoid any magic strings. Create a new enumeration named `CookieDataKeys` in the root of the `Controllers` projects:

```
namespace Agathas.Storefront.Controllers
{
    public enum CookieDataKeys
    {
        BasketItems,
        BasketTotal,
        BasketId
    }
}
```

With the mechanism to set and retrieve cookies in place, you can create the BaseController. Add a new class named BaseController within the Controllers folder of the Controllers project, as shown in the listing that follows:

```
using System;
using System.Web.Mvc;
using Agathas.Storefront.Controllers.ViewModels;
using Agathas.Storefront.Infrastructure.CookieStorage;

namespace Agathas.Storefront.Controllers.Controllers
{
    public class BaseController : Controller
    {
        private readonly ICookieStorageService _cookieStorageService;

        public BaseController(ICookieStorageService cookieStorageService)
        {
            _cookieStorageService = cookieStorageService;
        }

        public BasketSummaryView GetBasketSummaryView()
        {
            string basketTotal = "";
            int numberOfItems = 0;

            if (!string.IsNullOrEmpty(_cookieStorageService.Retrieve(
                            CookieDataKeys.BasketTotal.ToString())))
                basketTotal = _cookieStorageService.Retrieve(
                                    CookieDataKeys.BasketTotal.ToString());

            if (!string.IsNullOrEmpty(_cookieStorageService.Retrieve(
                            CookieDataKeys.BasketItems.ToString())))
                numberOfItems = int.Parse(_cookieStorageService.Retrieve(
                                    CookieDataKeys.BasketItems.ToString()));

            return new BasketSummaryView
            {
                BasketTotal = basketTotal,
                NumberOfItems = numberOfItems
            };
        }

        public Guid GetBasketId()
        {
            string sBasketId = _cookieStorageService
                                .Retrieve(CookieDataKeys.BasketId.ToString());
            Guid basketId = Guid.Empty;

            if (!string.IsNullOrEmpty(sBasketId))
            {
                basketId = new Guid(sBasketId);
            }

            return basketId;
        }
    }
}
```

You can now update the controllers that handle the product browsing functionality so that they implement the correct base constructor call to provide an instance of the `ICookieStorageService`. Update the existing `ProductCatalogBaseController` controller to inherit from the new `BaseController` class:

```
using Agathas.Storefront.Infrastructure.CookieStorage;

namespace Agathas.Storefront.Controllers.Controllers
{
    public class ProductCatalogBaseController : BaseController
    {
        private readonly IProductCatalogService _productCatalogService;

        public ProductCatalogBaseController(
                        ICookieStorageService cookieStorageService,
                        IProductCatalogService productCatalogService)
            : base(cookieStorageService)
        {
            _productCatalogService = productCatalogService;
        }

        ...

    }
}
```

This change causes the `HomeController` and the `ProductController` to break. Therefore, update the constructors of both of these classes, as shown in the following code listing:

```
using Agathas.Storefront.Infrastructure.CookieStorage;

namespace Agathas.Storefront.Controllers.Controllers
{
    public class HomeController : ProductCatalogBaseController
    {
        private readonly IProductCatalogService _productCatalogService;

        public HomeController(IProductCatalogService productCatalogService,
                        ICookieStorageService cookieStorageService)
            : base(cookieStorageService, productCatalogService)
        {
            _productCatalogService = productCatalogService;
        }

        public ActionResult Index()
        {
            HomePageView homePageView = new HomePageView();
            homePageView.Categories = base.GetCategories();
            homePageView.BasketSummary = base.GetBasketSummaryView();

            GetFeaturedProductsResponse response =
                        _productCatalogService.GetFeaturedProducts();
            homePageView.Products = response.Products;

            return View(homePageView);
        }
    }
}
```

```
    }

    using Agathas.Storefront.Infrastructure.CookieStorage;

    namespace Agathas.Storefront.Controllers.Controllers
    {
        public class ProductController : ProductCatalogBaseController
        {
            private readonly IProductCatalogService _productService;

            public ProductController(IProductCatalogService productService,
                                    ICookieStorageService cookieStorageService)
                : base(cookieStorageService, productService)
            {
                _productService = productService;
            }

            ...

            private ProductSearchResultView GetProductSearchResultViewFrom(
                                    GetProductsByCategoryResponse response)
            {
                ProductSearchResultView productSearchResultView =
                                    new ProductSearchResultView();

                productSearchResultView.BasketSummary = base.GetBasketSummaryView();
                productSearchResultView.Categories = base.GetCategories();
                productSearchResultView.CurrentPage = response.CurrentPage;
                productSearchResultView.NumberOfTitlesFound =
                                                    response.NumberOfTitlesFound;
                productSearchResultView.Products = response.Products;
                productSearchResultView.RefinementGroups = response.RefinementGroups;
                productSearchResultView.SelectedCategory = response.SelectedCategory;
                productSearchResultView.SelectedCategoryName =
                                                    response.SelectedCategoryName;
                productSearchResultView.TotalNumberOfPages =
                                                    response.TotalNumberOfPages;
                return productSearchResultView;
            }

            ...

            public ActionResult Detail(int id)
            {
                ProductDetailView productDetailView = new ProductDetailView();
                GetProductRequest request = new GetProductRequest() {ProductId = id};
                GetProductResponse response = _productService.GetProduct(request);

                ProductView productView = response.Product;

                productDetailView.Product = productView;
                productDetailView.BasketSummary = base.GetBasketSummaryView();
                productDetailView.Categories = base.GetCategories();

                return View(productDetailView);
            }
        }
    }
```

To obtain a `BasketSummary` from a `BasketView`, add a new class named `BasketMapper` to the root of the `Controllers` project. The `BasketController` uses this mapping class to persist details of a `Basket` to a cookie:

```
using Agathas.Storefront.Controllers.ViewModels;
using Agathas.Storefront.Services.ViewModels;

namespace Agathas.Storefront.Controllers
{
    public static class BasketMapper
    {
        public static BasketSummaryView ConvertToSummary(this BasketView basket)
        {
            return new BasketSummaryView()
                    {
                        BasketTotal = basket.BasketTotal,
                        NumberOfItems = basket.NumberOfItems
                    };
        }
    }
}
```

As mentioned at the start of this section, interaction between the customer and the web service in terms of basket actions is conducted via Ajax. To pass complex information on the basket from the client to the server, you utilize JavaScript Object Notation (JSON) objects. As with the `ProductSearch Results` view that you worked on earlier, you use the `JsonModelBinder` to convert JSON arrays into .NET objects. The .NET objects that you will be working with are `JsonBasketItemUpdateRequest` and `JsonBasketQtyUpdateRequest`. Create both of these classes within the `JsonDTOs` folder of the `Controllers` project:

```
using System.Runtime.Serialization;
using System.Web.Mvc;

namespace Agathas.Storefront.Controllers.JsonDTOs
{
    [DataContract]
    [ModelBinder(typeof(JsonModelBinder))]
    public class JsonBasketItemUpdateRequest
    {
        [DataMember]
        public int ProductId { get; set; }
        [DataMember]
        public int Qty { get; set; }
    }
}

using System.Runtime.Serialization;
using System.Web.Mvc;

namespace Agathas.Storefront.Controllers.JsonDTOs
{
    [DataContract]
    [ModelBinder(typeof(JsonModelBinder))]
```

```
public class JsonBasketQtyUpdateRequest
{
    [DataMember]
    public JsonBasketItemUpdateRequest[] Items { get; set; }
}
}
```

You use these JSON objects when a customer is updating the quantity of ordered products in a basket line. To simplify the conversion of a collection of JsonBasketItemUpdateRequest to a BasketItemUpdateRequest, add a JsonDtoMapper mapping class to the JsonDTOs folder, which provides conversion method extensions:

```
using System.Collections.Generic;
using Agathas.Storefront.Services.Messaging.ProductCatalogService;

namespace Agathas.Storefront.Controllers.JsonDTOs
{
    public static class JsonDtoMapper
    {
        public static IList<ProductQtyUpdateRequest>
          ConvertToBasketItemUpdateRequests(
                    this JsonBasketQtyUpdateRequest jsonBasketQtyUpdateRequest)
        {
            return jsonBasketQtyUpdateRequest.Items
                        .ConvertToBasketItemUpdateRequests();
        }

        public static IList<ProductQtyUpdateRequest>
          ConvertToBasketItemUpdateRequests(
                    this JsonBasketItemUpdateRequest[] jsonBasketItemUpdateRequests)
        {
            int i = 0;
            IList<ProductQtyUpdateRequest> basketItemUpdateRequests =
                                    new List<ProductQtyUpdateRequest>();

            for (i = 0; i < jsonBasketItemUpdateRequests.Length; i++)
            {
                basketItemUpdateRequests.Add(
                    jsonBasketItemUpdateRequests[i]
                        .ConvertToBasketItemUpdateRequest());
            }

            return basketItemUpdateRequests;
        }

        public static ProductQtyUpdateRequest ConvertToBasketItemUpdateRequest(
                    this JsonBasketItemUpdateRequest jsonBasketItemUpdateRequest)
        {
            return new ProductQtyUpdateRequest
                        {
                            ProductId = jsonBasketItemUpdateRequest.ProductId,
                            NewQty = jsonBasketItemUpdateRequest.Qty
                        };
        }
    }
}
```

You can now finally create the `BasketController`. Again, this is a fairly lengthy class, but it is simple:

```csharp
using System;
using System.Web.Mvc;
using Agathas.Storefront.Controllers.JsonDTOs;
using Agathas.Storefront.Controllers.ViewModels;
using Agathas.Storefront.Controllers.ViewModels.ProductCatalog;
using Agathas.Storefront.Infrastructure.CookieStorage;
using Agathas.Storefront.Services.Implementations;
using Agathas.Storefront.Services.Interfaces;
using Agathas.Storefront.Services.Messaging.ProductCatalogService;

namespace Agathas.Storefront.Controllers.Controllers
{
    public class BasketController : ProductCatalogBaseController
    {
        private readonly IBasketService _basketService;
        private readonly ICookieStorageService _cookieStorageService;

        public BasketController(IProductCatalogService productCatalogService,
                                IBasketService basketService,
                                ICookieStorageService cookieStorageService)
            : base(cookieStorageService, productCatalogService)
        {
            _basketService = basketService;
            _cookieStorageService = cookieStorageService;
        }

        public ActionResult Detail()
        {
            BasketDetailView basketView = new BasketDetailView();
            Guid basketId = base.GetBasketId();

            GetBasketRequest basketRequest = new GetBasketRequest()
                                                {BasketId = basketId};
            GetBasketResponse basketResponse =
                        _basketService.GetBasket(basketRequest);

            GetAllDispatchOptionsResponse dispatchOptionsResponse =
                        _basketService.GetAllDispatchOptions();

            basketView.Basket = basketResponse.Basket;
            basketView.Categories = base.GetCategories();
            basketView.BasketSummary = base.GetBasketSummaryView();
            basketView.DeliveryOptions = dispatchOptionsResponse.DeliveryOptions;

            return View("View", basketView);
        }

        [AcceptVerbs(HttpVerbs.Post)]
        public JsonResult RemoveItem(int productId)
        {
            ModifyBasketRequest request = new ModifyBasketRequest();
            request.ItemsToRemove.Add(productId);
```

```
        request.BasketId = base.GetBasketId();

        ModifyBasketResponse response = _basketService.ModifyBasket(request);

        SaveBasketSummaryToCookie(response.Basket.NumberOfItems,
                                  response.Basket.BasketTotal);

        BasketDetailView basketDetailView = new BasketDetailView();

        basketDetailView.BasketSummary = new BasketSummaryView()
                          {
                               BasketTotal = response.Basket.BasketTotal,
                               NumberOfItems = response.Basket.NumberOfItems
                          };

        basketDetailView.Basket = response.Basket;
        basketDetailView.DeliveryOptions =
                    _basketService.GetAllDispatchOptions().DeliveryOptions;

        return Json(basketDetailView);
    }

    [AcceptVerbs(HttpVerbs.Post)]
    public JsonResult UpdateShipping(int shippingServiceId)
    {
        ModifyBasketRequest request = new ModifyBasketRequest();
        request.SetShippingServiceIdTo = shippingServiceId;
        request.BasketId = base.GetBasketId();

        BasketDetailView basketDetailView = new BasketDetailView();

        ModifyBasketResponse response = _basketService.ModifyBasket(request);

        SaveBasketSummaryToCookie(response.Basket.NumberOfItems,
                                  response.Basket.BasketTotal);

        basketDetailView.BasketSummary = new BasketSummaryView()
        {
            BasketTotal = response.Basket.BasketTotal,
            NumberOfItems = response.Basket.NumberOfItems
        };

        basketDetailView.Basket = response.Basket;
        basketDetailView.DeliveryOptions =
                    _basketService.GetAllDispatchOptions().DeliveryOptions;

        return Json(basketDetailView);
    }

    [AcceptVerbs(HttpVerbs.Post)]
    public JsonResult UpdateItems(
                    JsonBasketQtyUpdateRequest jsonBasketQtyUpdateRequest)
    {
        ModifyBasketRequest request = new ModifyBasketRequest();
```

```csharp
        request.BasketId = base.GetBasketId();
        request.ItemsToUpdate = jsonBasketQtyUpdateRequest
                                .ConvertToBasketItemUpdateRequests(); ;

        BasketDetailView basketDetailView = new BasketDetailView();
        ModifyBasketResponse response = _basketService.ModifyBasket(request);

        SaveBasketSummaryToCookie(response.Basket.NumberOfItems,
                                response.Basket.BasketTotal);

        basketDetailView.BasketSummary = new BasketSummaryView()
        {
            BasketTotal = response.Basket.BasketTotal,
            NumberOfItems = response.Basket.NumberOfItems
        };

        basketDetailView.Basket = response.Basket;

        basketDetailView.DeliveryOptions = _basketService
                                .GetAllDispatchOptions().DeliveryOptions;

        return Json(basketDetailView);
    }

    [AcceptVerbs(HttpVerbs.Post)]
    public JsonResult AddToBasket(int productId)
    {
        BasketSummaryView basketSummaryView = new BasketSummaryView();
        Guid basketId = base.GetBasketId();
        bool createNewBasket = basketId == Guid.Empty;

        if (createNewBasket == false)
        {
            ModifyBasketRequest modifyBasketRequest =
                                new ModifyBasketRequest();

            modifyBasketRequest.ProductsToAdd.Add(productId);
            modifyBasketRequest.BasketId = basketId;

            try
            {
                ModifyBasketResponse response = _basketService
                                    .ModifyBasket(modifyBasketRequest);
                basketSummaryView = response.Basket.ConvertToSummary();
                SaveBasketSummaryToCookie(basketSummaryView.NumberOfItems,
                                    basketSummaryView.BasketTotal);
            }
            catch (BasketDoesNotExistException ex)
            {
                createNewBasket = true;
            }
        }

        if (createNewBasket)
```

```
        {
            CreateBasketRequest createBasketRequest =
                                new CreateBasketRequest();

            createBasketRequest.ProductsToAdd.Add(productId);

            CreateBasketResponse response = _basketService
                                .CreateBasket(createBasketRequest);

            SaveBasketIdToCookie(response.Basket.Id);
            basketSummaryView = response.Basket.ConvertToSummary();
            SaveBasketSummaryToCookie(basketSummaryView.NumberOfItems,
                                basketSummaryView.BasketTotal);
        }

        return Json(basketSummaryView);
    }

    private void SaveBasketIdToCookie(Guid basketId)
    {
        _cookieStorageService.Save(CookieDataKeys.BasketId.ToString(),
                        basketId.ToString(), DateTime.Now.AddDays(1));
    }

    private void SaveBasketSummaryToCookie(int numberOfItems,
                                    string basketTotal)
    {
        _cookieStorageService.Save(CookieDataKeys.BasketItems.ToString(),
                        numberOfItems.ToString(), DateTime.Now.AddDays(1));
        _cookieStorageService.Save(CookieDataKeys.BasketTotal.ToString(),
                        basketTotal.ToString(), DateTime.Now.AddDays(1));
    }
  }
}
```

Code snippet BasketController in project Agathas.Storefront.Controllers

You can now turn your attention to the .ASPX views of the `basket`. Create a new MVC User Control named `BasketSummary.ascx` in the folder `Views/Shared` of the `Web.MVC` project with the following markup:

```
<%@ Control Language="C#"
            Inherits="System.Web.Mvc.ViewUserControl<BasketSummaryView>" %>
<%@ Import Namespace="Agathas.Storefront.Controllers.ViewModels" %>

<div id="smoverlay" class="smoverlay"></div>
<div id="basketSummary">
<span class="basket-details">
    <%=Html.ActionLink("Your Basket", "Detail", "Basket")%>
    <span id="basket-summary-text">
  <% if(Model.NumberOfItems == 0 ) { %>
     is empty
  <% }
     else { %>
```

```
        <%=Model.NumberOfItems%> Item(s) at <%=Model.BasketTotal%>
    <% }%>
      </span>
  </span>
</div>
```

With the `BasketSummary.ascx` control built, you can include it within the `ProductCatalog.master` file, as shown in the highlighted section that follows:

```
<%@ Master Language="C#" MasterPageFile="Site.Master"
          Inherits="System.Web.Mvc.ViewMasterPage<BaseProductCatalogPageView>" %>
<%@ Import Namespace="Agathas.Storefront.Controllers.ViewModels.ProductCatalog" %>

<asp:Content  ID="TitleContent" ContentPlaceHolderID="TitleContent" runat="server">
    <asp:ContentPlaceHolder ID="TitleContent" runat="server">

    </asp:ContentPlaceHolder>
</asp:Content>

<asp:Content ID="MainContent" ContentPlaceHolderID="MainContent" runat="server">
    <asp:ContentPlaceHolder ID="MainContent" runat="server">

    </asp:ContentPlaceHolder>
</asp:Content>

<asp:Content  ID="headerBasketSummary"
          ContentPlaceHolderID="headerBasketSummary"
          runat="server">
    <% Html.RenderPartial("~/Views/Shared/BasketSummary.ascx",
                          ((BaseProductCatalogPageView)Model).BasketSummary); %>
</asp:Content>

<asp:Content ID="MenuContent" ContentPlaceHolderID="MenuContent" runat="server">
    <asp:ContentPlaceHolder ID="MenuContent" runat="server">
        <% Html.RenderPartial("~/Views/Shared/Categories.ascx",
            ((BaseProductCatalogPageView)Model).Categories); %>
    </asp:ContentPlaceHolder>
</asp:Content>
```

Add the following JavaScript to the `agatha-common-scripts.js` file within the `Scripts` folder. This piece of JavaScript will be used on the `Product` detail view as well as the `Basket` detail view to refresh the basket summary:

```
function updateBasketSummary(basketSummary) {

    if (basketSummary.NumberOfItems == 0) {
        $('#basket-summary-text').text('empty');
    }
    else {
        $('#basket-summary-text').text(basketSummary.NumberOfItems
                                  + ' Item(s) at ' +
                                  basketSummary.BasketTotal);
    }
}
```

Add a new folder within the `Views` folder of the `Web.MVC` project named `Basket`, and then add a new view to the `Basket` folder named `View.aspx`. This lengthy page contains all the functions for a customer to update his basket. All the operations happen via Ajax calls, so the `JTemplate` library is used again to data-bind the resulting Ajax callback JSON object to the markup:

```
<%@ Page Title="" Language="C#"
         MasterPageFile="~/Views/Shared/ProductCatalog.Master"
         Inherits="System.Web.Mvc.ViewPage<BasketDetailView>" %>
<%@ Import Namespace="Agathas.Storefront.Services.ViewModels" %>
<%@ Import Namespace="Agathas.Storefront.UI.Web.MVC.Helpers" %>
<%@ Import Namespace="Agathas.Storefront.Controllers.ViewModels.ProductCatalog" %>

<asp:Content ID="Content1" ContentPlaceHolderID="TitleContent"
            runat="server"> Your Basket
</asp:Content>

<asp:Content ID="Content2" ContentPlaceHolderID="MainContent" runat="server">

    <script type="text/javascript">

        function removeItem(productId) {

            var postData = { productId: productId };

            showOverlay("overlay", "main");
            showOverlay("smoverlay", "basketSummary");

            $.post('<%=Html.Resolve("/Basket/RemoveItem") %>', postData,
                                                updateBasket, "json");
        }

        function updateItemQtys() {

            showOverlay("overlay", "main");
            showOverlay("smoverlay", "basketSummary");

            var postData;
            var postArr = [];
            var index = 0;

            $("[id^='Qty-']").each(function() {

                itemElementId = $(this).attr('id');
                var productId = 0;
                productId = itemElementId.replace("Qty-", "");

                postArr[index] = { ProductId: productId, Qty: $(this).val() }
                index++;
            });

            postData = { Items: postArr };

            var jsonData = JSON.stringify(postData);

            $.post('<%=Html.Resolve("/Basket/UpdateItems") %>', jsonData,
```

```
                                                updateBasket, "json");
    }

    function updateShippingService(ddlShippingService) {

        var postData = { shippingServiceId: $(ddlShippingService).val() };

        showOverlay("overlay", "main");
        showOverlay("smoverlay", "basketSummary");

        $.post('<%=Html.Resolve("/Basket/UpdateShipping") %>',
                                   postData, updateBasket, "json");
    }

    function updateBasket(basketDetailView) {

        if (basketDetailView.BasketSummary.NumberOfItems == 0) {
            $("#basketDisplay").text("You have no items in your basket.");
        }
        else {
            $("#basketDisplay").setTemplate($("#basketTemplate").html());
            $("#basketDisplay").processTemplate(basketDetailView);
        }

        updateBasketSummary(basketDetailView.BasketSummary);

        hideOverlay("overlay");
        hideOverlay("smoverlay");
    }
</script>

<h2>Your Basket</h2>

 <% if (Model.Basket.Items.Count() > 0)
     {%>
 <div id="overlay" class="overlay"></div>
 <div id="basketDisplay">
 <table width="100%">
    <tr>
        <td>Product</td>
        <td>Qty</td>
        <td align="right">Price</td>
        <td align="right">Total</td>
    </tr>
    <tr>
        <td colspan="4"><hr /></td>
    </tr>
  <% foreach (BasketItemView item in Model.Basket.Items) { %>
     <tr>
        <td><%=Html.Encode(item.ProductName) %> -
            <%=Html.Encode(item.ProductSizeName) %><br />
            <a href="JavaScript:removeItem(<%=Html.Encode(item.ProductId) %>)">
                remove this item</a>
        </td>
```

```
            <td><%=Html.TextBox("Qty-" + item.ProductId.ToString(), item.Qty,
                           new { @class = "itemQtyBox" })%></td>
            <td align="right"><%=Html.Encode(item.ProductPrice) %></td>
            <td align="right"><%=Html.Encode(item.LineTotal) %></td>
        </tr>
      <% } %>
        <tr>
            <td></td>
            <td><a href="JavaScript:updateItemQtys();">update</a></td>
            <td></td>
            <td></td>
        </tr>
        <tr>
            <td colspan="4"><hr /></td>
        </tr>
        <tr>
            <td align="right" colspan="3">Basket: </td>
            <td align="right"><%=Html.Encode(Model.Basket.ItemsTotal) %></td>
        </tr>
        <tr>
            <td align="right"  colspan="3">Shipping:
                <select class="item-sortdropdown" name="ddlShippingService"
                        onchange="JavaScript:updateShippingService(this);"
                        id="ddlShippingService">
                <% foreach (DeliveryOptionView deliveryOption in
                                            Model.DeliveryOptions){%>
                    <option value="<%=Html.Encode(deliveryOption.Id) %>"
                    <% if (Model.Basket.DeliveryOptionId == deliveryOption.Id) { %>
                        selected
                    <%}%>>
                    <%=Html.Encode(deliveryOption.ShippingServiceDescription) %>
                    </option>
                 <%}%>
                </select>
        </td>
            <td align="right"><%=Html.Encode(Model.Basket.DeliveryCost) %></td>
        </tr>
        <tr>
            <td align="right" colspan="3"> Total: </td>
            <td align="right"><%=Html.Encode(Model.Basket.BasketTotal) %></td>
        </tr>
        <tr>
            <td colspan="3"></td>
            <td align="right">
              <%=Html.ActionLink("Check Out", "Checkout", "Checkout")%></td>
        </tr>
    </table>
</div>
<p></p>
<%
    }
    else
    {
%>
You have no items in your basket.
```

```
<%
    }%>


<script type="text/html" id="basketTemplate">
    <table width="100%">
        <tr>
            <td>Product</td>
            <td>Qty</td>
            <td align="right">Price</td>
            <td align="right">Total</td>
        </tr>
        <tr>
            <td colspan="4"><hr /></td>
        </tr>
        {#foreach $T.Basket.Items as record}
        <tr>
            <td>{$T.record.ProductName} - {$T.record.ProductSizeName}<br />
                <a href="JavaScript:removeItem({$T.record.ProductId})">
                remove this item</a>
            </td>
            <td><input class="itemQtyBox" id="Qty-{$T.record.ProductId}"
                       type="text" value="{$T.record.Qty}" /></td>
            <td align="right">{$T.record.ProductPrice}</td>
            <td align="right">{$T.record.LineTotal}</td>
        </tr>
        {#/for}
        <tr>
            <td></td>
            <td><a href="JavaScript:updateItemQtys();">update</a></td>
            <td></td>
            <td></td>
        </tr>
        <tr>
            <td colspan="4"><hr /></td>
        </tr>
        <tr>
            <td align="right" colspan="3">Basket: </td>
            <td align="right">{$T.Basket.ItemsTotal}</td>
        </tr>
        <tr>
            <td align="right"  colspan="3">Shipping:
                <select class="item-sortdropdown" name="ddlShippingService"
                        onchange="JavaScript:updateShippingService(this);"
                        id="ddlShippingService">
                {#foreach $T.DeliveryOptions as deliveryOption}
                    <option value="{$T.deliveryOption.Id}"
                      {#if $T.deliveryOption.Id ==
                                   $T.Basket.DeliveryOptionId} selected{#/if}
                      >{$T.deliveryOption.ShippingServiceDescription}</option>
                    {#/for}
                </select>
            </td>
            <td align="right">{$T.Basket.DeliveryCost}</td>
        </tr>
```

```
        <tr>
            <td align="right" colspan="3"> Total: </td>
            <td align="right">{$T.Basket.BasketTotal}</td>
        </tr>
        <tr>
            <td colspan="3"></td>
            <td align="right">
              <%=Html.ActionLink("Check Out", "Checkout", "Checkout")%></td>
        </tr>
    </table>
    </script>

</asp:Content>
```

Code snippet View.aspx in project Agathas.Storefront.UI.Web.MVC

Next, update the Product detail view named `Detail.aspx`, which you can find within the `Views/` `Product` folder. Update the markup to include the JavaScript highlighted next, along with the `onclick` handler of the Add to Basket button.

...

```
<asp:Content ID="Content2" ContentPlaceHolderID="MainContent" runat="server">

    <script type="text/javascript">
        function addProductToBasket() {

            showOverlay("smoverlay", "basketSummary", 5);

            var postData = { productId: $("#productsizes").val() };

            $.post('<%=Html.Resolve("/Basket/AddToBasket") %>',
                    postData, updateBasket, "json");
        }

        function updateBasket(basketSummaryView) {
            updateBasketSummary(basketSummaryView);
            hideOverlay("smoverlay");
        }
    </script>

    <h2><%=Model.Product.BrandName%> <%=Model.Product.Name%></h2>

    <div>
        <span style="float : left">
            <img src="<%=Html.Resolve("/Content/Images/Products/" +
                                Model.Product.Id.ToString() + ".jpg") %>" />
        </span>
        <div>
         <%=Model.Product.Price%><br />
            <%=Model.Product.BrandName%> <%=Model.Product.Name%><br />
            <p>

            <select id="productsizes">
            <% foreach (ProductSizeOption option in Model.Product.Products)
```

```
            {%>
                    <option value="<%=option.Id %>"><%=option.SizeName %></option>
            <%
                }%>
            </select>

            <input type="button"
                    onclick="JavaScript:addProductToBasket();"
                    value="+ Add to cart" />
            </p>
            <p>
            * - Rutrum mattis nulla sodales<br />
            * - Duis sodales tempor felis ac<br />
            * - Ut porta metus a metus<br />
            </p>
        </div>
    </div>

        ...
```

Lastly, you need to wire up the new classes with the BootStrapper class found at the root of the Web.MVC project. Amend the class, as shown in the following listing:

```
...
using Agathas.Storefront.Model.Basket;
using Agathas.Storefront.Model.Shipping;
using Agathas.Storefront.Infrastructure.CookieStorage;

namespace Agathas.Storefront.UI.Web.MVC
{
    public class BootStrapper
    {
        ...

        public class ControllerRegistry : Registry
        {
            public ControllerRegistry()
            {
                // Repositories
                ForRequestedType<IBasketRepository>().TheDefault.Is.OfConcreteType
                        <Repository.NHibernate.Repositories.BasketRepository>();
                ForRequestedType<IDeliveryOptionRepository>()
                        .TheDefault.Is.OfConcreteType
                        <Repository.NHibernate.Repositories
                        .DeliveryOptionRepository>();
                ForRequestedType<ICategoryRepository>().TheDefault.Is.OfConcreteType
                        <Repository.NHibernate.Repositories.CategoryRepository>();
                ForRequestedType<IProductTitleRepository>()
                        .TheDefault.Is.OfConcreteType
                        <Repository.NHibernate.Repositories
                        .ProductTitleRepository>();
                ForRequestedType<IProductRepository>().TheDefault.Is.OfConcreteType
                        <Repository.NHibernate.Repositories.ProductRepository>();
                ForRequestedType<IUnitOfWork>().TheDefault.Is.OfConcreteType
```

```
            <Repository.NHibernate.NHUnitOfWork>();

    // Product Catalog
    ForRequestedType<IProductCatalogService>()
            .TheDefault.Is.OfConcreteType
            <ProductCatalogService>();

    ForRequestedType<IBasketService>().TheDefault.Is.OfConcreteType
            <BasketService>();
    ForRequestedType<ICookieStorageService>()
            .TheDefault.Is.OfConcreteType
            <CookieStorageService >();

    // Application Settings
    ForRequestedType<IApplicationSettings>()
            .TheDefault.Is.OfConcreteType
            <WebConfigApplicationSettings>();

    // Logger
    ForRequestedType<ILogger>().TheDefault.Is.OfConcreteType
            <Log4NetAdapter>();

    // E-Mail Service
    ForRequestedType<IEmailService>().TheDefault.Is.OfConcreteType
            <TextLoggingEmailService>();
        }
    }
  }
}
```

Before you can run the solution, you need to enter some data into the database for the `Couriers`, `CourierServices`, and `DeliveryOptions` tables. When this is complete, you can to build the solution and browse the site. When you land on a product detail page, you can add products to the basket and then amend your products at the Basket Detail page, as can be seen in Figure 12-7.

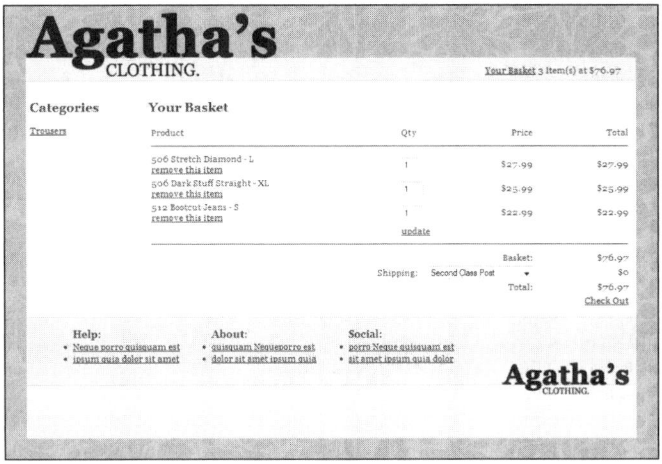

FIGURE 12-7

SUMMARY

You now have a site where customers can browse products and add them to their basket. In this chapter, you accomplished the following:

➤   You built the Basket domain model and the shipping delivery options aggregation to enable customers to select a delivery service.

➤   You updated the controllers and view models to inherit from new abstract base classes that gave functionality to retrieve and display a basket summary.

➤   You created an interface for the client-side storage service and applied the adapter pattern to adapt the `HttpContext` interface to that of the `ICookieStorageService`.

➤   You used AJAX to add a product to the basket and modify the actual basket.

The more eagle-eyed among you may have noticed the link to the checkout controller action that was placed on the Basket detail page. You will build the checkout and ordering facility in Chapter 14, but the next chapter focuses on the customer membership requirements.

13

Customer Membership

WHAT'S IN THIS CHAPTER?

➤ You will build the customer domain model and customer account section

➤ You will use the ASP.NET membership API to offer a local authentication service

➤ You will use a web-based authentication service provided by Janrain to allow customers to authenticate themselves on the site using existing accounts such as Google and Facebook

This chapter builds upon the solution from Chapter 12 by adding customer membership functionality. In this chapter, you tackle the requirements of customer membership, registration, and authentication.

CUSTOMER MEMBERSHIP

Figure 13-1 shows the site map for customer membership.

You will focus on the login and registration functionality as well as the customer and delivery address book management. The next chapter deals with the customer's order history.

Customer Model

The domain model for customer aggregation is simple and consists of only two classes: the `Customer` and the `DeliveryAddress`, as shown in Figure 13-2.

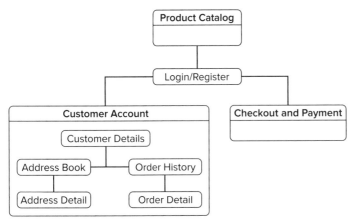

FIGURE 13-1

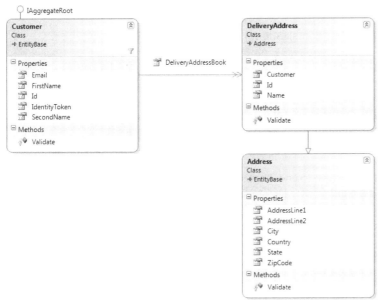

FIGURE 13-2

`Address` has been defined as a separate base class because it will be used with the order aggregation to represent the order dispatch address. Because customers and addresses can be created, it's important that they are created in a valid state. With this in mind, add a new class to the root of the `Model` project named `AddressBusinessRules`:

```
using Agathas.Storefront.Infrastructure.Domain;

namespace Agathas.Storefront.Model
{
    public class AddressBusinessRules
```

```
    {
        public static readonly BusinessRule AddressLine1Required = new
                        BusinessRule("AddressLine1",
                                    "The 1st line of an Address is required.");
        public static readonly BusinessRule CityRequired = new
                        BusinessRule("City", "An address must have a city.");
        public static readonly BusinessRule StateRequired = new
                        BusinessRule("State", "An address must have a state.");
        public static readonly BusinessRule CountryRequired = new
                        BusinessRule("Country", "An address must have a country.");
        public static readonly BusinessRule ZipCodeRequired = new
                        BusinessRule("ZipCode", "An address must have a zip code.");

    }
}
```

Next, create the Address class in the root of the Model project. This is a simple class that contains validation logic to ensure that an address adheres to the store's business rules:

```
using System;
using Agathas.Storefront.Infrastructure.Domain;

namespace Agathas.Storefront.Model
{
    public class Address : EntityBase<int>
    {
        public string AddressLine1 { get; set; }
        public string AddressLine2 { get; set; }
        public string City { get; set; }
        public string State { get; set; }
        public string Country { get; set; }
        public string ZipCode { get; set; }

        protected override void Validate()
        {
            if (String.IsNullOrEmpty(AddressLine1))
                base.AddBrokenRule(AddressBusinessRules.AddressLine1Required);

            if (String.IsNullOrEmpty(City))
                base.AddBrokenRule(AddressBusinessRules.CityRequired);

            if (String.IsNullOrEmpty(State))
                base.AddBrokenRule(AddressBusinessRules.StateRequired);

            if (String.IsNullOrEmpty(Country))
                base.AddBrokenRule(AddressBusinessRules.CountryRequired);

            if (String.IsNullOrEmpty(ZipCode))
                base.AddBrokenRule(AddressBusinessRules.ZipCodeRequired);
        }
    }
}
```

With the base Address class created, you can create the customer's DeliveryAddress class that will inherit from it. However, before you create the class, you need to add some more business rules to validate the extra information contained within a `DeliveryAddress`. Create a new folder within the `Model` project named `Customers`, and add a new class named `DeliveryAddressBusinessRules`:

```
using Agathas.Storefront.Infrastructure.Domain;

namespace Agathas.Storefront.Model.Customers
{
    public class DeliveryAddressBusinessRules
    {
        public static readonly BusinessRule NameRequired = new
            BusinessRule("Name", "A delivery address must have a name.");
        public static readonly BusinessRule CustomerRequired = new
            BusinessRule("Customer",
                    "A delivery address must be associated with a customer.");
    }
}
```

With the business rules defined, you can add the `DeliveryAddress` that inherits from `Address`. Add the new class to the `Customers` folder that you just created:

```
namespace Agathas.Storefront.Model.Customers
{
    public class DeliveryAddress : Address
    {
        public string Name { get; set; }
        public Customer Customer { get; set; }

        protected override void Validate()
        {
            base.Validate();

            if (String.IsNullOrEmpty(Name))
                base.AddBrokenRule(DeliveryAddressBusinessRules.NameRequired);

            if (Customer == null)
                base.AddBrokenRule(DeliveryAddressBusinessRules.CustomerRequired);
        }
    }
}
```

Visual Studio complains because you haven't defined a `Customer` class as yet. Fear not; you will see to this in just a second. Before you do, however, you must define the business rules for a `Customer`. A `Customer` will have an e-mail address. The address needs to be valid, so you will add a new specification for checking its validity, named `EmailValidationSpecification`, with the following listing:

```
using System.Text.RegularExpressions;

namespace Agathas.Storefront.Model.Customers
{
    public class EmailValidationSpecification
    {
        private static Regex _emailregex
                = new Regex(@"\w+([-+.]\w+)*@\w+([-.]\w+)*\.\w+([-.]\w+)*");

        public bool IsSatisfiedBy(string email)
```

```
            {
                return _emailregex.IsMatch(email);
            }
        }
    }
```

You can now define the set of rules pertaining to a customer in a class named `CustomerBusinessRules`:

```
using Agathas.Storefront.Infrastructure.Domain;

namespace Agathas.Storefront.Model.Customers
{
    public class CustomerBusinessRules
    {
        public static readonly BusinessRule FirstNameRequired = new BusinessRule(
                        "FirstName", "A customer must have a first name.");
        public static readonly BusinessRule SecondNameRequired = new BusinessRule(
                        "SecondName", "A customer must have a second name.");
        public static readonly BusinessRule EmailRequired = new BusinessRule(
                        "Email", "A customer must have a valid email address.");
        public static readonly BusinessRule IdentityTokenRequired = new
                        BusinessRule("IdentityToken",
                                        "A customer must have an identity token.");
    }
}
```

When a delivery address is added to a customer's delivery address book, it needs to be in a valid state. If it is not, an exception is thrown. The `InvalidAddressException` class is used when an invalid `DeliveryAddress` is added:

```
using System;

namespace Agathas.Storefront.Model.Customers
{
    public class InvalidAddressException : Exception
    {
        public InvalidAddressException(string message)
            : base(message)
        {
        }
    }
}
```

With the business rules defined, you can complete the model by adding the `Customer` class:

```
using System;
using System.Collections.Generic;
using System.Linq;
using System.Text;
using Agathas.Storefront.Infrastructure.Domain;
using Agathas.Storefront.Model.Orders;

namespace Agathas.Storefront.Model.Customers
{
    public class Customer : EntityBase<int>, IAggregateRoot
```

```
    {
        private IList<DeliveryAddress> _deliveryAddressBook =
                                        new List<DeliveryAddress>();
        public string IdentityToken { get; set; }
        public string FirstName { get; set; }
        public string SecondName { get; set; }
        public string Email { get; set; }

        public void AddAddress(DeliveryAddress deliveryAddress)
        {
            ThrowExceptionIfAddressIsInvalid(deliveryAddress);

            _deliveryAddressBook.Add(deliveryAddress);
        }

        private void ThrowExceptionIfAddressIsInvalid(
                                    DeliveryAddress deliveryAddress)
        {
            if (deliveryAddress.GetBrokenRules().Count() > 0)
            {
                StringBuilder deliveryAddressIssues = new StringBuilder();
                deliveryAddressIssues.AppendLine(
                    "There were some issues with the address you are adding.");

                foreach (BusinessRule rule in deliveryAddress.GetBrokenRules())
                    deliveryAddressIssues.AppendLine(rule.Rule);

                throw new InvalidAddressException(
                                deliveryAddressIssues.ToString());
            }
        }

        public IEnumerable<DeliveryAddress> DeliveryAddressBook
        {
            get { return _deliveryAddressBook; }
        }

        protected override void Validate()
        {
            if (String.IsNullOrEmpty(FirstName))
                base.AddBrokenRule(CustomerBusinessRules.FirstNameRequired);

            if (String.IsNullOrEmpty(SecondName))
                base.AddBrokenRule(CustomerBusinessRules.SecondNameRequired);

            if (!new EmailValidationSpecification().IsSatisfiedBy(Email))
                base.AddBrokenRule(CustomerBusinessRules.EmailRequired);

            if (String.IsNullOrEmpty(IdentityToken))
                base.AddBrokenRule(CustomerBusinessRules.IdentityTokenRequired);
        }
    }
}
```

To retrieve and persist `Customer` entities, you need a customer repository. Define a new `ICustomerRepository` interface that matches the following definition:

```
using Agathas.Storefront.Infrastructure.Domain;

namespace Agathas.Storefront.Model.Customers
{
    public interface ICustomerRepository : IRepository<Customer, int>
    {
        Customer FindBy(string identityToken);
    }
}
```

Notice that the `ICustomerRepository` contains an extra method to find Customers by their `IdentityToken`. The authentication service that you will create later in this chapter provides the `IdentityToken`.

That completes the customers domain model; next, you will create the data model.

Customer Data Tables

You will now update the database by adding data tables to store the customer and delivery address details. Within the `Web.MVC` project, open the database `Shop.mdf` database and add the following tables, as shown in Figure 13-3. Ensure that you set all the primary key fields as identity fields. This will mean that the database is in charge of creating the entity's identity.

FIGURE 13-3

After the data model is created, you need to set up the mapping files so that NHibernate can retrieve and persist the customer and his delivery addresses.

Customer NHibernate Mappings

There are two mapping files for the customer aggregation to match the two entities. The mapping files are similar to what you have seen before. The first mapping file to create is `DeliveryAddress.hbm.xml`, which maps delivery address data rows to delivery address entities:

```
<?xml version="1.0" encoding="utf-8" ?>
<hibernate-mapping xmlns="urn:nhibernate-mapping-2.2"
    namespace="Agathas.Storefront.Model.Customers"
```

```
               assembly="Agathas.Storefront.Model">

    <class name="DeliveryAddress" table="CustomerDeliveryAddresses" lazy="false" >

      <id name="Id" column="DeliveryId" type="int" unsaved-value="0">
        <generator class="native" />
      </id>

      <property name="Name">
        <column name="Name" sql-type="nvarchar(50)" not-null="true" />
      </property>

      <property name="AddressLine1">
        <column name="AddressLine1" sql-type="nvarchar(50)" not-null="true" />
      </property>

      <property name="AddressLine2">
        <column name="AddressLine2" sql-type="nvarchar(50)" not-null="true" />
      </property>

      <property name="City">
        <column name="City" sql-type="nvarchar(50)" not-null="true" />
      </property>

      <property name="State">
        <column name="State" sql-type="nvarchar(50)" not-null="true" />
      </property>

      <property name="ZipCode">
        <column name="ZipCode" sql-type="nvarchar(50)" not-null="true" />
      </property>

      <property name="Country">
        <column name="Country" sql-type="nvarchar(50)" not-null="true" />
      </property>

      <many-to-one name="Customer"
                       class="Customer"
                       column="CustomerId"
                       not-null="true"
                       lazy="false" />

    </class>
  </hibernate-mapping>
```

Remember that you need to change the build action for the `DeliveryAddress.hbm.xml` file. Right-click on the `DeliveryAddress.hbm.xml` XML file and bring up its properties from the context-sensitive menu. Once the Properties dialog is displayed, change the build action to Embedded Resource. This ensures that the XML data is embedded when the assembly is built. Ensure that you do the same for the `Customer.hbm.xml` file that follows:

```
<?xml version="1.0" encoding="utf-8" ?>
<hibernate-mapping xmlns="urn:nhibernate-mapping-2.2"
    namespace="Agathas.Storefront.Model.Customers"
```

```
                       assembly="Agathas.Storefront.Model">

    <class name="Customer" table="Customers" lazy="false" >

      <id name="Id" column="CustomerId"  type="int" unsaved-value="0">
        <generator class="native" />
      </id>

      <property name="IdentityToken">
        <column name="AuthenticationToken" sql-type="nvarchar(250)"
                not-null="true" />
      </property>

      <property name="FirstName">
        <column name="FirstName" sql-type="nvarchar(100)" not-null="true" />
      </property>

      <property name="SecondName">
        <column name="SecondName" sql-type="nvarchar(100)" not-null="true" />
      </property>

      <property name="Email">
        <column name="Email" sql-type="nvarchar(100)" not-null="true" />
      </property>

      <bag name="DeliveryAddressBook"  access="field.camelcase-underscore"
           inverse="true" cascade="all" lazy="true" >
        <key column="CustomerId"/>
        <one-to-many class="DeliveryAddress"></one-to-many>
      </bag>

    </class>

</hibernate-mapping>
```

After you have mapped both of the entities that form the Customer aggregation, you need to implement the ICustomerRepository. Create a new CustomerRepository within the Repositories folder of the NHibernate project, as shown in the following listing:

```
using System.Collections.Generic;
using System.Linq;
using Agathas.Storefront.Infrastructure.Querying;
using Agathas.Storefront.Infrastructure.UnitOfWork;
using Agathas.Storefront.Model.Customers;
using NHibernate;
using NHibernate.Criterion;

namespace Agathas.Storefront.Repository.NHibernate.Repositories
{
    public class CustomerRepository : Repository<Customer, int>,
                                      ICustomerRepository
    {
        public CustomerRepository(IUnitOfWork uow)
            : base(uow)
```

```
        {
        }

        public Customer FindBy(string identityToken)
        {
            ICriteria criteriaQuery = SessionFactory.GetCurrentSession()
                    .CreateCriteria(typeof(Customer))
                    .Add(Expression.Eq(PropertyNameHelper
                    .ResolvePropertyName<Customer>
                    (c => c.IdentityToken), identityToken));

            IList<Customer> customers = criteriaQuery.List<Customer>();

            Customer customer = customers.FirstOrDefault();
            return customer;
        }
    }
}
```

The base repository that you developed in Chapter 11 can take care of most of the requirements of the
ICustomerRepository interface, apart from the extra method you added that retrieved a customer via
his IdentityToken. For this method, you had to define a new criteria object, because it's not the default
identity property of the Customer entity. As mentioned before, the need for retrieving the Customer
entity via the IdentityToken will become apparent when you look at implementing the Authentication
mechanism a little later.

Customer Service

Customerservice returns a view of the customer aggregation, as displayed in Figure 13-4.

FIGURE 13-4

Create a new class within the ViewModels of the Services project with the following definition:

```
namespace Agathas.Storefront.Services.ViewModels
{
    public class DeliveryAddressView
    {
        public int Id { get; set; }
        public string Name { get; set; }
        public string AddressLine1 { get; set; }
        public string AddressLine2 { get; set; }
```

```
        public string City { get; set; }
        public string State { get; set; }
        public string Country { get; set; }
        public string ZipCode { get; set; }
    }
}
```

Next, add a class named `CustomerView` to represent the default view of a `customer`:

```
using System.Collections.Generic;

namespace Agathas.Storefront.Services.ViewModels
{
    public class CustomerView
    {
        public string IdentityToken { get; set; }
        public string FirstName { get; set; }
        public string SecondName { get; set; }
        public string Email { get; set; }
        public IEnumerable<DeliveryAddressView> DeliveryAddressBook { get; set; }
    }
}
```

To convert a `Customer` entity into a `CustomerView`, you will again use AutoMapper. Open the `AutoMapperBootStrapper` class found at the root of the `Services` project, and update it to include the extra maps bolded in the following code snippet:

```
    ...

using Agathas.Storefront.Model.Customers;

namespace Agathas.Storefront.Services
{
    public class AutoMapperBootStrapper
    {
        public static void ConfigureAutoMapper()
        {
            ...

            // Customer
            Mapper.CreateMap<Customer, CustomerView>();
            Mapper.CreateMap<DeliveryAddress, DeliveryAddressView>();
            ...

        }
    }

    ...
}
```

The process of converting a `customer` entity into a `CustomerView` is performed in an extension method contained in a class named `CustomerMapper` that you can place in the `Mapping` folder:

```
using Agathas.Storefront.Model.Customers;
using Agathas.Storefront.Services.ViewModels;
```

```
using AutoMapper;

namespace Agathas.Storefront.Services.Mapping
{
    public static class CustomerMapper
    {
        public static CustomerView ConvertToCustomerDetailView(
                                        this Customer customer)
        {
            return Mapper.Map<Customer, CustomerView>(customer);
        }
    }
}
```

Similarly, the `DeliveryAddress` has a corresponding `DeliveryAddressMapper` class to provide a method extension that is responsible for the conversion:

```
using Agathas.Storefront.Model.Customers;
using Agathas.Storefront.Services.ViewModels;
using AutoMapper;

namespace Agathas.Storefront.Services.Mapping
{
    public static class DeliveryAddressMapper
    {
        public static DeliveryAddressView ConvertToDeliveryAddressView(
                                        this DeliveryAddress deliveryAddress)
        {
            return Mapper.Map<DeliveryAddress,
                            DeliveryAddressView>(deliveryAddress);
        }
    }
}
```

As with the `IProductCatalogService` and `IBasketService` service contracts, you communicate via the request-response messaging pattern. The creation of a customer requires a request-response pair named `CreateCustomerRequest` and `CreateCustomerResponse`, as shown in the following listing. Create both of these classes and all the other customer messaging classes in a new folder named `CustomerService` that sits under the `Messaging` folder:

```
namespace Agathas.Storefront.Services.Messaging.CustomerService
{
    public class CreateCustomerRequest
    {
        public string CustomerIdentityToken { get; set; }
        public string Email { get; set; }
        public string FirstName { get; set; }
        public string SecondName { get; set; }
    }
}

using Agathas.Storefront.Services.ViewModels;

namespace Agathas.Storefront.Services.Messaging.CustomerService
```

```
    {
        public class CreateCustomerResponse
        {
            public CustomerView Customer { get; set; }
        }
    }
```

To obtain a view of the customer aggregation from the service layer, create a request-response pair named GetCustomerRequest and GetCustomerResponse, as shown in the following listing:

```
namespace Agathas.Storefront.Services.Messaging.CustomerService
{
    public class GetCustomerRequest
    {
        public string CustomerIdentityToken { get; set; }
    }
}

using System.Collections.Generic;
using Agathas.Storefront.Services.ViewModels;

namespace Agathas.Storefront.Services.Messaging.CustomerService
{
    public class GetCustomerResponse
    {
        public bool CustomerFound { get; set; }
        public CustomerView Customer { get; set; }
    }
}
```

The classes ModifyCustomerRequest and ModifyCustomerResponse communicate modifications to a customer's details:

```
namespace Agathas.Storefront.Services.Messaging.CustomerService
{
    public class ModifyCustomerRequest
    {
        public string CustomerIdentityToken { get; set; }
        public string FirstName { get; set; }
        public string SecondName { get; set; }
        public string Email { get; set; }
    }
}

using Agathas.Storefront.Services.ViewModels;

namespace Agathas.Storefront.Services.Messaging.CustomerService
{
    public class ModifyCustomerResponse
    {
        public CustomerView Customer { get; set; }
    }
}
```

To add a new `DeliveryAddress` to a customer's `DeliveryAddressBook` collection, use the classes `DeliveryAddressAddRequest` and `DeliveryAddressAddResponse`:

```
using Agathas.Storefront.Services.ViewModels;

namespace Agathas.Storefront.Services.Messaging.CustomerService
{
    public class DeliveryAddressAddRequest
    {
        public string CustomerIdentityToken { get; set; }
        public DeliveryAddressView Address { get; set; }
    }
}

using Agathas.Storefront.Services.ViewModels;

namespace Agathas.Storefront.Services.Messaging.CustomerService
{
    public class DeliveryAddressAddResponse
    {
        public DeliveryAddressView DeliveryAddress { get; set; }
    }
}
```

`DeliveryAddressModifyRequest` and `DeliveryAddressModifyResponse` communicate the modification of an existing `DeliveryAddress`:

```
using Agathas.Storefront.Services.ViewModels;

namespace Agathas.Storefront.Services.Messaging.CustomerService
{
    public class DeliveryAddressModifyRequest
    {
        public string CustomerIdentityToken { get; set; }
        public DeliveryAddressView Address { get; set; }
    }
}

using Agathas.Storefront.Services.ViewModels;

namespace Agathas.Storefront.Services.Messaging.CustomerService
{
    public class DeliveryAddressModifyResponse
    {
        public DeliveryAddressView DeliveryAddress { get; set; }
    }
}
```

Create the contract for `CustomerService` in the `Interfaces` folder of the `Services` project, and name it `ICustomerService`:

```
using Agathas.Storefront.Services.Messaging.CustomerService;

namespace Agathas.Storefront.Services.Interfaces
{
```

```
public interface ICustomerService
{
    CreateCustomerResponse CreateCustomer(CreateCustomerRequest request);
    GetCustomerResponse GetCustomer(GetCustomerRequest request);
    ModifyCustomerResponse ModifyCustomer(ModifyCustomerRequest request);

    DeliveryAddressModifyResponse ModifyDeliveryAddress(
                                DeliveryAddressModifyRequest request);
    DeliveryAddressAddResponse AddDeliveryAddress(
                                DeliveryAddressAddRequest request);
}
}
```

The `ICustomerService` interface defines a simple create, read, update, and delete (CRUD)-like API for working with the `customer` aggregation.

Before you create the implementation of the `ICustomerService` interface, define a new exception named `CustomerInvalidException`. The `CustomerInvalidException` is thrown if an attempt is made to save or add a `customer` who is not valid:

```
using System;

namespace Agathas.Storefront.Services.Implementations
{
    public class CustomerInvalidException : Exception
    {
        public CustomerInvalidException(string message) : base (message)
        {
        }
    }
}
```

With the supporting code in place, you can now create the implementation of `ICustomerService` named `CustomerService`. Create the `CustomerService` class in the `Implementations` folder with the following listing:

Available for download on Wrox.com

```
using System.Linq;
using System.Text;
using Agathas.Storefront.Infrastructure.Domain;
using Agathas.Storefront.Infrastructure.UnitOfWork;
using Agathas.Storefront.Model.Customers;
using Agathas.Storefront.Services.Interfaces;
using Agathas.Storefront.Services.Mapping;
using Agathas.Storefront.Services.Messaging.CustomerService;
using Agathas.Storefront.Services.ViewModels;

namespace Agathas.Storefront.Services.Implementations
{
    public class CustomerService : ICustomerService
    {
        private readonly ICustomerRepository _customerRepository;
        private readonly IUnitOfWork _uow;

        public CustomerService(ICustomerRepository customerRepository,
```

```
                          IUnitOfWork uow)
{
    _customerRepository = customerRepository;
    _uow = uow;
}

public CreateCustomerResponse CreateCustomer(CreateCustomerRequest request)
{
    CreateCustomerResponse response = new CreateCustomerResponse();
    Customer customer = new Customer();
    customer.IdentityToken = request.CustomerIdentityToken;
    customer.Email = request.Email;
    customer.FirstName = request.FirstName;
    customer.SecondName = request.SecondName;

    ThrowExceptionIfCustomerIsInvalid(customer);

    _customerRepository.Add(customer);
    _uow.Commit();

    response.Customer = customer.ConvertToCustomerDetailView();

    return response;
}

private void ThrowExceptionIfCustomerIsInvalid(Customer customer)
{
    if (customer.GetBrokenRules().Count() > 0)
    {
        StringBuilder brokenRules = new StringBuilder();
        brokenRules.AppendLine("There were problems saving the Customer:");
        foreach (BusinessRule businessRule in customer.GetBrokenRules())
        {
            brokenRules.AppendLine(businessRule.Rule);
        }

        throw new CustomerInvalidException(brokenRules.ToString());

    }
}

public GetCustomerResponse GetCustomer(GetCustomerRequest request)
{
    GetCustomerResponse response = new GetCustomerResponse();

    Customer customer = _customerRepository
                                .FindBy(request.CustomerIdentityToken);

    if (customer != null)
    {
        response.CustomerFound = true;
        response.Customer = customer.ConvertToCustomerDetailView();

    }
    else
```

```
            response.CustomerFound = false;


        return response;
    }

    public ModifyCustomerResponse ModifyCustomer(ModifyCustomerRequest request)
    {
        ModifyCustomerResponse response = new ModifyCustomerResponse();

        Customer customer = _customerRepository
                                    .FindBy(request.CustomerIdentityToken);

        customer.FirstName = request.FirstName;
        customer.SecondName = request.SecondName;
        customer.Email = request.Email;

        ThrowExceptionIfCustomerIsInvalid(customer);

        _customerRepository.Save(customer);
        _uow.Commit();

        response.Customer = customer.ConvertToCustomerDetailView();

        return response;
    }

    public DeliveryAddressModifyResponse ModifyDeliveryAddress(
                                    DeliveryAddressModifyRequest request)
    {
        DeliveryAddressModifyResponse response =
                                    new DeliveryAddressModifyResponse();

        Customer customer = _customerRepository
                                    .FindBy(request.CustomerIdentityToken);

        DeliveryAddress deliveryAddress = customer.DeliveryAddressBook
                        .Where(d => d.Id == request.Address.Id)
                        .FirstOrDefault();

        if (deliveryAddress != null)
        {
            UpdateDeliveryAddressFrom(request.Address, deliveryAddress);

            _customerRepository.Save(customer);
            _uow.Commit();
        }

        response.DeliveryAddress = deliveryAddress
                                    .ConvertToDeliveryAddressView();

        return response;
    }

    public DeliveryAddressAddResponse AddDeliveryAddress(
```

```
                                        DeliveryAddressAddRequest request)
    {
        DeliveryAddressAddResponse response = new DeliveryAddressAddResponse();
        Customer customer = _customerRepository
                                   .FindBy(request.CustomerIdentityToken);

        DeliveryAddress deliveryAddress = new DeliveryAddress();

        deliveryAddress.Customer = customer;
        UpdateDeliveryAddressFrom(request.Address, deliveryAddress);

        customer.AddAddress(deliveryAddress);

        _customerRepository.Save(customer);
        _uow.Commit();

        response.DeliveryAddress = deliveryAddress
                              .ConvertToDeliveryAddressView();

        return response;
    }

    private void UpdateDeliveryAddressFrom(
                            DeliveryAddressView deliveryAddressSource,
                            DeliveryAddress deliveryAddressToUpdate)
    {
        deliveryAddressToUpdate.Name = deliveryAddressSource.Name;
        deliveryAddressToUpdate.AddressLine1 =
                                    deliveryAddressSource.AddressLine1;
        deliveryAddressToUpdate.AddressLine2 =
                                    deliveryAddressSource.AddressLine2;
        deliveryAddressToUpdate.City = deliveryAddressSource.City;
        deliveryAddressToUpdate.State = deliveryAddressSource.State;
        deliveryAddressToUpdate.Country = deliveryAddressSource.Country;
        deliveryAddressToUpdate.ZipCode = deliveryAddressSource.ZipCode;
    }
}
}
```

Code snippet CustomerService.cs in project Agathas.Storefront.Services

The `CustomerService` class is straightforward and simply updates the customer aggregation based on requests from the client.

With the customer membership taken care of, you will now look at how you can authenticate users on the site.

Authentication Service

The requirements for authentication state that there should be two forms of authentication available for customers. Customers who already have web-based accounts at sites such as Facebook or Google should be able to use these accounts when registering or signing on to the site so that there is no need for them to have to remember another username and password combination. Customers without or who do not want to use an existing web-based account can use a local authentication service that the site supplies. In this section, you create the local authentication service before implementing a web-based authentication service.

Both of the authentication types supply a `User` object after verifying a user's profile. Create a new class named `User` within the `Authentication` folder of the `Infrastructure` project with the following code listing:

```
namespace Agathas.Storefront.Infrastructure.Authentication
{
    public class User
    {
        public string AuthenticationToken { get; set; }
        public string Email { get; set; }
        public bool IsAuthenticated { get; set; }
    }
}
```

Local Authentication with ASP.NET Membership

The local authentication method uses the built-in ASP.NET membership provider to register and verify users. To make the membership API testable and to keep your code loosely coupled, define an interface for the membership API to implement via an adapter.

Create a new interface named `ILocalAuthenticationService` with the following contract:

```
namespace Agathas.Storefront.Infrastructure.Authentication
{
    public interface ILocalAuthenticationService
    {
        User Login(string email, string password);
        User RegisterUser(string email, string password);
    }
}
```

Next, add an adapter class named `AspMembershipAuthentication` that adapts the membership API to your interface:

```
using System;
using System.Web.Security;

namespace Agathas.Storefront.Infrastructure.Authentication
{
    public class AspMembershipAuthentication : ILocalAuthenticationService
    {
        public User Login(string email, string password)
        {
            User user = new User();
            user.IsAuthenticated = false;

            if (Membership.ValidateUser(email, password))
            {
                MembershipUser validatedUser = Membership.GetUser(email);
                user.AuthenticationToken = validatedUser
                                          .ProviderUserKey.ToString();
                user.Email = email;
```

```
                    user.IsAuthenticated = true;
                }

                return user;
            }

            public User RegisterUser(string email, string password)
            {
                MembershipCreateStatus status;
                User user = new User();
                user.IsAuthenticated = false;

                Membership.CreateUser(email, password, email,
                                    Guid.NewGuid().ToString(),
                                    Guid.NewGuid().ToString(),
                                    true, out status);

                if (status == MembershipCreateStatus.Success)
                {
                    MembershipUser newlyCreatedUser = Membership.GetUser(email);
                    user.AuthenticationToken = newlyCreatedUser
                                                    .ProviderUserKey.ToString();
                    user.Email = email;
                    user.IsAuthenticated = true;
                }
                else
                {
                    switch (status)
                    {
                        case MembershipCreateStatus.DuplicateEmail:
                            throw new InvalidOperationException(
                                    "There is already a user with this email address.");
                        case MembershipCreateStatus.DuplicateUserName:
                            throw new InvalidOperationException(
                                    "There is already a user with this email address.");
                        case MembershipCreateStatus.InvalidEmail:
                            throw new InvalidOperationException(
                                    "Your email address is invalid");
                        default:
                            throw new InvalidOperationException(
                            "There was a problem creating your account. " +
                            "Please try again.");
                    }
                }

                return user;
            }
        }
    }
```

You will build the .ASPX views later, but that's all there is to creating the local authentication service. The built-in membership API creates a local ASPNETDB.MDF database the first time it is used. The ASP.NET membership API is out of the scope of this book, but for a good resource on this feature of ASP.NET, check out the Wrox book *Beginning ASP.NET Security* by Barry Dorrans.

Web-Based Authentication with Janrain

To authenticate customers using existing web-based accounts, you will use a third party service from `www.janrain.com/`. Figure 13-5 shows the flow of using the Janrain service.

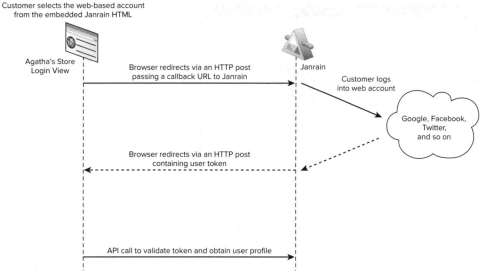

FIGURE 13-5

The Janrain service acts as a proxy to a host of third-party sites. An iframe is embedded on Agatha's sign-in and registration page, allowing a customer to select a web-based account to authenticate. Upon selecting a provider, the customer is asked to log in to that site. The response is then redirected via Janrain, and an authentication token is supplied to Agatha's callback page. Lastly, a check is made to validate the token and obtain the user profile before authentication is set and the user is allowed to check out or manage her account.

To start working with Janrain, you need to create an account. Navigate to `www.janrain.com/`, and create a free basic account. After you have created an account, Janrain asks you to create a new application, as shown in Figure 13-6. Add `ASPDesignPatterns_<YourName>` for the name of the account, and click Next.

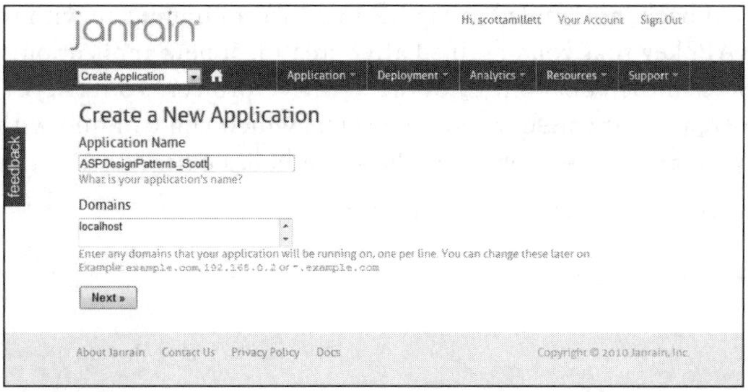

FIGURE 13-6

After creating an application, you are taken to the homepage for that application, as can be seen in Figure 13-7.

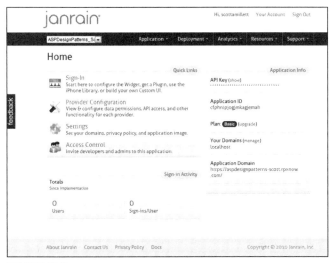

FIGURE 13-7

Make a note of your API key, which can be obtained by clicking on the API Key (shown) link in the top-right corner of the page, as shown in Figure 13-7.

To work with a web-based authentication service, first define an interface to work against. Add a new interface named `IExternalAuthenticationService` to the `Authentication` folder of the `Infrastructure` project:

```
namespace Agathas.Storefront.Infrastructure.Authentication
{
    public interface IExternalAuthenticationService
    {
        User GetUserDetailsFrom(string token);
    }
}
```

The `IExternalAuthenticationService` service obtains a user's profile from the token that you receive from the Janrain HTTP Post callback, as detailed in Figure 13-5. To communicate with the Janrain service, you need to pass the API key that you obtained after creating a new application, as shown in Figure 13-7. The key is stored in the `web.config` of the `Web.MVC` project. To retrieve it, you must add a new property to the `IApplicationSettings` interface, which you can find within the `Configuration` folder of the `Infrastructure` project, as shown in bold next:

```
namespace Agathas.Storefront.Infrastructure.Configuration
{
    public interface IApplicationSettings
    {
```

```
        int NumberOfResultsPerPage {get; }

        string LoggerName { get; }

        string JanrainApiKey { get;  }
    }
}
```

With the `IApplicationSettings` interface updated, you need to update the `WebConfigApplication`
`Settings` implementation, as bolded in the following code listing:

```
namespace Agathas.Storefront.Infrastructure.Configuration
{
    public class WebConfigApplicationSettings : IApplicationSettings
    {
        public string LoggerName
        {
            get { return ConfigurationManager.AppSettings["LoggerName"]; }
        }

        public string NumberOfResultsPerPage
        {
            get { return ConfigurationManager
                            .AppSettings["NumberOfResultsPerPage"]; }
        }

        public string JanrainApiKey
        {
            get { return ConfigurationManager
                            .AppSettings["JanrainApiKey"]; }
        }
    }
}
```

Finally, add an entry into the `web.config` of the `Web.MVC` project, replacing the XXXs with your
Janrain API key:

```
<appSettings>
  <add key="NumberOfResultsPerPage" value="9"/>
  <add key="JanrainApiKey" value="xxxxxxxxxxxxxxxxxxxxxxxxxxxxxxxxxxxxxxxx" />
  <add key="LoggerName" value="AgathaLogger"/>
</appSettings >
```

With the Janrain API key in the configuration data, you can create an implementation of the
`IExternalAuthenticationService` interface. Add a new class named `JanrainAuthentication`
`Service` with the following listing:

```
using System;
using System.Linq;
using System.Net;
using System.Xml.Linq;
using Agathas.Storefront.Infrastructure.Configuration;

namespace Agathas.Storefront.Infrastructure.Authentication
```

```
    {
        public class JanrainAuthenticationService : IExternalAuthenticationService
        {
            public User GetUserDetailsFrom(string token)
            {
                User user = new User();

                string parameters = String.Format("apiKey={0}&token={1}&format=xml",
                        ApplicationSettingsFactory.GetApplicationSettings()
                                            .JanrainApiKey,token);
                string response;
                using (var w = new WebClient())
                {
                    response = w.UploadString("https://rpxnow.com/api/v2/auth_info",
                                                                    parameters);
                }
                var xmlResponse = XDocument.Parse(response);
                var userProfile = (from x in xmlResponse.Descendants("profile")
                                    select new
                                    {
                                        id = x.Element("identifier").Value,
                                        email = (string)x.Element("email") ?? "No Email"
                                    }).SingleOrDefault();

                if (userProfile != null)
                {
                    user.AuthenticationToken = userProfile.id;
                    user.Email = userProfile.email;
                    user.IsAuthenticated = true;
                }
                else
                    user.IsAuthenticated = false;

                return user;
            }
        }
    }
}
```

As mentioned before, this `GetUserDetailsFrom` method takes a token supplied via the callback HTTP Post, which occurs after the customer has signed in to a web-based account. The token is then used with the Janrain API key to retrieve an XML file with details on the user's profile. The `GetUserDetailsFrom` method uses LinqToXML to pull the user's e-mail and ID from the XML response before populating the `User` object that you defined earlier. The code snippet that follows shows the XML response from the Janrain call:

```
<?xml version='1.0' encoding='UTF-8'?>
<rsp stat='ok'>
<profile>
    <displayName>JohnSmith</displayName>
    <email>JohnSmith@googlemail.com</email>
    <identifier>https://www.google.com/accounts/o8/idid=XXXXXXX</identifier>
    <name>
```

```
            <givenName>John</givenName>
            <familyName>Smith</familyName>
            <formatted>John Smith</formatted>
        </name>
        <preferredUsername>JohnSmith</preferredUsername>
        <providerName>Google</providerName>
        <verifiedEmail>JohnSmith@googlemail.com </verifiedEmail>
        <googleUserId>00000000000000000</googleUserId>
    </profile>
    </rsp>
```

This is all the work you need to do for the web-based authentication service for the moment. You will return to the Janrain service when you implement the .ASPX views later in this chapter.

Authentication Cookie

For the site to know that a user has logged in and verified his membership, you need some kind of flag to tell the site that this user has been authenticated. To meet this requirement, you use the ASP.NET forms-based authentication. To make the forms-based authentication testable and loosely coupled, you again create an interface and add an adapter. Start by adding a new interface named IForms Authentication to the Authentication folder of the Infrastructure project:

```
namespace Agathas.Storefront.Infrastructure.Authentication
{
    public interface IFormsAuthentication
    {
        void SetAuthenticationToken(string token);
        string GetAuthenticationToken();
        void SignOut();
    }
}
```

Next, add an implementation of this interface named AspFormsAuthentication to the same folder:

```
using System.Web;
using System.Web.Security;

namespace Agathas.Storefront.Infrastructure.Authentication
{
    public class AspFormsAuthentication : IFormsAuthentication
    {
        public void SetAuthenticationToken(string token)
        {
            FormsAuthentication.SetAuthCookie(token, false);
        }

        public string GetAuthenticationToken()
        {
            return HttpContext.Current.User.Identity.Name;
        }

        public void SignOut()
```

```
                {
                    FormsAuthentication.SignOut();
                }
            }
        }
```

And that's all there is to do to for the authentication functionality at this point. Next, you turn your attention to the customer and account controllers.

Customer Controller

You can see the .ASPX views and view models that make up the Customer Account section in Figure 13-8.

You will now create the two strongly typed views for the .ASPX views for the Customers section. Both of the views inherit from a common base class named `BaseCustomerAccountView`. Create this class within a new folder named `CustomerAccount`, which you can create within the `ViewModels` folder of the `Controllers` project:

```
namespace Agathas.Storefront.Controllers.ViewModels.CustomerAccount
{
    public abstract class BaseCustomerAccountView
    {
        public BasketSummaryView BasketSummary { get; set; }
    }
}
```

The `CustomerDeliveryAddressView` that also lives within the `CustomerAccount` folder is strongly typed to an .ASPX view that displays a customer's list of delivery addresses:

```
using Agathas.Storefront.Services.ViewModels;

namespace Agathas.Storefront.Controllers.ViewModels.CustomerAccount
{
    public class CustomerDeliveryAddressView : BaseCustomerAccountView
    {
        public CustomerView CustomerView { get; set; }
        public DeliveryAddressView Address { get; set; }
    }
}
```

The `CustomerDetailView` is strongly typed to a view that displays details about a customer:

```
using Agathas.Storefront.Services.ViewModels;

namespace Agathas.Storefront.Controllers.ViewModels.CustomerAccount
{
    public class CustomerDetailView : BaseCustomerAccountView
    {
        public CustomerView Customer { get; set; }
    }
}
```

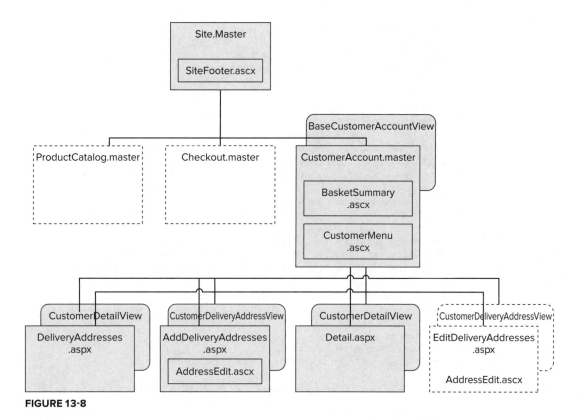

FIGURE 13-8

With the views in place, you can create the customer's controller. Add a new class to the Controllers folder of the Controllers project named CustomersController with the following listing:

```
using System.Linq;
using System.Web.Mvc;
using Agathas.Storefront.Controllers.ViewModels.CustomerAccount;
using Agathas.Storefront.Infrastructure.Authentication;
using Agathas.Storefront.Infrastructure.CookieStorage;
using Agathas.Storefront.Services.Interfaces;
using Agathas.Storefront.Services.Messaging.CustomerService;
using Agathas.Storefront.Services.ViewModels;

namespace Agathas.Storefront.Controllers.Controllers
{
    [Authorize]
    public class CustomerController : BaseController
    {
        private readonly ICustomerService _customerService;
        private readonly IFormsAuthentication _formsAuthentication;

        public CustomerController(ICookieStorageService cookieStorageService,
                                  ICustomerService customerService,
                                  IFormsAuthentication formsAuthentication)
```

```
        : base(cookieStorageService)
    {
        _customerService = customerService;
        _formsAuthentication = formsAuthentication;
    }

    [Authorize]
    public ActionResult Detail()
    {
        GetCustomerRequest customerRequest = new GetCustomerRequest();
        customerRequest.CustomerIdentityToken =
                        _formsAuthentication.GetAuthenticationToken();

        GetCustomerResponse response =
                        _customerService.GetCustomer(customerRequest);

        CustomerDetailView customerDetailView = new CustomerDetailView();
        customerDetailView.Customer = response.Customer;
        customerDetailView.BasketSummary = base.GetBasketSummaryView();

        return View(customerDetailView);
    }

    [Authorize]
    [AcceptVerbs(HttpVerbs.Post)]
    public ActionResult Detail(CustomerView customerView)
    {
        ModifyCustomerRequest request = new ModifyCustomerRequest();

        request.CustomerIdentityToken =
                    _formsAuthentication.GetAuthenticationToken();
        request.Email = customerView.Email;
        request.FirstName = customerView.FirstName;
        request.SecondName = customerView.SecondName;

        ModifyCustomerResponse response =
                    _customerService.ModifyCustomer(request);

        CustomerDetailView customerDetailView = new CustomerDetailView();

        customerDetailView.Customer = response.Customer;
        customerDetailView.BasketSummary = base.GetBasketSummaryView();

        return View(customerDetailView);
    }

    [Authorize]
    public ActionResult DeliveryAddresses()
    {
        GetCustomerRequest customerRequest = new GetCustomerRequest();
        customerRequest.CustomerIdentityToken =
                        _formsAuthentication.GetAuthenticationToken();
```

```csharp
        GetCustomerResponse response =
                    _customerService.GetCustomer(customerRequest);

    CustomerDetailView customerDetailView = new CustomerDetailView();

    customerDetailView.Customer = response.Customer;
    customerDetailView.BasketSummary = base.GetBasketSummaryView();

    return View("DeliveryAddresses", customerDetailView);
}

[Authorize]
public ActionResult EditDeliveryAddress(int deliveryAddressId)
{
    GetCustomerRequest customerRequest = new GetCustomerRequest();
    customerRequest.CustomerIdentityToken =
                    _formsAuthentication.GetAuthenticationToken();

    GetCustomerResponse response = _customerService
                                .GetCustomer(customerRequest);

    CustomerDeliveryAddressView deliveryAddressView =
                                new CustomerDeliveryAddressView();

    deliveryAddressView.CustomerView = response.Customer;
    deliveryAddressView.Address =
        response.Customer.DeliveryAddressBook
                        .Where(d => d.Id == deliveryAddressId)
                        .FirstOrDefault();
    deliveryAddressView.BasketSummary = base.GetBasketSummaryView();

    return View(deliveryAddressView);
}

[Authorize]
[AcceptVerbs(HttpVerbs.Post)]
public ActionResult EditDeliveryAddress(
                            DeliveryAddressView deliveryAddressView)
{
    DeliveryAddressModifyRequest request =
                new DeliveryAddressModifyRequest();
    request.Address = deliveryAddressView;
    request.CustomerIdentityToken =
                _formsAuthentication.GetAuthenticationToken();

    _customerService.ModifyDeliveryAddress(request);

    return DeliveryAddresses();
}

[Authorize]
public ActionResult AddDeliveryAddress()
{
```

```
                   CustomerDeliveryAddressView customerDeliveryAddressView =
                                             new CustomerDeliveryAddressView();

                   customerDeliveryAddressView.Address = new DeliveryAddressView();
                   customerDeliveryAddressView.BasketSummary =
                                             base.GetBasketSummaryView();

                   return View(customerDeliveryAddressView);
               }

               [Authorize]
               [AcceptVerbs(HttpVerbs.Post)]
               public ActionResult AddDeliveryAddress(
                                         DeliveryAddressView deliveryAddressView)
               {
                   DeliveryAddressAddRequest request = new DeliveryAddressAddRequest();
                   request.Address = deliveryAddressView;
                   request.CustomerIdentityToken =
                               _formsAuthentication.GetAuthenticationToken();

                   _customerService.AddDeliveryAddress(request);

                   return DeliveryAddresses();
               }
           }
       }
```

Code snippet CustomerController in project Agathas.Storefront.Controllers

Notice how each of the methods of the `CustomerController` is decorated with the `Authorize`
attribute, meaning that a customer can only access this URL if he has been authenticated. Note also
that the `CustomerController` uses the `IFormsAuthentication` to retrieve the token that identifies
the `customer` when talking to the `CustomerService` — hence the need for the extra method of the
`ICustomerRepository` contract.

You will now create the account controller to handle user registration and verification.

Account Controllers

Figure 13-9 shows the two .ASPX views that you will be creating later in the chapter. Both of the
views are strongly typed to a `AccountView` and have an `JanrainLogin.ascx` partial view embedded,
which in turn is strongly typed to the `CallBackSettings` view. The `JanrainLogin.ascx` partial view
corresponds to the Internet-based authentication that you created an account for earlier in the chapter.

Before you create the view models and the controllers, you need some supporting classes to keep the
system loosely coupled. When using forms-based authentication, you need to retrieve and work with
query string parameters. To keep the controllers clean from calls, you will wrap the query string
parameters in an action arguments class.

Create a new folder named `ActionArguments` within the `Controllers` project, and add a new enumeration to the folder named `ActionArgumentKey`:

```
   namespace Agathas.Storefront.Controllers.ActionArguments
   {
```

```
public enum ActionArgumentKey
{
    ReturnUrl
}
}
```

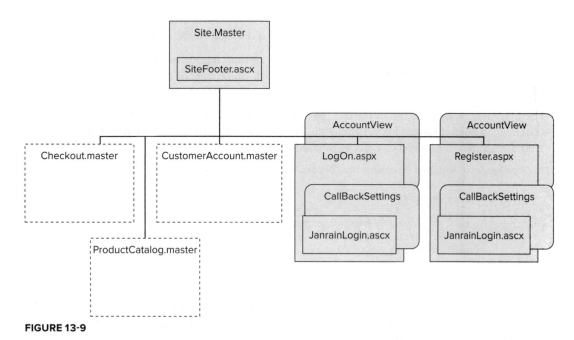

FIGURE 13-9

Forms authentication uses the `ReturnUrl` to instruct the authentication service to navigate the user to that location after a successful login.

To retrieve query string parameters, define an `IActionArguments` interface that has a single method that resolves an `ActionArgumentKey` enumeration value:

```
namespace Agathas.Storefront.Controllers.ActionArguments
{
    public interface IActionArguments
    {
        string GetValueForArgument(ActionArgumentKey key);
    }
}
```

The implementation for the `IActionArguments` interface uses the `HttpContext` to return the value for the given key from the query string dictionary:

```
using System.Web;

namespace Agathas.Storefront.Controllers.ActionArguments
{
    public class HttpRequestActionArguments : IActionArguments
    {
```

```
        public string GetValueForArgument(ActionArgumentKey key)
        {
            return HttpContext.Current.Request.QueryString[key.ToString()];
        }
    }
}
```

This enables the code to be tested, because there is no reliance on the `HttpContext` run time.

You will now create the strongly typed view that the account logon and account register .ASPX views will be bound to. Add a new folder named `Account` to the `ViewModels` folder of the `Controllers` project.

The first view model to create is the `CallBackSettings` view, which will be bound to the `Janrain Login.ascx` partial view. This view tells the Janrain authentication service which URL to return to after a customer has logged into his web-based account:

```
namespace Agathas.Storefront.Controllers.ViewModels.Account
{
    public class CallBackSettings
    {
        public string ReturnUrl { get; set; }
        public string Controller { get; set; }
        public string Action { get; set; }
    }
}
```

The view that the account .ASPX views will be bound to is represented by the `AccountView`. The view will be used mainly to provide information on an unsuccessful login or a failed attempt to register a new customer account:

```
namespace Agathas.Storefront.Controllers.ViewModels.Account
{
    public class AccountView
    {
        public AccountView()
        {
            CallBackSettings = new CallBackSettings ();
        }
        public CallBackSettings CallBackSettings { get; set; }
        public bool HasIssue { get; set; }
        public string Message { get; set; }
    }
}
```

When registering customers, you require some details that will be posted to an action on a controller. To retrieve the values from the forms dictionary collection, use an enumeration so you don't rely on magic strings.

Create a new enumeration at the root of the `Controllers` project named `FormDataKeys`, with the following definition:

```
namespace Agathas.Storefront.Controllers
{
```

```
    public enum FormDataKeys
    {
        Password,
        Email,
        FirstName,
        SecondName,
    }
}
```

Again, to remove the need for magic strings, update the `ActionArgumentKey` enumeration to include two new values. These values will determine where to send a customer after a successful login/registration:

```
namespace Agathas.Storefront.Controllers.ActionArguments
{
    public enum ActionArgumentKey
    {
        ReturnUrl,
        GoToAccount,
        GoToCheckout
    }
}
```

With the supporting classes created, you can now add the account controllers. Figure 13-10 shows the two account controllers: `AccountLogOnController` and `AccountRegisterController`. Both of the controllers inherit from a common `BaseAccountController` class.

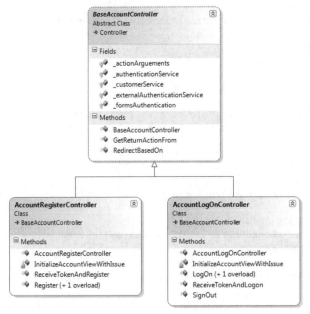

FIGURE 13-10

Add a new class to the `Controllers` folder named `BaseAccountController` with the following listing:

```
using System;
using System.Web.Mvc;
using Agathas.Storefront.Controllers.ActionArguments;
using Agathas.Storefront.Infrastructure.Authentication;
using Agathas.Storefront.Services.Interfaces;

namespace Agathas.Storefront.Controllers.Controllers
{
    public abstract class BaseAccountController : Controller
    {
        protected readonly ILocalAuthenticationService _authenticationService;
        protected readonly ICustomerService _customerService;
        protected readonly IExternalAuthenticationService
                                        _externalAuthenticationService;
        protected readonly IFormsAuthentication _formsAuthentication;
        protected readonly IActionArguments _actionArguments;

        public BaseAccountController(
                        ILocalAuthenticationService authenticationService,
                        ICustomerService customerService,
                        IExternalAuthenticationService
                                            externalAuthenticationService,
                        IFormsAuthentication formsAuthentication,
                        IActionArguments actionArguments)
        {
            _authenticationService = authenticationService;
            _customerService = customerService;
            _externalAuthenticationService = externalAuthenticationService;
            _formsAuthentication = formsAuthentication;
            _actionArguments = actionArguments;
        }

        public ActionResult RedirectBasedOn(string returnUrl)
        {
            if (returnUrl == ActionArgumentKey.GoToCheckout.ToString())
                return RedirectToAction("Checkout", "Checkout");
            else
                return RedirectToAction("Index", "Home");
        }

        public ActionArgumentKey GetReturnActionFrom(string returnUrl)
        {
            if (!String.IsNullOrEmpty(returnUrl) &&
                                returnUrl.ToLower().Contains("checkout"))
                return ActionArgumentKey.GoToCheckout;
            else
                return ActionArgumentKey.GoToAccount;
        }
    }
}
```

With the base controller added, you can now inherit from it and create the `AccountLogOnController`, which handles all functionality related to logging in and logging out:

```
using System;
using System.Web.Mvc;
using Agathas.Storefront.Controllers.ActionArguments;
using Agathas.Storefront.Controllers.ViewModels.Account;
using Agathas.Storefront.Infrastructure.Authentication;
using Agathas.Storefront.Services.Interfaces;
using Agathas.Storefront.Services.Messaging.CustomerService;

namespace Agathas.Storefront.Controllers.Controllers
{
    public class AccountLogOnController : BaseAccountController
    {
        public AccountLogOnController(
                        ILocalAuthenticationService authenticationService,
                        ICustomerService customerService,
                        IExternalAuthenticationService
                                            externalAuthenticationService,
                        IFormsAuthentication formsAuthentication,
                        IActionArguments actionArguments)
            : base(authenticationService, customerService,
                    externalAuthenticationService,
                    formsAuthentication, actionArguments)
        {
        }

        public ActionResult LogOn()
        {
            AccountView accountView = InitializeAccountViewWithIssue(false, "");

            return View(accountView);
        }

        [AcceptVerbs(HttpVerbs.Post)]
        public ActionResult LogOn(string email, string password, string returnUrl)
        {
            User user = _authenticationService.Login(email, password);

            if (user.IsAuthenticated)
            {
                _formsAuthentication.SetAuthenticationToken(
                                                    user.AuthenticationToken);

                if (!String.IsNullOrEmpty(returnUrl))
                    return Redirect(returnUrl);
                else
                    return RedirectToAction("Index", "Home");
            }
            else
            {
                AccountView accountView = InitializeAccountViewWithIssue(true,
                                "Sorry we could not log you in. " +
```

```
                                "Please try again.");
            accountView.CallBackSettings.ReturnUrl =
                            GetReturnActionFrom(returnUrl).ToString();

            return View("LogOn", accountView);
        }
    }

    public ActionResult ReceiveTokenAndLogon(string token, string returnUrl)
    {
        User user = _externalAuthenticationService.GetUserDetailsFrom(token);

        if (user.IsAuthenticated)
        {
            _formsAuthentication.SetAuthenticationToken(
                                            user.AuthenticationToken);

            GetCustomerRequest getCustomerRequest = new GetCustomerRequest();
            getCustomerRequest.CustomerIdentityToken =
                                            user.AuthenticationToken;

            GetCustomerResponse getCustomerResponse =
                        _customerService.GetCustomer(getCustomerRequest);

            if (getCustomerResponse.CustomerFound)
            {
                return RedirectBasedOn(returnUrl);
            }
            else
            {
                AccountView accountView = InitializeAccountViewWithIssue(true,
                        "Sorry we could not find your customer account. " +
                        "If you don't have an account with us " +
                        "please register.");
                accountView.CallBackSettings.ReturnUrl = returnUrl;

                return View("LogOn", accountView);
            }
        }
        else
        {
            AccountView accountView = InitializeAccountViewWithIssue(true,
                                "Sorry we could not log you in." +
                                " Please try again.");
            accountView.CallBackSettings
                .ReturnUrl = returnUrl;

            return View("LogOn", accountView);
        }
    }

    public ActionResult SignOut()
    {
        _formsAuthentication.SignOut();
        return RedirectToAction("Index", "Home");
```

```
        }

        private AccountView InitializeAccountViewWithIssue(bool hasIssue,
                                                           string message)
        {
            AccountView accountView = new AccountView();
            accountView.CallBackSettings.Action = "ReceiveTokenAndLogon";
            accountView.CallBackSettings.Controller = "AccountLogOn";
            accountView.HasIssue = hasIssue;
            accountView.Message = message;

            string returnUrl = _actionArguments
                                .GetValueForArgument(ActionArgumentKey.ReturnUrl);
            accountView.CallBackSettings.ReturnUrl =
                                GetReturnActionFrom(returnUrl).ToString();

            return accountView;
        }
    }
}
```

Finally, add the `AccountRegisterController`, which handles new customer registrations:

```
using System;
using System.Web.Mvc;
using Agathas.Storefront.Controllers.ActionArguments;
using Agathas.Storefront.Controllers.ViewModels.Account;
using Agathas.Storefront.Infrastructure.Authentication;
using Agathas.Storefront.Services.Implementations;
using Agathas.Storefront.Services.Interfaces;
using Agathas.Storefront.Services.Messaging.CustomerService;

namespace Agathas.Storefront.Controllers.Controllers
{
    public class AccountRegisterController : BaseAccountController
    {
        public AccountRegisterController(
                        ILocalAuthenticationService authenticationService,
                        ICustomerService customerService,
                        IExternalAuthenticationService
                                            externalAuthenticationService,
                        IFormsAuthentication formsAuthentication,
                        IActionArguments actionArguments)
            : base(authenticationService, customerService,
                   externalAuthenticationService,
                   formsAuthentication, actionArguments)
        {
        }

        public ActionResult Register()
        {
            AccountView accountView = InitializeAccountViewWithIssue(false,
                                                           string.Empty);

            return View(accountView);
```

```
    }

    [AcceptVerbs(HttpVerbs.Post)]
    public ActionResult Register(FormCollection collection)
    {
        User user;

        string password = collection[FormDataKeys.Password.ToString()];
        string email = collection[FormDataKeys.Email.ToString()];
        string firstName = collection[FormDataKeys.FirstName.ToString()];
        string secondName = collection[FormDataKeys.SecondName.ToString()];

        try
        {
            user = _authenticationService.RegisterUser(email, password);
        }
        catch (InvalidOperationException ex)
        {
            AccountView accountView = InitializeAccountViewWithIssue(
                                                true,  ex.Message);

            return View(accountView);
        }

        if (user.IsAuthenticated)
        {
            try
            {
                CreateCustomerRequest createCustomerRequest =
                                new CreateCustomerRequest();
                createCustomerRequest.CustomerIdentityToken =
                                user.AuthenticationToken;
                createCustomerRequest.Email = email;
                createCustomerRequest.FirstName = firstName;
                createCustomerRequest.SecondName = secondName;

                _formsAuthentication.SetAuthenticationToken(
                                                user.AuthenticationToken);
                _customerService.CreateCustomer(createCustomerRequest);

                return RedirectToAction("Detail", "Customer");
            }
            catch (CustomerInvalidException ex)
            {
                AccountView accountView = InitializeAccountViewWithIssue(
                                                true,  ex.Message);

                return View(accountView);
            }
        }
        else
        {
            AccountView accountView = InitializeAccountViewWithIssue(true,
                        "Sorry we could not authenticate you. " +
                        "Please try again.");

            return View(accountView);
```

```
            }
        }

        public ActionResult ReceiveTokenAndRegister(string token, string returnUrl)
        {
            User user = _externalAuthenticationService.GetUserDetailsFrom(token);

            if (user.IsAuthenticated)
            {
                _formsAuthentication.SetAuthenticationToken(
                                                user.AuthenticationToken);

                // Register user
                CreateCustomerRequest createCustomerRequest =
                                        new CreateCustomerRequest();
                createCustomerRequest.CustomerIdentityToken =
                                        user.AuthenticationToken;
                createCustomerRequest.Email = user.Email;
                createCustomerRequest.FirstName = "[Please Enter]";
                createCustomerRequest.SecondName = "[Please Enter]";

                _customerService.CreateCustomer(createCustomerRequest);

                return RedirectBasedOn(returnUrl);
            }
            else
            {
                AccountView accountView = InitializeAccountViewWithIssue(true,
                                    "Sorry we could not authenticate you.");
                accountView.CallBackSettings.ReturnUrl =
                                        GetReturnActionFrom(returnUrl)
                                        .ToString(); ;

                return View("Register", accountView);
            }
        }

        private AccountView InitializeAccountViewWithIssue(bool hasIssue,
                                                    string message)
        {
            AccountView accountView = new AccountView();
            accountView.CallBackSettings.Action = "ReceiveTokenAndRegister";
            accountView.CallBackSettings.Controller = "AccountRegister";
            accountView.HasIssue = hasIssue;
            accountView.Message = message;

            string returnUrl = _actionArguments
                    .GetValueForArgument(ActionArgumentKey.ReturnUrl);
            accountView.CallBackSettings.ReturnUrl =
                    GetReturnActionFrom(returnUrl).ToString();

            return accountView;
        }
    }
}
```

Code snippet AccountRegisterController.cs in project Agathas.Storefront.Controllers

You will now finish the chapter by creating the .ASPX views for the Customer Membership and Account Login and Register sections.

Customer Membership Views

The views for the Customer Membership pages are fairly straightforward. To enable customers to navigate their account, first create a new partial view named `CustomerMenu.ascx` that contains links to the various sections within a customer's account. Create the `CustomerMenu.ascx` within the `Views/Shared` folder:

```
<%@ Control Language="C#" Inherits="System.Web.Mvc.ViewUserControl" %>

<h2>Menu</h2>
    <ul class="refine-attributes">
    <li><%=Html.ActionLink("Your Details", "Detail", "Customer") %></li>
    <li><%=Html.ActionLink("Delivery Address Book", "DeliveryAddresses",
                        "Customer")%>
    </li>
</ul>
```

Next, create a new master page that uses the existing `Site.Master` as its master page. Name the new master page `CustomerAccount.Master`, and again create it within the `Views/Shared` folder:

```
<%@ Master Language="C#" MasterPageFile="Site.Master"
    Inherits="System.Web.Mvc.ViewMasterPage<BaseCustomerAccountView>"  %>
<%@ Import Namespace="Agathas.Storefront.Controllers.ViewModels.CustomerAccount" %>

<asp:Content  ID="TitleContent" ContentPlaceHolderID="TitleContent" runat="server">
    <asp:ContentPlaceHolder ID="TitleContent" runat="server">

    </asp:ContentPlaceHolder>
</asp:Content>

<asp:Content ID="headerBasketSummary" ContentPlaceHolderID="headerBasketSummary"
            runat="server">
    <% Html.RenderPartial("~/Views/Shared/BasketSummary.ascx",
                        ((BaseCustomerAccountView)Model).BasketSummary); %>
</asp:Content>

<asp:Content runat="server" ID="Content1" ContentPlaceHolderID="MenuContent">
<% Html.RenderPartial("~/Views/Shared/CustomerMenu.ascx"); %>
</asp:Content>

<asp:Content ID="MainContent" ContentPlaceHolderID="MainContent" runat="server">
    <asp:ContentPlaceHolder ID="MainContent" runat="server">

    </asp:ContentPlaceHolder>
</asp:Content>
```

Both editing and adding an address require a set of text boxes matching the properties of an address, so create a partial view that displays this markup named `AddressEdit.ascx`. Once more, create this within the `Views/Shared` folder:

```
<%@ Control Language="C#"
    Inherits="System.Web.Mvc.ViewUserControl<DeliveryAddressView>" %>
```

```
<%@ Import Namespace="Agathas.Storefront.Services.ViewModels" %>
        <%= Html.Hidden("Id", Model.Id) %>
        <p>
            <label for="Name">Name:</label><br />
            <%= Html.TextBox("Name", Model.Name) %>
        </p>
        <p>
            <label for="AddressLine1">AddressLine1:</label><br />
            <%= Html.TextBox("AddressLine1", Model.AddressLine1) %>
        </p>
        <p>
            <label for="AddressLine2">AddressLine2:</label><br />
            <%= Html.TextBox("AddressLine2", Model.AddressLine2) %>
        </p>
        <p>
            <label for="City">City:</label><br />
            <%= Html.TextBox("City", Model.City) %>
        </p>
        <p>
            <label for="State">State:</label><br />
            <%= Html.TextBox("State", Model.State) %>
        </p>
        <p>
            <label for="Country">Country:</label><br />
            <%= Html.TextBox("Country", Model.Country) %>
        </p>
        <p>
            <label for="ZipCode">ZipCode:</label><br />
            <%= Html.TextBox("ZipCode", Model.ZipCode) %>
        </p>
```

With the partial views and master pages created, you can add the four views of the customer account. Add a new folder within the `Views` folder named `Customer`, and add to it a new view named `Detail.aspx` with the following markup:

```
<%@ Page Title="" Language="C#"
    MasterPageFile="~/Views/Shared/CustomerAccount.Master"
    Inherits="System.Web.Mvc.ViewPage<CustomerDetailView>" %>
<%@ Import Namespace="Agathas.Storefront.Controllers.ViewModels.CustomerAccount" %>

<asp:Content ID="Content1" ContentPlaceHolderID="TitleContent" runat="server">
    Customer Details
</asp:Content>

<asp:Content ID="Content2" ContentPlaceHolderID="MainContent" runat="server">

    <h2>Your Details</h2>

    <% using (Html.BeginForm()) {%>
        <p>
            <label for="FirstName">FirstName:</label><br />
            <%= Html.TextBox("FirstName", Model.Customer.FirstName) %>
        </p>
        <p>
```

```
                <label for="SecondName">SecondName:</label><br />
                <%= Html.TextBox("SecondName", Model.Customer.SecondName)%>
            </p>
            <p>
                <label for="Email">Email:</label><br />
                <%= Html.TextBox("Email", Model.Customer.Email)%>
            </p>
            <p>
                <input type="submit" value="Save" />
            </p>
        <% } %>
</asp:Content>
```

The `Detail.aspx` displays the customer's name and e-mail and enables this information to be updated. Next, add a view that displays the list of delivery addresses a customer has. Name this view `DeliveryAddresses.aspx`, and update it to match the following markup:

```
<%@ Page Title="" Language="C#"
        MasterPageFile="~/Views/Shared/CustomerAccount.Master"
        Inherits="System.Web.Mvc.ViewPage<CustomerDetailView>" %>
<%@ Import Namespace="Agathas.Storefront.Services.ViewModels" %>
<%@ Import Namespace="Agathas.Storefront.Controllers.ViewModels.CustomerAccount" %>

<asp:Content ID="Content1" ContentPlaceHolderID="TitleContent" runat="server">
    Customer Delivery Address Book
</asp:Content>

<asp:Content ID="Content2" ContentPlaceHolderID="MainContent" runat="server">

    <h2>Delivery Addresses</h2>

    <%=Html.ActionLink("Add new address", "AddDeliveryAddress", "Customer")%>

    <ul>
    <% foreach (DeliveryAddressView deliveryAddress in
                                    Model.Customer.DeliveryAddressBook)
      {
    %>
        <li><%=Html.ActionLink(deliveryAddress.Name, "EditDeliveryAddress",
                            "Customer",
                            new { deliveryAddressId = deliveryAddress.Id }, null)%>
        </li>
    <% }%>
    </ul>

</asp:Content>
```

The `AddDeliveryAddress.aspx` view adds a new address and uses the `AddressEdit.ascx` partial view that you created earlier within the shared folder:

```
<%@ Page Title="" Language="C#"
        MasterPageFile="~/Views/Shared/CustomerAccount.Master"
```

```
               Inherits="System.Web.Mvc.ViewPage<CustomerDeliveryAddressView>" %>
<%@ Import Namespace="Agathas.Storefront.Controllers.ViewModels.CustomerAccount" %>

<asp:Content ID="Content1" ContentPlaceHolderID="TitleContent" runat="server">
    Add Delivery Address
</asp:Content>

<asp:Content ID="Content2" ContentPlaceHolderID="MainContent" runat="server">

    <h2>AddDeliveryAddress</h2>

    <% using (Html.BeginForm()) {%>

        <% Html.RenderPartial("~/Views/Shared/AddressEdit.ascx", Model.Address); %>
        <p>
            <input type="submit" value="Save" />
        </p>
    <% } %>

</asp:Content>
```

Lastly, add an `EditDeliveryAddress.aspx` view, which enables a customer to modify an existing delivery address:

```
<%@ Page Title="" Language="C#"
    MasterPageFile="~/Views/Shared/CustomerAccount.Master"
    Inherits="System.Web.Mvc.ViewPage<CustomerDeliveryAddressView>" %>
<%@ Import Namespace="Agathas.Storefront.Controllers.ViewModels.CustomerAccount" %>

<asp:Content ID="Content1" ContentPlaceHolderID="TitleContent" runat="server">
    Edit Address
</asp:Content>

<asp:Content ID="Content2" ContentPlaceHolderID="MainContent" runat="server">

    <h2>Address Detail</h2>

    <% using (Html.BeginForm()) {%>

            <% Html.RenderPartial("~/Views/Shared/AddressEdit.ascx",
                            Model.Address); %>
        <p>
            <input type="submit" value="Save" />
        </p>
    <% } %>

</asp:Content>
```

You will now build the views that enable customers to authenticate themselves and gain access to the customer account area and later the checkout.

Authentication Views

Before you can create the LogOn and Register views, you need to log back into www.janrain.com/ using the account you created earlier. When you have logged back in, click on the Sign-In Setup link. Then on the next screen, click on the Get the Widget link to bring up the screen shown in Figure 13-11.

FIGURE 13-11

Choose Embedded from the drop-down list for the Widget Style, and enter **localhost** for the token URL, because you will be changing this later. After you have entered the token URL, click the Generate Code button. You then see a section of code that matches the following listing:

```
<iframe
   src="http://aspdesignpatterns-scott.rpxnow.com
      /openid/embed?token_url=http%3A%2F%2Flocalhost"
   scrolling="no" frameBorder="no" allowtransparency="true"
   style="width:400px;height:240px"></iframe>
```

The bolded sections are replaced with the name that you gave for the application. Save the code to your Clipboard, and flip back to Visual Studio and create a new partial view within the Views/Shared folder named JanrainLogin.ascx with the following listing, copying the Janrain iframe into the new partial view as shown here:

```
<%@ Control Language="C#" Inherits="System.Web.Mvc.ViewUserControl<CallBackSettings>" %>
<%@ Import Namespace="Agathas.Storefront.Controllers.ViewModels.Account" %>
<%@ Import Namespace="Agathas.Storefront.UI.Web.MVC.Helpers" %>

<iframe
   src="http://XXXXXXXXXXXX.rpxnow.com/
   openid/embed?token_url=
```

```
    <%=Server.UrlEncode(
        Html.Resolve("/" + Model.Controller +"/" + Model.Action + "/?returnUrl=" +
        Model.ReturnUrl))%>"
scrolling="no" frameBorder="no" allowtransparency="true"
style="width:400px;height:240px"></iframe>
```

You can now create the `LogOn` and `Register` views. Add a new folder named `AccountLogOn` within the `Views` folder, and add a new view named `LogOn.aspx` with the following markup:

```
<%@ Page Language="C#"
        MasterPageFile="~/Views/Shared/Site.Master"
        Inherits="System.Web.Mvc.ViewPage<AccountView>" %>
<%@ Import Namespace="Agathas.Storefront.Controllers.ViewModels.Account" %>

<asp:Content ID="loginTitle" ContentPlaceHolderID="TitleContent" runat="server">
    Log On
</asp:Content>


<asp:Content ID="loginContent" ContentPlaceHolderID="MainContent" runat="server">
    <h2>Log On</h2>
    <% if (Model.HasIssue) { %>
    <p>
    <div style="color: #D63301; background-color: #FFCCBA;
                padding:15px 10px 15px 50px;" >
        <%=Html.Encode(Model.Message)%>
    </div>
    </p>
    <% } %>
    <p>
        Please enter your username and password.
        <%= Html.ActionLink("Register", "Register", "AccountRegister") %>
        if you don't have an account.
    </p>

    <h2>Login with your existing account associated with this site</h2>
    <% Html.RenderPartial("~/Views/Shared/JanrainLogin.ascx",
                        Model.CallBackSettings); %>

    <h2>Login with an account created with us</h2>
    <% using (Html.BeginForm()) { %>
        <div>
            <p>
                <label for="username">Email:</label><br />
                <%= Html.TextBox("email") %>
            </p>
            <p>
                <label for="password">Password:</label><br />
                <%= Html.Password("password") %>
            </p>
            <p>
                <input type="submit" value="Log On" />
            </p>
        </div>
    <% } %>
</asp:Content>
```

Add a second new folder within the `Views` folder named `AccountRegister`, and add to it a new view named `Register.aspx` with the following markup:

```
<%@ Page Language="C#"
        MasterPageFile="~/Views/Shared/Site.Master"
        Inherits="System.Web.Mvc.ViewPage<AccountView>" %>
<%@ Import Namespace="Agathas.Storefront.Controllers.ViewModels.Account" %>

<asp:Content ID="registerTitle" ContentPlaceHolderID="TitleContent" runat="server">
    Register
</asp:Content>

<asp:Content ID="registerContent" ContentPlaceHolderID="MainContent"
              runat="server">
  <% if (Model.HasIssue) { %>
  <p>
  <div style="color: #D63301; background-color: #FFCCBA;
              padding:15px 10px 15px 50px;" >
      <%=Html.Encode(Model.Message)%>
  </div>
  </p>
  <% } %>

  <h2>Associate an existing account with us</h2>
  <% Html.RenderPartial("~/Views/Shared/JanrainLogin.ascx",
                        Model.CallBackSettings); %>

  <h2>Don't have an internet account? Create an account with us</h2>

  <% using (Html.BeginForm()) { %>
      <div>
            <p>
                <label for="email">Email:</label><br />
                <%= Html.TextBox("email") %>
            </p>
            <p>
                <label for="password">Password:</label><br />
                <%= Html.Password("password") %>
            </p>
            <p>
                <label for="confirmPassword">Confirm password:</label><br />
                <%= Html.Password("confirmPassword") %>
            </p>
            <p>
                <label for="email">First Name:</label><br />
                <%= Html.TextBox("FirstName")%>
            </p>
            <p>
                <label for="email">Second Name:</label><br />
                <%= Html.TextBox("SecondName")%>
            </p>
            <p>
                <input type="submit" value="Register" />
            </p>
        </div>
    <% } %>
</asp:Content>
```

To complete the views, you need to update the `Site.Master` page to include some markup to show whether the customer has been authenticated. Add the bolded markup in the following listing to the `Site.Master` page:

```
<div id="headerSummary">
        <span class="basket-details">
        <% if (Request.IsAuthenticated) {%>
            <%= Html.ActionLink("Your Account", "Detail", "Customer") %> /
            <%=Html.ActionLink("Log Off", "SignOut", "AccountLogOn")%>
        <% }
           else { %>
            <%= Html.ActionLink("Create Account", "Register",
                            "AccountRegister")%> /
            <%=Html.ActionLink("Log On", "LogOn", "AccountLogOn")%><br />
        <%  } %>
        </span>
        <asp:ContentPlaceHolder ID="headerBasketSummary" runat="server">
        </asp:ContentPlaceHolder>
    </div>
```

The last step before you can run your solution is to wire up the dependencies within the `BootStrapper` class that can be found in the `Web.MVC` project. Update the `BootStrapper` class with the bolded code shown in the following listing:

```
using Agathas.Storefront.Controllers.ActionArguments;
using Agathas.Storefront.Infrastructure.Authentication;
using Agathas.Storefront.Model.Customers;

namespace Agathas.Storefront.UI.Web.MVC
{
    public class BootStrapper
    {
        ...

        public class ControllerRegistry : Registry
        {
            public ControllerRegistry()
            {
                // Repositories
                ForRequestedType<ICustomerRepository>()
                        .TheDefault.Is.OfConcreteType
                        <Repository.NHibernate.Repositories.CustomerRepository>();

                ...

                // Services
                ForRequestedType<ICustomerService>().TheDefault.Is.OfConcreteType
                        <CustomerService>();

                // Authentication
                ForRequestedType<IExternalAuthenticationService>().TheDefault.Is
                        .OfConcreteType<JanrainAuthenticationService>();
                ForRequestedType<IFormsAuthentication>().TheDefault.Is
                        .OfConcreteType<AspFormsAuthentication>();
```

```
        ForRequestedType<ILocalAuthenticationService>().TheDefault.Is
                .OfConcreteType<AspMembershipAuthentication>();

        // Controller Helpers
        ForRequestedType<IActionArguments>().TheDefault.Is.OfConcreteType
                <HttpRequestActionArguments>();
        …

            }
        }
    }
}
```

The customer membership and authentication functionality is now complete. You can fire up a browser from within Visual Studio and see a Create Account / Log On link on the homepage. Click on the Create Account link to be taken to insert the `Register` view, as shown in Figure 13-12.

If you register with a web-based account such as Google, a pop-up box appears, as shown in Figure 13-13.

After you log in to the web-based account, your account is created and you are redirected to the homepage. The links on the top of the homepage are changed to Your Account / Log Off. Click on the Your Account link to be taken to the Customer Detail page, as shown in Figure 13-14.

From here, you can update your details and navigate to your address book. Click on the Address book link and create a new address. Your address book should now look similar to Figure 13-15.

FIGURE 13-12

FIGURE 13-13

FIGURE 13-14

FIGURE 13-15

SUMMARY

In this chapter, you tackled the customer membership and authentication requirements of the site. The customer membership involved creating a domain model of a customer with a delivery address book. This was simple and had a standard set of views, service layer, and controller similar to what you have seen up until this point.

The authentication service was a lot more interesting. The first authentication method utilized the built-in ASP.NET membership API. You first created an interface for a local authentication service and implemented an ASP.NET membership adapter to adhere to the contract.

You then implemented a web-based authentication service using a Janrain service that enables customers to use existing Internet accounts to authenticate themselves with the site.

You applied the forms authentication method for establishing that a customer is authenticated after a successful login or register. Again, you created an interface and then implemented an ASP.NET forms-based adapter to keep the code loosely coupled and highly testable.

In the final chapter of this case study, you will implement the checkout using PayPal and the order history views within the customer account.

14

Ordering and Payment

➤ Creating the checkout and using PayPal as the payment merchant

➤ Creating an order history section within the customer account

➤ Using domain events to trigger workflow

In this final case study chapter, you will complete Agatha's online store by adding the facility for customers to place an order and pay for it using PayPal. You will also add screens to the customer account area to enable customers to view their order history.

CHECKOUT

Figure 14-1 shows the screens you will be creating in this chapter. The Customer Account section will include new screens for customers to view their order history. The checkout section will enable customers to order products placed in their basket. The payment merchant you will be using is PayPal, but the system will be designed to allow any payment merchant who uses the post callback method to take payments.

As with the previous three chapters, you will begin by designing the domain model of the order aggregation.

Order Model

Figure 14-2 shows the domain model for the order aggregation. As you can see, an order contains a collection of order items. It also contains a payment object that represents details of the transaction made to pay for the order. The order also contains a property of type IOrderState, which defines the order's state. The states of an order are open and submitted. An order in the open state has been created but not paid for. When an order is paid, it changes to the state of submitted.

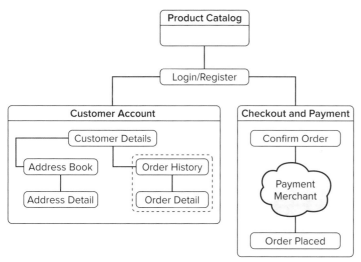

FIGURE 14-1

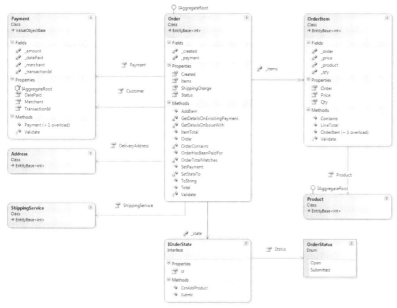

FIGURE 14-2

Figure 14-3 shows the classes that are required for the order state framework. The order state classes follow the State Design Pattern. Refer to Chapter 5 for more details on this pattern.

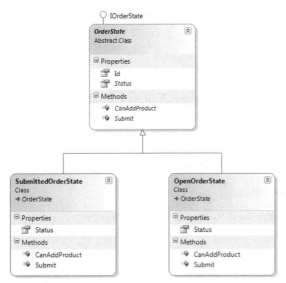

FIGURE 14-3

Before you start work on creating the order entities, you need to build a framework for handling events that occur within the domain model, known as domain events. *Domain events* are events that occur in your model that can be published for other services inside and outside the model to respond to. The domain event that you will be modeling in the order aggregation is that of an order changing state from open to submitted after a successful payment is made. When the change in state occurs, a domain event is fired. A handler in the service layer responds by sending the customer an e-mail informing him that his order has been paid for and therefore will be processed.

The domain events framework you will create is based on the framework designed by Udi Dahan (www.udidahan.com), who is a great domain-driven design (DDD) evangelist with a blog that is well worth reading. Create a new folder within the Domain folder of the Infrastructure project named Events, and add to it a simple interface named IDomainEvent that will identify domain events within the model:

```
namespace Agathas.Storefront.Infrastructure.Domain.Events
{
    public interface IDomainEvent
    {
    }
}
```

Create a second interface named IDomainEventHandler. This is the interface that handlers of the events must implement:

```
namespace Agathas.Storefront.Infrastructure.Domain.Events
{
```

```
        public interface IDomainEventHandler<T> where T : IDomainEvent
        {
            void Handle(T domainEvent);
        }
    }
```

Next, add a third interface named `IDomainEventHandlerFactory`. You will use this to obtain the collection of domain event handlers for a given domain event:

```
using System.Collections.Generic;

namespace Agathas.Storefront.Infrastructure.Domain.Events
{
    public interface IDomainEventHandlerFactory
    {
        IEnumerable<IDomainEventHandler<T>> GetDomainEventHandlersFor<T>(T domainEvent)
                                            where T : IDomainEvent;

    }
}
```

Add an implementation of the `IDomainEventHandlerFactory` named `StructureMapDomainEvent HandlerFactory`, as shown in the following listing. The `StructureMapDomainEventHandlerFactory` provides the list of `IDomainEventHandlers` for a given domain event:

```
using System.Collections.Generic;
using StructureMap;

namespace Agathas.Storefront.Infrastructure.Domain.Events
{
    public class StructureMapDomainEventHandlerFactory : IDomainEventHandlerFactory
    {
        public IEnumerable<IDomainEventHandler<T>> GetDomainEventHandlersFor<T>
                                      (T domainEvent) where T : IDomainEvent
        {
            return ObjectFactory.GetAllInstances<IDomainEventHandler<T>>();
        }
    }
}
```

After you obtain the collection of `IDomainEventHandlers`, their handle method is called and given the domain event as an argument to action. To keep the code fluid, add a new extension method to handle the invocation of the `IDomainEventHandlers`. Add a new class named `IEnumerableExtensions` to the `Events` folder with the following listing:

```
using System;
using System.Collections.Generic;

namespace Agathas.Storefront.Infrastructure.Domain.Events
{
    public static class IEnumerableExtensions
    {
        public static void ForEach<T>(this IEnumerable<T> source, Action<T> action)
        {
```

```
                foreach (T item in source)
                    action(item);
            }
        }
    }
```

To raise an event, you will create a static `DomainEvents` class that is called by the domain entities from within the `Model` project. The code for this class is shown in the following listing:

```
namespace Agathas.Storefront.Infrastructure.Domain.Events
{
    public static class DomainEvents
    {
        public static IDomainEventHandlerFactory DomainEventHandlerFactory { get; set; }

        public static void Raise<T>(T domainEvent) where T : IDomainEvent
        {
            DomainEventHandlerFactory.GetDomainEventHandlersFor(domainEvent)
                                    .ForEach(h => h.Handle(domainEvent));
        }
    }
}
```

This completes the framework to support domain events. You will now build the order aggregation model.

The first class you will create is the `Payment` value object. Create a new folder within the `Model` project named `Orders`, and add a class that contains the rules of a `Payment` value object named `PaymentBusinessRules`:

```
using Agathas.Storefront.Infrastructure.Domain;

namespace Agathas.Storefront.Model.Orders
{
    public class PaymentBusinessRules
    {
        public static readonly BusinessRule TransactionIdRequired =
            new BusinessRule("TransactionId", "A payment must have a transaction id.");
        public static readonly BusinessRule MerchantRequired =
            new BusinessRule("Merchant", "A payment must have a Merchant.");
        public static readonly BusinessRule AmountValid =
            new BusinessRule("Amount", "A payment must be for a non negative amount.");
    }
}
```

Next, add the `Payment` value object, ensuring that you inherit from the `ValueObjectBase` that you created within the `Infrastructure` project in Chapter 10.

```
using System;
using Agathas.Storefront.Infrastructure.Domain;

namespace Agathas.Storefront.Model.Orders
{
```

```csharp
public class Payment : ValueObjectBase
{
    private readonly DateTime _datePaid;
    private readonly string _transactionId;
    private readonly string _merchant;
    private readonly decimal _amount;

    public Payment()
    {
    }

    public Payment(DateTime datePaid, string transactionId,
                   string merchant, decimal amount)
    {
        _datePaid = datePaid;
        _transactionId = transactionId;
        _merchant = merchant;
        _amount = amount;

        base.ThrowExceptionIfInvalid();
    }

    public DateTime DatePaid
    {
        get { return _datePaid; }
    }
    public string TransactionId
    {
        get { return _transactionId; }
    }
    public string Merchant
    {
        get { return _merchant; }
    }
    public decimal Amount
    {
        get { return _amount; }
    }

    protected override void Validate()
    {
        if (string.IsNullOrEmpty(_transactionId))
            base.AddBrokenRule(PaymentBusinessRules.TransactionIdRequired);

        if (string.IsNullOrEmpty(_merchant))
            base.AddBrokenRule(PaymentBusinessRules.MerchantRequired);

        if (_amount < 0)
            base.AddBrokenRule(PaymentBusinessRules.AmountValid);
    }
}
```

To make it easier to create `payments`, you will add a `PaymentFactory` class, as shown in the following listing:

```
using System;

namespace Agathas.Storefront.Model.Orders
{
    public class PaymentFactory
    {
        public static Payment CreatePayment(string paymentToken,
                                      decimal amount, string paymentMerchant)
        {
            return new Payment(DateTime.Now, paymentToken, paymentMerchant, amount);
        }
    }
}
```

The next class to create defines the business rules that govern `OrderItem` entities. Add a new class named `OrderItemBusinessRules` with the following listing:

```
using Agathas.Storefront.Infrastructure.Domain;

namespace Agathas.Storefront.Model.Orders
{
    public class OrderItemBusinessRules
    {
        public static readonly BusinessRule OrderRequired =
            new BusinessRule("OrderRequired",
                            "An order item must be associated with an order.");
        public static readonly BusinessRule PriceNonNegative =
            new BusinessRule("Price",
                            "An order item must have a non negative price value.");
        public static readonly BusinessRule QtyNonNegative =
            new BusinessRule("Qty", "An order item must have a positive qty value.");
        public static readonly BusinessRule ProductRequired =
            new BusinessRule("Product",
                            "An order item must be associated with a valid product.");
    }
}
```

With the business rules for the `OrderItem` defined, you can create the class. Add a new class named `OrderItem` with the following listing. You will receive a complier warning because you have not created the `Order` object yet. Don't worry; you will create this class shortly:

```
using Agathas.Storefront.Infrastructure.Domain;
using Agathas.Storefront.Model.Products;

namespace Agathas.Storefront.Model.Orders
{
    public class OrderItem : EntityBase<int>
    {
        private readonly Product _product;
        private readonly Order _order;
```

```csharp
private readonly int _qty;
private readonly decimal _price;

public OrderItem()
{
}

public OrderItem(Product product, Order order, int qty)
{
    _product = product;
    _order = order;
    _price = product.Price;
    _qty = qty;
}

public Product Product
{
    get { return _product; }
}

public int Qty
{
    get { return _qty; }
}

public decimal Price
{
    get { return _price;  }
}

public Order Order
{
    get { return _order;}
}

public decimal LineTotal()
{
    return Qty*Price;
}

protected override void Validate()
{
    if (Order == null)
        base.AddBrokenRule(OrderItemBusinessRules.OrderRequired);

    if (Product == null)
        base.AddBrokenRule(OrderItemBusinessRules.ProductRequired);

    if (Price  < 0)
        base.AddBrokenRule(OrderItemBusinessRules.PriceNonNegative);

    if (Qty < 0)
        base.AddBrokenRule(OrderItemBusinessRules.QtyNonNegative);
```

```
        }

        public bool Contains(Product product)
        {
            return Product == product;
        }
    }
}
```

Again, you will create a factory class to take responsibility for creating valid instances of an `OrderItem`. Name this class `OrderItemFactory`, and update it to match the following listing:

```
using Agathas.Storefront.Model.Products;

namespace Agathas.Storefront.Model.Orders
{
    public static class OrderItemFactory
    {
        public static OrderItem CreateItemFor(Product product, Order order, int qty)
        {
            return new OrderItem(product, order, qty);
        }
    }
}
```

Before you create the `Order` class, you will define the business rules and some custom exceptions that it will use when attempts are made to put it into an invalid state. Add a new class named `Order BusinessRules`, as shown in the following listing:

```
using Agathas.Storefront.Infrastructure.Domain;

namespace Agathas.Storefront.Model.Orders
{
    public class OrderBusinessRules
    {
        public static readonly BusinessRule CreatedDateRequired =
            new BusinessRule("CreatedDate", "An order must have a created date.");
        public static readonly BusinessRule PaymentTransactionIdRequired =
            new BusinessRule("PaymentTransactionId", "If an order is set as paid " +
                             "it must have a corresponding payment transaction id.");
        public static readonly BusinessRule CustomerRequired =
            new BusinessRule("Customer", "An order must be associated with a customer.");
        public static readonly BusinessRule DeliveryAddressRequired =
            new BusinessRule("DeliveryAddress", "An order must have a valid " +
                                                "delivery address.");
        public static readonly BusinessRule ItemsRequired =
            new BusinessRule("Items", "An order must contain at least one order item.");
        public static readonly BusinessRule ShippingServiceRequired =
            new BusinessRule("ShippingService",
                                        "An order must have a shipping service set.");
    }
}
```

Next, add three custom exceptions — PaymentAmountDoesNotEqualOrderTotalException, CannotAmendOrderException, and OrderAlreadyPaidForException — that will be used if an action on an order breaks some business logic:

```
using System;

namespace Agathas.Storefront.Model.Orders
{
    public class PaymentAmountDoesNotEqualOrderTotalException : Exception
    {
        public PaymentAmountDoesNotEqualOrderTotalException(string message)
            : base(message)
        {
        }
    }
}

using System;

namespace Agathas.Storefront.Model.Orders
{
    public class OrderAlreadyPaidForException : Exception
    {
        public OrderAlreadyPaidForException(string message) : base (message)
        {
        }
    }
}
using System;

namespace Agathas.Storefront.Model.Orders
{
    public class CannotAmendOrderException : Exception
    {
        public CannotAmendOrderException(string message) : base(message)
        {

        }
    }
}
```

You can finally add the Order class. As with the OrderItem class, you will receive some compiler errors because of the nonexistence of the IOrderState interface. Don't worry; you will create this next:

```
using System;
using System.Collections.Generic;
using System.Linq;
using System.Text;
using Agathas.Storefront.Infrastructure.Domain;
using Agathas.Storefront.Model.Customers;
using Agathas.Storefront.Model.Orders.States;
using Agathas.Storefront.Model.Shipping;
using Agathas.Storefront.Model.Products;

namespace Agathas.Storefront.Model.Orders
```

```csharp
{
    public class Order : EntityBase<int>, IAggregateRoot
    {
        private IList<OrderItem> _items;
        private DateTime _created;
        private Payment _payment;
        private IOrderState _state;

        public Order()
        {
            _created = DateTime.Now;
            _items = new List<OrderItem>();
            _state = OrderStates.Open;
        }

        public DateTime Created
        {
            get { return _created; }
        }

        public decimal ShippingCharge { get; set; }

        public ShippingService ShippingService { get; set; }

        public decimal ItemTotal()
        {
            return Items.Sum(i => i.LineTotal());
        }

        public decimal Total()
        {
            return Items.Sum(i => i.LineTotal()) + ShippingCharge;
        }

        public Payment Payment
        {
            get { return _payment; }
        }

        public void SetPayment(Payment payment)
        {
                if (OrderHasBeenPaidFor())
                    throw new OrderAlreadyPaidForException(
                                            GetDetailsOnExisitingPayment());

                if (OrderTotalMatches(payment))
                    _payment = payment;
                else
                    throw new PaymentAmountDoesNotEqualOrderTotalException(
                                            GetDetailsOnIssueWith(payment));

                _state.Submit(this);
        }

        private string GetDetailsOnExisitingPayment()
```

```
    {
        return String.Format("Order has already been paid for. "+
                             "{0} was paid on {1}. Payment token '{2}'",
                             Payment.Amount, Payment.DatePaid,
                             Payment.TransactionId);
    }

    private string GetDetailsOnIssueWith(Payment payment)
    {
        return String.Format("Payment amount is invalid. " +
                             "Order total is {0} but payment for {1}." +
                             " Payment token '{2}'",
                             this.Total(), payment.Amount, payment.TransactionId);
    }

    public bool OrderHasBeenPaidFor()
    {
        return Payment != null && OrderTotalMatches(Payment);
    }

    private bool OrderTotalMatches(Payment payment)
    {
        return Total() == payment.Amount;
    }

    public Customer Customer { get; set; }

    public Address DeliveryAddress { get; set; }

    public IEnumerable<OrderItem> Items
    {
        get { return _items; }
    }

    public OrderStatus Status
    {
        get { return _state.Status; }
    }

    public void AddItem(Product product, int qty)
    {
        if (_state.CanAddProduct())
        {
            if (!OrderContains(product))
                _items.Add(OrderItemFactory.CreateItemFor(product, this, qty));
        }
        else
            throw new CannotAmendOrderException(String.Format(
            "You cannot add an item to an order with the status of '{0}'.",
                                                    Status.ToString()));
    }

    private bool OrderContains(Product product)
    {
        return _items.Any(i => i.Contains(product));
```

```
        }

        protected override void Validate()
        {
            if (Created == DateTime.MinValue)
                base.AddBrokenRule(OrderBusinessRules.CreatedDateRequired);

            if (Customer == null)
                base.AddBrokenRule(OrderBusinessRules.CustomerRequired);

            if (DeliveryAddress == null)
                base.AddBrokenRule(OrderBusinessRules.DeliveryAddressRequired);

            if (Items == null || Items.Count() == 0)
                base.AddBrokenRule(OrderBusinessRules.ItemsRequired);

            if (Items == null || Items.Count() == 0)
                base.AddBrokenRule(OrderBusinessRules.ItemsRequired);

            if (ShippingService == null)
                base.AddBrokenRule(OrderBusinessRules.ShippingServiceRequired);

        }

        internal void SetStateTo(IOrderState state)
        {
            this._state = state;
        }

        public override string ToString()
        {
            StringBuilder orderInfo = new StringBuilder();

            foreach (OrderItem item in _items)
            {
                orderInfo.AppendLine(String.Format("{0} of {1} ",
                                item.Qty, item.Product.Name));
            }

            orderInfo.AppendLine(String.Format("Shipping: {0}", this.ShippingCharge));
            orderInfo.AppendLine(String.Format("Total: {0}", this.Total()));

            return orderInfo.ToString();

        }
    }
}
```

Code snippet Order.cs in project Agathas.Storefront.Model

The logic contained within the Order class is straightforward. In most cases, any business rules are delegated to the order's IOrderState instance, which you will create now.

Because the IOrderState implementation raises a domain event, it makes sense to create this now. Add a new folder within the Orders folder named Events, and add a new class named OrderSubmitted Event that will contain a property holding the Order instance that has just been submitted:

```
using Agathas.Storefront.Infrastructure.Domain.Events;

namespace Agathas.Storefront.Model.Orders.Events
{
    public class OrderSubmittedEvent : IDomainEvent
    {
        public Order Order { get; set; }
    }
}
```

Now you can tackle the IOrderState implementation. Add a new folder within the Orders folder named States, and to this folder add a new interface named IOrderState with the following code listing:

```
namespace Agathas.Storefront.Model.Orders.States
{
    public interface IOrderState
    {
        int Id { get; set; }
        OrderStatus Status { get; }
        bool CanAddProductTo(Order order);
        void Submit(Order order);
    }
}
```

The IOrderState interface references an enumeration named OrderStatus. Add this to the States folder as well:

```
namespace Agathas.Storefront.Model.Orders.States
{
    public enum OrderStatus
    {
        Open = 1,
        Submitted = 2
    }
}
```

To provide a base class for all the states of an order, create an OrderState abstract class. Add this with the following listing to the States folder:

```
namespace Agathas.Storefront.Model.Orders.States
{
    public abstract class OrderState : IOrderState
    {
        public virtual int Id { get; set; }
        public abstract OrderStatus Status { get;  }
        public abstract bool CanAddProduct();
        public abstract void Submit(Order order);
    }
}
```

The initial state of an order will be OpenOrderState, as displayed in the following listing. Note that when the Submit method is called and if an order has been paid, the OrderSubmittedEvent that you created earlier will be raised. Later in the chapter, you will create a handler for this event that sends an e-mail to customers letting them know that their order has now been submitted:

```
using Agathas.Storefront.Infrastructure.Domain.Events;
using Agathas.Storefront.Model.Orders.Events;

namespace Agathas.Storefront.Model.Orders.States
{
    public class OpenOrderState : OrderState
    {
        public override OrderStatus Status
        {
            get { return OrderStatus.Open; }
        }

        public override bool CanAddProduct()
        {
            return true;
        }

        public override void Submit(Order order)
        {
            if (order.OrderHasBeenPaidFor())
                order.SetStateTo(OrderStates.Submitted);

            DomainEvents.Raise(new OrderSubmittedEvent() {Order = order});
        }
    }
}
```

You will receive a compiler error due to the missing OrderStates class. Don't worry; you will add this shortly.

The second state an order can be in is SubmittedOrderState. Once an order is in this state, you cannot modify it:

```
using System;

namespace Agathas.Storefront.Model.Orders.States
{
    public class SubmittedOrderState : OrderState
    {
        public override OrderStatus Status
        {
            get { return OrderStatus.Submitted; }
        }

        public override bool CanAddProduct()
        {
            return false;
        }

        public override void Submit(Order order)
```

```
            {
                throw new InvalidOperationException(
                    "You cannot submit this order as it has already been submitted.");
            }
        }
    }
```

To change state efficiently, you will use the Singleton pattern. Because an instance of the `IOrderState` interface contains no state, it's safe to use the Singleton pattern. Create the `OrderStates` helper class with the following listing:

```
namespace Agathas.Storefront.Model.Orders.States
{
    public class OrderStates
    {
        public static readonly IOrderState Open =
                    new OpenOrderState() {Id = 1};
        public static readonly IOrderState Submitted =
                    new SubmittedOrderState() {Id = 2};
    }
}
```

Now that you have the order aggregation complete, you can update the `Customer` entity to include a property that exposes its order history. Open the `Customer` entity and add the `Orders` property, which is bolded in the following listing:

```
using Agathas.Storefront.Model.Orders;

namespace Agathas.Storefront.Model.Customers
{
    public class Customer : EntityBase<int>, IAggregateRoot
    {
        ...

        public IList<Order> Orders { get; set; }

        ...
    }
}
```

The final act of creating the `Order` aggregation is to define an `IOrderRepository`, which will be used to retrieve and persist `Orders`:

```
using Agathas.Storefront.Infrastructure.Domain;

namespace Agathas.Storefront.Model.Orders
{
    public interface IOrderRepository : IRepository<Order, int>
    {
    }
}
```

With the domain model complete, you can now create the data model that will be used to save the state of the order aggregation.

Order Data Tables

Within the `Web.MVC` project, open the `Shop.mdf` database and add the following tables, as shown in Figure 14-4, except the `CourierServices` table, which you created in Chapter 12. Ensure that you set all the primary key fields as identity fields apart from the `OrderStates` table. This will mean that the database is in charge of creating the entity's identity.

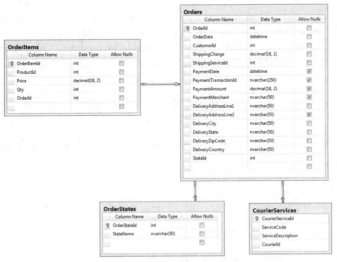

FIGURE 14-4

Once the data model is created, enter the data as shown in Figure 14-5 into the `OrderStates` table.

With the data model in place, you can now turn your attention to mapping the domain model to the data model via the NHibernate mapping files.

	OrderStateId	StateName
▶	1	Open
	2	Submitted
*	NULL	NULL

FIGURE 14-5

Order NHibernate Mappings

Three mapping files for the `Order` aggregation map to the `Order`, `OrderItem`, and `IOrderState` classes. The `IOrderState.hbm.xml` mapping file, as shown in the following listing, uses NHibernate's inheritance mechanism and discriminator column to hydrate the correct instance of the `IOrderState`:

```xml
<?xml version="1.0" encoding="utf-8" ?>
<hibernate-mapping xmlns="urn:nhibernate-mapping-2.2"
    namespace="Agathas.Storefront.Model.Orders.States"
        assembly="Agathas.Storefront.Model">

    <class name="IOrderState" table="OrderStates" lazy="false" >

        <id  name="Id" column="OrderStateId" >
            <generator class="native" />
```

```
        </id>

        <discriminator column="StateName" type="string" />
        <subclass name="OpenOrderState" discriminator-value="Open" />
        <subclass name="SubmittedOrderState" discriminator-value="Submitted" />
      </class>
  </hibernate-mapping>
```

Remember that you need to change the build action for the `IOrderState.hbm.xml` file. Right-click on the `IOrderState.hbm.xml` XML file, and bring up its properties from the context-sensitive menu. Once the Properties dialog is displayed, change the build action to Embedded Resource. This ensures that the XML data is embedded when the assembly is built. Do the same for the rest of the mapping files in this section.

The remaining mapping files are straightforward and similar to what you have already seen in previous chapters.

Create a new mapping file named `Order.hbm.xml` for the `Order` entity with the following definition:

```
<?xml version="1.0" encoding="utf-8" ?>
<hibernate-mapping xmlns="urn:nhibernate-mapping-2.2"
    namespace="Agathas.Storefront.Model.Orders"
        assembly="Agathas.Storefront.Model">

  <class name="Order" table="Orders" lazy="false" >

    <id name="Id" column="OrderId" type="int" unsaved-value="0">
      <generator class="native" />
    </id>

    <property access="field.camelcase-underscore" name="Created">
      <column name="OrderDate" sql-type="datetime" not-null="true" />
    </property>

    <property name="ShippingCharge">
      <column name="ShippingCharge" sql-type="decimal" not-null="true" />
    </property>

    <many-to-one cascade="all" not-null="true" lazy="false"
                 fetch="join" name="State" column="StateId"
                 access="field.camelcase-underscore" />

    <many-to-one name="ShippingService"
                  class="Agathas.Storefront.Model.Shipping.ShippingService"
                  column="ShippingServiceId"
                  not-null="true" />

    <component access="field.camelcase-underscore" name="Payment" class="Payment">
      <property access="field.camelcase-underscore"
                 column="PaymentDate" name="DatePaid"/>
      <property access="field.camelcase-underscore"
                 column="PaymentTransactionId" name="TransactionId"/>
      <property access="field.camelcase-underscore"
```

```
                  column="PaymentMerchant" name="Merchant"/>
    <property access="field.camelcase-underscore"
                  column="PaymentAmount" name="Amount"/>
  </component>

  <component name="DeliveryAddress" class="Agathas.Storefront.Model.Address">
    <property column="DeliveryAddressLine1" name="AddressLine1"/>
    <property column="DeliveryAddressLine2" name="AddressLine2"/>
    <property column="DeliveryCity" name="City"/>
    <property column="DeliveryState" name="State"/>
    <property column="DeliveryCountry" name="Country"/>
    <property column="DeliveryZipCode" name="ZipCode"/>
  </component>

  <many-to-one name="Customer"
                  class="Agathas.Storefront.Model.Customers.Customer"
                  column="CustomerId"
                  not-null="true"/>

  <bag name="Items" access="field.camelcase-underscore"
        inverse="true" cascade="all-delete-orphan" lazy="true" >
    <key column="OrderId"/>
    <one-to-many class="OrderItem"></one-to-many>
  </bag>
  </class>
</hibernate-mapping>
```

Create a new mapping file named `OrderItem.hbm.xml` for the `OrderItem` entity with the following definition:

```
<?xml version="1.0" encoding="utf-8" ?>
<hibernate-mapping xmlns="urn:nhibernate-mapping-2.2"
    namespace="Agathas.Storefront.Model.Orders"
        assembly="Agathas.Storefront.Model">

  <class name="OrderItem" table="OrderItems" lazy="false" >

    <id  name="Id" column="OrderItemId" unsaved-value="0">
      <generator class="native" />
    </id>

    <property access="field.camelcase-underscore" name="Qty">
      <column name="Qty" sql-type="int" not-null="true" />
    </property>

    <property access="field.camelcase-underscore" name="Price">
      <column name="Price" sql-type="decimal" not-null="true" />
    </property>

    <many-to-one access="field.camelcase-underscore" name="Product"
                    class="Agathas.Storefront.Model.Products.Product"
                    column="ProductId"
                    cascade="none"
```

```
                                  not-null="true"/>

        <many-to-one access="field.camelcase-underscore" name="Order"
                        class="Order"
                        column="OrderId"
                        not-null="true"/>

    </class>

</hibernate-mapping>
```

Because you updated the `Customer` entity class within the `Model` project, you must now update the `Customer` mapping file to include information on the `Customer` order history. Open the `Customer` `.hbm.xml` file, and update it to include the bolded section shown in the following code listing:

```
<?xml version="1.0" encoding="utf-8" ?>
<hibernate-mapping xmlns="urn:nhibernate-mapping-2.2"
    namespace="Agathas.Storefront.Model.Customers"
        assembly="Agathas.Storefront.Model">

  <class name="Customer" table="Customers" lazy="false" >

    ...

    <bag name="Orders" inverse="false" cascade="all-delete-orphan" lazy="true" >
      <key column="CustomerId"/>
      <one-to-many class="Agathas.Storefront.Model.Orders.Order"></one-to-many>
    </bag>

  </class>

</hibernate-mapping>
```

The final act in allowing the `Order` aggregation to be persisted and retrieved is to create an implementation of the `IOrderRepository`. As with previous chapters, this is trivial due to the work you did in Chapter 11 with the `NHibernate` base repository class:

```
using Agathas.Storefront.Infrastructure.UnitOfWork;
using Agathas.Storefront.Model.Orders;

namespace Agathas.Storefront.Repository.NHibernate.Repositories
{
    public class OrderRepository : Repository<Order, int>, IOrderRepository
    {
        public OrderRepository(IUnitOfWork uow)
            : base(uow)
        {
        }
    }
}
```

With the domain model and the repository constructed, it's time to turn your attention to the classes that will make up the service layer.

Order Service

Figure 14-6 shows the view models that the order service implementation will return. The Order SummaryView gives a history of a collection of orders that a customer places, whereas the OrderView and OrderItemView are used to view the details of an Order.

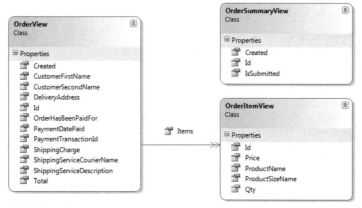

FIGURE 14-6

Create a new class named OrderSummaryView within the ViewModels folder of the Services project:

```
using System;

namespace Agathas.Storefront.Services.ViewModels
{
    public class OrderSummaryView
    {
        public int Id { get; set; }
        public DateTime Created { get; set; }
        public bool IsSubmitted { get; set; }
    }
}
```

To represent an OrderItem, create a class named OrderItemView with the following listing:

```
namespace Agathas.Storefront.Services.ViewModels
{
    public class OrderItemView
    {
        public string ProductName { get; set; }
        public string ProductSizeName { get; set; }
        public int Id { get; set; }
        public int Qty { get; set; }
        public string Price { get; set; }
    }
}
```

To represent an `Order`, create a class named `OrderView` again with the following listing:

```
using System;
using System.Collections.Generic;

namespace Agathas.Storefront.Services.ViewModels
{
    public class OrderView
    {
        public DateTime PaymentDatePaid { get; set; }
        public string PaymentTransactionId { get; set; }
        public bool OrderHasBeenPaidFor { get; set; }
        public IEnumerable<OrderItemView> Items { get; set; }
        public DateTime Created { get; set; }
        public string ShippingCharge { get; set; }
        public string ShippingServiceCourierName { get; set; }
        public string ShippingServiceDescription { get; set; }
        public string Total { get; set; }
        public int Id { get; set; }
        public DeliveryAddressView DeliveryAddress { get; set; }
        public string CustomerFirstName { get; set; }
        public string CustomerSecondName { get; set; }      }
}
```

With the views defined that the order service will return, you can now work on the messaging objects using the Request-Response pattern as detailed in Chapter 6.

Create a new folder named `OrderService` within the `Messaging` folder of the `Services` project. Add a pair of classes that will be used to create an order from a `Basket` named `CreateOrderRequest` and `CreateOrderResponse`:

```
using System;

namespace Agathas.Storefront.Services.Messaging.OrderService
{
    public class CreateOrderRequest
    {
        public int DeliveryId { get; set; }
        public Guid BasketId { get; set; }
        public string CustomerIdentityToken { get; set; }
    }
}

using Agathas.Storefront.Services.ViewModels;

namespace Agathas.Storefront.Services.Messaging.OrderService
{
    public class CreateOrderResponse
    {
        public OrderView Order { get; set; }
    }
}
```

To retrieve an order, the pair of classes named `GetOrderRequest` and `GetOrderResponse` are used:

```
namespace Agathas.Storefront.Services.Messaging.OrderService
{
    public class GetOrderRequest
    {
        public int OrderId { get; set; }
    }
}

using Agathas.Storefront.Services.ViewModels;

namespace Agathas.Storefront.Services.Messaging.OrderService
{
    public class GetOrderResponse
    {
        public OrderView Order { get; set; }
    }
}
```

For a customer to pay for an order, the classes `SetOrderPaymentRequest` and `SetOrderPayment Response` are required:

```
namespace Agathas.Storefront.Services.Messaging.OrderService
{
    public class SetOrderPaymentRequest
    {
        public string PaymentToken { get; set; }
        public decimal Amount { get; set; }
        public string PaymentMerchant { get; set; }
        public int OrderId { get; set; }
    }
}

using Agathas.Storefront.Services.ViewModels;

namespace Agathas.Storefront.Services.Messaging.OrderService
{
    public class SetOrderPaymentResponse
    {
        public OrderView Order { get; set; }
    }
}
```

Now that a `Customer` is related to her `Orders`, the Request-Response class pair needs to be modified to allow the client to specify if this information is loaded when a customer is retrieved. Amend the classes `GetCustomerRequest` and `GetCustomerResponse` found within the `Messaging/Customer Service` folder, as shown in the bolded sections of the following code listing.

```
namespace Agathas.Storefront.Services.Messaging.CustomerService
{
    public class GetCustomerRequest
    {
```

```
        public string CustomerIdentityToken { get; set; }
        public bool LoadOrderSummary { get; set; }
    }
}

using System.Collections.Generic;
using Agathas.Storefront.Services.ViewModels;

namespace Agathas.Storefront.Services.Messaging.CustomerService
{
    public class GetCustomerResponse
    {
        public bool CustomerFound { get; set; }
        public CustomerView Customer { get; set; }
        public IEnumerable<OrderSummaryView> Orders { get; set; }
    }
}
```

You will also need to update the `CustomerService` implementation to include the new `LoadOrder Summary` flag, as shown in bold in the following code listing:

```
namespace Agathas.Storefront.Services.Implementations
{
    public class CustomerService : ICustomerService
    {
        ...

        public GetCustomerResponse GetCustomer(GetCustomerRequest request)
        {
            GetCustomerResponse response = new GetCustomerResponse();

            Customer customer =
                _customerRepository.FindBy(request.CustomerIdentityToken);

            if (customer != null)
            {
                response.CustomerFound = true;
                response.Customer = customer.ConvertToCustomerDetailView();
                if (request.LoadOrderSummary)
                    response.Orders = customer.Orders
                    .OrderByDescending(o => o.Created).ConvertToOrderSummaryViews();
            }
            else
                response.CustomerFound = false;


            return response;
        }

        ...
    }
}
```

Because you set the customer's orders to be lazy loading in the NHibernate mapping file, there is no overhead in retrieving a customer without his orders. For a more detailed view of the Lazy Loading pattern, take a look at Chapter 7.

You will receive a compiler error because currently there is no ConvertToOrderSummaryViews extension method, so let's fix that.

To convert Order entities into ViewModels, you need to configure the AutoMapperBootStrapper class located at the root of the Services project. Update the AutoMapperBootStrapper class so that it includes the bolded lines, as shown in the following listing:

```
...
using Agathas.Storefront.Model.Orders.States;
using Agathas.Storefront.Model.Orders;
using Agathas.Storefront.Model;

namespace Agathas.Storefront.Services
{
    public class AutoMapperBootStrapper
    {
        public static void ConfigureAutoMapper()
        {

            ...

            // Orders
            Mapper.CreateMap<Order, OrderView>();
            Mapper.CreateMap<OrderItem, OrderItemView>();
            Mapper.CreateMap<Address, DeliveryAddressView>();
            Mapper.CreateMap<Order, OrderSummaryView>()
                .ForMember(o => o.IsSubmitted,
                             ov => ov.ResolveUsing<OrderStatusResolver>());

        }
    }

    public class OrderStatusResolver : ValueResolver<Order, bool>
    {
        protected override bool ResolveCore(Order source)
        {
            if (source.Status == OrderStatus.Submitted)
            {
                return true;
            }
            else
            {
                return false;
            }
        }
    }

    ...
}
```

The actual action of converting `Orders` is the responsibility of a mapper class. Add a new class named `OrderMapper` to the `Mapping` folder of the Services project:

```
using System.Collections.Generic;
using Agathas.Storefront.Model.Orders;
using Agathas.Storefront.Services.ViewModels;
using AutoMapper;

namespace Agathas.Storefront.Services.Mapping
{
    public static class OrderMapper
    {
        public static OrderView ConvertToOrderView(this Order order)
        {
            return Mapper.Map<Order, OrderView>(order);
        }

        public static IEnumerable<OrderSummaryView> ConvertToOrderSummaryViews(
                                          this IEnumerable<Order> orders)
        {
            return Mapper.Map<IEnumerable<Order>,
                        IEnumerable<OrderSummaryView>>(orders);
        }
    }
}
```

To create an `Order` from a `Basket`, you need to amend the `BasketMapper` class, as shown in the bolded code in the following listing:

```
using Agathas.Storefront.Model.Orders;

namespace Agathas.Storefront.Services.Mapping
{
    public static class BasketMapper
    {
        public static BasketView ConvertToBasketView(this Basket basket)
        {
            return Mapper.Map<Basket, BasketView>(basket);
        }

        public static Order ConvertToOrder(this Basket basket)
        {
            Order order = new Order();

            order.ShippingCharge = basket.DeliveryCost();
            order.ShippingService = basket.DeliveryOption.ShippingService;

            foreach(BasketItem item in basket.Items()) {
                order.AddItem(item.Product, item.Qty);
            }
            return order;
        }
    }
}
```

Next, add a contract for the order service in the `Interfaces` folder named `IOrderService`, as shown in the following code listing:

```
using Agathas.Storefront.Services.Messaging.OrderService;

namespace Agathas.Storefront.Services.Interfaces
{
    public interface IOrderService
    {
        CreateOrderResponse CreateOrder(CreateOrderRequest request);

        SetOrderPaymentResponse SetOrderPayment(SetOrderPaymentRequest paymentRequest);

        GetOrderResponse GetOrder(GetOrderRequest request);
    }
}
```

The implementation of the `IOrderService` that should be created within the `Implementations` folder is shown in the following listing. Again, this class is similar to what you have seen before in previous chapters:

Available for download on Wrox.com

```
using System.Linq;
using Agathas.Storefront.Infrastructure.Logging;
using Agathas.Storefront.Infrastructure.UnitOfWork;
using Agathas.Storefront.Model.Basket;
using Agathas.Storefront.Model.Customers;
using Agathas.Storefront.Model.Orders;
using Agathas.Storefront.Services.Interfaces;
using Agathas.Storefront.Services.Mapping;
using Agathas.Storefront.Services.Messaging.OrderService;

namespace Agathas.Storefront.Services.Implementations
{
    public class OrderService : IOrderService
    {
        private readonly ICustomerRepository _customerRepository;
        private readonly IOrderRepository _orderRepository;
        private readonly IBasketRepository _basketRepository;
        private readonly IUnitOfWork _uow;

        public OrderService(IOrderRepository orderRepository,
                            IBasketRepository basketRepository,
                            ICustomerRepository customerRepository,
                            IUnitOfWork uow)
        {
            _customerRepository = customerRepository;
            _orderRepository = orderRepository;
            _basketRepository = basketRepository;
            _uow = uow;
        }

        public CreateOrderResponse CreateOrder(CreateOrderRequest request)
        {
            CreateOrderResponse response = new CreateOrderResponse();
            Customer customer = _customerRepository
```

```
                            .FindBy(request.CustomerIdentityToken);
        Basket basket = _basketRepository.FindBy(request.BasketId);

        DeliveryAddress deliveryAddress = customer.DeliveryAddressBook
                    .Where(d => d.Id == request.DeliveryId).FirstOrDefault();

        Order order = basket.ConvertToOrder();

        order.Customer = customer;
        order.DeliveryAddress = deliveryAddress;

        _orderRepository.Save(order);
        _basketRepository.Remove(basket);
        _uow.Commit();

        response.Order =  order.ConvertToOrderView();

        return response;
    }

    public SetOrderPaymentResponse SetOrderPayment(
                                    SetOrderPaymentRequest paymentRequest)
    {
        SetOrderPaymentResponse paymentResponse = new SetOrderPaymentResponse();

        Order order = _orderRepository.FindBy(paymentRequest.OrderId);

        try
        {
            order.SetPayment(
                PaymentFactory.CreatePayment(paymentRequest.PaymentToken,
                                        paymentRequest.Amount,
                                        paymentRequest.PaymentMerchant));

            _orderRepository.Save(order);
            _uow.Commit();
        }
        catch (OrderAlreadyPaidForException ex)
        {
            // Out of scope of case study:
            // Refund the payment using the payment service.

            LoggingFactory.GetLogger().Log(ex.Message);
        }
        catch (PaymentAmountDoesNotEqualOrderTotalException ex)
        {
            // Out of scope of case study:
            // Refund the payment using the payment service.

            LoggingFactory.GetLogger().Log(ex.Message);
        }

        paymentResponse.Order = order.ConvertToOrderView();

        return paymentResponse;
```

```
        }

        public GetOrderResponse GetOrder(GetOrderRequest request)
        {
            GetOrderResponse response = new GetOrderResponse();

            Order order = _orderRepository.FindBy(request.OrderId);

            response.Order = order.ConvertToOrderView();

            return response;
        }
    }
}
```

Code snippet OrderService.cs in project Agathas.Storefront.Services

The final class for the `Services` project is required to handle the `OrderSubmittedEvent` that you
defined in the `Model` project. Create a new folder named `DomainEventHandlers`, and add a new class
named `OrderSubmittedHandler`, as shown in the following listing. You will use this class to send
e-mails to customers informing them that their order has been submitted:

```
using System;
using System.Text;
using Agathas.Storefront.Infrastructure.Domain.Events;
using Agathas.Storefront.Infrastructure.Email;
using Agathas.Storefront.Model.Orders.Events;

namespace Agathas.Storefront.Services.DomainEventHandlers
{
    public class OrderSubmittedHandler : IDomainEventHandler<OrderSubmittedEvent>
    {
        public void Handle(OrderSubmittedEvent domainEvent)
        {
            StringBuilder emailBody = new StringBuilder();
            string emailAddress = domainEvent.Order.Customer.Email;
            string emailSubject = String.Format("Agatha Order #{0}",
                                                domainEvent.Order.Id);

            emailBody.AppendLine(String.Format("Hello {0},",
                                 domainEvent.Order.Customer.FirstName));
            emailBody.AppendLine();
            emailBody.AppendLine(
              "The following order will be packed and dispatched as soon as possible.");
            emailBody.AppendLine(domainEvent.Order.ToString());
            emailBody.AppendLine();
            emailBody.AppendLine("Thank you for your custom.");
            emailBody.AppendLine("Agatha's");

          EmailServiceFactory.GetEmailService()
           .SendMail("orders@Agatha.com",emailAddress,
                   emailSubject, emailBody.ToString());
        }
    }
}
```

In a full production system it makes sense to store the e-mail template in a database or XML file. A great template engine is NVelocity, found at `www.castleproject.org/others/nvelocity/index.html`.

With the ability to create and retrieve orders taken care of, you now need to be able to obtain payment. That's what you will look at next.

Taking Payment with PayPal

To get started with PayPal, you need to create a PayPal sandbox account at `https://developer .paypal.com/`, as shown in Figure 14-7.

FIGURE 14-7

Once your account is created, log in and create a test buyer and seller account by clicking on the Create a Preconfigured Buyer or Seller Account, as shown in Figure 14-8.

FIGURE 14-8

Make a note of the password and e-mail addresses of both of these accounts, because you will need them later. Figure 14-9 shows an account with a buyer and seller profile created.

FIGURE 14-9

PayPal has numerous products and ways to work with them. You will be using the express checkout and the Name-Value Pair API. Figure 14-10 shows the journey a customer will take when checking out and paying for an order.

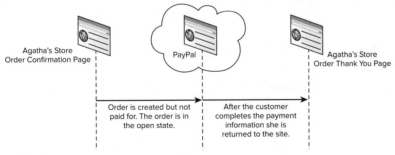

FIGURE 14-10

When the customer wants to place an order, she is presented with a confirmation screen on Agatha's site. When the customer clicks to confirm, data is posted to the PayPal site, where the customer fills out her payment information. Once the information is complete, the customer returns to Agatha's storefront.

In a separate action displayed in Figure 14-11, PayPal sends an Instant Payment Notification (IPN) detailing the transaction via an HTTP Post. Agatha's site uses this notification to verify the details of the transaction the customer made.

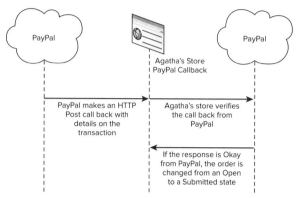

FIGURE 14-11

To work with any payment merchant, abstract away the details of the PayPal implementation. Figure 14-12 shows the data transfer objects you will create to communicate with the payment service.

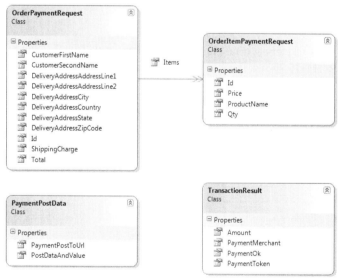

FIGURE 14-12

Create a new class named `OrderItemPaymentRequest` within the `Payments` folder of the `Infrastructure` project:

```
namespace Agathas.Storefront.Infrastructure.Payments
{
```

```
public class OrderItemPaymentRequest
{
    public int Id { get; set;}
    public string ProductName { get; set;}
    public decimal Price { get; set;}
    public int Qty { get; set; }
}
}
```

Next, create a class named `OrderPaymentRequest` with the following code listing:

```
namespace Agathas.Storefront.Infrastructure.Payments
{
    public class OrderPaymentRequest
    {
        public decimal Total { get; set;}
        public string CustomerFirstName { get; set; }
        public string CustomerSecondName { get; set; }
        public decimal ShippingCharge { get; set; }
        public string DeliveryAddressAddressLine1 { get; set; }
        public string DeliveryAddressAddressLine2 { get; set; }
        public string DeliveryAddressCity { get; set; }
        public string DeliveryAddressState { get; set; }
        public string DeliveryAddressCountry { get; set; }
        public string DeliveryAddressZipCode { get; set; }
        public int Id { get; set; }
        public IEnumerable<OrderItemPaymentRequest> Items { get; set; }
    }
}
```

The data that will be posted to PayPal after the customer confirms her order will be supplied by the payment service in the form of a `NameValueCollection` collection. Create a new class with the `Payments` folder named `PaymentPostData` that will contain this information and a URL on where to post it:

```
using System.Collections.Specialized;

namespace Agathas.Storefront.Infrastructure.Payments
{
    public class PaymentPostData
    {
        public string PaymentPostToUrl { get; set;}
        public NameValueCollection PostDataAndValue { get; set; }
    }
}
```

The result that the payment service returns after verifying a notification callback is returned as a `TransactionResult`:

```
namespace Agathas.Storefront.Infrastructure.Payments
{
    public class TransactionResult
    {
        public string PaymentMerchant { get; set; }
```

```
            public bool PaymentOk { get; set; }
            public string PaymentToken { get; set; }
            public decimal Amount { get; set; }
        }
    }
```

The contract for the payment service, IPaymentService, as can be seen in the following listing, deliberately abstracts away any implementation-specific details relating to PayPal. This allows it to be reused with other payment merchants:

```
using System.Web.Mvc;

namespace Agathas.Storefront.Infrastructure.Payments
{
    public interface IPaymentService
    {
        PaymentPostData GeneratePostDataFor(OrderPaymentRequest orderRequest);
        TransactionResult HandleCallBack(OrderPaymentRequest orderRequest,
                                         FormCollection collection);
        int GetOrderIdFor(FormCollection collection);
    }
}
```

Before you create a PayPal implementation of the IPaymentService, you need to modify the IApplicationSettings interface that can be found in the Configuration folder of the Infrastructure project to expose two new properties, as shown in bold in the following code listing:

```
namespace Agathas.Storefront.Infrastructure.Configuration
{
    public interface IApplicationSettings
    {
        ...

        string PayPalBusinessEmail { get; }
        string PayPalPaymentPostToUrl { get; }
    }
}
```

You now need to modify the WebConfigApplicationSettings implementation to include the two new properties, as can be seen in the following listing:

```
using System.Configuration;

namespace Agathas.Storefront.Infrastructure.Configuration
{
    public class WebConfigApplicationSettings : IApplicationSettings
    {
        ...

        public string PayPalBusinessEmail
        {
            get { return ConfigurationManager.AppSettings["PayPalBusinessEmail"]; }
```

```
        }

        public string PayPalPaymentPostToUrl
        {
            get { return ConfigurationManager.AppSettings["PayPalPaymentPostToUrl"]; }
        }
    }
}
```

Finally, update the web.config file in the Web.MVC project as illustrated in bold in the following listing to include your PayPal seller account e-mail that you generated when creating a seller and buyer PayPal account. The other property is used when you are ready to go live. Here you substitute the real PayPal checkout from the sandbox checkout:

```
<appSettings>

    …

    <add key="PayPalBusinessEmail"
        value="XXXXX@XXXXXX.XXXX"/>
    <add key="PayPalPaymentPostToUrl"
        value="https://www.sandbox.paypal.com/cgi-bin/webscr"/>

</appSettings >
```

You can now create the PayPal implementation of the IPaymentService. The workings of PayPal are out of scope for this book, but I have commented all methods to give you an idea of what's going on. Please look at the PayPal developer documentation for more information:

```
using System;
using System.Collections.Specialized;
using System.IO;
using System.Net;
using System.Text;
using System.Web.Mvc;
using System.Web;
using Agathas.Storefront.Infrastructure.Configuration;

namespace Agathas.Storefront.Infrastructure.Payments
{
    public class PayPalPaymentService : IPaymentService
    {
        public PaymentPostData GeneratePostDataFor(OrderPaymentRequest orderRequest)
        {
            PaymentPostData paymentPostData = new PaymentPostData();
            NameValueCollection postDataAndValue = new NameValueCollection();

            paymentPostData.PostDataAndValue = postDataAndValue;

            // When a real PayPal account is used, the form should be sent to
            // https://www.paypal.com/cgi-bin/webscr.
            // For testing use "https://www.sandbox.paypal.com/cgi-bin/webscr"
            paymentPostData.PaymentPostToUrl = ApplicationSettingsFactory
```

```
            .GetApplicationSettings().PayPalPaymentPostToUrl;

// For shopping cart purchases.
postDataAndValue.Add("cmd", "_cart");
// Indicates the use of third-party shopping cart.
postDataAndValue.Add("upload", "1");

// This is the seller's e-mail address.
// You must supply your own address here!!!
postDataAndValue.Add("business", ApplicationSettingsFactory
    .GetApplicationSettings().PayPalBusinessEmail);

// This field does not take part in the shopping process.
// It simply will be passed to the IPN script at the time
// of transaction confirmation.
postDataAndValue.Add("custom", orderRequest.Id.ToString());

// This parameter represents a currency code.
postDataAndValue.Add("currency_code", "GBP");

postDataAndValue.Add("first_name", orderRequest.CustomerFirstName);
postDataAndValue.Add("last_name", orderRequest.CustomerSecondName);

postDataAndValue.Add("address1", orderRequest.DeliveryAddressAddressLine1);
postDataAndValue.Add("address2", orderRequest.DeliveryAddressAddressLine2);
postDataAndValue.Add("city", orderRequest.DeliveryAddressCity);
postDataAndValue.Add("state", orderRequest.DeliveryAddressState);
postDataAndValue.Add("country", orderRequest.DeliveryAddressCountry);
postDataAndValue.Add("zip", orderRequest.DeliveryAddressZipCode);

// This parameter determines whether the delivery
// address should be requested.
// "1" means that the address will be requested; "0" means
// that it will be not.
//postDataAndValue.Add("no_shipping", "0");

// This is the URL where the user will be redirected after the payment
// is successfully performed. If this parameter is not passed, the buyer
// remains on the PayPal site.
postDataAndValue.Add("return",
            Helpers.UrlHelper.Resolve("/Payment/PaymentComplete"));

// This is the URL where the user will be redirected when
// he cancels the payment.
// If the parameter is not passed, the buyer remains on the PayPal site.
postDataAndValue.Add("cancel_return",
            Helpers.UrlHelper.Resolve("/Payment/PaymentCancel"));

// This is the URL where PayPal will pass information about the
// transaction (IPN). If the parameter is not passed, the value from
// the account settings will be used. If this value is not defined in
// the account settings, IPN will not be used.
postDataAndValue.Add("notify_url",
            Helpers.UrlHelper.Resolve("/Payment/PaymentCallBack"));

int itemIndex = 1;
```

```
    foreach(OrderItemPaymentRequest item in orderRequest.Items )
    {
        postDataAndValue.Add("item_name_" + itemIndex.ToString(),
                                        item.ProductName);
        postDataAndValue.Add("amount_" + itemIndex.ToString(),
                                        item.Price.ToString());
        postDataAndValue.Add("item_number_" + itemIndex.ToString(),
                                        item.Id.ToString());
        postDataAndValue.Add("quantity_" + itemIndex.ToString(),
                                        item.Qty.ToString());

        itemIndex++;
    }

    postDataAndValue.Add("shipping", orderRequest.ShippingCharge.ToString());

    return paymentPostData;
}

public TransactionResult HandleCallBack(OrderPaymentRequest orderRequest,
                                        FormCollection collection)
{
    TransactionResult transactionResult = new TransactionResult();

    string response = ValidatePaymentNotification(collection);

    if (response == "VERIFIED")
    {
        string sAmountPaid = collection["mc_gross"];
        string transactionId = collection["txn_id"];

        Decimal amountPaid = 0;
        Decimal.TryParse(sAmountPaid, out amountPaid);

        if (orderRequest.Total == amountPaid)
        {
            transactionResult.PaymentToken = transactionId;
            transactionResult.Amount = amountPaid;
            transactionResult.PaymentMerchant = "PayPal";
            transactionResult.PaymentOk = true;
        }
        else
        {
            transactionResult.PaymentToken = transactionId;
            transactionResult.Amount = amountPaid;
            transactionResult.PaymentMerchant = "PayPal";
            transactionResult.PaymentOk = false;
        }
    }

    return transactionResult;
}


private string ValidatePaymentNotification(FormCollection formCollection)
```

```
        {
            formCollection["cmd"] = "_notify-validate";

            string paypalUrl = ApplicationSettingsFactory
                            .GetApplicationSettings().PayPalPaymentPostToUrl;

            HttpWebRequest req = (HttpWebRequest)WebRequest.Create(paypalUrl);

            // Set values for the request back
            req.Method = "POST";
            req.ContentType = "application/x-www-form-urlencoded";

            byte[] param = HttpContext.Current.Request
                        .BinaryRead(HttpContext.Current.Request.ContentLength);
            string strRequest = Encoding.ASCII.GetString(param);

            StringBuilder postFormData = new StringBuilder();

            foreach (string key in formCollection.Keys)
            {
                postFormData.AppendFormat("&{0}={1}", key, formCollection[key]);
            }

            strRequest = postFormData.ToString();
            req.ContentLength = strRequest.Length;


            string response = "";
            using (StreamWriter streamOut = new StreamWriter(req.GetRequestStream(),
                                                System.Text.Encoding.ASCII))
            {

                streamOut.Write(strRequest);
                streamOut.Close();
                using (StreamReader streamIn =
                        new StreamReader(req.GetResponse().GetResponseStream()))
                {
                    response = streamIn.ReadToEnd();
                }
            }

            return response;
        }

        public int GetOrderIdFor(FormCollection collection)
        {
            return int.Parse(collection["custom"]);
        }
    }
}
```

Code snippet PayPalPaymentService.cs in project Agathas.Storefront.Infrastructure

The PayPal payment service is now complete, so you can turn your attention to the `Controllers` project that will coordinate the checkout, payment, and customer order history actions.

Order, Payment, and Checkout Controllers

Figure 14-13 shows the views and view models that you will be using in this section.

Create a new folder within the `ViewModels` folder of the `Controllers` project, and name it `Checkout`. Add a new class to this folder named `OrderConfirmationView`. This view is tied to the order confirmation .ASPX view:

```
using System.Collections.Generic;
using Agathas.Storefront.Services.ViewModels;

namespace Agathas.Storefront.Controllers.ViewModels.Checkout
{
    public class OrderConfirmationView
    {
        public BasketView Basket { get; set; }
        public IEnumerable<DeliveryAddressView> DeliveryAddresses { get; set; }
    }
}
```

Next, add a view within the `CustomerAccount` folder. This folder is in the `ViewModels` folder of the `Controllers` project named `CustomersOrderSummaryView`, which will be strongly typed to the .ASPX view that shows a customer's order history:

```
using System.Collections.Generic;
using Agathas.Storefront.Services.ViewModels;

namespace Agathas.Storefront.Controllers.ViewModels.CustomerAccount
{
    public class CustomersOrderSummaryView : BaseCustomerAccountView
    {
        public IEnumerable<OrderSummaryView> Orders { get; set; }
    }
}
```

The `CustomerOrderView` view is strongly typed to the .ASPX order detail view, which will be found within the customer account section:

```
using Agathas.Storefront.Services.ViewModels;

namespace Agathas.Storefront.Controllers.ViewModels.CustomerAccount
{
    public class CustomerOrderView : BaseCustomerAccountView
    {
        public OrderView Order { get; set; }
    }
}
```

Figure 14-14 shows the three controllers that coordinate the logic for the customer account order history, payment, and checkout sections of the site.

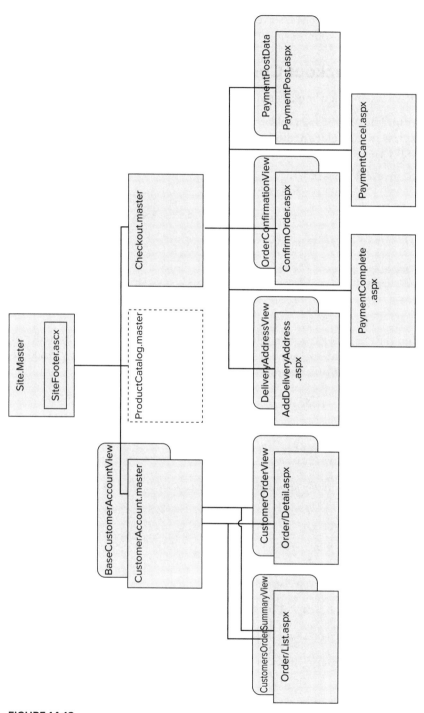

FIGURE 14-13

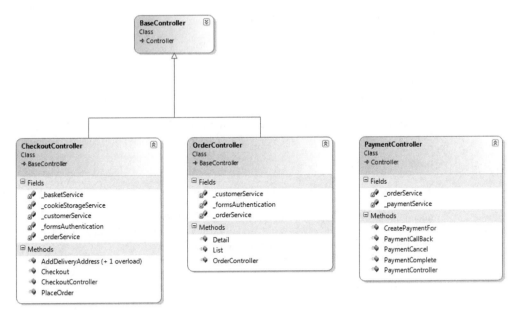

FIGURE 14-14

Add a new class to the `Controllers` folder of the `Controllers` project named `OrderController` with the following listing. The `OrderController` is simple and just retrieves lists of order summaries or an order's detail:

```
using System.Web.Mvc;
using Agathas.Storefront.Controllers.ViewModels.CustomerAccount;
using Agathas.Storefront.Infrastructure.Authentication;
using Agathas.Storefront.Infrastructure.CookieStorage;
using Agathas.Storefront.Services.Interfaces;
using Agathas.Storefront.Services.Messaging.CustomerService;
using Agathas.Storefront.Services.Messaging.OrderService;

namespace Agathas.Storefront.Controllers.Controllers
{
    [Authorize]
    public class OrderController : BaseController
    {
        private readonly ICustomerService _customerService;
        private readonly IOrderService _orderService;
        private readonly IFormsAuthentication _formsAuthentication;

        public OrderController(ICustomerService customerService,
                               IOrderService orderService,
                               IFormsAuthentication formsAuthentication,
                               ICookieStorageService cookieStorageService)
            : base(cookieStorageService)
        {
```

```
            _customerService = customerService;
            _orderService = orderService;
            _formsAuthentication = formsAuthentication;
        }

        [Authorize]
        public ActionResult List()
        {
            GetCustomerRequest request = new GetCustomerRequest(){
              CustomerIdentityToken = _formsAuthentication.Get AuthenticationToken(),

              LoadOrderSummary = true};

            GetCustomerResponse response = _customerService.GetCustomer(request);

            CustomersOrderSummaryView customersOrderSummaryView =
                                            new CustomersOrderSummaryView();
            customersOrderSummaryView.Orders = response.Orders;
            customersOrderSummaryView.BasketSummary = base.GetBasketSummaryView();

            return View(customersOrderSummaryView);
        }

        [Authorize]
        public ActionResult Detail(int orderId)
        {
            GetOrderRequest request = new GetOrderRequest() {OrderId = orderId};
            GetOrderResponse response = _orderService.GetOrder(request);

            CustomerOrderView orderView = new CustomerOrderView();
            orderView.BasketSummary = base.GetBasketSummaryView();
            orderView.Order = response.Order;

            return View(orderView);
        }
    }
}
```

The next controller you will create is the `CheckoutController`. Part of the checkout process is to select a delivery address for an order. If one does not exist, the customer is redirected to enter one before continuing the checkout. To facilitate this and update an order with the correct delivery address, you need to add a new value to the `FormDataKeys` enumeration, as shown in bold in the following listing:

```
namespace Agathas.Storefront.Controllers
{
    public enum FormDataKeys
    {
        DeliveryAddress,
        Password,
        Email,
        FirstName,
        SecondName,
    }
}
```

Create the `CheckoutController` with the following code definition:

```
using System;
using System.Linq;
using System.Web.Mvc;
using Agathas.Storefront.Controllers.ViewModels.Checkout;
using Agathas.Storefront.Infrastructure.Authentication;
using Agathas.Storefront.Infrastructure.CookieStorage;
using Agathas.Storefront.Services.Interfaces;
using Agathas.Storefront.Services.Messaging.CustomerService;
using Agathas.Storefront.Services.Messaging.OrderService;
using Agathas.Storefront.Services.Messaging.ProductCatalogueService;
using Agathas.Storefront.Services.ViewModels;

namespace Agathas.Storefront.Controllers.Controllers
{
    public class CheckoutController : BaseController
    {
        private readonly ICookieStorageService _cookieStorageService;
        private readonly IBasketService _basketService;
        private readonly ICustomerService _customerService;
        private readonly IOrderService _orderService;
        private readonly IFormsAuthentication _formsAuthentication;

        public CheckoutController(ICookieStorageService cookieStorageService,
                                  IBasketService basketService,
                                  ICustomerService customerService,
                                  IOrderService orderService,
                                  IFormsAuthentication formsAuthentication)
            : base(cookieStorageService)
        {
            _cookieStorageService = cookieStorageService;
            _basketService = basketService;
            _customerService = customerService;
            _orderService = orderService;
            _formsAuthentication = formsAuthentication;
        }

        [Authorize]
        public ActionResult Checkout()
        {
            GetCustomerRequest customerRequest = new GetCustomerRequest(){
                CustomerIdentityToken = _formsAuthentication.Get AuthenticationToken()};

            GetCustomerResponse customerResponse =
                        _customerService.GetCustomer(customerRequest);
            CustomerView customerView = customerResponse.Customer;

            if (customerView.DeliveryAddressBook.Count() > 0)
            {
                OrderConfirmationView orderConfirmationView =
                                    new OrderConfirmationView();
                GetBasketRequest getBasketRequest = new GetBasketRequest() {
```

```
                                            BasketId = base.GetBasketId()};

        GetBasketResponse basketResponse =
                            _basketService.GetBasket(getBasketRequest);

        orderConfirmationView.Basket = basketResponse.Basket;
        orderConfirmationView.DeliveryAddresses =
                            customerView.DeliveryAddressBook;

        return View("ConfirmOrder", orderConfirmationView);
    }

    return AddDeliveryAddress();
}

[Authorize]
public ActionResult AddDeliveryAddress()
{
    DeliveryAddressView deliveryAddressView = new DeliveryAddressView();
    return View("AddDeliveryAddress", deliveryAddressView);
}

[Authorize]
[AcceptVerbs(HttpVerbs.Post)]
public ActionResult AddDeliveryAddress(DeliveryAddressView deliveryAddressView)
{
    DeliveryAddressAddRequest request = new DeliveryAddressAddRequest();
    request.Address = deliveryAddressView;
    request.CustomerIdentityToken =
            _formsAuthentication.Get AuthenticationToken();

    _customerService.AddDeliveryAddress(request);

    return Checkout();
}

[Authorize]
public ActionResult PlaceOrder(FormCollection collection)
{
    CreateOrderRequest request = new CreateOrderRequest();
    request.BasketId = base.GetBasketId();
    request.CustomerIdentityToken =
            _formsAuthentication.Get AuthenticationToken();
    request.DeliveryId =
        int.Parse(collection[FormDataKeys.DeliveryAddress.ToString()]);

    CreateOrderResponse response = _orderService.CreateOrder(request);

    _cookieStorageService.Save(CookieDataKeys.BasketItems.ToString(),
                        "0", DateTime.Now.AddDays(1));
    _cookieStorageService.Save(CookieDataKeys.BasketTotal.ToString(),
                        "0", DateTime.Now.AddDays(1));

    return RedirectToAction("CreatePaymentFor", "Payment",
```

```
                                    new { orderId = response.Order.Id});
            }
        }
    }
```

To work with the payment service, you must convert an order to an `OrderPaymentRequest`. You achieve this by using AutoMapper. Create a new class named `AutoMapperBootStrapper` in the root of the `Controllers` project with the following listing:

```
using AutoMapper;
using Agathas.Storefront.Services.ViewModels;
using Agathas.Storefront.Infrastructure.Payments;

namespace Agathas.Storefront.Controllers
{
    public class AutoMapperBootStrapper
    {
        public static void ConfigureAutoMapper()
        {
            Mapper.CreateMap<OrderView, OrderPaymentRequest>()
                .ForMember(o => o.Total,
                           ov => ov.ResolveUsing<OrderTotalResolver>())
                .ForMember(o => o.ShippingCharge,
                           ov => ov.ResolveUsing<ShippingChargeResolver>());

            Mapper.CreateMap<OrderItemView, OrderItemPaymentRequest>()
                .ForMember(o => o.Price, ov => ov.ResolveUsing<ItemPriceResolver>());
        }
    }

    public class OrderTotalResolver : ValueResolver<OrderView, decimal>
    {
        protected override decimal ResolveCore(OrderView source)
        {
            return decimal.Parse(source.Total.Substring(1, source.Total.Length -1));
        }
    }

    public class ShippingChargeResolver : ValueResolver<OrderView, decimal>
    {
        protected override decimal ResolveCore(OrderView source)
        {
            return decimal.Parse(source.ShippingCharge
                            .Substring(1, source.ShippingCharge.Length - 1));
        }
    }

    public class ItemPriceResolver : ValueResolver<OrderItemView, decimal>
    {
        protected override decimal ResolveCore(OrderItemView source)
        {
            return decimal.Parse(source.Price.Substring(1, source.Price.Length - 1));
        }
    }
}
```

The `AutoMapperBootStrapper` simply defines how to convert the `OrderView` to an `OrderPayment`
`Request` object. To make this conversion, create a new class named `OrderMapper` to provide an
extension method:

```
using Agathas.Storefront.Infrastructure.Payments;
using Agathas.Storefront.Services.ViewModels;
using AutoMapper;

namespace Agathas.Storefront.Controllers
{
    public static class OrderMapper
    {
        public static OrderPaymentRequest ConvertToOrderPaymentRequest(
                                                  this OrderView order)
        {
            return Mapper.Map<OrderView, OrderPaymentRequest>(order);
        }
    }
}
```

You can now create the `PaymentController` that coordinates the taking workflow with the `IPayment`
`Service`. Notice that there are no specific details relating to PayPal; this is intentional so that a new
payment merchant can be swapped in for PayPal at a later date if necessary:

```
using System;
using System.Web.Mvc;
using Agathas.Storefront.Infrastructure.Logging;
using Agathas.Storefront.Infrastructure.Payments;
using Agathas.Storefront.Services.Interfaces;
using Agathas.Storefront.Services.Messaging.OrderService;

namespace Agathas.Storefront.Controllers.Controllers
{
    public class PaymentController : Controller
    {
        private readonly IPaymentService _paymentService;
        private readonly IOrderService _orderService;

        public PaymentController(IPaymentService paymentService,
                             IOrderService orderService)
        {
            _paymentService = paymentService;
            _orderService = orderService;
        }

        [AcceptVerbs(HttpVerbs.Post)]
        public void PaymentCallBack(FormCollection collection)
        {
                int orderId = _paymentService.GetOrderIdFor(collection);
                GetOrderRequest request = new GetOrderRequest() {OrderId = orderId};

                GetOrderResponse response =  _orderService.GetOrder(request);

                OrderPaymentRequest orderPaymentRequest =
```

```
                response.Order.ConvertToOrderPaymentRequest();

            TransactionResult transactionResult =
                _paymentService.HandleCallBack(orderPaymentRequest, collection);

            if (transactionResult.PaymentOk)
            {
                SetOrderPaymentRequest paymentRequest =
                                        new SetOrderPaymentRequest();
                paymentRequest.Amount = transactionResult.Amount;
                paymentRequest.PaymentToken = transactionResult.PaymentToken;
                paymentRequest.PaymentMerchant = transactionResult.PaymentMerchant;
                paymentRequest.OrderId = orderId;

                _orderService.SetOrderPayment(paymentRequest);
            }
            else
            {
                LoggingFactory.GetLogger().Log(String.Format(
                 "Payment not ok for order id {0}, payment token {1}",
                    orderId, transactionResult.PaymentToken));
            }
        }

        public ActionResult CreatePaymentFor(int orderId)
        {
            GetOrderRequest request = new GetOrderRequest() {OrderId = orderId};

            GetOrderResponse response = _orderService.GetOrder(request);
            OrderPaymentRequest orderPaymentRequest =
                        response.Order.ConvertToOrderPaymentRequest();

            PaymentPostData paymentPostData =
                        _paymentService.GeneratePostDataFor(orderPaymentRequest);

            return View("PaymentPost", paymentPostData);
        }

        public ActionResult PaymentComplete()
        {
            return View();
        }

        public ActionResult PaymentCancel()
        {
            return View();
        }
    }
}
```

The last thing you need to do is add an entry in the Web.config file found within the Web.MVC project as shown next, so that when a customer who is not logged in tries to check out they will be redirected to the login page:

```
...
<authentication mode="Forms">
```

```
                <forms loginUrl="~/AccountLogOn/LogOn" timeout="2880"/>
    </authentication>
    ...
```

With the model, services, and controllers in place, you are left only with the task of creating the .ASPX views.

Order and Checkout Views

Create a master view named `Checkout.master` that inherits from the `Site.Master` and provides the layout for the checkout views:

```
<%@ Master Language="C#" MasterPageFile="Site.Master" %>

<asp:Content ID="TitleContent" ContentPlaceHolderID="TitleContent" runat="server">
    <asp:ContentPlaceHolder ID="TitleContent" runat="server">

    </asp:ContentPlaceHolder>
</asp:Content>

<asp:Content ID="headerBasketSummary" ContentPlaceHolderID="headerBasketSummary"
            runat="server">

</asp:Content>

<asp:Content runat="server" ID="Content1" ContentPlaceHolderID="MenuContent">

</asp:Content>

<asp:Content ID="MainContent" ContentPlaceHolderID="MainContent" runat="server">
    <asp:ContentPlaceHolder ID="MainContent" runat="server">

    </asp:ContentPlaceHolder>
</asp:Content>
```

Create a new folder within the `Views` folder named `Checkout`. The first view you will create within the `Checkout` folder is `ConfirmOrder.aspx`. The markup for this view is shown in the following listing:

```
<%@ Page Title="" Language="C#"
        MasterPageFile="~/Views/Shared/Checkout.Master"
        Inherits="System.Web.Mvc.ViewPage<OrderConfirmationView>" %>
<%@ Import Namespace="Agathas.Storefront.Services.ViewModels" %>
<%@ Import Namespace="Agathas.Storefront.Controllers.ViewModels.Checkout" %>

<asp:Content ID="Content1" ContentPlaceHolderID="TitleContent" runat="server">
    ConfirmOrder
</asp:Content>

<asp:Content ID="Content2" ContentPlaceHolderID="MainContent" runat="server">

    <h2>Confirm Order</h2>

        <%using (Html.BeginForm("PlaceOrder", "Checkout")) {%>

        Delivery Address
```

```
        <select id="DeliveryAddress" name="DeliveryAddress">
    <%
            foreach (DeliveryAddressView deliveryAddress in Model.DeliveryAddresses)
            {
    %>
            <option value="<%=Html.Encode(deliveryAddress.Id)%>">
              <%=Html.Encode(deliveryAddress.Name)%></option>
    <%
            }%>
    </select>

    - <%=Html.ActionLink("Create new address", "AddDeliveryAddress", "Checkout")%>

    <ul>
    <% foreach(BasketItemView item in Model.Basket.Items) {%>
        <li><%=Html.Encode(item.Qty) %> of <%=Html.Encode(item.ProductName) %> at
            <%=Html.Encode(String.Format("{0:F}", item.ProductPrice))%></li>
    <% }%>
    </ul>

    <p>Total: <%= Html.Encode(String.Format("{0:F}", Model.Basket.ItemsTotal)) %>
    </p>

    <p>DeliveryCharge: <%= Html.Encode(String.Format("{0:F}",
                                    Model.Basket.DeliveryCost)) %></p>

    <p>Total: <%= Html.Encode(String.Format("{0:F}",
                            Model.Basket.BasketTotal )) %></p>

    <input id="Submit" type="submit" value="Place Order" />
        <% }%>
</asp:Content>
```

If a customer wants to create a new delivery address or does not have a delivery address at checkout, he is presented with the AddDeliveryAddress.aspx view whose markup can be seen in the following listing:

```
<%@ Page Title="" Language="C#" MasterPageFile="~/Views/Shared/Checkout.Master"
        Inherits="System.Web.Mvc.ViewPage<DeliveryAddressView>" %>
<%@ Import Namespace="Agathas.Storefront.Services.ViewModels" %>

<asp:Content ID="Content1" ContentPlaceHolderID="TitleContent" runat="server">
    Add Delivery Address
</asp:Content>

<asp:Content ID="Content2" ContentPlaceHolderID="MainContent" runat="server">

    <h2>Add DeliveryAddress</h2>

    <% using (Html.BeginForm("AddDeliveryAddress", "Checkout")) {%>

        <% Html.RenderPartial("~/Views/Shared/AddressEdit.ascx", Model); %>
        <p>
            <input type="submit" value="Create Address and Checkout" />
```

```
        </p>
    <% } %>

    <div>
        <%=Html.ActionLink("Check Out", "Checkout", "Checkout")%>
    </div>

</asp:Content>
```

Create a new folder within the `Views` folder named `Order`. This folder contains the two views to display a customer's order history. Add the first `List.aspx` to the folder with the following markup:

```
<%@ Page Title="" Language="C#"
        MasterPageFile="~/Views/Shared/CustomerAccount.Master"
        Inherits="System.Web.Mvc.ViewPage<CustomersOrderSummaryView>" %>
<%@ Import Namespace="Agathas.Storefront.Services.ViewModels" %>
<%@ Import Namespace="Agathas.Storefront.Controllers.ViewModels.CustomerAccount" %>

<asp:Content ID="Content1" ContentPlaceHolderID="TitleContent" runat="server">
    Your Order History
</asp:Content>

<asp:Content ID="Content2" ContentPlaceHolderID="MainContent" runat="server">

    <h2>Your Orders</h2>

    <ul>
    <% foreach(OrderSummaryView order in Model.Orders)
       {
    %>
            <li><%=Html.Encode(order.Created.ToLongDateString()) %>
                <% if (order.IsSubmitted == false){ %>
                <%=Html.ActionLink("Pay", "CreatePaymentFor", "Payment",
                                        new { orderId = order.Id}, null)%>
                <% } %>
                <%=Html.ActionLink("View Detail", "Detail", "Order",
                                        new { orderId = order .Id}, null)%>
            </li>
    <% }%>
    </ul>

</asp:Content>
```

Add the `Detail.aspx` view, which displays the full detail of an order:

```
<%@ Page Title="" Language="C#"
        MasterPageFile="~/Views/Shared/CustomerAccount.Master"
        Inherits="System.Web.Mvc.ViewPage<CustomerOrderView>" %>
<%@ Import Namespace="Agathas.Storefront.Services.ViewModels" %>
<%@ Import Namespace="Agathas.Storefront.Controllers.ViewModels.CustomerAccount" %>

<asp:Content ID="Content1" ContentPlaceHolderID="TitleContent" runat="server">
    Your Order Detail
```

```
</asp:Content>

<asp:Content ID="Content2" ContentPlaceHolderID="MainContent" runat="server">

    <h2>Order #<%= Html.Encode(Model.Order.Id)%> placed on
            <%=Html.Encode(Model.Order.Created.ToLongDateString()) %> at
            <%=Html.Encode(Model.Order.Created.ToShortTimeString())%></h2>

    <% if (Model.Order.OrderHasBeenPaidFor == false) {%>
        <p>This order has not been paid.
          <%=Html.ActionLink("Pay", "CreatePaymentFor", "Payment",
                            new { orderId = Model.Order.Id }, null)%>  </p>
    <% }
       else
       {
     %>
        <p>Paid on <%=Html.Encode(Model.Order.PaymentDatePaid)%>.
            Payment ref <%=Html.Encode(Model.Order.PaymentTransactionId)%></p>
     <%
        }%>

    <ul>
    <% foreach (OrderItemView item in Model.Order.Items)
       {%>
        <li><%=Html.Encode(item.Qty) %> of <%=Html.Encode(item.ProductName) %>
           (<%=Html.Encode(item.ProductSizeName)%>) at
            <%=Html.Encode(String.Format("{0:F}", item.Price))%></li>
    <% }%>
    </ul>

    <p>Shipping Charge: <%= Html.Encode(String.Format("{0:F}",
                                Model.Order.ShippingCharge))%></p>
    <p>Shipping Via: <%=Html.Encode(Model.Order.ShippingServiceCourierName)%> -
                   <%=Html.Encode(Model.Order.ShippingServiceDescription)%></p>
    <p>Total: <%= Html.Encode(String.Format("{0:F}", Model.Order.Total))%></p>

    <p>Delivery Address</p>

    <%=Html.Encode(Model.Order.DeliveryAddress.AddressLine1)%><br />
    <%=Html.Encode(Model.Order.DeliveryAddress.AddressLine2)%><br />
    <%=Html.Encode(Model.Order.DeliveryAddress.City)%><br />
    <%=Html.Encode(Model.Order.DeliveryAddress.State)%><br />
    <%=Html.Encode(Model.Order.DeliveryAddress.ZipCode)%><br />
    <%=Html.Encode(Model.Order.DeliveryAddress.Country)%><br />

</asp:Content>
```

For a customer to navigate to his order history, you need to update the `CustomerMenu.ascx` partial view that can be found in the `Views/Shared` folder:

```
<%@ Control Language="C#" Inherits="System.Web.Mvc.ViewUserControl" %>

<h2>Menu</h2>
```

```
<ul class="refine-attributes">
<li><%=Html.ActionLink("Your Details", "Detail", "Customer") %></li>
<li><%=Html.ActionLink("Delivery Address Book",
                       "DeliveryAddresses", "Customer")%></li>
<li><%=Html.ActionLink("Your Orders", "List", "Order")%></li>
</ul>
```

Create another new folder named `Payment` within the `Views` folder to hold all the views related to payments. The first is `PaymentPost.aspx`, which posts the values defined by the `PaymentService` to the payment merchant's website:

```
<%@ Page Title="" Language="C#"
        MasterPageFile="~/Views/Shared/Checkout.Master"
        Inherits="System.Web.Mvc.ViewPage<PaymentPostData>" %>
<%@ Import Namespace="Agathas.Storefront.Infrastructure.Payments" %>

<asp:Content ID="Content1" ContentPlaceHolderID="TitleContent" runat="server">
    Payment Post
</asp:Content>

<asp:Content ID="Content2" ContentPlaceHolderID="MainContent" runat="server">

    <h2>Payment Post</h2>

    <script type="text/javascript">

    $(document).ready(function() {

            $('#paymentForm').submit();

            });
    </script>


    <form id="paymentForm" name="paymentForm"
          action="<%=Html.Encode(Model.PaymentPostToUrl) %>" method="post">

    <% foreach (String postDataKey in Model.PostDataAndValue.AllKeys) {%>
            <%=Html.Hidden(postDataKey, Model.PostDataAndValue[postDataKey])%>
    <% } %>

    <input id="Submit" type="submit"
           value="Click here if the page doesn't auto redirect in 5 seconds" />

    </form>

</asp:Content>
```

The final two views to create within the `Payment` folder are static views that confirm the placement of an order or the cancellation of a payment transaction.

Add the first view named `PaymentComplete.aspx` with the following markup:

```
<%@ Page Title="" Language="C#"
    MasterPageFile="~/Views/Shared/Checkout.Master"
```

```
    Inherits="System.Web.Mvc.ViewPage" %>

<asp:Content ID="Content1" ContentPlaceHolderID="TitleContent" runat="server">
    Payment Complete
</asp:Content>

<asp:Content ID="Content2" ContentPlaceHolderID="MainContent" runat="server">

    <h2>Payment Complete</h2>

    Thank you, please allow up to 10 minutes for the payment
    to be confirmed before your order becomes active.

</asp:Content>
```

Add the second view named `PaymentCancel.aspx` with the following markup:

```
<%@ Page Title="" Language="C#"
    MasterPageFile="~/Views/Shared/Checkout.Master"
    Inherits="System.Web.Mvc.ViewPage" %>

<asp:Content ID="Content1" ContentPlaceHolderID="TitleContent" runat="server">
 Payment Cancel
</asp:Content>

<asp:Content ID="Content2" ContentPlaceHolderID="MainContent" runat="server">

    <h2>Payment Cancel</h2>

    You cancelled your payment. You can always
    <%=Html.ActionLink("pay for you order at a later date", "List", "Order")%>.

</asp:Content>
```

With all the views complete, you need only to configure the new services and repository in the `BootStrapper` class and amend the `Global.asax` file to configure the new AutoMapper code in the service layer. Open the `BootStrapper` class found at the root of the `Web.MVC` with the new code bolded here:

```
using Agathas.Storefront.Infrastructure.Payments;
using Agathas.Storefront.Model.Orders;
using Agathas.Storefront.Model.Orders.Events;
using Agathas.Storefront.Services.DomainEventHandlers;

namespace Agathas.Storefront.UI.Web.MVC
{
    public class BootStrapper
    {
        ...

        public class ControllerRegistry : Registry
        {
            public ControllerRegistry()
            {
                // Repositories
                ForRequestedType<IOrderRepository>().TheDefault.Is.OfConcreteType
```

```
                              <Repository.NHibernate.Repositories.OrderRepository>();

             ...

             // Order Service
             ForRequestedType<IOrderService>().TheDefault.Is.OfConcreteType
                   <OrderService>();

             // Payment
             ForRequestedType<IPaymentService>().TheDefault.Is.OfConcreteType
                   <PayPalPaymentService>();

             // Handlers for Domain Events
             ForRequestedType<IDomainEventHandlerFactory>().TheDefault
                   .Is.OfConcreteType<StructureMapDomainEventHandlerFactory>();
             ForRequestedType<IDomainEventHandler<OrderSubmittedEvent>>()
                   .AddConcreteType<OrderSubmittedHandler>();
          }
       }
    }
}
```

Finally, amend the Global.asax file to include the call to configure the AutoMapperBootStrapper of the Controllers project, as shown in the following listing:

```
namespace Agathas.Storefront.UI.Web.MVC
{

    public class MvcApplication : System.Web.HttpApplication
    {
        ...

        protected void Application_Start()
        {
            RegisterRoutes(RouteTable.Routes);

            BootStrapper.ConfigureDependencies();

            Controllers.AutoMapperBootStrapper.ConfigureAutoMapper();
            Services.AutoMapperBootStrapper.ConfigureAutoMapper();

            ApplicationSettingsFactory.InitializeApplicationSettingsFactory
                             (ObjectFactory.GetInstance<IApplicationSettings>());

            LoggingFactory.InitializeLogFactory(ObjectFactory.GetInstance<ILogger>());

            EmailServiceFactory.InitializeEmailServiceFactory
                             (ObjectFactory.GetInstance<IEmailService>());

            ControllerBuilder.Current.SetControllerFactory(new IoCControllerFactory());

            LoggingFactory.GetLogger().Log("Application Started");
        }
    }
}
```

With the solution complete, you can run the site and view your latest additions. Figure 14-15 shows the order confirmation view.

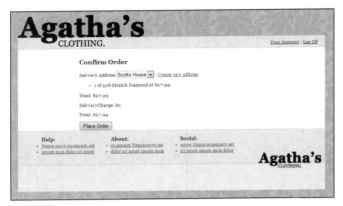

FIGURE 14-15

Figure 14-16 shows the login screen at PayPal.

FIGURE 14-16

Figure 14-17 shows the payment review after logging in to PayPal.

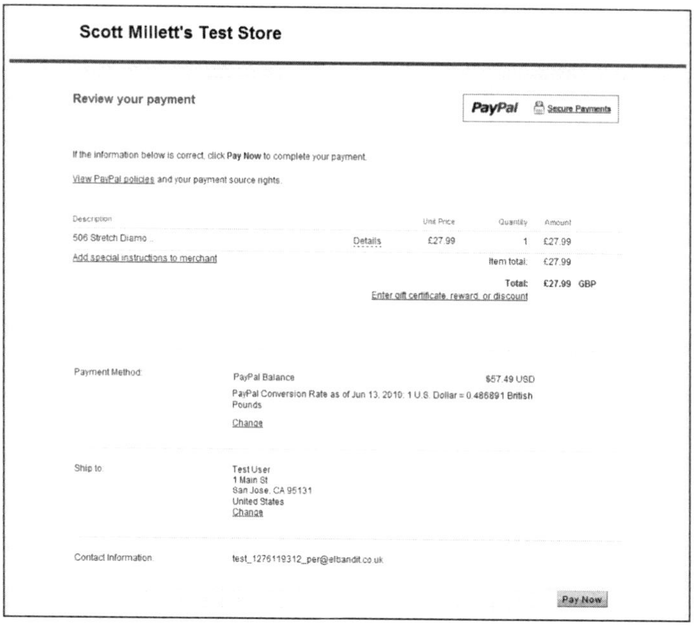

FIGURE 14-17

Figure 14-18 shows the confirmation of the payment transaction.

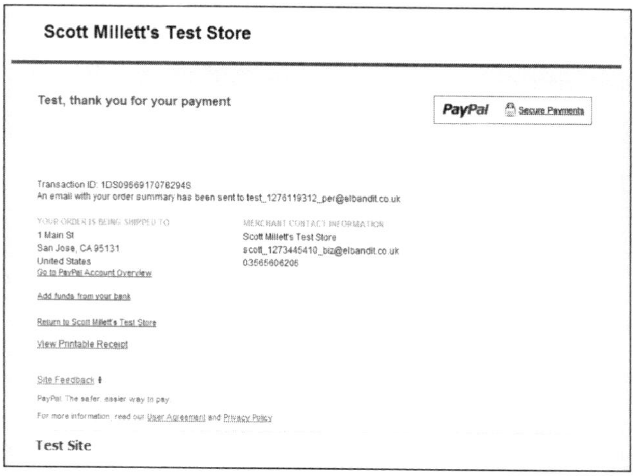

FIGURE 14-18

Figure 14-19 shows the payment complete confirmation view after returning to Agatha's site from PayPal.

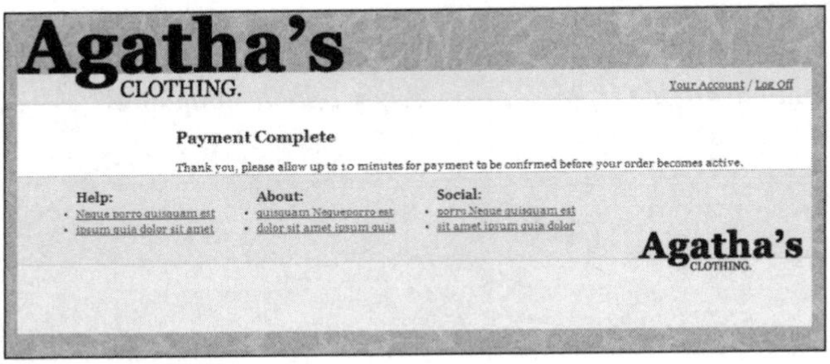

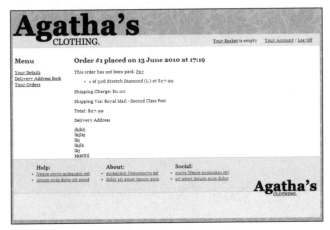

FIGURE 14-19

Figure 14-20 shows the order history for a customer.

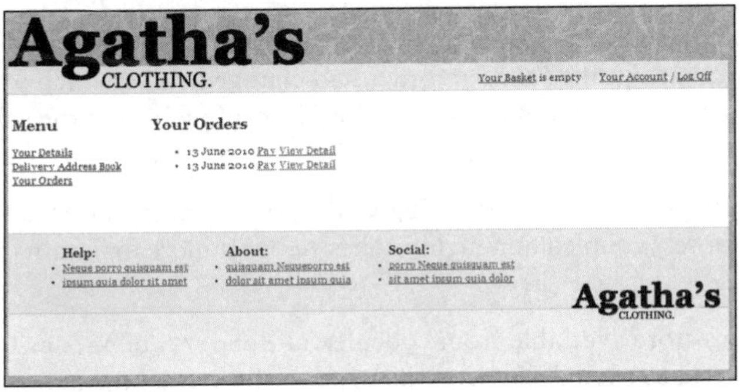

FIGURE 14-20

Figure 14-21 shows the detail of a customer's order.

FIGURE 14-21

> *You can find the product caching layer in the project named* Agathas.Storefront
> .Services.Cache *in the download available from* www.wrox.com *that accompanies*
> *this book.*

SUMMARY

In this chapter, you finished Agatha's e-commerce store. You added the checkout and payment sections using PayPal as the payment merchant. However, the PayPal implementation was abstracted away so that no service or controller directly referenced PayPal; this means it will be easier to change payment merchants and to test the logic of the site.

You also added to the Customers section by including the customer's order history. You utilized the Domain Events pattern to raise an event that signified that an order had changed state, which was handled by the service layer, which in turn sent an email to the customer informing him of the submitted order.

In all, you have created a fully functioning e-commerce site using well-known design patterns and principles, you have kept the code base loosely coupled and highly cohesive, for a more maintainable and testable application.

There is a project homepage for Agatha's store available from codeplex at http://aspnetdesign patterns.codeplex.com/ that will be used to extend the case study and to show you how more patterns and principles can be used in an enterprise-level site. These extensions include the following:

➤ Product Catalog Management

➤ Content Management System

➤ Order Processing

➤ Order Management

➤ Customer Vouchers

If you want to see more features in the future, please stop by and add a suggestion.

INDEX

C

N